Cypress Branch Library

5331 Orange Ave.

Cypress, CA 90630

D0501313

THE GIFTED GENERATION

BY THE SAME AUTHOR

The American Journey: A History of the United States

America Aflame: How the Civil War Created a Nation

Black, White, and Southern: Race Relations and Southern Culture, 1940 to the Present

Still Fighting the Civil War: The American South and Southern History

Twentieth-Century America

Region, Race, and Cities: Interpreting the Urban South

THE
GIFTED
GENERATION

. . . .

WHEN GOVERNMENT
WAS GOOD

DAVID GOLDFIELD

BLOOMSBURY

NEW YORK · LONDON · OXFORD · NEW DELHI · SYDNEY

Bloomsbury USA
An imprint of Bloomsbury Publishing Plc

1385 Broadway	50 Bedford Square
New York	London
NY 10018	WC1B 3DP
USA	UK

www.bloomsbury.com

BLOOMSBURY and the Diana logo are trademarks of Bloomsbury Publishing Plc

First published 2017

© David Goldfield, 2017

All rights reserved. No part of this publication may be reproduced or transmitted in any form or by any means, electronic or mechanical, including photocopying, recording, or any information storage or retrieval system, without prior permission in writing from the publishers.

No responsibility for loss caused to any individual or organization acting on or refraining from action as a result of the material in this publication can be accepted by Bloomsbury or the author.

ISBN: HB: 978-1-62040-088-3
ePub: 978-1-62040-089-0

LIBRARY OF CONGRESS CATALOGING-IN-PUBLICATION DATA

Names: Goldfield, David R., 1944– author.
Title: The gifted generation: when government was good / David Goldfield.
Other titles: When government was good
Description: New York: Bloomsbury USA, [2017] | Includes bibliographical references.
Identifiers: LCCN 2017020004 | ISBN 9781620400883 (hardcover: alk. paper)
Subjects: LCSH: United States—History—1945- | United States—Social conditions—1945- | Social change—United States—History—20th century. | United States—Politics and government—1945–1989. | United States—Politics and government—1989- | Baby boom generation—Attitudes. | Federal government—United States—Public opinion. | Public investments—United States—Public opinion. | Public opinion—United States.
Classification: LCC E741 .G65 2017 | DDC 320.97309/04—dc23
LC record available at https://lccn.loc.gov/2017020004

2 4 6 8 10 9 7 5 3 1

Typeset by Westchester Publishing Services
Printed and bound in the U.S.A. by Berryville Graphics Inc., Berryville, Virginia

To find out more about our authors and books visit www.bloomsbury.com. Here you will find extracts, author interviews, details of forthcoming events, and the option to sign up for our newsletters.

Bloomsbury books may be purchased for business or promotional use. For information on bulk purchases please contact Macmillan Corporate and Premium Sales Department at specialmarkets@macmillan.com.

For Abigail Sofia

CONTENTS

GOOD GOVERNMENT

THIS BOOK IS ABOUT THE FIRST boomers—the gifted generation—born into America in the 1940s and early 1950s, and the gifts they received from government. Thanks to federal policies that eased the way for their parents and made achievement more realizable for themselves, they were twice as likely as their parents to attend college, also aided by the federal government. The boom economy after World War II hummed along in great part because of their needs: food, clothing, education, electronics, toys, and housing and everything that could go into a home from air-conditioning units to dishwashers to vacuum cleaners. Their educational attainments fueled the transformation of the nation's economy and spurred innovation and invention. The gifts kept on giving, not only to the gifted generation and their offspring, but also to the commonwealth.

What I call the commonwealth ideal defined governance in the United States during the first two decades after World War II. The ideal followed three basic principles of governance. First, government should enhance opportunities for all Americans. By benefiting individuals, public policy enhanced the commonwealth, in turn freeing its citizens to pursue their dreams. Second, the ideal charged government with the responsibility of balancing competing interests—individuals, business and industry, and government itself—to benefit the nation. Third, the commonwealth ideal required obedience to the rule of law. The constitution, as interpreted by the federal judiciary, serves as the ultimate guarantor of equality before the law.

The ideal worked best when citizens believed the government kept their interests paramount. That was the case during the Great Depression and World War II. Once those crises ended, maintaining the commonwealth ideal became more difficult. Yet, for a remarkable twenty-year period following the war, the federal government did just that. Three presidents—Harry S. Truman, Dwight D. Eisenhower, and Lyndon B. Johnson, of similar family and geographic backgrounds, and each shaped by depression and war, expanded opportunities for a broad cross section of Americans, who, in turn, produced an era of prosperity and innovation. Public policy provided the gifts, and Americans, especially those of the gifted generation, ran with them.

Government responded to the changing circumstances of American life: the baby boom, an economy transitioning to a postindustrial society, and the growing awareness that significant segments of the population—the poor, women, African Americans, and ethnic and religious minorities—encountered too many obstacles on the journey toward reaching their full potential. Major government initiatives in education, research, civil rights, welfare, and immigration followed. These were not merely top-down measures. Consciousness-raising books on gender, the environment, and poverty spurred federal action as well. Key legislation involved collaborations among organizations, individual citizens, and the government. Their combined efforts, marshaled by forward-looking presidents, created a more equitable, inclusive, and educated America. Government was indeed good. It was hardly surprising that, by the mid-1960s, nearly 80 percent of Americans believed that to be the case, compared with less than 20 percent in 2015. The gifted generation was indeed blessed.[1]

"Generation" is an amorphous concept. The two most common dictionary definitions—"a group of individuals born and living contemporaneously" or "the span of time between the birth of parents and that of their offspring"— are, respectively, vague and fluid. The phrase *baby boom generation* is similarly indeterminate. The U.S. Census Bureau set the boundaries of that generation between 1946 and 1964, supposedly based on birthrate statistics. But those born at the beginning of the boom and those toward the end grew up in very different circumstances.[2]

The baby boom actually began in the early 1940s, perhaps as soon as 1940, when births spiked. Popular magazines at the end of World War II were already touting an ongoing boom, which they traced back to 1941. By 1943, demographers were identifying a baby boom, citing that year's record crop of babies, which followed high birthrates the previous three years. They attributed the rapid rise in the birth rate to the return of prosperity and the exigencies of war.[3]

Recently, demographers have further challenged the Census's 1946 starting year for the boom by questioning the usual explanation for the boom: prosperity and the pent-up demand for marriage and family. Prosperity was already evident by 1940 as the United States geared up for the war. Marriages spiked as well in the early 1940s, indicating the desire to begin a family before men went off to war. The boom, in other words, began well before 1946. Walter T. K. Nugent, who has studied the boomers perhaps more than any other historian, concluded, "Conventional wisdom starts the baby boom in 1946.

That's erroneous . . . Bedroom behavior changed at the beginning of World War II, not after it ended."[4]

The first boomers were more than a cohort of a larger group. They were distinctive in numbers, experience, and impact. Thirty-two million babies were born during the 1940s, a 25 percent increase over the previous decade, the largest jump in American history to that point. Their influence on culture, the economy, and, ultimately, the political process announced the emergence of a new generation, a term I use with the caveats noted above, but also because the size and influence of the early boomers justify the designation.

The first wave of baby boomers had very different trajectories from the boomers born from the mid-1950s onward. The early boomers grew up in the 1950s, entered college at the beginning of the 1960s, and by the end of that decade embarked on a variety of careers, many of which did not exist at the time they were in high school. Journalists and demographers have abandoned any pretense that the early boomers and the late boomers shared anything except the Census definition of the boomer generation.[5]

Journalist Richard Pérez-Peña argued that the boomer generation had two distinct halves: Boomer Classic and Boomer Reboot, with the latter born in the mid-1950s and after, and coming of age in the early 1970s, a very different time from the early 1960s, when the postwar idealism of limitless progress and equality prevailed. Boomer Reboot also faced three recessions between 1973 and 1982, two energy crises, inflation, and high unemployment. Teacher Jean O'Brien, recalling her students at Palisades High School in Santa Monica, California, between 1965 and 1975, termed that decade "the saddest years of the century." The expectations of the students were as high as their predecessors', perhaps even higher, she related. But the promise of the early years dissolved.[6]

The unbounded belief carried by the early boomers—the gifted generation—that they would find not only meaningful work but also a fulfilling life began to recede by the 1970s. The early boomers took a prosperous economy for granted, which enabled them to pursue nothing less than the reformation of the nation in civil rights, immigration, medical care, gender equity, and environmental protection. Federal policies that expanded the economy and encouraged broader participation from heretofore marginalized groups helped to fuel both prosperity and confidence.

The federal role was crucial. The stories and successes of the gifted generation—and of the nation—are inseparable from the activist state. The New Deal had provided a model of how government could help a struggling population in the midst of the worst economic crisis in its history. But the

New Deal was narrow in other respects, particularly with regard to race. The administrations of Truman, Eisenhower, and Johnson not only preserved the gains of the New Deal, but they also expanded its programs, added new ones, and welcomed the participation of people whose race, ethnic or religious backgrounds, and gender had restricted success for themselves and, therefore, for the nation.

The expansive view of federal power did not come easily. Franklin D. Roosevelt entered office a strong advocate of balanced budgets. But the exigencies of the Great Depression required the abandonment of traditional economic views. Truman and Johnson came to Washington during the 1930s and observed firsthand the benefits of an active government for common men and women. Eisenhower, serving in the military, cheered Roosevelt's New Deal as an opportunity to cleanse the government of forces inimical to the nation's well-being. The positive results fixed their belief that a modern economy required some government direction and involvement.

British economist John Maynard Keynes argued during the 1920s and 1930s that government spending increased demand and boosted consumption, creating a cycle of prosperity. That cycle kept wages from falling, enabling workers to maintain strong demands for goods and services. In this view, wages were less a cost than an asset. A strong labor market ensured a healthy national economy.[7]

Keynes's insights derived from his understanding of the modern economy. It had grown so complex and interconnected globally that the operation of the market alone could not guarantee prosperity or even a measure of equity. Government intervention was necessary to balance competing interests and maintain a strong level of employment. To achieve this balance, Keynes advocated major public works investments as a strategy to keep wages level. He understood that such activities would create deficits. But the ensuing prosperity would overcome the debt.

Keynes also believed, without contradiction, in free markets. The tendency of modern business and capital was toward concentration and away from competitive free enterprise. Government's role was to maintain a competitive economy, which meant guarding against concentration. While consolidation brought efficiencies, it also created the danger of wage decline and inflation, both of which would harm the overall economy. Keynes's thinking on this point would find resonance with a young American political historian and presidential adviser, Arthur Schlesinger Jr., who compared government to an umpire. Government would not direct play, but would enforce the rules ensuring a level playing field for everyone, from the great corporation to the minimum-wage earner.[8]

The balance between public and private enterprise would ultimately be a political decision. Its resolution went to the heart of a democratic society. As Keynes noted, "The political problem of mankind is to combine three things: economic efficiency, social justice and individual liberty." In the two decades after World War II, the nation's political leadership, particularly the three presidents, sought to create and perpetuate this combination. Keynes's "three things" were, of course, interconnected. Individual liberty would flourish in a strong economy that tilted toward social justice.[9]

The architects of deregulation from Ronald Reagan forward assumed that unfettered capitalism produced a vibrant economy. To the contrary, it generated instability and, eventually, serious disruption. As Keynes asserted, "When the capital development of a country becomes a by-product of the activities of a casino, the job is likely to be ill-done." He became a staunch proponent of government regulations to rein in unfettered capitalism. Keynes wrote, "The important thing for Government is not to do things which individuals are doing already, and to do them a little better or a little worse; but to do those things which at present are not done at all." Eighty years earlier, Abraham Lincoln said much the same thing: "The legitimate object of government is to do for a community of people whatever they need to have done, but cannot do at all, or cannot so well do, for themselves, in their separate and individual capacities." Dwight D. Eisenhower employed the Lincoln quote often, usually to fend off conservative critics. Truman and Johnson practiced it. And all employed the standard to expand the role of government.[10]

Princeton sociologist Paul Starr argued that democracy relies on "the ability of political power to control strictly economic forces." In other words, a good government not only promotes prosperity but also preserves liberty. It balances the people's interest with the corporate sector's. Citing the Progressive period, Starr noted that the era's legislation "was a common recognition— a collective revulsion against the privileges of great wealth allied with great power." Government became the countervailing power on behalf of the people.[11]

What government became in the decades after the 1970s was a partner in a coalition with corporations and Wall Street, providing deregulatory cover and a favorable tax structure. The commonwealth ideal disappeared. The Keynesian view adopted by Truman, Eisenhower, and Johnson understood that the era of small businesses and cottage industries had long disappeared, and that an active government was necessary to rein in "the formidable power of the corporation" and protect the interests of the people by keeping the doors of opportunity open. Their administrations bolstered labor unions and promoted the Keynesian management of the economy, and they undertook great projects such as the interstate highway system, the conquest of disease, and the guarantee of civil rights. The government expanded educational, scientific, and technological opportunities and, through its regulatory initiatives, ensured safe food and drugs and cleaner air and water. These enterprises were beyond the capability and means of individuals and corporations. They were, therefore, appropriate projects for government. The federal government during these postwar years seemed to be following city planner Daniel Burnham's dictum "Make no little plans." Government was bold; government was innovative; government was good.[12]

The three presidents played a major role in moving the government to extend the pursuit of happiness to a broader population. They often worked against members of their respective parties. The presidents also sometimes pulled against prevailing public opinion, particularly with respect to their civil rights and immigration initiatives. A majority of Americans did not clamor for civil rights in the years immediately following World War II. They did not demand gender equity, a clean environment, or medical care for the aged. They voiced strong disapproval to loosening immigration laws and expressed concerns about federal intrusion into elementary and secondary education. The presidents used their pulpit, their influence with lawmakers, and their rhetoric to place these issues on the legislative agenda.

All three presidents were nineteenth-century men, though Johnson was born in 1908. They grew up in economically troubled families, in small towns and on farms in borderland areas, and with strong, well-educated, and doting mothers. The basic history they learned at school shaped their views. For Truman and Johnson, William Jennings Bryan, the Great Commoner from Nebraska, was a hero. For Eisenhower it was Abraham Lincoln. The three presidents had a clear sense of what government could do, and, more important, what it ought to do. They preferred to look forward, not back to some golden era. Nostalgia irritated them, though they were keen students of history. And because of that historical knowledge, they had a good sense of where America ought to be heading.

The presidents had long careers in public service before entering the White House. Two of the presidents attained the highest office initially by accident, and the other entered the White House with no experience in elective office. These circumstances likely enhanced the freedom they felt to engage in visionary thinking and in advocating policies that looked ahead to a more inclusive nation rather than back to a more recognizable but restrictive past. They drew upon values from their own pasts to forge a future befitting a modern and diverse society.

The gifts of a good government stimulated innovation, freedom, and upward mobility for millions of Americans in the postwar era. Not equally, but sufficiently so that America in 1970 bore little resemblance to the nation emerging from World War II in 1945. An accessible and affordable college education, a cornucopia of new jobs in a vibrant, transforming economy, universal health care for the elderly, and the conquest of the summer scourge of polio created the best educated, most affluent, most inclusive, and healthiest Americans ever. The results were beneficial for the gifted generation and for the nation as a whole. Individual success enhanced the collective. They were mutually reinforcing. That was one of the key features of the commonwealth ideal.[13]

The federal government did not guarantee success for the gifted generation. But it opened opportunities for Americans first and foremost by securing the basic needs of food, security, jobs, and shelter. The government created the beneficial context within which individuals could reach their greatest potential. Striving for what was now suddenly attainable, these early boomers closed the gap between what was and what ought to be. Their horizons expanded and so did their accomplishments. A sense of liberation accompanied these advances—liberation from traditional stereotypes and taboos; liberation from norms that prescribed specific roles for different groups; and liberation from orthodoxy, be it political, cultural, or religious, that constrained human actions and interactions.[14]

THE BRIEF INTERVIEW EXCERPTS in this book derive primarily, but not exclusively, from Brooklyn's Samuel J. Tilden High School class of 1961. Class members were born between 1943 and 1945, squarely in the time frame of the gifted generation. The interviews do not comprise a scientific sample, but are merely examples of first- and second-generation American kids who benefited from the gifts of the postwar era. They excelled not only in academics but also in artistic and musical pursuits, which they combined with their professional careers. They applied that creativity to those careers, innovating in science, technology, and finance.

The high school was named after failed Democratic presidential candidate Samuel J. Tilden. In typical Brooklyn fashion, that failure had been spectacular. Tilden won the popular vote in the 1876 presidential election, but through Republican chicanery lost the electoral vote. Tilden, therefore, was not merely a loser, but a tragic casualty of the Reconstruction era. I can never recall an instance when either faculty or students ever referred to his Republican opponent other than as Rutherfraud B. Hayes. For long-suffering Dodger fans and for all of us who experienced the condescension of Manhattanites, this unusual historical event generated a melancholy pride.

Tilden High was firmly rooted in the East Flatbush section of Brooklyn. Many of the students' parents had moved to the area just after World War II. It was part of the odyssey that Russian Jewish and Italian immigrants or their offspring undertook from New York's Lower East Side to Brownsville in Brooklyn, and then to East Flatbush. It was an aspirational middle-class to lower-middle-class neighborhood, and it included some public housing as well. The Dutch Reformed Church, where we held our Cub Scout meetings, was a lingering remnant of a time when the area comprised larger homesteads and farms. Synagogues, Jewish community centers, and Roman Catholic schools and churches became the dominant institutions of the district, along with Tilden High.

A few Protestants attended Tilden High, and I met one during my three years of attendance. Of the five thousand students who enrolled in Tilden in the early 1960s, 97.9 percent were either Jewish or Italian, by one estimate. By the time we reached high school, and likely before, all of us understood that white Protestant men ran the country—dominated its politics, its major corporations, its elite educational institutions, and the clubs that perpetuated that power. Many of us knew firsthand how these folks discriminated against blacks, Jews, and Italians, which is why we understood that we had to be not only as good, but better. Which fit in well with the chip-on-their-shoulder attitude of Brooklynites.

I recall many of us crowding into a square near Eastern Parkway and Utica Avenue in Brooklyn on a cool fall evening in 1960 to hear and see candidate John F. Kennedy campaign for the presidency. It was exhilarating to contemplate the possibility that one of us—for that is how we viewed Kennedy—could actually become president of the United States. There, on the makeshift wooden platform, sat Congressman Victor Anfuso, born in Sicily, and Congressman Manny Celler, whose grandparents were respectively Jewish and Catholic German immigrants. These were our people, and it suddenly seemed as if a barrier had been breached. It was the beginning of many such breaches in that wonderful decade. We did our part. But we also had an active and resourceful government at our backs.[15]

In 2006, the New York City Department of Education declared Tilden High a failed school and it ceased to exist as a high school. It was a cruel irony considering how important it was for the strivers of the postwar era and how many notables it turned out, such as labor leader Victor Gotbaum, White House counsel Leonard Garment, baseball star Willie Randolph, civil rights leader Al Sharpton, and the numerous less well-known but equally accomplished former students whose stories appear in this book. Three smaller experimental schools filled the space, but in 2010, Tilden closed its doors for good.

Tilden is a metaphor for what has happened since those promising years in the two decades after World War II. Experts explain such events in terms of demographic changes, disintegrating family structures, and economic transformations not only in Brooklyn, but across urban America. But it is also an indictment of our public policy during the past forty years.[16]

By the late 1960s, the great surge of government programs, expanded opportunities, and the confidence they generated were subsiding. The commonwealth ideal did not go uncontested during the preceding twenty years, and challenges increased significantly in the 1960s. Since FDR's second term, a coalition of Southern Democrats and conservative Republicans had battled federal initiatives. Southern Democrats fought to keep the definition of citizenship in their jurisdictions to whites only. Conservative Republicans, perennially suspicious of government and wary of ethnic and religious diversity, joined in opposition to the commonwealth ideal. They supported restrictions on immigration and labor and opposed many federal initiatives such as the G.I. Bill, major infrastructure projects, health-care assistance, aid to education and scientific research, and environmental protection on both budgetary and philosophical grounds. Religious conservatives rebelled at perceived assaults on traditional gender roles, the banishment of religion from public life, and court decisions against school prayer. Ultimately these factions would coalesce in a restructured Republican Party by the 1970s.

The racial disturbances that rocked the nation's major cities between 1964 and 1968, and the growing opposition to the Vietnam War from 1965 onward, deepened the growing national divide and expanded the opposition to an activist federal government and diminished trust in that government. Older, conservative Americans, including the white working class that, initially at least, did not identify either with Southern Democrats or conservative Republicans, reacted sharply to what they saw as a descent into chaos and a threat to patriotism.

The very size and consequent influence of the early boomers also grated on some older Americans. In education, income, and homeownership, the gifted generation exceeded their predecessors, especially in the nation's metropolitan areas. The declension of the industrial heartland, the growing assertiveness and visibility of blacks, women, and religious minorities, and the loosening (or disappearance) of cultural standards fueled the conservative backlash. Rather than a momentary flare of resentment, these sentiments would persist into the next century. The Republicans exploited it, and the Democrats did little to heal it.

In January 1967, *Time* magazine honored the "Under-25 Generation" as its Man of the Year. From the vantage point of a half century later, the magazine's predictions that the gifted generation would "land on the moon, cure cancer and the common cold, lay out blight-proof, smog-free cities, help end racial prejudice, enrich the underdeveloped world, and write an end to poverty and war" seem a bit over the top. But *Time*'s editors were likely playing it straight. Only the moon landing would come true, but the other milestones seemed within reach based on what had occurred over the previous twenty years. Well into the second decade of the twenty-first century, these other objectives remain elusive, but the saddest assessment is that we seemed to have stopped trying.[17]

The road map to recapture the faith in good government exists. Consider a sampling of what public policy has accomplished since the end of World War II in expanding and creating vast opportunities: supporting medical, scientific, and technological innovation, improving the environment, providing safeguards against discrimination in the workplace and housing, guaranteeing security for seniors, and mandating improvements in workplace, car, and aviation safety. These and other initiatives have made America a better place and made many in America more hopeful. An optimistic nation is a nation that will thrive. The proof is in the past.

The gifted generation grew up in this era of confidence, embracing the disruption of change, not the leaden weight of a static past. They grew up in a nation expanding both economically and morally. The old precept of "work hard and get ahead" moved from proverb to promise. None of the stories chronicled here concern individuals born into privilege. What they were born into were families (typically whole and extended), religious institutions, neighborhoods, good public schools, and an activist federal government. These were the first of many gifts they received. Upward mobility was not a dream; it was an expectation.

In 1931, historian James Truslow Adams published a one-volume history of the United States, *The Epic of America*, in which he coined the phrase *the American dream*. He defined it as "a dream of a social order in which each man and each woman shall be able to attain to the fullest stature of which they are innately capable, and be recognized by others for what they are, regardless of the fortuitous circumstances of birth or position." In 1945 this noble ideal was not yet a reality in America. Adams himself admitted that the dream "has been realized . . . very imperfectly . . . among ourselves."[18]

Minorities confronted varying obstacles toward fulfilling that dream. Gays could remain hidden, Jews and Catholics could change names or life stories, women faced legal and cultural constraints not so easily circumvented, and black Americans lived the most confined lives, limited by the racism that resided at the core of many of our institutions, including the government, and in the actions of white Americans. By 1970, many barriers to full participation in American life for all citizens were lowered, and some erased entirely. Although many individuals contributed to this outcome, the major engine of this transformation was the federal government.

The gift Americans and their government passed along to their children was what journalist George Packer called "the great leveling," the creation of opportunities for a wider portion of the American population than had heretofore been the case. As Packer noted, state universities, progressive taxation, interstate highways, collective bargaining, health insurance for the elderly— all realized in the twenty years after World War II—distributed the nation's gifts to the general population. By doing so, these efforts enhanced individual attainment, or at least made attainment more possible, and, therefore, benefited the nation as well.[19]

The expansion of federal responsibilities ignited the dreams of individuals. The era attained a balance between individualism and community that enabled both to flourish, an important element of the commonwealth ideal. Arthur Schlesinger Jr. called this balance the "vital center." Presidents Truman, Eisenhower, and Johnson believed they governed under that standard.[20]

It was not an easy standard to maintain, especially since the conservative coalition opposed such a role for the federal government. The government's job, Schlesinger explained, was to "order society so that it will subdue the tendencies of industrial organization, produce a wide amount of basic satisfaction and preserve a substantial degree of individual freedom." Had Thomas Jefferson's arcadian republic come to fruition, a strong government would have been superfluous. But the industrial revolution created conditions that were "chilling the lifeblood of society." The state, Schlesinger argued, "had to expand its authority in order to preserve the ties which hold society together." His analysis echoed Keynes's emphasis on the necessity of government to combine "economic efficiency, social justice and individual liberty."[21]

The transformation of the government's role did not violate the nation's founding ideals. The founders had been wise enough to allow for a change in circumstances that they could neither predict nor imagine. That was the genius of their creation. Vice Admiral Hyman Rickover made this point in 1963 when he chronicled the transformation in the national government from the role of "night watchman" to that of "service agency." Though the expanded role of the federal government may not have been exactly what the founders contemplated, their language provided for it. As Rickover explained, "The Declaration of Independence states that 'it is the right of the people' to alter the powers of government in such a way 'as to them shall seem most likely to effect their safety and happiness.'"[22]

But the growth of government contained dangers, especially if a party rose to power and used government to benefit the few instead of the many. This is why the vital center, the balance between the individual and the community, had to be maintained. Franklin D. Roosevelt, though he supported strong government intervention to solve the Depression and win World War II, nevertheless held serious reservations about federal activism: "We have built up new instruments of public power. In the hands of a people's government this power is wholesome and proper. But in the hands of political puppets of an economic autocracy such power would provide shackles for the liberty of the people."[23]

What, then, is the true function of the state? Schlesinger was fond of base-ball metaphors, so he put it this way: "The function of the state . . . is to define the ground rules of the game; not to pitch, catch, hit homers or (just as likely) pop up or throw to the wrong base." The government should maximize options—opportunities—for individuals, but should not guarantee results. The "vital center" reunited "individual and community in fruitful union."[24]

The importance of government in leveling the playing field—to continue the metaphor—was not a new idea. John Quincy Adams asserted in his first message to Congress in 1825, "The great object of the institution of civil government is the improvement of the condition of those who are parties to the social compact, and no government, in whatever form constituted, can accomplish the lawful end of its institution but in proportion as it improves the condition of those over whom it is established."[25]

For those concerned about a government that might be *too* active, economists explained that in an industrialized and increasingly urbanized society, citizens were much more "interdependent" than formerly, and therefore, govern-ment and the private sector needed to work in tandem. The commonwealth ideal posits a balance between government, the individual, and business to ensure that all citizens have the opportunity to succeed: that one person's success redounds to the nation's success. The reality sometimes fell short of the ideal, as prejudice and nostalgia continued to block the path for some. But participation in the benefits of American life grew broader during the two decades following World War II than in any previous era in American history. More Americans than ever were pursuing, and attaining, happiness.

The commonwealth ideal represented a passion for government action to maximize individual achievement for the benefit of the whole. It was not an intellectual creation of the postwar era. The idea of government promoting the general welfare to ensure individual welfare appeared in the economic policies of Alexander Hamilton, Henry Clay's American system, and his disciple Abraham Lincoln's nationalist measures during the Civil War. The commonwealth ideal flourished in the early twentieth century during the Progressive era, the administration of Woodrow Wilson, and, most of all, in Franklin D. Roosevelt's New Deal. President Wilson stated that it was the obligation of the federal government to regulate the economy to protect ordinary Americans "from the consequences of great industrial and social processes which they cannot alter, control, or singly cope with."[26]

World War II demonstrated what we could accomplish with nearly all of our diverse population contributing to the general welfare. The challenge of postwar life was to carry this model forward. And just as the federal government, in partnership with public and private institutions, orchestrated the successful war effort, so too would that partnership build a more inclusive, more just society.

Did America move too fast to build an inclusive society? Did Washington outrun public opinion? Did the disjunction between what America had been earlier in the twentieth century and the nation it was becoming by the late 1960s stimulate the ascendancy of regressive forces already embedded in the political system?

What we know for certain is that political leaders from Richard Nixon forward were willing not only to exploit the divide, but also to broaden and deepen it. Good government became exclusive government. Washington worked for the few, not for the many. Both political parties were complicit in moving government away from the commonwealth ideal. Yes, economic forces contributed to the turbulence. But the economy had been undergoing a transformation since the end of World War II. Government's response in the ensuing two decades was to invest in education, infrastructure, and scientific and technological research—in human capital, in other words. And it worked.

America has, undeniably, experienced significant progress over the past sixty years in expanding the basic rights of citizenship. But progress has slowed and, in some cases, regressed. It is not the economy, globalization, and imperfect trade agreements that have altered the arc of generations following the gifted generation. It is public policy.

THE 1961 TILDEN HIGH SCHOOL graduates sampled here enjoyed an array of options. Rare was the student who had a specific game plan. Pursue what was interesting. The serendipity occasionally led to dead ends, but so what? New roads were opening all the time. Confidence and curiosity marked the graduates' lives; they flourished in an environment that encouraged both. They knew the distance they had traveled from the lives of their parents, who had grown up in very different circumstances. Their parents and teachers had given them the gift of freedom—to choose, to think, to dream. And their government gave them the gift of opportunity, which reinforced that freedom. The success of the gifted generation was a paean of gratitude to the government that required no loud exclamations of patriotism and even called for, on occasion, a little rebellion. For that was what freedom was about.

The Tildenites specialized in creativity, not convention. They had little regard for traditional boundaries, mixing art, music, science, technology, finance, and business, sampling widely different careers. Their musical tastes reflected their upbringing as the first rock 'n' roll generation, an amalgam of musical styles that took them from Buddy Holly to Bob Dylan to B.B. King. Arnie Fleischer joined a bluegrass band and played with some of the greatest artists of the late twentieth century. He also served his country in the Judge Advocate General's Corps of the U.S. Navy and continued his public service for thirty years in the New York Attorney General's Office.[27]

Lew Coopersmith played jazz piano on the radio and acted with Candice Bergen. He also served in the navy in the Public Health Service, got a degree in operations research, opened a consulting firm, and taught for many years at Rider University in New Jersey while maintaining a steady schedule as a chamber music performer. Jane Goren loved biology; she also enjoyed drawing and, for a time, dabbled in medical illustration, then moved on to designing sets for Broadway shows including *Jesus Christ Superstar*. Jane relocated to Los Angeles and began an art career that has taken her all over the world for shows and installations.[28]

Ed Goodgold touched off the national trivia craze with tournaments at Columbia University in the mid-1960s and was instrumental in forming the nostalgia rock group Sha Na Na. He introduced Peter Gabriel and Genesis to American audiences in the early 1970s and went on to become an educator and administrator at New York University. Tony Scarfone studied to be an accountant, but loved art and became one of the leading exhibit designers in the New York metropolitan area, partnering with another Tilden graduate.[29]

Jill Considine planned to be a research scientist and worked in a biology lab conducting pioneering work on DNA and RNA. She left for a year in France and lost her interest in science. Quite by accident, she landed a job with Bankers Trust in New York as a systems programmer, a new field in which she had no training. But Jill's broad liberal arts education prepared her well for

*Jill Considine sworn in as New York State Superintendent of Banks October 1985
while expecting her first child.*

the challenge, and she learned quickly. Eventually, Jill became president of
First Women's Bank in New York, and then banking superintendent for the
State of New York.[30]

Jerry Rosenbaum also had numerous career shifts, starting out with a
degree from Columbia in 1965 in mathematical methods in engineering and
operations research, what today we would call computer science. Like Jill,
Jerry trained for a career that did not exist when he graduated from Tilden in
1961. He went into academia, teaching in Denmark and Sweden, before
returning to the United States for a job at the National Aeronautics and Space
Administration, working on aircraft simulation. He started his own consulting
business in Baltimore, working on, among other projects, computer-animated
design.[31]

Heni Nunno, a divorced single mom, went back to school in 1972. By the
time she finished her studies, she had a doctoral degree in molecular biology
and went to work on a project cloning genes to produce interferon, a protein
effective in protecting cells from bacteria and cancer. Eventually, Heni's
research focused on inactivating viruses, such as those causing AIDS and
hepatitis, in blood products. She earned nineteen patents. Then she became a
lawyer and joined the Innocence Project, an organization that uses DNA
testing to exonerate individuals wrongly accused of crimes. Her legal work led

Heni back to the lab, where she was instrumental in developing the rape kit now used by law enforcement agencies across the country.[32]

These members of the gifted generation benefited from federal support for their education and career advancement. None of these individuals began life in privileged circumstances. Tony Scarfone grew up in the projects—public housing—and his father worked as a meat cutter. Heni Nunno had to go to work at age fourteen to help her family. Jerry Rosenbaum's father worked in a factory making sockets and switches. Jane Goren's dad was an ex-boxer who worked in a used-car lot. Ed Goodgold's father sold army surplus clothing. Jill Considine's father worked for a newspaper. These were not silver-spoon children. But they grew up in a golden era.

They succeeded because of their families, their teachers, and their peers. But they also succeeded because their government created opportunities in infrastructure, education, and work that provided them with the tools and the confidence to take and leave careers until they found what was right for them. Most of them left college and graduate school with no debt, benefiting from an array of federal programs that advanced their education. Some entered professions that did not exist just a few years earlier, but emerged because of federal research grants.

These members of the gifted generation came to adulthood confidently, in a confident nation. They possessed the freedom to learn, to experiment, even to fail. Ultimately, they each discovered a life that provided a livelihood and fulfilled a passion. Their stories were told many times over across the country. Good government aided that process of discovery. Together, they helped to build the nation. This is their history and that of their government.

PART I

CROSSING THE MERIDIAN

CHAPTER 1

MOVING

PEACE. SUCH A LOVELY and loving word. After fifteen years of depression and war the word augured possibility and hope. Returning servicemen had no time for lengthy explanations of what they sought. As one responded to a reporter, he simply wanted to "make up for lost time." Time taken from getting married and starting a family. Time taken from education. Time taken from getting ahead at the office or on the farm. A sailor just off his transport in Seattle blurted to a reporter's question about his plans, "Raise babies and keep house!" Their dreams were simple, but their very simplicity indicated the dislocations that had affected their lives.[1]

Concerns tempered the euphoria of peace. With over 15 million returning veterans and 10 million civilian employees of defense industries soon out of work, would the country lapse into an economic depression? Would inflation rob returning vets and their families of prosperity? Would reconversion stretch out to thwart a swift return to a normal civilian life? Would shortages of food, housing, and durable goods turn anticipation into despair? Would international tensions resume quickly as the Soviet Union replaced Nazi Germany as a threat to the security of America and its allies?

The national mood during the first year after the war was an odd cross between somber and hopeful. One exasperated writer complained that the United States was "too full of worries . . . We worry about politics and about Congress and about the conduct of the government . . . We worry about foreign affairs. We worry about prices. And we worry a lot about production and about labor."[2]

The government had spent the United States into prosperity during World War II. Defense industries, infrastructure projects such as roads, airports, and water and sewer systems, poured billions into the pockets of workers and corporations. As early as 1943, economists worried about "economic chaos" after the war ended. Reconverting war plants to peacetime needs, the layoff of millions of workers as defense industries wound down, and the simultaneous influx of millions of returning soldiers into the job market presaged a reversion to difficult economic times.[3]

Peace and prosperity energized the conservative coalition. Labor troubles were a certainty as unions sought to build upon their wartime gains and management tried to restore some of its former power when labor surpluses existed. Conservatives hoped to curtail labor's might. The stupendous national debt incurred by the war would likely result in higher taxes. Expected bonuses for veterans would make paring down that debt more difficult. The federal government would probably need to launch major infrastructure projects to absorb the unemployed. And shortages would send inflation skyrocketing at a time of projected high unemployment. Deficits, tax hikes, and inflation were an unholy trinity for conservatives. A major cut in federal spending, conservatives believed, would remedy all three dangers. In late 1944, writer Bernard DeVoto observed "a fear of the coming of peace" due to the economic uncertainty. Conservatives, however, viewed peace as an opportunity to take back their government. They had succeeded in stalling New Deal initiatives between 1937 and 1941, threatening the modest economic recovery. Now, they sought a broader reversal.[4]

The Cold War, emerging so soon after the defeat of the Axis powers, scarcely gave Americans time to celebrate their hard-won victories. And now, at the dawn of the nuclear age, the perils of conflict multiplied. The Communist insurgency in China contributed to national jitters. For a generation of Americans, many of whom had lived through the prosperous 1920s only to witness a near-total economic collapse and then a bloody war, neither peace nor prosperity were sure things. A group of MIT professors scolded cities for their lack of preparedness in the event of nuclear war and presented a plan that is laughable only in retrospect.[5]

The economy proved more resilient than the pundits. As early as February 1946, experts expressed surprise that the physical reconversion of war plants seemed to be going well and quickly, unemployment was far less than government economists had predicted, and income and retail sales had risen. The threat of inflation lingered as did persistent shortages, and both the Truman administration and Congress miscalculated on price controls. But there were hopeful signs these issues were manageable once production satisfied consumer demand. And consumers had cash. High wages and full employment during the war had put money into the pockets of millions of Americans, though there was precious little they could buy. With peace, the dam burst. As one editor put it in 1946, "Never before has the average man been so ready and able to buy things."[6]

During the Christmas shopping season of 1946, Macy's department store in New York City set an all-time daily sales record on December 5 of nearly $1.5 million, a record broken two weeks later. A headline trumpeted, "Shoppers Overrun New York Stores in History's Biggest Buying Spree." By early 1947, as production ratcheted up, the threat of inflation moderated. W. S. Woytinsky, an economist for the 20th Century Fund, attributed some of the good economic news to government policy, particularly the G.I. Bill, which pumped money into the housing market and new businesses, as well as seed funds for educating former soldiers, who could improve their incomes with a college degree. In October 1948, *Life* magazine's editor crowed, "Production stands on its greatest peacetime pinnacle, a height no other nation in all the years of the world has ever scaled."[7]

The median income of nonfarm families rose 66 percent between 1947 and 1957, the greatest decadal increase in American history. The broad affluence opened up experiences heretofore reserved for the wealthy, such as travel to Europe, which reached record numbers in 1949. As one writer noted, "Globetrotting is no longer the privilege of the well-to-do: the butchers and bakers and students and farmers now far outnumber and outspend the merchant chiefs." An increase in patronage of local orchestras, museums, and libraries, and the popularity of garden clubs and of reading the Great Books, also received notice in the press. Sports fans packed stands, especially in the baseball parks to watch Jackie Robinson of the Dodgers, Joe DiMaggio of the Yankees, Ted Williams of the Red Sox, and Stan "the Man" Musial of the St. Louis Cardinals. Americans were learning "that prosperity, once the primary needs of life are cared for, is only good as underpinning for the good life."[8]

In 1950, *Scientific American* calculated that, even allowing for inflation, Americans spent 96 percent more on books than in 1940, 140 percent more for toys and sports equipment, 219 percent more for photo developing, 129 percent more for flowers and seeds, and 263 percent more for phonographs and records, musical instruments, radios, and television sets. Much of this increase reflected the baby boom and the movement to the suburbs, but also the widespread prosperity of the American population. In the 1920s the top 5 percent income earners accounted for 38 percent of the total national income; by 1950, they accounted for only 17 percent. Which meant that many more Americans could afford the durable goods such as automobiles, refrigerators, washing machines, air conditioners, and power mowers. Economists agreed that the government played an important role in raising "the purchasing power of the formerly poor." The result was not only the rapid expansion of a middle class, but also the enrichment of civic life. By helping people become more independent, government assisted strengthening the bonds of the nation.[9]

Government spending lit the economic fires of the postwar era. Outlays for the G.I. Bill and higher education, and housing, mortgage, and tax subsidies, boosted consumer spending. Federal spending under the Truman administration dwarfed the outlays of the New Deal. In 1948, federal expenditures, which had reached as high as $95.2 billion in fiscal 1945, had shrunk to $36.5 billion, mostly from a decline in defense spending. But that latter figure far exceeded the $9.4 billion the New Deal spent in 1939.[10]

By 1952, the last year of the Truman administration, the economic numbers confirmed the extended reach of the nation's prosperity. The gross national product was $16 billion more than at its peak during the war (1944). Unemployment stood at 2 percent, below the figure most economists would call full employment. In 1952 alone, per capita income increased by 8 percent. America was building—houses, roads, utilities, and commercial and industrial buildings.[11]

Prosperity spread more evenly across the land. The South, identified as the nation's "Number One economic problem" in a 1938 government report, had, within a decade, become a promising region for economic development. Building on wartime industries, such as the Bell bomber plant in Atlanta, that had raised the skill levels of workers and drawn farmers from unproductive agriculture into the cities, the New South appeared to be poised to make good on its publicity. Businesses expanded, such as Malcolm McLean's trucking company in Winston-Salem, which grew from one to one thousand trucks between the beginning of the war and 1949. Republic Steel's new plant at Gadsden, Alabama, rolled out steel pipe for natural gas lines in the burgeoning subdivisions of the region. Furniture plants in High Point, North Carolina, could barely keep up with orders to furnish new homes. Hopeful articles appeared that the South's prosperity would eventually ameliorate its troubled race relations.[12]

The Pacific Northwest, long identified as a "colonial" economy dependent on lumber, fishing, and agriculture, underwent a transformation as the federal government harnessed the Columbia River's power to produce one third of the nation's hydroelectric power. The Grand Coulee and Bonneville dams added to the region's capacity. The Grand Coulee was the biggest project ever built, four times bigger than the Great Pyramids when it was completed in 1942. The Northwest received more government funds for industrial development during the war than any other region, the largest share of which—$347 million—went to the Hanford Engineering Works in central Washington State, where scientists produced plutonium from uranium for the first atomic bomb. Government subsidies poured into shipyards, aircraft factories, and electrochemical plants, most of which declined after the war, but the Boeing company refitted to produce aircraft for the growing commercial air market. The diversity of the Northwest's economy reduced dependence on the lumber industry and enabled the federal government to place the Northwest's forests on a sustained-yield basis.[13]

All of these developments resulted in what the National Bureau of Economic Research (NBER) called in 1951 "one of the greatest social revolutions in history." At the core of this revolution was the dramatic change in the distribution of income. By 1951, one half of the nation's families were classified by the NBER as middle-class. Fifty years earlier, that figure stood at 25 percent. Adjusting for inflation, the annual income of a factory worker went up sixfold during that half century, even after taxes. The transformation broadened people's horizons and allowed them to fulfill aspirations for education, jobs, homes, and leisure.[14]

Management consultant Peter F. Drucker wrote in 1952 that the expansion of the middle class also resulted from a change in attitude by corporate executives. Earlier in the century, Drucker explained, American businessmen believed that regard for the social and economic well-being of workers and the nation were irrelevant to the corporate mission, a philosophy best summarized by President Calvin Coolidge's statement "The business of this country is business." Drucker believed that the corporation at midcentury would phrase its philosophy as "The business of this business is the country"—in other words, the commonwealth ideal of interdependence. Drucker believed that management was coming to understand that treating workers with dignity would lead to greater productivity.[15]

The workforce itself was changing. Demand increased for positions requiring greater skills, training, and education. As Drucker noted, "An American youngster starting out on his career has at least two chances out of three that he will end up in a skilled, professional or executive job paying a middle-class wage or better, or as his own boss in his own business." This was the economy that the gifted generation would grow into.[16]

The achievement of this broad prosperity occurred when the top income bracket in 1949 paid a marginal tax rate of 82 percent, a figure that would climb to 91 percent in the 1950s. Taxes on corporate profits were two times as large as they were in 2017. The tax on large estates rose to more than 70 percent. Not only did businesses operate under a relatively high tax burden, but they also confronted a labor force where one third of the workers were unionized and bargained with executives as equals. From the conservatives' perspective, that such a tax structure produced great prosperity seemed counterintuitive.

But it merely confirmed Keynes's economic theories of how an activist state could generate wealth in a transforming economy and create spheres of mutual interest across disparate elements of the national economy. Corporations in the early 1950s, economist Paul Krugman observed, served "an array of 'stakeholders' as opposed to merely serving stockholders."[17]

Frank W. Abrams, chairman of Standard Oil of New Jersey, articulated this notion of "stakeholder capitalism," a corporate form of the commonwealth ideal that balanced the interests of all members in the firm's family. "The job of management," Abrams explained, "is to maintain an equitable and working balance among the claims of the various directly affected interest groups," which he defined as "stockholders, employees, customers and the public at large." Other executives shared this view, such as Earl S. Willis at General Electric: "The employee who can plan his economic future with reasonable certainty is an employer's most productive asset." Both median family income and productivity nearly doubled between 1948 and 1973.[18]

Labor unions pioneered the concept of "living" or "family" wages, and corporations bought into the philosophy, sometimes grudgingly. The relative weakness of foreign competition only partially accounted for the prosperity of the late 1940s and 1950s. Companies were responsible not only to their shareholders, but also to their employees. Henry Ford had discovered as far back as 1914 that higher wages had a palliative effect on turnover and absenteeism. When he began to pay an unprecedented wage of $5 a day, productivity and profits rose.[19]

Any company at which a majority of workers voted to join a union in a federally supervised election had to sit down at the bargaining table and negotiate a contract that included clear rules and procedures and protected workers from arbitrary treatment by management. Union workers could rely on regular wage increases that allowed them to purchase cars, appliances, and homes. They also wielded political muscle to sustain regular increases in the minimum wage. Jack Metzgar, who grew up as a son of a steelworker, recalled, "If what we lived through in the 1950s was not liberation, then liberation never happens in real human lives."[20]

In the postwar years, corporate leaders formed the Committee for Economic Development (CED), which helped to forge a consensus supporting strong unions, bigger government, and the welfare state. For example, the CED called for higher taxes to fund the Korean War effort. As corporate analyst Mark Mizruchi noted of the CED, "They believed that in order to maintain their privileges, they had to insure that ordinary Americans were having their needs met."[21]

In 1955, *Fortune* magazine published an article on the lifestyles of that year's top executives compared with the opulent lives led by the barons of finance and industry early in the twentieth century. The typical executive in 1955 lived in a relatively modest suburban house, employed part-time help, and usually owned a small boat. Data supported this portrait. By 1955, the incomes of the top 0.01 percent of Americans were less than half of what they had been in the late 1920s, and their share of total income was down by 75 percent. In 1950, the income gap between the least paid and best paid workers diminished to its lowest point in the twentieth century. In the 1950s, the corporate CEO received twenty times as much as the firm's typical employee; by 2016, CEOs averaged more than two hundred times that of the average worker.[22]

Economists called it "the virtuous circle of growth": well-paid workers fueled consumer demand, which, in turn, generated business expansion and hiring, raising corporate profits to induce higher wages and more hiring. The American social structure changed its shape from a pyramid to a diamond. In 1929, 80 percent of American families earned less than $4,000 a year (in 1950 dollars); by 1953, more than 58 percent had annual incomes ranging from $4,000 to $10,000. Factory workers saw their paychecks double between 1945 and 1970. That told only part of the story as companies also provided health insurance and generous pensions.[23]

A consumer culture flourished and, therefore, so did the economy. Everyone, it seemed, had money to spend, and there were so many more things to spend it on. A writer in *Fortune* in 1956 remarked, "Never has a whole people spent so much money on so many expensive things in such an easy way as Americans are doing today." *Fortune* noted that middle-class families— those earning more than $5,000 annually by the mid-1950s—were increasing by 1.1 million a year. By 1956, there were 16.6 million such families.[24]

The baby boom fueled economic growth. In 1940 fewer than 11 million Americans were under the age of five; by 1950 it was 16 million. The five- to seventeen-year-old age group increased by only fifty-two thousand during the 1940s, but exploded by 8.3 million in the 1950s. Economists talked about "prosperity by population." Diapers were a $32 million industry by 1947, and $50 million a decade later. One out of every ten Americans consumed baby food, at a rate of 1.5 billion jars a year, in 1953; in 1940, it was a modest 270 million jars. And toys? Every year after 1940, the toy industry set records. Bicycle sales doubled each year; parents spent $75 million on cowboy regalia. The kids market drew in $33 billion annually by the early 1950s.[25]

Those new homes that housed growing families required furnishings and appliances. The average suburban family income in 1950 was $6,500 ($65,000 in 2016 dollars). Two-car families increased by at least 750,000 a year after 1951. In that year, 40.3 million cars were registered to 39.9 million families. In 1945, new car sales totaled 69,500; in 1955, consumers purchased 7.9 million automobiles. Many of these autos could be found parked at suburban shopping malls. The nation's first enclosed mall opened outside Minneapolis in 1956.[26]

Prosperity was broad but not yet pervasive. In 1947, 30 percent of the population was poor by government standards. One third of American homes had no running water, two fifths had no flush toilets, and three fifths lacked central heating. Almost half of Americans toiled at manual labor on farms or in factories, mines, or construction. Nearly one out of five Americans worked on the land.[27]

It was not long—maybe five years after the end of World War II—that the combination of consumer buying power and automobiles generated new types of entrepreneurial activities. In the summer of 1953, Eugene Ferkauf drove through farmland near Westbury, Long Island. He envisioned a large store that would sell everything, and everything at a discount. The service in these stores would be minimal, and the ambience would hardly evoke Saks Fifth Avenue. He called his new retail establishment E. J. Korvette. Legend had it that the name derived from "eight Jewish Korean War veterans," but although he was indeed a vet and Jewish, the name came from the first-name initials of Ferkauf and his Samuel J. Tilden High School buddy Joe Swillenberg. *Korvette* was a derivation of the Canadian submarine chaser, the corvette. Ferkauf just liked the name.[28]

Ferkauf had retail experience, having worked in his father's two luggage stores in midtown Manhattan. For ambitious Jews in the 1930s, retail was one of the relatively few avenues of work open to members of their faith. Ferkauf recalled one of his dad's regular customers, an executive at Texaco, who, in response to the elder Ferkauf's question about a summer job for young Gene at the oil company, said, "Harry, you know how I feel about you and Gene, but Texaco doesn't hire Jews." So, young Gene struck out on his own by opening a discount store in Manhattan and, in 1951, a second store in the city before he headed for suburbia.[29]

On December 2, 1953, opening day and just in time for the Christmas shopping season, more than one thousand customers burst through the doors of the Westbury store, completely overwhelming the sales staff. It was the beginning of a suburban retail empire. By 1959, E. J. Korvette had annual sales of $157.7 million in over twenty-five suburban stores. While Ferkauf did not invent discounting, he took it down to a new level, sometimes reducing items more than 40 percent below what traditional stores sold them for. Ferkauf sold his share in Korvette for $20 million in 1966, when the brand had forty-five department stores and sixty supermarkets. He then gave away most of his fortune to cultural and Jewish charities.[30]

During the early years of the Great Depression, the textile industry of New England collapsed, and two brothers, Dick and Maurice McDonald, took off for California. They opened a hot dog stand in 1937 near the Santa Anita race-track, a profitable endeavor until the racing season ended. Their next venture was a small drive-in restaurant in San Bernardino in 1940, which was considerably more profitable.[31]

Southern California led a trend that would take hold after the war: more mobility and greater distances between work and home. Lingering over a meal and spending a great deal of money on it were not options for young families stressed between home and work. The McDonalds pared down their menu to just hamburgers, which enabled them to mechanize their preparation, and they eliminated plates and silverware and, thus, the need for a dishwasher. By the mid-1950s, the brothers were clearing $100,000 a year, an impressive sum considering their hamburgers cost fifteen cents each.

In 1954, Ray Kroc, a high school dropout, was selling Multi-Mixers, a machine that spun five spindles from a single motor and made great milk shakes. But the soda fountain was a vanishing institution, and sales were sluggish, except, that is, for a small hamburger place in San Bernardino, which could not get enough of them. Kroc arrived before lunch on a visit one day, and already a long line had formed. Once inside, he saw a clean establishment that slung cheap hamburgers for each customer in about fifteen seconds. There was no tipping. The brothers were looking for someone to handle franchising for them. Ray Kroc took the job and made McDonald's a national brand. By 1960, Kroc was opening one hundred restaurants a year, and he had bought out the brothers.[32]

THE DOOMSDAY SCENARIO FORECAST by some economists as early as 1943 never occurred. There was some inflation, labor unrest in 1946, and shortages that lasted, in some cases, to the end of the decade. The Truman administration, by extending the New Deal, loosening credit for home purchases, expanding grant programs under the G.I. Bill for education, and maintaining a progressive tax system enabled Americans to improve their lives and their bank accounts. Above all, consumers drove the economy. The demand for goods and services, particularly as a result of the baby boom, touched off a decade of economic expansion the size of which had never before occurred in American history. When Harry Truman left the White House in January 1953, Americans had gained 11 million new jobs in the previous seven years.

By then, it seemed as if labor, capital, and government were in equilibrium, attaining the balance implicit in the commonwealth ideal, which drove postwar policy. The U.S. government operated on a system of checks and balances. So did the economy. These elements functioned, according to economist John Kenneth Galbraith, as "countervailing powers," preventing excess and ensuring prosperity.[33]

In his influential book *The Affluent Society* (1958), Galbraith was one of the first economists to write about the emergence of a "New Class" and the gifted progeny of that class—gifted in the sense that they would reap the benefits of their parents' upward mobility. As Galbraith wrote, "The New Class is not exclusive . . . Any individual whose adolescent situation is such that sufficient time and money are invested in his preparation, and who has at least the talents to carry him through the formal academic routine, can be a member." In the 1850s, this New Class, Galbraith explained, numbered only a few thousand; a century later, the figure was in the millions.[34]

Membership bestowed certain advantages, noted Galbraith: "Exemption from manual toil; escape from boredom and confining and severe routine; the chance to spend one's life in clean and physically comfortable surroundings; and some opportunity for applying one's thoughts to the day's work." The expansion of the middle class involved, then, more than an economic improvement. It consisted of an enhanced quality and style of life as well. The gifted generation would enter a society with better opportunities than any previous generation.[35]

JERRY ROSENBAUM'S FATHER CAME to the United States from Poland in 1928; his mother's family emigrated from Bessarabia (now part of Moldova and Ukraine), with a stop in Montreal. Jerry's father was a trained machinist, but due to anti-Semitism in New York's machinist union, he could not get a job in his field during the 1920s, so, with only a eighth-grade education, he worked in a luncheonette until he found a better-paying job at a company that manufactured sockets. Jerry's mother had a high school degree and secured employment at the New York State Department of Labor.

Their lives were improving. When the Rosenbaums first arrived in the United States, they settled, like so many other Jewish immigrants, in the Lower East Side of Manhattan. The Rosenbaums followed the mobility pattern of fellow Jewish immigrants, moving to Brownsville in Brooklyn and, in 1952, to an apartment in East Flatbush. The family had moved up to "the higher end of the lower class," Jerry recalled.[36]

Henrietta Nunno's grandparents came from Russia and Romania, but fled to Turkey during the pogroms of the late-nineteenth and early-twentieth centuries, emigrating to the United States in the early 1920s. Escaping one tragedy, Henrietta's family experienced another. Settling in Brooklyn, Henrietta's paternal grandparents had four children. One Sunday afternoon enjoying a picnic at a lake in upstate New York, two of their children drowned, the older sister while trying to save her brother. Henrietta was named after that girl.

Henrietta's maternal grandparents were, compared to her father's family, relatively well-off. Her mother's father was a tailor, and his wife worked at home as a seamstress. By the time Henrietta's parents married, they could afford a walk-up apartment in East Flatbush, where Heni, as everyone called her, shared a bedroom with her parents while her older brother slept on the sofa. Then, in 1957, the family made the "big move" to a two-bedroom apartment in the same building.

Heni's father had difficulty working as he battled depression through most of his life. Her mother got a part-time job as a bookkeeper in her brother's business. Heni remembers her family as being poor, the last in her building to have a television set and never able to purchase a car like her other neighbors. Necessity forced Heni into the workforce at the age of fourteen, as a secretary to a rabbi after school.[37]

Neither of these family moves involved great distances in geography, but they did signal a step upward in status. These newer urban neighborhoods teemed with children of the gifted generation. They used the wide streets of East Flatbush and public school yards as stickball courts, touch-football fields, and baseball diamonds. These were improvised venues, as were the games, often with quirky rules always applied seriously and equally to all. They reflected newly prosperous circumstances generated by hard work, better education, a growing economy, and government programs such as Federal Housing Administration (FHA) mortgages and loans from the G.I. Bill.

The American dream manifested itself in these modest moves. They enabled families and their children to contemplate even greater dreams. They were not so naïve as to believe there were no barriers to overcome—their economic condition, their religion, their ethnicity—but they believed these obstacles mattered less than merit. Their new surroundings were first testimonials to that belief. They were inveterate optimists: optimistic for themselves, their families, and their country.

CHAPTER 2

PIONEERS

THE RETURN OF 15 MILLION VETERANS had created fears of mass unemployment that never materialized. By September 1947, 92 percent of veterans were working or in school. Seven out of every ten college students were veterans. Dean Mabry of Trinidad, Colorado, was typical of many returning GIs. Mabry was married and had a three-year-old daughter. When he was drafted in 1941, he was about to enter law school. Twenty-seven years old when he returned from the war, he enrolled in the University of Colorado. He was surprised to find that 90 percent of his entering class were veterans and the average age was thirty-one.[1]

Finding housing was much more difficult than obtaining a place in the university, but he finally found a basement apartment for his young family. Through the G.I. Bill he received $90 a month, which covered half of the family's expenses. Mabry estimated that about 50 percent of his fellow vets would not be going to school without the government's help. In an era when a high school education was sufficient to guarantee a relatively well-paying, stable job, a college degree ensured a higher income in the new white-collar economy. In turn, the higher salaries fueled consumer buying, which buoyed the economy.[2]

Sam Marchesi had an eighth-grade education, dropping out of school to help support his mother and eight siblings when his father died. With American entrance into World War II, Marchesi enlisted in the army. When he was discharged at the end of the war, he used the benefits of the G.I. Bill to pay for vocational training in architectural drawing and carpentry. He went on to a successful career as a custom-home builder. "I think it was a great thing that the government did, to give us this opportunity to pick up where we left off . . . Thank God the government had the doors open for us."[3]

There was a sense that, regardless of an individual's origins, the benefits of education, housing, and work were within reach of anyone. John Mink, who owed his education to the G.I. Bill, looked back on the postwar years: "Those who became the movers and shakers came from backgrounds that had been oppressed before the war. It created a whole new United States. It really changed the dynamics."[4]

G.I. Bill business loans also helped to launch ambitious enterprises for returning veterans. Mary Connelly and Mary Ransone, two former sergeants from Connecticut, each had prewar experience in sales, accounting, and advertising. They put together a business plan for a dress shop and secured a bank loan guaranteed by the Veterans Administration. By late 1946, Mary Kay of Wilton, Inc., was a thriving business.[5]

Stories like these convinced Peter F. Drucker to single out the G.I. Bill as transformative in moving the country toward a "knowledge society." By 1956, white-collar workers outnumbered blue-collar workers for the first time. The Servicemen's Readjustment Act, as the G.I. Bill was formally called, applied only to war veterans, but it served as a national insurance policy. Guaranteeing loans with no down payment, it fueled the growth of the crucial housing industry. The bill's education provisions absorbed several million of the 15 million returning veterans into institutions of higher education.[6]

None of this was foreordained. The American Legion proposed a G.I. Bill of Rights to the Roosevelt administration late in 1943. The proposal encountered rough going in the House of Representatives, particularly from Mississippi's John E. Rankin, chairman of the Committee on World War Veterans' Legislation.[7]

Since the 1930s, Southern lawmakers had dominated committee chairmanships in Congress. Most legislation had to go through committees. A coalition of Southern Democrats and conservative Northern (mainly Midwestern) Republicans restricted New Deal legislation after 1937 when President Roosevelt attempted to expand the number of Supreme Court justices to ensure favorable rulings on the constitutionality of his New Deal measures. Republicans perceived the move as an attempt to bypass Congress, thus upsetting the balance of powers. Southern Democrats feared that a more liberal court could strike down the South's voting and segregation statues aimed at maintaining white supremacy.

Congressman Rankin believed that higher education held dubious benefits anyway, producing an "overeducated and undertrained" population. Besides, professors invariably held views well to the left of mainstream America. "I would rather send my child to a red schoolhouse," Rankin explained, "than to a red schoolteacher." Since the G.I. Bill also provided unemployment insurance for veterans, Rankin also feared the legislation would encourage his state's black population to remain idle. But overwhelming public support for the returning veterans overcame the South's parochial concerns. After considerable debate, the G.I. Bill of Rights passed in late 1944.[8]

Rankin was not the only skeptic. Some university educators worried about diluting the quality of their student bodies with returning veterans. Translated, this sentiment reflected a fear of the sons and daughters of Catholic and Jewish immigrants entering the hallowed halls of elite institutions. Robert Maynard Hutchins, president of the University of Chicago, predicted that tens of thousands of soldiers would matriculate "only because they cannot get jobs." They would convert universities "into educational hobo jungles." Hutchins instead recommended that those veterans seeking a college education through the G.I. Bill submit to an entrance exam first.[9]

But universities liked the government money that accompanied each veteran, and the GIs flocked to campuses across the country. More than 50 percent of eligible veterans, or nearly 8 million former soldiers, took advantage of the bill's educational provisions. This number was more than twice the figure projected by the G.I. Bill's authors.[10]

The seriousness of these students reflected their diversity in age and family circumstances. Nearly one third had spouses, and one in ten had children. The bill covered outright the cost of tuition plus a modest living stipend that relieved most veterans from the necessity of having to balance full-time employment with obtaining a college degree, thus broadening the class diversity of campuses across the country.[11]

Isaac Gellert grew up during the Great Depression. Struggles in the family's small business led to his father's premature death. After serving in the war, Isaac took advantage of the G.I. Bill: "I had the opportunity to go to Columbia University for the simple reason that the G.I. Bill paid everything . . . Columbia was essentially free." Anthony Miller became a Catholic priest on the G.I. Bill. Had the legislation not existed, "I would have kept working for the insurance company" that employed him prior to the war. The bill allowed him to obtain a college degree that led him to the seminary. "I think the two most influential moments in the American Catholic Church," he recalled years later, "were the Second Vatican Council [and] also the G.I. Bill." Indeed, the bill encouraged large numbers of working-class Jewish and Catholic war veterans to go to college.[12]

Heinz Kissinger was one of the veterans who went to college on the G.I. Bill. Born in Fürth, Germany, in 1923, young Heinz and his family escaped the Nazis in 1938, settling in New York City. Now known as Henry, he entered City College, a free institution at the time, to pursue a degree in accounting. But the war interrupted his studies. Sergeant Kissinger resumed his education after the war at Harvard, using the G.I. Bill of Rights to afford what would have been impossible on his own. He graduated in 1950 at the top of his class with a Phi Beta Kappa key and admission to Harvard's doctoral program in international relations.[13]

The G.I. Bill was a federal initiative that provided opportunity, but did not guarantee results. Individual veterans had to take advantage of the legislation, or not. In an era when a high school education was sufficient to sustain an adequate wage and working life, one might assume that the compulsion for a college education would not resonate widely, particularly among working-class veterans. This was not the case, however.

The elusiveness of college for working-class Americans derived both from cultural factors—few family members and friends went to college—and from financial exigencies. Even if the cost of college was relatively reasonable, postponing an income was not an option for many returning veterans. What the G.I. Bill accomplished was to remove or at least lighten the immediate economic burden in exchange for future economic rewards. And it changed the culture as well. Most of the veterans who took advantage of the G.I. Bill were the first in their families to attend college. Many, in turn, passed down the habit to their children, the children of the gifted generation. A college education became contagious. As one beneficiary noted, the G.I. Bill "gave our family a 'boost' that has allowed us to help our children to college more than I had expected, i.e., G.I. Bill benefits have been passed to a second generation!"[14]

Also changed was the national attitude toward education. In 1950, colleges and universities awarded 496,000 degrees, the highest number in American history. As the nation moved away from an industrial economy, institutions of higher learning were turning out a workforce well suited to smooth the economic transition. Arthur Schlesinger Jr. praised the G.I. Bill as "the most underrated national turning point" because it "contributed enormously to the release of economic and intellectual energy that carried postwar America to the summit of the world." Of the many gifts to the gifted generation, this federal policy was among the finest. It fulfilled both the short-term economic needs of the nation and the long-term educational needs of a transforming economy.[15]

The G.I. Bill provided a path of upward mobility to a greater extent than probably any other single piece of legislation in American history to that point. The son of a shoe salesman became the chief of seismological services for the U.S. government; the upholsterer's son became a teacher; the longshoreman's son became an attorney; the coal miner's son became a geologist; the shoemaker's son became an engineer; and the window cleaner's son became a chemist. In turn, many of these beneficiaries of the G.I. Bill passed along to their offspring both their new status and the opportunity to build upon that success. They were pioneers for their families, their communities, and their country.[16]

Although the G.I. Bill provided unprecedented opportunities for a college education, it often did not cover the entire cost. The rising cost of college was a growing concern in the immediate postwar years and raised fears that such inflation could "make higher education a luxury available only to the wealthy class."[17]

The average single veteran could get by on the $65 a month the government provided for his subsistence, and married veterans living on campus could afford food and residence on the $90 a month offered by the government. But campuses had precious few available rooms for the large numbers of veterans, single or married, and by 1947 80 percent of veterans enrolled in institutions of higher education lived off campus. Their costs were at least $105 per month.[18]

The Truman administration sought to address the veterans' financial squeeze. Harry Truman would be the last president without a college degree. He had had both the desire and the intellectual ability to attend college, but not the finances. Perhaps for that reason, he valued all the more affordable higher education. Seeing the rush of veterans to colleges, Truman established the President's Commission on Higher Education in the summer of 1946. Leading educators and laymen joined the panel. The thirst for a college degree among Americans who had never before thought they could obtain one surprised the experts. With this in mind, the commission developed a series of proposals by the end of 1947 and presented them to the president.

After the Civil War, most states provided free public secondary education for their youngsters. Truman's commission wanted to extend that benefit to the college level. The G.I. Bill had, in effect, made higher education free to tens of thousands of veterans. Why not offer that aid to all qualified citizens? "The American people," the commissioners advised, "should set as their ultimate goal an educational system in which at no level—high school, college, graduate school or professional school—will a qualified individual in any part of the country encounter an insuperable economic barrier to the attainment of the kind of education suited to his aptitudes and interests."[19]

To accomplish this, the commission advanced three proposals: the federal government would eliminate tuition fees for freshmen and sophomores at public institutions, reduce the fees to 1939 levels for juniors and seniors, and extend the G.I. Bill to all eligible college students by offering scholarships for enrollment at state-approved public or private institutions. Those students who qualified as "needy" would receive a maximum of $800 a year (nearly

$9,000 in today's dollars; the maximum federal Pell Grant for low-income students today is $5,730). Since these inducements and the students who obtained them would burden the physical plants and faculty of most institutions, the third recommendation of the panel was to subsidize buildings, salaries, and operating expenses for public universities. The bill would initially cost at least $1 billion, eventually rising to $2 billion.[20]

An editorial in *Life*, a publication often skeptical of major federal initiatives, argued that, in the case of higher education, logic should outweigh ideology. States alone could not bear the burden of educating their youth, especially in poorer states. The commission's proposals would equalize college education, not only for the states, but also for "all races, colors, and creeds." Neither states nor students could fund such an enterprise. A family with an income of $7,500 ($75,200 today) had a 30 percent chance of sending their children to college; however, a family with an income of $2,500 ($25,100 today) had only a 10 percent chance due to the cost of a higher education. The editorial concluded, "Federal aid need not turn into federal control . . . A basic principle of American democracy is the more education, the better. We cannot indefinitely afford not to have it. A high-school education is a U.S. civil birthright. Why not college, too?" The commission's recommendations, however, went nowhere in the Eightieth Congress, with a Republican majority and Southern Democrats controlling key committees. The Southerners feared potential federal incursions on white supremacy, and the conservative Republicans recoiled at the proposals' budget implications. Besides, they viewed education as strictly a state and local matter.[21]

States were more receptive to higher-educational initiatives inspired by the G.I. Bill. New York State, for example, began to create a statewide system of low-tuition colleges and universities in the 1940s. Buoyed by federal dollars, courtesy of the G.I. Bill, other states expanded and improved their higher education systems. For those students who could not take advantage of the G.I. Bill, tuition was relatively low, and work-study arrangements were abundant. Prior to World War II, the quality of state universities rarely rose above the mediocre. After the war, this was no longer the case, especially in generous states such as New York, California, Michigan, and North Carolina. In the 1950s, for example, more graduates of the University of Michigan were listed in *Who's Who in America* than those from Harvard and Yale. The University of California, Berkeley, led the nation in Guggenheim Fellowships awarded to its faculty in 1960. Whether it was the cyclotron on the Berkeley campus that revolutionized physics or the pioneering research in antibiotics at Rutgers, the state university came into its own in the decade after World War II. Permit the hyperbole of an Iowa State professor in 1960, when he observed, "The view of the state university is: expand Heaven. Bring the people into a larger room."[22]

By 1965, veterans' annual income of $5,100 compared to $3,200 for non-vets, as well their substantially lower unemployment rate, attested to the economic boost of a college degree. To say the G.I. Bill changed lives, and not only in the here and now, but for generations, is not an exaggeration. As Herbert Edelman of Brooklyn noted of his college experience, "Only God knows what would have become of me if it had not been for the G.I. Bill." Such testimonials were common, and the bounty from the bill was extraordinary: fourteen future Nobel laureates, two dozen Pulitzer Prize winners, three Supreme Court justices, three presidents, and hundreds of thousands of professionals in a wide array of fields.[23]

But an embrace of a less traditional student body would come slowly for elite institutions such as the Ivies. Harvard's 1946 entering class was the most diverse in its history as a result of veteran enrollment. By the following year, the university's freshman class more closely resembled its traditional white, affluent Protestant clientele. Not until the early 1960s would the Ivies crack open the door to ethnic diversity. Despite the financial rewards to these colleges from the G.I. Bill, they remained uncomfortable with the mix of students suddenly appearing on their campuses. Harvard dean Wilbur J. Bender complained, "There is a kind of unhealthy determination to get ahead, a grim competitive spirit, an emphasis on individual careerism and success which is disturbing . . . the lights are burning very late and there is not much leisurely talk or fellowship or group spirit." In another context, such seriousness and purpose among students would have been praiseworthy. But it did not take much reading between the lines to figure out that the good dean was objecting less to the manner than to the man.[24]

The Truman Commission report both detailed and condemned racial and religious barriers to higher education in the United States. "Federal legislation," the report demanded, "should end discrimination based on race, ethnicity, gender, and income." A college degree was becoming ever more essential for the transforming American economy and was the key to upward mobility. Therefore, the report concluded, "it is obvious . . . that free and universal access . . . in terms of the interest, ability, and need of the student" must be the major objective for American higher education.[25] This recommendation was also dead on arrival in Congress. Southern Democrats rebelled against any antidiscrimination legislation, and conservative Republicans harbored doubts about ethnic equity and a federal role in higher education more generally.

Still, the G.I. Bill had planted the notion that college was within reach of almost anyone. From a primarily elite activity prior to World War II, the halls of higher education became open to a much wider constituency, enabling the nation to compete better in an increasingly global economy and to make the transition out of an industrial economy less painful and more prosperous.

GIS WERE MORE LIKELY to find a place at a top-notch university than a place to live. They were hardly the only Americans in such a bind. By April 1946, the nation faced "the worst housing shortage in its history." Many Americans, particularly returning veterans and their young and now-growing families, had no place to live. Over 2.5 million families lived with relatives in 1946. Those were the lucky ones. Some returning veterans camped out in trolley cars in Chicago, and unfinished airplane fuselages in California, crowded into army Quonset huts in numerous locations, or sat forlornly on sidewalks, their families and possessions clustered around them in scandalous testimony to a nation that fought a global war successfully but could not adequately house its people. Others found cheap rooming houses, barns, chicken coops, or a friend's basement. Some staked out funeral parlors to pounce on the addresses of the recently deceased. An Omaha newspaper ad offered a "Big Ice Box, 7 by 17 feet. Could be fixed up to live in." Eighty-five thousand veterans signed up for public housing in New York City in 1946, except no public housing was available.[26]

Housing starts, peaking at nearly 1 million units in 1925, plummeted during the Great Depression and continued to slump during the war. Homeownership dropped to 41 percent in 1945, the same level as in 1920. In the 1930s, the Roosevelt administration understood that only government action could resolve the housing problem and, not incidentally, put people back to work. The National Housing Act of 1934 created a mortgage-insurance program that guaranteed twenty-year loans for up to 80 percent of the home's value. Amendments soon lengthened the mortgage term and lowered the down payment. The program reduced the lender's risk significantly. But widespread unemployment limited consumer demand during the Depression.[27]

The experience of the war convinced many economists that public spending could sustain a consumer market once the national economy reoriented from military priorities to civilian needs. In 1946, Chester Bowles, a staunch New Dealer and soon to be the governor of Connecticut, wrote the handbook for government economic policy, *Tomorrow Without Fear*. Bowles argued that the construction industry was "perhaps our greatest single opportunity, not only to correct our shocking lack of decent homes, but to increase the purchasing power of our people." The government, in partnership with the private sector, had to reward innovative construction techniques, Bowles asserted, and provide financial incentives and security to attract builders. *Fortune* magazine was less sanguine about homebuilders' resolving the housing shortage. Only government action could overcome "an incompetent housing industry" in order to satisfy the "most valued and most studied demand of an American family"—a home.[28]

In 1946, President Truman appointed former Louisville mayor Wilson Wyatt to address the crisis, quoting Chicago's early-twentieth-century planner Daniel H. Burnham, to "make no little plans." Wyatt hoped to start 2.7 million units within the next two years, a daunting task considering materials shortages and strong opposition from building-industry lobbies. A *Fortune* poll indicated that a strong majority of respondents favored the government's embarking on a major building program. To accomplish his ambitious objectives, Wyatt contemplated site prefabrication. But he placed his reliance on an industry unaccustomed to such building methods.[29]

By the end of 1946, the housing shortage persisted and had become a political liability for the Truman administration. *Life* magazine's tenth anniversary issue in November selected "No Vacancies" as the year's most ubiquitous phrase. A picture accompanying the article showed a Mrs. Leonard Saar and her six children huddled on a park bench in Brooklyn with no place to go. Housing construction indeed accelerated in 1946, but the backlog was so great that the misery persisted.[30]

The shortage continued into 1947. The price of materials and labor, as well as traditional methods of construction, kept housing prices relatively high and beyond the reach of most Americans, including for those who qualified under the G.I. Bill or Federal Housing Administration (FHA) mortgage guarantees. By mid-1947, the nation was producing 13 percent fewer homes than by the midpoint of the previous year.[31]

There were a few exceptions, most notably William J. Levitt's experiment on Long Island. *Architectural Forum*, not typically concerned with building for the masses, praised the Levitt development as both big and good. Levitt priced his homes reasonably, and government subsidies enabled buyers to secure good terms on loans so that mortgage payments were manageable. The G.I. Bill enabled the former soldier to put up nothing as a down payment, move in, and then begin paying off the mortgage. For those who were not eligible for the G.I. Bill, the FHA guaranteed loans, freeing up banking capital, especially for first-time homeowners with little credit history. Homebuyers need only put down 10 percent of the total price. These were policies the banking industry could love. As housing expert Charles Abrams wrote in a glowing account of the federal government's policies, "The government function in housing is conceived to be to underwrite private losses and insure private profits."[52]

Levitt, the grandson of Russian Jewish immigrants, grew up in Brooklyn. During the 1920s, he dropped out of New York University to work in his father's construction company. Levitt served in the navy Seabees during World War II building homes and barracks for war-production workers. The work gave him an opportunity to experiment with new assembly techniques. His Seabee crew divided house construction into twenty-seven separate steps and assigned a team to each step. This strategy reduced the need for highly skilled workers.[33]

Toward the end of the war, Levitt foresaw the need for civilian housing and purchased 7.3 square miles of potato fields on Long Island, thirty miles from New York City, a broad canvas on which to apply his wartime experience. Building a dozen or so dwellings per year on this tract would not do. The housing shortage required new methods and, above all, new financing. Levitt acquired a partner in this endeavor.

The federal government had been in the real estate business since the nation's founding. Occasionally donating and often selling public lands at modest prices, the national government helped to populate a continent and fulfill the dreams of striving Americans who migrated to what they hoped would be something better. The government's efforts were returned many times over in the agricultural and industrial bounty generated from expanded settlement.

The suburb was the next frontier. A combination of the FHA, the G.I. Bill, and a beneficent tax code subsidized the dreams of homeownership for millions of Americans. Mortgages extended to thirty years reduced the monthly payments to a manageable size for homes that cost a total of $6,990 initially ($76,341 in 2016 dollars). For $56 a month ($611 in 2016 dollars) with no down payment, a GI could move into a two-bedroom, one-bath home built atop a twenty-five-by-thirty-foot concrete slab that contained copper coils providing the unit with radiant central heating. Levitt equipped his homes with a fireplace, electric range and refrigerator, washer, and even a television—at no extra cost. The price was about $1,500 less than a dwelling with comparable square footage, and it was less expensive than renting an apartment in the city: a one-bedroom apartment cost at least $60 a month.

Homeownership was cheaper still with federal and state tax incentives, most notably the mortgage-interest deduction. The government provided large builders (more than a hundred units per year) with billions of dollars in credit and insured loans up to 95 percent of the value of the house. Without these subsidies, large-scale homebuilding would have been considerably more difficult. It worked. By 1956, 60 percent of American families owned their home. Large-scale builders accounted for nearly two out of three new homes built during that period.[34]

These incentives would have mattered less had not Levitt pioneered construction techniques to deliver homes to eager buyers. Levitt's mechanized army swarmed over the potato fields. Trucks dumped identical bundles of building materials, while bulldozers attacked the soil. In thirteen minutes the machines prepared the lot for the slab, and along came cement trucks laying the four-inch-thick foundations. The laborers followed: teams laying bricks, painting, sheathing, then moving on to the next site. One workman marched along the line of soon-to-be homes caulking windows—three hundred per day; another traveled down the line installing venetian blinds; a work crew of forty-five nailed shingles all day, and another group installed bathtubs. It was Henry Ford's assembly line adapted to homebuilding.

Levitt became a master of vertical integration, circumventing materials and labor shortages. He employed his own workforce, manufactured and supplied his own materials—lumber came from Levitt's own company and was cut from his own timber with his own equipment to his own specifications—and coordinated workforces and materials with precision. Each laborer had an assigned task that he performed over and over, thus reducing the need for dear and scarce skilled labor. And it was quick. At their peak, Levitt's workers could put up a house every sixteen minutes. Levitt, and a handful of other major builders, constructed 14 million single-family homes between 1946 and 1960.

The media marveled at the transformation of the rural landscape: "Three years ago, little potatoes had sprouted from these fields. Now there were 10,600 houses inhabited by more than 40,000 people, a community almost as big as 96-year-old Poughkeepsie, N.Y. . . . Its name: Levittown." Housing starts in 1949 exceeded 1.4 million, in 1950, 1.9 million—more than twice the pre-1945 record.[35]

The homes and their occupants also supported appliance, automobile, and furniture industries. Home buying touched off a consumer spree that buoyed the postwar economy. New residents drew additional commercial development, feeding both local tax coffers and workers' salaries. Shopping malls, school construction, road building, and entertainment complexes filled out suburbia. The building itself required steel, lumber, glass, and textiles, and the construction of infrastructure and schools provided work for laborers and teachers. Nearly eight out of every ten homes built between 1945 and 1960 were erected in the suburbs. Throughout the country in 1960, one fourth of all of the homes had been built over the previous ten years.[36]

The Levitt house reflected the postwar emphasis on domesticity and aspiration. He placed the kitchen front and center, with bedrooms in the back. An unfinished attic stoked buyers' dreams for an additional bedroom or a study. For all the speed in their construction, Levitt built sturdy homes that would fare well over time. It was a home of the future, and the future lay bright ahead for the families comfortably settled in the homes and the community.

Levitt marketed the homes and communities creatively. As he noted, "Any damn fool can build homes. What counts is how many can you sell for how little." A week before the opening of Levittown on Long Island, Levitt placed an ad in the *New York Times*: "This is Levittown! Uncle Sam and the world's largest builder have made it possible for you to live in a charming house in a delightful community without having to pay for them with your eye teeth." When he went out to the site the following day, Levitt found thirty people already in line, unfazed that the sale would not begin for another six days.[37]

Levittown quickly became a community. The residents were pioneering a new (for them) type of settlement. Herbert Gans, a sociologist who purchased a Levitt house, wrote that everyone "was looking forward to occupying his new home and this engendered a spirit of optimism and the trust that other purchasers shared this spirit. After all, Levittown would be a new community, and newness is often identified with perfection in American culture."[38]

The suburb was a place of reinvention, especially for immigrant families and their sons and daughters. A place where Jews, Roman Catholics, and the occasional Protestant could mingle—their shared experience was the community itself and not the particular ethnicities of its parts. In 1955, emblematic of this reorientation, Molly and Jake Goldberg moved from their apartment in the Bronx to the fictional Long Island town of Haverville. *The Goldbergs* was among the more popular shows of early television, and the suburban hegira of the family was both an entertainment and a social phenomenon. Reflecting the blending action of suburban living, the name of the show changed to the less ethnic *Molly*.[39]

Hundreds of other suburban developments mirrored Levittown's success. Above all, they were communities for young working- and middle-class families. Prior to the end of World War II, suburbanization drew relatively affluent residents who could afford the land, floor space, and the commute to the city. What occurred after 1945 was nothing less than the democratization of the suburbs. Between 1950 and 1970, the population of American suburbs doubled from 36 million to 72 million. More people moved to the suburbs every year than had ever arrived at Ellis Island in a year.[40]

Alex and Alice Grunewald purchased a Levitt house in 1950 while still in college. Price was the great attraction. They could buy a home cheaper than they could rent an apartment in the city. The village had a swimming pool, schools, shopping centers, and plans for trees and shrubs. By 1956, the Grunewald family had grown by two children as well as by the arrival of Alice's mother and father. Clearly, the Levitt Cape Cod home could not contain the family comfortably. They could not afford to purchase a larger house in another town, and besides, they enjoyed the lifestyle of Levittown. By 1956, the trees that William Levitt's father, Abraham, had planted had added a leafy canopy to the erstwhile potato fields.[41]

By the end of the 1950s, many Levittown homeowners, including the Grunewalds, had availed themselves of the renovation option, so that a drive through the community yielded a view of architectural diversity and individuality scarcely imagined by the town's early critics. The homes and their subsequent renovations enabled many families, especially veterans who resided below or on the lower cusp of the middle class, to move into the middle class. After building bedrooms in the attic, homeowners often added formal dining rooms, a rare feature of working-class housing before the war. As the children grew, "rec" rooms also appeared.

PUNDITS PREDICTED THAT WITHIN a decade Levittown, and similar instant suburbs, would become slums, a vast sea of monotony unbroken by imagination, landscaping, or any deviation from the industrial design of the community. An aerial view of these communities as they emerged from the raw dirt confirmed the monotony, except that few residents perceived their new homes from the vantage point of two thousand feet aboveground. Architects, urban planners, and even songwriters derided the structures as "ticky-tacky," but they were well constructed and easily modified and expanded.[42]

Others—sociologists, academics, and journalists—dissected the alleged pathologies of suburban life. Just as an earlier generation of urban theorists and planners had expended considerable energy chronicling the alleged debilities of urban life, a new generation of experts offered equally dire diagnoses of the suburbs. Sociologist David Riesman in *The Lonely Crowd* (1950) complained about low suburban densities with the same fervor as earlier sociologists had condemned high urban densities. Low densities, Riesman claimed, destroyed diversity and rendered the suburb sterile.[43]

Picking up that theme, journalist William H. Whyte, in his profile of Park Forest, a Chicago suburb, in his book *The Organization Man* (1956), found a stifling conformity, from the designs of the homes to the people within them— "organization men," trained to work within large corporations. Their wives functioned primarily to establish a comfortable home environment for their husbands, with few outside interests except their children's recreational and school activities. Other works on suburban life in the early 1950s, bearing titles such as *The Split-Level Trap* and *The Crack in the Picture Window*, advanced similar themes. Popular television shows of the 1950s such as *Ozzie and Harriet*, *I Love Lucy*, and *Father Knows Best* merely confirmed commentators' views on the vacuity of suburban life.[44]

Sure, the suburbs lacked the diversity of a Greenwich Village, the élan of gritty urban neighborhoods, the mixed land uses competing for limited space, the bustle of sidewalks at all times of day and night, and the proximity of great cultural attractions. But young families with children had other priorities, and the suburban home, its space, and the congenial neighbors and amenities such as schools and nearby recreational facilities counted more than the urban moil. Besides, city dwellers often sought to insulate themselves from diversity as much as possible, congregating in neighborhoods of similar social class, ethnicity, or religion. In some respects, the suburb blended ethnic and religious distinctions more than many city residential districts.

The suburb captured the popular imagination in the years immediately after World War II. Here was a place to realistically fulfill the dream of homeownership, to experience the feeling of pioneers heading for the wide-open spaces and the anticipation of adventure, new friends, new members of the family, and new institutions in which to immerse oneself. For the most part, these pioneers did not escape cities to escape people of color; they left to find something better. Aided by federal policies, they believed they did.

These moves obviously had consequences in the race and the health and wealth of cities, but it would be unfair to insist that the early suburban migrants dwelled on the sociology of their actions as opposed to their dreams of owning a home, raising a family in a nurturing environment, and relating, to some degree, to a natural landscape. The home became at once a symbol of their advance, a means to accumulate wealth, and a place to help shape their children's futures to be better than their own.[45]

Robert and Dorothy Kirsch moved with their first child, Bobby, to Levittown from Queens in 1955. They had a daughter that year, and another girl four years later. The eldest daughter, Susan, recalled living in the neighborhood, popping over to borrow food, play with other children, or just hang out. "Levittown," she reminisced forty years later, "gifted us with beautiful apple trees, with wonderful gnarled branches that were perfect for climbing." Susan and her brother navigated the neighborhood on bicycles. Though critics chastised suburbs as being too car-centric, automobiles rarely disturbed bicyclists or pedestrians. Most families possessed only one car, and typically, Dad drove off in the morning, leaving the town car-free except for the occasional delivery truck or mail van. Sidewalks encouraged walking and visiting neighbors. The

Kirsch children walked to school and to St. Bernard's Roman Catholic Church. On their bicycle excursions Susan and Bobby "discovered many wonders of nature . . . tadpoles and fish swimming in the stream along the willow-shaded bicycle trail."[46]

Critics of the suburbs often charged that such children, the members of the "gifted generation," received too much sheltering from their parents. A Harvard anthropologist sniffed that suburban kids lived through "filtered experience." They lived in unrealistic environments and rarely experienced "how the other half lives." Critics charged that these children were "inbred," that they lived in "neatly manicured, fumeless, pleasantly monotonous bedroom towns," as if, deprived of chaos, carbon monoxide, and clutter, they were somehow disadvantaged in moving forward in life. Yet, as one critic admitted, if you talked to the youngsters, "just about every kid likes it there. To him it is a near-utopia with plenty of room, friendly faces, unlimited hordes of playmates and no major menaces." Which is what most parents wanted for their children. They were pioneers, moving to new places and raising aspirations for themselves and their families.[47]

CHAPTER 3

THE PLOWBOY

HARRY TRUMAN WAS A PLOWBOY, rolling up Missouri loam. Twenty-two in 1906, an age when many young men in Independence, Missouri, were embarking on careers, Harry was stuck behind a mule. This was not his choice. He had enjoyed school, excelling at history, Latin, and math. But his labor was necessary to save the family farm.[1]

Harry was born into a middle-class family in 1884. His mother, Martha Ellen Young Truman, was college educated in an era where such credentials were relatively rare for women. She imparted her love of classical music, books, and the theater to Harry. Her father had resided in Independence since the town had served as the gateway to the Oregon Trail in the 1840s. He sold provisions to the wagon trains that wound their way westward every spring.

Independence in the 1880s had the usual complement of small town institutions, especially churches. But it still included remnants of its frontier past as a key provisioning point for the Oregon Trail. Saloons flanked the courthouse, and the streets were unpaved and muddy quagmires when it rained or dusty trails when it did not. The Union Army had desolated the area during the Civil War, a conflict that here outlasted Appomattox as William Quantrill's Confederate guerrillas continued the struggle. The town's heritage turned more to the South than the West, although Truman considered himself "a good old Middle Westerner."[2]

But the pull of the South was strong, and of its memory stronger still. Harry's mother, Martha Ellen, blamed the struggles her family and Jackson County endured after the war on Republicans in general and Abraham Lincoln in particular. She proudly related the story of how she once literally stomped on a copy of Harriet Beecher Stowe's *Uncle Tom's Cabin*. Independence was Democratic territory.

Racial violence was rare, but racial segregation prevailed. The black section of Independence was universally known as Nigger Neck. The Confederate cause evoked homage with a thriving chapter of the United Daughters of the Confederacy and blood connections to Confederate heroes. The father of one of Harry's teachers had been wounded no fewer than three times during General George E. Pickett's ill-fated charge at Gettysburg in 1863. Portraits of Robert E. Lee and Thomas "Stonewall" Jackson adorned the walls of numerous Independence homes of whites. But if Southern heritage implied fealty to white supremacy, then that is where Harry and the South would eventually part ways.

The aspirations of mother and son were no match for the poor business decisions of Harry's father, John A. Truman. John dabbled in wheat futures only to see the market crash in 1902, wiping out the family's modest wealth and the farm Martha Ellen had inherited from her father.

With college now out of the question, Harry moved to Kansas City and became a clerk with the National Bank of Commerce. Kansas City was a prosperous, growing center of a vast wheat empire. Financial services, insurance companies, railroads, and agricultural-equipment firms spurred the economy. Kansas City was a regional cultural center that offered an array of plays and concerts. The city was sufficiently prominent to draw the 1900 Democratic National Convention. It was an exciting time to be in Kansas City, and Harry took advantage of its cultural attractions as much as his modest income and family financial obligations allowed.

Harry's job supported the family. To minimize living costs, he shared a boardinghouse with several other bank employees, including Arthur Eisenhower, whose brother Dwight and their family lived west of Kansas City in Abilene, Kansas. Harry thrived in banking, and within a few years he was making $100 per month as an assistant teller ($2,800 in today's dollars). But his father's persistent financial misfortunes ended Harry's upward mobility.

Hoping to regain his economic footing, John Truman had rented a farm after the wheat-trading debacle. But a flood wiped out his entire corn crop, and the family moved to his mother-in-law's farm, a sprawling six-hundred-acre property, and entrusted John with running it. He called Harry home to help out. Harry's life in Kansas City was suddenly over. For the next ten years, the bookish bank teller would work behind a mule. He would also court Bess Wallace, whom he had known since he was six years old. Although her mother disapproved of the match—she felt her daughter deserved better—Bess and Harry became engaged in November 1913. Harry wrote to Bess, presumably in jest, "How does it feel to be engaged to a clodhopper who has ambitions to be Governor of Montana and Chief Executive of the U.S.?" He had no money to buy her an engagement ring.[3]

The farm prospered modestly, but Harry wanted more than a rural life could offer. America's entrance into World War I provided the opportunity to escape the farm and reinvent himself or, more properly, to discover his true

self. The war would provide a chance to prove both his manhood and patriotism. His intelligence and maturity placed Harry in a leadership position, a
Southern Baptist commanding a battery of Irish Catholics in France. At the
first glimpse of their new leader, the men wondered if, somehow, a college
professor had gotten lost and wound up in France. As one soldier remembered
of Captain Truman, "You could see that he was scared to death." Years later,
Harry confirmed that observation. But he performed superbly during the
Meuse-Argonne Offensive of September 1918 that hastened the armistice two
months later. Harry had discovered he was a leader.[4]

Back home in Independence, lauded for his service, Harry looked forward
to new opportunities. His first decision was to marry Bess in June 1919. They
lived with her mother. He resolved to go back to Kansas City and resume a
business career. He wanted no more of life on a farm. Harry entered a business partnership with fellow veteran Eddie Jacobson, son of a moderately
successful Jewish family in Kansas City. Truman's partnership with Bess
would last considerably longer than his business arrangement with Jacobson.
Truman & Jacobson, a haberdashery, went under in 1922. All he had from the
business was a burdensome debt he would carry for twenty years.

Jim Pendergast, like Eddie Jacobson, forged a wartime friendship with
Harry. This connection would prove more portentous. Pendergast was the
namesake of the legendary "Big Jim" Pendergast, who came to Kansas City in
1876. The son of Irish Catholic immigrants, he made his way in the gritty
industrial district of the city, creating a tidy fortune through slick business
deals and investments in gambling and liquor enterprises. He built a powerful
Democratic political machine that embraced immigrants and African Americans. Few city bosses of the era wielded the comprehensive power of the
Pendergast machine in Kansas City. It controlled saloons, illegal liquor sales,
brothels, and the police. As one journalist noted, "If you want to see some
sin, forget about Paris and go to Kansas City . . . probably . . . the greatest sin
industry in the world."[5]

After Big Jim's death in 1911, younger brothers Tom and Mike took over the
organization and built an empire of saloons and a thriving concrete business
that benefited from city contracts as Kansas City boomed during the first two
decades of the twentieth century. Tom was a master of retail politics, passing
out warm clothing and food to the needy during the brutal Missouri winters,
with the only "payment" expected at the polls, his supporters sometimes
voting four or five times each on election day.

At young Jim's behest, Mike visited with Harry during the winter of 1921
and asked him if he would run for eastern judge of Jackson County. The
position had nothing to do with jurisprudence. The office was equivalent to

a county commissioner. The eastern judge's jurisdiction was primarily rural. The western judge represented Kansas City. A presiding judge completed the three-member panel. The judges controlled the county budget, making them powerful figures in the allocation of construction contracts and county employment, and, not incidentally, a mechanism to reward Pendergast allies. It was machine politics through and through, and Truman was an ideal candidate because of his sterling reputation as a war hero. From Harry's perspective, the offer was a godsend. As he noted succinctly, "I have to eat."[6]

Harry had always harbored a keen interest in politics. The highlight of Harry's political life prior to Mike Pendergast's invitation was attending the 1900 Democratic National Convention in Kansas City, where young Harry thrilled to the oratory of William Jennings Bryan. Even when he became president, Truman's speeches would invoke the cadences and causes of the Great Commoner from Nebraska.

But, in 1922 it was less political passion than economic necessity that drew Harry to Mike. The position paid $3,465 a year (roughly $42,000 in today's dollars), enough for Harry and Bess to live on and to begin to pay down his business debt. As Harry wrote in a private memoir, "Went into business all enthusiastic. Lost all I had and all I could borrow. Mike Pendergast picked me up and put me into politics and I've been lucky." Harry added, "I loved him as I did my own daddy."[7]

Harry campaigned on the need for more road construction and the importance of sound fiscal policy, an interesting but ultimately effective juxtaposition. Despite opposition from the Ku Klux Klan, who charged, mistakenly, that Truman was Jewish, Harry won the post and plunged into his work with great diligence. He both improved the county's credit rating and satisfied the Pendergasts.

The balancing act between integrity and contract leasing took its toll on Harry, though. Every once in a while, he would experience blinding headaches and stomach pains, likely psychosomatic, and repair to a hotel room in Kansas City to convalesce. There he wrote a diary chronicling his actions and contrasting them with the corruption he witnessed around him. The diary would serve as an exculpatory record should his own integrity come into question. He admitted that his job was "sometimes hard on head and nerves."[8]

Despite his periodic "disappearances," Truman reveled in the political life and the socializing that accompanied it. Playing poker and drinking bourbon (Prohibition notwithstanding) with his friends were both politic and relaxing. Nearly forty, he had found his life's work: politics. In 1925, he became presiding judge of the county and remained in that position for two terms.

He traveled throughout the county determining infrastructure needs and how to preserve the area's beauty. He authored a book of his findings, *Results of County Planning: Jackson County Missouri*. The book focused on good roads for farmers to transport their crops to market. Translating his theories into action, he prevailed on his colleagues to vote for bond issues totaling $10 million for major and secondary roads, the latter to take visitors "through miniature canyons . . . every now and then the traveler coming upon distant views of the finest natural landscaping." The Pendergasts delighted in Harry's projects, of course—county voters approved upward of $50 million in bond issues—but the county judge always insisted he accomplished these works without resorting to graft or corruption even if he did hire some of his boss's political allies.[9]

What Truman gained from his county political experiences was that government could accomplish a great deal, not only in terms of public works, but also in helping those who could not help themselves. He compiled a notable record in the field of mental health and in ensuring equality for the provision of services in the African American community, an effort that black voters would remember.

TRUMAN LEFT COUNTY POLITICS in 1934 having served the maximum number of terms allowed by law. He was fifty years old and had no business prospects or any desire to resume farming. He toyed with the idea of running for governor, but Tom Pendergast discouraged that hope. Instead, he asked Truman to run for the U.S. Senate. Jumping from county official to U.S. senator was not the usual political trajectory, but he was broke. Pendergast staked him to $500 in campaign funds.

Truman won the Democratic primary, rolling up a large majority in Pendergast-controlled Jackson County, and easily bested the Republican candidate in the fall general election. Tom Pendergast's parting advice: "Work hard, keep your mouth shut, and answer your mail." Harry would spend his first few years in the Senate following that plan to the letter.[10]

Truman's election flabbergasted both the national press and his peers in the Senate. The *New York Times*, which referred to him as "Henry" Truman, dismissed the new senator as "a rube from Pendergast land." Harry received a lukewarm reception from his Senate colleagues. Many in that body viewed him as "the senator from Pendergast." Republican senator George W. Norris of Nebraska, a noted reformer, characterized Harry as "poison" and refused to speak to him.[11]

Despite this difficult initiation, he never disavowed the Pendergast connection. He owed his position to Tom Pendergast, and whatever anyone else thought, that was not Truman's problem. More important was to support Franklin D. Roosevelt's New Deal, which he did right on down the line from labor legislation to the Works Progress Administration (WPA), Social Security, and, most important to his constituents, rural electrification. Nine out of ten farms in Missouri had no electricity in 1935. He funneled $74 million of WPA money into Missouri, and so what if this bonanza also benefited the Pendergasts.

Three years into his Senate term, the opposition to Harry began to recede. His votes had solidified his New Deal credentials, and his unassuming manner contrasted favorably with that of some of the oversize egos in the chamber. Perhaps his closest friendship was with U.S. Supreme Court associate justice Louis D. Brandeis, a pairing one would not predict for this former Missouri plowboy, but one that came readily from their mutual loathing of corporate avarice. Invitations to Brandeis's Sunday teas had become much sought after in Washington, and one of Truman's staffers, Max Lowenthal, helped to secure one. The justice, then in his eighties, returned Harry's admiration. Truman's first major speech on the Senate floor in December 1937 bore echoes of Brandeis's own battles on the Court. Truman attacked Wall Street and greed in a Brandeis-Bryan amalgam that he feared would "probably . . . catalogue me as a radical, but it will be what I think."[12]

Everyone should have the same opportunity, a level playing field, Truman asserted. Money, status, or connections should not privilege one person or one institution over another. Truman continued:

> We worship money instead of honor . . . It is a pity that Wall Street, with its ability to control all the wealth of the nation and to hire the best law brains in the country, has not produced some statesmen, some men who could see the dangers of bigness and of the concentration of the control of wealth. Instead of working to meet the situation, they are still employing the best law brains to serve greed and self-interest. People can stand only so much, and one of these days there will be a settlement.[13]

Here were sentiments Truman would articulate for the rest of his political career. He believed that Wall Street had caused the Great Depression (as well as his own business failures), and that government's role was to ensure that investment bankers and oligarchs would never again play the economic system to the detriment of the common man.

Despite his New Deal credentials and his service to Missouri, Harry's reelection bid in 1940 looked like a long shot. In 1938, the federal government indicted Tom Pendergast for income-tax evasion. Truman refused to abandon his mentor, and the connection hurt him in Missouri. The *St. Louis Post-Dispatch* warned, "Should Truman be nominated, there would be shrill rejoicing among all the forces of evil in Missouri."[14]

Without the support of Pendergast, and with no endorsement from President Roosevelt, Truman launched what pundits believed was a futile reelection campaign. It would not be the last time that experts underestimated him. He had little money for the campaign, occasionally sleeping in his car because he could not afford a hotel room. But his growing coterie of Senate friends came to his aid, visiting Missouri to promote his candidacy. South Carolina's Senator Jimmy Byrnes prevailed upon his close friend the financier Bernard Baruch to send a generous donation to the Truman campaign. The unions and farmers chipped in as well.

Surprising some of his supporters, Truman also spoke out about race relations, a subject many felt would only hurt the senator in the Democratic primary. Though he made clear his opposition to social equality, his voting record revealed a progressive streak on racial issues. Truman had opposed the poll tax and favored an antidiscrimination amendment to the Selective Service Act. In 1938, he was one of only sixteen Democrats to vote to end the filibuster against federal antilynching legislation. Even on relatively minor bills such as preserving the office of Recorder of Deeds for the District of Columbia—an office that hired hundreds of African Americans—Truman supported the concept of fairness.

Speaking to an audience composed mainly of white farmers in Sedalia, Missouri, during the primary campaign, he avowed, "I believe in the brotherhood of man, not merely the brotherhood of white men, but the brotherhood of all men before the law . . . If any class or race can be permanently set apart from, or pushed down below the rest, in political and civil rights, so may any other class or race when it shall incur the displeasure of its more powerful associates, and we may say farewell to the principles on which we count our safety." In the commonwealth, unfairness to one race threatened all.[15]

Truman won a close primary race by slightly more than 8,000 votes out of 665,000 cast. He did it mostly on his own. To the extent that the Pendergast connection still existed, it hurt him in Jackson County, but he made up for it elsewhere in the state. Truman went on to win the general election. At the least, he was still employed, and maybe he could save enough to purchase back his mother's farm, which had lapsed into foreclosure and was auctioned off during the campaign.

Confident after his victory, Truman proposed that the Senate establish a special committee to look into the awarding of defense contracts. As the country moved closer to war footing in early 1941, Truman felt that congressional oversight of such contracts was necessary, remembering his days on the Jackson County Court. The Senate agreed, and though the Special Committee to Investigate the National Defense Program, or the Truman Committee, as it came to be called, did not uncover any major scandals, it found numerous instances of waste, poor workmanship, cheating by both labor and management, and persistent shortages throughout the system. The committee revealed and ended the cozy business relationship of Alcoa Aluminum and Standard Oil of New Jersey with the I. B. Farben Company of Germany on the development of new technologies.

Truman also cited the lack of government oversight on steel production, where the shortages were most critical. In response, the Roosevelt administration established the War Production Board, placing all contracts and oversight under one administrative roof. Truman's work proved essential to the nation's relatively quick mobilization after Pearl Harbor in December 1941. His fellow senators evinced a new respect for the Pendergast crony. Florida's liberal Democratic senator Claude Pepper confessed, "The man from Missouri had dared to say 'show me' to the powerful military-industrial complex and he had caught many people in the act."[16]

Truman now had a national profile, appearing on the cover of *Time* magazine in March 1943, and was the subject of flattering profiles in newspapers and in journals such as *Business Week*, which called Truman's committee "the [country's] first line of defense." This slight, soft-spoken, bespectacled man of dubious provenance had become one of the nation's most respected politicians. Estimates after the war indicated that the Truman Committee had saved the nation as much as $15 billion, or about $206 billion in today's dollars.[17]

BY THE SUMMER OF 1943 rumors began circulating among the political cognoscenti of Truman as a potential vice-presidential candidate for the following year's presidential election. Henry A. Wallace, the current vice president, had numerous enemies within the Democratic Party, including the urban Democratic bosses, who distrusted the Iowan and former Republican, and Southern Democrats, who disdained his open liberalism on race.

South Carolina's Jimmy Byrnes was probably the leading candidate to replace Wallace should Roosevelt have concurred that a new vice-presidential nominee was essential for the ticket. But the big-city bosses found him unacceptable. Byrnes had left his Catholic faith when he married, becoming an Episcopalian, and his hostility toward organized labor sealed Northern opposition. And Byrnes, like most Southern senators, was a fierce protector of white supremacy.

Such a position threatened turnout among the growing numbers of African Americans in the North who had supported Roosevelt and the New Deal.

Harry Truman, on the other hand, had done nothing to rile the urban bosses. With them, the Pendergast connection was hardly a negative. His work on the Truman Committee and his relative progressivism on race marked him as acceptable. Truman could also draw in more conservative Democrats from border states such as Missouri. Southern Democrats found him acceptable as well, despite his pro-labor and pro–civil rights votes in the Senate. His closest friends in the Senate were Southerners, and they understood that some of his votes reflected the importance of 130,000 black ballots in Missouri, something Southern Democrats never worried about in their home states. In conversations with his Southern colleagues he casually used the N-word or participated in the racial jokes that made the rounds of the capital in those days. He was one of them, they believed, with Confederate ancestors to boot.

Perhaps the greatest resistance to Truman's candidacy came from Truman himself. He denied to friends and to anyone who asked that he harbored vice-presidential ambitions. That may have been politic, but he was also concerned about the president's health and what that might mean for a vice president. The prospect frightened him.

Roosevelt had remained aloof from the vice-presidential sweepstakes until union leader and presidential confidant Sidney Hillman, and Ed Flynn, the powerful Bronx Democratic boss, convinced the president that Harry Truman would do the least damage to the ticket and might actually help it among farmers and moderate voters generally. Their sense of Truman's political proclivities was mostly correct. Despite his Bryanesque rhetoric, Harry was a man of the center, positioned between the "radicals" in his own party and the reactionaries among Republicans. Truman straddled the awkward coalition that was the Democratic Party of the 1930s. His background was thoroughly rural, mostly Southern by preference; yet he owed his political success to urban machine politics. Roosevelt seemed pleased with the selection, though he scarcely knew the senator.

Truman made a special effort to reassure black voters. When the *Pittsburgh Courier*, one of the nation's leading black newspapers, responded to Truman's selection with the headline "Democrats 'Sell' Race, Wallace, to 'Buy' South," the nominee sought out the editor to inform him, "I have always been for equality of opportunity in work, working conditions and political rights." Then he asked the paper's readers to take a broad perspective on the upcoming campaign: "Harry Truman isn't the important issue of the campaign. The real issue is the re-election of the greatest living friend of the Negro people, Franklin Roosevelt."[18]

Presidential campaigns rarely turn on a vice-presidential candidate, and the 1944 election was no exception. The old rumor of Truman's alleged Jewish ancestry flared again. Truman deflected it well, denying it, but also stating that if he were Jewish, he would "not be ashamed of it." In the strange alchemy of campaigns, allegations also surfaced that he had been a member of the Ku Klux Klan. And, of course, the Republicans and the press played the Pendergast connection. The conservative *Chicago Tribune* was especially pointed in this regard, observing that if Roosevelt died, the nation was "faced with the grinning skeleton of Truman the bankrupt, Truman the pliant tool of Boss Pendergast in looting Kansas City's county government."[19]

The Roosevelt-Truman ticket won thirty-six of the forty-eight states. Yet, the election was closer than the electoral vote indicated. A shift of three hundred thousand votes in key states would have thrown the election to the Republican candidates, New York governor Thomas E. Dewey and Ohio governor John W. Bricker.

Roosevelt and Truman communicated sparingly during the campaign and during the rest of the president's remaining months of life. Truman saw Roosevelt only two times before he died and discussed little of substance during those meetings. After one of those meetings, in late August 1944, Truman mentioned to a friend that the president had looked awful, his "hands were shaking and he talks with considerable difficulty . . . It doesn't seem to be any mental lapse of any kind but physically he's just going to pieces."[20]

Cut off from specific policy issues and from the president himself, Truman found the highlight of his typical day to be in House Speaker Sam Rayburn's room beneath the House floor at the end of the day's session. Conviviality and bourbon were the main agenda items at these small gatherings. At one of these affairs on an April afternoon in 1945, Truman received a call to come to the White House as "quickly and quietly" as possible. He asked the group to mention nothing about this. When Truman left the White House that evening and returned to his modest apartment on Connecticut Avenue, he was president of the United States.[21]

The news of Roosevelt's death and Truman's elevation touched off shock waves of grief and alarm. "Good God, Truman will be president" was a common sentiment. David Lilienthal, head of the Tennessee Valley Authority, cried, "The country and the world don't deserve to be left this way . . . God help us all." More ominously, the nation's leading military figures had grave doubts about Truman. General George S. Patton, stationed in Germany, complained, "It seems very unfortunate that in order to secure political preference, people are made Vice President who are never intended, neither by Party nor by the Lord to be Presidents." Those who met with Truman at the

White House that fateful evening remarked that he looked "absolutely dazed."[22]

Yet some believed that the man from Missouri was up to the job. John Nance Garner of Texas, former vice president and one of Truman's closest friends, wrote to fellow Texan Sam Rayburn, "Truman is honest and patriotic and has a head full of good horse sense. Besides, he has guts." Arthur Vandenberg, Republican senator from Michigan, believed Truman was "a *grand person* with every good intention and high honesty of purpose." Those who knew him well respected both his instincts and abilities.[23]

ON HIS FIRST FULL DAY as president, Truman journeyed to Capitol Hill to take lunch with his former colleagues. Confronted by reporters afterward, he asked them to "pray for me now. I don't know whether you fellows ever had a load of hay fall on you, but when they told me yesterday what had happened, I felt like the moon, the stars, and all the planets had fallen on me."[24]

He would need those prayers. Though the war was winding down in Europe, it was still raging in the Pacific. And peace, what would that look like? Would the nation lapse back into an economic depression? How would the economy absorb millions of returning servicemen? And would the advances of the New Deal shrivel in the face of a growing conservative reaction in Congress?

After more than two decades in public office, Harry Truman had a good idea of how to govern and of the priorities he should advance. These principles would ground his decisions in the difficult months transitioning from war to peace. Like Bryan and Brandeis, Truman had a visceral dislike for bigness, whether it was a corporation or a labor union. Bigness meant money, and money meant power. And concentration not only warped the playing field but also dominated it.

His experience in county government and in the New Deal and the war years confirmed the view that government had a legitimate interest in promoting both economic prosperity and individual opportunity, and that these two objectives reinforced each other. Fiscal probity never meant compromising New Deal initiatives. In fact, a sound national economy depended on consolidating and extending those programs and rendering them more equitable. He disdained privilege, especially unmerited privilege. As he wrote to a constituent in 1941, the business of government was "to see that everyone has a fair deal."[25]

Truman called his philosophy "progressive liberalism," a phrase perhaps redundant in today's political parlance, but one that fellow countrymen at the time associated with Woodrow Wilson, Franklin Roosevelt, and progressive

Republicans, who bequeathed numerous examples of government activism on behalf of "the people."[26]

When Truman suddenly ascended to the presidency, newspapers and magazines scrambled to publish profiles of the new chief executive. Seeking a common denominator for his background and politics, "Southerner" came up more often than not as shorthand for understanding Truman. *Life* magazine's first major profile of Truman noted his Jackson County roots, a place the editors called "the last frontier of the Old South." The managing editor of the *Kansas City Star* portrayed him as a rural Southerner, and the *Richmond Times-Dispatch* praised his speaking style as "especially pleasing to Southern ears." Several outlets even spread the incorrect story that the new president was the son of a Confederate veteran.[27]

Although Truman was not the first vice-presidential choice for Southern political leaders, his ascension to the presidency gave most of them at least guarded hope that white supremacy remained relatively safe. South Carolina's Senator Burnet Maybank, riding on Franklin D. Roosevelt's funeral train, reassured a Southern colleague, "Everything's going to be all right—the new president knows how to handle the niggers."[28]

So it seemed during the early weeks of Truman's presidency. When he named James K. Vardaman Jr. of Mississippi, the son of one of the most vicious white supremacists of the early twentieth-century South, to his White House staff, when he selected Tom Clark of Texas as attorney general, and when he nominated his former Senate colleague Jimmy Byrnes to become the next secretary of state, whom the *Pittsburgh Courier* called a "white supremacist of the first rank," black leaders expressed alarm. Prior to 1947, when Congress changed the order of presidential succession, the secretary of state was second in line behind the vice president to assume the presidency. Since Truman was president, there was no longer a vice president, which meant that Byrnes was the heir to the presidency.[29]

Southerners in Congress viewed public policy through the lens of white supremacy. Social Security was fine, but African Americans needed to be excluded from its benefits. Minimum-wage legislation was acceptable as long as domestic workers were exempt. Farm subsidies to prop up a weak agricultural sector were wonderful as long as enforcement did not require payments to trickle down to black farm laborers. If African Americans became dependent on the federal government, their white employers would exercise less control over them. Southern Democrats formed a compatible partnership with conservative Republicans, whose principles of a minimalist government and the dominance of Anglo-Saxon Protestants in the nation and its institutions dovetailed nicely with Southern priorities.

Besides, race was not only a Southern white preoccupation. The Great Migration of Southern blacks to the North and West accelerated during the war years as industries shorn of manpower called on African Americans and even women to set the rivets and solder the wires. Proximity could breed contempt. Racial violence flared in Detroit, Harlem, and Chicago over jobs and neighborhoods. These were portents. Black Americans would help win the war on the battlefields and in the factories. They would not be denied the fruits of peace. Harry Truman's accidental ascension to the presidency left blacks concerned.[30]

Franklin D. Roosevelt did not challenge Southern racial customs. But African Americans believed that, at heart, he shared their dreams of racial equality. The growing numbers of blacks in the federal government, their rising importance in Democratic Party ranks, the numerous New Deal programs that, even within the strictures of Jim Crow, blacks could access, produced the greatest outpouring of grief over the death of a president among African Americans since the assassination of Abraham Lincoln. Tens of thousands of blacks lined the tracks of the funeral train, many with tears flowing and hearts heavy.

Few black people had followed Truman's political career to know that he had not voted like a Southern senator, that even as a county politician he'd insisted on fairness for the county's African American population. Truman's first major policy decision was to recommend to Congress the restoration of funds for the Fair Employment Practices Committee (FEPC), a body white Southerners had consistently vilified since its inception in June 1941. Although relatively weak, its presence and occasional victories on behalf of fairness in hiring for defense and government work served as a talisman of unwanted federal intrusion into Southern racial traditions. As Truman wrote in his message to Congress on the issue, "The principle . . . of fair employment practice should be established permanently as a part of our national law."[31]

Given the Southern Democrats' control of key congressional committees and their coalition with conservative Republicans, ratification of Truman's request on the FEPC was unlikely. Truman, discouraged, noted privately that "he wished that there might be organized a liberal party in this country so that the Southern Democrats could go where they belonged into the conservative Republican party." He would have to wait twenty years for that political realignment. In the meantime, he seethed, but did not back down.[32]

That was the thing about Truman: he was tenacious. Not that he abjured compromise, but he seemed to relish battling against great odds. His actual legislative accomplishments during his nearly eight years in office were relatively modest. But during that time, he brought to the public forum issues that had scarcely surfaced in mainstream political discourse, but that, one by one, would become the law of the land in subsequent administrations. Some were issues that did not enjoy even moderate public support. Civil rights for African Americans were a concern of roughly 2 percent of the population in 1946.

Truman could have easily parsed his support for civil rights, spoken eloquently about equality, and done nothing. But his own biography had steeled him against inequality, regardless of race; it had taught him to be at least wary if not antagonistic toward privilege. His models were William Jennings Bryan and Louis D. Brandeis; Truman's cause was the underdog, hang public opinion and a troglodyte Congress.

At one of his first cabinet meetings a month after taking office, he related a story about Abraham Lincoln and the Emancipation Proclamation. Lincoln, according to Truman's version, polled the cabinet on the edict, and every member voted no. But Lincoln voted yes, and that was how it stood. "That is the way I intend to run this," Truman informed his colleagues.[33]

Civil rights was just the beginning. Barely five months in office, Truman put forward a wide-ranging agenda to expand the New Deal, to transform Franklin D. Roosevelt's eloquent call in 1944 for an Economic Bill of Rights into reality. But neither Congress nor the American people were in the mood for more crusades. Having just saved the world, they wanted to resume their lives, to make up for lost time, to start families, to begin or continue their education, to find a decent place to live. Although the government had rendered these pursuits more attainable for more people, the era of reform was drawing to a close. If not for the war, it might have closed much earlier. Besides, it seemed a month after V-J Day that the government was getting in the way as much as easing the way. Price controls, scarce goods, and housing shortages made the future look tentative for businesses and individuals alike.

Neither Congress nor the American people seemed amenable to continued change. As early as 1938, a Gallup poll indicated that 66 percent of Americans wanted Roosevelt to pursue more conservative policies. In that year's midterm elections, the Democrats lost six Senate seats and seventy-one House seats. Outside the South, the Republican vote was robust. The Democratic losses were primarily among Northern liberals. The conservative coalition of Southern Democrats and conservative Republicans could obstruct most progressive legislation, which they did for the next two decades. As political correspondent Arthur Krock observed, "The New Deal has been halted."[34]

As a member of the U.S. Senate during this period, Truman understood the political odds against pursuing a progressive agenda that neither the American people nor Congress seemed to endorse. But for Truman, the disciple of Bryan and Brandeis, doing what was right was more important than yielding to expediency. In the late summer of 1945, Truman advocated an increase in the minimum wage to account for inflation and a plan to build a million new units of public housing coupled with rent supplements to lower-income families. He stated his intention to broaden coverage of Social Security by including 3 million additional workers, to provide national health insurance, to reform immigration policy, and to expand educational opportunities. Continuing to poke his Southern colleagues in the Senate, Truman reintroduced legislation to abolish the poll tax, one of several mechanisms used by Southern states to suppress the African American vote, and he talked about ending racial discrimination in schools and public accommodations. The House minority leader, Joseph Martin, a conservative Massachusetts Republican, stood aghast: "Not even President Roosevelt asked so much at one sitting." For those who hoped Truman's ascendancy meant that the "Roosevelt nonsense" was over and that "the New Deal was as good as dead," the agenda came as a major shock. By December of that year, Congress had blocked or killed every proposal.[35]

Congress did indeed pass a tax reform program, but it gave relief to corporations and wealthy taxpayers, not to the middle class. The minimum wage stayed the same. No major housing legislation was enacted until the 1949 Housing Act, and even then, Congress strangled appropriations for it. Congress did not act on education proposals despite the growing evidence that baby boomers were poised to inundate classrooms around the country. Lawmakers grudgingly lifted some restrictions on refugees, but kept in place and even strengthened the bigoted quotas against Southern and Eastern European immigrants.[36]

Congress was not the only problem Truman confronted. Less than a year into his presidency, a rising chorus outside Washington questioned his abilities. Labor unrest, persistent shortages of housing, food, and durable goods, recurring fears of unemployment and inflation, and concerns of another war, this time with the Soviet Union, created a sense that Truman was in over his head. A prominent editor sighed, "We joined the nation in hoping that, by some alchemy, a Pendergast politician would become a statesman overnight," but "the little man from Missouri is a little man indeed."[37]

When Truman took office, his approval rating registered about 80 percent. A little more than a year later it had plunged to 32 percent. The blinding headaches and stomach pains that had plagued him in Jackson County returned. His response was to become even more pugnacious. He wrote to Bess, "I'm doing as I damn please for the next two years and to hell with all of them." That stance was not likely to quell the opposition. As he confessed, "Sherman was wrong . . . I find peace is hell."[38]

Truman had no road map to follow in providing a smooth transition to peacetime after fifteen years of depression and war. Releasing government controls risked rampant inflation that would erode the savings of war workers as well as the dreams of returning veterans. Retaining some price supports could create shortages, particularly in the food and housing sectors. It would do consumers little good to have money in their pockets but little to spend it on. Economists' opinions were divided, as were those of people in the government.

The Democratic-controlled Congress attempted to split the difference by renewing the Office of Price Administration (OPA), but with little enforcement power. The result was soaring prices, particularly for food, and even more particularly for meat. The *New York Daily News* headlined, "Prices Soar, Buyers Sore, Steers Jump over the Moon." The *Washington Times-Herald* noted sarcastically, "Only 87 Meatless Days Until Christmas." Going into the November 1946 off-year congressional elections, Truman had become a punch line: "Would you like a Truman beer? You know, the one with no head."[39]

Republicans had their own slogan: "Had Enough? Vote Republican." And Americans did. For the first time since 1930, the GOP took control of both houses of Congress. The *U.S. News & World Report* enthused that the new Congress was going to "rewrite the Truman legislative program, line by line." Some Democrats were so despondent that they pressed Truman to resign. Arkansas senator J. William Fulbright urged the president to let Secretary of State Jimmy Byrnes take over. Truman dismissed the suggestion, calling its bearer Senator "Halfbright."[40]

Truman now had to contend not only with Southerners within his own party, but also with an expanded conservative wing among Republicans. The combination would torment him until the end of his presidency in January 1953. The coalition would also frustrate his successor, the Republican Dwight D. Eisenhower. Truman would issue the third most vetoes of any president in American history, exceeded only by Franklin D. Roosevelt, who was in office for more than twelve years, and Grover Cleveland, who occupied the White House for eight years. A reflection of the toxicity of Truman's relationship with Congress was that lawmakers overrode twelve of his vetoes. Only Andrew Johnson, subject of an impeachment trial by Radical Republicans after the Civil War, suffered more reversals.[41]

GIVEN THE RISING PUBLIC DISCONTENT with his administration, expressed most vividly in the Democrats' defeat in the midterm elections, speculation was widespread on Truman's dwindling chances for the 1948 Democratic Party presidential nomination, let alone for his victory that fall. Even Truman began to question his own prospects for 1948. In a meeting in Berlin with General Dwight D. Eisenhower in 1946, Truman startled Ike by saying, "General, there is nothing you may want that I won't try to help you get. That definitely and specifically includes the presidency in 1948." Eisenhower recovered enough to reply, "Mr. President, I don't know who will be your opponent for the presidency, but it will not be I." The following year, as his political fortunes continued to plummet, Truman met with Eisenhower, again offering the presidency, with Truman as the vice presidential candidate. Ike, whose political-party preferences remained unknown to most at this time, declined once more.[42]

The two years before the 1948 presidential election were difficult for Truman, but he had been forewarned. James H. Rowe Jr., a Harvard-educated lawyer and an official at the Bureau of the Budget, wrote to Truman after the Republican congressional triumph and told him to expect obstruction for the remainder of his term. The Republicans wanted to make certain Truman's presidency would end in January 1949, and Southern Democrats in particular were in no mood to advance his domestic agenda given his stance on civil rights. Rowe advised that Truman "should first of all accept the inevitability that formal cooperation is unworkable."[43]

So what could the president do? Rowe recommended that Truman use his bully pulpit and speak out to the public. He should sound conciliatory (difficult for Truman) but never waver from his basic principle of fairness (an easier task). By stressing and repeating the themes of health care, civil rights, access to education, immigration reform, affordable housing, and decent wages, he embedded these issues in the public discourse. Most of Truman's domestic policy ideas would appear in the Democratic Party platform in 1948, and for several presidential cycles afterward. Eventually, all would become public policy in one form or another.[44]

Truman did not follow Rowe's advice entirely. Truman was too much of a partisan to play the role of conciliator. His duty, he explained, was to "get into the fight and help stem the tide of reaction. They [the Republicans] did not understand the worker, the farmer, the everyday person . . . Most of them honestly believed that prosperity actually began at the top and would trickle down in due time to benefit all the people."[45]

Republicans capitalized on their 1946 election victory immediately. Given the public's growing agitation with organized labor, the Republicans sought to reverse or seriously weaken the 1935 Wagner Labor Relations Act, which, among other provisions, guaranteed the right of workers in the private sector to organize and bargain collectively. The Wagner Act also established the National Labor Relations Board (NLRB) to adjudicate disputes and ensure that employers would not intimidate workers who wished to organize.[46]

Senator Robert A. Taft of Ohio, widely known as Mr. Republican, a leader of the party's conservative forces and a potential presidential candidate in 1948, joined together with another Republican conservative, New Jersey representative Fred Hartley, to pass a strong antilabor bill empowering the president to immediately end strikes for an eighty-day period, prohibit unions from contributing to candidates for federal office (thereby hurting Democrats), and outlaw the closed shop, a provision that would allow employers to hire nonunion workers at unionized factories and businesses.

Truman, who had his problems with organized labor, opposed the Taft-Hartley Act. It violated his sense of fairness, the balance between labor and management, of where the vital center of government power should fall in labor relations. Truman's veto message captured that balance: "The bill is deliberately designed to weaken labor unions . . . Unions exist so that laboring men can bargain with their employers on a basis of equality. Because of unions, the living standards of our working people have increased steadily until they are today the highest in the world . . . It [the bill] would take the bargaining power away from the workers and give more power to management."[47]

This restated his belief that the level playing field must be preserved. He concluded the veto message, "We must . . . construct a better America in which all can share equitably in the blessing of democracy." Congress overrode the veto, conservative Republicans combining with Southern Democrats to deliver a stunning rebuke to the president. It was the first and, as it turned out, the last major piece of legislation to originate from the Eightieth Congress.[48]

The Eightieth Congress continued to thwart the president's agenda for the next two years. Truman hoped to pass a national health insurance bill, given the inadequate and expensive health-care system controlled by private insurance companies. But the health-care industry and their friends in Congress hampered Truman's efforts to broaden coverage and lower costs.[49]

Truman's proposal was moderate, following the Social Security model of funding national health insurance through a 4 percent tax on personal income up to $3,600 ($47,000 in today's dollars). The average salary in 1946 was $3,150, so a majority of wage earners would pay into the plan. Government funds would finance health insurance for those individuals without an income or whose salary lay below the poverty line.

The American Medical Association (AMA) fought the proposal as socialistic, a charge echoed by Senator Taft, who called Truman's plan "the most socialistic measure this Congress has ever had before it." In the midst of a Cold War with the Soviet Union, such an accusation resonated with many

Americans and, particularly, with the conservative bloc in Congress. A Kansas City physician and friend wrote to the president complaining that the health-care initiative was creating a welfare state "where they guarantee everything from birth to the grave [and] incentive is destroyed." Truman responded sharply, concluding with a warning:

> When we find 34% of our young men and women unfit for military service because of physical and mental defects, there is something wrong with the health of the country and I am trying to find a remedy for it. When it comes to the point where a man getting $2,400.00 a year has to pay $500.00 for prenatal care and then an additional hospital bill on top of that there is something wrong with the system. Before I get out of this office I am going to find out what is wrong and I am going to try and remedy it. I'd suggest you Doctors had better be hunting for a remedy yourselves unless you want a drastic one.[50]

BUT TRUMAN'S CIVIL RIGHTS initiatives generated the most hostility, inside Congress and beyond. He was well aware that embracing civil rights estranged him from an important part of his heritage. That was difficult for a person steeped in family and place as was Truman. His commitment to racial fairness would become all the stronger for how much it went against the grain of his upbringing.[51]

CHAPTER 4

TO SECURE THESE RIGHTS

ISAAC WOODARD WAS A DECORATED black veteran, still in uniform, when he
boarded a Greyhound bus at Camp Gordon in Augusta, Georgia, on February
12, 1946, Abraham Lincoln's birthday. He was traveling to his home, near
Columbia, South Carolina. Sergeant Woodard and the bus driver had an
argument over the use of a restroom at one of the stops. The driver reported
the incident to the police, and in Batesburg, South Carolina, officers removed
Woodard from the bus, took him to a jail cell, and gouged out his eyes with a
blackjack. An all-white jury (jury pools were derived from voting lists and
blacks were disfranchised) deliberated for half an hour before acquitting the
town's police chief.[1]

On the evening of July 25, 1946, a white farmer was driving two black
couples back to his farm in Walton County, Georgia. One of the black men in
the car, Roger Malcom, had stabbed a white farmer in the arm over a wage
dispute and had been released on bond. His wife, as well as two of their friends,
George Dorsey, a navy veteran, and his wife, Mae Murray Dorsey, were the
other passengers. George Dorsey was rumored to be dating a white woman.

As they crossed a narrow bridge, a car blocked the road on the other side.
Another car pulled up behind them, then another and yet another. Thirty
white men armed with shotguns and rifles climbed out of their vehicles and
dragged the two black men out of their car. One of the women cried out the
name of a member of the mob—they had not bothered to disguise themselves.
Fearing that she could identify him and possibly others, the mob took the
women as well, lined up the couples, and emptied their guns into the victims,
who were mutilated beyond recognition.[2]

In the year following the end of the war in 1945, racial violence increased
in the South as whites sought to restore the strictures of white supremacy loos-
ened by war, and black Southerners hoped to bring the fight for freedom
abroad to the home front. These two incidents in particular caught Truman's
heart, and it would spur him to more substantive action on civil rights than
any other previous president.

A furious President Truman dispatched the Federal Bureau of Investigation (FBI) to Walton County, but residents would not talk with the agents. No indictments were ever handed down. Senator Richard B. Russell of Georgia, perhaps the most powerful Democrat in the Senate, lived about eleven miles from where the murders had occurred. He went on the floor of the U.S. Senate to speak against federal antilynching legislation. Russell asserted that the races got along harmoniously in the South and that, if trouble erupted, local law enforcement was better positioned to deal with it than a distant federal government. This was not a racial issue; it was a matter of states' rights. Truman, in disbelief, confided to a colleague in his typically earthy vocabulary, "There was a Georgia sheriff who took four niggers in a car, two men and two women, ordered them out of the car and shot them down, and nothing was done about it." In case the listener did not get the point, the president repeated, "Nothing was done about it."[3]

Truman found the brutality of these incidents hard to understand and harder to stomach. But federal authority was limited in the face of local resistance. After learning of the assault on Sergeant Woodard, Truman trembled, saying, "My God! I had no idea it was as terrible as that! We've got to do something." Truman would do "something" about it.[4]

In December 1946, in the wake of the midterm election debacle, Truman appointed fifteen distinguished Americans to the President's Committee on Civil Rights. He charged the committee to recommend specific policies to answer the question "How can State, Federal and local governments implement the guarantees of personal freedoms embodied in the Constitution?" He promised their work would not become another government report gathering dust on a distant shelf. This was Truman's response to his party's defeat at the polls.[5]

Though the Advisory Committee would not have an immediate impact on racial violence nor render justice in these particular cases, the ultimate objective was to enhance federal power where states and localities were unable or unwilling to protect their own citizens. Truman spoke with committee members and minced few words. As a Missouri Democrat, he respected states' rights; but he also recognized the necessity of federal action to enable fellow citizens to enjoy the protection of the Constitution. "There are certain rights under the Constitution of the United States which I think the Federal Government has a right to protect, and I want to find out just how far we can go." And so he told the committee, "Go to it."[6]

Some historians and critics at the time viewed Truman's advocacy of civil rights as politically motivated. A memorandum from two of his advisers, James H. Rowe Jr. and Clark Clifford, noted the growing political power of

African Americans in the North, and the declining influence of white votes in the South. As Rowe explained, "The northern Negro vote today holds the balance of power in Presidential elections for the simple arithmetical reason that the Negroes not only vote in a block [*sic*] but are geographically concentrated in the pivotal, large and closely contested electoral states such as New York, Illinois, Pennsylvania, Ohio, and Michigan." That vote, along with the traditionally Democratic urban ethnic vote, might swing some key Northern states into the Democratic column.[7]

The South was not essential to a Democratic presidential victory, nor had it been for some time. Franklin D. Roosevelt could have lost the entire South in his four election campaigns and still have won the presidency. Four Northern states—New York, Pennsylvania, Ohio, and Illinois—had more electoral votes than all of the states of the former Confederacy combined. These Northern states were also the recipients of tens of thousands of new black voters in the late 1940s and 1950s.[8]

Southern Democrats noticed the demographic shift well before 1948, which is why their reaction to Truman's initiatives was so furious. In 1943 journalist John Temple Graves, a native Georgian, wrote of "the cold arithmetic which makes the Northern Negro a more profitable object of political cajolery than the South." The Democratic Party was becoming a truly national party. In 1924, the South counted for nearly 93 percent of the party's presidential electoral total, but less than 24 percent in 1936. The transformation was not only a reflection of Franklin Roosevelt's popularity, but also of the increase of immigrant and African American voters in Northern cities. In 1918, the South accounted for twenty-six of the thirty-seven seats held by Democrats in the U.S. Senate. In 1936, the South held twenty-six of seventy-five Democratic seats. A similar shift occurred in the House of Representatives, where the South accounted for 107 of 131 Democratic seats in 1920, but 116 out of 333 Democrats in 1936.[9]

Still, Roosevelt and the Democratic Party were immensely popular in the South. Many Southerners considered the president their savior. The mere mention of his name during political campaigns provoked cheers in the deepest of the Deep South. But when he died in April 1945, that personal connection was severed. Harry Truman's early pronouncements on behalf of civil rights for African Americans hastened the dissociation between white Southerners and the Democratic Party. The solid Democratic South vanished after the 1944 election, never to return. The transformation was not instantaneous, but the direction was evident.

To take on a volatile issue that neither his party nor his country supported reflected Truman's heartfelt belief that this was the right thing to do.

Whatever the political or personal consequences—the loss of his Southern political friends or the disappointment of his family—they would not deter him from his determination to raise America to the standard of its ideals. If government could do anything, it should do this.

In 1947, just before he became the first president in history to address the National Association for the Advancement of Colored People (NAACP), he wrote to his sister, "I've got to make a speech to the Society for the Advancement of Colored People [sic] tomorrow and I wish I didn't have to make it . . . Mamma won't like what I have to say because I wind up by quoting Old Abe. But I believe what I say and I am hopeful we may implement it."[10]

The speech on June 29, 1947, was a brief both for racial equality and for the government's role in attaining that objective. His advisers told him to limit comments on civil rights to one paragraph. He ignored the advice. Walter White, executive secretary of the NAACP, would call the address "the hardest hitting and most uncompromising speech on the subject of race which any American President has ever delivered."[11]

For Truman, civil rights required federal action. The thin popular support and robust hostility of many citizens, North and South, precluded states and localities from addressing racial equality in the near term. "We must make the Federal Government a friendly, vigilant defender of the rights and equalities of all Americans. And . . . I mean *all* Americans." A system that placed artificial limitations on the dreams and opportunities of a people defied the principles of the nation's founding. "The only limit to an American's achievement should be his ability, his industry, and his character." Government was the umpire, assuring that the rules were applied equally.

But what must be done to achieve this noble end? "Our immediate task is to remove the last remnants of the barriers which stand between millions of our citizens and their birthright. There is no justifiable reason for discrimination because of ancestry, or religion, or race, or color." Waiting for the right moment was not an option: "We cannot wait another decade or another generation to remedy these evils. We must work, as never before, to cure them now . . . We cannot, any longer, await the growth of a will to action in the slowest State or the most backward community. Our National Government must show the way." At the conclusion of his speech, Truman turned to Walter White and blurted, "I mean every word of it—and I am going to prove that I do mean it."[12]

BY THE TIME OF THE PRESIDENTIAL election campaign of 1948, Truman had convinced many African American leaders, who were initially skeptical of his support, that they had a great friend, perhaps their greatest friend since

Lincoln, in the Oval Office. The NAACP's magazine, *Crisis*, was not, initially, an ally of the president's. But in September 1948, the editors praised Truman's actions on behalf of racial equality over the past three years:

> Mr. Truman's opponents are crying that his moves in the civil rights field are purely political . . . But no one has explained just how a man fighting to win the greatest prize, the highest office in America, can be insincere when he stubbornly and stoutly insists on a civil rights program that everyone knows is dynamite—and death—to political ambition in this country . . . His new orders represent a spirit and a courage on these issues as refreshing as they are rare.[13]

The President's Committee on Civil Rights released its report, *To Secure These Rights*, in October 1947. The report deserves to be counted among the nation's landmark documents. Its length—178 pages—has meant that many more honor the work than have read it. Nevertheless, it was an important milestone on the nation's journey toward racial equality. Inequality, the committee concluded, was "a kind of moral dry rot which eats away at the emotional and rational bases of democratic beliefs." Moreover, it damaged our credibility abroad at a time of intense competition with the Soviet Union.[14]

Such harmful consequences, both domestic and foreign, required epochal remedies. The committee proposed expanding the Civil Rights Section of the Justice Department and establishing a permanent commission on civil rights. The report urged a federal antilynching statute, the abolition of the poll tax, a law punishing police brutality, a law protecting the right to vote, and legislation forbidding discrimination in private employment and housing. The committee also called for the immediate end to segregation in the armed forces, in federal agencies, and in the District of Columbia. Eventually, all of these recommendations would come to pass, but few during the Truman years.

When the committee members sat down with the president to present their report on October 29, 1947, Truman had already read it. He told them, "I want you to know that not only have you done a good job, but you have done what I wanted you to." He predicted to an Oval Office visitor later that day that the report "will take its place among the great papers on freedom."[15]

The release of the report convinced many political experts that Truman had dealt a severe blow to the Democratic Party in the South. The mail from that region was virulently hostile. A Baptist minister from Jacksonville, Florida, warned the president, "If that report is carried out, you won't be elected dogcatcher in 1948," adding with some accuracy, "The South today is the South of 1861." A Virginia woman was both apoplectic and apocalyptic: "If you do away with segregation, allow negro children in white schools, churches, etc. you might as well drop a few bombs on us and not prolong the agony." Closer to home, friends from Missouri warned Truman to distance himself from the report.[16]

The president felt a need to respond to his neighbors. The reply captured his vision of a nation in which equal opportunity was color-blind. It underscored his belief in the possibilities of the future rather than in clinging to the detritus of the past. It also reflected his continued shock and sadness over the violence visited on African Americans in the South:

> The main difficulty with the South is that they are living eighty years behind the times and the sooner they come out of it the better it will be for the country and themselves. I am not asking for social equality . . . but I am asking for equality of opportunity for all human beings, and, as long as I stay here, I am going to continue that fight. When the mob gangs can take four people out and shoot them in the back, and everybody in the [surrounding] country is acquainted with who did the shooting and nothing is done about it, that country is in a pretty bad fix from the law enforcement standpoint . . . I am going to try to remedy it and if that ends up in my failure to be reelected, that failure will be in a good cause.[17]

Truman's civil rights program stood no chance of passage, or even of coming to a vote, and it jeopardized his other domestic initiatives as well. The power of Southern Democrats may have been eroding with the party, but not within the Congress. In 1949, the U.S. Senate had fifteen standing committees, of which thirteen directly related to public policy. Of those thirteen, Southerners and their allies chaired all but one committee. Committee chairs had unchallenged power to form, block, or delay legislation emanating from their committees. The more powerful Senate committees had a strong representation of Southerners. The most powerful, Appropriations, included thirteen Democrats, seven of whom were from the South. They were the sentinels for states' rights, and the most important of those rights was white supremacy.

Most Southern Democrats had been in the Congress for a long time. They rarely, if ever, faced Republican opposition at home, and as their seniority increased, so did the projects they bestowed on their districts, further solidifying their position. Longevity enabled Southern senators to master the rules, and if they needed a favorable interpretation, the Senate's parliamentarian was from Arkansas. The Southern Caucus, a group of twenty-two senators from the former states of the Confederacy, met frequently to discuss strategy concerning pending legislation. They gathered in the office of their leader, Georgia senator Richard B. Russell.[18]

In February 1948 Truman sent a special civil rights message to Congress including most of the report's recommendations as well as one of his own urging reparations for Americans of Japanese descent who were forced into internment camps during World War II "solely because of their racial origin." It was the most comprehensive civil rights legislative package a president had ever sent to Congress. Truman noted bitterly in his diary, "They no doubt will receive it as coldly as they did my State of the Union message. But it needs to be said."[19]

He also knew it would cut him off from his Southern friends, perhaps forever. Senator Tom Connally of Texas, a good friend of Truman's, termed the president's civil rights package, with no sense of irony, "a lynching of the Constitution." White Southerners compared Truman's assault on racial inequality to Northern attacks on Southern institutions in the 1850s. Jimmy Byrnes related that one of his fellow South Carolinians told him he was "much more afraid of Truman than of Russia."[20]

If the white South was furious, white Northerners were indifferent. According to a Gallup poll, only 6 percent of Americans supported the president's civil rights initiatives. Leaving out the South, the approval rating increased to 21 percent, but that was hardly a ringing endorsement. On the other hand, Americans' disapproval of Truman had grown from 18 percent in October 1947 to 57 percent by April 1948.[21]

To compound Truman's problems, the Democratic left was suddenly as unreliable as the party's conservative wing. In December 1947, Henry A. Wallace, the former vice president, announced his independent candidacy for president. Most Democrats found Wallace too radical on domestic policy and unquestioning about the motives of the Soviet Union abroad. He opposed the popular Marshall Plan for rebuilding Europe as too confrontational toward the Soviets. The Soviet takeover of Czechoslovakia in 1948 did not bother him in the least. Eleanor Roosevelt compared Wallace to former British prime minister Neville Chamberlain, whose name had become synonymous with appeasement. Wallace also championed racial equality and campaigned in the South at much personal peril. Despite such noble gestures, the longer Wallace campaigned, the more support he lost.[22]

Many in the party believed that Truman was a sure loser and cast about for a viable candidate to challenge the president. In March 1948, Elliott Roosevelt, one of Franklin D. Roosevelt's sons, publicly endorsed Dwight D. Eisenhower. In April the liberal magazine *The New Republic* featured a front-page editorial with the headline, "As a Candidate for President, Harry Truman Should Quit." By the time of the Democratic National Convention in Philadelphia in July, a Stop Truman movement had gained momentum. Some of these dissident Democrats favored Supreme Court associate justice William O. Douglas or the ever-popular Eisenhower, but both declined to run.[23]

While the Stop Truman movement fizzled, another threat to the president emerged on the convention floor. Truman, sensing the real possibility of a Southern boycott or walkout, supported a more moderate civil rights plank in the party platform than what he himself had called for earlier in the year. Ironically, the president's own activism on civil rights had given courage to Northern liberals, led by Hubert H. Humphrey, who was running for a U.S. Senate seat from Minnesota. As Minneapolis's youngest mayor in history at age thirty-four, Humphrey had championed a municipal Fair Employment Practices Commission, an advocacy that created great turmoil within the city, so much so that the city's leading black newspaper urged him to drop it in the name of restoring harmony. Humphrey brushed aside the suggestion: "To hell with that, it's right and it's going through." But the conflict highlighted that civil rights issues were not much more popular in the Deep North than in the Deep South.[24]

Humphrey would have none of Truman's sudden caution on civil rights. Victory in the Cold War, Humphrey insisted, would go to the nation that could live the strongest ideals. Humphrey mounted the stage and, like a Roman senator addressing the Forum crowd, cried out, "People! This is the issue of the twentieth century . . . In these times of world economic, political, and spiritual . . . crisis, we cannot and we must not turn back from the path so plainly before us. That path has already led us through many valleys of the shadows of death . . . Our land is now, more than ever before, the last best hope on earth. I know that we can—know that we shall—begin here the fuller and richer realization of that hope—that promise—of a land where all men were truly free and equal."[25]

The result of the electrifying address was the strongest civil rights plank in any party's platform ever. Humphrey's cry represented, Arthur Schlesinger Jr. noted, "the most basic challenge to the American conscience." Sixty million Americans heard the speech on radio and 10 million more viewed it on television. Humphrey's heartfelt words impressed many, and the delegates knew it.[26]

Democratic urban bosses, who typically had little patience for the party's liberal wing and who usually compromised with Southern conservatives to preserve party unity, joined Humphrey. It was less a moral commitment on their part than a political calculation. They recognized that the growing influence of black votes in their cities required a tougher stand on racial equality, especially since the Republicans also supported civil rights at their convention. Besides, as one urban boss noted, "I'd also like to kick those Southern bastards in the teeth for what they did to Al Smith in 1928."[27]

Most of the Deep South delegates walked out of the hall, led by Alabama delegate Eugene "Bull" Connor, carrying the state's standard as he exited. It was almost reminiscent of the procession out of the U.S. Senate when the lower-South states left the Union in January 1861, except the 1948 bolt lacked the solemnity of that earlier occasion. The gallery taunted the defectors, serenaded them with traveling music, and waved mock good-byes. Florida's liberal senator, Claude Pepper, who stayed, noted sadly, "We are witnessing the complete breakup of the Democratic Party. This might be Charleston, South Carolina, in 1860." Not yet; but it was a portent.[28]

There were exceptions. There, in a sea of empty metal folding chairs, in the place where the Alabama delegation had once held forth, sat a young man in a dapper dark suit, his black hair slicked back, and his jaw thrust forward in a profile the nation would soon become familiar with. George Corley Wallace would not desert his president over civil rights.

Still, as *Time* magazine put it graphically, "The South had been kicked in the pants, turned around and kicked in the stomach." With the desertion of some, but not all, of the Deep South states into the newly formed States' Rights Democratic Party (popularly known as the Dixiecrats) and with the Democratic Party fracturing on its left wing with the defection of Henry A. Wallace to the new Progressive Party, Truman's candidacy seemed doomed in the summer of 1948. The Dixiecrats understood they had no chance of winning a national election outright, but they hoped to pull enough Southern states into their electoral column to throw the election into the House of Representatives, where they stood a much better chance of brokering the selection of the next president.[29]

The polls showed Truman's Republican opponent, New York governor Thomas E. Dewey, winning handily. But the president came out of the convention fighting. He called the Eightieth Congress back into an unprecedented session—the first such call-up in an election year since 1856—to deal with the nation's housing crisis, inflation, education, and civil rights legislation, all of which the Republicans addressed in their own party platform, but now, in this special session, declined to support lest Truman share the credit. The enmity between Congress and the president was evident in this special session. In a significant departure from protocol, some senators and representatives did not rise from their seats when the president entered the chamber. "No," said

Republican senator Robert A. Taft, "we're not going to give that fellow anything."[30]

Which is what Truman expected. When the special session yielded nothing, Truman charged out over the country on a whistle-stop train tour attacking the "do-nothing" Eightieth Congress. *Life* called him "Li'l Abner Ozark Style," but journalists compared him to William Jennings Bryan. And Eleanor Roosevelt, who had once called Truman "a weak and vacillating person," now asserted, "There has never been a campaign where a man has shown more personal courage and confidence in the people of the United States." The message, as Mrs. Roosevelt implied, was bold and forward-looking, a sharp contrast to the fearmongering of the Republicans.[31]

Truman's whistle-stop campaign tour with his wife, Bess, was vintage Bryan. He had promised running mate Alben Barkley, "I'll mow 'em down . . . I'll give 'em hell." Which is precisely what he did. Typically speaking on a platform at the back of his train, he railed against "Wall Street reactionaries," "gluttons of privilege," "bloodsuckers," and "plunderers." He tapped Republicans in Congress as "tools of the most reactionary elements." At the end of the speech, Bess would toss a rose into the crowd.[32]

In Chariton, Iowa, on September 18, 1948, he reminded the rural audience that 123,000 farmers lost their farms in 1932; in 1947, only 800 farms were foreclosed. Truman used the past to contrast it with the present and warn about what Republicans would do to people's future. It was the future, most of all, that energized the Truman campaign: "I'm asking you just to read history, to use your own judgment," he told the Iowa crowd, "and to decide whether you want to go forward with the Democratic Party or whether you want to turn the clock back to the horse-and-buggy days." His optimistic message bet on a promising future instead of restoring a dubious past.[33]

It was good theater, but according to the pollsters, it was barely registering with the electorate. Two weeks before the election, most of the polling services stopped their surveys as Dewey had a failproof lead, winning the Roper poll by 52.2 percent to Truman's 37.1 percent, and Gallup by 49.5 percent to 44.5 percent. The *Chicago Tribune* was so certain of Dewey's victory on election night that at ten P.M. it published an election-night edition with the banner headline "DEWEY DEFEATS TRUMAN." When the final results were posted the following morning, Truman had received 49.6 percent of the popular vote to Dewey's 45.1 percent. Both the Dixiecrat candidate, Strom Thurmond, and the Progressive Party standard-bearer, Henry A. Wallace, fared poorly, garnering a combined 5 percent of the popular vote.[34]

Truman's margin in the Electoral College was a bit more comfortable, 303 to 189, but it was still a close race. The president carried the thirteen largest cities, precisely those locales where the immigrant and black vote were likely to be decisive. The Democratic Party regained control of both houses of Congress. As Truman's train pulled into Union Station in Washington, D.C., after the election, 750,000 people gathered to welcome him. When he and Bess stepped off the train, the band played "I'm Just Wild About Harry." In January 1949, Harry Truman was inaugurated for a full term as president of the United States. It was the first integrated inauguration in the nation's history.[35]

As political pundits wiped the omelet off their faces, the narratives they wove to explain the "greatest upset in American history" were equally off base. Some concluded that now the United States was "normally Democratic." Others accounted for the upset by stating Truman won "the urban masses" as well as the voters who lived on farms and in small towns. By that accounting Truman should have won by a landslide as few people did not live in one of these places. Other experts noted that Truman did especially well among voters of German descent in the Midwest who had deserted the Democrats because of Roosevelt's decision to go to war against Nazi Germany. They now returned to their ancestral political home. So Truman got the Nazi vote. He also somehow did incredibly well with Jewish voters.[36]

More accurately, Truman benefited from his enemies, specifically the Dixiecrats and the partisans of Henry A. Wallace. They allowed Truman to run from the center, away from the two extremes, even though his programs carried the New Deal much further than Roosevelt had contemplated. Truman won also because of the electoral power of Americans new to inclusion in the political process: African Americans, Jews, and Catholics, who parlayed their concentration in the cities of the Northeast and Midwest into power.

Republicans provided the other asset for President Truman. They rejected programs most Americans favored. Truman had asked for low-cost rental housing; Republicans responded by weakening rent controls. He sent a proposal for a national health program to Congress; the Republicans denounced it as socialistic, and nothing came of it. Truman had also requested federal funding for public schools; again, the Republicans did nothing. The president wanted to expand Social Security and increase the minimum wage; Republicans turned down both requests. Republican obstruction of the president's agenda might not have hurt the party much if its members had provided alternatives. But they did not. The only major measure to pass the Eightieth Congress was the Taft-Hartley Act, which seriously restricted labor unions. The Republicans had some help from Southern Democrats in rejecting many of the president's proposals, but since the GOP controlled both houses of Congress, they had to run on its record, which was meager.[37]

Thomas E. Dewey, governor of New York and the Republican presidential nominee, proved an unwitting foil for Truman. He had run a crisp presidential campaign against Roosevelt in 1944, and most experts predicted he would finally gain the White House in 1948. Though he was congenial in private, and a decent fellow overall, he came across as pompous when in public. Lillian Dykstra, a close friend of Senator Taft's wife's, quipped that Dewey "struts sitting down."[38]

Assured that he would win, Dewey took the high road during the campaign and mouthed platitudes rather than policy. The *Louisville Courier-Journal* distilled Dewey's campaign speeches into four sentences: "Agriculture is important. Our rivers are full of fish. You cannot have freedom without liberty. The future lies ahead." Dewey's stilted campaign suffered in comparison with Truman's combativeness. The *New Republic*, not a Truman fan, grudgingly admitted, "It was fun to see the scrappy little cuss come out of his corner fighting . . . being himself and saying a lot of honest things."[39]

The advice of Rowe and Clifford was well taken. Truman held enough of the South and gained more in the North to snatch the victory from Dewey. Truman became the first presidential candidate to venture into Harlem for a political rally, on October 29, where an enthusiastic crowd estimated at sixty-five thousand cheered his words on racial equality a few days before the general election. In his whistle-stop train tour across the country, he insisted on integrated seating at Rebel Stadium in Dallas and weathered boos in Waco when he shook hands with a black woman. Although he rarely mentioned civil rights during his whirlwind October campaign, he had issued two executive orders three months earlier initiating the desegregation of the armed forces. A second executive order established a Fair Employment Board to monitor ethnic and racial discrimination in federal hiring. He would have done more were it not for Congress, or as he termed it time and again from the back of his railcar, "the do-nothing Eightieth Congress."[40]

Some experts believed Truman had doomed his candidacy by flogging the South on civil rights. The Harlem excursion was the last straw, the final nail in his political coffin that, according to *Newsweek*, "all but dooms the candidacy of President Truman." The president indeed lost four Deep South states to the Dixiecrat ticket of South Carolina governor Strom Thurmond and Mississippi governor Fielding Wright. In addition to those two states, the Dixiecrats picked up Alabama and Louisiana. Remarkably, and fulfilling the prediction of the Rowe-Clifford memorandum, Truman held on to the rest of the South.[41]

Southern political leaders and their constituents were not yet ready to abandon the Democratic Party and the power they held in Congress. Besides, the likelihood of Truman's ever implementing his civil rights measures was dim. The pull of history—the Civil War and Reconstruction—persuaded many Southern white voters to either stay home or vote their memories.

The Republican postmortem was painful. Henry Cabot Lodge Jr., Republican senator from Massachusetts, attempted to explain the defeat. He also took some swipes at the Democratic Party that, ultimately, proved accurate. Lodge acknowledged that the Democrats effectively presented the GOP as "a rich man's club and as a haven for reactionaries." He admitted that some Republicans fit that description, though they did not represent the rank and file of the party. But there was no question, he noted, that the GOP had to broaden its appeal to more segments of the population. Lodge challenged the assertion that the Democratic Party was the sole party of progress. As evidence, he cited a substantial segment of that party—the South—as avowed opponents of civil rights.[42]

For the increasing numbers of voters who were married with young children, the Democratic Party presented a more hopeful agenda than the Republicans. Americans voted for tomorrow, not for yesterday. The United States was prosperous in 1948, both on the farms and in the cities. Incomes were at their highest peak in American history, people were buying homes, cars, household appliances, and the prospects for advancement through education never looked better.

There was hope for continued prosperity. There was hope in Truman's civil rights proposals for a more just society, not only for African Americans, but also for the sons and daughters of Southern and Eastern European immigrants, who swelled the voting rolls. As one Italian American voter stated, "The Dixiecrats made me think of Al Smith." The key lesson, perhaps, of the 1948 presidential election was, as political scientist Samuel Lubell opined, "the doctrine of too little government" became as frightening "as that of too much government." The Republicans would need to develop "their own concept of the positive role that government is to play in American life." Through Dwight D. Eisenhower, they would do that.[43]

IN 1949, HISTORIAN BERNARD DeVOTO wrote that America had crossed a meridian: "For more than a century we have provided Government assistance to business whenever business got into truly serious trouble. Now we have adopted a corollary. From now on the power of the Government will be used to combat unemployment and extreme private distress as well as breakdowns in industry and finance." Truman's surprising victory in the 1948 presidential election affirmed that principle.[44]

Truman carried a grudge against the Southern Democratic defectors. At the inauguration parade in January 1949, he turned his back on Strom Thurmond. Truman denied patronage and federal programs to former Dixiecrats. When Mississippi Democrat John Rankin asked the president to support the Tombigbee Waterway, a canal project to connect the Tennessee River with the Gulf of Mexico, Truman angrily rejected the notion: "The economy bloc, made up principally of Democrats and Southerners who have been against my program, have rather cooled me off on this subject. They are extremely on the economy side when Social Legislation is up but when it comes to 'pork barrel,' . . . they are right in the front line."[45]

Despite the opposition of the conservative coalition in Congress, in the realm of civil rights during his new term Truman could advance certain policies through executive action. He ordered the desegregation of Washington National Airport and named black law professor William Hastie to the U.S. Court of Appeals for the Third Circuit, the highest rank an African American had ever attained in the federal judiciary. And Truman continued to push for the array of civil rights proposals he had sent to Congress the previous year, though he knew this was a futile exercise. To keep the issue before the public and the press was worth the effort.[46]

Yet, even executive orders were not exempt from dilatory tactics. Truman's order desegregating the armed forces had specified that it must occur as rapidly as possible, "having due regard to the time required to effectuate any necessary changes without impairing efficiency or morale." General Omar Bradley, who would implement the policy, opposed integration and fastened on the "due regard" clause to delay it altogether. But when General Matthew Ridgway succeeded Douglas MacArthur as supreme commander in the Pacific during the spring of 1951, he ordered the desegregation of all troops in that theater, including those fighting in the Korean conflict. Complete desegregation of the armed forces would not occur, however, until Dwight D. Eisenhower pursued the issue when he became president in 1953. No officer would dare delay an executive order from the former general.[47]

TRUMAN COULD ALSO MOVE ON civil rights without going through Congress via the federal court system. The Hastie appointment was one example. The president also intervened in several federal cases challenging *Plessy v. Ferguson*, the 1896 U.S. Supreme Court ruling that established the principle that racial segregation did not violate the Constitution as long as the separate facilities (in that case, passenger railroad cars) were equal. The separate-but-equal formula enabled Southern states to codify racial segregation. The facilities were rarely if ever equal, be they railroad cars, schools, neighborhood services, parks, or any other place where citizens gathered. It was not only a system of separation, but also a pattern of humiliation—a daily reminder to African Americans that they were inferior.

The first case the Truman administration entered was that of George McLaurin, a sixty-three-year-old black doctoral student in education at the University of Oklahoma. In 1948, a federal district court ordered the university to admit McLaurin because none of the state's black colleges offered the doctoral degree in education. In other words, there was no equal facility available to African Americans; in fact, there was no facility at all. The university, forced to accommodate McLaurin, placed his desk in an anteroom outside his classroom, provided a segregated desk in a dingy corner of the library, and allowed him to use the cafeteria only at odd hours and to eat only at a specific table.

Truman directed his Justice Department to file an amicus brief on behalf of McLaurin. The University of Oklahoma, sensing an adverse ruling, modified its position and permitted McLaurin to sit in the classroom, but only in a seat railed off and marked RESERVED FOR COLORED. McLaurin could also enter the library's main floor and eat in the cafeteria at regular mealtimes, though still separate from whites.

White fellow graduate students, however, upset the university's bizarre plan by ripping down the railing and joining McLaurin for meals. The Supreme Court ruled unanimously in *McLaurin v. Oklahoma Board of Regents* (1950) that "the restrictions placed upon him [McLaurin] were such that he had been handicapped in his pursuit of effective graduate instruction . . . Those who will come under his guidance and influence . . . will necessarily suffer to the extent that his training is unequal to that of his classmates. State-imposed restrictions which produce such inequalities cannot be sustained." While the *Plessy* precedent remained intact, the Court had broadened the definition of what constituted inequality. More ominously for the forces of segregation, Chief Justice Fred M. Vinson, a conservative Kentuckian, delivered the Court's opinion.[48]

That same day, the Court handed down its decision in a companion case also joined by the administration. The University of Texas Law School had refused the admission of black applicant and veteran Heman Sweatt, contending that all-black Texas Southern University possessed a law school that complied with the separate-but-equal standard. At the time, Texas had 7,701 white lawyers and 23 black attorneys. The University of Texas student-body president and a large number of students rallied on behalf of

Sweatt, pointing out the contradiction between Sweatt's fight for the nation's democratic ideals abroad and his treatment at home.[49]

NAACP attorney Thurgood Marshall presented the case to the U.S. Supreme Court in April 1950. Marshall was a thorough integrationist. He had grown up in segregated Baltimore, convinced that integration was the key to resolving what Swedish economist Gunnar Myrdal called the "American dilemma" of race. The best way to accomplish integration was first to tackle education, Marshall believed. If children sat together in classes at a young age, they would grow up with one another, and integration in other venues would invariably follow. Marshall understood that a direct assault on *Plessy* would not work as judges were loath to overturn a precedent that had existed for over fifty years. If, however, he could expose how segregation was, in itself, unequal, he could base the case on *Plessy* while simultaneously narrowing if not eviscerating the legal logic on which it rested.[50]

Price Daniel, the Texas attorney general, used the domino defense, arguing that if Sweatt succeeded in the suit, then African Americans would have to be admitted to swimming pools, elementary schools, and hospitals. "All we ask in the South," he pleaded, "is the opportunity to take care of this matter and work it out [ourselves]." This was the common refrain of segregationists: we know best, so we can solve this without outside interference. The refrain repeated itself over the next fifteen years, demonstrating how little white Southerners knew about African Americans and how much they defined "work it out ourselves" as a tenacious embrace of the status quo.[51]

In another unanimous decision on behalf of a civil rights plaintiff delivered by Chief Justice Vinson, the Court in *Sweatt v. Painter* added some intangible distinctions to the definition of separate but equal: "The University of Texas Law School possesses to a far greater degree those qualities which are incapable of objective measurement but which make for greatness in a law school." The Court cited the school's prestige, the network of influential alumni, and the quality of the faculty. Excluding Sweatt from such perquisites would place him in an "academic vacuum" and at a singular disadvantage in the practice of law. Thurgood Marshall knew, of course, that no Jim Crow school could meet those criteria. He told an audience at Fisk University shortly after the ruling, "We now have the tools to destroy all governmentally imposed racial segregation." It was but a short step to declaring that segregation itself was unequal and, therefore, violated the equal protection clause of the Fourteenth Amendment.[52]

The Court may well have ruled in favor of the plaintiffs in both cases without the Truman administration's support. But the Court tilted to the moderate-conservative side of the political spectrum. The support given by the federal government made an impression on the justices, four of whom (including two Southerners) were Truman appointees.

By 1950, a few judges in the lower federal-court system were already contemplating overturning *Plessy*. A case emerged from South Carolina that, along with similar cases in four other jurisdictions, would change the landscape of race relations for all time. This time, however, the litigation involved a public school system in the Lower South, raising the stakes of the outcome considerably.

Harry Briggs was a navy veteran who, returning to his Summerton, South Carolina, home at the end of World War II, hoped for a better future for himself and his children. Like many other Southern blacks, Briggs believed that a war against racism abroad would resonate at home. His children went to school in a dilapidated structure. The school served grades one through twelve, and more than one hundred children crowded into a single classroom with desks spilling out into the hallway. A potbellied stove provided heat in the winter. The toilets were outdoors.[53]

The local white elementary school was a relatively new brick structure with modern fixtures, indoor plumbing, and sufficient space for youngsters' education and recreation. By any reading of *Plessy*, this was unconstitutional. Harry Briggs, however, was not prepared to press his case along those lines— this was, after all, rural South Carolina, and he had a family to support on his salary as a gas-station attendant. He merely wanted a school bus so his children would not need to walk nine miles around a lake or else row across it to get to school. Clarendon County's white schoolchildren had thirty buses at their disposal; black pupils had none. Briggs took his request to the county school board in 1947. The chairman, lumber merchant R. W. Elliott, responded succinctly, "We ain't got no money to buy a bus for your nigger children."[54]

Briggs took Elliott to court to get that school bus. But NAACP counsel Thurgood Marshall and federal district court judge J. Waties Waring, a prominent white Charlestonian, persuaded Briggs to alter his suit to launch a direct challenge to *Plessy*: whether segregation under any circumstances could be equal. The three-judge panel of the federal district court in Charleston in 1951 denied Briggs's petition in a two-to-one ruling with Judge Waring dissenting.[55]

Waring's dissent presaged the language of the *Brown* decision three years later: "Segregation in education can never produce equality and . . . is an evil that must be eradicated . . . All of the legal guideposts, expert testimony, common sense, point unerringly to the conclusion that the system of segregation in education adopted and practiced in the state of South Carolina must go and must go now. Segregation is *per se* inequality."[56]

In 1952, the Truman administration prepared an amicus brief on behalf of *Briggs* as the case went to the U.S. Supreme Court. Eventually, the Court decided to fold the *Briggs* case into four other similar cases then winding through the federal court system. By then, Dwight D. Eisenhower was president, and in an unusual move, his attorney general, Herbert Brownell, used the Truman brief, virtually intact, for the government's argument in favor of overturning the *Plessy* precedent. Truman left office with a parting vow to his erstwhile Southern Senate colleagues. He pledged that the fight against racial injustice "will never cease with me as long as I live."[57]

The Truman administration contributed mightily to the growing discourse on equality. By 1950, stories of African Americans appeared regularly in magazines. Jackie Robinson made the cover of *Life* in 1950, the first black person ever on the magazine's cover. One writer noted that, by this time, there was "a spreading sense of outrage that discrimination based solely on skin color was locking people out of jobs, housing . . ."[58]

It would have been relatively easy, especially during the postwar boom years, to sidestep subjects such as civil rights and ethnic equality. But Harry Truman's upbringing and his political genes did not allow for silence on subjects that Americans ought to know and act upon. His mostly futile persistence on civil rights placed that issue on the national agenda for all time. His advocacy of a permanent Fair Employment Practices Committee, his call for the abolition of the poll tax, his commissioning of a study that took its title— *To Secure These Rights*—from the Declaration of Independence, led to an extensive legislative agenda. When Southern congressional committee chairmen suppressed these initiatives, Truman turned to the courts, filing amicus briefs supporting the NAACP suits that would eventually bring down separate but equal. Thurgood Marshall concluded that President Truman had "done more . . . for civil rights than all other presidents put together."[59]

In the meantime, African Americans were voting with their feet. The great migratory stream that had begun in the early twentieth century resumed after World War II. Whether the North was the promised land was debatable. But in contrast to life in the South, African Americans could live without fear of random racial violence, with some prospect of making a decent living, and without the daily humiliations of racial segregation. At least that was the hope.

CHAPTER 5

SOUTH BY NORTH

SINCE THE EARLY 1900S, African Americans had left the South for cities in the North and West. By the early 1960s, more than 6 million had made that journey, nearly one third of them since the 1940s. They migrated for the same reason that propelled other diasporas worldwide: to make a better life for themselves and their families. They left the South to find work, a better place to live, and for dignity—to no longer live under a system that separated and humiliated them daily, where upward mobility was strictly a white-American dream.

But in their new home, they confronted old prejudices. The landscape was different, but opportunities were still hard to come by. Work, housing, and education—the stepping-stones to the fruitful pursuit of happiness—proved elusive and difficult to access. The attitudes of whites in the North turned out to be little different from those of whites in the South. Still, African Americans came and hoped.

David Blakely left Pensacola, Florida, in 1947 for New York City "because I was tired of not being able to vote and not being treated like a human being." Robert Joseph Pershing Foster, a physician, departed Monroe, Louisiana, for Los Angeles in 1953 because he "did not want to be paid with buttermilk or the side of a freshly killed hog and did not want to deliver babies in somebody's kitchen."[1]

Blakely and Foster, like most of the six million black migrants, set their sights on a city. Roughly 50 percent of the nation's African Americans were city dwellers by the 1940s, over 80 percent by the 1970s. Detroit's black population, for example, grew from 9 percent of the total population in 1940 to 45 percent by 1970.[2]

The economic opportunities may have been greater in the urban North, but the migrants' timing was problematic. Northern cities were beginning to lose manufacturing and retail jobs, an economic trend that would accelerate in the coming decades. These jobs were either gone forever or gone to the suburbs. Ford Motor Company shifted all engine production from its River Rouge plant, which was the largest employer of black workers in the Detroit area, to more automated plants in Cleveland and Dearborn. In 1945, the River Rouge factory employed eighty-five thousand workers, but only thirty thousand by 1960. In 1945, Chicago, Pittsburgh, and Gary, Indiana, produced 54 percent of the world's steel; by 1970, only about 20 percent.[3] Global competition and outsourcing contributed to the decline.

When blacks succeeded in landing jobs in the retail sector, it was almost always as "maids, elevator operators, and wrappers," not as salespeople. Such major department store chains as Kaufmann's, Sears, and Gimbels openly acknowledged their policy of excluding blacks from sales positions, arguing that white customers would refuse to conduct business with African Americans.[4]

If postwar America seemed like one large building site, black construction workers stayed mostly on the sidelines. Building-trades unions systematically excluded African Americans. They worked as common laborers, but not as electricians, carpenters, plumbers, or brick masons. The unions barred them from apprenticeship programs for skilled positions. In 1961, Philadelphia had seventy-three hundred members in its plumbers, electricians, and steamfitters unions. Only one of those members was African American.[5]

The Northern urban job market threw up obstacles for black women as well. Josephine McCloudy worked as the only custodian on the night shift at a Packard automobile factory in the Detroit area. In June 1945, the company fired her for attempting to use the whites-only restroom. Segregation did not only occur in the South. Her local United Auto Workers representative refused to take up her case with management. In 1946, a New York City cosmetics manufacturer housed its black and white female workers in two separate buildings and paid the white women $4 more per week. In 1950, 41 percent of black women workers in the North toiled in domestic service. These jobs were not subject to minimum-wage regulations, Social Security benefits, or unemployment compensation.[6]

Job discrimination existed at the higher end of the employment scale as well, often perpetuated by prominent civic institutions in Northern cities. Harry Smyles was one of the best classical oboists in postwar America. Serge Koussevitsky, the noted conductor and composer, said Smyles was "perfectly qualified to take a position in any orchestral organization in America." Yet Smyles could find no symphony to hire him. No major American symphony employed a black musician in the 1950s. African American conductor Dean Dixon won rave notices for his guest-conducting appearances but could never find a permanent place with an American orchestra. In 1953 he accepted a post as the permanent conductor of the Gothenburg Symphony in Sweden.[7]

* * *

AFRICAN AMERICANS ALSO FACED discrimination in finding a decent place to live. The G.I. Bill and other government-guaranteed loan programs favored new housing. By the mid-1950s, 50 percent of all new home construction benefited from federal subsidies, but only 2 percent of these developments accepted African American buyers. At a time when all Americans faced housing shortages, the situation was especially dire for African Americans. Their desperate need for shelter rendered them susceptible to practices that took advantage of them.[8]

Clyde Ross came to Chicago in 1947 and took a job as a taster for Campbell's soup. With a steady income and a young family, he purchased a house that year in the North Lawndale section of the city for $27,500 ($300,400 in 2016 dollars), or nearly four times as much as the cost of a new Levitt home at that time. The seller was not the previous owner but someone else who had bought the house for $12,000 six months earlier. Since it was unlikely that Ross could obtain a bank loan, he bought the home "on contract." That meant that the seller kept the deed until Ross paid the entire purchase price. In the meantime, Ross accrued no equity in the property, and if he missed a payment, he would forfeit both his $1,000 deposit and all of his monthly payments to that point. Plus, he and his family could be evicted, and the seller could start the process all over again with another black family. North Lawndale became a ghetto.[9]

Housing developments and neighborhoods had long possessed restrictive covenants barring black purchasers, but also Jewish and Catholic homebuyers as well. In 1948, however, the U.S. Supreme Court in a St. Louis case, *Shelley v. Kraemer*, outlawed restrictive covenants. Thurgood Marshall argued the case on behalf of the plaintiffs. In a rare action, three of the nine Supreme Court justices recused themselves from the case—they each owned properties with deeds that included racial covenants.[10]

The Truman administration joined Marshall in the case. Attorney General Tom Clark and Solicitor General Philip Perlman supported Marshall's effort. Perlman, a Baltimore native like Marshall, was Jewish. He knew about restrictive covenants from personal experience. Perlman gave a heartfelt, dramatic hour-long presentation to the Court, almost as if he were pleading his own case. White Americans, he informed the justices, were "under a heavy debt to colored Americans. We brought them here as slaves. Yet, after three quarters of a century, attempts are made by such devices as restrictive covenants to hold them in bondage, to segregate them, to hem them in so that they cannot escape from the evil conditions under which so many of them are compelled to live." The Court unanimously struck down restrictive covenants. That neighborhoods found other ways to discriminate against African Americans,

Jews, and Catholics did not diminish the importance of the decision and the wide publicity Perlman's oration received. The fight for equal rights was not only a political matter; once again, it was seen as a moral undertaking.[11]

Truman hoped that the 1949 Housing Act would provide a path around such discriminatory measures by establishing national programs for slum clearance and public housing for all tenants, regardless of race, religion, or national origin. Truman's stake in the housing debate was the same as in his efforts to promote civil rights legislation and immigration reform. The federal government had a key role to play when neither state governments nor the private sector could fill the role of ameliorating injustice.[12]

Working closely with the Truman administration were three senators—New Dealer Robert Wagner of New York, and two conservatives, Democratic senator Allen J. Ellender from Louisiana and Senator Robert A. Taft of Ohio. Together they crafted the Taft-Ellender-Wagner Act. The stated objective of the act was to "build enough houses, over a long enough period, to supply a decent home in a suitable living environment for every American in every income group in every section of the country." It was a fine statement of the commonwealth ideal: that the federal government's role was to help provide decent housing when the private sector did not or could not fill the requirements. The act offered federal funding to cities to acquire "blighted" areas for redevelopment. Cities would be rebuilt, providing more jobs, eliminating unsightly slums, and opening up the city to new activities, more space and light, and more private investment. The result was a two-tier approach to housing policy: publicly subsidized housing for the inner-city poor and a series of tax breaks and subsidies to private developers and homebuyers mainly in the suburbs.[13]

The real estate lobby opposed the new law vigorously, but bipartisan support in Congress overcame objections. Scarcely a member of Congress did not have some constituents strapped for housing choices in the years immediately following the war. Taft, whose leading role in the legislation might be surprising given his opposition to federal activism, was convinced that the private sector could not profitably fill the gap in low-income housing, thus opening the way for government to enter the market. It was a Keynesian and Lincolnian principle even some conservatives could embrace: that the government must do for the people that which they cannot do for themselves. "Not many people," Taft explained, "are complaining that they cannot find doctors. But many complain that they can't find homes."[14]

In one poll 69 percent of Americans favored the legislation. The act offered a seemingly simple solution to two major urban problems: not enough housing for the poor, and deteriorating inner-city neighborhoods. Construction of public housing and demolition of slums under the act would resolve both problems, its sponsors promised. That it did not quite work out in that manner is less an indictment of the legislation than a reflection of our federal system of government, which relies on local implementation of national legislation, and of the failure of Congress to fund the legislation it passed. These problems and the heavy Korean War expenditures limited construction to only about a quarter of the 810,000 public housing units authorized in 1949.[15]

THE DIFFICULTIES IN IMPLEMENTING the 1949 Housing Act to its fullest extent forced African Americans to seek housing in existing urban neighborhoods. The expansion of the black urban population in the North generated confrontations with white urban residents. As early as 1943, Detroit experienced a bloody race riot connected to housing and jobs, the worst civil disorder in the United States since the draft riots of the Civil War in 1863. When African Americans entered previously all-white neighborhoods in Northern cities, trouble often followed. Nearly three fourths of all violent racial incidents between 1945 and 1950 occurred over housing. Whites living in contested zones and who could afford to leave moved to the suburbs or to peripheral urban neighborhoods. But many working-class whites could not.[16]

An era of what one historian called "chronic urban guerilla warfare" unfolded. The war had lasting consequences: the racial divide widened, working-class whites took a more conservative turn in their politics, and neighborhoods and then the city deteriorated.[17]

Most of the contested neighborhoods housed white working-class families, often only one or two generations removed from Europe. As manufacturing began its long decline, the insecurities of employment compounded the fear of losing one of the few solid investments these workers had: a home. A 1951 survey of Detroit residents revealed these fears. One woman, who described herself as an "average American housewife," wrote, "What about us, who cannot afford to move to a better location and are surrounded by colored? . . . Most of us invested our life's savings in property and now we are in constant fear that the neighbor will sell its property to people of a different race." Only 18 percent of white respondents throughout the city expressed "favorable" views toward the "full acceptance of Negroes," and 54 percent opposed integration.[18]

When the survey asked respondents to comment on "the colored problem," some of the responses included, "80% of [blacks] are animals." "If they keep them all in the right place there wouldn't be any trouble." When asked, "What do you feel ought to be done about relations between Negroes and whites?,"

68 percent advocated some form of racial segregation, and a number of respondents referred favorably to the South's Jim Crow racial traditions.[19]

These responses had a distinct class inflection, with 85 percent of poor and working-class whites supporting racial segregation. But these whites had middle-class aspirations and many believed they had already attained that status through homeownership. These white families were on the front lines of transitional neighborhoods and schools. In Detroit, they formed neighborhood organizations—192 of them—to prevent black influx and, during the late 1940s, became a growing and powerful political force.[20]

From the 1940s to the 1960s Detroit had at least two hundred racial incidents involving African Americans moving into white neighborhoods, a reflection not only of the depth of racial antagonism but also of the speed with which neighborhoods could change—fewer than four years on average. Real estate brokers went door-to-door urging white residents to sell quickly, even at below-market prices, lest the value of their properties fall even more. Realtors often organized a "staging," where they ostentatiously showed houses in the neighborhood to a few black families, followed by a flurry of leaflets and phone calls urging whites to sell their homes while a relatively decent market existed.[21]

These events had profound political implications. In the 1949 Detroit mayoral race, Democrat George Edwards, a former activist with the United Auto Workers and a public housing administrator with a strong New Deal background, faced off against Albert Cobo, a Republican corporate executive and real estate investor. Normally, this would not have been much of a contest, with Edwards winning easily in the pro-union city. However, the clash over housing propelled Cobo to victory. A postelection analysis observed, "In these municipal elections we are dealing with people who have a middle class mentality. Even in our UAW, the member is either buying a home, owns a home, or is going to buy one."[22]

The white backlash that became a common theme of politics in the mid-1960s first emerged in Northern cities during the late 1940s. Cobo easily won reelection in 1951, 1953, and 1955. Working-class whites triumphed politically, but eventually lost the battle for their neighborhoods. By the mid-1950s, black residents comprised one third of Detroit's population, and the white population had fallen by 23 percent as families exited for the suburbs. African Americans rarely had that option. Approximately ten thousand African Americans worked in the Ford plant at suburban Dearborn in the mid-1950s; not one black person lived in Dearborn.[23]

African American families that pioneered in white neighborhoods often paid a price above their monetary debt. When three black families moved into the previously all-white Trumbull Park Homes in Chicago in 1953, they carried their belongings into their respective apartments under police guard. The police patrolled the property around the clock in three eight-hour shifts. White women hurled stones and tomatoes at the new tenants. A sixty-five-year-old white woman prostrated herself in front of a car carrying black tenants. The police dragged her away. Black families kept their children indoors, blinds drawn. Local shops that served black customers found windows smashed. The violence forced many to close. Resident black families avoided walking neighborhood streets and did their shopping at a considerable distance from the area. Eventually, the city assigned twelve hundred police to the houses, 15 percent of all the officers in Chicago, but it did not ease the tension.[24]

Even when prospective black tenants found white allies, efforts to break the de facto residential segregation in the North encountered major obstacles. In the spring of 1946, Lee Lorch returned to New York from the Pacific, where he had served with the Army Air Corps during the war. He obtained a job teaching math at the City College of New York. Lorch, his wife, and their young daughter set up a temporary home in a Quonset hut in Brooklyn while he looked for more permanent quarters in the city. After a two-year search, they finally moved into Stuyvesant Town, a sprawling apartment complex in lower Manhattan built by the Metropolitan Life Insurance Company in 1943. Lorch and his family were white, which was a good thing, since Frederick H. Ecker, the president of Met Life, stated in 1943, "Negroes and whites don't mix."[25]

In 1947, three black veterans brought suit against Met Life, an action cosponsored by the American Civil Liberties Union, the American Jewish Congress, and the NAACP. But the suit was unsuccessful since Met Life had not broken any laws. New York State, the city, and the federal government had no legislation prohibiting discrimination in housing. The city, in fact, was a partner with Met Life, providing the land and tax breaks, but leaving the selection of tenants entirely to the company.

Lee Lorch thought this was not right, especially since the aggrieved parties were veterans. Along with twelve other tenants, he formed the Town and Village Tenants Committee to End Discrimination in Stuyvesant Town. The group soon swelled to eighteen hundred tenants. Met Life refused to end the "no Negroes allowed" policy, and Lorch paid the price for his activism by being denied tenure and promotion at City College despite having the support of his department.

Lorch found a position at Penn State. The Lorches invited a black family, Hardine and Raphael Hendrix and their young son, to live in the Lorch apartment during the academic year. Met Life refused to accept the Lorches' monthly

$76 rent check and began maneuvering for their eviction. Penn State declined to reappoint Lorch. An administrator for the university told him that accommodating the Hendrixes was "extreme, illegal, and immoral, and damaging to the public relations of the college."[26]

But protests by Penn State students, Albert Einstein, the American Association of University Professors, the American Mathematical Society, and two newspapers—the New York Times and the communist Daily Worker—pushed Met Life to admit three black families in 1949. Yet Met Life persisted in its efforts to evict Lorch along with thirty-four other tenants who led the Tenants Committee. When they refused to move, the Teamsters Union mobilized to provide protection for the tenants to ensure they would not be forcibly evicted.

In the meantime, Lorch had obtained a teaching position at historically black Fisk University in Nashville, Tennessee, becoming one of two white professors at the school. A resolution of sorts was reached when Met Life, Lorch, and two other tenants agreed to move as long as the Hendrixes could stay. By 1957, only forty-seven black tenants lived among the twenty-five thousand residents of the complex.

Lorch continued his activism in Nashville on behalf of civil rights, a habit that resulted in his firing from Fisk. He found a job at another historically black institution, Philander Smith College in Little Rock, Arkansas. But he ran afoul of the administration there as well for his civil rights activities. No American college or university would hire Lorch, so he moved his family to Canada and secured a position at the University of Alberta, and then at York University in Toronto, where he remained until his retirement in 1985. Five years later, Lorch received an honorary degree from the City University of New York.

The Lorches' experience underscored the difficulties inherent in challenging residential segregation in Northern cities. African Americans and their white allies could expect little assistance from local governments, major employers, or most religious institutions. In some of the contested neighborhoods, supporting black housing aspirants could be dangerous, especially given the broad consensus in these districts to preserve the racial status quo.

Even when African Americans gained access to suburbs, the reception was likely to be as hostile as in cities. In 1957, Daisy and Bill Byers became the first black family to move into Levittown, Pennsylvania. Their neighbors protested against the couple and burned a cross on their lawn. One neighbor summarized the sentiment, acknowledging that Bill Byers was "probably a nice guy, but every time I look at him I see two thousand dollars drop off the value of my house."[27]

* * *

THE RACE-NEUTRAL G.I. BILL seemed to provide a path around systemic discrimination. A spokesman for the National Urban League in 1945 remarked that the G.I. Bill did not contain a "single loophole for different treatment of white and black veterans." But the guaranteed home-loan program required recipients to receive the loans via local banks. In the South, this proved nearly impossible for black applicants. In 1947, for example, of the 3,229 Veterans Administration–backed loans granted under the G.I. Bill in Mississippi cities, black vets received only two.[28]

When African American veterans managed to obtain loans, racial discrimination severely restricted their options of where to purchase a home. The legal demise of restrictive covenants notwithstanding, in Levittown, Long Island, for example, which had eighty-two thousand residents by 1960, none were black. As one observer noted about the G.I. Bill in 1945, "The white GI will be considered first a veteran, second and incidentally a white man; the Negro GI will often be considered first a Negro, second and incidentally a veteran."[29]

The broad consensus among federal bureaucrats, bankers, and real estate agents was that housing should be segregated, and black neighborhoods were, by definition, significant credit risks. In 1950, the National Association of Real Estate Board's code of ethics warned, "A Realtor should never be instrumental in introducing into a neighborhood . . . any race or nationality, or any individuals whose presence will clearly be detrimental to property values." While this admonition also implied discrimination against Jews and Catholics, it targeted primarily African Americans in the postwar years.[30]

Dubious sociology reinforced the idea that separation of the races was necessary for public order. A *Life* magazine editorial in 1946 warned, "Heterogeneous neighborhoods of conflicting social mores and races breed strife. Negroes do not mix well with the Irish; Poles, Hungarians, Czechs, Puerto Ricans each have their own racial characteristics." The writer attributed the alleged spike in juvenile delinquency to mixed urban neighborhoods.[31]

Redlining was the most notorious contribution of federal policy in the financing of homeownership that maintained and created segregated neighborhoods. The FHA routinely rejected loans in black neighborhoods. At its outset in 1934, the FHA correlated racial homogeneity with a property's quality. An early FHA manual explained, "If a neighborhood is to retain stability, it is necessary that properties shall continue to be occupied by the same social and racial classes." The FHA also encouraged restrictive covenants until *Shelley v. Kraemer* prohibited them in 1948, then looked the other way when neighborhood associations sprouted to accomplish much the same result.[32]

Redlining made the complaints of white homeowners that black families tended to depress housing prices a self-fulfilling prophecy. Failure to invest in a neighborhood almost guaranteed its decline. Thus the creation of the "second ghetto," a more sprawling, more isolated, and more troubled area of the city than the neighborhood's earlier incarnation. The ultimate consequence of the obstacles African Americans encountered in obtaining loans and homes was that during the postwar decades when millions of white families were able to build wealth through homeownership, African Americans lagged significantly behind, a gap that increased over time and remains to the present day.[33]

INSTITUTIONAL DISCRIMINATION SIMILARLY undermined the good intentions of the G.I. Bill with respect to education. In housing, city administrations and other federal agencies undercut the G.I. Bill. In education, private institutions maintained control over their admissions process, which meant African Americans faced exclusion in the South and quotas in the North. Nor were public institutions of higher education necessarily under the law's purview. A provision in the bill prohibited any federal agency from "exercising supervision or control over any state educational agency," meaning that, in the South, the federal government had no control over state-sanctioned segregation at public institutions. By 1947, about twenty thousand black vets could not find a place at any institution of higher education; it was likely that tens of thousands more did not bother to try. Not surprisingly, education gaps and, therefore, income gaps between blacks and whites increased during the late 1940s and early 1950s as college-educated whites spurted ahead.[34]

But the G.I. Bill was mostly responsible for one advance. Without it, black college enrollment would not have increased after the war given the financial exigencies of most black applicants. Where African Americans could enroll without obstacles—at historically black colleges and universities—attendance jumped from twenty-nine thousand in 1940 to seventy-three thousand by 1947. During the next two decades some of these black college graduates would play significant roles in the growing civil rights movement in the South.[35]

Discrimination in jobs, housing, and education were part of a broader pattern of racial exclusion confronting the rising black population of Northern cities in the decade after World War II, and color was more important than status. In 1947, blues singer Huddie Ledbetter, known as Lead Belly, had his first New York experience. After he performed at Sarah Lawrence College, a restaurant manager, a train conductor, and a cabdriver each either refused to provide service or did so discourteously. In each case, Lead Belly encountered the N-word. When world-renowned singer Josephine Baker visited New York the following year, things had not changed. She and her French husband were turned away at no fewer than thirty-six hotels before they found a place to stay. In the early 1950s, with the rapid expansion of commercial air travel, blacks who could afford it looked to the skies for relief from the indignities of segregated train travel. But the American Airlines travel manual for 1951 instructed ticket agents to segregate passengers by race.[36]

African Americans were no more likely to encounter better treatment from Northern law enforcement. New York City black councilman Benjamin J. Davis published a pamphlet in 1947, "Lynching Northern Style: Police Brutality," detailing twenty-six cases of unwarranted police assaults on African Americans. Seattle police justified racial profiling of blacks by claiming "all negroes carry knives" and "any Negro driving a Cadillac is either a pimp or a dope-peddler."[37]

The tools African Americans could employ to challenge discrimination were limited. In 1947, blacks boycotted the White Tower restaurant chain in Brooklyn's Bedford-Stuyvesant neighborhood and reversed the chain's stand against hiring black workers. In an awkward but revealing public statement about the resolution, the company declared it no longer believed "Negroes aren't capable of being good countermen and women."[38]

THE GREAT MIGRATION did not precipitate a great reinvention of black life in America after World War II. One black migrant who came North in 1947 admitted a decade later, "I tell myself all the time it's better than Mississippi, but I'm not always sure." Although gratuitous violence and daily humiliation were less likely in the North, blacks continued to encounter "walls of exclusion" and even racial violence in their new homes.[39]

A comprehensive approach was necessary to break down the barriers to housing, work, and education for African Americans. Harry Truman understood this. He would be the first of the gifted generation's presidents to go beyond his time and his background to forge a better America. And not only for African Americans.

CHAPTER 6

THE SCARLET LETTER

MOBILITY WAS A COMMON THREAD of the immediate postwar era. Soldiers returning home, African Americans migrating from the South, refugees hoping to come in, and millions of citizens moving out to the suburbs or over to the next neighborhood. Mobility implied confidence, a new place to live, a new job, a new family, and all brimming with possibilities. There was no sentiment for returning to the dreary days of the Depression or to the dislocations of war. But many hoped that mobility would not upend tradition: that Protestant white men would continue to dominate the nation's political, economic, and educational institutions, that African Americans would quietly slide into their accustomed economic and residential separateness, that Jews and Catholics would not push too ardently to enter institutions and neighborhoods where they were not wanted, and that women would stay home and embrace housekeeping and motherhood.

This age-old battle between progress and tradition was much more than a philosophical tug-of-war, as the racial violence, North and South, indicated, as the flaring anti-Semitism exposed, and as the contest for what a woman ought to be was fiercely joined. The results of these struggles were mixed in the immediate postwar years, reflecting divided public opinion. Government, beginning with the Truman administration, would open the national bounty to a much wider constituency than at any previous time in American history. The movement had already begun for African Americans, and for Catholics and Jews. But not yet for women.

Government policies helped to generate unprecedented prosperity and opportunities for building wealth and obtaining an education. In turn, individuals could aspire to greater accomplishments. Women could look forward to security, a family, and usually children. From this beneficent base, it was possible to build a career, if they so desired. While many Americans applauded the former aspiration, they questioned, even condemned, the latter. For some women, though, these objectives were not mutually exclusive; they were mutually reinforcing.[1]

Gwyned Filling came to New York City from St. Charles, Missouri, in June 1947. Like many young men and women arriving in the big city from small towns, she hoped for a rewarding career. Gwyned, recently graduated from the University of Missouri, borrowed $250 from a local bank, and, together with her college roommate, Marilyn Johnson, set off on her life's adventure. After a five-week search for work, during which her nest egg had dwindled to $30, she found a job at the Newell-Emmett Company, one of the city's largest advertising agencies. Her starting salary was $35 a week (nearly $400 per week in 2017 dollars). A male semiskilled factory worker in New York earned $67 a week ($730 in 2017 dollars).[2]

Budgeting became an occupation that rivaled her ad agency work. Gwyned had learned frugality during her college years, making her own clothes and rarely spending more than fifteen cents on breakfast. She and Marilyn found a furnished room, eleven by fifteen feet, on East Twenty-third Street at $75 a month, which they split. Attractive and friendly, Gwyned could usually count on one of her male officemates to take her out to dinner, which usually saved her $4 a week. After six months, Newell-Emmett promoted her and raised her salary to $52 a week. Gwyned did not escape financial straits, however, as she had to begin paying off her bank loan at the rate of $21.93 per month.

Despite the financial burdens, Gwyned reveled in the independence and the variety of life in New York. She enjoyed encountering the artists, musicians, and writers that populated lower Manhattan in the late 1940s. She became more politically engaged than she was back home. Discussions about anti-Semitism and the impending formation of the new state of Israel were major topics among her friends at the ad agency, she reported. Less than a year into her work, she found a boyfriend, Charlie Straus, a talented copywriter at the agency. She enjoyed his quick wit, though his shyness sometimes irritated the outgoing Gwyned. The most constant element of her life, though, was her great enthusiasm for her career. While she occasionally experienced homesickness, Gwyned knew she belonged in New York.

Gwyned married Charlie on November 3, 1948. They remained married for fifty-four years, until his death in November 2002. The marriage ended Gwyned's advertising career: Newell-Emmett did not allow married couples to work together, and typically the wife resigned. But she did not retire entirely to domestic life. In the ensuing years, she became involved in charitable work, ran a fabric business with her friends, engaged in fund-raising and development, and worked for environmental causes. By the 1960s, she was organizing fund-raising galas for the American Cancer Society, featuring such headliners as the violinist Isaac Stern and the Alvin Ailey dancers. Gwyned turned to politics in the 1980s, winning election to the South Dartmouth,

Massachusetts, Town Meeting. She also became much in demand as a speaker to college audiences and to women's studies departments, talking about how she refused to settle into an exclusively domestic life after World War II and, instead, entered a field—advertising—traditionally dominated by men.

Charlie became a successful copywriter, enabling the family to employ nannies for their two sons (born in 1951 and 1953) and the children to attend boarding school. The boys, members of the gifted generation, pursued successful careers in finance and the law. After Charlie's death, Gwyned moved to a retirement community in Tiverton, Rhode Island, on the eastern shore of Narragansett Bay, where she died in 2005 at the age of eighty.[3]

Gwyned's life was perhaps remarkable in its trajectory, but not in its ambition. The writer in *Life* magazine who profiled Gwyned in 1948 implied that for her and for other young women, a career and ambition were good things. The writer could not of course know of Gwyned's future with Charlie or the prosperity she would attain, so different from her financially strapped upbringing. The writer concluded the piece by observing Gwyned's great joy for her work and her choice "for the career she has well started. Whether it will also end well seems a remote matter to her—what is important is that she is doing what she has always wanted to do."[4]

Life's profile did not sit well with some of its readers. A woman from Detroit, noting Gwyned's often sleep-deprived pace of life in New York, concluded that her "tired too-old eyes, the tense posture all proclaim the barren gain from her frantic efforts to find self-expression . . . If your story can keep only a few girls in their small-town homes it will have done at least some small service to humanity. Big cities are a menace to the progress of civilization." A gentleman from Syracuse, New York, was more succinct: "Gwyned Filling would look much more appealing ironing diapers back in St. Charles, Mo."[5]

The contest between those who supported, even demanded, a more traditional role for women after World War II, and those who believed that independence and ambition were admirable traits, raged mightily in the postwar years. Although many credit Betty Friedan's *The Feminine Mystique* (1963) with launching the modern feminist movement, the frustrations she highlighted were evident two decades earlier. Far from wandering in a desert of domesticity, women in the immediate postwar years pursued a variety of options including marriage and childbearing, but also careers outside the home. They did so despite disapproval, ridicule, and hostility to their soaring ambitions.

WORLD WAR II BROUGHT record numbers of women into the workplace. The percentage of women in the workforce increased from 26 percent in 1940 to

36 percent in 1945. In 1940, most of the women workers were young, single, and working- or middle-class, doing "women's work" as housecleaners, farm laborers, waitresses, nurses, and elementary-school teachers. By the end of the war, married women made up three fourths of those newly entering the workforce. Some of the jobs they held, such as pipe fitter, welder, and carpenter, glamorized by "Rosie the Riveter" posters, were simply not open to women before the war.[6]

Such opportunities motivated high school girls to think of careers outside the home. A 1943 poll of thirty-three thousand female high school students found that 88 percent preferred a career other than housewife for at least some part of their lives. A May 1945 survey of female workers in Detroit found that 60 percent of the respondents who were housewives expressed the desire to remain employed once the war ended. Black women in particular benefited from the openings to female employment brought by the war. The number of African American women employed in government grew from sixty thousand to two hundred thousand between 1940 and 1945.[7]

The large numbers of women in the wartime workforce led experts to predict that the old equation of "career *or* marriage" would give way to "career *and* marriage" as women enjoyed the economic and social benefits of work outside the home. These predictions also forecast a change in the attitude of women toward marriage. Ray E. Baber, a prominent sociologist, wrote in 1943 that women's participation in the wartime workforce and their service in the auxiliary branches of the armed forces "strengthen[ed] the feeling of independence." He forecast that this sense of independence would actually enhance marriage as women's status as wage earners would permit them to marry, and at a younger age.[8]

But Baber was ambivalent about this newfound freedom. He warned that women's independence came at a cost as "a large number of mothers in war work have not provided adequate care and supervision for their children." Hence the rise in juvenile delinquency and "moral confusion." It harked back, Baber argued, to the "wild twenties," "flaming youth," and the loosening of social control.[9]

Demobilization resulted in 2.5 million women leaving their jobs voluntarily and another million being laid off. Most of the latter had toiled in industrial occupations, typically male work. Many rejoiced at returning to a "normal" life with husbands and families. Others did not. Women members of the United Automobile Workers threw up picket lines, hoisting placards stating FORD HIRES NEW HELP. WE WALK THE STREET, or STOP DISCRIMINATION BECAUSE OF SEX. It was a lost cause. The fear of sliding back into an economic depression combined with millions of veterans returning to civilian life rendered equal employment opportunity unattainable. The American public had little patience with women who wanted to retain their wartime jobs. In a 1946 poll only 22 percent of men thought women should have an equal chance at employment. Most women agreed, with only 29 percent favoring equal employment access.[10]

Despite the exodus, only about 1 million fewer women were working in 1950 than in 1945. For the first time in American history, in 1950 fully 50 percent of these workers were married. These working women believed that marriage and family and career were not mutually exclusive options. For most, paid work was an economic necessity. Still, young women such as Gwyned Filling bucked prevailing public opinion, as the letters to *Life* magazine indicated. The expectation was that young women would marry and devote the remainder of their lives to husband and children. A variety of sources cited work outside the home as incompatible with women's primary roles as wife and mother. One magazine's ominous headline warned, "Nearly Half the Women in *Who's Who* Are Single."[11]

This was not only the view of conservative public opinion, but also often of experts. In *Modern Women: The Lost Sex* (1947), sociologist Ferdinand Lundberg and psychoanalyst Marynia Farnham asserted, "The independent woman is a contradiction in terms." Women, they counseled, should strive instead for "receptivity and passiveness, a willingness to accept dependence without fear or resentment, with a deep inwardness and readiness for the final goal of sexual life—impregnation." They warned that women who veered from this advice were "sick, unhappy, neurotic, wholly or partly incapable of dealing with life." The authors also recommended that older unmarried women—spinsters, in the common parlance—should be barred from teaching, as they were obviously emotionally unstable.[12]

Helene Deutsch, a colleague of Sigmund Freud's, published the influential two-volume study *The Psychology of Women: A Psychoanalytical Interpretation* (1944–45), in which she equated "femininity" with "passivity" and "masculinity" with "activity" in all spheres of life. Sociologist Willard Waller claimed that women had "gotten out of hand" during the war because of the job options suddenly available to them and the absence of men on the home front. Now it was time to enforce two rules: "women must bear and rear children; husbands must support them." Instead of advancing the cause of women in the postwar world, social science, according to Betty Friedan, gave "old prejudices" new authority.[13]

Popular culture also reinforced the role of marriage for women, usually at the expense of "careerism." In the 1950 movie *All About Eve*, Bette Davis played a renowned actress who gave up a major role to marry. "I've finally got a life to live," she rejoiced, and something "to do with my nights." In *The Tender Trap* (1955), Debbie Reynolds's character won her first role on Broadway, but when Frank Sinatra congratulated her, she replied, "A career is just fine, but it's no substitute for marriage." Film critic Peter Biskind offered that the "scarlet letter *A*" in 1950s cinema stood for "ambition" rather than "adultery."[14]

THE ADVANCES OF WOMEN during wartime were taken back in the immediate postwar years. They did not last either at professional schools or at undergraduate institutions generally. With large numbers of men off to war in 1942, colleges actively recruited women and offered courses that challenged prevailing views of feminism. In the fall of 1942, the Sociology Department of Syracuse University offered the course "The Status and Responsibility of Women in the Social Order." The syllabus included a section on women in the defense industry and asked the students to consider women as "creative personalities outside the home." In 1930, women constituted 43 percent of all undergraduate students and 18 percent of doctoral recipients, the former figure rising to 55 percent by the end of the war. By 1960, however, women comprised 36 percent of all undergraduates and 10 percent of doctoral students.[15]

It was worse at elite colleges and universities. Women were less likely than African Americans to gain admission to the Ivies. More accurately, they were highly unlikely to attend. Yale did allow a few women to enroll in graduate school in 1950, but not at the undergraduate level. Harvard had Radcliffe as a sister institution, but few boundaries were crossed outside of socializing. Radcliffe's president informed freshmen that the school "would train them to be excellent wives and mothers and perhaps even to win the ultimate prize: marriage to a Harvard man." When Yale floated a proposal in 1956 to accept women as undergraduates, alumni rejection was swift. Undergraduate men opposed it as well.[16]

Some wondered whether it mattered for women to attend college at all given their preordained roles as wives and mothers. An article advocating federal aid to higher education in April 1949 profiled two fictional teenagers from a small Midwestern town, Eddie Burns and Susie Smith. Because Susie came from a relatively well-off family and Eddie did not, she went to Vassar and he was pumping gas at a local filling station. The writers asserted that there were "tens of thousands of Eddies in the U.S. who ought to go to college, and also tens of thousands of Susies who should probably stay at home." Susie "has no particular talents, except for marrying a nice man, but Eddie was a potential doctor, engineer or scientist."[17]

Some of the anxiety about women breaking from traditional roles related to sex, particularly the revelation that young, single middle-class women actually enjoyed sex and did not necessarily view chastity as a virtue. The sexualized female had been a concern in the buttoned-up Victorian era, but especially during the 1920s, the jazz age, when both skirts and libidos rose too high for critics. Combined with the newly won right to vote, the result in the minds of many was too much liberation is not a good thing.

Alfred Kinsey, an Indiana University scientist who had spent much of his early academic career studying insects, reignited the debate with *Sexual Behavior in the Human Female* (1953). The book easily outsold his previous bestseller, *Sexual Behavior in the Human Male* (1948), selling 250,000 copies. Kinsey's report on women, couched in scientific jargon, indicated that a shocking (to some) 50 percent of women had premarital sexual intercourse and that 26 percent of married women had committed adultery. The figures were higher for men—90 percent and 50 percent, respectively—and extramarital affairs were particularly rampant among successful businessmen, 80 percent of whom admitted to such behavior, causing the usually unflappable Kinsey to exclaim, "God, what a gap between social front and reality." The veil on many things would drop over the next two decades, creating a more honest if also a more discomfiting perception of society.[18]

Kinsey's book on women created a storm of controversy. Some libraries refused to purchase it, and several bookstores sequestered the volume, forcing buyers to ask for it specifically. A few commentators dismissed Kinsey's methods, though the studies were based on over eighteen thousand lengthy interviews and extensive research. Kathleen Norris, a novelist, did not believe the women Kinsey and his staff interviewed were telling the truth. "Believe me, Dr. Kinsey," she wrote, "the women who told you of such girlhood and postmarital sex experiences were of an easily recognized sort: the sort who wrote themselves letters from imaginary lovers, in high school days, and have gone right along into womanhood fabricating sensational affairs . . . But genuine women, with something in the past of which they are ashamed . . . don't talk about it." For this reason, Norris concluded, Kinsey's work was harmful. If the book convinced young and unmarried readers "that the purely physical side of wedlock is the all-important one, then they are doomed to alternating unsatisfactory matings and divorces."[19]

These were the mildest forms of criticism. The religious community, which consistently perceived a nation in moral decline, denounced the report. Billy Graham intoned, "It is impossible to estimate the damage this book will do to the already deteriorating morals of America." The Reverend Henry P. Van Dusen, president of the prestigious Union Theological Seminary in New York, charged that the report revealed "a prevailing degradation in American morality approximating the worst decadence of the Roman Empire." And everyone knew what happened to Rome. The Indiana Roman Catholic Archdiocese contended that Kinsey helped "pave the way for people to believe in communism," though the Church was vague on the precise connection between sex and Marx.[20]

But even liberal sources damned the report. Literary critic Lionel Trilling expressed alarm at Kinsey's conclusions, worrying that the scientist had used "facts" to celebrate an ideology of "liberation." The nerve. The Rockefeller Foundation ostentatiously announced it was withdrawing its financial support from Kinsey's research. An exhausted and dispirited Kinsey died in 1956 at the age of sixty-two.[21]

The emphasis on role conformity hardened by the mid-1950s. In a June 1947 issue of *Life* magazine, the writers took an evenhanded view of women balancing work and family. In a December 1956 number, the magazine tilted decidedly toward an exclusively homebound role for married women, which, demographically, more closely resembled their female readership than during the immediate postwar years. The 1956 issue included interviews with five psychiatrists (all men) who agreed that the rise in marital unhappiness, divorce, and unruly children owed to "wives who are not feminine enough and husbands [who are] not truly male." Wives leaving home to work emasculated husbands. Traditional ideas about the role and status of women were thus repackaged as scientific formulas for family life.[22]

By the early 1950s, men and women were marrying young—twenty-two for men, and twenty for women—the lowest yet in the twentieth century. In 1940, 24 percent of eighteen- to twenty-four-year-old women were married. By 1950, that figure had risen to 60 percent. The same pattern prevailed for men. In 1940, 15 percent of all women who reached their early thirties had never been married. Twenty years later, that figure had dropped to 7 percent. By the 1950s, 95 percent of all Americans of marriageable age were getting married, the highest rate in the developed world. It was not a matter of "want" or "choice," one young woman noted. "Why talk about things that are as natural and as routine as breathing?"[23]

Marrying so young, at the height of a woman's fertility, fueled the baby boom. By the mid-1950s, the median marriage age of women had dropped to a historic low of 20.1. One out of two brides was still in her teens, and more than half of these women had babies before they turned twenty. The percentage of men who married between the ages of twenty and twenty-four nearly doubled from 27 percent to 51 percent between 1940 and 1955. The median marriage age of men dropped to 22.5 by the mid-1950s.[24]

Experts agreed that marriage was a young woman's top and only priority. Dr. Emily Mudd, executive director of the Marriage Council of Philadelphia, assured her readers that "practically every woman wants to get married, or anyway, believes she does." Several university professors agreed that most of their female graduate students on track for careers "would drop their studies and get married in a minute, if the right man came along." Education, in fact, had a "deflating effect upon romance," since four out of five "spinsters now in their forties are women with college degrees." It was important for women to select occupations that would put them in contact with men. Nurses and schoolteachers rarely met eligible men; but secretaries did. "Air hostesses" were best positioned to meet men.[25]

THE EXPECTATION FOR WOMEN was not only to marry, but also to have children. The baby boom touched off loud hosannas. *Look* magazine was ecstatic: "The wondrous creature [woman] marries younger than ever, bears more babies and looks and acts far more feminine than the 'emancipated' girl of the twenties or thirties. If she makes an old-fashioned choice and lovingly tends a garden and a bumper crop of children, she rates louder Hosannas than ever before."[26]

The number of children per family increased by one child, from 2.27 to 3.2 children, within less than a generation. Single-child families became the exception by the late 1940s, and families with two or more children rose from 55 percent to 82 percent during this period. In 1940, fewer than 11 million children were under the age of five; by 1950, it was 16 million, and by 1960 it was 20 million. In the 1950s, the five- to seventeen-years age group, the heart of the gifted generation, which had increased by fifty-two thousand during the 1940s, jumped by an additional 8.3 million. By 1964, four out of every ten people in the United States were under the age of twenty. It was a cohort to be reckoned with—economically, culturally, and politically.[27]

The postwar generation of college women was unequivocal in defining success in terms of matrimony and children. A 1946 survey of students at fourteen universities found that "success" for four of every five girls interviewed meant "happiness in marriage." Male students were primarily concerned with success in their chosen fields. Such views were understandable, as an educated woman's primary avenue to security was to make a good marriage as early as possible, leave the workforce, and raise children. She derived her social standing from her husband. Marriage, therefore, was an implicit deal: in exchange for the security and social standing the husband provided, the wife offered sex, children, and care of the household. As late as 1961, a study of female college seniors revealed that the vast majority of the students "mostly wanted to be mothers of 'highly accomplished children' and wives of 'prominent' men."[28]

The idea had become so ingrained in American society by the early 1950s that Adlai E. Stevenson, a former and future Democratic candidate for president, could say in his commencement address in 1955 at Smith College, one of the most prominent women's institutions of higher education in the nation, "I want merely to tell you young ladies" that they could do much "in a great historic crisis" America faced in the Cold War by assuming "the humble role of housewife—which, statistically, is what most of you are going to be whether you like the idea or not just now—and you'll like it!"[29]

THE PROLIFERATION OF YOUNG marriages would not have occurred, cultural pressures aside, had it not been the case that young couples could now afford to get married, and young couples could afford to get by on one income once the children came. That, and government subsidies for loans in housing and education, eased financial burdens. The baby boom occurred most vigorously among white middle-class women whose husbands earned sufficient income to facilitate larger families cared for by stay-at-home moms. In the mix of personal choice, societal expectations, and general prosperity, the choice of homemaking was realistic, especially after depression and war. What increasing numbers of women challenged was the notion that "housewife" was the only acceptable choice and that the realm outside the home could not be less tilted in favor of men.

Betty Friedan borrowed a phrase from Nazi Germany for this postwar development. Society had confined women to their biological role: *Kinder, Küche, Kirche* (children, kitchen, church). In the late 1930s, Friedan noted, fiction in women's magazines often depicted career women as heroines. That was much less the case by the 1950s. The range of topics in these publications narrowed to home and family. The male editor of a popular women's magazine explained to Friedan, "Our readers are housewives, full-time. They're not interested in the broad public issues of the day . . . They are only interested in the family and the home . . . Humor? Has to be gentle, they don't get satire." It was an infantilization of women, or at least a thorough condescension.[30]

The new and ever-younger parents grasped for a manual. They found it in Dr. Benjamin Spock's *Common Sense Book of Baby and Child Care* (1946), which became immensely popular because its vagueness allowed for numerous interpretations suiting different parenting styles. As he noted in the book's preface, "I want to urge you not to worry or to decide that you have made a mistake with your child on the basis of anything that you read in this book (or anywhere else, for that matter) . . . We don't know all the answers yet." On one point, however, Dr. Spock was clear: mothers should devote all their time to rearing children, at least until they were three years old. Fathers, Spock suggested, had a relatively minor role during this period of nascent growth.[31]

Dr. Spock's book initially received little promotion and no reviews. Yet, by 1952, it had sold 4 million copies. Dr. Spock allowed mothers to feel good about themselves and raise children in a relaxed atmosphere. The rigid upbringing promoted by the Victorian model, which flourished through World War II, emphasized discipline and strict schedules for bottle-feeding and toilet training. The leading manual for the grandparents of boomers was John B. Watson's *Psychological Care of Infant and Child* (1928), which admonished mothers not to hug or kiss children or allow them to sit in an adult's lap.[32]

Spock challenged this approach, encouraging mothers to shower love on their children and advancing the then-radical principle that children were individuals who developed at different rates. Delays in speech or toilet training were not causes for alarm. By the 1960s, as Spock's boomers mounted campaigns against racism, sexism, and the war in Vietnam, conservative critics blamed some of the protests on the alleged "permissiveness" countenanced by Spock's widely read book. The critics assumed that permissive attitudes toward toilet training translated into antiestablishment behavior in teenagers and young adults. Spock's child-rearing suggestions did indeed encourage independence, but it was the questioning of authority, not sloppy toilet training, that most riled conservatives.[33]

The marriage bonanza among younger partners produced a spike in divorces. At the turn of the twentieth century, there was one divorce for every sixteen marriages. By 1946, it was one divorce for every three marriages and climbing. Psychiatrists and social workers blamed the soaring divorce rate on "the degree of emancipation attained by women," and women in 1946 did have more options to survive life as a single person than in 1900. But these experts also claimed that "many women who formerly thought of marriage as a permanent bond now marry with the idea that they can escape at the first sign of friction or unpleasantness and return to the office at $35 a week." They had entered into contingent marriages easily discarded when things got difficult. "Their dominant thought," these experts argued, "is not to 'give' and to be a partner in marriage, but to 'get' and to walk out if things don't go exactly the way they want." In other words, the scandalous divorce rate was the fault of women.[34]

Women's involvement in the business world was a particular culprit as it made "some of them aggressive to an extent far beyond normal conceptions of femininity which, in turn affects the marriage partnership adversely. They attain a feeling of self-sufficiency and independence, traits detrimental to the conception of marriage that placed men at the unequivocal head of the household." These traits allegedly also had negative effects on children, accounting for the sudden rise in juvenile delinquency, a development noted by many experts, despite statistics to the contrary.[35]

Working-class wives rarely had the luxury of following the proscriptive literature. In a society increasingly lured by the growing array of consumer products for the home, for leisure, and for children, two incomes were necessary for many families. In the Planko family of New Jersey, Stanley worked as a mechanic at an ordnance factory; his wife, Pauline, had a job at Johnson & Johnson's baby-products plant; their daughter, Debbie, spent the day with Pauline's grandmother. Pauline explained that although she disliked leaving her baby "even for a minute," the couple could not make it on just her husband's salary: "There is almost no place to cut it."[36]

Added to the economic stress of the Plankos was the implied disapproval of society toward working mothers. Even an enlightened writer such as Michael Harrington, who spoke movingly about urban poverty in his book *The Other America* (1962), felt that working mothers contributed to "the impoverishment of home life, of children who receive less care, love and supervision." Families improved their incomes with two working parents, but "at the cost of hurting thousands and hundreds of thousands of children." Harrington, to be sure, advocated higher wages and government child-care subsidies so working-class women would not need to work outside the home, but he also articulated the prevailing negative perceptions of working married women with children.[37]

By 1952 the United States had 19 million working women, or almost half as many as in 1940, and eight hundred thousand less than the all-time peak in 1945. By 1955, more women worked for wages than they had during the war. Despite the cultural opposition to married women working, they outnumbered single, divorced, or widowed women in the workplace. And half of the married women had young children. It was not only about buying a television set or a car, but of simply of making ends meet.[38]

IN 1948, SUSAN B. ANTHONY II, grandniece of the eponymous woman's rights pioneer, decried both the customary and legal barriers women confronted in the immediate postwar era. If custom shortchanged women in gender equity, prevailing state laws exacerbated the problem. In fifteen states, a mother could be a child's legal guardian only if her offspring was born out of wedlock. In sixteen states, a woman could not sign a legal document without her husband's consent. Thirteen states barred women from jury service. Ninety percent of the nation's school districts refused to hire married women, and 70 percent required female teachers to quit when they married.[39]

All of these legal debilities, Anthony charged, reflected women's political impotence. Only seven women served in Congress in 1948 compared with 524 men; and of the more than 7,500 state legislators in the country, fewer than 200 were women.[40]

Anthony called for a new women's movement that would campaign for universal nursery schools for preschool children, cooperative housecleaning and prepared-meal services, and professional shopping services. Anthony made clear she was not demanding identical rights for women with men; rather, if women were going to have children, then society should provide maternity benefits such as paid family leave to enable women to take time off for childbearing. Seventy years later, many of these goals remain elusive.[41]

Women's situation in American society after World War II was not nearly as dire as Anthony implied, nor were the 1920s a relative golden age. For example, women were beginning to increase their political visibility by the end of the 1940s. Part of this trend owed to the relationship between President Truman and India Edwards, the vice chairman of the Democratic National Committee, whom one commentator called "the most important woman in American politics." Because of Edwards's efforts, Truman appointed more women to top jobs than any other previous president, including nineteen to major national posts and the first woman ambassador, Eugenie Anderson, the envoy to Denmark. Other firsts included the appointment of the first female treasurer of the United States, Georgia Neese Clark, the first woman on the Federal Communications Commission, Frieda Hennock, and perhaps most surprisingly, in the male-dominated lair of the Defense Department, Anna Rosenberg as assistant secretary of defense.[42]

India Edwards's background prefigured her involvement in politics. She marched in a suffrage parade with her mother at the age of five and spent twenty-two years as a journalist with the *Chicago Tribune*, a conservative Republican newspaper, before joining the Democratic Party, where she became a persistent force (or thorn) to male colleagues on the issues of gender equity. A journalist profiling her was quick to add, "But she also is an excellent cook, she makes her own hats, she is happily married, and she is the most doting and meddlesome of grandmothers." In other words, despite her feminism and political acumen, she was still a woman.[43]

Edwards's primary role with the party was to get women out to vote for Harry Truman. To do that, she initiated local activities and educational forums to apprise women of their stake in the upcoming election. During the

1948 presidential campaign, Truman confided to her, "Sometimes, India, I think there are only two people who think I will win—you and I."[44]

The gains on the political front, however tenuous they might have seemed in view of prevailing public opinion and scientific commentary, provided impetus for a renewed assault on gender inequality. The Equal Rights Amendment emerged in 1923 in the heady aftermath of the woman's suffrage movement. Alice Paul, head of the National Woman's Party, along with such luminaries as Georgia O'Keeffe, Margaret Mead, Margaret Sanger, Pearl Buck, and Katharine Hepburn, led the postwar battle for its adoption. In 1946, the ERA passed the U.S. Senate by three votes, but fell far short of the two-thirds majority required for a constitutional amendment, despite President Truman's support for the measure. The *New York Times* rejoiced at its failure: "Motherhood cannot be amended, and we are glad the Senate didn't try."[45]

The resurrection of the ERA was another indication that during the first few years after World War II, the debate over gender roles was far from settled. The popular magazines presented a variety of views, which, given the magazines' dependence on advertisers and subscriptions, must have found resonance among a broad readership. Hila Colman, who wrote *Thoroughly Modern Millie*, among other books, fumed in an August 1947 piece she wrote for the *Saturday Evening Post*, "'Why don't you stay home and take care of your children?' If I hear that one more time I'll scream. Heaven knows there may be something to it, but the thing that gets me is that the men who have been so busy yapping for centuries about women's place seem to have quite forgotten that they also have something to do with a home and a family." Elizabeth Pope, a writer on women's issues, concluded in 1948 that there was "no excuse for the attitude of many American fathers that 'bringing up the children is the wife's department.'"[46]

Writer Margaret Moon Loutit's "Memorandum" responded to a gentleman's suggestion that "a home should be run like a well-organized office," and that a wife who was unsuccessful at this task was a failure. Loutit wholeheartedly agreed with the office analogy. She henceforth demanded better working conditions and new appliances and infrastructure to aid her work. She also announced new hours for her job, "8:15 am to 5:30 pm, Mondays through Fridays inclusive." In a side note, she reminded her male adversary that these hours excluded the preparation of both breakfast and dinner. Acknowledging that emergencies might arise requiring an extension of hours, Loutit demanded "the usual time-and-one-half fee as enjoyed by your staff." That rate would, of course, apply to all of Saturday and Sunday. As for vacation: "I am . . . arranging to be away from my duties for one month, as of THIS MINUTE."[47]

The popular magazines acknowledged, however tentatively, that something was wrong with prevailing gender stereotypes. If not often challenged in words, magazines made the point in cover art. A January 1949 cover of the *Saturday Evening Post* depicted a New Year's Eve scene with the wife sitting at the dining room table looking sadly at a pile of dishes in the kitchen, while the husband relaxed in an easy chair reading a newspaper. A July 1952 cover in the same magazine showed a cabin perched on the edge of a beach with the wife washing and drying a stack of dishes while the husband lounged in a beach chair and the kids played in the sand. To make the point clearer, a March 1954 cover of the magazine allowed the reader to peer into a lit bedroom at night where the father was feeding a bottle to his baby. In contrast with the other covers, this portrait did not portray tedium and resentment, but rather offered warm contentment that this was how it should be.[48]

The magazine covers were explicit statements that despite improvements in household technology, homemakers in the 1950s spent about the same amount of time on their housework as homemakers in the 1920s, and sometimes more. Appliances actually added to the housework load. If a woman had an electric mixer, she had to use it; an electric freezer meant that beans, raised in the garden, must be prepared for freezing. Betty Friedan estimated that the average housewife spent sixty hours a week on household chores including preparing meals, shopping, cleaning, and taking care of the children.[49]

After depression and war, the prospect of a stable and comfortable family life would be attractive to both women and men. That was not the issue. What was especially troubling, though, was that institutions of higher learning, the job market, and society's expectations leaned against women pursuing domestic lives and careers outside the home simultaneously. The irony was that prosperity, homeownership, a transitioning economy, and education enabled women to dream of other options at a time when society increasingly frowned on those choices. Soon, women, with a strong assist from government, would reconcile that irony. The "scarlet letter" of ambition would become a badge of honor.[50]

CHAPTER 7

THE ENDLESS FRONTIER

VANNEVAR BUSH WAS PROBABLY the most optimistic American in 1945 as he surveyed the future of his country and the technology that could transform it. A nineteenth-century man (born in Massachusetts in 1890), he had a twenty-first-century imagination. In the 1930s he had designed a powerful mechanical calculator that prefigured the digital computer, and in 1945 he predicted the technology that would give us the Internet. His skills helped immensely in the war effort, and his popularity was such that *Time* magazine placed him on its cover in 1944, dubbing him the "general of physics."[1]

After the war, Bush urged the federal government to expand its role in health, science, and technology research. Such investments would create jobs, improve the quality of life, and enhance national security. The effort would partner government, universities, and private enterprise—precisely the type of coalition implied in the commonwealth ideal. Bush initiated the nation's first Silicon Valley along Route 128 outside Boston, pioneering the close connection between university research and government funding. He believed that federal funds would unleash scientists from financial concerns and uncertain collaborations with the military or private enterprise. "The individual to me is everything," he wrote in 1938. "I would circumscribe him just as little as possible." While conservatives believed that government and individual autonomy were adversarial, Bush posited just the opposite.[2]

Bush's faith in government was in direct contrast to his suspicion of other institutions. His father was a pastor of a Universalist church. The local Young Men's Christian Association (YMCA) barred not only Catholics and Jews, but also liberal Protestants such as young Bush and his family. "As the net result of that," Bush recalled later, "my boyhood friends were the Catholics and the Jews. I was not only not a Boston Brahmin, I acquired a very considerable set of prejudices against them." The contrarian attitude suited his scientific curiosity well.[3]

Bush loved football, but in his college days at Tufts, he was too frail to play, so he became the team manager. One of his responsibilities was to schedule opponents, and he was particularly pleased when the U.S. Military Academy at West Point agreed to play Tufts. The only memorable aspect about the game was that one of the best players on the Army team severely injured his knee, thereby ending a promising football career. But Dwight D. Eisenhower would rebound to excel in other areas.[4]

Bush was an inveterate tinkerer. After joining the Tufts faculty in 1916, he founded the nation's second radio station, believing, correctly, that this new invention would soon reach millions of American households. Three years later, Bush moved to MIT. While there, he and a former Tufts classmate founded a company they eventually called Raytheon, where he perfected vacuum tubes used in radios and, later, in televisions. In 1931, he developed the first differential analyzer, a machine capable of solving certain differential equations, the foundation for calculus. The machine was huge, taking up most of a large room. Journalists called it a "mechanical brain."[5]

By the late 1930s, Bush had turned his attention to solar power and continued work on developing a machine that could store huge files of information. He called his primitive machine a "rapid selector," and it prefigured the personal computer and the Internet. By then, Bush had become a science administrator as president of the Carnegie Institution in Washington, D.C., which dispensed $1.5 million annually for scientific research. Bush also served on the board of the Smithsonian Institution, promoting closer cooperation between science and government.[6]

When the war broke out, President Roosevelt tapped him to head the National Defense Research Committee (NDRC), an agency whose creation was actually Bush's idea. The new agency would oversee technological developments, especially in aeronautics. Bush enticed leading scientists from MIT, Harvard, and Caltech and commandeered their laboratories as well. Perhaps the greatest triumph of Bush and his team was the development of advanced radar systems, one of the few areas where the Americans had a significant technological advantage over the Germans. The first fruit of radar research was the neutralization of Germany's U-boats. Within a two-month period in 1943, the Allies sank forty-five German submarines with the assistance of Bush's radar. In 1942, Collier's magazine hailed him as "the man who may win the war."[7]

The war institutionalized the close connection between government funding and technological innovation. Bush believed that the government's most effective use of its resources would be in basic or "pure" scientific research that neither private industry nor the military had the patience to pursue. Such research was essential for the creation of new scientific knowledge, which would ensure economic growth and maintain a strong national defense.

Toward the end of the war, President Roosevelt wrote to Bush asking him to prepare a report on how the wartime experience of government-science cooperation could "be used for the improvement of the national health, the creation of new enterprises bringing new jobs, and the betterment of the national standard of living." The possibility of a severe economic downturn following demobilization concerned Roosevelt, and he believed that scientific research could offer at least one hedge against that possibility.[8]

In response, Bush wrote *Science: The Endless Frontier* (1945). The frontier evoked a basic American characteristic—pushing boundaries, high energy, great mobility, and, above all, innovation. The actual frontier—the iconic West—had passed a half century earlier, according to historian Frederick Jackson Turner. Now, the frontier would be knowledge, especially scientific knowledge, and the pioneers would be trailblazing scientists. The book centered on Bush's proposal for the creation of a national research foundation that would sponsor research in medicine, the physical sciences, and national defense and coordinate other types of research carried on in the various federal agencies.[9]

Bush emphatically made the case for government's major role in this endeavor, writing, "Science is a proper concern of government." Moreover, there was considerable historical precedent for this role: "It has been the basic United States policy that Government should foster the opening of new frontiers. It opened the seas to clipper ships and furnished land for pioneers. Although these frontiers have more or less disappeared, the frontier of science remains." Bush concluded, "The federal Government should accept new responsibilities for promoting the creation of new scientific knowledge and the development of scientific talent in our youth." His proposed agency would be the vehicle to accomplish these noble ends.[10]

The conservative Eightieth Congress, however, aimed to curtail, not expand, the federal government and shelved Bush's recommendations. After the 1948 election and the restoration of a Democratic majority, Congress was more amenable to the idea of a federal agency to promote scientific research. In 1950, Congress passed and President Truman signed the legislation that created the National Science Foundation. By 1958, NSF had extended its funding apparatus to the social sciences. Bush's vision paid off in numerous scientific breakthroughs as a result of NSF support. These breakthroughs can be googled. Incidentally, Google was one of them.[11]

Agencies such as NSF and the National Institutes of Health (NIH) created jobs at universities and industries that had not existed prior to World War II. Many in the gifted generation would take advantage of these openings to build careers in research and development, computers, and teaching that had not existed prior to the 1940s.

For those who found work in computers and related fields, the early fruits of government-sponsored research were crucial in establishing the United States as the world's major technological innovator. Two young engineers, John Mauchly and Pres Eckert, created the first computer, ENIAC (for Electronic Numerical Integrator and Computer), during the war at the University of Pennsylvania under contract to the U.S. military. The problem with ENIAC, however, was bulk and excessive heat from the eighteen thousand vacuum tubes it required.

It was John von Neumann who advanced computer technology. He grew up in Budapest, but the virulent anti-Semitism in Hungary, even before the Germans arrived, forced him to leave for the United States, where he secured a position at Princeton. In June 1952, von Neumann unveiled his new computer, which would become the IBM 701. Thomas Watson Jr. of International Business Machines had received a government contract to develop a machine that could assist in aircraft design, nuclear development, and munitions manufacture. The great advantage of the new computer was its speed, faster than that of any previous computer. It began the evolution that led to the personal computer two decades later.[12]

INNOVATIONS IN THE STRUCTURE OF research facilitated innovations in science and technology. Bell Labs, an offshoot of the American Telephone and Telegraph Company (AT&T), began in 1909, charged with building a transcontinental phone line. The effort required the collaboration of engineers, physicists, metallurgists, and pure theoreticians. Bringing such diverse talent together was probably Bell Labs' greatest innovation, as it enabled everyone to achieve that proverbial thinking outside the box.[13]

During World War II, Bell Labs moved from New York to a campus in Murray Hill, New Jersey, and constructed an environment that consciously promoted interdisciplinary collaboration. The building featured extra-long halls, and it would be nearly impossible for someone walking down those corridors to avoid numerous colleagues, who would share problems and trade ideas. Above all, they had the freedom to fail—and there were many dead ends over the years. But that freedom proved essential for numerous breakthroughs.

Seeking to replace relay switches and vacuum tubes, both of which were bulky and often balky, with a much smaller system for their telephone exchanges, radios, and televisions, a thirty-one-member team developed a new device they called a transistor. The transistor proved useful beyond telephone circuits and radio and television receivers. It became essential to the digital revolution in computing and information technology.

Bell Labs research also led to the invention of the laser and to fiber optics. Bell scientists developed the silicon solar cell, the precursor of all solar-powered devices; they built the first communications satellites; and they created a device that formed the basis for digital photography. Today's computer operating systems and computer languages derived from innovations of its scientists. As Apple's Steve Jobs observed, the "most difficult and important thing to create was not an innovative product but a great organization that could continually create innovative products."[14]

HARVEY RUBIN SPENT FOUR DECADES at Bell Labs and participated in many of the technological innovations noted above. His story typified that of many of the gifted generation and the legacy of good government. Harvey's maternal grandparents came from Ukraine in the early 1920s. Because of new immigration quotas the United States barred their entry. They landed in Cuba instead, migrating to the United States several years later, probably illegally. His paternal grandparents also came to the United States in the 1920s, from South Africa. The Rubins settled in the tough area in Brownsville of Brooklyn. Harvey's father worked as a salesman for a sporting goods chain and his mother as a seamstress. Their dual income enabled them to leave Brownsville for East Flatbush in 1954.[15]

Harvey recalled that as a nine-year-old he picked up his older brother's book *The 1954 Radio Amateur's Handbook*. It presented various radio projects and explained the theory behind radio technology. From then on, Harvey wanted to be an electronics engineer, even though at the time he did not quite understand what that entailed.

Harvey's other passion was football, and he played tight end on a storied Tilden High School team that included all-American Ronnie Bly, who later played for Notre Dame and the New York Giants. Harvey received an inquiry from the football coach at Columbia University inviting him to apply. He received an Alfred P. Sloan Foundation scholarship, without which he could not have afforded Columbia. Harvey enrolled as an electrical engineering major. His class was the last to be taught out of a book that featured vacuum tubes.

Harvey received a doctoral degree from Columbia, financed by government grants from NSF and the National Aeronautics and Space Administration (NASA), and he secured a job at Bell Labs. He credits those federal grants with providing him with the skills to work on innovative projects at Bell Labs, especially his work in pioneering wireless technology. His son, David, who was born in 1974, is a computer-language specialist who currently works for Bloomberg as a software developer.

PERHAPS THE GREATEST TECHNOLOGICAL innovation of the postwar era in its cultural, political, and economic impact on the gifted generation was television. The events of the 1950s and '60s would unfold in their living rooms with an immediacy that newspapers, magazines, or books could not match. Television purveyed mass culture across the nation and connected Americans to that culture and to each other. In an era when there was no other comparable medium for the instantaneous visual delivery of news, television bound the nation together in a common culture.

By the 1940s, TV had been around for twenty years, but its technology was a work in progress. As late as 1946, its future looked uncertain. The *Saturday Evening Post* wondered whether television would be hailed as "the biggest coming attraction" or "the most resounding flop in the history of entertainment."[16]

Yet by 1947, there were seventeen broadcasting stations and 136,000 television sets. Television was still a curiosity confined to the major cities of the Northeast and California. As late as 1949, more than 50 percent of Americans resided outside telecasting range. What those who had sets were viewing, according to *Life* magazine, ranged from "mediocre to bad." Fred Allen, a radio personality, called television "a device that permits people who haven't anything to do to watch people who can't do anything."[17]

But Allen was sore because he could never adjust to the new medium. In 1947, experts projected that, by 1950, programs would reach an estimated 4 million viewers. That threshold was passed in 1948 when Americans possessed seven hundred thousand sets and fifty stations. That year, such film and stage stars as Raymond Massey, Jessica Tandy, Margaret Sullavan, and Paul Muni performed in small-screen dramas. Famed conductor Arturo Toscanini led the NBC Symphony Orchestra. Viewers savored the convenience and low cost of watching a play or a movie in the comfort of home. Products advertised on television turned higher profits, book sales lagged, and in cities with even just one station, movie attendance declined by 20 to 40 percent.[18]

The gifted generation would be the nation's first to grow up with television. Whether this was a gift or a curse may be debated, but it also brought news, the works of major playwrights, and shows about animals and distant lands that taught while entertaining. It also brought an instantaneous portrayal of events heretofore scrubbed in newsreels or described by journalists. The exposure of Senator Joseph McCarthy's thuggery by Edward R. Murrow on his CBS show *See It Now*, the assassination of John F. Kennedy, the brutality of police against civil rights demonstrators, and, most notably for the gifted generation, the horrors and futility of the Vietnam War testified to the new medium's power to move a nation. In 1949, *Redbook* warned potential television-set buyers that the seemingly innocuous piece of furniture—and it was designed as a piece of furniture—would "rearrange your home life and social activities for you. Your home will never be the same again." And maybe the viewer would change as well.[19]

MEDICINE ADVANCED ALONG WITH technology. World War II was the first war in American history in which more U.S. soldiers died in battle than from disease. The reason was the perfection or discovery of medicines such as penicillin and sulfa drugs that could combat infections. Vannevar Bush's team improved upon penicillin to the extent that, by 1945, it had likely saved more lives than any other drug in history. The new medications reduced the mortality of pneumonia victims from 24 percent to 0.6 percent by 1945, and of meningitis patients from 38 percent to 4 percent. A vaccine almost entirely eliminated tetanus as a cause of death. The use of plasma and whole blood saved the lives of thousands of soldiers who might otherwise have perished on the way to a field hospital. Researchers would soon perfect a vaccine to eradicate one of the most dreaded diseases of the time: polio.[20]

The conquest of polio was probably the most significant medical event of the immediate postwar era, particularly for the gifted generation.

> *Why did they send us to summer camp—were they*
>   *being parental?*
> *Swimming pools—and gathering places—were*
>   *considered plague central.*
> *Everywhere you went, billboards displayed the smiling*
>   *faces*
> *March of Dimes kids offered up to go with their metal*
>   *leg braces.*
>
> *Imagine being inside an iron lung and having to*
>   *swallow the rotten truth*
> *That life was going to be one long bad connection*
>   *inside a telephone booth,*
> *And that you'd been really unlucky and would never*
>   *walk*
> *Because it had happened before there was vaccine*
>   *from Jonas Salk.*
>
> *Truman was in the White House but polio was the*
>   *president . . .* [21]

In early June 1944, a boy in Hickory, North Carolina, lay sick with fever and a painful stiff neck. As his fever worsened, the boy's parents rushed him to the emergency room at Memorial Hospital in Charlotte, ninety minutes away. The doctors diagnosed polio. More cases followed from Hickory, until the hospital ran out of beds in its isolation ward. The National Foundation for Infantile Paralysis built an emergency facility on the grounds of a summer camp in Hickory in fifty-four hours. In the meantime, the town had become a pariah. Trains sped past the city without stopping, and people drove through with their car windows rolled up despite the intense summer heat. Hickory, known widely for its thriving furniture industry, now received the title Polio City.[22]

By the 1940s, when the Hickory epidemic occurred, agreement was widespread that a virus caused the disease. But the origin of the virus and how to combat it eluded researchers, though it seemed to thrive in polluted water, which is why swimming pools and beaches were among the first facilities to close when news of an outbreak emerged. It thrived also in the excrement and saliva of infected individuals, rendering it highly contagious, especially since the incubation period could be as little as three days and as long as thirty-five days.[23]

Prior to 1949, only twice in the twentieth century—in 1916 and 1946—were there more than twenty-five thousand cases of polio. In 1949 the number of afflicted jumped to forty-two thousand. The disease, it seemed, was more uncontrollable than ever. About 8 percent of polio victims died that year, and an additional 15 percent were crippled. The true extent of the epidemic that year will never be known as doctors understood by then that polio could mildly afflict a child and never be diagnosed. But that child could infect other children, who might not be so fortunate in battling the disease. There was no prevention or cure for polio, nor was there a sure means of early diagnosis, as a low fever and a stiff neck could indicate any number of ailments. And few children under two could describe their symptoms.[24]

July 4, 1953, was Millie Dalton's fifth birthday. She was part of the gifted generation, and her parents, residents of Charlotte, were enjoying the benefits of prosperity that they would pass along to her. Millie's birthday coincided with the family's annual trip to Pawleys Island in South Carolina. The Clark family from Lincolnton, North Carolina, joined the Daltons. At their shared beach house, the Clarks' toddler came down with an ear infection, a common affliction at that age. Millie contracted the same illness several days later. One late afternoon that week, Millie was on the beach building a sand castle. Soon, it was time for dinner. To get back to the house, she had to climb a long set of stairs over the dunes. Each step seemed harder than the one before, as if she were walking in a rising pool of molasses. In the morning, she got out of bed and one of her legs was useless. Millie had contracted polio.[25]

Millie's mom had vivid memories of the Hickory polio epidemic. She rushed her daughter to a doctor in nearby Georgetown, South Carolina. The doctor quickly grasped the gravity of her illness: "Your child has infantile paralysis, and I suggest you get out of town as quickly as possible, and don't contaminate the ambulance and I don't want my nurse contaminated." With her husband on a business trip in New England and unreachable, Millie's mom decided to drive the five hours back to Charlotte and admit Millie to the hospital.

A doctor placed her immediately in isolation, where she remained for two weeks. Millie was five years old and could not see or speak with her family. The health department's polio protocol required its agents to burn all of her toys and other items. Gone were her favorite stuffed Sleepy Dog and her baby blanket.

Millie remained in Charlotte's Memorial Hospital for nearly two months. By late October, her pain had subsided. Gone also were the involuntary muscle spasms, including face grimaces that often accompanied the disease as it ran its course. Millie suffered total paralysis of her left leg and abdominal muscles, and her right leg and right arm were partially paralyzed. Through a vigorous rehabilitation regimen at Warm Springs, Georgia (the resort frequented by the nation's most famous polio patient, Franklin D. Roosevelt), Millie got back the function of her abdominal muscles. Two months after she left Warm Springs, a preliminary announcement came that a vaccine had been developed to prevent polio. Millie never dwelled on her bad timing. Returning to Charlotte, she entered the first grade confined to a wheelchair. By 1958, she exchanged the wheelchair for braces and crutches. She went on to marry and have three children as well as a distinguished career as an educator and as the French consul in Charlotte.

Some writers have questioned the attention the media, foundations, and governments lavished on polio, considering the relatively low number of deaths compared with, say, heart disease or cancer. However, as late as 1954, disagreement was widespread on how victims contracted the disease, which made prevention difficult, if not impossible. It would strike suddenly and was no respecter of social class or neighborhood. Once someone contracted the disease, it was incurable, though it was possible to palliate the symptoms. But what fixed the disease in the public mind was that it afflicted children primarily, and the pain, the treatment protocols, and often the years of rehabilitation tugged at people's emotions, and rightly so. As the mother of one such stricken child noted, polio was "a word that strikes more terror in the hearts of parents than the atom bomb." And it struck down children who were active and in robust health.[26]

By the mid-1940s, parents across the country were giving their children a daily "polio test" during the summer months: "Did the neck swivel? Did the toes wiggle? Could the chin reach the chest?" It was not a panic, but rather a sword that hung over the heads of parents each summer.[27]

JONAS SALK WAS BORN in East Harlem in 1914 to Jewish immigrant parents from Russia. His father had less than an eighth-grade education and worked in New York City's garment district. Jonas's mother never attended school. They had three children: one would go on to become one of the world's greatest researchers, another a veterinarian, and the third a psychologist.

Jonas attended City College of New York, a tuition-free institution that has turned out more Nobel Prize winners and Ph.D. recipients than any other public college except for the University of California, Berkeley. It was a particular haven for Jewish students, who confronted quotas and financial burdens at topflight private universities. After graduation, Jonas entered New York University's College of Medicine. The tuition was relatively low for a medical school, and, equally important, it had no quotas for Jewish students. He had hoped to go to Yale Medical School, but in 1935, of two hundred Jewish students who applied, only five were accepted. The medical school dean's instructions were clear: "Never admit more than five Jews, take only two Italian Catholics, and take no blacks at all."[28]

Salk interned at New York's Mount Sinai hospital. To intern there was, as a Salk friend noted, "like playing ball for the New York Yankees." After Mount Sinai, he contacted Thomas Francis, a former NYU faculty member and now chairman of the Epidemiology Department at the University of Michigan's School of Public Health. Salk hoped to work with Francis on developing a flu vaccine. To fund his appointment at Michigan, Salk applied for a National Research Council fellowship. In his letter of recommendation, Francis wrote, "Dr. Salk is a member of the Jewish race but has, I believe, a very great capacity to get on with people."[29]

During World War II, Francis received a contract from the U.S. Army to test his flu vaccine. That was crucial to later polio research because he and Salk worked with a large population and could test their theory about the effectiveness of a "killed" strain of the flu virus. It turned out that the dead virus produced a strong antibody response that protected soldiers against the flu.

Salk wanted to run his own laboratory, and he received an offer from the University of Pittsburgh to do just that. Pitt, as a result of Mellon-family and Carnegie Foundation grants, had lured a number of top scientists to its medical school, including Dr. Benjamin Spock. There, in 1948, Salk embarked on his polio research.

In the summer of 1952, the nation was experiencing its worst polio epidemic in history. Eventually, a record fifty-seven thousand cases were diagnosed, reflecting the baby boom. More alarming, twenty-one thousand of those victims suffered permanent paralysis and three thousand died. Not only the high number of cases but the virulence of the disease alarmed public health experts. The National Foundation for Infantile Paralysis reported that the epidemic bankrupted five hundred of its three thousand chapters.[30]

Any hint of a potential cure or prevention was likely to generate considerable excitement. In February 1953, Salk gave a presentation in New York about his findings to date. Immediately, headlines appeared, such as "Polio Conquest Nearer" or the even bolder "Hint Polio Vaccine Ready." To calm the furor that erupted, the National Foundation convinced CBS radio to give Salk a fifteen-minute show, "The Scientist Speaks for Himself," on March 26, 1953. The message was that, while he had made considerable progress, "there will be no vaccine available for widespread use for the next polio season." Despite this disclaimer, the part about considerable progress received much more publicity: "A polio-free world may be at the fingertips of a Pittsburgh scientist."[31]

The federal government now became involved. To conduct massive trials and extensive manufacture of the purported vaccine, some government control and coordination was necessary. Joseph A. Bell from the National Institutes of Health (NIH) directed the process. But the National Foundation balked at the strict rules Bell laid out, particularly that the vaccine to be used in the trials should be "triple-tested": tested by Salk's lab, by a commercial manufacturer of the vaccine, and by the federal government through the Public Health Service. In the meantime, Albert Sabin, another polio researcher, denounced the rush to certify the Salk product, claiming that Sabin's live-virus vaccine could protect against the disease. By the time the Salk trials began in 1954, Bell had resigned and Sabin had cast doubt on the suitability of a dead-virus vaccine.[32]

Despite the controversy, Salk appeared on the cover of *Time* magazine, and a Gallup poll indicated that more people were aware of the field trials for the vaccine than the "full name of the President of the United States." The plan was to give three doses (for the three types of polio) to 650,000 schoolchildren in 211 counties across the nation, funded by the National Foundation. The vaccine had already been tested on five thousand volunteers, including Salk, his wife, and three young sons. What could go wrong?

Thomas Francis, Salk's mentor, led the team evaluating the trials. It was one of the earliest medical evaluations to rely on computers. Francis compiled nearly 15 million IBM cards punched with 144 million pieces of information. On April 12, 1955, the tenth anniversary of Franklin D. Roosevelt's death, Francis announced the results in Ann Arbor, and soon they were flashed to the nation on Dave Garroway's NBC show, *Today*. Sportswriter Frank Deford, then a fourth-grader in Baltimore, recalled the reaction in his class: "We were safe again. At our desks, we cheered as if the Orioles or the Colts had won a big game. Outside we could hear car horns honking and church bells chiming in celebration. We had conquered polio." The *Pittsburgh Press* headline blared, "POLIO IS CONQUERED."[33]

The Public Health Service issued a federal license for the Salk vaccine, allowing its distribution more widely. Salk had decided not to patent the formula, enabling the vaccine to reach a worldwide population at relatively low cost. But Oveta Culp Hobby, the secretary of Health, Education, and Welfare, had not made provisions to distribute the vaccine nationwide. After vigorous lobbying by drug companies, Hobby decided to shift distribution responsibilities to the private sector. But as the polio season of 1955 approached, the supply of the vaccine ran considerably short of the demand. It was a classic violation of the principle that government should do what the private sector could not. Fortunately, other federal agencies stepped up when even greater problems appeared.

A batch of the vaccine produced by Cutter Laboratories in Berkeley, California, caused polio in several children inoculated with their product. U.S. Surgeon General Leonard Scheele acted quickly to have the vaccine recalled, only to have new reports that vaccines from two other labs were also tainted with the live virus. The Public Health Service created a Polio Surveillance Unit to monitor the growing crisis. On May 8, 1955, Scheele ordered a halt to all vaccinations nationwide.[34]

Scheele's quick action had averted a tragedy. By mid-May, he had recertified the vaccine and inoculations resumed, but with much lower participation rates. Of the twenty-eight thousand polio cases in 1955, most might have been avoided had the government followed its original testing protocols. The episode resulted in the strengthening of federal oversight of drugs, their distribution, and their effectiveness. The NIH budget increased from $81 million in 1955 to $400 million by 1960. Henceforth all testing of drugs would come under the purview of the federal government.[35]

In 1957, only seven thousand cases of polio were reported, half the number of 1956. In August, the U.S. surgeon general approved Albert Sabin's live-virus vaccine for trial manufacture, and within a year, the Sabin formula became the vaccine of choice against polio. The scourge of polio was over. Its conquest was one of the great stories of postwar America, and one of the greatest gifts to the gifted generation.[36]

The conquest of polio highlighted the growing role of the federal government in national health, medicine, and science generally. The NIH played a critical role in ensuring that the polio vaccine was ultimately safe and widely available. By 1956, the NIH was already investigating rare and chronic diseases for which there were no cures. The NIH Clinical Center in Bethesda, Maryland, had three hundred patients from around the country with as-yet-incurable ailments such as heart disease, cancer, arthritis, epilepsy, and schizophrenia. Although the clinic would cure few of these patients, the purpose of their residence was to learn as much as possible about these diseases. The service to these patients was free, supported by federal funds. The clinic team was confident that these deadly diseases would be vanquished just like polio. Congress supported the initiative, generously beginning with a $29 million grant in 1948, increased to $98 million annually by 1956.[37]

Even prior to the conquest of polio, the gifted generation had already benefited from advances in medicine, many of them as a result of government-sponsored research during and immediately after World War II. Diphtheria annually infected twenty thousand people a year, mainly children. The development of a vaccine in 1945 virtually eliminated this dread childhood disease. Whooping cough, a feared child-killer, infected over 183,000 children in 1940—one out of every one hundred children died. A vaccine cut the number of cases to 15,000 by 1960.[38]

The conquest of polio let imaginations soar envisioning a world without disease or chronic illness. Up until the 1940s, when people got sick, doctors had relatively few medications. By 1956, 80 percent of the drugs on the market had been developed since the previous decade, as antibiotics accelerated cures and reduced the threat of epidemics. By the 1960s, vaccines to control mumps, measles, and rubella came on the market, the fruits of government-funded research in the 1950s. These advances paid off in longer lives. By 1960 life expectancy had risen to 69.7 years. It was 62.9 years in 1940. Government infrastructure and funding were in place to generate an array of scientific and technological breakthroughs in the coming decades. For the gifted generation, the frontier was indeed endless. They would repay the gifts many times over. In the meantime, others waited to contribute. And waited.[39]

CHAPTER 8

"To Hell with Jews, Jesuits, and Steamships!"

SELMA MOSES, AGE ELEVEN, sat on a stair step clutching a rag doll and a hat, with her suitcase by her side. It was the winter of 1946. Small for her age, she wore a thin dress and was bare legged. Little apprehension was in her face, but her eyes had a weariness far too old for her young years. She was at the Emigrant Assembly Center in Bremen, Germany, awaiting passage to America. Selma had lost both of her parents in the Holocaust, but she had survived Auschwitz. Her caregivers at the center noticed she did not cry, nor did she seem anxious, as if what she had witnessed had robbed her of emotions as it stole her childhood. She did not bestow any affection on the doll as most children would.[1]

Selma was lucky, her trials notwithstanding. The U.S. Committee for Care of European Children was a federal agency established in 1940 to evacuate English children from areas of actual and potential destruction during the Battle of Britain that year. American entrance into the war suspended such efforts, though the organization succeeded in rescuing a small number of German Jewish children. After the war, the committee toured displaced-persons camps and selected a number of orphans to pair with American adoptive parents, enabling them to emigrate to the United States. The effort of the federal government to rescue Jews, children or otherwise, during the war was paltry. Only in 1944 did the Roosevelt administration step up its activities to help European Jews find a home in America. But by then more than 80 percent of the Jews who would perish in the Holocaust had already died.[2]

Federal efforts did not improve significantly in the years immediately after the end of the war, as Americans opposed absorbing tens of thousands of refugees. There was little sentiment to change the 1924 Immigration Act, which severely restricted the number of immigrants from Southern and Eastern Europe—areas heavily Catholic and Jewish.

The 1924 Immigration Act (also known as the Johnson-Reed Act) codified the slogan of one of the nativist groups: "To Hell with Jews, Jesuits, and

Steamships!" Southern Democrats had generally supported liberal immigration policies because of their preference for white labor. But the growing threat of radicalism, the nationalism generated by World War I, and the emphasis on racial distinctions shifted Southern opinion. A national consensus formed that newcomers from Southern and Eastern Europe comprised culturally and biologically inferior races that would mongrelize the nation and undermine its republican institutions.[3]

The 1924 act was woefully inadequate to deal with the crisis generated by the aftermath of World War II. By the fall of 1946, more than 850,000 refugees crowded into displaced-persons camps. No country or even groups of countries wanted to absorb that large a number of migrants. Most were refugees from Eastern Europe, then coming under Soviet control, and therefore resistant to returning to an uncertain fate. A minority were Jewish. With Congress unwilling to act, President Truman sent consular officials to the U.S. zone in Germany to process immigration visas as quickly as possible. But the existing immigration law slowed the process as it prohibited more than 10 percent of the year's total quota to be admitted per month. The Greek quota, for example, allowed for 307 immigrants annually, compared with the United Kingdom's quota of 65,721. The U.K. had not fulfilled its maximum number since 1929. The requirement of documenting one's past—a difficult if not impossible hurdle for many of the Jewish refugees, whose homes and records no longer existed—added to the delay.[4]

Truman wanted to open the door to American ingress a little wider, a position that contributed to his plummeting approval ratings in late 1945 and 1946. In August of 1946, a poll indicated that 72 percent disapproved of the president's plan "to ask Congress to allow more Jewish and other European refugees to come to the United States to live than are allowed under the law now." Over 50 percent of respondents to the statement "about one million Polish people, Jews, and other displaced persons must find new homes in different countries" believed that the United States should not take any of them. Of the 43 percent that approved of welcoming some of the refugees into the country, most opted for a policy that would restrict the flow to roughly one quarter of the proposed number of immigrants.[5]

These figures were not surprising given the institutionalization of bigotry even within the federal government. Not until 1943 did the U.S. commissioner of immigration and naturalization remove the racial classification "Hebrew" from immigration forms, acknowledging, at least officially, that Jews were not a separate race. The elimination of that word generated fears that Jewish refugees would now inundate the nation. Even if every immigrant between 1943 and 1945 had been Jewish, the total number would not have exceeded forty thousand. The emigration of Jewish refugees to Canada and Latin America exceeded that to the United States during this period.[6]

Of the 850,000 displaced persons crowded into camps in western Germany in 1946, Jews comprised the largest group at 225,000 persons. Few could be repatriated to their former homes, either because of persistent religious prejudice, the confiscation of their property, or the destruction of their villages and neighborhoods. The 1924 immigration quotas would allow only 8,107 of these individuals into the country per year. At that rate most of the refugees would die of old age in the camps before they could be admitted to the United States.[7]

If Truman had his way, the quotas would be eliminated, but neither Congress nor the American public would tolerate it. The president urged that orphans like Selma Moses, and close family members of immigrants already in this country, receive priority. Truman hoped his directive would result in about three thousand immigrants per month, which would put the annual total within the thirty-nine thousand quota limit. But the deliberately slow pace of reviewing applications and trolling for any hint of potential subversion severely restricted the flow. Only 3,452 refugees came into this country through the first eight months of 1946. Both Sweden and Switzerland each took in more than the United States during the same period. The revived debate over immigration at the end of World War II occurred amid the persistent anti-Catholic and anti-Jewish prejudice that flourished among many white Protestants, businesses, and institutions.[8]

A POPULAR FILM IN 1947, *Gentleman's Agreement*, based on a bestselling book of that title, explored anti-Semitism. Gregory Peck goes undercover as Phil Greenberg to write a magazine article on anti-Jewish sentiment in New York City and Darien, Connecticut. One of his earliest encounters is with the secretary Elaine Wales (played by June Havoc), assigned to him by the magazine. She confides to Peck that she is Jewish and to get the job she has had to change her name from Estelle Wilovsky. Under her original name, the magazine denied her a position. Peck's childhood friend Dave Goldman (played by the Jewish actor John Garfield) arrives in New York with a new job and begins a difficult search for a place to live amid the combination of a postwar housing shortage and the unwillingness of some landlords to rent to Jewish tenants.[9]

In the film, Peck encounters a series of anti-Semitic incidents that reveal a cultural pattern of exclusion. His mother's doctor attempts to discourage Peck from taking her to a specialist who is Jewish because he will likely cheat Peck's mother. A widower, Peck becomes romantically involved with Kathy Lacy (played by Dorothy McGuire), the niece of the magazine's publisher. When they travel to an upscale resort outside the city, the receptionist refuses to register Peck and McGuire, but suggests another hotel that accepts Jewish guests. Peck's young son, Tommy, becomes the target of bullies in school who taunt him with the epithet "dirty Yid." When Dave Goldman is unsuccessful in finding an apartment in the city, Peck asks Kathy, who lives in Darien, Connecticut, to help Dave locate a home there. Kathy informs Peck that Darien has a "gentleman's agreement" not to sell homes to Jews.

The movie ends in Hollywood fashion with everyone more aware of anti-Semitism and resolved to combat it. The film garnered eight Academy Award nominations, winning three, including Best Picture. A reflection of the sensitivity of the subject matter was the warning Peck's agent gave him that the role would ruin his film career. It did not. Elia Kazan, the film's director, decided to make the movie after he was denied membership in the Los Angeles Country Club because they thought, mistakenly, he was Jewish.

The film touched off a broad discussion on the previously taboo subject of anti-Semitism. As a *Life* magazine editor noted, "The kind of anti-Semitism it [the film] deals with is a widespread feature of the American scene: the clannish snobbery which excludes Jews from certain jobs, country clubs and restricted suburbs and puts them on a quota basis in private and professional schools." The editor praised the movie for making non-Jews "uncomfortable." The film's inescapable conclusion was that "Jews in America are discriminated against and thus denied equality of opportunity." The editor reminded readers that this was one of the "basic" civil rights cited by President Truman's Committee on Civil Rights.[10]

Quoting Elliot Cohen, editor of the Jewish monthly *Commentary*, the *Life* editor advanced a historical argument to end exclusion based on race or religion: "America if I read the old documents aright, was not meant to be a country club for people 'just like us.' The 'exclusiveness' of the gentleman's agreement, collusive or legal, was no part of the picture . . . This was meant to be a free land for all kinds of people." While the statement glosses over the reality of late eighteenth-century America, the interpretation was something increasing numbers of Americans would ponder and subscribe to in the years after World War II. And the gifted generation would be its beneficiaries.[11]

The open discussion of anti-Semitism was itself a sign that Americans were beginning to confront ethnic and religious prejudices. The amalgam of war, the throwing together of young men, and women, from different parts of the country, from farms and large cities, and from varied economic backgrounds, softened stereotypes enough for such prejudices to become more glaring after the war. By 1945, Jewish applicants to professional schools had a 10 to 15 percent better chance of admission than they did in 1929. Catholics of Eastern or

Southern European backgrounds had less difficulty purchasing homes in upscale neighborhoods than in the 1920s. Better than two thirds of respondents in a 1942 poll indicated they could vote for a Catholic for president. During the war, a few stores hired black salesgirls with no falloff of business or complaints from customers.[12]

While Catholics were probably closer than other groups to inclusion in white Protestant America, the majority of Americans still viewed Asians, Jews, and blacks—in that order—as the "other." The internment of Japanese Americans during World War II, but not typically of German and Italian Americans, reflected then-current racial views. As late as 1946, only half of the respondents to a poll believed Japanese Americans were loyal to the United States. Harry Truman's plea for reparations on behalf of the interned was forty years too early.[13]

In another poll that year, 55 percent of those queried agreed with the statement "Jews have too much power in the United States." Anti-Semitism was much stronger among the thirty-five-to-forty-nine age group than among those between the ages of twenty-one and thirty-four. The latter cohort was more likely to have had direct contact with Jewish wartime comrades and some with wartime atrocities. But historian Sheldon Neuringer is probably correct in noting that "between 1924 and the early 1950s nothing had happened to weaken appreciably" in the minds of most Americans and their representatives in Congress "that there existed but one desirable national culture, the one that had been forged and nurtured by the original colonists and the 19th-century immigrants from Northern and Western Europe."[14]

ALL OF THIS WAS FAMILIAR to Jewish Americans, particularly outside the South. When the G.I. Bill made higher education economically feasible for Jewish veterans, some elite institutions expressed concern about a flood of Jewish students. At New York's Cornell University, a state institution, President Edmund Ezra Day reassured concerned alumni that Jewish students would not displace "legacy" admissions or unduly degrade the campus environment. He promised the alumni to keep Jewish enrollment not so large "as to make it unpleasant for first-class Gentile students." To enforce this policy, Cornell systematically rejected students from New York City high schools (which enrolled large numbers of Jewish students) and transfer students from New York University and Hunter College, two institutions with relatively high proportions of Jews.[15]

The Big Three—Harvard, Yale, and Princeton—had historically admitted students almost exclusively on academic criteria. That changed in the 1920s, however, when immigrants from Southern and Eastern Europe sought entrance. The new criteria included academics, but also "character," a feature that Protestant, but apparently not Catholic or Jewish, students displayed. Traits such as "manliness," "personality," and "leadership" defined character. What these schools were looking for, according to their admissions officers, was the "all-round man" (women were excluded from all three institutions), strong in body, character, and social class. Jewish applicants in particular were perceived as bookish, clannish, and rarely of social standing.[16]

The Big Three had Jewish students, just not many of them, and they were often segregated or excluded from participation in various aspects of campus life, not by choice, but by tradition. The top floor of a freshman dormitory at Harvard was known as Kike's Peak, as that floor housed Jewish freshmen. At Yale, Jewish students could not attain prominent positions in major student organizations. When Woodrow Wilson was president of Princeton, he attacked the religious exclusivity of the eating clubs. That, of course, was their point, and they successfully resisted Wilson.[17]

By the late 1940s, anti-Semitism was losing fashion, at least in its most public forms, assaulted on numerous fronts by Hollywood, the new medium of television, popular literature, and state law. Massachusetts enacted the Fair Educational Practices Law in 1949, targeting university admissions. Harvard vigorously but unsuccessfully opposed the law. Truman's Commission on Higher Education denounced quotas directed against African Americans and Jews as "un-American." Professional organizations such as the American Council on Education (ACE) published a major exposé of discrimination in college admissions in 1949.[18]

By 1949, several states in the Northeast and Northwest had passed antidiscriminatory legislation. Jewish enrollment began to move up ever so slightly, though the percentage of Jewish students at Harvard in 1953 was still less than it was in 1925. Both public opinion and the law were moving against restrictive practices. As one college president of that era stated, "Whenever colleges have become more liberal and wise in their selection of students other than those who are white and Gentile, they have done so, not because of a zeal for fair play and democracy, but because they were forced to by the pressure of organized and unorganized opinions upon their public relations policy."[19]

These were encouraging developments, but Jewish families in the 1950s could still drive through the hills and valleys of New England and point out all the hotels that were "restricted"—a euphemism for not allowing Jews and, in some cases, Italians—and the few that were not. They could do the same with certain neighborhoods in Chicago, Philadelphia, and New York and their suburbs. The prejudice against Jews was usually more subtle than that against African Americans, but no less hurtful.

The growing discourse on both ethnic and religious prejudice in press and film brought both attention and opprobrium to prejudice. Broadway joined the dialogue with *South Pacific*, a Rodgers and Hammerstein musical based on James Michener's Pulitzer Prize–winning novel, *Tales of the South Pacific* (1947), which dealt with interracial issues. The show made its Broadway debut in 1949. The leading man, Emile de Becque, a French plantation owner, had two biracial children, a situation that initially scuttled the romance between him and the female lead, Arkansas native Ensign Nellie Forbush. A parallel romance blossomed between a U.S. marine, Joe Cable, and a local island girl, Liat, but again, prejudice intervened as Joe, worried about what his friends and family back home might think of the union, broke off the relationship.[20]

In the meantime, de Becque and Cable go on a spy mission behind Japanese lines. The intelligence they collect results in an American victory, but Cable is killed. Nellie, seeing Liat's grief at the news of Cable's death, and believing that de Becque suffered the same fate, overcomes her prejudice and resolves to raise his children. When de Becque returns after all, an overjoyed Nellie agrees to marry him. The show won ten Tony Awards, including Best Musical.

THERE WAS LITTLE MUSIC in Washington, D.C., however, when Congress began to debate immigration legislation and the status of refugees in the years immediately following the end of World War II. Whatever Broadway and Hollywood illuminated, lawmakers seemed determined to extinguish. Congress wanted to cut the quotas from Southern and Eastern Europe even more. In the spring of 1946, Ed Gossett (D-TX) called for a 50 percent reduction in immigration, despite the long queues and the suffering in the displaced-persons camps. The bill lost, succumbing to pressure from Catholic and Jewish groups and labor unions. The American Legion led the support for the bill, going so far as to recommend a cessation of all immigration until every World War II veteran had a job and a place to live.[21]

Truman believed that the nation's immigration policy, especially toward refugees, was untenable and antithetical to American ideals. He worked with the interfaith Citizens Committee on Displaced Persons, an organization created primarily through the efforts of Jewish organizations to issue four hundred thousand visas (the total, more or less, of those unused during the war years). More than one hundred thousand Jewish refugees would be included in that number. Secretary of State George C. Marshall, author of the famous Marshall Plan that would help to rebuild Europe, strongly supported Truman's plan. Despite Marshall's endorsement, a Texas congressman denounced the idea as benefiting Jews whom the Soviets had planted to spread Communism across America.[22]

Truman found some satisfaction in the arrival of the army transport *General Black* when it steamed into New York harbor on October 30, 1948, after a ten-day crossing from Bremerhaven, Germany. On board were 813 passengers, most of whom were concentration-camp survivors or refugees from Soviet-occupied Eastern Europe. In the group were 161 Jews and 493 Catholics.[23]

They had arrived courtesy of the Displaced Persons Act, a measure that President Truman had championed, and Congress approved, but only after it had seriously weakened its provisions. The president signed it grudgingly as something better than nothing. He called it "flagrantly discriminatory" against Jews and Catholics. Although the *General Black* carried a good number of these immigrants to New York, its passengers would not be typical of those of the ships that followed.[24]

The measure sanctioned a modest expansion in the number of refugees entering the country, but processing delays built into the new system effectively mitigated its benefits. Arguments that the refugees would become an intolerable financial burden, engage in criminal behavior, or form a fifth column of Communist subversives stoked the opposition to allowing any of the refugees into the country. In fact, Catholic and Jewish agencies bore most of the costs in bringing the refugees to America and helping them to establish residences and find jobs. Many of the refugees were highly educated and adapted well and quickly.

Joachim and Irene Bronny survived a Nazi concentration camp in Poland. They arrived in the United States in 1948. Joachim was a doctor and worked as an intern in Chicago's Norwegian American hospital. He and his wife gave birth to a son in the summer of 1949. Once Joachim completed his residency, he stated, "I want to be a poor man's doctor." He came to the United States under the terms of the Displaced Persons Act, one of the relatively few who made it through the paperwork maze and the act's restrictive provisions, which stipulated that 30 percent of migrants must be farmers (impossible in the case of Jews), and 40 percent must come from the Baltic countries (as opposed to Southern and Eastern Europe). Truman pushed hard to amend the act, and in 1950 he succeeded in raising the immigration quota from 197,460 refugees to 341,000. Eventually, more than 400,000 displaced persons were admitted under the amended Displaced Persons Act.[25]

While Truman pushed in one direction, Congress pulled the opposite way. In 1950, Senator Pat McCarran (D-NV) obtained the passage of the Subversive Activities Control Act, ostensibly designed to tighten security against suspected Communists. Aside from its dubious incursions on civil liberties, the act sharply increased the waiting time for prospective immigrants, requiring each applicant to undergo intense interrogation at ports of entry such as Ellis Island on the East Coast and San Francisco on the West Coast. The nativists were not done, however.[26]

The McCarran-Walter Act of 1952 marked the high tide of nativism. Senator McCarran, despite his Irish Catholic ancestry, viewed immigration as both a security threat and an economic liability. The exceptions to his immigration-restriction program were Spanish Basque sheepherders employed by his rancher constituents. To provide intellectual heft to his bill, McCarran instructed an aide, Richard Arens—described by one congressional staffer as "one of the most prejudiced people I've ever known, a force for intellectual evil"—to undertake a comprehensive review of immigration.[27]

Arens's report unsurprisingly concluded that the continuation of the national-origins quota system was in the best interests of the country, "to best preserve the sociological and cultural balance of the United States." Arens took pains to emphasize that he was not against immigration per se. The quotas were generous to Northern Europeans as they were "more readily assimilable because of the similarity of their cultural background to those of the principal components of our population." The report also noted, somewhat gratuitously, that Jews constituted 4 percent of the nation's population but 14 percent of all immigrants between 1906 and 1943, clearly an imbalance that required correction.[28]

With the usual conservative coalition of Southern Democrats and Midwestern and Western Republicans, the bill passed. But on June 25, 1952, Truman vetoed the bill, condemning it in the strongest of terms: "It is incredible to me that we should again be enacting into law such a slur on the patriotism, the capacity, and the decency of a large part of our citizenry." The House overrode the President's veto easily, as did the Senate, in a much narrower vote. Most of the votes to sustain the veto came from lawmakers residing in the Northeast from both political parties.[29]

The Immigration and Nationality Act of 1952 did not so much replace the 1924 law as endorse its basic premises, tinkering with the quota formula, adding a few hundred immigrants to the annual total. The law gave preference to immigrants with skills, but only those skills that the secretary of labor certified were in short supply. These applicants would comprise the first 50 percent of the allotted immigrants, the next 30 percent would be parents of adult citizens, and the final 20 percent would be spouses and children of legal resident aliens. The new law also broadened the grounds for the exclusion of "immoral" or "subversive" applicants. As Arens explained, the law would thwart Communist "conquest by immigration." For all the discussion about national security, old racial prejudices guided McCarran-Walter Act. The act ensured that 85 percent or more of immigrants would come from Northern and Western Europe.[30]

By the time the law went into effect, the pressure caused by wartime dislocation had lessened. Combined with alternative entry possibilities as refugees or through special acts of Congress, less than one half of the immigrants to the United States in the 1950s arrived within the quota system. Truman, and Eisenhower after him, used their executive parole authority to admit seven hundred thousand political refugees between 1945 and 1960. Still, in those countries disfavored by the quotas—Southern and Eastern European nations—demand to emigrate remained high, and waiting lists strung out for years. Northern European nations meanwhile used only 45 percent of their quotas.[31]

About all Truman could do was to appoint a Presidential Commission on Immigration and Naturalization to counter the research of the Arens committee. It proposed a "blanket" quota without favoring any one group of nations, a recommendation attacked by the editor of the *Saturday Evening Post*. Though admitting that McCarran-Walter might be a bit "over-security conscious" in trying to vet former Communists, the editor argued that the law effectively reflected public opinion, an accurate assumption. The problem with Truman's recommendations, the editor explained, was that "the racial group with the best public relations setup and the tightest squeeze on politicians would win all the arguments"—a not-so-veiled reference to Jewish groups that had vigorously battled the quota system since World War II.[32]

The editor repeated the charge three years later, and if readers did not immediately get the connection, that later editorial prefaced its comments about "the seamy side of immigration," personified by "the rise of 'minority' pressure groups," by noting that David Sarnoff (head of the National Broadcasting Company, and Jewish) did not identify as a member of a minority group, but simply as an American. There is no record of Sarnoff ever saying such a thing, but clearly the editorial wanted to make a distinction between assimilable Jews and those who were not.[33]

On April 14, 1952, President Truman welcomed the last displaced persons under his watch, a husband, wife, and, as Truman wrote in his diary, "two sweet little girls"—to the United States. In all, the United States accepted 339,000 DPs through 1952, far more than many would have wanted or predicted at the end of World War II when upward of 1.2 million DPs resided in European camps. Truman celebrated the event, but resented the long fight to alleviate the suffering of people who lost family and homes during a brutal war.[34]

Truman's hope was that, with South America and the Commonwealth countries agreeing to take in four hundred thousand each, the United States would step up and invite four hundred thousand as well. The 339,000 who came were the best he could do given congressional hostility and public opposition. His failure to prevent McCarran-Walter especially rankled him. He closed his diary entry with a faint hope that "we will agree to 330,000 more. They are fine people and may be an addition to our blood stream that we need right now."[35]

THE TRUMAN ADMINISTRATION also grappled with Mexican migration. Congress had never assigned quotas to Mexicans, or to other Latin Americans. Mexican migration to the United States accelerated in the 1920s when the expanding agricultural economy of the West and Southwest drew hundreds of thousands of migrant laborers, many of whom crossed the border illegally. John Nance Garner, a Texas congressman and later vice president during Franklin D. Roosevelt's first two presidential terms, argued that the migrants had integrated well into southern Texas and the area's agriculture depended heavily on their labor: "They will do necessary labor that even a Negro won't touch."[36]

Garner's main adversary on Mexican immigration was John Box, a Democratic congressman from northern Texas who wanted the state preserved "as the future home of the white race." Box objected to Texas becoming a "dumping ground for the human hordes of poverty stricken peon Indians of Mexico." The restrictive 1924 immigration act limited U.S. citizenship to "free white" persons and those of African origins. The "science" of the era designated Mexicans as nonwhite and decidedly inferior.[37]

Their status as "guest" workers left them vulnerable to exploitation. Although Garner claimed that Mexicans had assimilated well into their respective local communities, the native-born whites in those settlements resisted any integration. NO MEXICANS signs were commonplace in restaurants and shops throughout the Southwest. The restrooms in the Cochran County, Texas, courthouse bore the sign FOR WHITES, MEXICANS KEEP OUT. Such exclusion even trapped the Mexican consul in Houston, who could only obtain a meal in a restaurant kitchen, not in the dining room. A Catholic church refused to baptize the child of another Mexican diplomat.[38]

Discrimination persisted despite the fact that nearly half a million soldiers of Mexican descent served in World War II, including one as General Dwight D. Eisenhower's personal cook. Some fourteen thousand Mexican immigrants were drafted and fought in the conflict. Those who had not become naturalized citizens had to prove they had entered the United States legally once they were discharged from the service. If they could not come up with the requisite paperwork, they were deported. At least several thousand of these ex-soldiers suffered that fate.[39]

The case of Felix Longoria indicated the depth of anti-Mexican sentiment in some parts of the country. Longoria, a Mexican American private, was killed in the Philippines during World War II. His remains could not be returned to his home in San Antonio until 1948. Longoria's widow hoped to bury him in a cemetery near that city. The funeral director refused her request, stating, "Other white people object to the use of the funeral home by people of Mexican origin." An organization of Mexican American veterans took up the matter with Senator Lyndon B. Johnson, who had appealed to the Hispanic vote in his recent election campaign. Johnson responded, "I deeply regret to learn that the prejudice of some individuals extends even beyond this life." He arranged for Longoria to be buried with honors at Arlington National Cemetery.[40]

Truman's disappointment about the path not taken to reform the immigration laws reflected his impatience with an outmoded vision of America that violated the nation's basic ideals. Opponents of immigration reform hoped to restore a lost America of white Protestant citizens, or at least ensure their continued dominance. Truman believed the nation's future depended on the immigration of new people with new perspectives, ideas, and talents. Rather than diluting American culture, immigration would add to it and make it stronger. Presidential action made a difference in the immigration debate. Truman's persistence pressured Congress to expand the numbers of war refugees admitted and to remove at least some of the discriminatory provisions of its initial legislation. But more comprehensive immigration reform would await the presidency of Lyndon B. Johnson.

IN 1951, LOOK MAGAZINE, no ally of Truman's, published an essay by historian Henry Steele Commager that hailed the outgoing Truman administration as a great success, a judgment that was not unanimous, as the rise of conservatism indicated. Business leaders chafed under the president's periodic attacks on greed and the private enterprise system in general. Fatigue with the Korean War, fears of Communism, and concerns about corruption among some of Truman's associates tarnished the administration. Yet, the economic indexes revealed an unprecedented era of prosperity, and the record of the Truman administration in protecting and, in some areas, extending the New Deal offered evidence that corresponded with Commager's judgment.[41]

The G.I. Bill put millions of Americans in homes, classes, and new businesses. Prosperity extended deeper into American society than at any previous time in the country's history. The young members of the gifted generation would grow up in a prosperous country of expanding opportunities and social justice. Social Security benefits doubled, and the minimum wage increased. White supremacy and the policies to eradicate it were on the public agenda and some genuine progress had occurred through the president's executive orders and amicus briefs to the U.S. Supreme Court. The effort to rid cities of slums and the poverty that fueled them began, imperfectly to be sure; the 1949 Housing Act was a precedent nonetheless. The United States became the world's leader in science and technology.

Harry Truman believed in the commonwealth ideal of mutual responsibility not only among citizens but also as a compact between citizens and a government that could and should ensure opportunity for all Americans. These principles were evident in William Jennings Bryan, in Woodrow Wilson, and in Franklin D. Roosevelt, all of whom Truman admired. They were also evident in his career as a county official and as a U.S. senator. What he detested was the lack of vision that could not see a nation beyond the small-town, white, Protestant, male-dominated society of the nineteenth century. This was the environment from which he came. But he understood that this America had receded in favor of a larger, more urban, more complex country that depended on the federal government to ensure equality and opportunity for all of its citizens to the benefit of the nation.

Truman had little patience for nostalgia. Sure, he thought about the Civil War and Reconstruction with a particular Southern filter, but they did not guide his policies. The vision of this nineteenth-century man was of the future. He chafed at World War I veterans' gatherings where the men "get together and talk about how brave and great they were forty years ago." "No one," he argued, "can live in the past and do his country any service . . . They should be using experience to meet present day problems."[42]

In his final year in office, Truman could not restrain himself from a parting shot at the Republicans. He believed that government in the mid-twentieth century not only had a right but also a responsibility to intervene on behalf of its citizens to level the playing field. A common tactic of Republicans was to denigrate legislation they opposed by labeling it "socialist." In the midst of the Cold War, the effect was to stop debate. Though mainstream Republicans never accused Harry Truman of disloyalty, they implied on several occasions that both he and the Democratic program were a near relative of a deeper red. Truman, combative as ever, eviscerated this illogic in a speech at the

Democratic Party's annual Jefferson-Jackson Day dinner on March 29, 1952, where he predicted that the Republicans would play the socialist card in the upcoming presidential campaign:

> They will go to the people and say, "Did you see that Social Security check you received the other day—you thought that was good for you, didn't you? That's just too bad! That's nothing in the world but socialism. Did you see that new flood-control dam the government is building over there for the protection of your property? Sorry—that's awful socialism! That new hospital that they are building is socialism. Price supports, more socialism for the farmers! Minimum-wage laws? Socialism for labor! Socialism is bad for you, my friend. Everybody knows that." And here you are, with your new car, and your home, and better opportunities for the kids, and a television set—you are just surrounded by socialism![43]

AS HARRY AND BESS TRUMAN made their way back to Independence, Missouri, in January 1953, the now-former president left behind a considerable amount of unfinished business. He had wanted to do more in the realm of public housing. He had failed to persuade Congress to pass universal health insurance. Immigration law remained mired in prejudice rather than inspired by compassion. Gender equity barely registered on the national radar, except to be ridiculed, though more women worked in high government office under the Truman administration than in any other previous presidency.

Truman's aspirations for civil rights fell considerably short of realization as well, though he had begun desegregating the armed forces and the federal civil service. Most of all, Truman had initiated a broad discussion on civil rights that would remain in the national dialogue, even though during his administration there was precious little public support for ameliorative legislation.

Harry Truman had lived by the principle that government "must be operated on the basis of the greatest good for the greatest number of its citizens." In a March 1952 address to the Columbia Scholastic Press Association in New York, Truman began by invoking his hero, William Jennings Bryan, and how, in 1900, Truman attended the Democratic National Convention in Kansas City to witness Bryan's nomination for president. Bryan, Truman explained, was ahead of his time. His ideas had more to teach the present generation. The core of Bryan's message, and of Truman's, was that "when our own government has looked after the average man first, we have grown and prospered.

But when those in power have used our government to increase the privileges of the few at the top, the life and spirit of our country have declined."[44]

For Truman, it was not merely the use of government power that had inspired Bryan or Wilson or Roosevelt; it was utilization of that power on behalf of the greatest number, the essence of the commonwealth ideal. Truman had tried to govern by that precept, even when it was not politically expedient to do so. In time, that would change, and it would change because Harry Truman placed these issues—health care, immigration reform, and, above all, civil rights—in the public forum. Few of the major victories of the Eisenhower and Johnson years derived from new ideas. Truman had championed most of them, and several had dated from the Progressive era of the early twentieth century. But the Truman administration placed these ideas front and center, and if he could not implement them, they would remain, and still remain, part of the national political discourse.

AT THE END OF WORLD WAR II, America was incomplete. Americans could bask for a while in the glow of victory and go about resuming or refashioning their lives, often with the assistance of the federal government. But for African Americans, for women, and for various ethnic and religious groups, obstacles remained along the path of attaining the promise of American life. In prior decades, these serious flaws in national life remained submerged for the most part, rarely part of daily discussions. But gradually in the late 1940s and in the 1950s, conversations emerged exposing some of the more serious contradictions in society: racism, anti-Semitism, xenophobia, and sexism. Popular magazines, which, for the most part, avoided cultural crusading, as did Hollywood, spoke out on some of these issues in the late 1940s. They discussed anti-Semitism, they depicted women in a variety of roles, they touted the benefits immigrants had brought to America, and they lectured readers on the importance if not of racial equality then of racial fairness.

Truman's seven years in the White House did not result in major legislation that significantly expanded the New Deal. But Truman both protected and advanced the gains in education, social services, and housing initiated during the Roosevelt years. Not a mean feat given the conservative resurgence after the war and the structure of Congress, controlled by Southern Democrats suspicious of expanding opportunities for the American people lest opportunities should also expand for African Americans. The modest advance engineered and overseen by the president included the growing role of the federal government in public health, education, civil rights, and housing, as well as the subsidizing of the dreams of homeownership for tens of thousands of American families.

Truman understood the Keynesian economic principle that government policy could grow the economy by putting money into consumers' pockets, thereby increasing the demand for goods and services. By the time Truman issued his final State of the Union address to Congress on January 7, 1953, the country had gained 11 million jobs since the end of World War II. Unemployment was at an all-time low, and farm and corporate income were at all-time highs. Banks were solvent. Millions of veterans had taken advantage of the G.I. Bill. Federal funds had cleared slums and subsidized new housing in cities and suburbs.

Truman placed before the American public the disparity between the Declaration of Independence and conditions in postwar America with respect to racial, religious, and economic inequality. The message would remain there for every subsequent election season until the Congress and the president could agree on a formula to implement policies to level the playing field for everyone. Some breakthroughs would come relatively quickly; for others, the wait continues.

Truman's class-based oratory, derided by contemporaries as both anachronistic and divisive, reflected a deep-seated sense that the nation's prosperity should be shared, not hoarded, and that government had a responsibility to use its portion of the profits to invest in the people, in their education, in their housing, in their jobs, and to ensure above all a fairness in enabling them to reach their utmost potential. Truman's Fair Deal was not merely a slogan; it was the basis of his governing philosophy. For those early baby boomers born just before or during his presidency, such objectives would define them as the gifted generation.

PART II

Settlement

CHAPTER 9

THE SWEDISH JEW

DWIGHT DAVID EISENHOWER WAS born into a struggling working-class family on October 14, 1890. The place was Denison, Texas, a railroad town, a way station on the family's downward journey to poverty. Dwight's father, David, worked for the Missouri, Kansas, and Texas Railroad as an engine wiper for $10 a week. Dwight was the third of seven sons. The family lived in a soot-stained shack near the tracks. After four difficult years in Denison, the family moved to Abilene, Kansas.[1]

It was hardly a portentous beginning. But four of the sons would go on to distinguished careers of leadership: Arthur, Harry Truman's erstwhile roommate, and Edgar became bank presidents; Milton held three university presidencies, the last one at Johns Hopkins; and Dwight became commander in chief of Allied forces during World War II, president of Columbia University after the war, and two-term president of the United States. How this could happen reveals as much about the United States during the early twentieth century as it does about parental influences. In this case, Dwight's mother, Ida.

Ida Stover's forebears settled in Pennsylvania, migrating from Swabia, a region in southwestern Germany, in the 1730s. They moved down the Great Wagon Road to Virginia's Shenandoah Valley, where Ida was born in 1862, one of eleven children. When she turned twenty-one, Ida set out for Kansas to join her brother and enter Lane College, where she met David Eisenhower and married him in 1885. David was descended from a German Protestant sect that had migrated from Pennsylvania to Kansas in the late 1870s.

Ida became a legend at Lane. She won a prize for memorizing 1,325 biblical verses.[2] Despite their mutual religiosity, Ida and David Eisenhower were an odd couple. He was quiet, humorless, and preternaturally pessimistic. His life would become a self-fulfilling prophecy. She was an extrovert and an eternal optimist. Ida would impart that outlook, as well as her love of books, to her sons.

Abilene was a railroad town, much like Denison, except that it was near some of the most fertile farmland in America. When the Eisenhowers arrived, hitching posts and watering troughs for horses lined the main street, which was unpaved until 1904. While Independence, Missouri, could claim significant connections to American history, as well as contacts with the cosmopolitan world of Kansas City, Abilene was more isolated.

By the time Dwight entered high school, Abilene residents enjoyed electricity and running water. The telegraph was the main source of immediate news from the outside world, such as results from the first World Series, played in 1903. Dwight's brother Milton recalled, "The isolation was political and economic as well as a prevailing state of mind." In this type of environment parents, pastors, and schoolteachers had an inordinate influence on young minds, and Dwight's mother played a crucial role in shaping his intellectual and personal ideals. Like Harry Truman, Dwight Eisenhower hailed from the nineteenth century, and like Truman, he absorbed the values of his town and family, which included an abiding faith in the future and its possibilities.[3]

The town functioned around its religious institutions, of which there were many. The Eisenhowers belonged to a splinter Mennonite sect, setting them off from their more conventional Protestant neighbors, but such denominational differences did not generate prejudice or exclusion. The key commonalty was a strong religious faith. That was what mattered.

Unlike Independence, Missouri, and its deep Confederate heritage, Abilene did not hold much for the Southern cause. About one hundred African Americans were among the little more than three thousand residents. Segregation existed, especially in the churches, but it was not as rigid as in Independence. Ida Stover insisted on equal treatment, and her Mennonite sect required it. Young Dwight internalized his mother's egalitarian principles. If any politics excited the sleepy village in the 1890s, it was populism. Any questions about the Eisenhowers' political leanings were dispelled by the fact that they named one of their sons Abraham Lincoln Eisenhower.[4]

David had no interest in farming. He opened up a clothing store with a partner, but became bored with the retail trade and set off for Texas, where Dwight was born. The move only worsened the family's economic situation. They returned to Kansas, where David worked six days a week at a creamery for wages that scarcely covered food and lodging for his growing family. "I found out later," Dwight recalled, "we were very poor, but we didn't know it at the time."[5]

David drifted from place to place and job to job, but he remained steadfast in his religion. He read Scripture to his family every morning, led prayers before each meal, and required the boys to read passages out loud in the evening. Perhaps this regimen is why none of the brothers maintained such religious devotion in their adulthood. Both parents were pacifists. Dwight did not follow that ideal either. When he left for West Point, his brother Milton reported, it was the first time he had ever heard his perpetually cheerful mother cry.[6]

With each setback, David became more reclusive. Dwight recalled that his father never played with him or took him hunting as the fathers of his friends did with their sons. "Mother was by far the greatest personal influence on our lives," Dwight recalled. Despite the family's travails, she always seemed upbeat. As brother Milton said, "She always had a song in her heart."[7]

Dwight found his studies mostly boring, but football kept him engaged with the school, and he obtained a free education, an important consideration due to the financial challenges of his family. A curious reference to Dwight in the West Point yearbook as "a terrible Swedish-Jew" has confounded historians as to its meaning. Rumors circulated about Dwight's alleged Jewish ancestry during his presidential years—primarily focusing on his dark-haired father, David Jacob Eisenhower—but there is no evidence to support that claim. The yearbook profiles were meant to be witty, even salacious—an inside joke rather than a sharp profile. Dwight's good looks or his diffident scholastic record may have accounted for the Swedish part, and his being known to hustle for every cent he could make—an endeavor necessary because of his family's poor finances—fed common stereotypes of the time. But the conundrum represented what would become a pattern with Dwight, a divergence between his private and public personae.[8]

Graduating from West Point in 1915, 61st out of 164 cadets, Dwight began his army career at Fort Sam Houston in San Antonio, Texas. There, he met his wife-to-be. They were married in July 1916. His bride, nineteen-year-old Mary Geneva Doud, called Mamie, came from a wealthy Denver, Colorado, family that wintered in San Antonio. Her father's family, originally from Connecticut, made a fortune in meatpacking. Her mother was the daughter of Swedish immigrants.

Dwight trained recruits after American entrance into World War I, but did not see action himself. Perhaps the most memorable adventure of his early years in the military occurred in 1919 when he led a truck convoy on a cross-country trip. The journey involved considerably more than merely moving equipment from the East Coast to the West Coast. The only realistic, safe, and relatively quick way to undertake a transcontinental trip in those days was by rail. But more Americans were purchasing automobiles. There were no maps, no highway network, and few road signs. Drivers navigated by compass. The roads were often unpaved. There were few vehicular bridges and nothing in the way of roadside service if your car broke down or you needed a place to eat or spend the night.

With much ceremony, the eighty-one-vehicle convoy embarked from the Ellipse in Washington, D.C., on July 7, 1919, headed for San Francisco, 3,251 miles away. Sixty-two days later (five days behind schedule), the convoy entered San Francisco. The route took the vehicles along a planned Lincoln Highway (what is now U.S. 30 and I-80). The wretched conditions the convoy encountered made a deep impression on Dwight, one that would drive his passion for a nationwide system of highways thirty-five years later, which became the largest government-sponsored public works project in American history.

For the next quarter century, Eisenhower built a distinguished military career, culminating in his selection as supreme commander of Allied forces in December 1943. Before then, he had honed his intellectual skills by writing a history of American involvement on the Western Front during World War I, under the direction of General John J. Pershing. During a stint in Panama in the 1920s, Eisenhower read widely in history and the classics, an education in the humanities that he did not receive at West Point. Although some critics considered him an intellectual lightweight, his brother Milton, who had an exceptional academic career, asserted that Dwight was "the real scholar of the Eisenhower family." Their correspondence supports this view.[9]

During his time in military service, it is speculative to assess Eisenhower's political philosophy given the traditional reticence of officers about (and strictures against) expressing partisan political viewpoints. He did not register a party affiliation, nor did he vote. But Eisenhower's service in the military clearly colored his view about government activism, which he came to view as positive, within prescribed boundaries. A rare glimpse into his philosophy came from his reaction to congressional approval of financial legislation in March 1933 that gave President Franklin D. Roosevelt authority over the nation's banking system at the height of the Great Depression. Eisenhower commented enthusiastically, "Yesterday Congress met and gave the President extraordinary power over banking. Now if they'll just do the same with respect to law enforcement, federal expenditures, transportation systems, there will be such a revival of confidence that things will begin to move."[10]

Eisenhower would eventually temper his enthusiasm for a hyperactive federal government, but decades of public service convinced him that Washington had an important role to play in guiding an increasingly complex nation to a prosperous and safe future. His military career, especially in coordinating the egos and temperaments of British and French political and military leaders during and immediately after World War II, enabled him to appreciate the benefits of compromise. His strengths were planning, public relations, and conciliation—good traits for both a military and a civilian leader.

AFTER EISENHOWER HELPED to save Western civilization, peace taxed his patience. He served a tour as army chief of staff, but presiding over demobilization was hardly a rewarding endeavor. In mid-1947, he accepted the presidency of Columbia University, a move that astonished his friends and the academic world in general. It was a good hire for Columbia, considering the financial exigencies of postwar private higher education, and from Eisenhower's perspective, it was a dignified "fade" for a military hero, now ensconced in the ivory tower of the Ivy League.

Eisenhower was so adept at concealing his political preferences in the years following 1945 that both political parties attempted to encourage his candidacy in 1948 and again in 1950, looking toward the 1952 presidential election. In February 1951, he served the Truman administration as head of the North Atlantic Treaty Organization (NATO), headquartered in Paris. He remained in public view, a larger-than-life figure of probity and devotion to country in the midst of an increasingly anxious Cold War with the Soviet Union.

After he assumed the presidency of Columbia in 1948, Eisenhower began to express his views more publicly. His speeches rarely focused on specific issues, but they provided some insight into the intellectual context within which he might address domestic policy. He emphasized the importance of a balanced society among citizens, business, and government. In these ruminations, little distinguished Eisenhower from Truman. As Eisenhower related in his presidential-installation address at Columbia in October 1948, "Danger arises from too great a concentration of power in the hands of any individual or group: the power of concentrated finance, the power of selfish pressure groups, the power of any class organized in opposition to the whole—any one of these, when allowed to dominate, is fully capable of destroying individual freedom." It was a classic restatement of the commonwealth ideal.[11]

In that same speech, Eisenhower, shielded by his military bona fides, suggested the importance of social policy over armaments as weapons in the Cold War: "We'll never have peace as long as there are hungry people in the world." The best way to fight Communism was through soft power, investing in people rather than arms.[12]

Eisenhower shared with Truman a studied disdain for those who embraced a vision of an alleged golden era of American life when what they really meant was a time before immigrants, women, and African Americans began pressing their cases for equal inclusion in the American enterprise. In another

Columbia address a year later, he dismissed "reactionaries" who "see no hope for us except in a vain attempt to return to the methods, practices, and circumstances of the late nineteenth century."[13]

Eisenhower's speech to the American Bar Association in September 1949 was especially instructive. He would return to the themes of this presentation on numerous occasions during his presidency. As a keen student of history, and, like Truman and Johnson, an eyewitness to the Great Depression, he was well aware that the power of "concentrated wealth" had become "a menace to the self-respect, opportunities, and livelihood of great groups of ordinary citizens" and had "compelled drastic action for the preservation of the laborer's dignity—for the welfare of himself and his family." This was the same concern Keynes had articulated in his brief for government activism. Truman expounded on this theme numerous times as well.

Eisenhower applauded the legislation of the Progressive and New Deal eras in ameliorating such social and economic imbalances, but class divisions remained a potentially serious problem in the United States: "Such divisions . . . inevitably become so clearly reflected in political organization and doctrine that they damage both our political and economic structures, thus enlarging and perpetuating initial effects." He warned against "the unbearable selfishness of vested interest." While Truman believed such class conflict already existed and imminently threatened American democracy, Eisenhower perceived such divisions as nascent and something government could control.[14]

In his private correspondence before Eisenhower formally entered the presidential campaign in 1952, he returned to the themes of the commonwealth ideal, particularly the interdependence of society's disparate groups: "Agriculture, labor, management frequently speak of themselves as if each were a separate and self-sufficient enterprise or community. Yet the simple fact is that each is helpless without the others; . . . no prosperity for one economic group is permanently possible except as all groups prosper." Eisenhower put this idea into practice at Columbia, creating the American Assembly to attract leaders of business, labor, government, and academia "to study and plan cooperatively for the future."[15]

THE REPUBLICAN PARTY was badly split in 1952 between the moderate wing, headed by the "Northeastern establishment," and the conservatives, led by Ohio senator Robert A. Taft. To complicate the Republicans' chances in the fall, Wisconsin Republican senator Joseph R. McCarthy was bullying his way through hearings on the alleged Communist infiltration of the U.S. government, the media, and educational institutions. The conservatives, for the most part, cheered on these efforts. The moderates, fearful of political fallout, remained mostly silent. But they believed that a Taft candidacy in the fall would doom the party to yet another defeat. The combination of a candidate who wished to eradicate the New Deal and withdraw from meaningful participation in the world, and the baggage of the fearmongering McCarthy, would not likely appeal to an electorate in the midst of prosperity.[16]

Both wings of the Republican Party agreed that limited government served the best interests of the country. The problem, as two-time failed presidential candidate Thomas E. Dewey noted, was that while "all middle-class citizens of education have a common belief that tendencies toward centralization and paternalism must be halted and reversed . . . no one who voices these views can be elected." In other words, Americans, regardless of their views on government activism, had embraced the New Deal, and going backward, or even halting its progress, was not a viable electoral strategy. But perhaps a stealth candidate with a limited public record could attain electoral success. Dewey advised, "We must look around for someone of great popularity and who has not frittered away his political assets by taking positive stands against national planning, etc., etc. Elect such a man to the Presidency, *after which* he must lead us back to safe channels and paths." It would be yet another of Dewey's miscalculations.[17]

Eisenhower, as Dewey knew, fulfilled those criteria well. He was an immensely popular leader who had not, beyond generalizations, expressed strong opinions on the major domestic issues of the day. But Eisenhower's political philosophy might have given Dewey some pause had he probed deeply into the public statements of the former general.

Eisenhower had no intention of dismantling the New Deal or of turning the federal government into a spectator, though his grasp of domestic issues was that of a relatively well-informed citizen rather than that of a politician. As he wrote testily to his brother Edgar, perhaps the most conservative member of the Eisenhower family, "Should any political party attempt to abolish social security, unemployment insurance, and eliminate labor laws and farm programs, you would not hear of that party again in our political history." Instead, the programs needed strengthening.[18]

Eisenhower was fond of quoting Abraham Lincoln's dictum "The legitimate object of government is to do for a community of people whatever they need to have done but cannot do at all or cannot so well do, for themselves, in their separate and individual capacities." Harry Truman and most Northern Democrats could endorse this statement. In fact, Democrats often quoted the same passage. The idea of the government as umpire, of seeking the "vital center" on issues, was at the core of Eisenhower's political beliefs, a core derived from both his military experience and his years growing up in Abilene.[19]

This was not what Thomas E. Dewey had in mind in March 1952 when he dispatched Herbert Brownell to Paris, where Ike was serving as the supreme commander of NATO. Brownell was a good choice. Like Eisenhower, he came from a small town on the Plains: Peru, Nebraska, about two hundred miles north of Abilene. Also like Eisenhower, he had a profound interest in and respect for Abraham Lincoln. Brownell had amassed an impressive Lincoln library and, by 1952, had become a serious scholar of the Fourteenth and Fifteenth Amendments to the Constitution, amendments that guaranteed the former slaves equal protection under the law and the right to vote, respectively. Both his upbringing and legal grounding molded Brownell into a strong advocate for civil rights.[20]

By the time Brownell met with Eisenhower in Paris, Ike had already won the New Hampshire primary against Robert A. Taft, even though Ike had not set foot in the state, a testament to the remarkable draw of his name and reputation. While Eisenhower agreed to have his name on the New Hampshire ballot, he insisted that he remain above the fray until such time as he made a definite decision. Which was the purpose of Brownell's trip.

Brownell's journey to Paris was all cloak-and-dagger as he flew to Paris under an assumed name. He checked into the George V Hotel on March 24, 1952, still using the fictitious name. A car and driver met him in front of the hotel and took him to NATO headquarters. Eisenhower's appointment log for the day did not list the meeting, though Brownell spent most of the day with the NATO commander. Brownell made his pitch that only Ike could save the country (and the Republican Party) from isolationism and reaction. He admitted he had little clue of Eisenhower's views on domestic issues. Ike referred him to his speech at the American Bar Association convention in September 1949, paraphrased his favorite Lincoln quote, and stated his belief in a balanced budget (a point Truman espoused). Eisenhower's responses were generic enough so that both wings of the Republican Party could read into them what they wished.

Brownell moved to a discussion of civil rights. Racial justice was a priority with Truman, though not yet with the American people, and certainly not with a majority in Congress. The Truman administration had bypassed both popular and political opinion by working through the federal courts supporting NAACP legal actions challenging segregation by law. Brownell understood that while civil rights would not be a compelling issue during the upcoming presidential campaign, it would likely emerge as such in the not-too-distant future. Brownell privately supported the NAACP initiatives, and

he hoped the Republican Party would take the lead on civil rights, particularly given the Democrats' reluctance to alienate the Southern wing of the
party in the upcoming election.

Eisenhower related his wartime record on civil rights. In March 1944 he
issued a confidential directive to the American forces holding officers responsible for "the scrupulous enforcement" of the principle "equal opportunities
of service and of recreation are the right of every American soldier regardless
of branch, race, color or creed." Eisenhower also engaged in heated discussions with the War Department to allow black soldiers in combat. A surprise
German offensive in the Ardennes in December 1944 left the general dangerously short of infantry. He complained to General George C. Marshall that
more than one hundred thousand black troops were performing "back-
breaking manual work" on roads and docks but were not allowed to fight on
the front lines. "I feel," General Eisenhower wrote, "that in existing circumstances I cannot deny the Negro volunteer a chance to serve in battle."
Marshall ultimately relented.[21]

But the War Department struck down Eisenhower's directive, included
in the mobilization order, that he would assign black soldiers "without regard
to color or race to the units where assistance is most needed." This policy,
if carried out, would end the military policy of segregating troops, thus
violating army regulations. Although Ike complied, he assigned all-black
platoons of about forty men each to white units on the front lines. The black
response to Eisenhower's invitation was overwhelming, some even accepting
a reduction in grade to qualify. With the Nazi surrender, this experiment with
quasi-integrated troops ended. But officers of such units reported that the
camaraderie was "far better than they had expected," including with those
African American soldiers assigned to mainly Southern white units, challenging arguments that integration would seriously damage troop morale.[22]

The public disputes reflected Ike's private views on racial justice. In 1946,
his brother Milton, then president of Kansas State University, asked him for
suggestions on a citizenship course Milton wanted to inaugurate at the school.
Ike responded, "In presenting the objectives of the course I should bear down
hard on *elimination of racial intolerance*." Eisenhower was born in Texas—in
Democratic House Speaker Sam Rayburn's home district—and grew up in a
border town. He had served his entire adult career in a segregated military,
often at bases in the South, and several of his closest friends were white
Southerners. Like Truman, he never disavowed his background, but he often
transcended it.[23]

After the war Eisenhower continued to fight for civil rights, especially in
the military. As chief of staff in 1946 and 1947, he attempted, unsuccessfully,

to partially integrate the army. Walter White, the executive secretary of the NAACP, who knew of Eisenhower's behind-the-scenes efforts, wrote in 1948 that "Eisenhower was implacable in his opposition to that system [segregation in the military]."[24]

By the late 1940s, African Americans looked upon Eisenhower with the same admiration they reserved for Truman. A story appeared in a black newspaper, which Ike later corroborated, that the center on Ike's high school football team refused to play that position as he would be lined up opposite a black player from the opposing school. Eisenhower stepped in to play center for the first and only time of his football career.[25]

EISENHOWER'S PRESIDENTIAL CAMPAIGN began in June 1952, relatively late, even in those days, and little more than one month before the Republican National Convention in July. By the time Ike got started, Taft had already built a strong delegate lead. Brownell reported that Eisenhower was not taking to the campaign routine well, especially the receiving of orders from party politicos. At a stop in Denver, Ike reportedly complained, "I don't like this business; these politicians are terrible." He then walked over to the corner of a rug, lifted it up, and said, "You see them crawling out from under there." He was particularly annoyed when party leaders booked him in Wisconsin. He despised Senator McCarthy, especially his insinuations about the loyalty of one of Ike's closest friends, General George C. Marshall. Once Ike received the nomination, he hired Brownell to serve as an intermediary between the party and himself so he would not have to deal directly with politicians.[26]

To mollify the conservative wing of the Republican Party, Eisenhower agreed on Richard M. Nixon, senator from California, as his running mate. In 1950, Nixon's notoriously virulent anticommunist Senate campaign against his Democrat opponent, Helen Gahagan Douglas, a former actress and congresswoman, endeared him to the party's conservative wing. Nixon was also young, thirty-nine in 1952, a good complement to the avuncular Ike.

The 1952 presidential campaign was notable for several reasons. First, television made its debut as a player in presidential politics. Eisenhower's acceptance speech at the Republican National Convention was televised to a nationwide audience. More innovative were the "spots" Ike's team employed. These were brief (usually one-minute) advertisements called "Eisenhower Answers America," which featured the candidate responding to a question from a voter. These were not random questions, nor were the questioners even in the same studio. Ike's responses were generic and shot before the ad agency filmed the questioners, despite the appearance that Ike was responding directly to the questioner. But the strategy enabled tens of thousands of viewers to see a presidential candidate, perhaps for the first time, and hear him not in a formal speech, but in a response to an average citizen. Although Eisenhower's performance was wooden and scripted, it was so novel that the delivery style mattered much less than the medium. Ike's Democratic opponent, Adlai Stevenson, hated the new medium and refused to use it.

Equally important in Ike's spots was the diversity of the questioners in an era when diversity was uncommon in political advertising. The spots included women and even an African American man, who asked Eisenhower not about civil rights—which would have been a controversial subject to air—but about the cost of living, an economic issue shared by millions of Americans. The black questioner was not dressed in identifiable work clothes, but as a middle-class citizen. At a time when *Amos 'n' Andy* was enormously popular on radio, and then on TV, this was a significant departure from stereotype.[27]

Another oddity of the 1952 campaign was that Eisenhower began it in Atlanta. Since the Civil War, no Republican candidate had had a remote chance of capturing the Deep South. Even the Catholic Al Smith won these states (South Carolina, Georgia, Alabama, Mississippi, Louisiana, and Arkansas) despite the strong opposition of the Ku Klux Klan and numerous evangelical ministers. And with the Dixiecrats back in the regular Democratic Party fold, a Republican breakthrough was unlikely. However, Eisenhower was immensely popular nationally, including in the South. He never wore his party affiliation on his sleeve, which caused consternation among party regulars, but suited the Southern white electorate. Although Ike could not crack the Deep South in the general election, he was competitive. And he did win four former Confederate states—Virginia, Tennessee, Florida, and Texas.[28]

Adlai Stevenson never had a chance against the wildly popular general, especially since his public positions on the major domestic and foreign affairs issues differed little from his opponent's. Stevenson's wealthy background, his Ivy League education, and his faintly effeminate manner—the *New York Daily News* referred to him as "Adelaide"—contrasted with Eisenhower's take-charge demeanor and his war-hero status. Stevenson was bright, articulate, but relatively unknown outside his home state of Illinois, where he had served as governor. His precise diction and highly intellectual discourses may have worked in a university classroom, but not in a political campaign. Commentators poked fun at his "fruity" voice and his use of "teacup words" that reminded one of a "genteel spinster who can never forget that she got an A in elocution at Miss Smith's finishing school."[29]

The election contained other troubling news for Democrats in that Catholic blue-collar whites, traditionally Democratic voters, preferred the former general over Stevenson. Eisenhower won a solid victory throughout the country, overwhelming Stevenson in the Electoral College, 442 to 89. Ike's coattails, though, were relatively short, resulting in a one-vote Republican majority in the Senate and a ten-vote majority in the House of Representatives. For the first time since 1930, Republicans controlled both Congress and the White House.

It was difficult to run a negative campaign against a war hero. Rumors of Eisenhower's Jewish ancestry resurfaced—"Ike the Kike"—but played no role in the outcome. More serious were allegations of Eisenhower's political leanings based on comments he made at a dinner at Washington's F Street Club in 1947. During a discussion on inflation—a major concern in the immediate postwar years—Ike stated that industrialists should do more to keep prices down, even if it sacrificed profits. The after-dinner comments became campaign fodder in an era when some perceived attacks on the private-enterprise system as Communist-inspired. Several journalists claimed that Eisenhower was at heart a socialist out to destroy capitalism. Ike dismissed such charges and repeated what he had said at the dinner. His head-on handling of the matter effectively ended it.[30]

Exit interviews indicated less of a smashing of the Democrats' New Deal coalition than a temporary desertion. Eisenhower did not run against the New Deal, which would have been a fatal strategy, as Dewey had noted. A Wisconsin teacher who voted for Ike told a reporter, "I wanted a change, but there are lots of good things the Democrats did I don't want undone." A Detroit worker, also an Eisenhower voter, stated he was "sick of politicians running the country." During the interview, his ten-year-old son asked him the difference between a Democrat and a Republican. The worker replied without irony, "The Republicans are for people with money, and the Democrats are for us poor people." The 1952 election was a victory for Eisenhower and not necessarily the Republican Party, as the rest of the decade would prove.[31]

The 1952 election was also the first campaign that drew tens of thousands of suburban voters. The idea of preserving the New Deal, but not going any further so taxes and inflation would remain in check, had a great appeal for this group. The suburbs rolled up hefty majorities for Eisenhower. His victories in the South occurred in states with substantial urban and, especially, suburban populations.[32]

Finally, voters were tired of the Korean War and concerned about the Cold War, two international issues that a former general would be well qualified to address. Foreign affairs rarely swing elections in the United States. But, combined with Ike's popularity and the satisfaction of the country with the status quo, his route to the presidency became easier. Political scientist Samuel Lubell analyzed Eisenhower's victory in January 1953 and concluded, "It was not a vote for a twenty-year rollback of history. To the contrary, the impression left was that the dominant concern of the voters was how to preserve the gains of those years."[33]

Civil rights played a subordinate role in the 1952 campaign as there was little public support for initiatives on race. But the differences between the parties were notable. The Democrats retreated from their strong support of civil rights in the 1948 platform. The Republicans were more ambitious, including a warning that the federal government could "take supplemental action within its constitutional jurisdiction to oppose discrimination against race, religion or national origins." The party also pledged to support anti-lynching and anti-poll-tax legislation and advocated an end to segregation in the District of Columbia. Ike pounded away at the disgrace of racial segregation in the nation's capital, a clear contrast between himself and his Democratic opponent. Most noteworthy was the Republican Party's promise "to further just and equitable treatment in the area of discriminatory employment practices," implying that Republicans would support a version of the Fair Employment Practices Committee, a body that was anathema to Southern Democrats. The National Council of Negro Democrats endorsed Eisenhower over Stevenson.[34]

Thomas E. Dewey had succeeded in drafting a candidate and placing him in the White House. The Republican Party, divided between those who wanted to send the New and Fair Deals to oblivion and those who favored a moderate pruning, were each hopeful. Eisenhower was their empty vessel within whom each faction placed their fondest hopes. Democrats were more wary—they had lost control of Congress and now had to work with not only a Republican majority but also a Republican president. Southern Democrats hoped mainly to retain the status quo of white supremacy. Whatever other policies the new president supported would be immaterial compared to that one large issue. Liberal Democrats hoped to at least hold the line on the gains of the previous two decades. They were the most fearful group in January 1953.

CHAPTER 10

THE WHEELS OF JUSTICE

PRESIDENTS NEVER TAKE OFFICE with a clean slate. Inevitably, issues hang over from the previous administration that the new chief executive must deal with, often immediately. The school-desegregation cases for which the Truman administration had filed amicus briefs remained before the Supreme Court. And just as Eisenhower took the oath of office, a federal circuit court ruled in *District of Columbia v. John R. Thompson Co., Inc.* that Washington, D.C.'s 1872 law banning racial discrimination was unconstitutional. During the campaign, Eisenhower had pledged to end racial segregation in the District.

In March 1951, Frank Willard, a New York investment banker, sent an op-ed piece from the *New York Herald Tribune* to Eisenhower. The column, written by Edward L. Bernays, an attorney, expressed concern that the Soviets were winning the propaganda war because of racial inequality in the United States. Bernays argued that "domestic activity . . . affects our standing in foreign countries as much as foreign activity." To counter negative perceptions, he recommended the establishment of a federal Fair Employment Practices Commission, an antilynching law, and legislation banning poll taxes—initiatives persistently but futilely promoted by the Truman administration. Such legislation, Bernays pointed out, would make the United States "conform as closely as possible in deeds both at home and abroad to the words we use to enlist favorable interest for it."[1]

Eisenhower responded to the Bernays column with agreement and exasperation: "The *real* fact that our propaganda should be able to emphasize is that there is no lynching in the United States, that no worthwhile citizen is really kept from voting . . . and that no man is kept out of employment merely because of race or religion or other factor of this kind." Eisenhower's opposition to segregation in the District of Columbia was of a piece with this viewpoint. Now that a federal court had placed a government imprimatur on racial discrimination in Washington, Eisenhower faced a dilemma.[2]

Circumscribed by what he could do in the District beyond encouraging the city's governing board (appointed by Congress) to desegregate the city's

Jane Goren surrounded by her artwork in her Studio City, California, home. 2012.

Heni Nunno receiving her Ph.D. degree from the CUNY Graduate Center, June 1978, with her parents and her two children, Wayne and Lara. Heni went on to earn numerous patents and perfect the rape kit used by law enforcement agencies today.

Martha Ellen Truman on her wedding day, December 28, 1881. Harry Truman's mother had a significant impact on his upbringing, particularly through her interests in literature and music. HARRY S. TRUMAN LIBRARY & MUSEUM

Harry Truman riding a cultivator on the family farm, ca. 1910. Truman disliked farm life, but family obligations drew him back for a ten-year period. World War I and politics rescued him. HARRY S. TRUMAN LIBRARY & MUSEUM

Jackie Robinson, 1947.
GETTY IMAGES (FROM BETTMANN)

Truman speaks to the thirty-eighth annual conference of the National Association for the Advancement of Colored People (NAACP) from the steps of the Lincoln Memorial, June 29, 1947. Truman was the first president to address the organization. ABBIE ROWE, NATIONAL PARK SERVICE, HARRY S. TRUMAN LIBRARY & MUSEUM

Truman receiving the report *To Secure These Rights* from his Committee on Civil Rights, October 29, 1947. Truman, much to the dismay of his Southern friends, made civil rights a top, if futile, priority. INTERNATIONAL NEWS SERVICE. HARRY S. TRUMAN LIBRARY & MUSEUM

India Edwards, Executive Director, Women's Division, Democratic National Committee, helping President Truman during his 1948 presidential campaign, October 1948. HARRY S. TRUMAN LIBRARY & MUSEUM

Truman in Morehead, Kentucky, during his famous "Whistle Stop" campaign, October 1, 1948.
HARRY S. TRUMAN LIBRARY & MUSEUM

Black children standing in front of a half-mile concrete wall in Detroit, August 1941. The wall separated a black neighborhood from a white housing development going up on the other side. Such strict patterns of residential segregation were common in northern cities. When extensive migration of African Americans into the urban North occurred during and after World War II, racial conflict often followed. LIBRARY OF CONGRESS, PRINTS & PHOTOGRAPHS DIVISION

Betty Friedan holding an infant child, possibly son Daniel, 1950. Friedan found her "assigned" role in society limiting. During the early 1950s, her ideas about feminism and the expectations of society took shape. COURTESY SCHLESINGER LIBRARY, RADCLIFFE INSTITUTE, HARVARD UNIVERSITY

An angry Truman inquires, "What Happened to the One We Used to Have?" October 9, 1946.

WASHINGTON POST, HERBLOCK COLLECTION, LIBRARY OF CONGRESS, PRINTS & PHOTOGRAPHS DIVISION

schools, Eisenhower worked to end segregation in federal facilities, such as shipyards and veterans hospitals, where his authority to issue executive orders did not require congressional action or judicial approval.[3]

A few weeks after taking office, Eisenhower declared in his State of the Union address, "I propose to use whatever authority exists in the office of the President to end segregation in the District of Columbia, including the Federal Government, and any segregation in the Armed Forces." The city of Washington, in Senator Hubert Humphrey's words, was "more Southern than the Southern cities." African Americans in 1953 could not check in at a good hotel, eat at a restaurant, attend a theater performance, or find a restroom in the downtown area without assiduous research. Eisenhower had requested an integrated inauguration, but most Washington establishments ignored him.[4]

Eisenhower appointed Herbert Brownell attorney general, and together they made certain to stock the Justice Department with civil rights advocates. Revealingly, one of the few attorneys they retained from the Truman administration was Philip Elman, who had argued Truman's amicus brief in the *Brown* case then before the U.S. Supreme Court. Ike also wanted to appoint a black cabinet member, but relented when his aides pointed out that Southern Democrats would likely filibuster the nomination to death and bottle up all legislation in the meantime.

But other administration openings did not require confirmation, and the president appointed more than two dozen African Americans to these posts. Lois Lippman, for example, became a White House secretary, the first black person to serve in the Executive Mansion in a capacity other than janitor or messenger. Eisenhower also appointed J. Ernest Wilkins Sr., a black Chicago attorney, as assistant secretary of labor for international affairs, the highest subcabinet post ever for an African American.[5]

The *Thompson* case stood in the way of Eisenhower's fulfilling his campaign promise and a personal commitment. He ordered Attorney General Brownell to appeal that decision to the U.S. Supreme Court. The Washington, D.C., *Afro-American* printed a banner headline, "Ike Redeems Rights Pledge." Southern Democrats denounced the move. Congressman James C. Davis (D-GA) accused Ike of trying to "outdeal the New Deal" by "appeasing radicals to get votes."[6]

On June 8, the Supreme Court ruled unanimously for the administration, with Associate Justice William O. Douglas writing the majority opinion validating the Reconstruction-era statue prohibiting discrimination in the city's restaurants. Mary Church Terrell, the veteran civil rights leader, commented, "I will be ninety on the twenty-third of September and will die happy that children of my group will not grow up thinking they are inferior because they are deprived of rights which children of other racial groups enjoy." An early victory for the gifted generation, with more to come.[7]

Eisenhower seconded Terrell's celebratory statement in a June 1953 speech: "We have taken substantial steps toward insuring equal civil rights to all of our citizens regardless of race or creed or color. These actions have been designed to remove terrible injustices rather than to capture headlines. They are being taken, quietly and determinedly, wherever the authority of the Federal Government extends." The *Afro-American* stated simply to its readers, "Eat anywhere!"[8]

The chains of racial segregation were loosening in the nation's capital. Mamie Eisenhower ordered the integration of the annual White House Easter egg roll. In May 1953, Eisenhower quietly enlisted the help of Jack Warner of Warner Bros. studios to integrate the District's movie theaters. The deal was accomplished with such little publicity that when a group of pickets showed up at a downtown theater, they were welcomed to purchase tickets. The protesters were so surprised they could not decide whether to go in or go home. By late May 1953, the District had outlawed segregation in parks, swimming pools, and other public facilities and merged the separate black and white fire companies. All U.S. attorneys and FBI agents now received a course on civil rights law enforcement as part of their training. The White House staff Christmas party included, for the first time, African American employees.[9]

The *Chicago Defender*, one of the nation's leading African American newspapers, had supported Harry Truman in 1948 and Adlai Stevenson in 1952. But by mid-1954, Eisenhower had moved on so many civil rights fronts, including his amicus briefs before the U.S. Supreme Court, that the editor wrote with conviction, "The reason for the unprecedented move in cleaning up the capital and for making so many Negro political appointments is not so much from a political motive, while this may not be discounted, but more from the deep-seated moral and spiritual convictions of the President."[10]

Eisenhower established the President's Committee on Government Contracts (PCGC) to use federal authority to end discrimination on government-funded projects. Ike would have preferred legislation to make compliance mandatory, but he hoped that the committee's members would use their powers of "cooperation, persuasion, education, and negotiation" to change the culture of segregation. To invest the committee with as strong a membership as possible, he selected Vice President Nixon to chair it, with J. Ernest Wilkins as vice chair.[11]

Nixon would remain, along with Brownell, Eisenhower's major advocate for civil rights on Capitol Hill. The vice president sent out a series of letters under his signature stating, "All firms dealing with government contracts must hire personnel disregarding discrimination." Given the absence of enforcement powers, the PCGC accomplished relatively little in the South, but by the time the Republican administration left office in 1961, the committee had taken corrective action on 96 percent of the one thousand discrimination complaints that had come before it.[12]

Another piece of unfinished business from the Truman administration was the integration of the armed forces. Truman had issued the order, but military brass had dragged their feet in implementing it. Eisenhower would finish the job, despite the persistent opposition of some high-ranking officers who continued to insist that morale would suffer as a result of integration. On October 24, 1954, twenty-one months after Eisenhower issued the order, the last racially segregated unit in the armed forces received black troops. Full integration of military facilities, especially in the South, would take a little longer, but those too succumbed.[13]

Eisenhower made no exceptions. Schools on military bases in the South were segregated and usually run by local school boards, but the president ordered their desegregation fifteen months prior to the *Brown* decision. When some local boards refused to comply, the federal government took control of the base schools. By the beginning of the 1955 school year, all schools on military posts were integrated.

The facilities at Southern navy yards proved more difficult to desegregate. Robert Anderson, Eisenhower's secretary of the navy, lobbied the president that the navy had to "recognize the customs and usages prevailing in certain geographic areas of our country." Ike overruled him, letting it be known, "We have not taken and we shall not take a single backward step. There must be no second class citizens in this country." The navy yard at Charleston, South Carolina, was the last holdout. The state's governor and Eisenhower friend, Jimmy Byrnes, pleaded with the president that "not even President Truman deemed [desegregation] necessary at such an installation." By January 1954, the Charleston navy yard had no segregated facilities.[14]

African American leaders offered unstinting praise for Ike's first year in office. The National Negro Council presented him with its 1953 Civil Rights Award of Honor, citing his "distinguished leadership and unprecedented statesmanship in enforcement for the first time in eight years of the District of Columbia Civil Rights Laws" and his "executive action in outlawing segregation in the armed services and discrimination in Government contracts." Adam Clayton Powell Jr., Democratic congressman from Harlem and one of the strongest proponents of racial equality in Congress, concluded, "The Honorable Dwight D. Eisenhower has done more to eliminate discrimination and to restore the Negro to the status of first class citizenship than any President since Abraham Lincoln."[15]

THE CONSTITUTION ALLOWED the president to accomplish these advances without deferral to the courts or Congress. A much more difficult issue loomed in the school-desegregation cases before the U.S. Supreme Court. The Court bundled five cases, including the *Briggs* case, into one: *Brown v. Board of Education of Topeka, Kansas*. Truman's Justice Department had already filed an amicus brief supporting the NAACP case against the various school boards. Brownell and Eisenhower filed their own brief, the text of which differed little from the Truman document.

Through the summer of 1953, his Southern friends probed Eisenhower to seek his views on the pending case. To prime his thinking, they depicted scenarios of disruption and violence should the Supreme Court overturn *Plessy*. Eisenhower remained noncommittal, as he should have, but made it clear that he had little patience with discrimination or defiance of the law. South Carolina governor Jimmy Byrnes used his access to the president to convey his region's concerns. In July, Eisenhower and Byrnes had a lengthy lunch together, and in August, the president sent the governor his thoughts on the federal government's responsibilities in this area. Eisenhower confided that he had been thinking about "equality of opportunity," and the relation of the *Brown* case to that concept. Eisenhower then made a declaration that Byrnes probably found chilling: "I believe it is incumbent upon us to make constant and distinct progress toward eliminating those things that all of us would class as unjust and unfair."[16]

Thurgood Marshall would argue the *Brown* case on behalf of the NAACP before the Supreme Court. Despite his steadfast passion for racial integration, he maintained cordial relations with his adversaries. Prior to presenting his brief to the Supreme Court, Marshall had lunch with his opponent in the *Briggs* case, John W. Davis. Davis would be arguing on behalf of the South Carolina school district in front of the Court.

Davis, a white-haired, seventy-nine-year-old Virginian, had argued more cases before the Supreme Court than any other attorney except for Daniel Webster. Impeccably dressed, he cut a distinguished swath through legal and social circles. He was also the Democratic nominee for president in 1924, a candidacy endorsed by the Ku Klux Klan in that year's tumultuous Democratic National Convention. Among his honors included a stint as U.S. ambassador to Great Britain and the presidency of the American Bar Association. He had grown wealthy practicing private law with a major New York City law firm. His good friend Jimmy Byrnes convinced him to take on the *Briggs* case (now folded into *Brown*) before the Supreme Court. It would be Davis's 140th, and last, case before the court.[17]

Davis's argument to the justices on December 9, 1952, stressed the *Plessy* ruling, knowing the Court's historic reluctance to overturn a precedent, especially one that had existed for nearly sixty years. He also deftly quoted the great black leader W. E. B. Du Bois: "We shall get a finer, better balance of spirit, an infinitely more capable and rounded personality, by putting children where they are wanted and where they are happy and inspired, than in thrusting them into the hells where they are ridiculed and hated."[18]

Marshall disagreed, stating to the justices that the issue was not whether states had the right to segregate as determined in *Plessy*, but whether racial segregation itself violated the Fourteenth Amendment, which guaranteed every American equal protection. Segregation was, in effect, exclusion, as it had taken African Americans "out of the mainstream of American life."[19]

On June 8, 1953, the justices surprised everyone by not issuing a decision. Instead, they presented each side with five historical questions, three of which were particularly crucial to the case: Did the framers of the Fourteenth Amendment intend to end school segregation? Did the Supreme Court have the power to abolish school segregation? How would school integration be managed? The delay proved portentous.

On September 8, 1953, as both sides were gathering research to respond to the Court, Chief Justice Fred Vinson died. It is difficult to speculate how the case might have turned out if Vinson had lived. The Court would likely have overturned the *Plessy* precedent anyway, but a sweeping unanimous decision would have been less likely. When Associate Justice Felix Frankfurter, a religious skeptic, heard the news of Vinson's death, he blurted to his clerk, "This is the first indication I have ever had that there is a God."[20]

The *Brown* case suddenly became Eisenhower's responsibility. The individual he would nominate for chief justice would exert a significant influence on the Court. The president selected California governor Earl Warren. For a president to appoint a politician to the Court was not unusual in those days. As with all appointments to the federal bench, especially to the highest court, the selection told as much about Eisenhower as it did about Warren.

In his political campaigns, Warren had characterized himself as a "progressive Republican," akin to fellow Republican progressives Teddy Roosevelt, the La Follettes, and Eisenhower himself. Warren had run as the Republican candidate for vice president in 1948, but had enjoyed bipartisan support through most of his political career. Both the Democratic and Republican parties nominated him for governor of California in 1946. Before then, Warren had served as a district attorney and battled corruption and the Ku Klux

Klan in the 1920s. During the 1930s, he prosecuted union thuggery on the Oakland docks. By the late 1940s, he became an outspoken critic of Wisconsin Republican senator Joseph McCarthy.[21]

As governor Warren had asked the California legislature to pass a bill authorizing a state Fair Employment Practices Commission to fight discrimination in job hiring. He also proposed prepaid medical care. The California Medical Association charged it was "socialized medicine," but Warren won a partial victory for his plan. The oil and gas industry unsuccessfully fought his attempt to raise taxes on gas and oil to fund a highway program in the rapidly growing state.[22]

The reaction to Warren's appointment was favorable in Democratic circles, except for the most liberal, who remembered the governor's evacuation of Japanese Americans from the West Coast after Pearl Harbor; mixed among moderate Republicans; and downright hostile from conservatives. Barry Goldwater, Republican senator from Arizona, grumbled that Warren "hadn't practiced law in twenty-five years and was a socialist." Ironically, Walter George and Richard Russell, the two Democratic senators from Georgia, supported Warren, for the same reason very liberal Democrats opposed him: if Warren acquiesced in the internment of Japanese Americans, he would not look unkindly on racial segregation.[23]

The Warren nomination troubled Senate Republicans, now the majority. Eisenhower knew this and confided to his diary, rather dramatically, that if the Senate did not confirm Warren, he would "leave the Republican Party and try to organize an intelligent group of independents, no matter how small." It was an extraordinary vow for a president toward his own party, but one that Franklin D. Roosevelt had also contemplated.[24]

The conservative wing of the Republican Party hoped for a nominee that would move the Court rightward, particularly with respect to the powers of the federal government. William Langer (R-ND) dispatched investigators to California to check on rumors that Warren was an alcoholic, had connections to the Mafia, refused to prosecute bookies, knowingly appointed corrupt judges, and was an outright Marxist. None of these allegations could be corroborated.[25]

These investigations delayed Warren's confirmation. Not until March 1, 1954, did the Senate confirm Earl Warren as chief justice of the U.S. Supreme Court by a unanimous voice vote. However, because Eisenhower had been wily (or devious, depending on one's perspective) and nominated Warren when Congress was in recess, Warren had already taken his seat as a recess appointment and performed his functions.[26]

*   *   *

THE COURT CONVENED ON December 7, 1953, to hear the responses to the five questions, but would not decide the case until May 17, 1954. In the meantime, rumors swirled that some Southern states were prepared to shutter their public school systems if the Court ruled against them. Jimmy Byrnes lobbied Eisenhower, warning that some districts in his state and in other Southern states had such overwhelming majorities of black students that segregation was necessary both for security and pedagogy. Eisenhower remained unmoved.[27]

At 12:52 P.M. on May 17, Chief Justice Warren began reading the Court's decision. His first comments were encouraging: "In approaching this problem we cannot turn the clock back to 1868 when the [14th] Amendment was adopted or even to 1896 when *Plessy v. Ferguson* was written. We must consider public education in the light of its [current role] in American life." Then he uttered his famous pronouncement: "We conclude that in the field of public education, the doctrine of 'separate but equal' has no place. Separate educational facilities are inherently unequal." The decision was unanimous. John W. Davis was the first to congratulate Marshall.[28]

The ruling was especially noteworthy for including a good deal of sociological and psychological evidence to supplement the legal reasoning. The willingness of the Court to consider such evidence reflected the relatively weak constitutional foundation for integrated education. Must a black child sit next to a white child in order to receive a decent education? Black psychologist Kenneth Clark provided crucial evidence that black children had lower self-esteem in a segregated environment. In fact, the opposite would turn out to be the case, but at the time, Clark's research was one of the few studies on the psychological impact of segregation.[29]

At the victory party that night, colleagues told Marshall that it would now be just a matter of time before every public school was integrated. Marshall warned, "I don't want any of you to fool yourselves; it's just begun, the fight has just begun." The Court had issued a momentous decision, but the justices had not set a means or a timetable by which the ruling should be implemented.[30]

More ominous was the Southern reaction. Senator Eastland, the ranking Democrat on the Senate Judiciary Committee, stated, "The South will not abide by or obey this legislative decision by a political court." Senator Russell asserted in equally emphatic terms that the ruling "strikes down the rights of the states, as guaranteed by the Constitution, to direct their most vital local affairs."[31]

African Americans saw the decision differently. New York's *Amsterdam News* editorialized, "The Supreme Court decision is the greatest victory of the Negro people since the Emancipation Proclamation."[32]

Scholars have pondered Eisenhower's reaction to *Brown* as ranging from quiet endorsement to studied indifference. Ike preferred to make limited public statements but work vigorously behind the scenes to achieve his objectives, a method that served him well in the military, but may have lessened his influence as president. Privately, there was no mistaking his support of the Warren Court. Eisenhower and Brownell worked closely together on the amicus brief responding to the justices' questions. They both concurred on selecting Earl Warren, whose views on civil rights and other matters were well-known, as chief justice.

Contributing to the impression that Eisenhower had, at best, mixed feelings about the decision was a story that appeared in an Eisenhower biography. It concerned a stag dinner hosted by the president in April 1954, just prior to the *Brown* decision. Earl Warren was among those invited, and Ike sat him next to John W. Davis. This may have been a questionable pairing from an ethical standpoint. After dinner and after Ike had praised Davis, the story goes, he put his arm around Warren and allegedly told the chief justice that Southerners such as Davis were "not bad people. All they are concerned about is to see that their sweet little girls are not required to sit in school alongside some big overgrown Negro." As it turned out, there was no evidence that such a conversation ever took place.[33]

Although Eisenhower's public statements on the *Brown* decision were muted, probably a mistake given the significance of that moment, the president's actions demonstrated his full commitment to the letter of the ruling. Fearful of Southern overreaction and the damage that might do to both the judicial system and to American standing abroad, he framed his response to *Brown* as an issue of compliance with the law rather than as a moral imperative. For six decades *Plessy* was the law, and now, suddenly, it was not. But Eisenhower did not merely leave *Brown* in suspended animation. Immediately following the decision, he ordered the desegregation of Washington, D.C., public schools.[34]

Five months after the *Brown* ruling, Eisenhower had another opportunity to express his commitment to civil rights. Justice Robert Jackson died in October, and Ike nominated Judge John Marshall Harlan II of the U.S. Court of Appeals for the Second Circuit, as his replacement. If the president wanted to use a powerful symbol to point where he thought the Court ought to go, Harlan was an excellent avatar for that purpose. His grandfather had offered the lone dissent nearly sixty years earlier in *Plessy v. Ferguson*. Harlan was a former law-firm colleague of Herbert Brownell's, a connection that obviously helped Harlan's cause.[35]

Southern Democrats attempted to delay the confirmation, but even Republican conservatives, with an off-year election looming, did not wish to challenge their popular president. The Senate confirmed Harlan on March 16, 1955, 71–11, just in time for him to sit in on a second crucial civil rights decision of the Warren Court.[36]

The Court had deliberately demurred from setting a timetable for the implementation of the *Brown* decision. The justices knew the Southern reaction would be fierce enough against the striking down of *Plessy*. Warren may also have used the delay to generate the unanimous vote that was necessary for such a momentous decision.

The NAACP submitted a brief arguing against delay. Thurgood Marshall urged the Court to "reiterate in the clearest possible language that segregation in public education is a denial of the equal protection of the laws." Specifically, the justices should place "an outer time limit by which desegregation must be completed." He recommended no later than September 1956.[37]

The Eisenhower Justice Department also filed a brief. Eisenhower's Southern friends lobbied him extensively during the year between *Brown I* and *Brown II*. Governors Allan Shivers of Texas and Robert Kennon of Louisiana wrote to Ike, pleading the case for delay in their states. Through his brother Milton, Eisenhower solicited the opinions of leading educators concerning the administrative complexities of implementing desegregation in Southern school districts.[38]

Brownell worked closely with the president to draft the brief. As a marker of how scholars should tread carefully interpreting Ike's public statements, when a reporter asked him if he had any personal views on the brief, he replied, "Not particularly." The draft actually contained Ike's own handwriting and, Brownell later acknowledged, Ike's own ideas as well. Eisenhower entrusted the final preparation of the document to Simon E. Soboloff, the solicitor general and, like Marshall, a native of Baltimore and a longtime advocate of civil rights causes.[39]

The Eisenhower administration's brief was not as far-reaching as the NAACP document, but it urged the Court not to be timid in enforcing the law, arguing, "Where there are no solid obstacles to desegregation, delay is not justified and should not be permitted." As a result of Eisenhower's consultation with educators, many of whom felt that redrawing school district lines and building new educational facilities that must accompany effective school desegregation would take some time, Brownell argued that immediate compliance was not possible.[40]

But Brownell warned the justices not to issue an order that "might have the practical effect of slowing down desegregation where it could be swiftly

accomplished." The Court "should make it clear that any proposal for desegregation over an indefinite period of time will be unacceptable and there can
be no justification anywhere for failure to make an immediate and substantial start toward desegregation, in a good-faith effort to end segregation as
soon as feasible." Just in case the Court did not understand the urgency,
Brownell concluded forcefully, "Delay solely for the sake of delay is
intolerable."[41]

Brownell did not offer a specific timetable as had Thurgood Marshall. But
he proposed that once plaintiffs filed a lawsuit in the lower courts, defendants
must submit a plan for ending racial segregation in the public schools within
ninety days. If the defendants failed to comply with that timetable, the lower
courts would issue an order "directing admission of the plaintiffs and other
children similarly situated to non-segregated public schools at the beginning
of the next school term."[42]

Earl Warren, a veteran politician, understood the import of *Brown II*, the
implementation ruling issued on May 31, 1955. The Court's credibility, its
ability to enforce a controversial decision, and the threat of plunging the
nation into turmoil in the midst of the Cold War all weighed on the chief
justice's mind. For these reasons, the Court rejected the specifics of Marshall's
and Brownell's arguments in favor of more general terms. Warren required
segregated districts to "make a prompt and reasonable start toward full
compliance" with *Brown*.[43]

Brown II mainly favored "reasonable" over "prompt." The justices even
presented offending districts with a list of excuses to coax additional time
from lower courts. Acceptable issues for delay included "the physical condition of the school plant, the school transportation system, personnel, revision
of school districts and attendance areas," and necessary "revision of local laws
and regulations." Concluding, the Court issued its famous contradictory order
that desegregation must proceed "with all deliberate speed." School desegregation would henceforth be deliberate, but not speedy.[44]

Thurgood Marshall translated this odd phrase as "S-L-O-W." Brownell,
equally disappointed, viewed the order to mean "some indefinite date in the
future." For the rest of his life, he believed that the Court's refusal to set a timetable for compliance was a serious mistake that undermined the moral force of
the original *Brown* decision. As the 1955–56 school year opened, only three of
the eleven former states of the Confederacy had made any moves toward integrating their schools, and those efforts were token. In the eight other states, the
total number of black children in integrated schools was zero.[45]

*   *   *

THE COURT DID NOT DECIDE *Brown II* in a vacuum. Racially motivated violence was increasing in the South, as were threats of resistance to any court-ordered implementation schedule. The two trends advanced together. In Belzoni, Mississippi, in May 1955, the Reverend George W. Lee, inspired by the *Brown* decision, registered to vote, along with about thirty other African Americans. When it came time to pay the poll tax, a voting requirement in Mississippi, the sheriff refused to accept payment and ordered Lee to "get the niggers to take their names off the book." Lee refused. Shortly, a car pulled alongside Lee's vehicle, and one of the occupants fired a shotgun at him at point-blank range, killing him instantly.[46]

Emmett Till was a fourteen-year-old black boy from Chicago visiting relatives in Money, Mississippi, in the summer of 1955. As a city boy, he enjoyed impressing his cousins and their friends with how different life was in the big city up North. To support his boast, he entered a store one morning and, allegedly, addressed a young white woman too familiarly. Several nights later, the woman's husband, Ray Bryant, and her brother-in-law, J. W. Milam, went to the home of Emmett's uncle, took young Till at gunpoint, and eventually shot and beat him to death. Till's battered and mutilated body was discovered the next day floating in the Tallahatchie River, attached to a cotton-gin fan. Bryant and Milam stood trial for murder. A jury of twelve white men deliberated one hour and acquitted both.[47]

The Till case frustrated the Eisenhower administration, which could do little. Brownell lamented that he "could never find any evidence that would allow us to act under any federal statute." Truman had faced the same dilemma after the spate of lynchings in the South in 1946. Truman's limited recourse at the time was to form a presidential commission on civil rights to recommend legislation that would enable the federal government to act in such cases. Nine years later, there was still no legal foundation for federal intervention, and the prospect of such action given the leadership of Senate committees was dim.[48]

The Supreme Court also understood that *Brown I* fell disproportionately on the South. The gifted generation in other parts of the country attended segregated schools for the most part. Few Northern whites or political leaders wished to address de facto segregation—school segregation based not on the law, as in the South, but on residence. The consequences of neighborhood geography created separate and unequal schools in the North. In 1955, most of New York City's all-black elementary schools reported enrollments at or over building capacity, while predominantly white schools had eighty thousand vacant seats. The New York City Board of Education refused to transfer black students to the white schools.[49]

In the meantime, Southern political leaders forged a movement of defiance against *Brown I* and *Brown II*. North Carolina senator Sam Ervin was not an inveterate race-baiter like some of his Southern colleagues, but he was a strong supporter of racial segregation. He sometimes tempered his views with sharp wit and constitutional acumen, but the style did not alter the substance of his loyalty to white supremacy. Early in 1956, Ervin drafted a "Declaration of Constitutional Principles" that circulated in both houses of Congress and drew the signatures of nearly all Southerners. The declaration, which came to be known as the Southern Manifesto, condemned the *Brown* decision as "contrary to the constitution" by usurping the states' control over public education. The 101 signatories (out of 128 Southern congressmen and senators) pledged to employ "all lawful means to bring about a reversal of this decision," and to ensure that the federal government would not use force to implement desegregation.[50]

Eisenhower, in his usual low-key manner, responded to the manifesto in a press conference four days after its release. He commended the signers for pledging to use legal means to challenge the Court's decision, but warned against nullification if the courts rejected Southern white claims. The president promised, "I am sworn to defend and uphold the Constitution of the United States, and I can never abandon or refuse to carry out my own duty." He would have to act upon the phrase the following year.[51]

By the time the Southern Manifesto appeared, the South's "massive resistance" to school integration was well under way. A coalition of the "best" people in the South—school board members, legislators, ministers, and the press—rallied to preserve racial segregation. The individuals and organizations always abjured violence, usually with a knowing wink accompanied by warnings that efforts to upend the racial customs of the South could lead to violence. The Southern Manifesto did not draw the battle line; it deepened the trench.

The so-called moderate white Southerner was mostly invisible during this time, except calling for patience or lecturing federal authorities that white folks in the South could take care of the problem themselves without outside interference. Yet, when a Northern reporter asked one of the more progressive white Southerners when desegregation would eventually come to the Deep South, he said, "Never . . . It looks utterly impossible."[52]

William Faulkner, whose novels had exposed the ironies and tragedy of Southern race relations, sent an open "Letter to the North" in March 1956. As massive resistance rose in the South, so did Faulkner's concern for his region. He had consistently opposed "the forces in my native country which would keep" African Americans as second-class citizens. But now, he stated, "I must go on record as opposed to the forces outside the South which would use legal or police compulsion to eradicate that evil overnight. I was against compulsory segregation. I am just as strongly against compulsory integration." Faulkner believed that coercion would never work in the South. His message to "all the organizations who could compel immediate and unconditional integration: 'Go slow now. Stop now for a time, a moment.'" He did not specify when it would be appropriate to take up the implementation of the Court's decision, but the implication was that it would not be in the near future, or maybe even in the far future.[53]

Faulkner lectured, "The rest of the United States knows next to nothing about the South." Southerners, white and black, knew one another best and were, therefore, best positioned to resolve the situation together without outside interference. The familiar argument, with a lineage back to the Reconstruction era, had failed in the earlier period and would collapse nearly a century later. It turned out white Southerners did not know their black neighbors at all.[54]

The white evangelical churches, so central to the cultural, political, and spiritual life of the South, ignored the issue, except when they provided scriptural support for the segregationists. Billy Graham, the South's most prominent evangelist and a racial moderate, counseled, "The church should not answer questions the people aren't asking. We've become advisers, social engineers, foreign policy experts, when we should be answering the questions of the Soul."[55]

AFRICAN AMERICANS WERE NOT waiting for Southern whites; they were taking matters into their own hands, despite the danger. *Brown I* and *Brown II* may not have altered the landscape of school segregation in the South, but it emboldened African Americans to challenge Jim Crow, and not only in the schools. In October 1955, a black teenaged girl in Montgomery, Alabama, refused to yield her seat to a white passenger. Arrested, she pleaded guilty and paid a $5 fine.[56]

On December 1, Rosa Parks, a forty-two-year-old seamstress at a Montgomery department store, boarded a bus bound for the housing project she lived in with her disabled husband. When a few whites boarded the bus, the driver, who controlled seating on the city's buses, shouted, "Niggers, move back!" Parks, seated in the first row of black passengers, refused to move. The driver stopped the bus and came over to Parks and repeated his demand. Parks remained seated. The driver, following procedure, called the police, who arrested and jailed her.

The incident might have ended there, as it had in October, and indeed the *Montgomery Advertiser* the following morning made light of the incident in a small column headlined, "Negro Jailed Here for 'Overlooking' Bus Segregation." But this was no random protest by an exhausted black woman supporting a household on a salary of $23 a week. It was a planned civil disobedience. Parks was one of the city's few African Americans who had attained a high school diploma, yet she could not obtain any jobs that matched her intellectual abilities and skills. She was a member of the local NAACP chapter and had attended a workshop at the interracial Highlander Folk School in Tennessee that previous summer, learning techniques for challenging racial segregation.

Parks and Jo Ann Robinson, an English professor at the black college in Montgomery, gathered other African American leaders and announced a bus boycott beginning that Monday, December 5. But both Robinson and E. D. Nixon, head of the NAACP in Montgomery, were too militant to attract broad support in the black community. Ministers were either reluctant to step forward or too jealous to choose one of their own. At a mass meeting that Monday evening, Martin Luther King Jr., a minister at the Dexter Avenue Baptist Church, was selected to lead the boycott.

King was a recent arrival in Montgomery so he had not made any enemies among the intensely competitive black ministers. He was finishing his doctoral dissertation at Boston University and took the position at Dexter Avenue because he thought it would be a quiet place to work while he completed his manuscript. Reluctantly, King accepted the new assignment.

EISENHOWER FEARED THAT the growing confrontational atmosphere in the South would wreck his domestic agenda and damage America's image abroad. It would also set back the timetable for reaching racial reconciliation on a broad range of issues. Conciliation and persuasion, he hoped, could rescue a deteriorating situation. The problem was how to go about it and whom he should enlist in the cause. In March 1956, Eisenhower reached out to Billy Graham, wondering if ministers could promote "both tolerance and progress in our race relations problems." Ike set out a possible strategy that focused on increasing the number of black elected officials, particularly on school boards, city councils, and county commissions. The president felt that the guarantee of voting rights was a key component of racial progress in the South.

Eisenhower asked Graham if universities in the South might admit students strictly on merit. At the time, a court had ordered the enrollment of Autherine Lucy, a black graduate student, at the University of Alabama. Her appearance on campus in February 1956 touched off a riot, which led the university's trustees to suspend Lucy "for her own safety and that of others at the university." In 1956, the Ivies did not admit students strictly on merit either.[57]

Eisenhower was not only sharing his thoughts, but also hoping for some action from Graham on these issues: "It would appear to me that things like this could properly be mentioned in a pulpit." Ike also asked Graham to "express some admiration for Louisiana's Catholic Archbishop, Joseph Francis Rummel, who had the courage to desegregate his parochial schools." But the opprobrium visited on Rummel when he desegregated New Orleans's Catholic schools convinced Graham that such praise would hurt his own ministry.[58]

Graham's response emphasized the political minefield inherent in Eisenhower's suggestions. The evangelist was sensitive to political ramifications, while the president was concerned about the moral import of the racial conflict. An interesting juxtaposition. All Graham would commit to was to recommend fellow clergy "to call upon the people for moderation, charity, compassion and progress toward compliance with the Supreme Court decision." In other words, to urge their congregations to obey the law. Hardly a heroic stance, though in the South of that time, white church members fired ministers for less.[59]

The Graham correspondence reflected Eisenhower's typical mode of operation: using surrogates to carry out his policies while he remained above the fray, especially in controversial issues such as race relations. He also encouraged his cabinet members to hire African Americans for their departments, something they might be inclined to do since all the cabinet members were businessmen, except for the secretary of labor. They had no political alliances or electoral constituencies to worry about. Ike targeted the Post Office Department as the most likely candidate for additional African American hires and had charged Arthur Summerfield, his postmaster general (and auto dealer), with carrying out that policy.

In March 1956, Summerfield reported that he had increased the number of African Americans in high-level positions at the headquarters in Washington, D.C., from two to four. He also noted the upgrading of "more than 300 colored employees to supervisory positions in post offices throughout the country" in 1955. The African American press picked up on Summerfield's actions, stating that they represented "real progress" in carrying out the president's "program for minority groups." Summerfield also asked Ike to "move more aggressively" in this area, as it could be to the president's advantage in Northern cities for the upcoming presidential election. Eisenhower praised Summerfield's effort: "Your record of solid accomplishment in placing Negroes in executive positions on the basis of merit and ability is another firm step forward."[60]

These were important, though incremental, steps toward racial justice in federal hiring. Considering mounting Southern white intransigence,

Eisenhower believed something more comprehensive was necessary to guarantee civil rights for African Americans. Herbert Brownell had stood helpless before the violence in Mississippi in 1955 and 1956. Perhaps Southern white resistance and the nonviolent demonstrations of African Americans in the South would move public opinion to favor a Truman-like initiative in Congress.

A softening of public opinion was evident in the positive stories about blacks that appeared in the popular press. The greater coverage of black athletes, musicians, and actors was one manifestation, as was the widespread revulsion following Emmett Till's death and the rigged trial that followed. A mocking editorial in *Life* magazine on the defense attorney's outlandish statements was widely circulated.[61]

Small acts of kindness in the South also belied the solidarity boasted by the massive resisters. In the summer of 1955, Augusta, Georgia, canceled the local Soap Box derby because two black youngsters entered the competition. The *Charlotte News* invited all of the Augusta participants, including the two African Americans, to come to Charlotte to compete in that city's Soap Box derby. Nine of the youngsters did, including the two African Americans. Overall, twenty-two blacks competed in the Charlotte race, which was won by a white Augusta boy.[62]

In his January 1956 State of the Union address, Eisenhower announced "in the Executive Branch operations throughout the nation, elimination of discrimination and segregation is all but completed." It was time to move on to the next challenge: "Negro citizens are being deprived of their right to vote and are likewise being subjected to unwarranted economic pressures." As a remedy, he called for a bipartisan commission to investigate these violations. He also expressed his determination "to assure our citizens equality in justice, in opportunity and in civil rights." Then, the president announced that "there will soon be recommended to the Congress a program further to advance the efforts of the Government, within the area of Federal responsibility, to accomplish these objectives." Like Truman, he would send civil rights legislation to Congress, and as in Truman's experience, there was little prospect of its ever becoming law.[63]

Undeterred, Brownell worked with the president to craft a civil rights bill. It contained four parts. The first two sections would create a federal Civil Rights Commission and elevate the civil rights section of the Justice Department to divisional status headed by an assistant attorney general. The provisions would establish both a monitoring and an enforcement mechanism within the federal government. Part III of the bill gave the attorney general power to seek injunctions against actions by the states that segregated schools and public places. The final section dealt with voting rights, extending federal jurisdiction over primary and special elections (the Democratic primary in most Southern states was the only election that mattered), as well as general elections. Realizing how difficult (and dangerous) it would be for aggrieved African Americans to sue for their voting rights, this provision allowed the attorney general to sue on their behalf.[64]

These were relatively modest proposals, as Eisenhower saw them. The president felt that a moderate bill was more likely to attract Republican votes in the Senate. In combination with support from Northern and Western Democrats, perhaps the bill would stand a chance. Southern Democrats would vehemently oppose any civil rights legislation regardless of how toothless it might be.[65]

The House of Representatives easily passed the measures, 276–126, on July 23, 1956. Conservative Republicans who might have opposed the bill did not want to desert their president in an election year. Besides, civil rights legislation had no chance in the Senate and they knew it. There had been no civil rights legislation since the Reconstruction era, and there would be none in 1956.[66]

In September, Supreme Court justice Sherman Minton announced his retirement, effective October 15, the beginning of the Court's new term. The 1956 presidential election was less than two months away, and Eisenhower had political considerations in mind when he told Brownell to help him come up with a nominee who was a Catholic Democrat and a moderate on the bench. Ike hoped to make inroads with this staunch Democratic group.

Brownell delivered on one of the two criteria Eisenhower had requested. In fairness, it is sometimes difficult to make assumptions about a nominee's tendencies once on the Supreme Court, but Brownell's candidate had an established judicial record. The choice, William J. Brennan Jr., was the son of an Irish immigrant labor organizer from New Jersey. Brennan graduated from Harvard Law School and eventually became a distinguished member of the New Jersey Supreme Court. He was a Catholic Democrat and highly qualified for a position on the High Court. But he was not a moderate, though the *New York Times*, trying to be helpful, called him a "moderate liberal." Eisenhower liked him personally, and that was that.[67]

Justice Brennan took his place on the Supreme Court on October 15 (he was confirmed the following spring) and remained there until July 1990, compiling a record as one of the most liberal justices on the postwar Court. He reinforced mightily the pro-civil-rights direction of the Warren Court. Had Eisenhower wished to forestall the budding civil rights movement in the South or provide more judicial cover for white Southerners, he would have nominated someone else. On October 19, Harlem congressman Adam Clayton Powell Jr. announced Independent Democrats for Eisenhower at a news conference.[68]

As Eisenhower received praise for his court appointments, his executive orders, and his legislative initiatives with respect to civil rights, he characteristically downplayed his record publicly. As he explained on October 12, 1956, "We have been pursuing this [civil rights] quietly, not tub-thumping, and we have not tried to claim political credit. This is a matter of justice, not of anything else."[69]

This leadership style characterized his presidency generally. As one observer noted, Eisenhower perfected "the art of leading while leaving no trace." This "hidden hand" style grabbed few headlines—indeed, by 1956, most journalists viewed his presidency as "bland and boring," but the style avoided airing contentious issues in a public forum that, he believed, would only harden positions or, as in the case of Wisconsin senator Joseph McCarthy, lend dignity to an undignified politician. Besides, Eisenhower had a number of other domestic policy objectives in addition to civil rights that he did not want to jeopardize.[70]

CHAPTER 11

YESTERDAY

WHEN DWIGHT D. EISENHOWER entered the White house in January 1953, he was a dedicated centrist committed to balanced budgets, but also to government action where the private sector could not or would not provide the necessary services for an increasingly prosperous mixed economy. While fellow Republicans controlled Congress, they did not share the president's enthusiasm for a range of federal domestic initiatives.

The assumption of many Republicans (and their constituents) was that a Republican administration would not only halt the New Deal, but also begin to reverse it. They looked forward to a legislative agenda comparable to the Taft-Hartley Act, which took down organized labor, and the McCarran-Walter Act, which protected the United States from stealth Communists among Catholic and Jewish immigrants. Eisenhower had other ideas. His pledge was to hew to the middle road "between the unfettered power of concentrated wealth . . . and the unbridled power of statism or partisan interests." This left considerable room for government action where he thought it could benefit the most people and reduce gaps in opportunity. For conservative Republicans, Eisenhower represented Truman's third term.[1]

Eisenhower's centrist politics particularly frustrated a young, acerbic, and articulate Yale graduate, William F. Buckley Jr. In 1955, he founded the *National Review* as a medium to purvey pure conservatism. Buckley condemned Ike's "middle way" politics: "Middle-of-the-Road, qua Middle-of-the-Road is politically, intellectually, and morally repugnant." Younger conservatives would rally to Buckley's views and coalesce to promote the presidential candidacy of Arizona senator Barry Goldwater in the following decade. In the shorter term, conservative Republicans would battle against Eisenhower's legislative agenda. Southern Democrats were happy to join them.[2]

As Eisenhower would prove time and time again, he was not one of "them," meaning conservative Republicans, for whom he harbored a deep distaste even before his biggest legislative imbroglios. Ike was closer to the progressive Republican traditions of Teddy Roosevelt and the La Follettes of

Wisconsin, but mostly he was happiest in the center, except the "center" shifted depending on changing circumstances—the economy and defense, for example. He was not a professional politician, and his background, his years of public service, and his ideals expressed in speeches during the late 1940s were replete with words and phrases such as "balance" and "the common good." He firmly believed that government's role was to achieve the former and ensure the latter. These were not the principles of conservative Republicans, or certainly of Southern Democrats. But Northern Democrats and most moderate Republicans shared Eisenhower's commonwealth views. Ike's greatest legislative successes occurred, particularly in his second term, through this bipartisan coalition.

In his first State of the Union, Eisenhower promised to revise the immigration laws (as in McCarran-Walter), amend Taft-Hartley, expand Social Security, and increase the minimum wage. This was hardly an agenda Republicans were likely to embrace, and in the first six months of the 1953 legislative session, Congress made no progress on any of these policies. But by the time the second session of the Eighty-third Congress met in January 1954, Eisenhower was pressuring lawmakers to act. He held a series of meetings with select lawmakers at the White House, beginning at eight thirty each morning and continuing until late evening.

The hands-on approach, however, did not move the agenda. Six months later, his domestic agenda remained either in committee limbo or discarded entirely. Ike got testy with his party, saying unless it could "develop and enact . . . a progressive, dynamic program enhancing the welfare of the people of our country . . . it does not deserve to remain in power." Sure enough, the voters returned the Democrats to majorities in both houses of Congress in the 1954 midterm elections. Republicans had no record to run on.[3]

Returning Congress to the Democrats did not help Eisenhower's agenda much. It meant that Southern Democrats once again gained control of key committees. Education policy was merely one example. Eisenhower asked Congress for a $200 million school-construction program in 1955 and again in 1956, to accommodate the burgeoning gifted generation. The president prepared the ground for this measure, calling a White House conference on education to address the need for 203,000 additional classrooms and 140,000 more teachers in the nation's public schools. Two thousand delegates from across the country attended the four-day conference.

The final report gave "a ringing two-to-one conference endorsement of federal financial aid to education." HEW secretary Marion B. Folsom promised "this Administration will present to Congress a broadened and improved program of federal assistance to help erase the classroom deficit." Which

Eisenhower did the following month. But concerns about church-state issues over grants to Catholic schools stalled the debate. Southern lawmakers' fears of federal intrusion into any aspect of education as well as Republican concern about possible federal control of the curriculum scuttled the initiatives.[4]

Eisenhower was equally unsuccessful in addressing environmental issues. In 1955 he asked Congress to renew the 1948 Water Pollution Control Act, which authorized the Public Health Service (PHS) to conduct research and provide research grants to the states. The administration not only promoted the renewal but also suggested some strengthening amendments, the strongest of which would have allowed the federal government to intervene without the consent of a state and, also, enabled the PHS to set water-quality standards for interstate streams if the states did not do so. Vigorous lobbying from industry groups, as well as the states, against these amendments proved successful. Not until the Nixon administration in 1972 did these amendments become law.

Nor was there much progress on other environmental issues such as air pollution. For three weeks in October 1954, a dangerous smog enveloped Los Angeles, a city that was no stranger to the toxic blanket. Fall was an especially conducive season for smog as a combination of fumes from nearby refineries and exhaust from 2 million cars and 1.5 million backyard incinerators became trapped under a layer of warm air that remained stationary between the San Gabriel Mountains and the ocean. Without a strong breeze and a good rain, the affliction would remain.

The extended smog touched off widespread protests in the Los Angeles area, including a rally of forty-five hundred residents who filled the Pasadena Civic Auditorium, and an Optimist Club luncheon where all the guests donned gas masks to protest the lack of enforcement of the city's smog ordinances. Signs such as IT HAS COME TO OUR CHILDREN'S HEALTH OR OIL, SO OIL MUST GO and SMOG HAS CHANGED SAN GABRIEL VALLEY TO DEATH VALLEY reflected the anger of residents. But the strong opposition of the Manufacturing Chemists' Association derailed congressional action on clean air regulations.[5]

The first Eisenhower term was not a total blank for environmental legislation. The administration was aware that the nation's parks and recreational areas demanded attention. With larger families, more affluence, and more leisure time, pressure on these domains increased. A series of articles in the *New York Times* in April 1954 exposed the deteriorating roads and facilities, and the woeful understaffing in the national parks. Yellowstone National Park, for example, had twice as many visitors in 1954 as in 1937, yet seventeen fewer park rangers.[6]

Eisenhower assigned his White House aide Sherman Adams to take the lead in upgrading the national parks. Adams developed a comprehensive program that the president approved as Operation Outdoors. Eisenhower hoped not only to improve conditions in the national parks, but also to ban development from wide swaths of the national forests. This initiative, however, ran up against powerful commercial interests, such as the American Mining Congress, the American Pulpwood Association, and the American National Cattleman's Association. Republicans in Congress would not go along with their president in sequestering public lands.[7]

Eisenhower also failed to overturn the discriminatory McCarran-Walter Act. It was a "blasphemy against democracy that only certain groups of Europeans are welcome on American shores," he declared during the 1952 campaign. In his first State of the Union address in February 1953, he urged Congress "to enact a statute that will at one and the same time guard our legitimate national interests and be faithful to our basic ideas of freedom and fairness to all." But Congress would not cooperate.[8]

The president received some solace when Congress passed the Refugee Relief Act of 1953 (RRA), though it slashed the total number of refugees to slightly above two hundred thousand and required certification of a job and housing in the United States before allowing entry, a difficult standard since few in the United States knew anything about the refugees. Under the old and now defunct Displaced Persons Act, churches, synagogues, and unions simply gave blanket guarantees to a specific number of refugees. The RRA mandated an elaborate screening process requiring potential refugees to supply documents dating from at least two years prior to the application attesting to their status. Many refugees had to spend nearly two years in a detention camp just to acquire that history. As one journalist observed, the Refugee Relief Act "instead of being a testament to American compassion has become a sardonic travesty." By April 1954, one year after enactment of this legislation, a grand total of eight thousand visas had been granted, while fewer than two thousand refugees had actually emigrated to the United States. One commentator called it "an evil law."[9]

Eisenhower, frustrated by the bureaucratic red tape, asked for ten amendments to the law in a special message to Congress in May 1955. Nothing happened. In his 1956 State of the Union message, the president cited "the urgent need" to revise McCarran-Walter substantially—he had given up trying to overturn it—and called for approval of the ten amendments to the Refugee Relief Act. Secretary of State John Foster Dulles seconded the effort, stating McCarran-Walter's impact "is felt in our relationships with friendly nations every day." Mississippi Democrat James O. Eastland, chairman of the

Senate Judiciary Committee, rejected the overtures. Representative Francis Walter (D-PA) accused the president of "seeking political dividends by catering to groups representing special interests." That was code for Italian American and Jewish groups that advocated scrapping the quota system entirely. Again, Congress failed to act.[10]

PEI-CHAO LI AND GRACE WANG LI were married in Shanghai on August 10, 1946. Two years later, Pei-Chao left to study at Columbia University in New York. He had planned to teach on his return to China. But the Communists took control of Shanghai, and Pei-Chao stayed in New York. Grace fled to Hong Kong, then a British protectorate. She applied for a visitor's visa to go the United States, typing on the document, "to visit my husband, who is a student at Columbia University in New York." Her visa was denied. The reason listed: the Immigration Act of 1924, which set varying quotas for countries. There was no further explanation.

Grace succeeded in obtaining a visa to Canada, and Pei-Chao persuaded Columbia to admit Grace as a student starting in the fall of 1952. From Canada, she reapplied for a U.S. visa and was rejected again. The solution to their now-four-year separation seemed to be for him to go to Montreal to be with his wife. However, because he had not returned to his homeland, technically he was without "status" in any country. The immigration authorities warned him that if he went to Canada, he might not be able to return to the United States. He went anyway, spent two weeks with Grace, and returned safely to the United States. But the following month when he attempted to enter Canada again to see his wife, Canadian authorities detained him and returned him to the United States. Their explanation: Canada had no assurance that the United States would allow him reentry.

The couple's hopes rose with the passage of the Refugee Relief Act in 1953, specifically designed by help refugees from Communist countries enter the United States. Grace obtained a sponsor and secured proof of a place to live and a job. But a minor provision of the act required her to obtain a readmission certificate from the government of Canada. The United States did not want to be burdened with an undesirable refugee. Canada, however, refused to issue that certificate, claiming she was only a visitor to that country.

The story had a happy ending when, as a last resort, the House of Representatives approved a resolution granting a group of seven hundred aliens from Communist nations resident in the United States permanent status. Pei-Chao Li was included in that group. Except for the two weeks in Montreal, he and his wife had not seen each other for seven years. On June 20, 1956, twenty-nine-year-old Grace flew from Montreal to Costa Rica and then to Miami to reunite with her husband, who had obtained a doctorate and was teaching at the School of Business and Public Administration at the City College [now University] of New York.[11]

By 1960, McCarran-Walter, combined with the restrictive quota-based Immigration Act of 1924, which it codified, resulted in the lowest percentage of immigrants in the U.S. population in the twentieth century, 5.4 percent. Immigration remained insignificant during the 1950s, averaging only 250,000 a year. Ellis Island, synonymous with the massive immigration from Southern and Eastern Europe earlier in the century, closed in 1955. With many fewer immigrants, immigration no longer was much of an issue. In fact, some speculated that within the not-too-distant future ethnicity would not matter either culturally or politically. Will Herberg, a prominent theologian, advanced this view in *Protestant Catholic Jew* (1955), arguing that ethnic loyalties were rapidly weakening. In an era when the commonwealth ideal remained a strong ethic, such projections were not surprising. But they were premature.[12]

The primary argument for maintaining quotas was that Southern and Eastern European immigrants would "upset the balance among racial and national groups which now exists." As one editorial noted in April 1957, "We must hold fast to our policy so that the cultural characteristics of our population will not be materially altered." But American culture had already been "materially altered" by the immigrants of the late nineteenth and early twentieth centuries. What supporters of immigration quotas really meant was that they wanted to perpetuate white Protestant Northern European economic, political, and cultural dominance.[13]

A second argument favoring immigration restriction was economic: "To open wide the floodgates of immigration could well depress our standard of living." Newcomers required housing, health, welfare, and educational benefits that would be an undue burden on the American people. A third argument related to national security: "What too many Americans fail to realize is that the restrictions in the immigration laws constitute the first line of defense in keeping out of the country subversives, criminals, and other utterly unfit elements." The assertion assumed that Southern and Eastern Europeans were more likely to fall into these categories than immigrants from Northern Europe.[14]

In some respects, these were shadow battles by the late 1950s. The pressure of immigration no longer came from Southern and Eastern Europe. Thanks to the Marshall Plan, Southern Europe enjoyed a degree of prosperity. Eastern Europe was now fully imprisoned in the Soviet bloc, rendering migration from those countries difficult. The fight was really over what America was coming to be: a nation where the sons and daughters of those Southern and Eastern

European immigrants, along with Asians, and eventually African Americans, would compete and fully participate in national life. In the battle in this ever-changing country between yesterday and tomorrow, tomorrow usually won, though rarely without struggle. Both Truman and Eisenhower recognized their responsibility was not to restore some lost idyll, but to prepare America for a better future. The conservative coalition in Congress felt otherwise.

IN A MEMO TO HIS BUDGET DIRECTOR in November 1953, Eisenhower allowed how he wanted to pursue "broad and liberal objectives in certain fields that affect our whole country." He was less interested in legislation targeting certain groups or regions than in promoting policies that would benefit the entire commonwealth. It fit well with his ideas of government's role in promoting the common good. To that end, he listed three areas of immediate need: slum clearance and public housing, utilization of America's water resources, and extension of Social Security and old-age benefits.[15]

Although the nation's housing shortage had eased by the time Ike took office, the migration of African Americans to Northern cities, where they encountered discrimination, created new housing problems. Truman's Housing Act of 1949 was supposed to address this issue, but congressional reluctance to fund it fully as well as the costs of the Korean conflict resulted in the construction of only about one quarter of the 810,000 planned public housing units. Anticipating some pushback from conservative Republicans, Eisenhower emphasized, "I should like to see *no* reduction—possibly even a slight increase—in housing appropriations." His motivation was "to put ourselves clearly on record as being forward-looking and concerned with the welfare of all our people." But many of his fellow Republicans believed that the federal government should "get out of the home-building business."[16]

The president's counterargument to Republicans' wariness of public housing was that if the federal government invested "in the low cost housing and slum clearance field—that is the kind of thing that would be very valuable in helping prevent unemployment." In other words, public housing was a public works project. If Congress would not authorize sufficient funding to build a large number of public housing units, then, Eisenhower believed, it should promote the conservation and the improvement of existing housing. He recommended an amendment to the 1949 Housing Act authorizing the FHA to ensure private credit for the rehabilitation of units in declining neighborhoods, precisely the types of loans the FHA had rejected since the 1930s. This policy, Ike believed, in conjunction with the construction of a modest 140,000 new public housing units, could address the housing crunch in the cities' poorest neighborhoods.[17]

But when Congress passed the 1954 Housing Act, its emphasis was on "urban renewal," a phrase that now entered the policy lexicon. It focused on destroying slums and erecting new structures—not necessarily new housing—to regenerate the flagging tax base of cities experiencing industrial decline, middle-class abandonment, and the influx of a much poorer and more dependent population. The new housing act also slashed the president's request to thirty-five thousand units reserved only for low-income families losing their homes to slum clearance.[18]

Congress did not deserve all of the blame. Lawmakers heard from their constituents. The real estate lobby was particularly effective at the local level in beating back public housing initiatives. By 1953, the lobby was victorious in rejecting federal housing funds in forty of sixty referenda. Their biggest victory occurred in Los Angeles, where the *Los Angeles Times* denounced the "Socialistic goals" of public housing.[19]

City leaders were more interested in destroying unsightly slums and, in partnership with private developers, erecting tax-revenue-generating entertainment and sports facilities, office and retail complexes, and midmarket and high-end residential properties than in housing the poor. The Great Migration continued through the 1950s, and without new public housing, pressure on existing neighborhoods persisted as well. The migrants, the neighborhoods, the school systems, and, ultimately, the cities suffered the consequences.

Blockbusting—in which Realtors panicked white homeowners into selling their properties below value before a black invasion wiped out their equity entirely, then flipped the homes to African Americans at inflated prices—precipitated this downward process. Blockbusters had numerous allies. In Chicago, the Board of Education wrote off a neighborhood school once it began to change. Pleas to address overcrowding, shortages of qualified teachers, and the absence of counselors went unaddressed.

The Chicago Urban League estimated that blockbusting was a $1-million-a-month business in that city. The inevitable neighborhood decline fed into the belief that African Americans lowered property values. When a neighborhood slipped into "transition," money for renovations dried up, shops and services closed and fled, and churches sold their buildings. Eventually, the neighborhood became part of the expanding black ghetto, crippling the chances of hard-pressed but hardworking African Americans to build equity and a decent life for their families.[20]

These conditions led to a vicious cycle of failure that would bedevil policymakers and analysts into the next century. Deteriorating neighborhoods, failing schools, rising numbers of teenagers, declining security, and inadequate services accelerated neighborhood disintegration. When federal funds for public housing increased in the 1960s, cities built those dwellings in existing impoverished neighborhoods, reinforcing their isolation and committing the new residents to the same baleful existence as their neighbors.

The perception of the outside world, of both whites and the African Americans who were fortunate to live elsewhere, was that these were communities of pathology. Even those who acknowledged the roles of public policy, finance, and prejudice in shaping these ghettos believed that the residents themselves shared some of the responsibility for their disintegration. Scholars began to talk about a "culture of poverty" that created a debilitating set of values making extrication from these environments much more difficult.[21]

Carl Rowan, an African American journalist who would serve in the Lyndon B. Johnson administration, was among the earliest commentators on the culture of poverty. In 1960, under the provocative title "Are Negroes Ready for Equality?," Rowan cataloged the growing public unease over stories and statistics concerning "Negro crime," "Negro social diseases," and "Negro delinquency." He was concerned that many whites were coming to believe that if black people "behave as an inferior," they must be inferior.

Rowan took "Negro leaders" to task for failing to address the culture of poverty, specifically that black people "are being killed and maimed, street gangs are spreading terror in big cities, young girls are bearing an increasing number of illegitimate children, and dope and gin mills are flourishing in our urban centers." He urged black leaders not to blame ghetto pathology only on segregation or to "pretend that integration will be a cure-all for every social problem in sight." Rowan praised the efforts of local churches that conducted family-life projects in the inner city, but he also noted their success was minimal.

Martin Luther King Jr. shared similar views: "We have not done all that we could do. It is possible that we have become so involved in trying to wipe out the institution of segregation, which certainly is a major cause of social problems among Negroes, that we have neglected to push programs to raise the moral and cultural climate in our Negro neighborhoods."

The press as well began to take more notice of these neighborhoods in unflattering portraits. An article in *U.S. News & World Report* showed that during one seven-month period in Washington, D.C., 185 girls under the age of sixteen became pregnant, of whom 169 were black. Such publicity fueled the perception of an "urban crisis," and it also touched off a debate on the respective roles of institutional racism and personal responsibility in contributing to the pathology of these neighborhoods.[22]

As Rowan implied, the turmoil in black urban neighborhoods in the North was not necessarily a figment of a hysterical press. Of the numerous confirmations by the late 1950s, one of the most heartbreaking occurred in Brooklyn. Public education had been the great assimilator in urban America. Education was a way out and up into the American mainstream. Children of immigrants first learned about the nation's history and culture in these diverse cauldrons of learning. And a good number of them repaid this experience by becoming teachers and school administrators themselves.

Such as George Goldfarb. George was the son of Jewish immigrants from Austria. He had taught in New York City schools for thirty-three of his fifty-five years. By 1958, he was in his fourth year as the popular principal of John Marshall Junior High School (grades seven through nine) in Brooklyn. Like many administrators, he had developed a proprietary interest in his school. It was the center of his life. And the school's recent descent deeply troubled him. John Marshall was in the "transitional" neighborhood of Crown Heights. By 1958, roughly one half of the students were African American, 40 percent white and the percentage declining, and 10 percent Puerto Rican. The security situation at the school had deteriorated during the school year, and Goldfarb contemplated having a police presence.[23]

Late in 1957, a black student at the school raped a thirteen-year-old blind white girl in a stairwell. Goldfarb's contemplation soon became a demand, but the city's Board of Education held firm to its policy of no police in the schools. The board feared that the public would conflate the image of police at an increasingly black school in Brooklyn with law enforcement officers blocking the entrance of African American students to public schools in the South. Called before a grand jury investigating the rape, Goldfarb again repeated his concern. While he was testifying, two more violent incidents occurred at his school, including another rape perpetrated by a black student.

Shaken by his inability to maintain order at his school and the lack of cooperation from educational administrators, Goldfarb, on the morning of January 28, 1958, climbed to the roof of his six-story apartment building in Brooklyn and jumped off. The Board of Education immediately changed its policy and assigned a policeman to the school.

The year after Goldfarb's death, George N. Allen, a reporter for the *New York World-Telegram & Sun*, landed a teaching job at John Marshall to conduct an undercover investigation of the school. Though he did not witness any violence during his two-month tenure, he found "defiant students and students who were ill-prepared for their classes." Among the incidents he recorded during his first two months at the school: "A 15-year-old girl was released from school to have her illegitimate baby; four boys who had been sexually molesting a girl and who had threatened her if she reported them, were given a lecture by the dean of boys—and kept in the school. And there was the time a teacher stopped me in the hall when the students were moving from class to class and pointed out a well-built, good-looking 15-year-old girl. 'Prostitute,' he said. 'When she plays hookey from school, the truant officer hotfoots it up to Harlem to pull her out of an apartment where she and some friends set up an establishment.' "[24]

Allen's experience confirmed his and the public's worst fears about John Marshall Junior High School. He found the classrooms and hallways "a tense battlefield for authority between teachers and students. Chronic truancy and little regard for student achievement permeated the school." Allen's series won the American Newspaper Guild's Heywood Broun Award for crusading journalism. One reviewer called the book derived from his articles a "penetrating portrait of a classroom when student lawlessness takes over." Allen went on to work for NBC covering the civil rights movement and the Vietnam War.[25]

Today, the John Marshall Junior High School is the Mary McLeod Bethune Academy. The student population is 82 percent African American and 1 percent white. Here is a recent comment on the school's web page from "Rachel," with the original spelling and syntax: "Dont go to this school is bad teachers screaming at children. and making them sit in auditoriums because kids had a fight . Theres fights almost evreyday there sometimes cockroaches evreywhere. Its ghetto dont come here also do not go to kipp the kids in this school go there. The kids curse out school aid throw f and stinkbombs. girls take over bathrooms theres bulling to particular people. Theres favortisim."[26]

It has happened in many cities since the 1950s. As neighborhoods change, so do schools, and as schools change, neighborhoods change. Education is also a housing problem, and the reverse is true as well. If the neighborhoods themselves are dysfunctional, schools cannot escape the dysfunction. New York City public schools were separate and unequal and becoming more so by the year. By 1954, nearly 75 percent of the city's schools were segregated. The buildings that housed black students suffered from deteriorating physical conditions and inexperienced teachers.

Readers were familiar with the tales of gratuitous violence coming out of the South. But they were also learning about a growing epidemic of violent behavior in the North. Early in 1957, a story circulated about a fifteen-year-old black student in Detroit who terrorized his classroom and then slashed the face of the principal with a straight razor. These episodes both horrified and scandalized Northern blacks, especially black professionals. One responded to the Detroit event, "Just when we think we've convinced these people that every Negro does not carry a switch-blade, we get a deluge of razor-totin' sharecroppers from Mississippi and Georgia." It was easy to blame the growing disorder of Northern cities on the newcomers, but studies indicated this was not often the case.[27]

African Americans who could afford to do so would have loved to escape to the suburbs, but given restrictive covenants and mortgage restrictions that was unlikely. Between 1950 and 1956, 178,000 new homes were constructed in Detroit suburbs. Blacks were permitted to purchase about 750, all in an African American community. A black social worker summarized, "Detroit is a woman with a Northern dress on and a Southern slip showing."[28]

The media churned out statistics and stories on the social disabilities of black urban residents. In New York City, African Americans had eight times as much illegitimacy as whites. In St. Louis, blacks represented 26 percent of the population, but 75 percent of the welfare cases, and they occupied 70 percent of public housing. Economic issues accounted for at least some of these figures, though they went unaddressed in the stories. Black per capita income in the late 1950s was only 53 percent of that for whites. Twice as many black mothers with preschool and school-age children worked.[29]

White political leaders in Northern cities tended to dismiss charges of racial discrimination. That was a problem for the South, not in Chicago or Detroit. As Chicago's Mayor Daley put it, "We feel we don't have segregation in Chicago." A black businessman agreed, sort of: "Of course there's no segregation in Chicago. I can go anywhere on the South Side that I desire." The policy focus in the late 1950s fixed on the South, but as Carl Rowan noted presciently, "The real desegregation showdown will come in the great cities of the North." When the explosion came, it would be those Northern cities erupting in rebellion and riot, not the urban South.[30]

WHETHER A COMPREHENSIVE PUBLIC housing program could have resolved some of these issues in Northern cities was doubtful. Housing was only one element, albeit an important one, in an array of problems confronting these neighborhoods, including schools, crime, services, family disintegration, and jobs. And even if Eisenhower had grasped the complexity of the problem, the congressional roadblock remained.

As *Time* magazine political correspondent James L. McConaughy Jr. summarized the Republican-controlled Congress in 1954, "While Eisenhower proposes the Old Guard disposes. Requests that were crucial to the over-all Administration program have been ignored, others have been turned down, and some allowed to get bogged down in a web of endless delays." Some of the fault, McConaughy admitted, rested with the president himself and his unwillingness to cajole fellow Republicans. As a former commanding general, the transition to politics, where colleagues did not necessarily follow orders, was a bit jarring. Yet Ike negotiated with the faculty and administration of Columbia University quite well.

The excuse of Eisenhower's Republican opponents was "I must vote my convictions." The implication was that the president did not share those convictions. Congressman Noah Morgan Mason, an Illinois Republican, protested, "I'm not voting against the administration at all, but I do vote against the program the Truman administration wanted, and since it's the same program, I am still against it." Congressman Wint Smith (R-KS) put his finger on what he thought the problem was: "There are a lot of people who've been giving him advice who are sympathetic to social progress ideas." Yes, Eisenhower favored social progress.[31]

After the Democrats took control of both houses of Congress in 1954, Eisenhower seemed to prefer the company of Senate Majority Leader Lyndon B. Johnson (D-TX) and House Speaker Sam Rayburn, also a Texas Democrat, who hailed from Denison, Ike's birthplace. Though Ike met regularly with the Republican leadership, he looked forward to his weekly evening sessions with Johnson and Rayburn over some good bourbon.[32]

Eisenhower's relationship with the Democratic leadership was so good that in a radio interview with Majority Leader Johnson in January 1955, the interviewer remarked that Eisenhower's recently delivered State of the Union address "had practically taken the Democrats over with various Democratic measures—health, schools, highways, reciprocal trade." Johnson welcomed the president's conversion and looked forward to working with him, a politic response, but one likely to displease Eisenhower's fellow Republicans.[33]

When Eisenhower had ileitis surgery in June 1956, Senator Johnson was especially solicitous. Johnson knew the fragility of life, having suffered a near-fatal heart attack in July 1955. The president wrote a confidential note to Johnson's close friend Sid Richardson to tell him "how wonderful Lyndon was to me while I was ill. His solicitude really touched me deeply." Ike added, "Also, during the past year when I have had to call on him for help on non-partisan issues, he has always done his best . . . Of course I have to write this on a confidential basis."[34]

Pundits, ignoring the deep ideological divisions in Congress because they existed within rather than between the political parties, complained about the prevailing bipartisanship—that is, it was increasingly difficult to discern whether a bill wending its way through the Congress was a Republican or a Democratic offspring. An editorial in the *Saturday Evening Post* in November 1954 warned that bipartisanship "is a very dangerous thing, because this state of affairs virtually disfranchises many voters." The system "rigs the game so that the minority is completely muzzled." Yet, nine months earlier, the same editor praised the president for his "natural gift for avoiding the doctrinaires on both sides of the fence and gearing his program to a generous concept of what the country needs, balanced by a shrewd appraisal of what congress and the public will accept." What the *Post* objected to in November was Eisenhower's cozy relationship with the Democrats, and how his personal popularity did not translate into Republican victories in the off-year elections, which returned control of Congress to the Democrats.[35]

What was happening was that moderate Republicans and Northern Democrats were frequently reaching across the aisle and collaborating on a number of issues the president supported. This four-party system had a conservative and a liberal wing in each of the two parties. Some lawmakers began to ponder party realignment, an idea floated periodically since the late 1930s. Senator Karl Mundt (R-SD), a great champion of realignment, believed that Midwestern Republicans and Southern Democrats shared more common interests with each other than with other members of their respective parties. The current party configuration, some charged, merely created confusion among the voters as it was difficult to figure out how candidates differed.[36]

William H. Grimes, editor of the *Wall Street Journal*, warned of where all of this was heading: "If the Democrats must always be more liberal, and if the Republicans must always be trying to win Democratic votes by following the Democrats, where do we end up? Apparently, we can only end up with two major parties tending toward a socialist form of government."[37]

Eisenhower remained true to his "Middle of the Road" course, as he explained to a correspondent in July 1954. That philosophy best suited a rapidly changing nation as it "preserves the greatest possible initiative, freedom and independence of soul and body to the individual, but does not hesitate to use government to combat cataclysmic economic disasters." It is "impossible for any durable governmental system to ignore hordes of people who through no fault of their own suddenly find themselves poverty stricken . . . Mass production has wrought great things . . . but it has created social problems that cannot be possibly met under ideas that were probably logical and sufficient in 1800." It was an eloquent restatement of the commonwealth ideal.[38]

CHAPTER 12

TOMORROW

IN NOVEMBER 1954, General Lucius D. Clay, former military governor of postwar Germany and Eisenhower confidant, met with the president. The midterm elections had just returned Congress to Democratic control. Clay asserted that the Republican Party required complete reformation into an "Eisenhower Republican Party." Ike did not care for the name, but endorsed the idea: "The Republican Party must be known as a progressive organization or it is sunk." Eisenhower dismissed advice to appease what he called "the reactionary fringe" of the party. He cited especially their attitude toward organized labor: "Labor is merely an item in their cost sheets, and labor is guilty of effrontery when it questions the wisdom or authenticity of any statement of management or of financiers." Clay proposed and Eisenhower agreed that they should focus their efforts on recruiting young people into the Republican Party and encouraging them to run for local offices. As for the older Republicans, "Their thinking is completely uncoordinated with the times in which we live."[1]

By the time of the 1956 presidential election, it was clear that there would be no retreat from the New Deal. During the two years following the 1954 midterm elections, Eisenhower's legislative agenda moved forward, if haltingly. Eisenhower had some success in strengthening several New Deal programs, thanks to the support of Majority Leader Lyndon B. Johnson and the moderate members of Eisenhower's own party. Congress supported the president in expanding Social Security benefits. Social Security was one of the measures conservative Republicans had in their sights to eliminate or drastically reduce. Eisenhower extended its coverage to an additional 10 million people. The program covered survivors, the disabled, farmers, and the self-employed, with a 16 percent increase in benefit levels. As part of the Social Security legislation, he convinced Congress to lower women's retirement age to sixty-two, and the age limit for permanently disabled benefits to fifty.[2]

The president increased the minimum wage in 1955 from seventy-five cents to $1 an hour, or $8.85 per hour in 2017 dollars. The federal minimum wage in

2017 was $7.25. He also established a new cabinet-level federal agency, the Department of Health, Education, and Welfare (HEW). He hoped to provide Americans with a national system of health care similar to what he enjoyed in the U.S. Army. As with Truman before him, the plan fell to intense lobbying and congressional indifference.[3]

His greatest triumph during his first term was for the nation's infrastructure. Eisenhower kept vivid memories of his cross-country tour in 1919 on behalf of the army. It was much easier to sail to Europe than to traverse the United States in a motor vehicle in the early 1950s. Unlike European nations, the United States had no federal highway system. The only highways the federal government actually built were on public lands, such as in national parks. Some highways, such as U.S. 1, bore federal designation, but they received only a relatively small amount of federal funding.

As early as 1939, Thomas H. MacDonald, chief of the Bureau of Public Roads in the Department of Agriculture, recognized both the practical and economic benefits of constructing a national highway network, which would help create jobs and boost the struggling economy. But President Roosevelt did not promote the idea.

Then came World War II, which required the massive movement of men and matériel. The overtaxed rail system could not adequately handle all the traffic. But even if it could, trucks had to get to and from rail depots sometimes at considerable distance from a defense facility or training base. Traffic on roads near defense plants backed up for miles. MacDonald reintroduced his plan for constructing a forty-thousand-mile national expressway network. Congress authorized such a system in 1944, but did not appropriate funds to build it. By 1950, it was even more evident that the absence of decent long-haul roads was limiting economic development. Automobile registrations meanwhile had climbed from 31 million in 1945 to 49 million five years later.[4]

Less than a month after he took office, in February 1953, Eisenhower reignited discussions on MacDonald's plan. To pay for it and protect the budget, Eisenhower suggested federally guaranteed bonds. But the Republican-controlled Congress remained unmoved.[5]

To increase pressure on Congress, Eisenhower in 1955 appointed a committee headed by General Clay to study the nation's highways and suggest strategies of improvement. Of course, Ike already knew the condition of the highways, as did General Clay. The committee's recommendations came with a price tag of $101 billion to be spent over the next decade. Congress, though now under Democratic control, recoiled from the expenditure.[6]

Senator Harry F. Byrd, a Virginia Democrat and chairman of the Senate Finance Committee, charged that Clay's plan would create "fiscal confusion and disorder." More ominously, it raised the specter of the "iron hand of the federal bureaucracy." In 1955, that specter shadowed white supremacy. Byrd and his fellow Southern Democrats had no intention of testing that slippery slope. Fiscal conservatives in Ike's own party supported Byrd's position.[7]

But 1956 was an election year, and the prospect of pumping large sums of money into multiple jurisdictions, with the jobs that money would create, moved Congress to reconsider. Also, after the *Brown II* decision in May 1955, the threat of federal intervention to desegregate Southern schools receded. In January 1956, Eisenhower tried again, asking Congress for an eye-popping $25 billion to fund a ten-year highway construction program, a figure that represented one third of the federal government's annual income. It was the biggest single expense, aside from World War II, that any president had ever requested.[8]

The need was obvious. The country's main highways were "narrow, acutely curved, dangerously graded, frequently intersected, and narrowly shouldered or shoulderless." Stories of "slaughter on the highways," economic waste, and potential disaster in the event of a national emergency added a sense of urgency. One article estimated that within a decade there would be three vehicles on the same highway area that carried one vehicle in 1941. At that point, the author quipped, "We will all get out and walk."[9]

The National System of Interstate and Defense Highways legislation that Eisenhower sent to Congress proposed a limited-access highway network of forty thousand miles, per MacDonald's initial proposal. It would connect 209 of the 237 cities having fifty thousand inhabitants or more. Though it would represent about 1 percent of the nation's total highway mileage, the system would carry 20 percent of the country's out-of-city traffic. It would be completed by 1965 and designed to handle highway traffic based on 1974 projections. The federal government would allocate 90 percent of the total cost and the states 10 percent. The program, projected out over fifteen years, would eventually cost $50 billion, not including maintenance costs. A four-cents-per-gallon gasoline tax would pay for the system, costing each driver about $7 annually. The current federal fuel tax is 1.4 cents per gallon. The payment plan obviated the need for a bond issue or federal expenditures. Constructing the network would employ a labor force of nine hundred thousand.[10]

Aside from its obvious benefits in moving people and goods more efficiently, the interstate highway system would become a significant economic generator not only during its construction, but also in the development that would occur because of it, just as Keynes would have predicted. The result belied the concerns of fiscal conservatives, who saw only the short-term expenditure, not the long-term benefits. The roads made travel easier and quicker. Vacations to relatively distant destinations, heretofore the province of the wealthy, became more accessible to middle-class Americans. Just load the car, hop in, and drive off on a road trip. No worries about where to eat or stay along the way as the network gave birth to an entirely new hospitality industry. The president believed the project could flatten out economic cycles: "Our whole industrial activity," he wrote to General Clay on January 26, 1955, must be "geared to a purpose of steady and stable expansion. The 'peak and valley' experience can make for us many serious and even unnecessary difficulties."[11]

Comparisons to enormous public works projects of the past only served to highlight the gargantuan nature of the interstate highway program. Imagine if the Panama Canal, the Grand Coulee Dam, and the St. Lawrence Seaway were combined into one large construction project. Then multiply the cost for that one project by twenty-nine times, and the result would equal the payout for the highway system. Or, if all the crushed stone utilized as the base of the roads constructed under the program were to be dumped into pyramid form, the outcome would be five hundred pyramids, each the size of the Pyramid of Cheops, which covered the equivalent of four square city blocks and rose to the height of a forty-story building.[12]

More than 75 percent of the new system would involve new highway construction, not the widening of existing routes. Engineers also predicted that within its first ten years of operation, the interstate system would save thirty-five thousand lives. On June 29, 1956, Eisenhower signed the bill after it passed Congress with only one negative vote. The change in funding from bonds to a gas tax played a role in bringing fiscal conservatives on board. It was also an election year.[13]

THE BENEFITS OF THE INTERSTATES, both personal and national, would come quickly in improved productivity and saved lives. The new highways would also help transform American leisure. In 1951, Kemmons Wilson, a home-builder in Memphis, Tennessee, decided to drive his wife and five children to Washington, D.C., for their summer vacation. The trip did not go well. The accommodations and restaurants along the way were few and wretched, and a car full of children at various stages of hunger and exhaustion did not improve Wilson's temperament. When he finally returned to Memphis, he vowed to get into the hotel business.[14]

Wilson asked a Memphis friend and draftsman, Eddie Bluestein, to draw up plans for a hotel. Bluestein delivered the sketches and wrote along the top of the drawings, "Holiday Inn," a name he had filched from a Bing Crosby movie, *Holiday Inn*, which he had seen on television the night before he completed the plans. The first Holiday Inn opened in Memphis in August

1952, exactly a year after Wilson's ill-fated trip to the nation's capital. The 120-room hotel included a restaurant and a swimming pool, and each room had a television and an air conditioner, a blessing in the humid Memphis summers. A single cost $4 a night (or $35.70 in 2017 dollars), a double $6. Children stayed for free, an unusual bonus in those days.

Over the next two years, Wilson built three more hotels located on the major highways leading to Memphis. When interstate highway construction began in 1956, Wilson expanded and franchised the property. By the early 1970s, Holiday Inns had over two hundred thousand rooms across the country, or three times as many as its nearest competitor.

Soon, Holiday Inn had competition. Howard Johnson barely finished eighth grade. He grew up in Boston, the only son of a Swedish immigrant father and a Scotch Irish mother. The family's fortunes crashed when his father's cigar-import business collapsed just before American entrance into World War I. After serving in the war, Johnson returned to the Boston area and went heavily into debt purchasing a run-down drugstore whose main attraction was a soda fountain. He purchased an ice cream recipe from an elderly German Jewish peddler that used natural, rather than synthetic, flavoring. The ice cream was a great hit, and by 1935, Johnson had twenty-five roadside restaurants throughout Massachusetts.[15]

But not until the upgrade of the national highway system in the 1950s did Howard Johnson create a national brand. By 1958, he had 550 establishments, most of them restaurants just off the major highways, and twenty-eight flavors of his popular ice cream. Tens of thousands of boomers flocked to the orange-roofed, white clapboard restaurants for fried clams and ice cream. This was not fast food, but meals served courteously by uniformed waitresses "hired not for their beauty or bust measurements but for their manners and deportment." Some of the restaurants had "motor lodges" (as Johnson called them) attached, with all of the amenities of the Holiday Inn, plus two washbowls in the bathroom, a major bonus for families. Getting to the vacation destination was now at least half of the fun.

EISENHOWER EMBRACED MAJOR PUBLIC WORKS projects not only for the economic value and for jobs, but also because they comported with his idea that an expanding country generated opportunities for its people. The nation should embrace the modern and build for the future. This was evident not only in Ike's promotion of the interstate highway system, but also in the construction of the St. Lawrence Seaway. The project did not capture the national imagination like the highway system, but it was emblematic of the president's expansive view of America ahead.

By the 1950s, the St. Lawrence Seaway had been part of the public policy discussion for thirty years, but Eisenhower was the first president who invested time and energy into making the project a reality. Its benefits were undeniable: It would provide a continuous route for oceangoing vessels from the Atlantic Ocean to the Great Lakes cities. The project would also generate electricity under a public authority more cheaply than by private companies. The seaway also had strategic benefits: in case of war, it provided a direct route to the Minnesota iron range.[16]

At the president's urging, Congress established the St. Lawrence Seaway Development Corporation, a wholly owned government corporation, in May 1954. The price tag was $1.1 billion ($9.7 billion in 2017 dollars), another huge public works project. On June 26, 1959, Eisenhower and Queen Elizabeth II opened the seaway to traffic. Large, deep-draft oceangoing vessels now sailed into the heart of the upper Midwest, providing a significant stimulus for the economy of that region and lower prices for the consumers of iron ore and other building materials.[17]

For Eisenhower, major infrastructure projects not only boosted the economy but also modernized America. From his military experience, he understood how technology could both improve and save lives. And how the federal government could assume responsibilities that the private sector was not capable of fulfilling. This was especially the case with commercial air travel, which required huge investments, not only in airplanes, but also in airport infrastructure and safety equipment as technologies evolved. In such circumstances, federal partnership with local governments and with the airlines could increase the mobility, and the economy, of the people of the vast American continent.

In February 1956, Eisenhower appointed Edward P. Curtis, a vice president of Eastman Kodak, to draw up a blueprint for America's entry into the age of jet travel. The immediate stimulus to this appointment was the deteriorating safety of air travel, much as the condition of America's roads had finally prompted Congress to act on Eisenhower's interstate system proposal. Curtis had already assembled his staff and begun research for the project when two airliners collided over the Grand Canyon in June, sending 128 passengers to their deaths, the worst commercial aircraft accident in American history to that point.[18]

To the Air Transport Association, this was tragic, but predictable. An average of four near collisions a day occurred in 1956. As one veteran pilot told a reporter four days before the Grand Canyon crash, "The trouble with civil aviation today is simply this: We are operating four-hundred-mile-an-hour aircraft under a control system that was designed to handle the DC-3, which flew at a hundred and sixty-five. We are using DC-3 communications under a control system that is twenty years old, ten years out-of-date, and totally unworkable three years from now, when the six-hundred-mile-an-hour jet transports come into service."[19]

The five years prior to 1956 had seen sixty-five midair collisions, nearly all in bad weather. As on the highways below, there was too much congestion above, and the state of technology could not effectively sort out that traffic. A safer air traffic control system and more efficient and larger airports would emerge from Curtis's recommendations.[20]

As early as October 1955, Pan American airlines ordered $269 million worth of jetliners capable of cruising speeds in excess of 550 miles per hour. Many airports were not equipped to handle such aircraft. Idlewild Airport (now JFK) in New York City was the nation's busiest international airport by the mid-1950s. Its buildings were drab, overcrowded boxes. But in December 1957, the New York Port Authority dedicated a terminal building designed for the jet age. The sleek, three-story expanse of glass, aluminum, and stainless steel had cost $30 million. It was probably the finest jet terminal in the world at the time. Idlewild benefited from a new Civil Aeronautics Authority program encouraging cities to modernize their airports by providing matching funds on a fifty-fifty basis.[21]

On October 26, 1958, Pan Am flight 114 took off from Idlewild to Paris on a Boeing 707. The flight took eight hours and forty minutes, shaving at least three hours off the fastest nonjet flights. The forty travelers who sat in the "de luxe" section in the front of the airplane paid $909 for the round-trip ($7,570 in 2016 dollars). They sat in comfortable wide seats, ate a multicourse dinner with an extensive selection of wines, and concluded the meal with brandy. The seventy-one passengers who sat in economy experienced "cramped" conditions, and their meal consisted of a sandwich and coffee. They paid $489.60 ($4,077) for the experience.[22]

AMERICANS HAD ALWAYS INDULGED in wanderlust, and now they could not keep still. It was a reflection of their optimism and abiding faith in the future. The frontier was endless, and the next turn was the most promising. "I was halfway across America, at the dividing line between the East of my youth and the West of my future," wrote Jack Kerouac in On the Road (1957), capturing the essence of the American migration dream as much as Walt Whitman's "Song of the Open Road" epitomized the confidence of nineteenth-century Americans, the West beckoning like the light at the end of Jay Gatsby's dock. The West was the future. When Kerouac reached California, driving down from Truckee to Sacramento, the elation and anticipation merged with the "warm, palmy air—air you can kiss," the river, the hills again, and then "the vast expanse of a bay" just before dawn with the lights of San Francisco sparkling in the mist.[23]

The geography, though, could not compensate for Kerouac's loneliness. Hanging out in Los Angeles, he called it "the loneliest and most brutal of American cities; New York gets god-awful cold in the winter but there's a feeling of wacky comradeship." But Los Angeles also epitomized the free-wheeling independence that remained subdued in the rest of "settled" America. The city was a huge desert encampment. Kerouac breathed in the aroma of marijuana, chili beans, and beer, the sound of strange music mixtures, a kind of "cowboy and boogie woogie." It was a careless New York, as in "care less." Nothing seemed to be serious, as if the farther one traveled from the Puritan bed of New England, the less anything mattered but the senses.[24]

Kerouac returned to New York, but could not stay still; he made a second cross-country trip, "leaving confusion and nonsense behind and performing our one and noble function of the time, move." He captured the excitement of the West's newness, and in the new, the possibilities for America. In Tucson, "the city was one big construction job; the people transient, wild, ambitious, busy, gay; washlines, trailers; bustling downtown streets with banners; altogether very Californian." Tucson had all the frenetic activity of Times Square without the furtiveness of its people. New York seemed already built, occupied, and settled. The West was a blank slate, quickly filling in, but yet with room for people to become part of the picture.[25]

Then, back out to the Bay Area, and the same wonderment as at first sight: "stretched out ahead of us the fabulous white city of San Francisco on her eleven mystic hills with the blue Pacific . . . and goldenness in the late after-noon of time." Who would not want to be there, to see and experience these natural wonders and the alabaster cities they caressed? And the freedom. It was the end of the continent, and as Kerouac wrote, "They didn't give a damn."[26]

For Kerouac and his fellow Beats, as they were called, it was the journey and not the destination that mattered. *On the Road* was the twentieth-century version of *Huckleberry Finn*, of "lighting out for the territory." Kerouac, through his character in the novel, Sal Paradise, was much less introspective than Huck, and it was not clear at the end of the book if the journeys had shaped or reshaped Sal. The Beats—such as Allen Ginsberg and Neal Cassady, appearing in the book as Carlo Marx and Dean Moriarty respectively—were the creative rebels of the 1950s. They seemed a welcome diversion from the alleged conformity of the period. The gifted generation enjoyed the journey too, but seemed more eager to take advantage of the possibilities that flourished at the destination.

And that destination was often the West, as the residents of Brooklyn ruefully discovered. To Brooklynites, the Dodgers were less a baseball team than part of the family. The most diverse of all the diverse boroughs of New York, Brooklyn's rallying point of unity was its baseball club. The players lived scattered about the borough among their fans. Like Brooklynites themselves, the Dodgers were zany, occasionally brilliant, and often underdogs, especially when it came to the New York Yankees. The Dodgers were blue-collar, like many of their fans. They pioneered the integration of baseball, while their Bronx rivals sat on their corporate fannies and only hired their first African American player, catcher Elston Howard, in 1955, a full eight years after Jackie Robinson broke baseball's color barrier. The most heated battles of Brooklyn's gifted generation occurred in discussions of who was the best center fielder in baseball: the Dodgers' Duke Snider, the Yankees' Mickey Mantle, or the Giants' Willie Mays.[27]

The Dodgers' fiercest rivalry was with their National League cohorts the New York Giants. But the saddest day in the history of the borough was October 3, 1951. The Giants tied the Dodgers on the last day of the season, setting up a three-game playoff to determine which team would meet the Yankees in the World Series. The teams split the first two games, and in the final game, the Dodgers took a 4–1 lead into the bottom of the ninth. Don Newcombe, the Dodgers' starting pitcher, was still on the mound, but he was tiring and gave up a run. Ralph Branca relieved Newcombe with runners on second and third and one out. Bobby Thomson, who had had a torrid September at the plate, stepped up to bat. After a first-pitch strike, Thomson lofted a fly ball on the next pitch that just cleared the short left-field wall of the Giants' Harlem field, the Polo Grounds. The Giants won the pennant, Bobby Thomson hit the "Shot Heard Round the World," and millions of hearts broke in Brooklyn.

Redemption would not come until 1955. The National League Dodgers played the American League Yankees solely in the World Series, which they did in 1952, 1953, 1955, and 1956, and in an annual exhibition game for the Mayor's Trophy. Only in that magical year of 1955 did the Dodgers manage to beat the omnipresent and omnipotent Yankees. Traffic stopped, horns blew, confetti flew, and church bells rang. Brooklyn was agog for the Bums, as they were affectionately known. Two years later, the Dodgers left for Los Angeles.

The Dodgers were family, and family members do not just pick up and leave for no reason. But there were plenty of reasons as it turned out, and it reflected a transition from East to West, and from city to suburb. By the mid-1950s, New

York could not support three major league baseball teams. On August 20, 1957, the Giants announced they were moving to San Francisco. The national pastime would at last be truly national.

Even though the Dodgers had the most populous borough to themselves, they had also experienced an attendance decline. Their white fan base was moving to Long Island, and Ebbets Field, which opened in 1913, was small and decrepit. Dodgers owner Walter O'Malley did not initially plan to move the team, hoping to arrange a deal with Robert Moses, in charge of the New York City's planning and development, for a tract of land at Brooklyn's Atlantic Yards, where the current Barclays Center sits, which would enable him to build a modern stadium. Moses nixed the deal.

While it was disconcerting to learn that baseball was a business, the moves of the Dodgers and the Giants to the West Coast (and of the Boston Braves to Milwaukee in 1953 and the Philadelphia Athletics to Kansas City in 1955) reflected the changing demographics of East Coast cities and the population shift westward. The St. Louis Browns did move to Baltimore in 1953, but St. Louis had already begun its lengthy decline in population and economic base. Its profile was similar to Brooklyn's. The borough was hemorrhaging jobs, white families were moving to Long Island, and African Americans and Puerto Ricans were moving in. Ebbets Field was demolished in 1960, and public housing, the Ebbets Field Apartments, replaced the hallowed greensward that had housed the dreams of Brooklyn boys and girls and their gods at play.[28]

The transformation did not work out well, reflecting the chronic underfunding of public housing and the overwhelming challenges of addressing urban poverty. Journalist Wright Thompson visited the apartments in 2007 and talked with Brenda Scott, head of the tenants association. She was in the midst of a battle against drugs and violence in the project. The previous year someone had fired a bullet through her front door as a warning. This was not the legacy Jackie Robinson had in mind. She sighed. "It should have stayed a ballpark."

Letitia James, the city councilwoman whose district included the apartments, acknowledged, "It's a very scary place at night." James added: "Jackie Robinson would be rolling over in his grave if he saw the conditions at Ebbets Field. We're doing a disservice to his memory." No lights, standing water, rats, exposed wires, trash, and drug dealers. Pee Wee Reese, the great Dodgers shortstop of the 1950s, went back for a documentary and recalled the field that stood there and wept. Brenda Scott thought about moving back to North Carolina, from where her parents had come with few possessions and much hope.[29]

It happened all over Brooklyn. By 1964, the *New York Times* reported, "Coney Island Slump Grows Worse." The physical decline of the iconic Brooklyn amusement fixture was evident during the 1950s, and it corresponded to the drop in visitors. A survey of concessionaires turned up a general agreement that "the growing influx of Negro visitors discouraged some white persons to the area." Three years later, Steeplechase Park, the first of Coney Island's great amusement parks, closed. It was happening all over the urban North. Chicago's Riverview Park began its descent in the 1950s as well. Demographics changed, and it too closed.[30]

On the other hand, Disneyland in Anaheim, California, south of Los Angeles, opened in 1955 and flourished immediately. Walt Disney had visited Coney Island in the early 1950s to get some ideas for his own project, but he recoiled from "its tawdry rides and hostile employees." Main Street in Disneyland would evoke an earlier world before large cities and complicating diversity coarsened American society. Disney did not bar any ethnic or racial groups from his park, but some were startlingly portrayed in his treatment of American history. Park brochures described Frontierland as "a land of hostile Indians and straight shooting pioneers." There, one could also find Aunt Jemima's Pancake House, a re-creation of a plantation where a black woman, dressed as "Aunt Jemima . . . was on hand everyday to welcome visitors warmly." Visitors to Adventureland would experience "the sound of native chants and tom-tom drums" and a Jungle Cruise featuring "wild animals and native savages [that] attack your craft." Once back to the safety of Main Street, visitors could experience "great moments with Mr. Lincoln." There, an "Audio Animatronic" Lincoln recited a patriotic speech that made no mention of slavery or the Civil War.[31]

The Dodgers and Giants were journeying to the newest place in a new country. New houses, new roads, new schools, new infrastructure, and new lives. More babies were born in California in the 1950s than in any other state. By 1960, one out of every ten schoolchildren in the United States was attending school in California. They would set trends in fashion, the drive-in culture, and media. More people—2,964,000—moved to California between 1950 and 1960 than came to the United States from the rest of the world.[32]

The population surge would play out in numerous ways, but most immediately in political power. The thirteen Western states gained ten new House of Representatives seats, eight in California alone as a result of the 1960 census, while the East, Midwest, and the South lost representatives. California gained from a national brain drain as the state became the residence of 16 Nobel Prize winners and 138 members of the National Academy of Sciences. New York

State came in a distant second with 6 Nobel laureates and 106 Academy members.[33]

California in the 1950s was America writ large. Wallace Stegner, a prominent Western novelist, wrote about the state:

> In a prosperous country, we are more prosperous than most; in an urban country, more urban than most; in a gadget-happy country, more addicted to gadgets; in a tasteless country, more tasteless; in a creative country, more energetically creative; in an optimistic society, more optimistic; in an anxious society, more anxious. Contribute regionally to the national culture? We *are* the national culture, at its most energetic end.[34]

ENERGY WAS WHAT PRESIDENT Eisenhower hoped to unleash nationally, not only in the West. Unfetter all Americans from prejudice, exclusion, and ignorance and a torrent of productivity and innovation would follow. Individual freedom was the handmaiden of collective prosperity. And both depended on a wise and active government. Ike had overcome the congressional inertia during the first two years of his presidency and compiled a strong legislative record, and now he was ready to place those accomplishments before the people as he ran for a second term.

Adlai Stevenson was again the Democratic candidate, but only the resurrection of Franklin D. Roosevelt could have defeated Eisenhower in 1956. Immensely popular nationwide—he had a 79 percent approval rating in early 1956—his strength transcended regional and racial divisions. Republicans were confident they could build on their 1952 incursions in the South, particularly in the growing cities and suburbs, where purity on racial issues was less important than economic development and prosperity. And Ike's record on civil rights could peel away enough black votes in the North to draw some of those states into the Republican column.

Indeed, Eisenhower's showing among black voters portended a potential fracturing of the Democratic coalition built during the Roosevelt era. In Harlem, Republicans were typically fortunate to receive 10 percent of the presidential vote; in 1956, Ike received 34 percent of the vote. In Chicago's South Side, the president received 36 percent of the black vote. Richard Nixon campaigned in Harlem, the only candidate to do so among the four running for the highest offices from the two major parties. Urging African Americans to vote Republican across the board, Nixon told black audiences that civil rights legislation "cannot pass . . . as long as the filibuster exists in the Senate." He reminded black voters that Mississippi Democrat James O. Eastland stood astride the Senate Judiciary Committee as a powerful sentinel against any civil rights legislation seeing the light of the Senate floor. Nixon vowed that if Eisenhower was reelected, "we are going to have performance on civil rights, not just promises." Eisenhower received a majority of the black vote in ten Northern and twelve Southern cities.[35]

The result was an Eisenhower landslide. He bested Adlai Stevenson in the Electoral College by a margin of 457–73. If there was any solace in the outcome for Democrats, it was that Ike's victory was more personal than for the Republican Party. The Democrats retained control of both the House and the Senate. It was the first time since 1848 that a presidential candidate (in that case, Zachary Taylor) had won without carrying either house of Congress with him. A residual benefit for Eisenhower was that several of his most conservative Republican adversaries went down to defeat, raising his hopes for a more productive second term. Political columnist Stewart Alsop, sampling postelection sentiment around the country, said he "heard the same phrase repeated in one form or another with metronomic regularity: 'Eisenhower is a good man, and I don't go too much for Stevenson, but the Republicans are for the big shots, and the Democrats are more for us little guys.' "[36]

Still, the electoral math was troubling for Democrats from another perspective. Eisenhower carried Texas for the second time in four years. Without Texas, the South's electoral vote total was 104. The nine states in the North with significant black populations totaled 223 electoral votes. "Give us a civil rights bill," a Republican leader pledged, "and by 1960 we will break the Roosevelt coalition of the large cities and the South, even without Eisenhower."[37]

Perhaps the most prescient analysis of the 1956 presidential contest came from Massachusetts Democratic senator John F. Kennedy. He had figured prominently at the 1956 Democratic National Convention as a possible running mate for Adlai Stevenson. But he lost out to Tennessee senator Estes Kefauver. Considering the Eisenhower landslide, it was a good thing for the junior senator to have avoided the debris from such a loss. Kennedy asserted that Eisenhower had blurred the distinctions between the Democrats and the Republicans. It was a point others had made, but Kennedy demonstrated how that created fissures in the Democratic coalition. Exit polls indicated that young voters, women voters, union families, immigrant families, blacks, big-city voters, independents, and Southerners switched to Eisenhower in great numbers. These voters had formed the core of Roosevelt Democrats.[38]

How could the Democrats regain the White House in 1960? Voters had clearly opposed upending the New Deal in the 1956 election. Their strong vote for Ike and their rejection of Republican conservatives implied a strong endorsement of the center. The dilemma, Kennedy noted, was that Democrats could not afford to move to the right of Republicans and oppose Eisenhower's progressive policies on federal aid to education, public housing, and immigration reform. Moving left was out of the question as well since that would alienate moderate and independent voters. And if the Democrats stayed in the middle, that would hardly distinguish them from Republicans. Adding to the conundrum was the continued factionalism between Northern and Southern Democrats.

Kennedy's solution was for congressional Democrats to take the lead in resolving key national issues such as federal aid to education, medical care for the elderly, expanded unemployment insurance, removal of urban blight, and immigration reform. These proposals differed little from Eisenhower's agenda, but Ike would not be a candidate in 1960, and if the Democratic-controlled Congress realized these policy objectives, Democrats could take credit for their success.

Kennedy concluded his analysis with a discussion of civil rights, an issue that, by 1957, neither party could ignore. He argued that the Democratic Party was uniquely positioned to solve "the sensitive, complex issue of race relations" because it included within its ranks the majority of the nation's African Americans, as well as the majority of Southern whites. What that solution would look like, Kennedy did not say, though it seemed more obvious for Republicans to take the lead in this area as they did not depend on Southern white support.

EISENHOWER'S CAMPAIGN OF 1956 adopted a national strategy aimed at independent voters and African Americans in Northern cities. This forward-looking plan succeeded in garnering the electoral-vote-rich states of the Northeast and the Midwest. Ike had not yet banished yesterday from public policy, but the light of tomorrow was shining through more clearly than it had at the beginning of his administration.

CHAPTER 13

STEPS

THE SLOW PROGRESS ON civil rights resulted from the American system of government, which in that era placed inordinate power in the hands of Southern white lawmakers. The Truman and Eisenhower administrations used executive orders, court appointments, and legal challenges to expand, however modestly, the rights of African Americans. As for substantive legislation, the U.S. Senate was the graveyard of civil rights. Southern Democrats were still fighting the Civil War and treated proposals with even a whiff of racial equality as an assault by Union forces bent on destroying white civilization. They turned on Truman, one of their own, and would even more readily oppose a president from the party of Lincoln who attempted to attack the fortress of white supremacy.

If, by some stroke of fortune, a civil rights bill could actually emerge from a committee chaired by a Southern Democrat, it would be talked to death on the floor. It was highly unlikely that the Senate could muster the two-thirds vote necessary (called cloture) to cut off debate and take a vote. Harry Truman tried numerous times to breach the Senate fortress, but he failed. In doing so, he jeopardized the rest of his domestic program. Eisenhower knew this history and understood the consequences of recommending civil rights legislation to a Congress averse to it. He did so anyway in 1956, and its rejection was swift and, it appeared, final.

But Eisenhower pressed the issue once again at the beginning of the new year. On January 1, 1957, the headline in the *New York Times* read, "President Pushes Civil Rights Plan at G.O.P. Parley." He reiterated his commitment to civil rights legislation in his State of the Union address ten days later: "I urge that the Congress enact this [civil rights] legislation." Eisenhower believed that the bill was a moderate effort, well within his ideal of the "middle way."[1]

In June 1957, the House passed a civil rights bill with a few minor amendments. But the House had passed a similar bill in 1956. As columnist Drew Pearson noted, the administration's proposals "were facsimiles of the very bills which we had introduced here in the Senate in every session of the Congress since 1949."[2]

A key difference in the summer of 1957 was Majority Leader Lyndon B. Johnson. At breakfast one day in the early spring of 1957, Johnson, in between bites of venison sausage, startled a reporter when he stated matter-of-factly, "A civil rights bill is going to be passed by this Congress. There's no getting around it." Although he had remained on the periphery of massive resistance to civil rights, Johnson had supported his Southern colleagues on burying or talking to death any civil rights measures. But he harbored presidential ambitions. The public's perception of him as a Southerner, he understood, reduced the possible fulfillment of those ambitions substantially. Southern senators shared his ambition, to some degree, figuring that if one of their own could get into the White House, the likelihood of a cascade of civil rights measures descending upon them would diminish. Richard Russell admitted, "We can never make him [Johnson] president unless the Senate first disposes of civil rights." If Russell came on board, the other Southern Democrats would follow.[3]

Johnson had to make the biggest sale of his life: convince fellow Southerners to accept an abomination—a civil rights bill—and persuade President Eisenhower to accept a watered-down version of what he had been promising since early 1956 or else risk certain defeat. On top of that, Johnson had to urge Southern Democrats not to employ their most precious parliamentary weapon, the filibuster, to kill the bill. The consequences of employing that weapon could be the death knell for the filibuster and a much stronger civil rights bill in the not-too-distant future, he warned.

Johnson would snooker both Southern Democrats and President Eisenhower, the former because there were likely not enough votes in the Senate to break a Southern filibuster. In addition to its Southern lawmakers, the Senate had a number of conservatives who so revered its unique rule that they would probably not vote for cloture even if it meant defying their president. Marshaling the required sixty-four votes would be an enormously difficult task. But even in getting the Southern Democrats to go along with him, Johnson was careful to make certain they knew that, in spirit at least, he was with them. He kept on railing about "the nigger bill," and the Hobson's choice that confronted him and them, and how, with appropriate safeguards, it could be possible to minimize the bill's impact.[4]

Johnson also convinced Eisenhower to moderate the attorney general's power to enjoin discrimination in education and public accommodations— Section III—or the entire bill would fail, either on direct vote or on a Southern filibuster. As Herbert Brownell would point out later, these were problematic assumptions. But Eisenhower was so invested in civil rights legislation that he convinced himself that some bill, as a historic precedent if nothing else, was better than no bill. It was not a compromise he took well, but he took it nonetheless.[5]

The other major sticking point for Southern Democrats was the power the bill gave to the attorney general in Section IV to haul individuals or jurisdictions into civil court to punish those who violated the right to vote or the right to attend desegregated schools under federal court order. Southern Democrats hoped to eviscerate this power in Section IV by insisting on a trial by jury. Of course, an all-white jury (jury pools consisted of registered voters, and in many places in the South, few or no African Americans qualified) would likely find for the defendant and against the federal government.

After the civil rights bill passed the House, the Senate was the next stop, literally. The likely fate was that Senator James O. Eastland's Judiciary Committee would bury the bill, and that would be the end of it. But Vice President Nixon, who presided over the Senate, and the Republican minority leader, William F. Knowland (R-CA), employed an arcane parliamentary maneuver to bypass Eastland's committee and bring the bill directly to the Senate floor.[6]

A Southern filibuster loomed, and it was unlikely that the administration could muster the two-thirds vote to end debate. For Southern Democrats, it was as if the Reconstruction era, or at least the one they imagined, had suddenly come back to life. They viewed the bill's provisions "as the measures proposed by Sumner and Stevens in Reconstruction days in their avowed drive 'to put black heels on white necks.'" Majority Leader Johnson now insisted to Eisenhower that unless he dropped Part III completely, the entire bill was doomed. Whether Johnson had the votes to kill the bill remains unclear. But he could be very persuasive.[7]

Southern Democrats next insisted on a jury trial in Part IV of the bill. The move infuriated Eisenhower, who raged, "Rarely in our entire legislative history have so many extraneous issues been introduced into the debate." He vigorously opposed the jury trial amendment claiming that "placing a jury trial between a court order and the enforcement of that order" would mean that "we are really welcoming anarchy."[8]

Jimmy Byrnes wrote to Eisenhower urging acceptance of the jury trial provision as a brake against an overly aggressive federal attorney general. The South Carolinian characterized a comment Brownell allegedly made to him (which Brownell denied) that "juries in the South would not convict" violators of the civil rights act as "an insult to the men and women of the South." Ike, in response, attempted to educate Byrnes, explaining, "It seems to me that the public interest in the protection of voting rights is at least as great as the public interest in the maintenance of minimum wages, or in the truthfulness of financial and other statements in connection with securities." In those cases, Eisenhower noted, "the Attorney General may enjoin violations of the law (for which criminal penalties are also provided), and violations of such injunctions are tried without a jury." Eisenhower added, "The right to vote is more important in our way of life than are the regulations cited above."[9]

The Senate passed the jury trial amendment 51–42, with the help of some liberal Democratic senators such as Minnesota's Hubert Humphrey, Idaho's Frank Church, and Illinois's Paul Douglas, who felt the sanctity of a jury trial outweighed any concerns about local perversions of that ideal. The amendment received the support of only twelve Republicans.

Frank Church, Idaho's liberal Democratic senator who supported the jury trial amendment, reasoned, "Our work in safeguarding civil rights cannot be accomplished in a single stroke." He urged the Senate to take the long view, that this bill would be but the first step to more comprehensive measures. A few months earlier, at a cocktail party, Majority Leader Johnson had chatted with Church's wife, Bethine, who confided her lifelong desire to visit South America. Two weeks after the jury trial vote, Johnson selected her husband to represent the Senate at an Organization of American States conference in Buenos Aires. He could take Bethine. Johnson also gave Church a coveted seat on the Senate Foreign Relations Committee.[10]

As the clerk announced the results of the jury trial amendment, Minority Leader Knowland broke down and wept. Richard Nixon called the vote "one of the saddest days in the history of the Senate because it was a vote against the right to vote." Later that evening, encountering Johnson in the Senate cloakroom, the vice president taunted the senator that although he had won this fight, in the long run Nixon's view would prevail. Eisenhower was equally distressed: "We've taken political defeats in [the] past four years, but this one is the worst." He predicted that "many fellow Americans will continue, in effect, to be disenfranchised." It would prove a fitting epitaph of the act's ineffectiveness.[11]

Eisenhower and Brownell worked to salvage something from the jury trial amendment, successfully proposing that a federal judge could bypass the provision if the projected punishment for abrogating voting rights did not exceed a fine of $300 or imprisonment for more than ninety days. Johnson cajoled his Southern colleagues to vote in favor of the compromise, and on August 7, 1957, the U.S. Senate passed the amended bill, 72–18, with all of the negative votes coming from Southern Democrats. After the House ratified the new version, the Senate passed the bill on August 29, 1957. For the first time in eighty-two years the nation had a civil rights bill.

IT WAS AN IMPORTANT BILL, but only a step nevertheless. The federal government would still be unable to assist African Americans battling segregation in schools and in public facilities. Few blacks could afford protracted legal battles and the threats to jobs and their personal safety such suits could generate. The NAACP could not take up hundreds if not thousands of cases throughout the South; logistically and financially, this was impossible.

Several black leaders urged Eisenhower not to sign the bill. Jackie Robinson fired off a telegram: HAVE WAITED THIS LONG FOR BILL WITH MEANING—CAN WAIT A LITTLE LONGER. Civil rights veteran A. Philip Randolph despaired, "It is worse than no bill at all." But once the initial frustration wore off, other black leaders and white liberals adopted a more sober perspective. A civil rights bill had passed the Senate. That was a historic accomplishment. As Roy Wilkins observed, "Once Congress had lost its virginity on civil rights, it would go on to make up for what had been lost." Martin Luther King Jr., who by the summer of 1957 was emerging as a major leader for racial justice in the South, wrote to Richard Nixon acknowledging the act's weakness, but noted, "After considering all angles I have come to the conclusion that the present bill is far better than no bill at all."[12]

If the federal government enforced the bill's provisions, the results in the South would be significant. But it did not. The fourth part of the legislation, which aimed to expand black voting rights in the South, received little use. The Justice Department had by 1960 filed only ten lawsuits against Southern registrars for "arbitrary refusals to register" qualified blacks. By then the net increase of black voters since the bill's passage was zero.[13]

Despite the disappointing outcome, many Americans, as King's remarks indicated, appreciated the breakthrough, symbolic or otherwise. The *New York Times* characterized the act as "incomparably the most significant domestic action of any Congress in this century." Shortly before his death in June 1956, IBM chairman Thomas J. Watson anointed Eisenhower "the greatest President since Lincoln" for advancing the cause of civil rights.[14]

On the day the civil rights bill finally passed the Senate, Carol Beane, a thirteen-year-old black girl, wrote to the president expressing her renewed faith in the promise of the Declaration of Independence: "America has built a great nation with these words and others as its foundation. If we destroy the equality of men for a little thing such as color . . . you could well say the America that we know today has begun her downfall." Eisenhower thanked her for the letter and assured her, "America will never tolerate the things you fear, though I admit that we do have many imperfections in our society. But the important thing to remember is that we are making progress toward their correction." He also acknowledged that progress was "painfully slow."[15]

Overlooked in the heated debate over Sections III and IV of the bill was the establishment of the Civil Rights Commission and the Civil Rights Division in the Justice Department. The latter would be especially active in the coming decades in enforcing civil rights laws and court rulings once stronger measures were on the books. Perhaps most important, the logjam had been broken. The first civil rights act would make those future measures more likely.

Lyndon B. Johnson was the big winner in the tortuous process, which irked Eisenhower. Upon the bill's final passage on August 29, Clarence Mitchell of the NAACP sent a telegram to Johnson thanking him for his efforts. Southern historian C. Vann Woodward wrote, "Moving between the incorrigible right and the immovable left, Senator Johnson worked mainly in the shifting center to shape and mold a . . . workable compromise to replace a futile stalemate." Another commentator compared Johnson to Henry Clay, the Great Compromiser. Although liberals were not thrilled with Johnson's maneuverings, he had gained some respect in their circle.[16]

Johnson's work may have enhanced his presidential credentials, but it did not resonate well in Texas. A Houston resident wondered why Johnson wouldn't do for Texas what "other Southerners are doing so well for their constituents" in opposing the bill. Other constituents threatened him with "impeachment" for treason. Even those outside Texas attacked the senator. A woman from Norfolk, Virginia, asked Johnson, "Why are you selling the south down the river?" A few weeks after Eisenhower signed the bill into law, Johnson received a telegram from a constituent in Houston: NIGGER LOVER.[17]

That such a mild bill could stir such animosity was not surprising. The new law, most understood, was a portent of things to come. The domino theory of white supremacy enjoyed wide credence in the South. As one barrier fell, others were sure to follow. Yet, Southern senators, though they hated the bill, were not vindictive toward the majority leader. They understood the changing political landscape. If they wished to see one of their own in the White House, this was a necessary sacrifice. Mississippi senator John Stennis recalled, "We knew that he had presidential ambitions, and most of us wanted to see him become president."[18]

BY THE TIME EISENHOWER SIGNED the bill on September 9, 1957, another racial crisis was hurtling toward the White House. The school board of Little Rock, Arkansas, one of the South's more progressive cities, had proposed a modest desegregation plan to comply with the *Brown* decision and a local court order.

The plan called for integration of the city's schools over a number of years, starting with Central High School and working down through the elementary grades. Nine black children would attend previously all-white Central High School in that city when the academic year began in September. Few expected trouble with the plan's implementation. By that time Arkansas led the South in the number of desegregated school districts, and five of the six state-supported white colleges and universities had already admitted black students. L. C. Bates, publisher of the state's major African American newspaper, the *Arkansas State Press*, predicted that Little Rock "will take school integration as just another going to school."[19]

In August, however, the Mothers' League of Little Rock filed suit to block the federal-court-ordered desegregation and asked Governor Orval Faubus for assistance. The governor had spent most of his political life as a champion of Arkansas's poor white and black populations. He hailed from the hill country, the son of a poor farmer who traveled the depressed communities in and around Madison County delivering speeches tinged with socialist doctrines. The father's political beliefs rubbed off on the boy, who became a liberal editorial writer for a hill-country weekly before casting his fortunes with the popular and progressive postwar governor Sid McMath.

In 1954, Faubus ran for governor as McMath's political heir. Though opponents tagged him a Communist sympathizer, a weighty epithet in that era, he won the Democratic primary, and hence the election. In his first term as governor, Faubus instituted a wide range of reforms, eclipsing even McMath's record. One of his first acts was to expand the state's Democratic Party central committee by six members and to appoint African Americans to all of the new positions. He also secured a $22 million tax increase to improve the state's lagging educational system, and he established the Children's Colony, a model facility for the mentally retarded.

Nothing in his background indicated that he would not be supportive of Little Rock's forthcoming efforts to desegregate its schools. As he ran for reelection in 1956 (Arkansas governors served two-year terms), he repeated often that "desegregation [was] an issue that should be left to local choice." The primary results, however, jolted Faubus. He barely fended off the challenge of former state senator Jim Johnson, who charged that the governor was "soft" on integration. Fearing increased opposition to his legislative program as well as for his political future, Faubus began to reassess his position on integration during the early months of 1957.[20]

The choice of Central to receive nine black students was unpopular among the city's white working class. The school board's integration plan seemed to single out their children for the experiment in interracial education. The board had "sold" the integration plan to the city's white leadership by noting that the construction of another all-white high school on the fashionable west side of town would be completed by the time the plan went into effect in the fall of 1957. The children of the city's elite could attend a high school segregated by both class and race.

Faubus joined the Mothers' League's cause. But NAACP legal counsel Thurgood Marshall obtained a ruling from federal district court Judge Ronald N. Davies on August 30 that the desegregation of Central High School must proceed as scheduled. Faubus ignored the court order and sent Arkansas national guardsmen to block the admission of the nine black students to Central High. He defended his action on the grounds that "blood will run in the streets" if black pupils entered Central High. In his increasingly absurd theater, he compared his decision to the choice forced upon Robert E. Lee—whether to serve his country or protect his home.[21]

On September 9, the U.S. district court, responding to this defiance, asked Eisenhower's Justice Department to enjoin Faubus and the National Guard from blocking a court order and to show cause why he should not be cited for contempt. Two days later, Arkansas Democratic congressman Brooks Hays, a moderate, offered to mediate and suggested a meeting between the president and Faubus at Eisenhower's vacation retreat in Newport, Rhode Island.

The meeting occurred on September 14, and as the president had hoped, it seemed to resolve the impasse. Ike announced that Faubus had agreed "to respect the decision of the United States District Court" and his "inescapable responsibility . . . to preserve law and order in this state." As a face-saving gesture, Eisenhower would allow Faubus to keep the National Guard in place, but instead of preventing the desegregation of Central High, they would allow the black students to enter the school.[22]

By September 19, however, it was clear that Governor Faubus was going to renege on his promise to comply with the court order. The following day Faubus removed the National Guard from Central High and urged the black students not to attend classes until a "cooling-off period" had elapsed. On Monday, September 23, the African American students showed up at Central High only to be confronted by a violent mob. The students left. When an even-larger hostile crowd gathered the following day, Little Rock's mayor, Woodrow Wilson Mann, sent a frantic telegram to the president stating the situation was "out of control," and pleading with Eisenhower that "in the interest of humanity, law and order," he should send federal troops immediately.[23]

The president had already discussed deploying federal troops with his military and civilian staffs as early as September 4. The time had now come. Calling the governor's actions "disgraceful," and stating that federal law could not be "flouted with impunity by any individual or any mob of extremists," Eisenhower called on the 101st Airborne Division. Mann's telegram provided the trigger, and Ike pulled it. As if to offer Ike grace for sending troops against American citizens, Billy Graham assured the president, it was "the only thing you can do."[24]

The following day, residents of Little Rock heard what appeared to be distant drums. As the sound grew louder, the ground began to vibrate, as if an earthquake were building. The 101st Airborne Division, the Screaming Eagles, in full battle gear, was crossing the Arkansas River into Little Rock. For the first time since the Civil War, federal troops were invading the South. The president also federalized ten thousand members of the Arkansas National Guard to prevent conflict between state and federal commands. The commander in chief had decided that open defiance of a federal court order would, if unaddressed, lead to anarchy and a permanent defacement of America's reputation abroad.

In an address to the nation on radio and television that evening, Eisenhower justified the deployment as a simple constitutional responsibility that a president must initiate to uphold the authority of federal courts: "When large gatherings of obstructionists made it impossible for the decrees of the Court to be carried out, both the law and the national interest demanded that the President take action." Ike would call it his toughest decision since D-day.[25]

A strong majority of Americans stood behind their commander in chief, with 68.4 percent of the country (77.5 percent outside the South) approving his decision to send troops to Little Rock. African Americans were especially supportive. Jazz great Louis Armstrong telegraphed the president, DADDY, IF AND WHEN YOU DECIDE TO TAKE THOSE LITTLE NEGRO CHILDREN PERSONALLY INTO CENTRAL HIGH SCHOOL ALONG WITH YOUR MARVELOUS TROOPS, TAKE ME ALONG . . . YOU HAVE A GOOD HEART. Jackie Robinson wired, PLEASE ACCEPT MY CONGRATULATIONS, I SHOULD HAVE KNOWN YOU WOULD DO THE RIGHT THING AT THE CRUCIAL TIME. Even some of Ike's Southern friends congratulated him on restoring law and order in Little Rock. Texas oil man Monty Moncrief assured the president, "The overwhelming majority of American people are in full accord with the determined action you have taken."[26]

Other white Southerners decried the deployment as a grievous violation of states' rights, a familiar cry from the South whenever federal authorities attacked white supremacy. Richard Russell was livid about the presence of federal troops in Little Rock. He complained to Eisenhower that the troops were pushing around unarmed citizens and holding some in jail without formal charges. The president sent a telegram in immediate reply defending his actions: HAD THE POLICE POWERS OF THE STATE OF ARKANSAS BEEN

UTILIZED NOT TO FRUSTRATE THE ORDERS OF THE COURT BUT TO SUPPORT THEM, THE ENSUING VIOLENCE AND OPEN DISRESPECT FOR THE LAW AND THE FEDERAL JUDICIARY WOULD NEVER HAVE OCCURRED. Had he failed to act, it would have been TANTAMOUNT TO ACQUIESCENCE IN ANARCHY AND THE DISSOLUTION OF THE UNION.[27]

But what particularly angered Eisenhower was Russell's comparison of the 101st Airborne Division to "Hitler's storm troopers." The former general shot back, I COMPLETELY FAIL TO COMPREHEND YOUR COMPARISON . . . IN ONE CASE MILITARY POWER WAS USED TO FURTHER THE AMBITIONS AND PURPOSES OF A RUTHLESS DICTATOR, IN THE OTHER TO PRESERVE THE INSTITUTIONS OF FREE GOVERNMENT.[28]

Lyndon B. Johnson had hoped that the passage of the 1957 Civil Rights Act would lay to rest at least for a while a divisive issue, both for the nation and for his presidential ambitions. Eisenhower's deployment of troops to Little Rock upended that hope. While not as intemperate as Russell, Johnson expressed his "regret that the President has taken this extremely drastic step without exploring the alternatives." Johnson's statement did not offer what alternatives the president should have considered.[29]

While the poll numbers were strong for Eisenhower, they did not mask the unease about sending soldiers against fellow Americans. The *Saturday Evening Post*, normally a pro-Republican magazine and a champion of the president's, expressed concern about the "invasion of Arkansas." The *Post* protested that school integration "is both right and inevitable," but it "cannot be forced over-night." The analogy the *Post* employed was Prohibition, which, in its analysis, proved "the impossibility of reforming the habits and attitudes of men by force." Except that the protection of the rights of citizens to equality before the law was a bit different from protecting the right to drink alcohol.[30]

Elements of the 101st Airborne stayed until late November, gradually replaced by the federalized Arkansas National Guard. The Guard would remain on duty until the end of May 1958. In the meantime, the nine black students were attending Central High. Just as the last federal troops were leaving Little Rock on November 25, 1957, the president's personal secretary, Ann Whitman, walked into the Oval Office and found him slumped over his desk. He had suffered a stroke. Little Rock had taken its toll.[31]

The Little Rock crisis played on in a perverse loop with no apparent resolve. Governor Faubus stalled and filed lawsuits to stall some more, citing the potential for violence and the difficulty of maintaining law and order in a highly volatile situation. In early September 1958, an exasperated Eisenhower wrote to Ralph McGill, editor of the *Atlanta Constitution*, "There doesn't seem to be any solution in sight—for the simple reason that not even the principles

of political and economic equality will be accepted in some of our states."
There was even talk of another military intervention.[32]

Relief of sorts would come a little more than a week later. The U.S. Supreme
Court, in *Cooper v. Aaron*, a case the Eisenhower administration joined with
the NAACP, unanimously ruled that community opposition was no excuse
for delaying integration and ordered the school board to proceed with the
plan. The NAACP's Roy Wilkins applauded the decision as it created a precedent that the "right of individual citizens cannot be abridged or denied,
because of threats or violent acts of those who uphold racial discrimination
and segregation." Richard Russell announced that the South would not
"surrender to the dictates of the N.A.A.C.P." Of course, this was not an edict
from the NAACP, but for the purposes of white Southerners such as Russell,
the Supreme Court had become a branch of that civil rights organization.[33]

Faubus, his legal options played out, closed the city's high schools as the
state legislature had empowered him to do earlier that year. Adolphine Fletcher
Terry, from one of Little Rock's most prominent families, sat in her living
room with about thirty other like-minded women beneath a portrait of her
Confederate-general ancestor to form the Women's Emergency Committee to
Open Our Schools. The economic leadership followed, and the governor
rescinded his order, but not until the 1958–59 academic year had been lost.
Faubus was reelected overwhelmingly in 1958 and would go on to serve three
more terms as governor.[34]

The Little Rock episode did not portend well for school desegregation
efforts across the South. Little Rock's moderate reputation, its institutional
support for peaceful desegregation, from the mayor to the clergy to business
leaders, counted for less than the political ambitions of a governor and the
strong popular approbation he received in the rest of the state.

AT A DECEMBER 10, 1958, news conference, the president, with both the
midterm elections (which returned a Democratic Congress) and Little Rock
resolved, returned to civil rights. He stated his intention of asking Congress
to extend the life of the Civil Rights Commission and called out the State of
Alabama for refusing to cooperate with the commission's investigation of
voting rights irregularities in that state. Eisenhower continued to believe that
if the federal government could protect African American voting rights,
many of the racial problems in the South could be resolved, including school
desegregation. The lack of political power shut out Southern blacks from an
equitable public policy. Could a new civil rights initiative be brewing?[35]

Eisenhower and Attorney General William P. Rogers, who had replaced
Herbert Brownell (who returned to private practice in New York), drafted a

civil rights bill in late January 1959. It set severe criminal penalties for "preventing, obstructing, impeding or interfering" with federal court orders protecting both the right to vote and the admission of children to schools. The bill would also deny federal aid to school districts that converted public school buildings to private academies. Most surprising was the revival of Part III of the 1957 civil rights bill, granting the attorney general significant powers to sue in court on behalf of persons denied equal protection of the laws under the Fourteenth Amendment.[36]

Eisenhower's civil rights bill was not something the American public clamored for. But the Little Rock crisis had annealed Ike's views to the point where his attitude toward defiance of the rule of law had significantly hardened. This evolving view was evident in his public reaction to the lynching of Mack Parker, a twenty-three-year-old black man, in Poplarville, Mississippi, on April 24, 1959. Parker had been charged with raping a white woman, and forty-eight hours before his trial, a mob of masked men dragged him from his jail cell, shot him, and threw his body into a river. In 1955, after the notorious lynching of Emmett Till, Eisenhower made no public statement. As Eisenhower well knew, the federal government was powerless to seek justice for Parker, and as in the Emmett Till case, the defendants went free. Attorney General Rogers called it a "travesty on justice," but, like Brownell before him, could do nothing.[37]

Eisenhower and Rogers decided they had to try to do something and took the unprecedented step of convening a federal grand jury in Biloxi, Mississippi, to investigate the denial of Parker's federal civil rights based on a Reconstruction-era law. The federal grand jury refused to indict, but a precedent had been set.[38]

Eisenhower would be equally unsuccessful with his latest civil rights initiative. The predictable opposition from Southern Democrats aside, he could no longer count on Republican Party unity to carry the day. Republican Party discipline, a key factor in the passage of the 1957 civil rights bill, would matter less in the new Senate, where Democrats now held a thirty-vote majority. Greater reliance on Democratic votes meant greater administration reliance on Majority Leader Johnson. Both Eisenhower and Rogers knew of Johnson's presidential ambitions and hoped that would propel him to support the bill and convince fellow Democrats to do the same. But Johnson did not want a civil rights bill passed in 1959. Without his Democratic partner, Eisenhower's bill stood no chance, though Congress allowed the extension of the Civil Rights Commission.

Eisenhower's State of the Union address on January 7, 1960, was redolent with phrases of racial equality: "In all our hopes and plans for a better world, we all recognize that provincial and racial prejudices must be combated." Particularly, "the right to vote has been one of the strongest pillars of a free society. Our first duty is to protect this right against all encroachment." Ike returned to the theme of the Fourteenth Amendment on three separate occasions in the speech, noting "bias still deprives some persons in this country of equal protection of the laws." And he challenged Congress to reconsider the civil rights legislation he'd introduced the previous year. He expressed confidence that "Congress will thus signal to the world that our Government is striving for equality under the law for all our people."[39]

On February 8, 1960, Illinois Republican senator and Minority Leader Everett Dirksen reintroduced the president's civil rights bill to the Senate. One section had been added to the proposal submitted the previous year. Following the recommendation of the Civil Rights Commission, Attorney General Rogers added a provision allowing the attorney general to appoint temporary voting registrars in states deemed to have discriminated against African American voting. The stipulation was sure to arouse the ire of Southern Democrats.[40]

By February 1960, the context within which the civil rights debate proceeded in Washington had changed. On the night of January 31, four freshmen sat in a dormitory room at historically black North Carolina A&T College (now University) in Greensboro, North Carolina. Earlier that day, one of the students, Joseph McNeil, had been denied counter service at the Greyhound bus terminal in Greensboro. The rebuff was typical in the South of that era, but McNeil, looking for sympathy and support, took up the issue with his friends that evening. As one of them, Franklin McCain, recalled, the discussion eventually centered on the question of "At what point does the moral man act against injustice?" Once they agreed that they had reached that point, the question became what to do about it. They decided on a sit-in at the Woolworth lunch counter in downtown Greensboro the next day.[41]

The sit-ins were quiet, nonviolent actions (though they often provoked a violent response) geared to the philosophy that unmerited suffering was redemptive. As McCain noted, "The most powerful and potent weapon that people have literally no defense for is love [and] kindness." They were unaware that the Congress of Racial Equality (CORE) had employed the sit-in in Chicago twenty years earlier and that as recently as 1958 and 1959 students had successfully desegregated some lunch counters in Tulsa and Miami. The lunch counter was an obvious target because it highlighted the preposterous and humiliating nature of segregation. African Americans could purchase toothpaste and underwear at Woolworth's, but could not buy a soft drink.[42]

The four freshman entered Woolworth's the following day, February 1, sat down with their schoolbooks, ordered, and were refused service. Within two weeks sit-ins had spread to fifteen other Southern cities. By April, demonstrations were occurring in fifty-four cities in nine Southern states. By the end of the year, seventy thousand students had sat in at lunch counters in one hundred Southern cities. The gifted generation was taking matters into their own hands.[43]

When a reporter asked Eisenhower's opinion on the sit-ins, the president replied, "My own understanding is that when an establishment belongs to the public, opened under public charter and so on, equal rights are involved." On the protest tactic—the sit-in—Eisenhower stated, "As long as they are in orderly fashion, [they] are not only constitutional, they have been recognized in our country as proper since we have been founded."[44]

Ernest ("Fritz") Hollings, Democratic governor of South Carolina, fired off a telegram to the president charging that his comments DID GREAT DAMAGE TO PEACE AND GOOD ORDER IN SOUTH CAROLINA. Normally, Eisenhower responded to such comments from government officials. This time he ignored it. Ike also received a telegram from Martin Luther King Jr.: SUCH AN AFFIRMATION GIVES NEW HOPE TO MEN SEEKING TO MOVE FROM THE LONG NIGHT OF OPPRESSION INTO THE BRIGHT DAY BREAK OF FREEDOM AND HUMAN DIGNITY.[45]

Two weeks after the sit-ins began, Senate Majority Leader Johnson exercised a parliamentary maneuver in partnership with Senator Dirksen to liberate the civil rights bill from Senator Eastland's committee. It was an election year, and Johnson's political ambitions overcame his earlier reluctance to advance civil rights legislation. But it might not have been mere political cynicism that motivated Johnson's cooperation with the administration. In January 1960, he promised a group of civil rights leaders that he would try to pass a civil rights bill because it "is the moral responsibility to protect every person's constitutional rights." The following month, he told a North Carolina reporter, "I do not believe that we can continue indefinitely without coming to some sensible resolution [on civil rights]."[46]

Johnson attached the sections of the civil rights bill to a bill already being considered by the full Senate that would permit the U.S. Army to lease a barracks as a temporary replacement for a burned-out school in Missouri. Southern Democrats, outfoxed, launched a filibuster. The bipartisan team of Dirksen and Johnson devised a counterstrategy, ordering the Senate to stay in session around the clock beginning on February 29. It was a gamble; the Senate had never broken a full Southern filibuster against any civil rights measure.

After a record 125 hours and 31 minutes, Johnson called for a break in the debate on March 6. The bill would have to be modified or else it was dead. What emerged was a mild voting rights bill that provided only for the controversial temporary registrars in states that violated African Americans' right to vote. Southern Democrats considered this limited bill a victory and ended their filibuster. On April 8 it passed the Senate, 71–18. All of the negative votes came from Southern Democratic senators. The three architects of the 1960 Civil Rights Act—Johnson, Dirksen, and Eisenhower—called the law "a step forward," a metaphor the administration had used when the Senate passed the 1957 bill. Steps forward were good, but the strides toward justice were small.[47]

In practice, the law barely advanced the cause of voting rights in the South beyond the 1957 Civil Rights Act. Still, the newly reconstituted Civil Rights Division within the Justice Department processed forty-three hundred voting rights complaints and succeeded in registering 1,377 African Americans. With the ability of federal courts to appoint "voting referees" when district courts "found a discriminatory 'pattern of practice,'" the 1960 act was more effective than its predecessor. The department demanded voting records in seventeen Southern counties and filed suits to compel compliance. But the burden remained on black registrants to step forward, a significant hurdle. Attorney General Rogers immediately requested voting records from one county each in South Carolina, Louisiana, Georgia, and Alabama, but little came from those requests. The act did not account for the culture of violence and intimidation that existed in the Deep South.[48]

Eisenhower believed that, eventually, the courts would compel the racial changes the legislation only weakly advanced. As Truman had turned from a recalcitrant Congress to the courts, Eisenhower, through his appointment powers, assured an integrationist majority on the U.S. Supreme Court and, equally important, on the federal district courts. Although Eisenhower never announced a litmus test for a Supreme Court nominee, all of his appointments were integrationists. This was the case with both Earl Warren and William J. Brennan.

When Associate Justice Harold Burton announced his retirement due to ill health in the fall of 1958, the president named Potter Stewart, originally from Michigan, now resident in Ohio, to replace him. Stewart was serving on the Sixth Circuit Court of Appeals and, like Brennan, brought impeccable juridical qualifications to the position. Senator Richard Russell led the futile opposition to Stewart's confirmation after Stewart, in an unusual moment of candor for a judicial nominee, told the Southerners on James O. Eastland's Senate Judiciary Committee that "they should not vote for him if they assumed he was 'dedicated to the cause of overturning that decision [*Brown*].' 'Because,' Stewart declared, 'I am not.'"[49]

Eisenhower also appointed three judges, Elbert Parr Tuttle of Georgia, John R. Brown of Texas, and John Minor Wisdom of Louisiana, all supporters of the *Brown* decision, to the U.S. Court of Appeals for the Fifth Judicial Circuit, which served Alabama, Florida, Georgia, Louisiana, Mississippi, and Texas, states that were the most contentious venues for civil rights litigation. In October 1955, Eisenhower appointed Frank M. Johnson Jr. to the Alabama Middle District Court, a trial court subordinate to the Fifth Circuit. Johnson served on the panel that issued the court order striking down segregated seating on Montgomery's buses in 1956 and that, nine years later, would order Alabama governor George C. Wallace not to interfere with the voting rights march from Selma to Montgomery.[50]

By the time the 1960 Civil Rights Act passed the U.S. Senate, the national discourse on race had changed from what it was in 1957. Although white violence against African Americans in the South was hardly a new vogue, incidents received broader coverage. Wider reporting of violence increased support for the 1960 Civil Rights Act. An editorial in *Redbook* in February 1959 was typical, citing bombings of schools and places of worship associated with school desegregation, concluding, "This session of Congress will have to face the challenge of protecting the rights of all minority groups."[51]

Little Rock had exposed to a national audience the venality of segregationist politics and the unseemly violent side of racial segregation. The Old South might linger for a while, but events in Washington and in the South had exposed its decrepitude. This was not 1861, no matter the analogies Southern Democrats drew in the Senate. Conservative Republicans could no longer abide their convenient coalition with Southern Democrats. And Northern Democrats could no longer ignore the festering sore in their midst. Morality may have figured into the growing revulsion against the South, but economic and especially political considerations would drive meaningful change.

WHILE THE SOUTH WRESTLED with schools and voting rights, the racial flash point in the North centered on housing and neighborhoods. These latter conflicts remained outside the realm of federal legislation and litigation, at least for the time being. But they reflected Northern whites' determination to maintain the color line as much as Southern whites' efforts to bar African Americans from schools and polling booths. The decade of the 1960s would illuminate the truth that white supremacy was no respecter of latitude in the United States.

CHAPTER 14

CONFIDENCE

THIS MOMENT TESTED THE WILL and judgment of the president. In the midst of the Little Rock imbroglio, on October 4, 1957, the Soviet Union launched a satellite into orbit around the earth. The Russians called it *Sputnik*, or "fellow traveler." The small satellite was just over 180 pounds and no bigger around than a beach ball. But it circled the earth every ninety-two minutes at eighteen thousand miles per hour. To compound the surprise and embarrassment to the United States, the Soviets launched a larger craft one month later, with scientific instruments and a dog that had medical instruments strapped to its body. Worse still, in December, the United States launched its response, a Vanguard missile. It rose two feet off the launching pad and then crumbled to the ground in flames. People called it Flopnik or Stay-putnik. Ike wrote ruefully to Ralph McGill that the Abilene High School Yearbook of 1909 predicted that his brother Edgar would become president of the United States and that Dwight would be a history professor at Yale. "There are many times when I certainly wish *that* particular prophecy had come true."[1]

The launch of *Sputnik* highlighted two issues: the technological superiority of the Soviet Union, and the military consequences of such superiority. Under enormous pressure from the military, members of Congress, and many American citizens, Eisenhower had to decide how best to respond to the new threat. Rather than request significant increases in military spending, the president instead emphasized the need to expand the nation's educational capabilities, especially, though not exclusively, in the sciences. Investing in people rather than in hardware, Ike believed, was the best way to ensure the nation's security in the long term.

Remaining calm in the midst of a political and media storm stoked by fear was one of the president's more significant contributions. Secret overflights of Russia by high-altitude U-2 planes reassured him that the United States had a commanding lead in warheads and missiles. Majority Leader Johnson, who was quick to offer military solutions for almost any foreign threat, announced that *Sputnik* was "a disaster . . . comparable to Pearl Harbor." The *New*

Republic, a liberal journal, compared *Sputnik* to "the discovery by Columbus of America" and cited its launch as "proof . . . the Soviet Union has gained a commanding lead." Physicist Edward Teller disagreed with Senator Johnson's likening of *Sputnik* to Pearl Harbor. *Sputnik* was worse: the United States had lost "a battle more important and greater than Pearl Harbor."[2]

Eisenhower's military background played well in the crisis. He realized that the military significance of *Sputnik* was minimal. Sure, the Soviets' rockets had more thrust than any developed in the United States, but they lacked accuracy. In the delivery of nuclear warheads, this would be a serious handicap, as the president understood. Added to this, the United States had superior nuclear-missile capacity. At a news conference five days after the *Sputnik* launch, Eisenhower downplayed its strategic significance, prompting a question from Hazel Markel of NBC: "Mr. President, in light of the great faith which the American people have in your military knowledge and leadership, are you saying that at this time with the Russian satellite whirling around the world, you are not more concerned nor overly concerned about our nation's security?" Ike replied calmly that the satellite "does not raise my apprehensions not one iota," adding, "We have no enemies on the moon." As for developing more bombs and missiles, Ike asked, "What is going to be done with this tremendous number of enormous weapons?" How many times "could [you] kill the same man?"[3]

He dismissed calls for increased defense expenditures. His rationale was that these appropriations would come at the expense of civilian needs. Reminding Americans of the broader picture, the president noted, "We must remember that we are defending a way of life." Turning America into a "garrison state" would mean taking the risk that "all we are striving to defend . . . could disappear."[4]

This was not a new philosophical bent for the president. Many recall the now-famous remarks warning about the military-industrial complex from his farewell address in 1961. But it was a theme he advanced early in his presidency. In a speech before the American Society of Newspaper Editors in April 1953, Eisenhower declared:

> Every gun that is made, every warship launched, every rocket fired, signifies, in the final sense, a theft from those who hunger and are not fed, those who are cold and are not clothed . . . It is spending the sweat of its laborers, the genius of its scientists, the hopes of its children. The cost of one modern heavy bomber is this: a modern brick school in more than thirty cities . . . This is not a way of life at all, in any true

sense. Under the cloud of threatening war, it is humanity hanging from a cross of iron.[5]

EISENHOWER WOULD REFUSE to nail America to that cross of iron. In the days immediately after the Soviet launch, he gave two televised speeches designed to both calm public fears and outline a policy response. He cited "glaring deficiencies" in scientific and engineering fields. To address these short-comings, Eisenhower promised, "The federal government . . . must and will do its part." He had tried unsuccessfully over the previous four years to secure a federal aid-to-education act. He hoped to use *Sputnik* to break the stalemate.[6]

Eisenhower's first response was to sponsor the National Defense Education Act (NDEA) of 1958 to strengthen education in the sciences, foreign languages, and area studies in universities. It was the most important national education legislation in nearly one hundred years. The NDEA provided scholarships for college students, with preference to those in defense-related fields, and aid to universities to improve instruction in those fields. It represented an important breakthrough for the federal government with respect to direct aid for college students. The preamble to the act emphasized that precedent: "The national interest requires . . . that the federal government give assistance to education for programs which are important to our national defense." Here was another area where the federal government responded to the changing economic and technological landscape by assuming broader responsibilities. Between the passage of the NDEA in 1958 and the time Neil Armstrong walked on the moon, eleven years later, 1.5 million men and women of the gifted generation had gone to college on NDEA's student loan program, and fifteen thousand of those had earned doctoral degrees.[7]

Some of the educational reforms generated by the NDEA legislation had already emerged in public schools by the time *Sputnik* launched. Credit the boomers' own curiosity about natural science and their parents' belief in the importance of foreign languages. Enrollment in these subjects soared in the postwar era. As one educator noted, "Let's not worry about keeping up with the Russians. Let's just keep up with the children." Science fairs became ubiquitous across the country before *Sputnik*, but participation increased by nearly 20 percent following the Soviet launch. What the NDEA accomplished was to fund and boost the trend rather than initiate it. It also performed the valuable service of relieving parents and students from financial stress. Scientifically minded youngsters became the stars of their communities and "the objects of fond and anxious national attention." Houston held a parade to honor star students. Federal funding leveraged local support as Houston's top science students received $100 savings bonds for their efforts.[8]

Unfortunately, Eisenhower could not get Congress to solve the crisis in school construction and teacher salaries at the primary and secondary school levels. The church-state issues, the concerns about federal control of education, and the controversy over school segregation scuttled legislative efforts, despite widespread public support.[9]

Shortly after submitting his proposal for the NDEA to Congress, Eisenhower named the first special assistant for science and technology, James R. Killian Jr., president of MIT. Killian formed and chaired the President's Science Advisory Committee (PSAC), which included representatives from the nation's scientific and academic elites. Glenn Seaborg, chancellor of the University of California, Berkeley, chaired a PSAC panel that, in 1960, issued recommendations concluding that strengthening basic research and graduate studies was a federal responsibility. That responsibility involved funding both research and infrastructure, including buildings, labs, and equipment. The report was clear on the government's role: "Whether the quantity and quality of basic research and graduate education in the United States will be adequate depends primarily upon the government of the United States. From this responsibility the Federal Government has no escape." By 1963, the federal government had, in fact, assumed primary responsibility for supporting basic research. Equally striking, but much less publicized, was the rapid growth of federal funding of "nonscience" research through HEW.[10]

Federally funded research across all disciplines grew dramatically after 1958. It was rarely a case of elevating science at the expense of social science and the humanities. An editorial in *Life* magazine in February 1958 called the juxtaposition of science and the humanities "in separate, self-sealing compartments" nonsense. The problem was that the two areas were estranged from each other in the classroom. The editor called for more integration and cited Rachel Carson's *The Sea Around Us* (1951) as an exemplar of combining "good science and good literature."[11]

To place the postwar federal efforts in a broader perspective, federal support accounted for more than 50 percent of all U.S. research and development funding between the 1950s and the 1970s, exceeding the total R&D funds expended by other OECD (Organisation for Economic Co-operation and Development) countries combined over this period. Federal funding for R&D increased from less than 0.7 percent of the gross domestic product in 1953, or $17 billion, to 1.8 percent of the GDP by 1959, or $40 billion. Research spending as a percentage of the GDP would peak in 1964 and decline thereafter. By 2004 federal research spending as a percentage of the GDP was roughly at the 1953 level. These initiatives in the Eisenhower administration provided prime examples of government stepping in when private industry cannot assume the risk or the high initial outlay for research, especially basic research. Federal funding not only assumed the risk but also often leveraged private industry and universities to engage in research, as such spending increased as well.[12]

Eisenhower's efforts corresponded with economists' views on the government's role in this new age of technology. John Kenneth Galbraith in *The Affluent Society* (1958), an influential postwar analysis of the American economy, heralded the growing importance of technological advance and the government's robust response to this new reality. It was a mistake, Galbraith noted, to believe that nowadays "brilliant, isolated, and intuitive inventions are still a principal instrument of technological progress." To the contrary, innovation "has become a highly organized enterprise," hence the need for government investment.[13]

Eisenhower increased by twentyfold the amount the federal government spent on space-related research and then sent a bill to Congress to authorize the National Aeronautics and Space Agency (NASA) to manage the nation's space and missile technology. It was instructive that Eisenhower entrusted this important role to a civilian agency rather than folding it into the armed forces.[14]

But the president did involve the Defense Department in his education and research strategy. Shortly after the Soviet's second launch, the Pentagon established what would become the Defense Advanced Research Projects Agency (DARPA). This agency laid the foundation for today's information economy, as it helped develop the Internet, chip design, and artificial-intelligence software. The federal government provided the seed money for Silicon Valley.[15]

The NDEA and subsequent legislation that boosted appropriations for NSF and NIH benefited major research universities, continuing a tradition that began during World War II, when scientists helped to develop radar and physicists at the University of Chicago experimented with controlled nuclear fission. By 1954, federal agencies accounted for 69 percent of total university research budgets. In the 1960s, universities outside the elite institutions would also participate in this partnership, and not only in the sciences.[16]

The gifted generation that began enrolling in universities from 1960 forward were the major beneficiaries of this expanded federal support. Harvey Rubin, for example, credited NSF and NASA grants with enabling him to complete his doctorate at Columbia University during the 1960s. At Bell Labs, his team helped to develop many of the innovations in computer technology that are commonplace today.[17]

Eisenhower would pay a political price for keeping the lid on defense spending and his seeming indifference to the exploration of outer space. An editorial in *Life* magazine emphasized this latter point, stating in italics, "*Space has no real friends at the top,*" and concluding with a serious yet ultimately silly dictum: "Who controls the moon may control the political lot of mankind."[18]

The alleged missile gap, as much a myth as the strategic importance of the moon, would become an issue in the 1960 presidential campaign when Democratic candidate John F. Kennedy charged the administration (of which his opponent, Vice President Richard M. Nixon, was a part) with leaving the United States dangerously vulnerable to attack.

Little Rock and *Sputnik* set America back. Stanley High, editor of *Reader's Digest*, wrote to Eisenhower in October 1957 to commiserate on these twin bolts of misfortune. He noted "a vast amount of unjustified defeatism abroad in the land." What the country needed most was "a heartening, inspiring word." More by his actions than by his words, Eisenhower calmed public fears, restored American confidence, and promoted specific policies to address the causes of the problems in the first place.[19]

The president set a good example. The nation quickly regained its confidence, in itself and in its future. That was the key, the future. Most of the nation looked forward, not back to some mythical past. The broad prosperity, the massive public works projects, and the recognition that racial equality was attainable had much to do with presidential leadership. Other forces were obviously involved, but it would have been easy to follow along with the status quo. Instead, Eisenhower envisioned the future and shaped it.

THE 1960 PRESIDENTIAL ELECTION centered more on the candidates than on the issues. The Democratic and Republican Party platforms differed little on domestic or foreign affairs, with both parties affirming civil rights for African Americans and a moderately active federal government. Demography had moved the Democratic Party further to the left on civil rights. Democratic senators in the North and the West who supported the 1960 Civil Rights Act resided in states that accounted for 70 percent of the presidential vote. The Democratic platform promised to assure "equal access . . . to . . . voting booths, schoolrooms, jobs, housing, and public facilities." The platform also praised the sit-ins, and it promised to create a fair employment practices commission, a body Southern Democrats condemned. Since the platform required only a majority vote, Southern delegates' objections could not block the plank. If they chose to walk out, the precedent of 1948 offered little solace as to the result of that departure.[20]

The Republicans met in late July in Chicago, two weeks after the Democrats. They had no concerns about an obstreperous Southern wing. Their president had signed two civil rights laws, and their leading candidate, Vice President Richard M. Nixon, was closely identified with that legislation. Ike's positive response to the sit-ins and his steadfastness in the Little Rock crisis, along with the violence and other forms of resistance in the South, guaranteed a strong civil rights plank as well. The Republican plank also promised fair employment and to "end the discriminatory membership practices" in labor unions. The two parties had fashioned the strongest civil rights platforms in their respective histories.[21]

John F. Kennedy was the Democratic nominee, besting two-time loser Adlai Stevenson and Southern favorite Lyndon B. Johnson. Kennedy's was a historic nomination, the second Roman Catholic presidential candidate for a major party. Well before the convention, his religion became a concern. Under the headline "Should a Catholic Be President?" the Right Reverend James A. Pike, an Episcopal bishop in San Francisco, raised the issue in a December 1959 article in *Life* magazine. He questioned the "first allegiance" of Senator Kennedy and where he stood on the relationship between church and state.[22]

A convocation of two hundred cardinals, archbishops, and bishops in Washington, D.C., the previous month concerned Pike when it condemned using federal funds to promote birth control in economically underdeveloped countries. Pike chaired the clergymen's national advisory committee of Planned Parenthood and asked Senator Kennedy whether the convocation's ruling would be binding on him. Kennedy's response of "not necessarily" did not satisfy Pike. While Pike was fairly confident that Rome would not issue orders to an American president, its influence in national affairs with a Catholic president remained unclear. "To ask questions about this subject," Pike explained, "and to weigh a particular candidate's stand on it is not bigotry, but responsible citizenship."[23]

Pike was one of the more liberal clergymen. Kennedy traveled to Houston to meet with more conservative Protestant clergymen, mainly evangelical Christians, to assure them that he would not take directives from the pope. He stated that the United States was a nation where the "separation of church and state is absolute—where no Catholic prelate would tell the president how to act, and no Protestant minister would tell his parishioners for whom to vote." More personally, "I am not the Catholic candidate for president . . . I do not speak for my church on public matters—and the church does not speak for me."[24]

A little more than three decades earlier, Democratic presidential candidate Al Smith faced similar questions, and his Catholic religion undoubtedly cost him millions of votes. Any Democrat would probably have lost to Herbert Hoover in 1928, but the religious vitriol against Smith revealed a strong strain of anti-Catholic bigotry in the country. Had the nation changed sufficiently in the ensuing thirty-two years?

Several factors hurt the Republican cause. A mild recession occurred early in 1960. Though productivity increased, employment did not. The long downward slope of manufacturing jobs in the United States was beginning to accelerate. Tens of thousands of men (and they were mostly men) laid off were not rehired. Kennedy ran best in those areas with the highest unemployment. Also, the first televised presidential debates had some impact, though it was hard to quantify. Kennedy looked at ease, Nixon looked tired at times, occasionally scowling, and inadequate makeup failed to cover his five o'clock shadow. Those who heard the debate on radio concluded that Nixon won. But television viewers felt the opposite.

The men differed little on domestic public policy. CBS commentator Eric Sevareid complained that they were "tidy, buttoned-down men . . . completely packaged products. The Processed Politician has finally arrived." Harry Truman was scathing in his assessment of the candidates: "They seem improbable, skillful technicians. The ideas are too contrived . . . These two . . . bore the hell out of me."[25]

The forty-three-year-old Kennedy epitomized change as the youngest presidential candidate in American history. He also had wily campaign advisers. Two weeks prior to the election, Kennedy called Coretta Scott King, Martin Luther King Jr.'s wife. Atlanta police had arrested King for attempting to integrate an Atlanta department store dining room. Kennedy wanted to extend his sympathy to Mrs. King and assure her that his brother, Bobby, was speaking with Georgia authorities about her husband's release, which occurred shortly thereafter. The connection between Bobby's calls and King's release was not clear, but the key point was that John had reached out to King's family, and that made a significant impression on African American voters in the North, who gave Kennedy 68 percent of their vote, providing a crucial lift in key Northern states in a tight race.[26]

Voters' affection for Eisenhower did not transfer to Nixon, or to other Republicans. Eisenhower's backing of Nixon was lukewarm at best. During the campaign, Nixon had boasted that he advised Eisenhower on a number of key decisions. At a news conference in August, a reporter asked the president to cite an example of a major idea of Nixon's that the administration had adopted. Ike replied, "If you give me a week, I might think of one. I don't remember."[27]

An important and, at the time, surprising decision to select Texas senator Lyndon B. Johnson as Kennedy's running mate helped secure Texas for the

Democrats. Many in Kennedy's circle despised the Texan as uncouth and devious. But they needed Texas. They also hoped his presence on the ticket would allay fears in the rest of the South.

The election was one of the closest in American history. Kennedy received 49.7 percent of the popular vote to Nixon's 49.6 percent. The Democrat held a comfortable majority in the Electoral College—303 to 219—reflecting the growing power of Northern metropolitan areas in the national electorate.[28]

Like Eisenhower, Kennedy had negative coattails. The Democrats lost twenty seats in the House and one in the Senate. They still held a 263–174 advantage in the House and a strong 65–35 lead in the Senate. But voting on key issues often defaulted to a conservative/liberal axis rather than a Democrat/Republican split. And Southern Democrats still controlled key Senate committees.[29]

Whether Kennedy would follow through on Eisenhower's initiatives, especially in civil rights, was uncertain. His primary interest was in foreign, not domestic, policy. And he was mindful of the long shadow cast by Southern Democrats in the U.S. Senate. With a Republican no longer in the White House, he could not count on GOP senators to support his initiatives, which meant greater reliance on Southern Democrats. Truman ignored the damage done to his overall domestic program by pushing civil rights in Congress. Kennedy would not.

DURING THE 1956 PRESIDENTIAL campaign, the columnists Stewart and Joseph Alsop set out on a cross-country trip to assess the political climate. That President Eisenhower was popular among the voters was hardly a major scoop. But what impressed the Alsops most during their tour was "how nice Americans are." They accounted for the graciousness as a reflection of the people's "unquestioning confidence in the American future . . . an innate sense of personal equality, personal dignity and personal freedom" that transcended class and region. The gifted generation would grow up in a confident nation, not only prosperous but also broadening inclusiveness, even if by small steps. The direction was unmistakable. If Americans had crossed the meridian in accepting an active government during and immediately after World War II, they had established a settlement over that divide by 1960.[30]

Everything was up. The gross national product increased from $355.3 billion in 1950 to $487.7 billion by 1960, or a 37 percent increase for the decade. More important, the wealth was widespread. The median family income doubled between 1945 and 1960. By 1960, the middle 60 percent of Americans earned nearly 55 percent of the national income. By contrast, in 2013, they earned 45 percent of the nation income.

As Keynes had predicted, government spending, such as funding the inter-state highway network, supporting research and development programs, and subsidizing homeownership, would repay itself by putting money into consumers' pockets. By 1960, the median family income was 30 percent higher in purchasing power than in 1950. Nearly 62 percent of the nation's homes were owner occupied in 1960, compared to 43.6 percent in 1940. The baby boom accounted for a good deal of this growth, which, in turn, generated more babies. During a decade when immigration was relatively low, the American population grew by 19.1 percent, the highest of any decade in the twentieth century, except for the 1900s. The babies, then children, then teen-agers, spurred demand for homes, household gadgetry, cars, radios and tele-visions, clothing, and toys. And it would get better. The federal government made it easier to buy a home, and anything, it seemed, could be bought on time, or even with a credit card, which made its debut in 1950. It was an era seemingly without limits. Scientists had conquered polio and were training their sights on heart disease and cancer.[31]

Social critics scarcely knew what to make of this brimming confidence. Some claimed it made for generic blandness; if everyone were happy, the creative edginess of society would disappear. It was a consensus society, they argued, with little dissent, and even in rebellion on the screen or in books, the target, if any, remained unclear. John Gardner, one of the nation's leading educators, warned in 1960, "We seem in danger of losing our bearings, of surrendering to a 'cult of easiness.'" The individual seemed to be in retreat, subsumed under the national quest for things instigated by advertising and the comfort of conformity. But other critics claimed that instead of becoming an undifferentiated blob, Americans were spinning off into their own indi-vidual pursuits, ruining the sense of society as an organic mutually depen-dent whole. There was no great purpose around which people could unite.[32]

But the dichotomy between the individual and the communal was false. They were both part of a larger whole: individuals with the means to pursue opportunities will create a more integrated and mutually respectful society. What was going on in the 1950s was the building of a more inclusive society. The media, the people themselves, and the federal government, particularly the president, insisted that the bounty of American life be shared in a wider arc, not only among white Protestant men. In 1960, poet and playwright Archibald MacLeish called for a rededication to our national purpose, which was "to liberate from domination; to set men free." But a rededication was not necessary. We were already on that path with the young men who sat down at a lunch counter and with a president who insisted that education was a better investment than missiles.[33]

The federal government would be the major architect of this new society. This was not an abandonment of American tradition, but rather its fulfillment. Eisenhower expressed impatience with Republican conservatives who were obsessive about that alleged American golden era. In May 1960, he vented this frustration to his sister-in-law Lucy Eisenhower, the wife of his conservative brother, Edgar, who had exasperated Ike on numerous occasions. He stated emphatically that "this country is *not* going to the right," and that "the economic and political affairs of our people are not going to be so conducted as to take our nation back to the days of the 1890s." Returning to his favorite theme of a cooperative commonwealth, he stated (as Truman had) that America had become an urban, industrial nation and could no longer afford a philosophy of government rooted in a nineteenth-century nation: "Our nation has become not only highly industrialized but highly interdependent among its several parts and classes."

Perhaps Eisenhower's singular accomplishment as president was to extol the virtues of government action in those areas private enterprise could not reach, a key principle of the commonwealth ideal. By 1960, a strong majority of Americans supported an activist government. In a survey that year, 58 percent of respondents agreed with the statement "The government in Washington ought to see to it that everybody who wants to work can find a job." While some were neutral on the idea, only 16 percent disagreed with the statement. On the question of federal aid to public schools, a particular cause of the president's, 65 percent approved, even if it meant higher taxes, and only 25 percent opposed. Still, William Buckley's view of limited government and the imminence of Barry Goldwater's rise to prominence indicated that the consensus was hardly universal.[34]

The battles over civil rights, in Congress, in the courts, and in the streets, began to register in polling by 1960. The Survey Research Center found agreement among 62 percent of respondents to the statement "If Negroes are not getting fair treatment in jobs and housing, the government should see to it that they do." There was less support, however, for government involvement in school desegregation, as 45 percent favored that strategy and 41 percent opposed. Substantial majorities of respondents favored Medicare and efforts to preserve wilderness areas in national parks, forests, wildlife refuges, and other public lands. That such government activity would increase federal spending did not elicit much concern among the respondents, though they favored a balanced budget. But when it came to cutting specific programs to achieve that goal, voters drew back.[35]

Surveys indicated a high level of trust in the government. During the late 1950s, 90 percent of respondents agreed that they "usually have confidence that the government will do what is right." In 1960, 76 percent of respondents agreed that the results of government intervention in domestic affairs were positive. Other polls reflected great pride in the nation's political institutions.[36]

Redbook magazine, which rarely commented on politics, editorialized favorably about an activist government. The editors assumed that their readers felt the same way. In a February 1959 editorial, the magazine urged an agenda that "will touch the lives of the nation's young families most intimately." The editors scolded Congress for not passing the administration's $2.5 billion housing bill for the construction of new homes.[37]

Civil rights was another *Redbook* priority, an issue the magazine would not have touched editorially a few years earlier. But the persistent violence and resistance in the South, as well as the debates over the new federal legislation, had raised the national consciousness. Calling it "the most complex and explosive issue facing the nation today," the editors lectured, "Congress will have to face the challenge of protecting the rights of all minority groups."[38]

In addition to these priorities, the editors noted several other areas they hoped Congress would address with legislation, including federal aid to education, measures to mitigate the costs of health care, economic aid to depressed areas of the country, and protection for workers from colluding unions and employers. For those Americans who hoped the New Deal would topple with the end of the Truman administration, such an agenda must have been dispiriting. *Redbook* was merely ratifying what many Americans, and especially the president, already believed: government action on behalf of Americans now living in a much more complex society than they had earlier in the century was not a choice but a necessity.[39]

Eisenhower had convinced a good number in his party to remove their longing gaze from the 1920s and focus on the possibilities of America's future. Most of the great achievements of his administration came with bipartisan support, of necessity. The establishment of the Department of Health, Education, and Welfare, a project that had eluded Truman, reflected the expansion of government in those respective areas. The Eisenhower administration also succeeded in garnering extensive increases in Social Security, funding for the NDEA, and major infrastructure projects such as the St. Lawrence Seaway and the interstate highway network. The president approved antirecessionary stimulus spending, raised the minimum wage, and extended unemployment compensation. Ike's 1958 budget was a landmark of sorts and reflected how far the nation had increased federal expenditures. It nearly doubled the federal budget from the Truman years and raised the national debt by billions of dollars.[40]

Eisenhower's handling of Little Rock and *Sputnik* played to the nation's highest ideals of the importance of the rule of law, and the refusal to give in to fear. Most important were the admittedly small steps taken to redress the greatest gap between American ideal and reality: race relations. The civil rights measures of 1957 and 1960 did not usher in a new era of racial equality, but they did mark a procedural trail through Congress that could pave the way for more extensive legislation in the future. And Eisenhower's executive actions on behalf of civil rights in the District of Columbia, within the armed forces, and at military installations reflected his commitment to racial justice. He used the law and the federal judiciary—which he had a hand in shaping— to reinforce that commitment. When Eisenhower left the White House in January 1961, the fate of the New Deal and the philosophy of government activism on behalf of the commonwealth were secure.

As the *Redbook* editorial indicated, problems existed in the midst of plenty. With prosperity and widespread confidence, these issues might easily be over-looked. But they were not. In 1960, noted political scientist Clinton Rossiter cataloged the crisis amid plenty. He identified "the steadily widening gap between the richness of our private lives and the poverty of our public services, between a standard of living inside our homes that is the highest in the world and a standard of living outside them that is fast becoming a national disgrace." He observed that the U.S. economy was able to satisfy the demands of its rapidly growing (and young) population for food, clothing, entertainment, housing, private transportation, and technology, but it did a poor job alleviating urban blight, environmental pollution, traffic congestion, and inadequate public education.[41]

How to solve these issues? Rossiter's prescription: "These public problems will never be handled in the style of a great nation until we rid our minds of threadbare prejudices about the role of government, value the things we buy with our taxes as highly as those we buy with what is left after taxes, and distribute our richest treasure—men and women of intelligence and character—more judiciously among the callings and professions." Americans would meet these challenges during the 1960s, with the government taking an active role in expanding the umbrella of full citizenship and in ensuring the gender, ethnic, and racial equity that implied.[42]

PART III

GIFTS

CHAPTER 15

THE COWBOY

LYNDON BAINES JOHNSON SHARED many of the hardships that characterized the early lives of Harry Truman and Dwight Eisenhower, only worse. His parents, Rebekah and Sam Ealy Johnson Jr., were a poor match. Sam Ealy, temperamental and domineering, contrasted with the refined and highly intelligent Rebekah Baines. Home was a battleground. Sam Ealy's ill-fated business ventures in cotton futures and other speculative enterprises pushed the family to the brink of financial ruin. By the time Lyndon was born in 1908, the Johnson clan had reached a plateau of futility.[1]

Sam Ealy's ancestors had come to Texas from Alabama by way of Georgia. The hill country was not particularly kind to agriculture, though its abundant grasses could feed cattle. The Johnsons went into the livestock business, only to see their investment crash when the supply of cattle far exceeded the demand for beef after the Civil War. The Buntons, in-laws of Sam Ealy's father, fortunately owned a subsistence farm in the hill country where the Johnsons moved. Sam Ealy was born there in 1877. Following his father's example, Sam Ealy entered politics as an "agrarian liberal." But financial difficulties ended his political career.[2]

Rebekah came from a different social stratum. She was the granddaughter of the founder of Baylor University. Rebekah was a voracious consumer of Victorian literature and the arts. She attempted to impart her cultural tastes to Lyndon, a difficult task in the raw hill country of Texas, where she moved after marrying Sam Ealy. Stonewall, Texas, was only fifty miles west of the capital at Austin, but centuries removed, it seemed, from the civilization Rebekah craved. Lyndon was a twentieth-century baby, but he grew up in a nineteenth-century environment.

Raising Lyndon in a ramshackle house without any running water or electricity was difficult for Rebekah. Lyndon would be her compensation. As he related, "The first year of her marriage was the worst year of her life. Then I came along and suddenly everything was all right again. I could do all the things she never did." She refused to be defined by her straitened financial circumstances, nor would she allow her son to be so identified either. Just as strong women shaped the lives of Harry Truman and Dwight Eisenhower, so Lyndon benefited from an educated and ambitious mother. All three men grew up with problematic fathers, financial reverses, and, courtesy of their mothers, a deep appreciation of the value of formal education.[3]

Stonewall, Texas, derived its name from the Confederate general, and Lyndon would spend a good deal of his political career both embracing and rejecting the Southern portion of his heritage. He would be most comfortable hobnobbing with the Southern Senate grandees, but would insist to the press and his Northern colleagues that he was just a Texas cowboy and prove it by riding around his ranch on a horse. His politics veered back and forth as well, until, finally, he adopted the nation rather than a region as his political guiding star.

At the age of sixteen, Lyndon struck out for California, where he picked up work that he would not have found at home. He returned to Texas sixteen months later and enrolled at Southwest Texas State Teachers College at San Marcos in 1927, much to his mother's delight. The school trained public school teachers, though even in that task it was a marginal institution academically. But for a bright and ambitious country boy, it was a place to shine.

Lyndon worked as a janitor's assistant to cover the modest tuition, practicing political oratory like a budding Bryan while he swept the halls at night. Despite a mediocre academic record his first year, he excelled as a debater and was elected editor of the campus newspaper. But he needed money and left the college to take a grade-school teaching position in Cotulla, Texas. The school, just sixty miles north of the Mexican border, enrolled mostly Mexican American students. This was a defining experience for Lyndon that he would draw upon many years later.[4]

Most of his students lived in shanties with their families, who, according to Lyndon's observation, were treated "just worse than you'd treat a dog." The Mexicans toiled on nearby ranches for a pittance. Lyndon recalled that the students were "mired in the slums . . . lashed by prejudice . . . [and] buried half alive in illiteracy." They came to school "without any breakfast, most of them hungry," with a look in their eyes and a "quizzical expression on their faces" that asked, "Why don't people like me? Why do they hate me 'cause I am brown?" Johnson, then only twenty years of age, not only served as a teacher, but also as the school principal. "I was determined," he recalled, to help "those poor little kids . . . Those little brown bodies had so little and needed so much. I was determined to spark something inside them."[5] Juan Gonzales, a student, who escaped Cotulla and was working as a well-paid civil servant at Fort Sam Houston in San Antonio, remembered that Lyndon "respected the kids more than any other teacher we ever had." It would be a hallmark of his career: whatever he set out to do, he did it thoroughly, and usually beyond anyone's expectations.[6]

The money from teaching enabled Johnson to return to college the following year. In August 1930, he graduated with a degree in history and education. Then he entered politics as a twenty-one-year-old campaign manager for a state Senate candidate. His candidate won by a landslide, but with the election season over, Johnson needed a job and received an appointment at a Houston high school teaching public speaking—a subject for which his debate experience had prepared him well—and business math, for which he had little background. Johnson elevated the debate team to one of the best in the state, but the political siren called again, as this time he worked for the election of Richard Kleberg to fill the congressional seat of Harry M. Wurzbach, who had just died. Kleberg won and hired Johnson as his secretary. In November 1931, Lyndon B. Johnson's career in Washington began.

Kleberg was not the most conscientious representative, more interested in golf, poker, and trips to Mexico than in the daily details of representing his district. That fell to the twenty-three-year-old Johnson, who had no clue about running a congressional office or serving the needs of constituents. To receive a quick education, he took four showers every morning for a week in the communal bathroom where congressional aides washed and he brushed his teeth five times at ten-minute intervals. By the end of the week, he had selected the best young men to help him understand his responsibilities. He also accosted congressmen and other staffers for advice, especially fellow Texan Sam Rayburn.

Much as the young Harry Truman thrilled to hear the oratory of William Jennings Bryan, Johnson would steal into the Senate chamber whenever Huey Long, the Louisiana Kingfish, took the Senate floor. Long "entranced" Johnson. "I thought he had a heart for the people. He hated poverty with all his soul and spoke against it until his voice was hoarse." Long advocated redistributing the nation's wealth through taxation, especially on the wealthy, and then applying those tax proceeds to guarantee every family a $5,000-a-year income, or nearly $90,000 per year in current dollars. He established Share Our Wealth clubs, which were especially popular in the South and believed the federal government had both the right and the moral responsibility to assure a living wage for all of its citizens.[7]

As Bryan influenced Truman, Long had an impact on Johnson's thinking, both about the role of the federal government and its responsibility toward the middle and working classes of ensuring a level playing field. The commonwealth ideal that fueled the political philosophy of both Truman and

Eisenhower inspired Johnson as well. The government's task, Johnson believed, was to assume "the positive role of eliminating the special interests," and that "neither misery nor squalor is inevitable so long as the government and the people are one." Johnson became an avid New Dealer and a devoted acolyte of President Franklin D. Roosevelt, signing up farmers in Kleberg's district for the cotton-reduction and farm-loan programs of the Agricultural Adjustment Act (AAA).[8]

Johnson's early attraction to Huey Long and Roosevelt's New Deal did not necessarily indicate a radical view of government activism. Like Truman's and Eisenhower's, it was more of a situational philosophy. A fellow student at San Marcos called Lyndon's philosophy "rational progressivism—adapting our institutions to changing conditions to attain the ideals of democracy." It resembled Eisenhower's "middle way." A co-worker in Kleberg's office thought that Johnson was not "a conservative or a liberal. I think he was whatever he felt he needed to be." He would retain that protean stance through his political career, confounding pundits and biographers as to where he really stood. He was perhaps, as his colleague noted, "happiest when he was in the center." For Johnson, it was the deal, not necessarily the ideology, that mattered most.[9]

From the outset of his tenure in Washington, Johnson was clearly a man in a hurry. His dedicated work ethic reflected an overwhelming ambition. It even extended to his personal life. On a visit to Austin in September 1934, he met Claudia Alta (Lady Bird) Taylor and married her after a ten-week courtship. She came from conservative East Texas, the daughter of a wealthy planter whose wife descended from equally well-off Alabama plantation owners. Lady Bird favored her mother, who often fled Texas for the Chicago opera season and enjoyed an eclectic range of fine literature. Lady Bird enrolled at the University of Texas in Austin, earning two degrees, in education and journalism, with plans to leave Texas upon graduation. She viewed her marriage to Lyndon as less an end to her career ambitions than a realization of her talents for supporting and informing the political career of someone obviously destined for great things.

The first great thing that came his way was a gift from President Roosevelt, who appointed Johnson in July 1935 as Texas state director for a new federal agency, the National Youth Administration (NYA), designed to help youngsters to remain in school or obtain job training. At twenty-seven, Lyndon was the youngest state director in the nation.[10]

Johnson's brief tenure at the Texas NYA revealed his talent for steering a middle course between Southern racial traditions and national efforts to promote equality. NYA regulations required state administrators to establish an advisory board representative of the population, meaning, in Texas, the inclusion of African Americans. The objective was to ensure that black citizens received education and training as did the white residents. Johnson, however, wrote to John Corson, the assistant director of the NYA in Washington, stating it was not "feasible" to have "a negro on the Texas State Advisory Board."[11]

That was not his personal preference, Johnson went on to reassure Corson, but Johnson was certain that the nine white members of the Texas board would resign immediately, that Johnson would likely be "run out of Texas," and that the state's black community would likely not trust an African American nominee who would agree to serve on the board. Instead, Johnson had a better idea: he established a separate black advisory board of men "who enjoy the confidence of white people." He was proud to inform Corson that the black board had already met once. Then Johnson made a final plea: "The racial question during the last 100 years in Texas . . . has resolved itself into a definite system of mores and customs which cannot be upset overnight. So long as these are observed there is harmony and peace between the races in Texas." This defense of state prerogative over federal policy would become increasingly common over the next three decades. Corson wrote back, "I have read your communication with especial care and note your strong objections to it. Accordingly, you may rest assured that I will not insist upon it at this time."[12]

Lyndon was good to his word and probably helped more African Americans with NYA funds than any other state director, certainly in the South, and perhaps nationally. He launched NYA projects at thirteen black colleges in the state and shifted funds to these institutions when white colleges received donations of educational equipment. A black leader in the North recalled, "We began to get word up here that there was one NYA director who wasn't like the others. He was looking after Negroes and poor folks, and most NYA people weren't doing that." Mary McLeod Bethune, the director of the Division of Negro Affairs for the NYA, and a notable African American leader, "held Johnson in far greater esteem than she did some of our other southern youth administrators." She described Lyndon as "a very outstanding young man" who was "going to go places."[13]

Overall, by early 1937, the Texas NYA was a great success, enrolling 428,000 students in its programs and an additional 190,000 on public works projects. Thirty years later, Johnson recalled that he often met constituents around Texas, "responsible and productive citizens . . . doctors, businessmen, teachers, and skilled craftsmen," who had benefited from Johnson's administration of the Texas NYA.[14]

But Johnson was in a hurry, consumed by a burning ambition that never seemed quenched. When a congressional seat in the Austin district came open through a death in February 1937, he declared his intention to run, even though he was not well known in that area. He excelled at retail politics, the glad-handing, backslapping aspects of political campaigning. While all of his Democratic primary opponents embraced President Roosevelt and the New Deal, Lyndon gave both a bear hug. He received 28 percent of the vote in a crowded field, sufficient to win the Democratic primary (and, therefore, the election).

With only ten months until he would need to run for a full term, LBJ threw himself into his congressional work. When the *Austin American* endorsed him for reelection, the editor listed an impressive array of accomplishments: Johnson completed financing of the Colorado River project, providing electricity and conservation for his constituents; funded public buildings for Austin and other cities in his district; directed federal funds to CCC and NYA projects in Texas; and provided money for slum clearance and farm-tenant benefits. It was a remarkable record for only ten months' work, and for a freshman lawmaker at that.[15]

He was a Roosevelt favorite, almost a son. Roosevelt informed two colleagues, "This boy could well be the first Southern president." Johnson hung out with a group of progressive young Southerners on Capitol Hill, including House majority leader and fellow Texan Sam Rayburn. This last connection proved fruitful both politically and socially, as Rayburn invited young Lyndon to join the "Board of Education," the Speaker's private club that met in his office for after-session drinks with like-minded comrades such as Harry Truman and Vice President John Nance Garner.[16]

Like Truman, Johnson followed the New Deal down the line, but not on civil rights issues, such as antilynching and poll-tax measures, which Roosevelt did not push for anyway. Yet Johnson secured loans for black farmers. As one Farm Security Administration official recalled, he "was the first man in Congress from the South ever to go to bat for the Negro farmer."[17]

African Americans were not the only beneficiaries of Johnson's congressional work. In an era when anti-Semitism thwarted efforts to rescue tens of thousands of Jews from Europe before and during World War II, Johnson began arranging for phony visas and passports to spring several hundred Polish and Austrian Jews from their respective countries for emigration to Mexico and Cuba, and from there to Texas. Operation Texas, as the clandestine program was called, remained a secret for nearly two decades.

The most numerous beneficiaries of Johnson's congressional career were the hill-country farmers, through AAA subsidies and FSA (Farm Security Administration) loans. In the 1937–38 congressional session alone he obtained millions of dollars in Works Progress Administration (WPA) grants for his district. Austin became one of the first three cities to receive U.S. Housing Administration loans to build public housing, despite cries of "socialism" in Texas. Austin constructed 186 units with the money—forty for Mexicans, sixty for African Americans, and eighty-six for white tenants. Johnson also obtained money for a dam on the Lower Colorado River to generate cheap power and conserve water resources. He was easily reelected. But he was restless, and in a hurry. He eyed the U.S. Senate.

Death again played a fortuitous role in Johnson's career when Texas senator Morris Sheppard died in April 1941, and Johnson, with the support of President Roosevelt, who funneled several hundred thousands of dollars in WPA money to Texas, declared for the seat. With 96 percent of the votes counted, Johnson led his nearest competitor, W. Lee "Pappy" O'Daniel, by over five thousand votes. But roughly eighteen thousand votes from rural East Texas remained to be counted. These districts were not particularly favorable for O'Daniel, yet, somehow, he won them, and with them, the election to the U.S. Senate. It was a lesson Johnson would remember.

When the war came, Johnson joined the navy and demanded a combat role, which the navy refused to approve, though he convinced General Douglas MacArthur to allow him to accompany a raid on Japanese forces in New Guinea. Returning safely, he now had a "war record," and even a medal to burnish his political credentials when he resumed his congressional career.

Unlike many of his Southern colleagues, Johnson continued to embrace the federal activism of the Roosevelt administration. He vowed "to vote for whatever legislation is necessary to let the federal government do it. If that be enlarging the power of the federal government, and if that be centralizing more power in Washington, make the most of it." Eisenhower would say much the same thing several years later.[18]

After Roosevelt's death, Johnson supported Truman's initiatives in health care, public housing, and farm electrification, but not in civil rights. He voted against the administration on antilynching and anti-poll-tax legislation as well as its efforts to extend the Fair Employment Practices Committee. His rationale was that these bills would fail anyway and he needed to vote with his Southern colleagues to ensure their support for other progressive legislation.

Johnson could show remarkable insensitivity toward selected African Americans when it suited his political purposes. During the mid-1940s, He secured a post office job for Robert Parker, a black sharecropper's son. Johnson occasionally asked Parker to work as a servant for dinner parties and cocktail receptions, assignments that Parker took for the money, but dreaded for the humiliation: "In front of his guests Johnson would often 'nigger' at me. He especially liked to put on a show for [Mississippi] Sen. [Theodore G.] Bilbo . . . I used to dread being around Johnson when Bilbo was present, because I knew it meant that Johnson would play racist."[19]

Johnson was clearly eyeing the 1948 Senate race, polishing his anti-civil-rights credentials, as well as his opposition to organized labor, as evidenced by his support for the Taft-Hartley bill—all of which set him up well with the conservative chorus in Texas as he stumped once again for a U.S. Senate seat. His campaign-opening speech in Austin in July of that year denounced Truman's civil rights program as "a farce and a sham—an effort to set up a police state in the guise of liberty." Coke Stevenson, his main opponent in the Democratic primary, received the endorsement of the state's American Federation of Labor (AFL), an indication of Johnson's lurch to the right. Stevenson bested Johnson in the primary, 40 percent to 34 percent, necessitating a runoff.[20]

The runoff election in August apparently favored Stevenson as well, until late results from south Texas, a region known for vote manipulation, came in. LBJ won the runoff by eighty-seven votes. The result called to mind a statement by Alvin J. Wirtz, a former Texas state senator and a prominent Austin attorney, that "no Texas election was over until the last crooks finished changing the votes in their counties." Stevenson hauled Johnson into federal court. But Truman's attorney general, Tom Clark, a Texan, was a friend of Johnson's, as was U.S. Supreme Court justice Hugo Black, who ordered the dismissal of Stevenson's suit. Johnson took his seat. Years later, he appointed Clark's son, Ramsey, attorney general.[21]

Though derided as "Landslide Lyndon," he took pride in the epithet. He was fond of telling the story about a Mexican boy sitting on a curb in Alice, Texas, with tears rolling down his face: "A passerby asked, 'Son, are you hurt?' The boy said, 'No, I no hurt.' . . . 'Are you sick?' . . . 'No, I no sick.' . . . 'Are you hungry?' . . . 'No, I no hungry.' 'What's the matter? What are you crying for?' 'Well, yesterday, my papa, he been dead four years, yesterday he come back and voted for Lyndon Johnson, didn't come by to say hello to me.' "[22]

When he entered the U.S. Senate in 1949, Johnson ingratiated himself with one of the most erudite and powerful members of that body, Georgia Democratic senator Richard Russell. Even closer than the father-son connection Johnson cultivated with Roosevelt was the friendship with Russell. Russell was a lonely man, unmarried, with few interests outside Senate politics. Lyndon and Lady Bird took him in almost as a family member. But aligning himself closely with Russell meant that Johnson's Senate colleagues would identify him with the Southern wing of the Democratic Party, if not its captive.

The relationship with Russell paid immediate dividends when, after less than two years in the Senate, Johnson told the Georgia Democrat that he wanted a leadership position. Russell arranged for Johnson, a forty-two-year-old junior senator from Texas, who had scarcely been in the body long enough to learn everyone's name, to become assistant Democratic leader, known as the majority whip. His main qualification was his friendship with Russell.[23]

As with all of his previous positions, Johnson threw himself into the job: what had been a mundane vote-counting role. He funneled campaign funds to non-Texas senators, he organized the calendar to bring up favored bills, and he transformed vote counting from a rough-estimate activity to a precise science. He was a quick study of men and knew how to get them over to his side, even if they were initially dead set against a bill. It was how he would cajole Southern senators into supporting civil rights legislation or convince Northern liberals that a weaker bill was better than no bill at all.

Hubert H. Humphrey, among the leading Democratic voices for civil rights in the Senate during the 1950s, forged an unlikely friendship with Johnson. Humphrey marveled at Johnson's intuitive grasp of political affairs. Watching Johnson maneuver the floor, buttonhole senators (literally), or pluck an obscure rule to benefit his cause was both education and entertainment. Humphrey explained:

> He was like . . . a psychiatrist. He knew how to appeal to every single senator and how to win him over. He knew how to appeal to their vanity, to their needs, to their ambitions . . . He knew Washington as no other man in my experience. He understood the structure and pressure points of the government, and the process and problems of legislation . . . I was always fascinated by his knowledge of politics. If you liked politics, it was like sitting at the feet of a giant.[24]

Humphrey attributed the friendship to his own sense of humor, something Johnson believed liberals generally lacked. But perhaps, as Johnson biographer Robert Caro noted, it was the Minnesota senator's "fundamental sweetness" and his willingness to never carry a grudge over differing opinions and lost causes. It might also have been that Johnson saw Humphrey as a useful bridge to the liberal camp, someone Johnson might need not only for a bill, but also for a future leadership position or a presidential bid.[25]

Johnson's political acumen and his diligence as majority whip led him to the next promotion—minority leader in 1953, and, finally, to majority leader in 1955. He was the youngest to serve in both capacities. LBJ would transform the latter position into the most powerful office in the Senate's history. He used his power to occasionally bypass the seniority system of committee chairmanships and install those whom he felt he could count on. Johnson also allocated offices; the largest suites went to allies. In return for favors and to reward his favorites, Johnson prioritized their bills on the Senate calendar.

In an era when the composition of both parties typically required bipartisan support for initiatives, Johnson became a master at reaching across the aisle and especially, as noted, clasping hands with President Eisenhower. It was old-fashioned horse-trading taken to an unprecedented level. That Congress passed the first civil rights bills since Reconstruction owed to Eisenhower's initiative, but also to Johnson's skill at maneuvering the senatorial maze of egos, regions, and rules.

When Johnson ran out of arguments, persuasion, and perks to bestow, there was always "the Treatment." The subject (or *victim*, more properly) was cornered, as political columnists Rowland Evans and Robert Novak reported:

> Its tone could be supplication, accusation, cajolery, exuberance, scorn, tears, complaint, the hint of threat. It was all of these together. It ran the gamut of human emotions. Its velocity was breathtaking, and it was all in one direction . . . He moved in close, his face a scant millimeter from his target, his eyes widening and narrowing, his eyebrows rising and falling . . . Mimicry, humor, and the genius of analogy made The Treatment an almost hypnotic experience and rendered the target stunned and helpless.[26]

JOHNSON'S LEGACY AS MAJORITY LEADER was broader than just coaxing civil rights legislation out of a reluctant Senate, important as that was, even in its modest iteration. His support for President Eisenhower's policy agenda was more than merely necessary cooperation with the chief executive. Johnson remained steeped in New Deal ideals that viewed the federal government as a vehicle to improve the lives of citizens and generate prosperity for all. He expressed his core philosophy in remarks to the Senate Democratic Conference in January 1959: "The capabilities of government must keep pace with the capabilities of the people it serves. For this we know with certainty: there is no expense of government more costly or more intolerable than the burden of laggard government." Both Truman and Eisenhower believed the complexities of modern America required a constant reassessment of the role of government to balance the nation's competing elements.[27]

Johnson's cooperation with Eisenhower derived from this philosophy. He helped the Eisenhower administration increase public housing subsidies and expand the Social Security system. Johnson played a key role in the Senate's bipartisan censure of Joseph McCarthy in December 1954, and he blocked legislation from his fellow Southerners that would have curbed the power of the U.S. Supreme Court in civil rights cases. All the while, he kept his eye and heart on his presidential ambitions, protecting his Texas flank—a state that Eisenhower carried both in 1952 and 1956—and building his credentials with Northern Democrats.

In this difficult balancing act, Johnson convinced himself that walking in the "middle of the road" was the most likely route toward consensus. And getting things done was what mattered, not venting a particular ideology. As Johnson explained to a journalist in 1954, "I have always liked to walk in the middle of the road because I believe that is where the majority of the American people are, and those are the kind of politics that I think the Democratic Party should follow."[28]

The middle was also the only possible course for a presidential bid, he believed. But, in the divided Democratic Party, as a Southerner, or at least in the public perception if not precisely corresponding ideologically to that geographic fact, his odds were long. He remembered folding his six-foot-four-inch frame into the backseat of Sam Rayburn's chauffeured limousine for the drive up to Capitol Hill during the 1940s. Affixed to the back of the front seat was a plaque placed there by some of Rayburn's colleagues: TO OUR BELOVED SAM RAYBURN—WHO WOULD HAVE BEEN PRESIDENT IF HE HAD COME FROM ANY PLACE BUT THE SOUTH.[29]

And that was a shame. There were talented Southerners, brilliant men such as Richard Russell, and caring men such as Alabama senators Lister Hill and John Sparkman, loyal New Dealers who fought for health care for the poor and public works projects that would light the darkness of their constituents with electricity. And young men such as Lyndon Johnson. Beyond Dixie, though, these men were dinosaurs. Changing demographics shifted Democratic Party power to the North, and Republicans resisted the temptation to abandon civil rights for the votes of disaffected Southern Democrats. Some in the party of Lincoln would vote with the Southern Democrats in Congress. But in national contests, Republicans focused their efforts on the North and West. Southern whites were not yet prepared to abandon their ancestral political home. That time was coming, though.

Something else marginalized Dixie. The two decades after World War II were America's confident years. Although Communist aggression, threats of nuclear destruction, and memories of the tenacious economic depression of the 1930s were unsettling, Americans for the most part approached their lives and their country not with fear but with optimism. Rather than march back to some mythic past, they moved forward, rarely rapidly, but inexorably, toward a better and more just society. If polio was the summertime scourge of the baby boom, we would conquer it. If the Soviets put a man in space, we would expand science and technology research and education. If pesticides and pollution threatened the air we breathed, the water we drank, and the natural beauty we enjoyed, we would rescue our patrimony. If women, African Americans, and immigrants confronted obstacles to full equality, we would remove those barriers. We would build a nation of homeowners. We would build the best higher education system in the world. We would build great highways to traverse a continent. We would build magnificent airports to transport people and goods farther and faster than ever before. We would conquer poverty, disease, and ignorance. We would do it because we could, and because we had to. Our government, in partnership with our people, would do it.

These prospects frightened Southern leaders: too much migration; too much government; too many opportunities for Catholics, Jews, blacks, and women to insert their alien ideas into an inert region. These men made their lives out of yesterday. And many in other parts of America knew it. In 1957, Massachusetts senator John F. Kennedy, contemplating his run for the 1960 Democratic nomination for president, dismissed the chances of his Texas rival, Lyndon Johnson: "It's too close to Appomattox for Johnson to be nominated and elected." "Too close to Appomattox," and this after ninety-two years. The past was not even past. And it tortured Johnson.[30]

So he tried to be a border man—to be both a Southerner and a Westerner—to maintain his attachment to the South to win votes in Texas, and to buff his national credentials when he could. Where Johnson's heart lay, one rarely knew. As a congressman and as a senator, he had never, until 1957, voted in favor of a civil rights measure. His maiden Senate speech in 1949 was a screed of states' rights oratory and of the goodness of Southern race relations, a performance that won the mind and the heart of Richard Russell. In September 1957 Johnson attacked President Eisenhower for sending troops to Little Rock. Yet he had been a faithful New Dealer, and in administering NYA funds in Texas, he had worked with black leaders to ensure African Americans received their due.[31]

He played on his ambiguous hill-country background. The region had opposed secession, and it stood astride the Balcones Fault, a geologic dividing line. To the east lay the flatlands and Big Cotton. To the West, the "broken country, the grasslands, the long stretches of nothingness," the land of Big Gas and Big Oil. On his campaign swings around the state, he hauled a western band that played "Home on the Range" and "Sioux City Sue." On occasion, the singing cowboy, Gene Autry, would join him.[32]

Johnson purchased a ranch in 1951, though he was not much of a rancher. The property gave him an opportunity to get on a horse, wear a big hat and cowboy boots, and talk about cattle futures as if he really knew the business. He was a cowboy. The act was enough to convince Hubert H. Humphrey: "He [Johnson] was a Westerner at heart." Thurgood Marshall saw "no problem at all" in the Democrats nominating Johnson in 1960 "because in my book Texas is not the South; it's Southwest." The West, of course, was America's optimistic future; the South, its troubled past. The gifted generation loaded up on western paraphernalia: coonskin caps, cap pistols, cowboy hats, tassels on skirts and vests. And for Johnson, the man on the move, the West, ever changing and rich in future prospects, suited his personality, not the lugubrious South.[33]

The cowboy image he cultivated notwithstanding, he seemed most comfortable in the Southern milieu. His close friendship with Dick Russell may have been opportunistic, but it was also heartfelt and derived from an unstated regional affinity. He often expressed his desire to rescue the South from its antediluvian social system and its imprisonment in the past. He viewed the racial customs of the South as a great albatross weighing down the region from attaining its ultimate potential. Johnson would rather have white Southerners move the revolution than have it imposed. Most of all, it was the right thing to do. As he explained to his aide Horace Busby in 1949, "The Negro fought in the war, and now that he's back here with his family, he's not gonna keep taking the shit we're dishing out. We're in a race with time. If we don't act, we're gonna have blood in the streets."[34]

Perhaps this was his most genuine connection to the South, a tough love that sought to drag the region into the twentieth century. He returned to this theme in the troubled last months of his presidency when he campaigned for Hubert Humphrey at the Houston Astrodome, just prior to the 1968 presidential election. By then, the South was emerging as the Sunbelt. While Northern cities erupted in race riots, the South was calm, going about its business building a biracial society. He reminded the audience of how the Democratic Party, within a relatively short time, had brought the South into the mainstream of American economic life, and only with that merger "could the South 'rise again'—as a vigorous, progressive part of America." It was a noble thought, and at the time, it seemed to reflect well the advances the region had made. No longer the keeper of a discredited past, but the portent of a dynamic, progressive future. Just like America.[35]

He understood the perceptions about him and how, apart from what he could control in the Senate, the signs of racial progress were unmistakable. Johnson moaned about the *Brown* decision, "I'm damned if I do and damned if I don't. The Dixiecrats, and a lot of my people at home, will be on me like stink on shit if I don't stand up and bray against the Supreme Court's decision. If I do bray like a jackass, the red hots and senators with big minority blocs in the East and the North will gut shoot me." His constituents' virulent responses to his support for both the 1957 and 1960 civil rights acts, as mild as those measures were, provided a good indication of the pressure he felt.[36]

The balancing act tore Johnson apart. He suffered through depression and consumed large amounts of antidepressants during the mid-to-late 1950s. His mother wrote long letters beseeching him to seek professional help and end his self-medication. There was nowhere Lyndon could be himself. But the question was, did he really know who he was? Perhaps his only respite from the stage was the room beneath the House chamber where Sam Rayburn held forth. There, Johnson could nurse his drink and his dream. Beyond, the judgment of Eleanor Roosevelt about his presidential future seemed the most accurate: "He's from the South, and it's impossible."[37]

Johnson probably knew it, which made his despair even deeper. Political columnist Stewart Alsop wrote a flattering profile of the majority leader in the *Saturday Evening Post* in January 1959. It was the sort of piece that helps to build support for a potential presidential candidate. Alsop called Johnson "the second most powerful man in the nation," and a close second at that. Praising his organizational skills and his tact in bringing together a divided party, Alsop credited LBJ with both the Senate's censure of Joseph McCarthy and the passage of the 1957 Civil Rights Act. Johnson's occasionally bullying tactics aside, Alsop depicted him as "good company," witty and brilliant. He portrayed Johnson as a man of the frontier, only two generations removed from Indian predations. Acknowledging his Southern leanings, Alsop argued for a Western interpretation. But LBJ must have found Alsop's conclusion chilling. The general perception of Johnson as a Southerner "is the central reason why, bar a miracle, LBJ will never be President."[38]

BY THE TIME OF THE DEMOCRATIC National Convention in 1960, Johnson had gathered more than 500 delegates to his presidential cause, but 385 of them came from the South. When his name was placed in nomination, the band played "Dixie." LBJ concluded that prejudice against Southerners was actually worse than prejudice against Catholics. He also realized that Massachusetts senator John F. Kennedy had the nomination sewn up.[39]

It was an unhappy time for Johnson. He had grown tired of being majority leader, with its arm-twisting, the need to satisfy two increasingly disparate wings of a party, and at the same time to mollify his restless Texas constituents growing ever more hostile toward civil rights. Now, with the presidency blocked, it seemed he had nowhere to go. But, for once, his Texas connection paid off at the national level.

Over the past thirty years or so, it has been commonplace for potential presidential nominees to prepare a short list of potential vice-presidential candidates well before the nominating conventions. The idea is to vet these individuals and consult with party leaders and key constituent groups. This is a relatively recent development. Although John F. Kennedy had prepared a list of vice-presidential candidates, neither he nor party leaders had vetted or settled upon one candidate. LBJ was on that list, but few thought he would relinquish his powerful Senate position for the vice presidency. Once Kennedy received the nomination, he had twenty-four hours to make that choice or throw the selection open to the convention.

The key for the Democrats was to present a united party in the fall. The problem was the persistent estrangement between the Northern and Southern branches of the party. City bosses, such as Chicago's Mayor Richard Daley and Carmine DeSapio of New York City, believed Lyndon Johnson solved many of the party's problems going into the general election. He was from a state— Texas—that the Democrats required in the fall, but had gone to Eisenhower in the two previous elections. Second, his presence on the ticket might mitigate Kennedy's Catholicism, which was unpopular among many Southern voters. Finally, Johnson could rally key Southern politicians to support the ticket and, therefore, keep at least part of the South within the Democratic column. The party's platform supported its most extensive civil rights plank ever, making Southern electoral support uncertain even with LBJ, but less likely without him.

Bobby Kennedy vigorously opposed the recommendation, but JFK's team of advisers believed political expediency trumped the lack of personal compatibility. Although some historians have claimed that Johnson reluctantly accepted the vice-presidential nomination, that was not the case. With the help of Sam Rayburn, Johnson made it look as if he were taking one for the team when, in fact, he viewed it as the best alternative available to him. Besides, it was not out of the realm of possibility that a vice president could ascend to the highest office.

Johnson's selection paid immediate dividends. At a meeting of leading Southern Democrats in Nashville after the convention, LBJ encouraged his

Southern colleagues to "vote for Kennedy and me despite all this bunk about ending racial segregation, the Supreme Court decision on integration of the schools, busing, and the rest. You have to elect Kennedy in order to have me in the administration so I, your fellow Southerner, can defeat his integration proposals." Johnson portrayed himself as the firewall against the collapse of white supremacy. The irony was that Johnson never had to fend off Kennedy's integration proposals. There were none. And LBJ, rather than being the guardian of white supremacy, became its destroyer.[41]

Johnson's ability to talk the language of Southern white political leaders was a significant asset, as the Republicans hoped to build on Eisenhower's success in peeling off several Southern states in 1952 and 1956. Even though Ike had sent troops to Little Rock and sponsored two civil rights laws, he had awakened a moribund Republican Party in the region, especially in the prosperous cities. Richard Nixon, the Republican nominee, received an "unbelievable welcome" in Atlanta, with supporters standing eight deep along his motorcade route. *Atlanta Constitution* editor Ralph McGill called it "the greatest thing in Atlanta since the premiere of *Gone with the Wind*." If Georgia might be in play, then Texas was certainly vulnerable.[42]

Johnson deposited another dividend in September when Kennedy addressed a group of Protestant ministers in Houston. Johnson played a significant role in arranging the meeting. Prior to his appearance in Houston, Kennedy, joined by LBJ, spoke in El Paso and San Antonio. At the latter venue, signs proclaiming WE WANT THE BIBLE AND THE CONSTITUTION and WE DON'T WANT THE KREMLIN OR THE VATICAN greeted the candidates. Johnson embarrassed the demonstrators by noting that when Kennedy was saving those Americans on PT-109, "they didn't ask what Church he belonged to." Then, Johnson listed the names of Catholic Texans who had died at the Alamo.[43]

Kennedy returned the favor, inviting Johnson to Boston. LBJ commandeered a policeman's horse and galloped around Copley Square for a while, mainly to quizzical looks from the locals. In Massachusetts, he was parading his Western bona fides.

But in the South, he was as Southern as could be. Following the advice of Harry Truman, Johnson boarded an eleven-car train in Virginia in October to barnstorm through the South. Reporters covering the journey, with a bit of help from LBJ's staff, rarely referred to the procession by its formal name, the LBJ Victory Special, but rather as the Cornpone Special. Touring eight Southern states, with aides clad in overalls and women dressed in blue blazers, white pleated skirts, and blouses, and with loudspeakers blaring country tunes, LBJ assured the assembled of the ticket's goodwill toward the South, particularly to the white South, as he compared attacks on Kennedy's Catholicism to prejudice against the South. At a stop in Salisbury, North Carolina, he abandoned any pretense of a Western bent. "I want to be remembered by how I live, not where I live, but the longer I stay in North Carolina, the more sectional I'm likely to become." Whenever he pulled into a station, a local band invariably struck up "Dixie," and he would remind the crowd that he was a grandson of a Confederate soldier. Lady Bird, just being herself, had a deep drawl and favored Southern idioms such as "We sho' do appreciate it," as one North Carolina newspaper reported.[44]

The caravan was not all moon pies and magnolias. The entourage met occasional resistance. Johnson's presence on a ticket with a New England Roman Catholic did not play well in certain parts of the South. Besides, rumor had it that Kennedy opposed the oil-depletion allowance, a matter of faith in Texas. Also, Southern whites recalled Johnson's central role in shepherding two civil rights bills through Congress while other Southern lawmakers steadfastly resisted.

The most serious incident occurred in Dallas, a fertile breeding ground for extreme right-wing racist sentiment. Four days before the presidential election, pickets confronted LBJ and Lady Bird at a Dallas hotel with signs denouncing Johnson as a CARPETBAGGER CONTROLLED BY YANKEE SOCIAL- ISTS. Entering the Adolphus Hotel to attend a dinner, the Johnsons encountered a "Mink Coat Mob" of Junior League women in the lobby who verbally and physically attacked them, including hitting Lady Bird on the head with a picket sign. Normally, the walk across the lobby to the dining room would have taken two minutes at most. But Johnson realized the unruly scene could work in his and JFK's favor. He asked the police to leave the scene: "If the time has come when I can't walk through the lobby of a hotel in Dallas with my lady without a police escort, I want to know it." So he and Lady Bird, holding on to each other, inched through the lobby, dodging placards and spittle while being subjected to verbal abuse. The procession consumed nearly thirty minutes, and all the while cameras were rolling and flashing, and reporters were furiously jotting down notes.[45]

The assault on Lady Bird moved Richard Russell to stump for the ticket in Texas and South Carolina in the final days before the election. But the virulence of the lobby crowd had another effect. As Rowland Evans and Robert Novak wrote of the confrontation, "In one sudden revelation, it portrayed Johnson to the critical North in a wholly new light . . . Suddenly a 'new Johnson' appeared." The attack also "outraged thousands of Texans and many more thousands of Southerners in other states." Johnson had accomplished the seemingly impossible with his slow walk through the lobby of the

Adolphus Hotel: he had drawn both Northerners and Southerners to his side and, more important, to the Democratic ticket.[46]

The 1960 election may have been an exception to the rule that vice-presidential candidates rarely swing elections. The Democratic ticket carried seven of the former Confederate states, including Texas, which the Kennedy-Johnson team won by the narrow margin of forty-six thousand votes out of over 2.3 million votes cast.[47]

Johnson was not, of course, the only reason for Kennedy's narrow national victory. The calls to Coretta Scott King and to the Georgia judge about releasing the imprisoned Martin Luther King Jr.—calls that Johnson approved—moved Northern black votes to Kennedy's column. The televised debates may have swayed some voters for Kennedy, and in a close election that was important. But Johnson likely also played an important role in the victory.

What should have been a moment of triumph for LBJ, or at least of satisfaction that he had pulled more than his own weight in the contest, was buried in one of his periodic bouts of despair. His secretary reported that when the final results became known, LBJ "looked as if he'd lost his last friend on earth . . . I don't think I ever saw a more unhappy man." Johnson was not accustomed to a subordinate role. He would play the apprentice, as he had as majority whip, provided the next step up was easily within his grasp. But at least for the next four and possibly eight years, that was out of the question. Not only that, but he was well aware that the Kennedy entourage looked down upon him in their mildest moments and utterly despised him the rest of the time. The adoring crowd and press that circled around Jack and Jackie ignored him. He was invisible. He was miserable.[48]

"Hoping it will hold."
In 1919, Eisenhower embarked on a trip transferring military equipment from Washington, D.C., to the West Coast. The obstacles he and his convoy encountered would inspire his later vision for an interstate highway network.
DWIGHT D. EISENHOWER PRESIDENTIAL LIBRARY & MUSEUM

Eisenhower and his mother, Ida Stover Eisenhower, 1938. Ike was very close to his mother. She possessed a love of learning and a consistent optimism, passing on both traits to her son.
DWIGHT D. EISENHOWER PRESIDENTIAL LIBRARY & MUSEUM

Eisenhower dedicates Columbia University's new cyclotron, April 2, 1950. Also present left to right are John R. Dunning, dean of the School of Engineering; Rear Admiral Thorvald A. Solberg, USN; and Isidor Isaac Rabi, professor of physics. As he had at Columbia, Ike promoted the partnership between the federal government and research institutions to develop new technologies. DWIGHT D. EISENHOWER PRESIDENTIAL LIBRARY & MUSEUM

Three white pickets protesting integration of a white neighborhood, possibly in Los Angeles, ca. 1951–1958. LIBRARY OF CONGRESS, PRINTS & PHOTOGRAPHS DIVISION, VISUAL MATERIALS FROM THE NAACP RECORDS

People awaiting American citizenship papers. President Eisenhower, Chief Justice Earl Warren, Attorney General Herbert Brownell, and WAC Gertrude Ernst (left to right) at a citizenship ceremony, November 10, 1954. Miss Ernst entered the United States as a displaced person in 1952 from Bratislava, Czechoslovakia. GETTY IMAGES (FROM BETTMANN/CORBIS)

Presentation of citation to Basil O'Connor and Dr. Jonas Salk, April 22, 1955, on the eve of the eventual conquest over polio. DWIGHT D. EISENHOWER PRESIDENTIAL LIBRARY & MUSEUM

Eisenhower meeting with Arkansas Governor Orval Faubus, September 14, 1957. Ike came away from this meeting with a sense that the Little Rock school crisis was solved. It turned out to be only the beginning of a wrenching episode that lasted over a year. DWIGHT D. EISENHOWER PRESIDENTIAL LIBRARY & MUSEUM

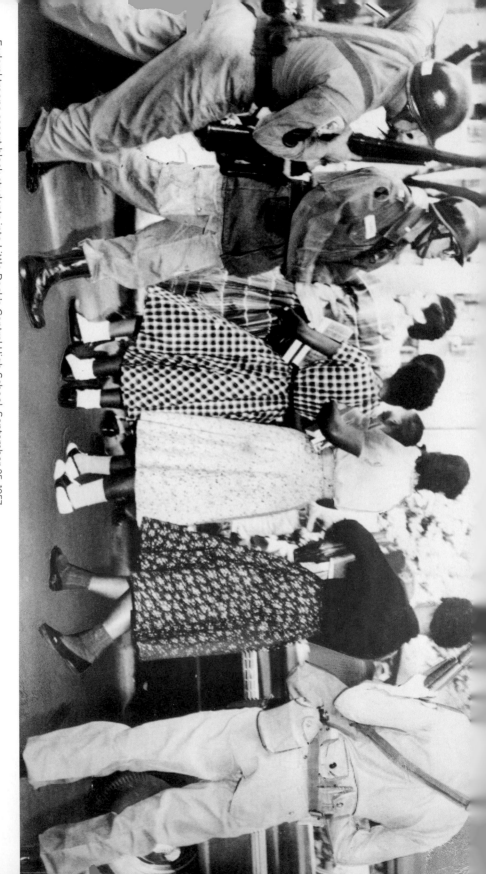

Federal troops escort black students into Little Rock's Central High School, September 25, 1957.
NEW YORK WORLD TELEGRAM & SUN COLLECTION, LIBRARY OF CONGRESS, PRINTS & PHOTOGRAPHS DIVISION

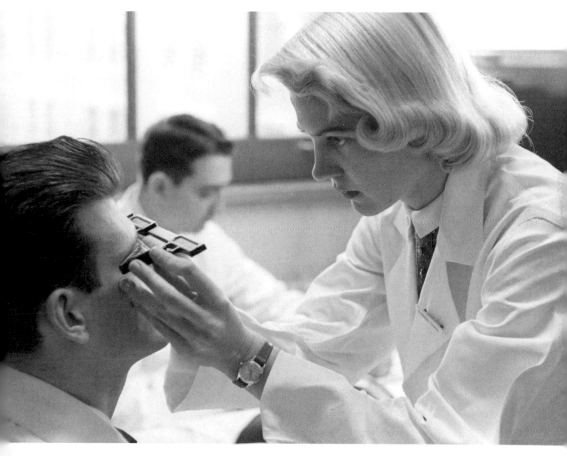

Twenty-four-year-old Susan Cook, a senior at the University of Chicago's medical school, examining a patient, November 18, 1959. It was a relatively rare sight in the 1950s to see female medical students. This would change in the following decade thanks to the pioneering efforts of individuals such as Dr. Cook. CHARLOTTE BROOKS, PHOTOGRAPHER, *LOOK* MAGAZINE PHOTOGRAPH COLLECTION, LIBRARY OF CONGRESS, PRINTS & PHOTOGRAPHS DIVISION

Harvey Rubin, far right, played left end on Tilden's storied 1960 football team. Rubin credited NSF and NASA grants with enabling him to complete his doctorate at Columbia University during the 1960s. At Bell Labs, his team helped to develop many of the innovations in computer technology commonplace today. HARVEY RUBIN

When America was new: the TWA Flight Center at New York International Airport (now JFK), 1962. One of many major infrastructure projects initiated during the Eisenhower administration.
MILSTEIN DIVISION OF U.S. HISTORY, LOCAL HISTORY & GENEALOGY, NEW YORK PUBLIC LIBRARY, ASTOR, LENOX AND TILDEN FOUNDATIONS

CHAPTER 16

INTERLUDE

THE DAY AFTER THE 1960 presidential election, Southern writer Willie Morris wondered, "Liberated now from his Texas constituency, will he [Johnson] have the vision to rise above the provincial interests which have so often seemed to enclose him and become . . . a genuine national leader?"[1]

A good question, but John F. Kennedy turned out to be the real provincial in the administration in domestic policy. More invested in foreign policy than in domestic issues, he nearly made a mash of both. Cold War tensions—the Bay of Pigs invasion and the Cuban missile crisis, among other conflicts—consumed much of his time. Overly concerned not to antagonize Southern Democrats, both to protect his domestic agenda and to gain their support for his 1964 reelection bid, Kennedy effectively conceded the debate on racial equality to the Southerners.

By 1963, however, events in the South pushed him to move on civil rights. He was also putting together a domestic agenda on education, gender equity, and the environment. But his assassination left an inchoate legacy. JFK, unlike his vice president, did not seem to be in a hurry. LBJ's early success after assuming the presidency occurred primarily with Kennedy's agenda. The major difference was that Johnson possessed both the political skills and the will to carry it out.[2]

During the 1960 election campaign, neither Kennedy nor his surrogates mentioned the words *civil rights*. When Richard Nixon's running mate, Henry Cabot Lodge Jr., suggested that Nixon, if elected, would appoint an African American to the cabinet, Kennedy termed the promise "racism at its worst." When JFK called Coretta Scott King, a crucial episode in the tight campaign, brother Bobby was furious at the campaign aides who had suggested it: "You bomb throwers have lost the whole campaign."[3]

Despite the key role black voters played in electing Kennedy, his inaugural address focused almost exclusively on the Cold War. His only allusion—and it was fleeting—to civil rights occurred in a sentence concerning America's commitment to human rights, a sentence inserted at the last moment.

Kennedy was not ignoring public sentiment. Among white Americans there was not a significant constituency for civil rights in 1961.[4]

The Freedom Rides confirmed this last point. In 1946, the U.S. Supreme Court in *Morgan v. Virginia* banned segregated seating on interstate bus routes. The Chicago-based Congress of Racial Equality (CORE) decided to test the decision the following year, but the Interstate Commerce Commission (ICC) declined to issue an order forcing bus companies to abide by the ruling. There the matter rested until 1961, when CORE returned to the issue, buoyed by a December 1960 Supreme Court ruling in *Boynton v. Virginia* that extended the *Morgan* precedent to include terminal facilities.[5]

On May 4, 1961, seven blacks and six whites divided into two interracial groups and boarded a Greyhound and a Trailways bus respectively, heading south from Washington, D.C. Their destination was New Orleans, which meant they would travel through the Deep South. The previous evening, the thirteen riders had enjoyed a farewell Chinese dinner in Washington. John Lewis, one of the young riders (now a congressman from Atlanta), called it "the Last Supper."

Aside from two ugly but brief encounters in Chapel Hill, North Carolina, and Rock Hill, South Carolina, the Riders arrived safely in Atlanta on May 13 and headed to Alabama. The Trailways bus pulled into an eerily quiet Birmingham terminal on Mother's Day, May 14. Approximately forty whites, including a few journalists, lined the terminal bay. No policemen were in sight. The whites, mostly Klansmen, descended on the Riders and beat them severely. After twenty minutes, the police arrived and the mob retreated unmolested. When reporters later questioned Public Safety Commissioner Eugene "Bull" Connor why no policemen were at the terminal, he replied that they were visiting their mothers.

To this point Kennedy had remained aloof from the Freedom Riders. In fact, prior to the Birmingham fracas, he had not heard of them and had no idea why they were in Alabama. A front-page *New York Times* photograph of the bus terminal violence in Birmingham the day after Mother's Day horrified the president. His main concern, however, was how this confrontation would play abroad. He would be meeting with Nikita Khrushchev in Vienna in three weeks, and as one journalist noted, Kennedy could see the Soviet leader "waving *The New York Times* in his face."[6]

Harris Wofford, Kennedy's adviser on civil rights, who had worked on getting out the black vote during the 1960 election, received an irate call from the president after news of Birmingham broke: "Can't you get your goddamned friends off those buses? Stop them." Of course, Wofford could do nothing of the sort.[7]

Burke Marshall, Kennedy's assistant attorney general for civil rights, had advised the president that he lacked the constitutional authority to protect the Freedom Riders; their safety rested in the hands of local authorities. That was a questionable interpretation, considering the matter involved interstate commerce, over which the federal government had the higher authority, as well as two U.S. Supreme Court decisions—the law of the land—that clearly prohibited the obstruction evident in the Riders' experience in Birmingham. All the administration would do was to negotiate with the governor of Alabama, John Patterson, to provide protection for the Riders to Montgomery, the state capital, and the next stop on their itinerary.

It seemed that Governor Patterson's promise to the Kennedy administration to protect the Riders would be fulfilled. An armada of buses, helicopters, and police cruisers escorted the riders for the two-hour journey to the state capital. When the bus neared the city, however, the escort vanished. As the bus pulled into the terminal, a mob surrounded the vehicle. Not a cop was in sight. The Montgomery thugs nearly killed two of the Riders and brutally assaulted John Seigenthaler, an emissary from Bobby Kennedy's Justice Department. Bobby dispatched four hundred U.S. marshals to Montgomery to ensure the safety of the Freedom Riders as they began the final leg of their troubled journey to Jackson, Mississippi. Per a prior arrangement with the Kennedy administration, the police in Jackson arrested the Riders, but there was no violence. The Freedom Rides were over.

Four months later, the ICC issued an order integrating interstate carriers and terminal facilities, though two previous U.S. Supreme Court decisions had supposedly accomplished that. The Kennedy administration's reluctance to intervene until the situation had escalated to violence would be repeated over the next two years. But the Kennedys read the polls, and they knew that 63 percent of Americans disapproved of the Freedom Rides. For a president concerned about reelection and about keeping most of the South in his column, the benefits of inaction outweighed the costs of intervention.

At a news conference in February 1962, Kennedy made clear that he would not press Congress for any civil rights legislation during the coming year. Also, during his 1960 election campaign, he had promised to sign an executive order barring discrimination in federally assisted housing. Now, JFK reneged on that pledge. The New York Times criticized the moves, stating Kennedy "has not waited for Congress to convene before beginning a retreat from the more challenging elements of his domestic program." Roy Wilkins, executive secretary of the NAACP, called the president's announcement "a basic error."[8]

Even when Kennedy took a step forward on civil rights, it invariably led to backtracking. In his 1962 State of the Union address, JFK asked Congress to abolish the poll tax and literacy tests, two mechanisms Southern states employed to restrict or eliminate African American voting. But he set no timetable for these requests. Senate majority leader Mike Mansfield (D-MT) introduced a bill to make a sixth-grade education the only literacy requirement for federal elections. Although Kennedy favored the bill, he did little to promote it. The president feared the inevitable conflict over the measure would threaten other pending legislation, especially tariff reductions with the European Common Market (later the European Union).[9]

Yet events in the South continued to challenge Kennedy's inaction on civil rights legislation. In 1962, black student James Meredith attempted to enroll at the University of Mississippi. Instead of sending soldiers or federalizing the Mississippi National Guard to protect Meredith, the Kennedy administration dispatched federal marshals, who were unable to prevent the melee that unfolded nor the deaths of two bystanders. Kennedy then ordered in the U.S. Army and federalized the National Guard. But again, the intercession occurred after violence and open defiance of court orders.[10]

Kennedy's inactions frustrated Martin Luther King Jr., who had supported Kennedy's candidacy in 1960. On May 17, 1962, the eighth anniversary of the *Brown* decision—a ruling that remained fixed on paper but barely visible in reality—King sent a sixty-four-page manifesto to the White House. With the hundredth anniversary of the Emancipation Proclamation less than seven months away, King challenged JFK to issue a second Emancipation Proclamation outlawing segregation. The president received the document politely, but did nothing. In January 1963, he avoided all centennial celebrations of the original document.[11]

That his administration initially failed to invite any black speakers for that commemorative event underscored how tone-deaf it was to African American aspirations. At the last minute Kennedy corralled Thurgood Marshall for the assignment. Occasionally a meanness surfaced in Kennedy's views on black leaders. His nickname for gay writer and civil rights advocate James Baldwin, for example, was Martin Luther Queen.[12]

IN SEPTEMBER 1962 COLUMNIST Stewart Alsop went off on one of his cross-country tours to take the political pulse of American voters. He found that black voters were disappointed in the president. A Chicago waitress who had voted for him in 1960 stated she would not do so in 1964 because he "hasn't pushed hard enough" on civil rights. Among whites, Alsop found an ambivalence concerning racial equality, best summarized by a Baltimore homemaker:

"They [African Americans] got rights, just like anybody else. They ought to vote and have just as good schools and all that, but I don't see why we got to mingle together."[13]

Much as Eisenhower had employed his vice president, Richard Nixon, as the point person for civil rights, Kennedy invested Johnson with the civil rights portfolio, selecting LBJ to chair the President's Committee on Equal Employment Opportunity (PCEEO). In that capacity, Johnson drafted an executive order for Kennedy requiring government contractors to take "affirmative action" to ensure equal employment opportunity in their operations. Johnson assumed, correctly, that such a measure would never pass Congress, but since it was confined to government contractors, it would fall under the president's executive powers.[14]

Kennedy issued the order. In practical terms, this meant that federal agencies were required to initiate special recruiting efforts to boost employment of minority groups. Simply not discriminating was insufficient. Agencies had to actively ensure minority representation by, say, recruiting on black college campuses and advertising in the black press.[15]

Johnson was aware that his leadership as chairman of the PCEEO could very well enhance his ability to attract Northern support for a future presidential bid. He used the committee to lean on federal agencies and companies doing government business that failed to hire and promote qualified African Americans. As one reporter noted, Johnson "speaks softly . . . and carries big Government contracts." After just one year on the job, Johnson had signed up nearly fifty major companies that agreed to drop barriers in hiring and promoting blacks, as well as promising equal use of plant facilities for all employees.[16]

By 1963, the results of Johnson's efforts were impressive. Federal jobs held by African Americans increased 17 percent in fiscal 1962 and another 22 percent in 1963. His committee ruled in favor of nearly seventeen hundred black employees who filed complaints between 1962 and 1963, doubling the rate of corrective actions in one year.[17]

EVENTS IN ALABAMA DURING what would be the last months of Kennedy's presidency went far beyond his ability to solve them through executive order. Martin Luther King Jr., and his Southern Christian Leadership Conference (SCLC), launched demonstrations in Birmingham on April 3, 1963. The Kennedy administration begged King to postpone the campaign as a new, moderate government had recently taken office in Birmingham. But the power of the new city administration was not clear as the old government challenged the legality of the election and refused to leave office.[18]

The demonstrations went forward and King was arrested on Good Friday. Sitting in his prison cell, he responded to an open letter from Birmingham's white clergy criticizing him for leading untimely demonstrations. King's reply encapsulated the essence of his nonviolent philosophy and the daily assault on the dignity of African Americans:

> We have waited for more than 340 years for our constitutional and godgiven rights . . . Perhaps it is easy for those who have never felt the stinging darts of segregation to say, "Wait." But when you have seen vicious mobs lynch your mothers and fathers at will and drown your sisters and brothers at whim, when you have seen hate-filled policemen curse, kick, and even kill your black brothers and sisters; when you see the vast majority of your twenty million Negro brothers smothering in an airtight cage of poverty in the midst of an affluent society; when you suddenly find your tongue twisted and your speech stammering as you seek to explain to your six-year-old daughter why she can't go to the public amusement park . . . and see tears welling up in her eyes . . . when your first name becomes "nigger," your middle name becomes "boy" . . . and your last name becomes "John," and your wife and mother are never given the respected title "Mrs."; . . . when you are forever fighting a degenerating sense of "nobodiness"—then you will understand why we find it difficult to wait.[19]

KING'S "LETTER FROM BIRMINGHAM JAIL," eloquent as it was, would not open the restaurants, theaters, parks, playgrounds, and city hall for blacks. The demonstrations resumed, and the city's police chief, Eugene "Bull" Connor, was ready. On May 3, 1963, one thousand schoolchildren gathered at the Sixteenth Street Baptist Church to march out into the downtown area. Connor's men barred the exits from the church, trapping roughly one half of the demonstrators inside. Another contingent of police pursued those who had left the church across the street to Kelly Ingram Park, where they loosed their German shepherd dogs on the children and beat demonstrators and onlookers alike. When adults in the park tried to ward off the attacking police with bricks and bottles, Connor ordered the firemen to turn their high-pressure hoses on the crowd. The sudden thrust of water knocked people to the ground, ripped off their clothes, and sent children skittering down the street. The scene was repeated on May 6. By then the nation, through television, had witnessed the debacle. On May 7, the downtown businesses removed their segregation signs.

A month earlier, William Moore, a thirty-five-year-old white mailman, set out from Baltimore determined to walk to Mississippi to protest racial segregation. Although he lived in upstate New York, he was born in Russell, Mississippi. He hoped to deliver a letter to Ross Barnett, the state's governor. Moore never got the chance. His bullet-riddled body was found along a road near Attalla, Alabama. He carried two placards with him: EAT AT JOE'S, BOTH BLACK AND WHITE and EQUAL RIGHTS FOR ALL—MISSISSIPPI OR BUST.[20]

Martin Luther King Jr. knew "it was the images of the bodies, not the constitutional logic of the case," that would capture Kennedy's attention. During the first two years of his administration, he offered no significant civil rights legislation. His judicial appointments to federal courts in the South ratified the segregationist recommendations of Southern senators, reversing the trend of moderate judges appointed by President Eisenhower.[21]

But the embarrassing images splayed over television screens and in newspapers around the world finally moved the Kennedy administration to address civil rights. On June 11, 1963, the president delivered a nationally televised address framing civil rights as a moral imperative: "We are confronted primarily with a moral issue . . . as old as the Scriptures and . . . as clear as the American Constitution." That very day, as if to underscore Kennedy's words, Alabama governor George C. Wallace stood in front of Foster Auditorium on the University of Alabama campus to prevent the enrollment of two black students, Vivian Malone and James Hood. Deputy Attorney General Nicholas Katzenbach, supported by the federalized Alabama National Guard—Kennedy had learned the lesson of his tardy response at Ole Miss the previous year—ordered the governor to step aside. After a brief speech on states' rights, Wallace departed and the students registered. That same night, Medgar Evers, NAACP field secretary for Mississippi, was gunned down in the driveway of his home. On June 19, the day of Evers's funeral at Arlington National Cemetery, Kennedy sent a civil rights bill to Congress.[22]

Although Kennedy's civil rights initiative was an important milestone in his administration, in practical terms the measure was weak, even more so than the two civil rights bills Congress had passed during the Eisenhower years. It focused on segregated public accommodations, a major target of the sit-ins and related civil rights demonstrations of the early 1960s. That was good. Not so good was that for the Justice Department to become involved in such cases, individuals had to initiate lawsuits. Considering the economic pressures and outright violence against those who openly challenged Southern racial customs in federal courts, that was an unrealistic procedure. Kennedy hoped that a moderate bill would attract enough Republicans to overcome Southern Democrats. It did not, and the bill went nowhere.[23]

LESS THAN TWO WEEKS before his televised address, Kennedy had the opportunity to deliver a strong endorsement of racial equality consistent with American ideals. On Memorial Day 1963, the Gettysburg National Battlefield hosted a commemorative event to mark the hundredth anniversary of Abraham Lincoln's famed address on that site (though the address occurred on November 19, 1863). It would have been an excellent venue for Kennedy to wrap himself in the mantle of Lincoln and establish himself firmly on the right side of history. He sent Lyndon Johnson instead.

Johnson's brief remarks connected Lincoln's immortal words to the current racial strife. "The Negro today asks justice," Johnson asserted. "We do not answer him—we do not answer those who lie beneath this soil—when we reply to the Negro by asking, 'Patience.'" Civil rights may have been an issue Democrats would have liked to kick down the road, especially as an election year approached, but Johnson would have none of it, invoking the commonwealth ideal: "The Negro says, 'Now.' Others say, 'Never.' The voice of responsible Americans—the voice of those who died here and the great man who spoke here—their voices say, 'Together.' There is no other way. Until justice is blind to color, until education is unaware of race, until opportunity is unconcerned with the color of men's skins, emancipation will be a proclamation but not a fact."[24]

That Lyndon Johnson would become the most outspoken advocate for civil rights in the Kennedy administration was not surprising given the president's assignment of those duties to LBJ. It relieved Kennedy of any direct involvement with sensitive issues that could hurt his political status not only in the South, but nationally as well. After the violence in Alabama and Mississippi in the spring of 1963, Kennedy's favorability ratings fell, not because he was slow responding to civil rights issues, but because he was moving too fast.[25]

Even the domestic policies that received congressional endorsement during the Kennedy years had minimal impact on the problems they were supposed to address. A housing act passed in 1961 did more to help construction unions, Democratic machine politicians, and developers than to provide housing for the poor. The Manpower Development and Training Act, a holdover from the Eisenhower administration, as finally constituted under Kennedy subsidized officials and businesses much more than the individuals who needed the training. Its impact on unemployment was minimal. Kennedy was fond of touting his New Frontier, but little about his domestic policies was cutting-edge. As the NAACP's Clarence Mitchell observed, the "New Frontier looks like a dude ranch with Senator Eastland as the general manager."[26]

Ted Sorensen, one of Kennedy's closest advisers, claimed that "the one domestic subject that mattered most to John Kennedy [was] education." But the record did not validate that assertion. Myer "Mike" Feldman, an aide to Sorensen, confided that the president had no deep personal commitment to public education aside from training the mentally retarded, a legacy of the experience with his disabled sister, Rosemary. Kennedy's own school history—he attended elite private schools from kindergarten through college—rendered him much less personally familiar with the issues of public education than his predecessors Truman and Eisenhower.[27]

As president-elect, Kennedy assigned Sorensen and Feldman to set up thirteen task forces to develop policies on as many issues. One task force focused on education, headed by Frederick L. Hovde, president of Purdue University. Hovde's recommendations bore a price tag of over $9 billion and included $1.46 billion for public schools, with poorer states (primarily in the South) receiving larger amounts of the aid. It also proposed a construction program for colleges (both public and private), expansion of the NDEA, and forgiving college loans to all teachers, not only public school teachers.[28]

Kennedy's response to the education task force report was at best lukewarm: "I don't know whether we have the resources immediately to take on the whole program, but we'll have to decide the degree of need and set up a list of priorities." Feldman recalled that the president was "quite annoyed, quite upset because it [the report] contained what he thought was a very unrealistic program." New York's Francis Cardinal Spellman weighed in, denouncing the Hovde recommendations: "It is unthinkable that any American child be denied the Federal funds allotted to other children which are necessary for his mental development because his parents chose for him a God-centered education."[29]

Cardinal Spellman need not have worried. The combination of the persistent church-state issue, the increasing intransigence of Southern Democrats against any federal role in education, and a rising tide of conservatism among Republican lawmakers doomed any Kennedy initiatives on education. He submitted a bill in 1961 based partially on the task force's recommendations, but he did not push it. Given the political opposition, it is not clear that, even if he had invested energy in promoting the legislation, the outcome would have been different. He submitted another education package to Congress in 1962, but as in the first instance, it went nowhere. When he did so again early in 1963, the focus was on the less controversial higher-education sector, with requests for construction funds for both private and public universities. But he would not live to see its passage in December 1963.[30]

Given Lyndon Johnson's skill with Congress, especially in the contentious Senate, why did Kennedy not take more advantage of the vice president's political talents? Congressional leaders often shook their heads at the amateurish lobbying of the administration and the apparent disarray in the ranks of the president's advisers. It was not that Kennedy marginalized LBJ. He gave the Texan responsibility for civil rights. He also sent him abroad on numerous occasions with discretion to bargain on behalf of the administration. But JFK's problems with Congress were less a matter of ineffectual negotiation than of a lack of commitment.

By the late summer of 1962, the public disillusionment with Kennedy's presidency grew. An editorial in August 1962 stated flatly, "The kind of inspiring leadership that the 1960 campaign promised has not materialized." The administration had a program, but did not seem to have much stomach to fight for it in a Congress that was more conservative than during the last years of Eisenhower administration.[31]

Congress shared some of the blame for the administration's domestic inertia. The coalition of Southern Democrats and conservative Republicans seemed impenetrable. In November 1963, the New York Times observed, "Rarely has there been such a pervasive attitude of discouragement around Capitol Hill and such a feeling of helplessness to deal with it. This has been one of the least productive sessions of Congress within the memory of most of its members." Truman could relate to that and transformed his frustration into a major campaign theme in 1948. Perhaps Kennedy could do the same.[32]

Still, Kennedy managed several notable achievements during his unfinished presidency. Maintaining the robust pace of economic growth and keeping inflation in check in the years following World War II was a challenge, especially with increased foreign competition and labor demands for higher wages. He successfully confronted the steel industry's efforts to raise prices by threatening that the federal government might purchase cheaper foreign steel. At the same time, he obtained an investment tax credit for new plants and equipment that encouraged productivity and investment.[33]

Kennedy believed in an active government to stimulate the economy. He favored a tax cut to put more money into consumers' pockets and, therefore, maintain economic growth. Normally, tax cuts are associated with Republicans. But JFK was a thorough Keynesian. The top marginal tax rate in 1962 was 91 percent, which Kennedy hoped to reduce to a "more sensible" 65 percent (it is 35 percent today). A tax cut could generate a budget deficit, but Kennedy, like Keynes, believed that planned deficits during a time of prosperity (as opposed to an era of depression and war) was a good public policy. Tax cuts would stimulate demand, "driving the economy from the bottom up." Coupled with increased spending, the economy would prosper. As JFK confided to his chief economic adviser eleven days before his assassination, "First we'll have your tax cut, then we'll have my expenditures program." The tax cuts would benefit the middle and working classes in particular. These were not conservative Republican principles.[34]

As with a number of his other domestic programs, the tax cut remained unrealized by the time of his death, but its effectiveness as an economic stimulant was proven in the Johnson administration. The concern about the elderly, raised by both the Truman and Eisenhower administrations, returned in the Kennedy presidency with a version of health insurance for retirees that would eventually become Medicare. He also advocated expanding Social Security benefits. These measures were efforts to fulfill his campaign pledge to wage a "War on Poverty," a phrase and an initiative that would become a hallmark of Lyndon B. Johnson's presidency.[35]

Acceding to Eleanor Roosevelt's persistent lobbying, Kennedy also established the Commission on the Status of Women, and he endorsed equal pay for equal work, child-care facilities for working women, and paid maternity leave—policy objectives that remain elusive to this day. Each subsequent president formed a similar in-house group until the Reagan administration discontinued the practice. As with the other domestic initiatives, the issues raised by the Commission on the Status of Women had been circulating since the 1930s, but JFK was the first president to seriously consider their implementation. None of these ideas received congressional consideration, however.[36]

Perhaps Kennedy's presidency reflected too-high expectations. The New Frontier, a young, attractive family in the White House, the first president born in the twentieth century, an avatar for the confidence and youthful exuberance of the postwar era. His timidity on civil rights and the meager accomplishments in other domestic policy areas inevitably produced a letdown. But he was banking on a victory in 1964 that would enable him to pursue and realize his policy aspirations. At the time of his death, he already had education and civil rights bills in the Congress, though their passage was uncertain.

Kennedy's June comments on civil rights as a moral issue were undoubtedly heartfelt. But the reaction in the South confirmed his worst fears that any move toward racial equality risked further alienation of Southern whites from his administration. By October 1963, Stewart Alsop stated simply, "The South hates Kennedy." That, and Arizona's conservative senator Barry Goldwater's gains among rank-and-file Republicans and restless Southern Democrats by the fall of 1963, left Kennedy's hope for winning the South in 1964 uncertain at best.[37]

Above all, he needed Texas, and the Democratic Party there was split between conservatives led by Governor John Connally, an old Johnson friend, and liberals led by Senator Ralph Yarborough. Kennedy believed, probably correctly, that the factions needed to reconcile if he was to prevail in that state in 1964. Johnson felt the rift was irreconcilable and advised Kennedy against the attempt. Texans knew that the president had submitted a civil rights bill to Congress. That was all the information they needed to oppose him.

The inevitable failure of a fence-mending mission would also redound to the detriment of Johnson. LBJ was already in one of his despairing moods, and the trip made it worse. His public visibility was minuscule. An article in the *Texas Observer* in the fall of 1963 asked, "What Is an LBJ?," as if he were a soon-to-be-extinct species. When the popular CBS show *Candid Camera* asked a random sample of Americans, "Who is Lyndon Johnson?," the question stumped many of the respondents. Some of the replies included, "No, I don't know him." "There's a lot of Johnsons around here." "He's not president. Am I getting close?" White House operatives noticed that Johnson was unusually quiet at meetings there that fall.[38]

Despite Johnson's advice to the contrary, Kennedy scheduled a visit to Texas in November. Johnson, accepting the decision, scheduled a lavish reception for John and Jackie at his ranch on the evening of November 22 following their visit to Dallas.[39]

JOHN F. KENNEDY'S ASSASSINATION was a dissonant event in the confident postwar narrative, not only for the gifted generation, but also for other Americans. By late 1963, the gifted generation had become accustomed to certain verities. The New York Yankees always won; the Chicago Cubs never did. On television, father knew best, and the good guys almost always triumphed. Summer jobs were easy to get, and a flip of a radio dial would get good music at any time of day or night. Inequality existed, to be sure, but like anything else in postwar America, it would be amenable to a solution. And presidents never got murdered.

The Kennedy assassination was not the end of American innocence, if, in fact, the country was ever thus. Nor was it the great divide between the postwar consensus and the contention and violence that would mark the rest of the decade. The gifted generation or anyone else could not foresee that in November 1963. The assassination did not transform them into a state of perpetual disillusionment. Many were in college, and many were the first of their family to attend an institution of higher education. The future still seemed bright. The feeling was more of a loss of promise, a wondering of what might have been, and that was not necessarily a universal perspective. Students in classrooms in parts of the South cheered when they heard the news from Dallas.

Five days after JFK's funeral, his wife, Jackie, called journalist Theodore White to the family compound in Hyannis Port, Massachusetts. White had written a bestselling account of the 1960 presidential campaign, *The Making of the President, 1960* (1961), and was fond of Kennedy. She told White that Jack had been sickly as a boy and spent hours reading about King Arthur and the knights of the Round Table. The Broadway musical *Camelot* was virtually simultaneous with his presidency. The popular show opened in December 1960 and closed in January 1963. She related how her husband often played the cast album before going to bed.

Jackie, still mourning her husband, told White that the Kennedy administration had been Camelot, "a magic moment in American history, when gallant men danced with beautiful women, when great deeds were done, when artists, writers, and poets met at the White House and the barbarians beyond the walls were held back." But "it will never be that way again . . . There'll never be another Camelot again."[40]

In some respects, Jackie Kennedy was correct. From afar, the White House family seemed like an ideal, and that such an attractive family was the nation's face to the world added to the image. The administration did indeed draw luminaries from the cultural world in an ever-rotating salon of brilliant minds and talents, fashionable dress, and consummate beauty. As *Camelot* was a tuneful re-creation of a fictional past, the Kennedy administration also projected an image based more on appearance than on substance. The city on a hill was, after all, a New England construct. A rider from the West was coming to take the nation out of the clouds toward a promised land of equal justice for all.

CHAPTER 17

BEING LINCOLN

ON NOVEMBER 22, 1963, Senator James Eastland and his wife were driving in Virginia, en route to Mississippi for the Thanksgiving holiday. He noticed flags flying at half-staff. Wondering why, he turned on the radio and heard the news of Kennedy's assassination in Dallas. "Good God, Lyndon's president," he exclaimed to his wife. "He's gonna pass a lot of this damn fool stuff."[1]

When Johnson ascended to the presidency, it liberated him from the bonds of regionalism. He was not Lyndon Johnson, Southerner or Westerner; he was Lyndon Johnson, American. In his first speech after taking office, Johnson vowed to carry on the legacy of JFK in civil rights. Considering Kennedy's meager record—a fine speech on the morality of racial equality and a bill ending segregation in public facilities submitted to Congress, but not acted upon—the reference was more rhetorical than real. As one Kennedy scholar noted, "The larger Kennedy strategy on civil rights was to pursue glacial change."[2]

A measured pace would not work for Johnson. He had always been in a hurry, and now that he had achieved his life's ambition, his pace accelerated. In a brief address to Congress on November 27, his first since Kennedy's assassination, LBJ listed the passage of a civil rights act as first among his "immediate tasks." "We have talked long enough in this country about equal rights. We have talked for one hundred years or more. It is time now to write the next chapter, and to write it in the books of law."[3]

African American leaders held their breath as the president spoke. His Texas drawl added to the unease. Black writer Louis Lomax recalled watching that address with friends and thinking "that he comes from a state that has had forty-seven lynchings since 1920. We could not recall a single time when he had spoken out against these murders of our brothers. As we listened to him talk, the cracker twang in this voice chilled our hearts." But when he called for civil rights legislation, they "whooped with surprised delight." Comedian

Dick Gregory quipped that after the address "twenty million of us unpacked." Johnson soon met with Martin Luther King Jr., who described his feeling: "As a Southerner, I am happy to know that a fellow Southerner is in the White House who is concerned about civil rights."[4]

Johnson did not undergo a philosophical transformation as much as a change in venue. Representing Texas, advocacy of civil rights legislation would have sent him home to his ranch quickly, where, as he noted several months after he had signed the 1964 Civil Rights Act, "I couldn't have done anything for anybody, white or Negro. Now I represent the whole country, and I can do what the whole thinks is right. Or ought to." But it was not clear that the "whole country" supported racial equality. The initiative came from Johnson, with considerable help from the young black and white men and women who had carried the movement to that moment.[5]

His Southern colleagues, who knew him longest and best, understood, even if they disapproved mightily of what he was doing. Richard Russell, like a father disappointed in his erstwhile prodigal son, confided to presidential aide Bill Moyers, "Now you tell Lyndon . . . I've been expecting the rod for a long time, and I'm sorry that it's from his hand the rod must be wielded, but I'd rather it be his hand than anybody else's I know. Tell him to cry a little when he uses it."[6]

When one of Kennedy's aides warned LBJ about wasting time and legislative capital on "the lost cause of civil rights," Johnson retorted, "Well, what the hell's the presidency for?" He sensed this was a historic moment. If he was thinking more about his legacy and showing up the Ivy Leaguers, so what? He was going to get it done.[7]

Here was Johnson's pride, insecurity, and narcissism on display. An element of payback was indeed in his new position—against the Texans who condemned his modest efforts on behalf of civil rights, and also against the Ivy League intellectuals who disdained him. Meeting with a group of Texas newspaper editors, LBJ growled, "You sons of bitches have got to find out that the world doesn't belong to all one group of people, that this is a black man's world as well as the white man's world." As for the New Englanders, his message was equally confrontational: "Those Harvards think that a politician from Texas doesn't care . . . Now I represent the whole country, and I have the power. I always vowed that if I ever had the power, I'd make sure every Negro had the same chance as every white man. Now I have it. And I'm going to use it." He would be a president for the ages. He would be Lincoln.[8]

Johnson, hardly a man of modest ambition, wanted nothing less than to secure his legacy as a modern-day Abraham Lincoln: "I'm going to be the president who finished what Lincoln began." In doing so, he would lift up the South to full participation in American life. "Those civil righters are going to have to wear sneakers to keep up with me," he vowed. When Roy Wilkins, executive secretary of the NAACP, asked LBJ why he had this sense of urgency on civil rights, the president replied, "Free at last, free at last." Indeed, Johnson was free from trying to appease his senatorial colleagues and his Texas constituents and from having to convince skeptical Yankees of his commitment to civil rights.[9]

In his first State of the Union address on January 8, 1964, LBJ challenged lawmakers to move on the stalled Kennedy civil rights bill: "Let this session of Congress be known as the session which did more for civil rights than the last hundred sessions combined . . . We must abolish not some, but all racial discrimination. For this is not merely an economic issue, or a social, political, or international issue. It is a moral issue, and it must be met by the passage this session of the bill now pending in the House." It was hyperbole, but he fully expected to attain it all.[10]

Johnson cleared the first obstacle relatively easily. Howard Smith, the chairman of the powerful House Rules Committee, told reporters he planned no hearings on the bill. But when Congressman Emanuel Celler (D-NY) filed a discharge petition, Johnson gave it his full support. Smith then promised to hold hearings early in January. Not good enough. The Rules Committee revolted. With unanimous Republican and Northern Democratic support, the discharge petition cleared the committee and went before the entire House where it passed easily, 290–130, all but twenty-two Republicans, and four Democrats from outside the South, supporting the bill. The margin reflected the administration's pressure and its utilization of civil rights groups to promote the legislation. Richard Russell, watching the spectacle, complained that the representatives were subjected to the "most intensive, extensive, and effective lobby assembled in Washington in many years." The bill went to the Senate, with Southerners armed for battle and prepared to use their most effective weapon, the filibuster.[11]

LBJ became the grand conductor of the civil rights chorus, on the phone continuously with Senate members, civil rights leaders, labor officials, and journalists to build the vote for cloture to break the expected Southern filibuster. In a call to the NAACP's Roy Wilkins in January 1964, Johnson ordered, "What I want you to do . . . is to get on this bill now, because . . . unless you get twenty-five Republicans, you're not going to get cloture." He directed one labor leader to "talk to every human you could," because "if we fail on this, then we fail in everything." Richard Russell observed what James

Eastland knew from the beginning: "You know, we could have beaten John Kennedy on civil rights, but not Lyndon Johnson."[12]

Illinois senator Everett Dirksen would be key in this process. He had worked with Johnson and President Eisenhower on the successful passage of both the 1957 and 1960 Civil Rights Acts. As Senate minority leader, Dirksen's cooperation in rallying Republicans to the bill was essential. LBJ explained to Wilkins, "You're going to have to persuade Dirksen on why this is in the interest of the Republican Party. I think a Republican [who] goes along with you on cloture, that y'all ought to tell him that you're going to go along with him and help him . . . If a fellow will stand up and fight with you, y'all can cross party lines." An unusual piece of advice from a Democratic president, but LBJ wanted this bill. The stakes were that high, he told Wilkins: "If we lose this fight, Roy, we're going back ten years."[13]

Johnson also assigned Hubert Humphrey to bring Dirksen around, sending him with specific instructions. Humor him, lavish praise on him: "He's got to look good all the time." Then you never let him alone: "You drink with Dirksen! You talk with Dirksen! You listen to Dirksen!" When Johnson thought Humphrey was not being persistent enough, the Minnesotan reported, "The president grabbed me by my shoulder and damn near broke my arm."[14]

Johnson was careful not to leave his fingerprints on his Senate strategy. He admonished Humphrey to emphasize that the bill was the Senate's business. Although LBJ did not play the "hidden hand" in his presidency as often as Eisenhower, he was sufficiently protean to assume that role when he felt it was necessary.[15]

The bill had been strengthened since Kennedy initially proposed it in June 1963. It provided for the desegregation of all state-licensed businesses (an expansion from the original version), and a fair-employment-practices section established an Equal Employment Opportunity Commission (EEOC) to ensure equal treatment in hiring, voting rights in both state and federal elections, and a mandatory cutting off of federal funds to activities and institutions engaged in discrimination. Although the voting rights section was weak—requiring individuals to initiate suits, a step that could be dangerous and, therefore, unlikely—the bill was a substantial improvement over the original measure.[16]

Southern Democrats made their last stand, a seventy-five-day filibuster, the longest in American history, and then LBJ broke it, with the help of Senator Dirksen. The president acceded to Dirksen's demand that the linkage between resistance to school desegregation and federal funding did not apply to school systems in the North. Aside from a few minor changes, the bill was virtually the same measure that passed the House. The key moment came when

Dirksen, suffering from a painful ulcer, stood in the Senate well and declaimed, "Stronger than all the armies is an idea whose time has come. The time has come for equality . . . in education and in employment. It will not be stayed or denied. It is here."[17]

Every vote would count. Johnson arranged for Democratic senator Clair Engle of California, who was dying of brain cancer and had lost the ability to speak, to attend the session. From his wheelchair, Engle pointed to his eye when his name was called, signaling a yes vote. The cloture vote was as dramatic as any tally in the Senate's history. Cloture passed, and so did the bill. The tally in favor of the bill, 73–27, reflected the bipartisan support. Only one Democrat from outside the South, Robert C. Byrd of West Virginia, voted against the bill, as did five Northern Republicans, including Arizona's Barry Goldwater.[18]

A little after five P.M. on June 19, 1964, LBJ learned that the Senate had passed the civil rights bill. His first call was to Roy Wilkins. "You're a mighty good man. You deserve all the credit," the president told him. Wilkins termed the bill's passage "absolutely magnificent."[19]

Lady Bird dictated into her diary, "June Teenth"—June 19—"and this is the day that the civil rights bill passed in the Senate! I wonder if anybody but me will remember that June Teenth was always celebrated by all the Negroes in Texas . . . because it was the day that the Emancipation Proclamation went into effect in Texas."[20]

The House passed the Senate's version of the bill on the morning of Thursday, July 2. At 6:45 P.M. on July 2, LBJ signed the Civil Rights Act of 1964. Among the more than one hundred present included Bobby Kennedy, Everett Dirksen, Hubert Humphrey, and Martin Luther King Jr. In his brief remarks, Johnson framed the legislation in the commonwealth ideal—that the new law "does not give special treatment to any citizens. It does say the only limit to a man's hope for happiness, and for the future of his children, shall be his own ability." The civil rights act provided opportunity; it did not guarantee results. The president also reminded the assembled, and the nation, that "an overwhelming majority" of Republicans and Democrats in Congress had voted for it and that "its purpose is not to divide, but to end divisions."[21]

The world did not end for white Southerners; attitudes would follow. As *Atlanta Constitution* editor Ralph McGill argued, "There was . . . a great prejudice against women being allowed to vote . . . Legislation at last succeeded. The end of this discrimination saw the decline of the prejudice." By the 1960s, few thought twice about or commented on a woman entering a polling booth. Eventually, many hoped, it would be that way with integration.

Novelty would become habit, and habit would become the natural order of things.[22]

EQUALLY IMPORTANT, SEGREGATION did not make sense from a business perspective. In Nashville, black shoppers were spending $50 million a year, $10 million of that in segregated downtown stores. These establishments desegregated quickly, as did theaters, restaurants, and hotels. Schools continued to resist, however, and voting rights remained illusory, especially in the Deep South.[23]

In the weeks following Johnson's signing of the 1964 Civil Rights Act, compliance was widespread and defiance was minimal. Some restaurants closed and reopened as private clubs, and Southern political leaders such as George Wallace condemned the federal intrusion. But for the most part, the fortress of segregation, that linchpin of white supremacy, crumbled, at least in public facilities. The events of the early 1960s had weakened its foundation considerably. Unlike their actions following the *Brown* decision, Southern senators did not release defiant manifestos. Both Richard Russell and Louisiana senator Allen J. Ellender called for compliance.[24]

A year after the act went into effect, Harry Golden, a Charlotte journalist and antisegregation gadfly, reminded Johnson White House aide Jack Valenti that Golden had predicted in the *Carolina Israelite* in 1959, "Only a Southerner will eventually smash the caste system of the South . . . I have a strong suspicion that the Majority Leader, Senator Lyndon B. Johnson might possibly be that man." Now, Golden related, blacks "sit on all the boards including the City Council, in all the restaurants, hotels, motels, theatres, as though it had never been any different."[25]

By the time the president signed the act in July, many outside the South had moved to a more positive views of civil rights legislation. In April 1964, as Southern senators battled Johnson's bill, 57 percent of respondents stated that they approved of the president's handling of civil rights. The small steps of the 1950s were becoming strides toward freedom. As Roy Wilkins summarized, the act "is a giant step forward, not only for the Negro citizens but for our country."[26]

OTHER AMERICANS DID NOT SHARE Wilkins's assessment of the legislation, and not only in the South. White America was not solidly behind civil rights for African Americans in the presidential election year of 1964. That same April, Alabama's segregationist governor, George C. Wallace, garnered 34 percent of the vote in the Wisconsin Democratic primary. Before the primary, the state's Catholic and Protestant clergy, Democratic Party officials, and organized labor condemned Wallace as a bigot and an "apostle of discord." Wisconsin's governor, a Democrat, predicted Wallace would receive less than 10 percent of the vote.[27]

In Maryland, Wallace carried 43 percent of the vote, and as he noted to an aide, "If it hadn't been for the nigger bloc vote, we'd have won it all." But by June, trailing Johnson badly in the number of pledged delegates, Wallace launched a third-party bid and got on the ballot in sixteen states. Not enough to win the presidency, but maybe sufficient to throw the election into the House of Representatives, where Southern Democrats held considerable power.[28]

A good deal of the Alabamian's success in Wisconsin occurred because the state allowed Republicans to cross over and vote in the Democratic primary. It was to the Republicans' advantage to embarrass President Johnson. However, in Maryland and in Indiana, only Democrats voted in their primary. In these states, working-class whites, concerned about declining industry, contested neighborhoods, and resentful of Washington's focus on African Americans, turned out for Wallace. It portended the defection of the Northern white working class to the Republicans later in the decade and from the 1970s onward.[29]

Johnson confronted another headache from a constituency he believed solidly behind his 1964 presidential campaign: African American voters. Bob Moses, a New York City math teacher with a graduate degree from Harvard, and Fannie Lou Hamer, the twentieth child of a sharecropping family, launched the Mississippi Freedom Democratic Party (MFDP). The MFDP sought to represent the state of Mississippi at the Democratic National Convention in Atlantic City that August. The regular Democratic Party, the all-white party, of Mississippi already occupied the delegate slots and informed the president that they would walk out of the convention if any MFDP delegates were seated. LBJ's Southern friends advised him not to compromise at all. A fellow Texan, the state's governor, John Connally, warned him, "You let those bugaboos march in, and the whole South will march out."[30]

Buffeted from both the right and the left, a bitter president, having just delivered the most significant civil rights law in the nation's history, contemplated withdrawing from the race. The self-pity emerged full force: "By God, I'm gonna go up there and quit. Fuck 'em all!" He confided to an aide that it was not possible for "a white Southerner . . . to unite this nation in this hour." He doubted "whether a man born where I was born, raised like I was raised, could ever satisfy the Northern Jews and Catholics and union people." He went so far as to draft a statement taking himself out of the race. Was he serious? It was impossible to tell.[31]

The Republicans had their own intraparty turmoil. Arizona Republican senator Barry Goldwater came to embody the growing unease with government activism, especially with respect to civil rights, property rights, and regulation. California's overwhelming rejection of that state's fair housing law in 1964 provided another indication that white resistance to racial equality was hardly confined to the Deep South. While this backlash should have encouraged Republicans, it also stoked the insurgency of Goldwater conservatives against the moderates that threatened to split the party. Between 1957 and 1965, the number of right-wing organizations more than doubled, with the largest number from Southern California. Thousands of evangelicals also flocked to Goldwater's cause, none more important than Robert Schuller, whose Garden Grove (CA) Community Church (and later the Crystal Cathedral) anticipated the rise of megachurches later in the twentieth century.[32]

Free-market, low-tax, and minimal-government conservatives combined with the religious right to support Goldwater's candidacy and remake the Republican Party in their own image. At the Republican National Convention in San Francisco in mid-July, Goldwater's bellicose acceptance speech made no compromises with the moderate wing of the party. He made clear he wanted to roll back the New Deal and drastically reduce the federal government's regulatory and fiscal power: "Let me remind you: Extremism in the defense of liberty is no vice! . . . Moderation in the pursuit of justice is no virtue." A reporter watching the spectacle declared, "My God, he's going to run as Barry Goldwater!" His nomination split the Republican Party as moderate stalwarts such as New York's Jacob Javits and Michigan's George Romney deserted the candidate.[33]

The coterie surrounding Goldwater astonished even veteran journalists. Richard Rovere described Goldwaterites as being "as hard as nails. The spirit of compromise and accommodation was wholly alien to them." They aimed at "a total ideological victory and the total destruction of their critics . . . They wished to punish as well as to prevail."[34]

Goldwater had enormous appeal in the South. He had voted against the 1964 Civil Rights Act, only one of six Republicans to do so. That was all white voters needed to know. That he did so on the grounds of states' rights and individual rights made no difference. As novelist Walker Percy explained, "It would not have mattered if Senator Goldwater had advocated the collectivization of the plantations and open saloons in Jackson; he voted against the Civil Rights Bill and that was that." Mississippi would give Goldwater 87 percent of its vote in November.[35]

Goldwater pursued a rigidly ideological campaign, unconcerned about alienating a good swath of the electorate, even groups to whom he was talking. He went to Appalachia to denounce federal antipoverty legislation. To the elderly he said he would dump Social Security, and to farmers he promised to end price supports. As he put it succinctly, "My aim is not to pass laws but to repeal them." His anger at the Republican establishment was so strong that he stated, "Sometimes I think this country would be better off if we could just saw off the Eastern Seaboard and let it float out to sea." Democrats spread his comments far and wide, even taking a riff on his campaign theme, "In Your Heart You Know He's Right," by changing it to "In Your Guts, You Know He's Nuts."[36]

Johnson's campaign emphasized this last point with voters. Perhaps the most effective attack involved a television ad of a girl picking daisies, interrupted by an explosion and a flash, with Johnson's voice warning, "These are the stakes—to make a world in which all of God's children can live, or go on into the dark." As it turned out, LBJ would be just as trigger-happy, though not with nuclear weapons.[37]

The Armageddon theme suited Johnson's view of the election as less a campaign than a crusade, a combination of religious revival and a strong dose of Huey Long and William Jennings Bryan. As Johnson worked with aides on his opening campaign speech in early September, Johnson instructed aide Bill Moyers, "Let's get a little of this Holy Roller populist stuff . . . A land where every child can have training to fit his abilities. A home to protect him from the elements. A church to kneel in. And throw at least two biblical quotations in . . . that every one of them have heard . . . It's what you Baptists just pour to them all the time!" For a man who had had presidential dreams most of his life, he would not overlook any theme, trick, story, or ideal. It mattered less what he thought personally of these issues than that his opponent opposed all of them.[38]

The *Saturday Evening Post*, usually a reliably Republican organ, endorsed Johnson in an editorial that was remarkable for the faith that even moderate publications had in the ability of government to oversee the complexities of the modern age, a position that Eisenhower had staked out in the 1950s. The editor noted, "We have strained every seam and fabric of our traditional habits and thinking to keep abreast of an age when all the supposed boundaries of man's environment are being broken, gravity defied, space penetrated, the moon reached, the riddle of the human cell being unraveled. Merely to understand, much less to master this surge and change . . . has required and will require government entry into areas never before imagined." Goldwater, the writer alleged, looked backward, with "his mind preoccupied with one—and only one—idea: somehow to shrink the Government back into the familiar and comfortable small proportions of his Arizona youth." He "is a grotesque burlesque of the conservative he pretends to be . . . A crushing defeat for Goldwater will drive the fanatic saboteurs of the Republican Party back into the woodwork whence they came." The *Post* editor would soon have his party back, but not for long.[39]

JOHNSON WOULD WIN IN a landslide and carry with him a Congress so strong in Northern and Western Democrats, plus a coterie of moderate Republicans, that an ambitious legislative agenda seemed within reach. LBJ won a resounding 61 percent of the popular vote, and an even greater share of the electoral vote: 486 to 52. The new House of Representatives of the Eighty-ninth Congress would include 295 Democrats and 140 Republicans, or a gain of thirty-seven Democrats, almost all of them from the North and West. The party acquired two additional seats in the U.S. Senate for a total of 68. It was the largest Democratic majority in Congress since the Roosevelt landslide of 1936. The South moved deeper into a minority position within the party, though Southerners still held key committee chairmanships. But it would now be easier to obtain cloture with the cooperation of moderate Republicans.

Still, LBJ was not totally satisfied. Goldwater won only six states, five in the lower South—South Carolina, Georgia, Alabama, Mississippi, and Louisiana—plus his home state of Arizona. Johnson was most upset at losing Georgia, as he complained to aides Bill Moyers and McGeorge Bundy the morning after the election: "I didn't care about the other Southern states. Louisiana's a bunch of crooks, and Mississippi's too ignorant to know any better, and Alabama's the same way. But Georgia knows better." For the first time in the state's history, it voted for a Republican candidate for president.[40]

Johnson understood the political ramifications of the 1964 Civil Rights Act. As he confided to Bill Moyers, "I think we just delivered the South to the Republican Party for a long time to come." The Republicans surged in the South for other reasons besides race, but the president's and the Democratic Party's position on civil rights became a major factor in precipitating "the great white switch" to the party of Lincoln.[41]

It was not the beginning of the South's defection to the Republican Party; that had begun in the 1940s when Thomas E. Dewey polled one third of the popular vote of the former Confederacy in both the 1944 and 1948 presidential elections. In 1952, Eisenhower captured 48.8 percent of Southern votes. In that year voters elected Republican congressmen Joel T. Broyhill and Richard Poff in Virginia and Charles Jonas in North Carolina. Race was not the predominant issue in these elections; these men ran in districts experiencing economic growth and urbanization more attuned to Republicans' ideals of limited government, fewer regulations, and pro-business policies. Broyhill's district was in northern Virginia and Jonas's in the Charlotte area. Poff hailed from southwest Virginia, a region that had often returned Republicans both during and since the Civil War.[42]

In 1956, Eisenhower won 51.1 percent of the Southern vote, and Republicans picked up two additional seats in the South for the House of Representatives. Nixon, not as popular as Ike, scored 47.7 percent of the South's popular vote in 1960. In 1962, Republicans elected five new congressmen from the South, two of them from districts the party did not bother to contest as late as 1958. Republican voters tended to be younger, urban, and more affluent than other Southern voters. But when the Democratic Party became indelibly associated with civil rights, a mass migration to the Republicans began in 1964, particularly in the Deep South.[43]

LBJ looked on civil rights as part of a larger program to finish what the New Deal had begun: to expand opportunities for all Americans so that everyone could share in the postwar dream. It reflected his belief in the commonwealth ideal. Effective racial equality involved more than civil rights. He also understood that the great Democratic majorities in Congress provided a brief two-year window to pass legislation that would change the nation for the better for all time. These initiatives evolved into his War on Poverty and the Great Society. But most important on his agenda was the right to vote.

SELMA IS A LOVELY SOUTHERN TOWN perched above the Alabama River, a place of front porches, generous shade trees, white frame houses, and iced tea. Selma was at its loveliest in the spring, in March, when the streets of the well-tended white neighborhoods came alive with color and fragrance, where muffled voices mixed with gentle breezes in an expectant air of renewed life.[44]

Hidden away from the consciousness of lovely Selma lay another town. There, Selma's blacks lived in shanties and drab rows of public housing streaked with diesel soot from the passing engines of the Louisville & Nashville Railroad, whose tracks skirted the district. In the spring of 1962, a few residents of this part of Selma launched a voting registration drive. By the beginning of 1965, they had managed to register ninety-three new voters. At that rate, it would take 103 years to register all of the eligible black voters in Dallas County, Alabama.

Selma and Dallas County were not alone in the struggle for black voting rights. That fight had gone on for more than twenty years in various parts of the South. Voting rights struck at the heart of white supremacy. The 1960 Civil Rights Act was supposed to make voter registration easier, or at least place the activity under federal protection. Other than outright obstruction, the response of the Deep South to the 1960 Civil Rights Act was to make its registration rules even stricter. The Georgia legislature, for example, stiffened its literacy qualification. A political science professor at the University of Georgia conceded that even he might have difficulty passing the test. The Mississippi state legislature considered a constitutional amendment to prohibit citizens convicted of vagrancy, perjury, child desertion, adultery, fornication, larceny, and gambling from voting. When some lawmakers suggested adding habitual drunkenness to the list, objections were raised that such a provision "might even get some of us."[45]

Sometimes new legislation was unnecessary. Louisiana conducted a review of its voting rolls and removed ten thousand black voters for various manufactured reasons. Mississippi short-circuited a voter registration drive in James Eastland's Sunflower County and in Leflore County, where Emmett Till was murdered, by cutting off the distribution of federal food surpluses.[46]

To combat these subterfuges, SCLC, CORE, the NAACP, SNCC, and the Urban League joined forces to form the Voter Education Project (VEP) in 1962. The assumption among VEP workers was that the federal government would protect them if trouble arose. SNCC drew Alabama and Mississippi primarily because, as one member recalled, "nobody else wanted 'em." SNCC had already been involved in Mississippi voter registration efforts in 1961 to little avail and much violence. SNCC leader Bob Moses received a vicious beating from whites after attempting to register black voters in Liberty, Mississippi. In nearby Amite County, a white state legislator shot and killed a black farmer for no other apparent reason other than that the farmer had attempted to register to vote. By the end of 1961, SNCC, its resources and nerves depleted, abandoned the campaign. The resources of the VEP in 1962 yielded paltry results and continued violence.[47]

But Bob Moses was not easily discouraged. Too many people were putting their bodies on the line for equal justice throughout the South. In late 1963, Moses and his colleague David Dennis planned a voter-registration drive for the summer of 1964 in Mississippi. This seemed to be nothing more than the resurrection of the earlier failed efforts. SNCC leaders, however, proposed to invite hundreds of Northern white college students to the state to assist in registering blacks. They knew that few African Americans would be registered that summer, but they hoped that the presence of white college students would provoke a reaction that would make voting rights a national priority. As Dennis calculated, "We knew that if we had brought in a thousand blacks, the country would have watched them slaughtered without doing anything about it. Bring a thousand whites and the country is going to react to that." Prior to

1964, sixty-three black registration workers had been murdered in Mississippi, and the media had generally ignored the killings.[48]

The Freedom Summer was less than a week old when news spread that three volunteers were missing near Philadelphia, Mississippi, in Neshoba County. Michael Schwerner was a twenty-four-year-old social worker from New York City who had been in the state since January running a SNCC community center in Meridian, Mississippi, with his wife, Rita. Andrew Goodman, twenty years old, was a student at Queens College in New York City. James Chaney, twenty-one, was a black Mississippian and a CORE volunteer. The three had come to Neshoba County to inspect the ruins of a black church recently burned and to reassure African Americans in the area that the voter registration drive would continue. On their way back to Meridian, they passed through Philadelphia, and just outside of that town Deputy Sheriff Cecil Price arrested them. They were never seen alive again.

Six weeks later, the FBI, dispatched by President Johnson, recovered three bodies from an earthen dam near Philadelphia. The FBI arrested twenty-one men, including the sheriff and deputy sheriff, for carrying out a Klan-inspired plot to murder the three workers. Three years later, an all-white jury returned a guilty verdict against seven of the defendants. Judge W. Harold Cox, a Kennedy appointee, meted out sentences, the most severe being a ten-year prison term. The wanton brutality of the Mississippi murders indeed shocked the nation, but as the college students filtered back North in August, the spotlight on voting rights dimmed. The tally for the Freedom Summer: thirty-five shooting incidents, thirty homes and other buildings bombed, eighty persons beaten; six murders, and twelve hundred blacks registered to vote across the state.[49]

Despite these unpromising results, Martin Luther King Jr. believed that Dallas County, Alabama, could serve as the Birmingham of the voting rights movement. The greatest voter suppression in the Deep South occurred in areas where African Americans were the majority, as in the Mississippi Delta. Selma, the county seat of Dallas County, was more than 50 percent black. Only 383 of 15,000 eligible black voters were registered.[50]

King hoped that as Eugene "Bull" Connor was his "ally" in the Birmingham drama, so the Dallas County sheriff Jim Clark would fill a similar role. Clark's racial views were straightforward: when a reporter asked him if a particular woman defendant was married, the sheriff replied, "She's a nigger woman and she hasn't got a Miss or a Mrs. in front of her name." Clark was most notable for the personal posse that he had raised and led to racial trouble spots around the state.[51]

On Sunday morning, March 7, 1965, white Selma was in a festive mood. Confederate battle flags decked downtown, and sales in firecrackers were brisk. Some families prepared picnic lunches to take to Edmund Pettus Bridge, a structure named after a Confederate general and which the demonstrators had to cross on the road to Montgomery. The marchers hoped to present their case personally to Governor George Wallace—a futile ambition, as they knew—but most of all to dramatize voting rights. Six hundred marchers filed out of Brown Chapel AME Church in the black section of town, walking double file, some clutching tiny American flags, turning onto Broad Street toward Pettus Bridge. Deployed across the four-lane expanse of Highway 80 on the opposite side of the bridge stood Major John Cloud and fifty Alabama state troopers in their black uniforms and black helmets, backed up by thirty of Sheriff Clark's mounted possemen. The troopers had goggles and tin-can snouts covering their faces. Governor Wallace had dispatched Major Cloud and his men to preserve public safety and enforce his order forbidding the march.

When the marchers passed the bridge's midpoint high above the Alabama River, Major Cloud stepped forward and announced, "This is an unlawful march. It will not be allowed to continue. You have three minutes to disperse." Some of the demonstrators knelt to pray, others stood in frozen, fearful silence. Scarcely a minute had passed when the major raised his black-gloved hand and ordered, "Troopers, advance!" On the signal, his men charged toward the demonstrators accompanied by shrieking rebel yells. Troopers, flailing away with bullwhips and nightsticks, descended on the marchers and fired tear gas canisters into the crowd. The ABC television network interrupted its popular *Sunday Night at the Movies* (the film was *Judgment at Nuremberg*) to bring viewers the scenes from Selma.[52]

Governor George Wallace visited the White House on Saturday, March 13, for a marathon three-hour session with the president. Johnson had to convince the governor that it was in his best interest to ensure the safety of the marchers, as they had vowed to carry out their pilgrimage to the state capital, despite the violence of March 7.

Johnson not only was the lead actor in this morality play, he also set the stage. He received the governor in the Oval Office and seated him on a sofa with soft cushions, so that the diminutive Wallace was almost swallowed by the upholstery and sat just above the floor. The president meanwhile positioned himself in a rocking chair and hulked over the nearly prostrate Wallace. LBJ allowed Wallace to speak first, and the governor presented his usual complaint of how outside agitators were disrupting the normally decent race relations in Alabama and that voting rights were a state matter, not a concern of the federal government.[53]

The president responded, inching even closer, "I know you're like me, not approving of brutality," and handed Wallace a newspaper with a picture of an Alabama state trooper kicking an African American demonstrator who had been knocked to the ground. Wallace replied that the troopers were only doing their duty to protect property and the citizens of Alabama as well as to ensure highway safety. Johnson ignored the reply and continued to pound at the issue of police brutality, finally getting the governor to acknowledge that some overzealous law enforcement might have occurred at the march.

LBJ moved on to the question of voting rights for Alabama blacks. Wallace protested that he had no power over local registrars to control the registration process. "Don't shit me about your persuasive power, George," LBJ shot back. "I saw you . . . attacking me [on television], George. And you know what? You were so damn persuasive that I had to turn off the set before you had me changing my mind."

LBJ then put a series of questions to Wallace, the answers to which he already knew, but he wanted to get the governor in a defensive frame of mind and fearing the worst. "Why don'tcha just desegregate all your schools?" Johnson asked. "You and I go out there in front of these television cameras right now, and you announce you've decided to desegregate every school in Alabama." The prospect agitated Wallace considerably: "Oh, Mr. President, I can't do that, you know. The schools have got school boards; they're locally run." Johnson roared, "Don't you shit me, George Wallace."

After nearly three hours of confrontational rhetoric, Johnson softened his tone. George, he implored, don't "think about 1968; you think about 1988. You and me, we'll be dead and gone then . . . Now you've got a lot of poor people down there in Alabama, a lot of ignorant people. You can do a lot for them, George. Your president will help you. What do you want left after you when you die? Do you want a great . . . big . . . marble monument that reads, 'George Wallace—He Built'? . . . Or do you want a little piece of scrawny pine board lying across that harsh caliche soil that reads, 'George Wallace—He Hated'?"

Wallace staggered out of the meeting remarking, "Hell, if I'd stayed in there much longer, he'd have had me coming out for civil rights." Although LBJ did not get a conversion, he convinced the governor to allow LBJ to federalize eighteen hundred Alabama national guardsmen when the voting rights marchers walked to Montgomery two weeks after "Bloody Sunday." LBJ knew that he could not get Wallace to come out for civil rights. But, by LBJ's suggesting a face-saving solution, it was, from Wallace's perspective, the least objectionable alternative. On March 15, federal district judge Frank Johnson, an Eisenhower appointee, ruled that Governor George Wallace had no legal right to block the march to Montgomery.

On the evening of March 15, 1965, President Johnson addressed a nation-wide television audience. It was probably LBJ's finest speech as president. He began by marking Selma as a turning point, much as Lexington and Concord and Appomattox were turning points. Selma demanded that the federal government once again take up the cause of freedom: "For the cries of pain and the hymns and protests of oppressed people have summoned into convocation all the majesty of this great government." Johnson made clear that race was not only a problem in Selma, or even the South more generally: "There is no Negro problem. There is no Southern problem. There is no Northern problem. There is only an American problem. And we are met here tonight as Americans—not as Democrats or Republicans—we are met here as Americans to solve that problem."[54]

Johnson vowed to send Congress a voting rights bill in two days. Its major features would include removal of all measures employed by states to restrict African American voting rights. This would apply to all elections—federal, state, and local. If a state still refused to register black voters, federal officials would enroll them. Addressing all Americans, the president declared, "Their cause must be our cause too. Because it is not just Negroes, but really it is all of us, who must overcome the crippling legacy of bigotry and injustice." At that moment, with his arms raised and with determination in his voice, he exclaimed, "And we *shall* overcome."

John Lewis, by then chairman of SNCC, watched the address on television. The president's citation of the movement's anthem left Lewis "deeply moved. Lyndon Johnson was no politician that night. He was a man who spoke from his heart. His were the words of a statesman and more; they were the words of a poet." Perhaps the most unexpected endorsement of the night came from a gesture made by several Supreme Court justices in the assemblage who became so carried away by this passage that they broke their traditional reserve and applauded.[55]

Martin Luther King Jr. viewed the president's address with some SCLC colleagues, one of whom recalled that when the president spoke those words, "we all cheered. I looked over toward Martin, and Martin was very quietly sitting in the chair, and a tear ran down his cheek. It was a victory like none other, it was an affirmation of the movement, it guaranteed us . . . that millions of people in the South would have a chance to be involved in their own destiny." That was what Johnson had hoped. The government would provide the legal framework and on-the-ground assistance if necessary, and the South's black population would do the rest.[56]

Southern senators in the chamber had a different reaction to Johnson's deliberate recitation of "we shall overcome." At a breakfast the following morning, Senator Spessard Holland of Florida sputtered to his Southern colleagues, "Did you hear ol' Lyndon say, 'We shall overcome'?" Strom Thurmond, equally exercised, replied, "The president betrayed the Southern cause." They realized that Lyndon Johnson was using the power of the federal government to transform the South in a way greater than at any time since the Civil War.[57]

A major theme running through the speech was that the civil rights bill was not a measure solely for African Americans. It benefited all Americans. Johnson invoked the commonwealth ideal—the principle that the fight for voting rights was not a regional or racial battle, but one that concerned all Americans. Opening the gates of freedom for one group expanded freedom for all. Removing the contradictions between American ideals and reality strengthened the nation. LBJ stressed he was presenting not merely a bill, but a program. "Its object is to open the city of hope to all people of all races." He talked about his time in Cotulla, Texas, at the Mexican American school. There, Johnson recalled, he found out "what poverty and hatred can do when you see its scars on the hopeful face of a young child." He said he never dreamed (a fib, to be sure) he would be in a position "to help the sons and daughters of those students and to help people like them all over the country." Then, pointing his finger at the members of Congress before him, he vowed, "But now I do have that chance—and I'll let you in on a secret—I mean to use it. And I hope that you will use it with me." Those who knew Lyndon also knew that this was a threat as much as it was a promise.

The pending legislation was no slapped-together, last-minute reaction to events in Selma. In December 1964, looking ahead to the next session of Congress, some of Johnson's advisers had urged him to postpone action on voting rights. After spending considerable political capital on the passage of the 1964 Civil Rights Act, it was time to move on to other domestic issues for a while. But Lyndon Johnson was in a hurry and brushed these cautions aside. In mid-December he ordered Attorney General Nicholas Katzenbach to "undertake the greatest midnight legislative drafting" session since the New Deal to secure black voting rights. LBJ added, "We need it pretty quick." The president kept Dr. King apprised of the bill, assuring him that voting rights legislation would be the "greatest achievement of my administration."[58]

On March 21, thirty-six hundred marchers, protected by eighteen hundred federalized Alabama national guardsmen and two thousand U.S. troops and marshals, took the familiar walk down Broad Street and onto the Edmund Pettus Bridge. Years later, John Lewis said that Barack Obama "was what comes at the end of that bridge." Four days later, after a thankfully uneventful journey, the marchers, now swelled to an interracial crowd of twenty-five thousand, entered Montgomery. Whites heckled from the sidelines, waving Confederate battle flags and singing "Dixie." The marchers broke out into "The Star-Spangled Banner."

In Montgomery, Martin Luther King Jr. mounted the capitol steps and stood on the star where Jefferson Davis took his oath of office as president of the Confederate States of America 104 years earlier. Across the way, he could see Dexter Avenue and the Baptist church where he preached as a young man and from where he had led the bus boycott that helped ignite the civil rights movement. The geographic distance between the church and the capitol was small, but the uplift in dignity and equality from then to now was immeasurable.

King had requested a meeting with George Wallace, which, of course, the governor refused. It hardly mattered. Amid the holiday atmosphere, King told the assembled, "I know some of you are asking today, 'How long will it take?' I come to say to you this afternoon, however difficult the moment, however frustrating the hour, it will not be long because truth pressed to earth will rise again." King concluded with a ringing declaration that connected the cause of justice both to the conflict a century earlier and to the struggle today, quoting the words of "The Battle Hymn of the Republic." "How long? Not long. Because mine eyes have seen the glory of the coming of the Lord . . . His truth is marching on!"[59]

SOUTHERN LAWMAKERS MOUNTED a futile filibuster, easily overcome with cloture on a 70–30 vote. The bill passed by lopsided majorities in the House, 328–74, and in the Senate, 79–18. All of the negative votes in the Senate came from Southern senators.

On August 6, 1965, an ebullient Lyndon B. Johnson went to Capitol Hill to sign the Voting Rights Act. A bust of Lincoln stood over his shoulder in the Rotunda. His remarks were a classic statement of the commonwealth ideal's quid pro quo: government will legislate to ensure equality of opportunity; it was up to the people to run with it. "Presidents and Congress, laws and lawsuits, can open the doors to the polling places and open the doors to the wondrous rewards which await the wise use of the ballot. But only the individual Negro, and all others who have been denied the right to vote, can really walk through those doors, and can use that right, and can transform the vote into an instrument of justice and fulfillment."[60]

The results were swift. Within nineteen days after Johnson signed the Voting Rights Act, 27,385 African Americans had registered to vote. In one recalcitrant district, Jefferson Davis County, Mississippi, the Justice

Department dispatched a team of federal examiners to ensure voting rights. But few Deep South districts failed to comply. In fifty Louisiana parishes, for example, registrars did not reject a single black registrant.[61]

By the end of 1966, only four former Confederate states had failed to register more than 50 percent of their eligible black voters. A year later, only Mississippi, with 45 percent of eligible black voters registered, failed to reach the 50 percent standard. By 1968, Mississippi had climbed to 59 percent.[62]

Black officeholders, a rarity, especially in the Deep South, grew along with the black vote. Between 1965 and 1969, the number of black elected officials increased sixfold in the six Deep South states. In 1972 Barbara Jordan of Houston and Atlanta's Andrew Young were elected to Congress. Young was the first black congressman from the Deep South since the nineteenth century.[63]

The new presence of African American voters boosted the political careers of white moderate governors such as Florida's Reubin Askew, Arkansas's Dale Bumpers, and Georgia's Jimmy Carter. Young voters, the white and black members of the gifted generation, were especially conspicuous in these campaigns, as when Bumpers defeated Orval Faubus in 1970. When Carter took over from Georgia's segregationist governor Lester Maddox that same year, he declared, "The time for racial discrimination is over . . . No poor, rural, weak, or black person should ever have to bear the additional burden of being deprived of the opportunity of an education, a job, or simple justice." That statement would have doomed a statewide political candidate in Georgia just a few years earlier.[64]

LBJ did not limit his civil rights program to legislation, as monumental as that contribution was to the cause of equality. He appointed more African Americans to high positions within the federal government than had any previous president. Significant "firsts" included the first black cabinet officer, Robert Weaver, as secretary of Housing and Urban Development; the first black governor of the Federal Reserve System, Andrew Brimmer; Carl Rowan, the first African American director of the U.S. Information Agency (later folded into the State Department); and the first black Atomic Energy Commission member, Samuel Nabrit. Perhaps the most significant appointment was LBJ's nomination of Thurgood Marshall to the U.S. Supreme Court in 1967. In the 178-year history of the U.S. Supreme Court to that point, all of the justices had been white.[65]

IN THE FALL OF 1965, the Reverend James Bevel, a close aide of Martin Luther King Jr.'s, pronounced, "There is no more civil rights movement. President Johnson signed it out of existence when he signed the voting rights bill." It was not a triumphal statement. Bevel was frustrated. Generational cracks in the civil rights coalition, divisions between militants and pacifists, between the middle-class and the poor, contributed to that frustration. The federal government had removed the barriers of exclusion and second-class citizenship, at least legally. What the future agenda of civil rights should be was unclear, as were the tactics on how to achieve it. By the time of Bevel's announcement, much had changed. Five days after Lyndon B. Johnson signed the Voting Rights Act, the Watts section of Los Angeles exploded in three nights of racial violence. If one had to put a specific date on when the civil rights movement ended, it would have been August 11, 1965.[66]

CHAPTER 18

PATRIMONY

WHEN PRESIDENT JOHNSON SIGNED the Clean Air Act Amendment in October 1965, he quoted the author of a book published three years earlier: "In biological history, no organism has survived long if its environment became in some way unfit for it, but no organism before man has deliberately polluted its own environment." The author was Rachel Carson, and her book *Silent Spring* (1962) alerted Americans to what, slowly but surely, was happening to the environment: we were not only losing our patrimony, we were in danger of killing ourselves.[1]

Concern about the environment became a national movement by the mid-1960s. Efforts grew to find solutions that would keep people and nature healthy. Two decades of postwar growth had taken their toll. In Chicago by 1966, an average of forty tons of sooty particles fell on each square mile of the city every month. New York City established a task force on air pollution that year, concluding, after a killer smog enveloped Manhattan, "More poisons are pumped into the air in New York than anywhere else in the United States."[2]

Writer Ed Christopherson decided he had had enough of urban living and decamped to the Big Sky Country of Missoula, Montana. "When I lived in New York, I used to watch the clinkers come down the air shaft and remember how great the pine-scented evening downdrafts smelled in Missoula." But Missoula, by 1966, was the country's second-worst smog area. Some Missoulans considered posting signs out on the highway: MISSOULA, MONTANA— DIRTY SKY COUNTRY.[3]

Denver was also once a fair pristine place now grown foul. A woman told a reporter in 1966 that when she moved into her house twenty years before "the yard had nice green grass and beautiful roses. The whole neighborhood was clean . . . you could see the mountains clearly most of the time, with snowcaps." But as the traffic worsened in and around her neighborhood, she and her husband began having eye and sinus trouble. "The roses all shriveled and died. The lawn began to go. Half the time you can't see the mountains anymore. I have to clean the house every day, and it's still gritty and greasy."[4]

In 1963, open fires, incinerators, chimneys, smokestacks, and tailpipes spewed 125 tons of chemicals into the American air; by 1965, that had climbed to 145 million, and with it respiratory diseases. Between 1955 and 1965, California recorded a 300 percent increase in emphysema cases.[5]

Although environmental issues had periodically surfaced since World War II, they had only occasionally pierced national consciousness before the early 1960s. The deteriorating air in major cities, concerns over radioactive waste from nuclear weapons testing, the fouling of waterways by industrial and agricultural wastes, and the destructiveness of suburban sprawl had built constituencies for federal regulations to protect both the environment and, therefore, human beings. Rachel Carson's book became the catalyst for a movement.

In June 1963, Carson sat before Senator Abraham Ribicoff (D-CT) and his Senate Committee on Commerce in a windowless hearing room on the ground floor of the New Senate Office Building in Washington, D.C. The senators were considering federal regulation of pesticides. Ribicoff looked at her and said, "You are the lady who started all this." It was reminiscent of Abraham Lincoln's remark to Harriet Beecher Stowe when the author of *Uncle Tom's Cabin* visited him at the White House in 1862: "So you are the little woman who wrote the book that started this great war." In fact, Senator Ernest Gruening (D-AK), a committee member, predicted that *Silent Spring* would change the course of history much like *Uncle Tom's Cabin*.[6]

Like Stowe, Carson was a middle-aged woman small in stature and large in passion about her work. As Stowe changed Americans' perceptions on the institution of slavery, so Carson altered our sense of how the environment and humans interacted, and how both were dependent upon the other for survival.[7]

RACHEL CARSON WAS BORN IN 1907 in Springdale, Pennsylvania, about sixteen miles northeast of Pittsburgh. She was the youngest of three children. Though the setting along the Allegheny River was bucolic, the region suffered from the air pollution of steel-mill furnaces that rose from the banks of the river. Carson did not recall Springdale fondly. It was a place of relentless ugliness. Her parents were of Scotch Irish descent. Her mother, Maria, and father, Robert, both came from middle-class families. Maria taught school, but had to resign when she married Robert Carson. They purchased a sixty-four-acre farm, where Rachel was born. Robert was not much of a farmer, and the family struggled financially.

Maria was an avid reader and nature lover. She passed along those passions to Rachel. If the sixty-four acres did not yield much profit, they were priceless as a natural laboratory. With her older siblings at school, Rachel and her mother explored the property and its rich botanic diversity. Rachel recalled that she was always "happiest with wild birds and creatures as companions." That connection would remain for the rest of her life.[8]

Above all, Rachel loved to write. *St. Nicholas* was a renowned children's magazine, founded by the noted American writer Mary Mapes Dodge. She devoted a section of the magazine to stories written by children. Among the precocious authors who appeared in the publication were William Faulkner, F. Scott Fitzgerald, Edna St. Vincent Millay, and in May 1918 eleven-year-old Rachel Carson. Within a year, Rachel had had four stories published in *St. Nicholas*, receiving a gold badge and $10 for her feat. A fifth story, the first about nature, appeared in July 1922 in the category of "My Favorite Recreation" and told of her meanderings in the woods with her dog and the birds and flora she discovered, notated, and photographed along the way.[9]

Rachel attended the Pennsylvania College for Women (PCW, now Chatham University). At PCW, she excelled in sports, playing field hockey and basketball, but avoided the college's social functions, especially those involving young men. She much preferred reading in her room, and writing, especially about nature. Although she had never been to the ocean, she wrote a short story, "The Master of the Ship's Light," that her English professor thought was excellent. She particularly complimented Rachel for translating technical information into brilliant prose: "Your style is so good because you have made what might be a relatively technical subject very intelligible to the reader."[10]

An introductory biology course taught by Mary Scott Skinker captured Rachel's imagination both for the subject matter and the instructor. But before Rachel's senior year at PCW, Skinker left to pursue a doctorate in zoology at Johns Hopkins University in Baltimore. Although Skinker would leave Hopkins to take a position as a researcher in parasitology at the zoological division of the U.S. Department of Agriculture in Washington, D.C., she remained in touch with Rachel, and the two spent long weekends at Skinker's cabin near Luray, Virginia, in the Shenandoah Valley.

When Rachel graduated from PCW in 1929, she received two pieces of good news: she had obtained a full-tuition scholarship at Hopkins and had won a seat at the world-famous Marine Biological Laboratory at Woods Hole, Massachusetts, for the summer. Woods Hole was a branch of what would become the U.S. Fish and Wildlife Service (FWS). Rachel's experience at Woods Hole was formative. Her sea books derived mainly from her research that first summer. Of the seventy-one investigators at the facility, thirty-one were women, a good example of the strides women were making in the sciences by 1930 and especially of the federal government's openness to their participation in research projects.

Carson received her M.A. from Johns Hopkins in 1932, but as her family's financial situation deteriorated in the midst of the Depression, she dropped out of the doctoral program to teach at the University of Maryland's Dental and Pharmacy School. But it was only a part-time position. Skinker encouraged Carson to take the federal civil service exam, and she found work with the U.S. Bureau of Fisheries, the forerunner of the FWS. Her task was to produce a public-education series of fifty-two brief radio programs on marine life called *Romance Under the Waters*. The job called for someone with expertise in marine biology who could make the subject interesting to the general public. Her superiors at Fisheries were so pleased with her work that she received a permanent appointment as a junior aquatic biologist, beginning a long and productive career as a government scientist.[11]

She eventually produced a book based on her government research, *Under the Sea-Wind*, "an intimate portrait of the sea and shore creatures whose world of air and water the reader enters," published by Simon & Schuster in 1941. What commanded the attention of reviewers was the eloquence of her writing. The *New York Times* found the book so "skillfully written as to read like fiction, but is in fact a scientifically accurate account of life in the ocean and along the ocean shore." But a month after its publication, the attack on Pearl Harbor shifted attention elsewhere and the book sold poorly.

Rachel continued to move upward through the federal pay-grade scale, receiving four promotions in two years. She prepared a series of detailed guides to the national wildlife refuge system for FWS, called *Conservation in Action*. The series broadened her thinking about the relationship between water, land, and humans. Her thoughts eventually became a book, *The Sea Around Us* (1951). Unlike her first book, this one sold well. It won the National Book Award for Nonfiction and was eventually translated into thirty-two languages.[12]

Despite its widespread popularity, *The Sea Around Us* elicited mixed reviews in the scientific community. Some of the negative reaction derived from Carson's status: she was outside academia, she dared to address a popular audience rather than only her scientific peers, and she was a woman. One reader thought Rachel Carson was a pen name: "I assume from the author's knowledge that he must be a man."[13]

The success of *The Sea Around Us* resulted in the reissue of *Under the Sea-Wind* in 1952, and it also reached the bestseller lists. The *New York Times* put Carson in exalted company: "Great poets from Homer, with his sonorous hexameters on the 'loud-sounding sea,' down to Masefield, with his poignant verses about sailing, have tried to evoke the deep mystery and endless fascinations of the ocean; but the slender, gentle lady who is editor of the US FWS seems to have the best of it. Once or twice in a generation does the world get a physical scientist with literary genius."[14]

The success of these books secured Carson financial independence for the first time in her life. She resigned from the FWS in June 1952 "to devote my time to writing." Her writing in the 1950s became increasingly related to public policy. She strongly opposed the federal government's plan to build a dam that would flood the national monument areas of Colorado and Utah, including Dinosaur National Monument. Carson spoke out against the "substitution of man-made ugliness—this trend toward a perilously artificial world," citing Levittown and the clear-cutting of trees for its development; she condemned the proposal to build a six-lane highway through the middle of Rock Creek Park in Washington, D.C. "Is it the right of this, our generation, in its selfish materialism, to destroy these things because we are blinded by the dollar sign?"[15]

In 1955, Carson published another bestseller, *The Edge of the Sea*, which established her as the nation's leading interpreter of marine science. She also wrote a television script on clouds for *Omnibus*, CBS TV's popular cultural and scientific show. She wrote articles for popular magazines, such as "Help Your Child to Wonder," in the July 1956 issue of *Woman's Home Companion*, asserting that communing with nature would enhance a child's emotional development.

In the fall of 1957, friends in the Audubon Society contacted Carson about the U.S. Department of Agriculture's plan to spray thousands of acres of crop- and forestland in the South with pesticides to eradicate the fire ant. The USDA was anxious to try out new chemical concoctions, dieldrin and heptachlor, that would not only control pests, but eliminate them altogether.

The fire ant was not a major problem. It had existed in the South for forty years prior to 1957, and aside from the problems farm machinery encountered with ant mounds, few paid much attention to the pests. Only two Southern states listed the fire ant among the twenty most important insect pests, and those states placed it near the bottom. According to Alabama scientists, "damage to plants in general is rare. No damage to livestock has been observed." An Alabama state health officer reported, "There has never been recorded in Alabama a human death resulting from the bites of imported fire ants," and medical cases resulting from bites he termed "incidental."[16]

The USDA, however, insisted that fire ants destroyed crops and attacked livestock. Besides, the USDA had new chemicals and was anxious to test them. The impact on poultry, livestock, pets, and wildlife in the treated areas was immediate. In one Alabama tract treated in 1959, half the bird population disappeared, and ground species suffered 100 percent mortality. The USDA advised farmers to keep milk cows out of treated pastures for up to ninety days. But there were no testing procedures to determine if the grazing areas were safe by that time. The Food and Drug Administration (FDA) eventually stepped in to ban dieldrin and heptachlor from any food, which effectively ended the program. In the meantime, Carson learned that Florida farmers had controlled fire ants for years merely by just treating the mounds with chemicals rather than spraying the poisons over fields.[17]

At the same time, a group of Long Island residents sought a restraining order against the USDA from spraying their property with DDT mixed with fuel oil. Carson, through her government connections, already knew about the spraying programs. She also knew that the pesticides were killing a wider array of species, and that the pests were becoming increasingly resistant to the chemicals.

Marjorie Spock, the eldest sister of Dr. Benjamin Spock, and one of the women involved in the Long Island suit, wrote to Carson, including a stack of documents on the impact of pesticides and the connections between the USDA and the chemical industry. In the early 1950s, Spock and her friend Mary Richards had purchased a home in Brookville, Long Island, where they practiced organic farming on a two-acre tract. This tract received the DDT/fuel-oil doses—fourteen times in one day—during the summer of 1957.

The object of the spraying was the gypsy moth, which in its larval stage attacked oak trees and other hardwoods. In the early-twentieth century the USDA imported thirteen parasites and predators from abroad to successfully combat gypsy moth outbreaks. But in 1957, the USDA in conjunction with local authorities decided to institute gypsy moth chemical spraying in the dense suburbs of Nassau County, Long Island, just outside New York City. The spraying was indiscriminate, including the drenching of a housewife who was desperately trying to cover up her flowers and shrubs before the onslaught. The insecticide fell on children at play and on commuters at a Long Island Rail Road station. In one town, a horse drank from a trough contaminated by the spray and died ten hours later.[18]

These incidents, and fear for their own food supply and dairy animals, prompted Spock and Richards to sue. The case eventually reached the U.S. Supreme Court in 1960, which declined to review it on a technicality, although Justice William O. Douglas wrote a strong dissent supporting the case. The adverse publicity and the Court's ambiguous ruling caused USDA to abruptly cancel the spraying program.

Carson's growing concern about pesticides received another jolt when an FWS study noted extensive collateral damage during another gypsy moth spraying program. Here was one government agency contradicting another government agency. Through her government contacts, Carson was again able to build up a thick file of research findings that, taken together, presented an alarming picture of USDA pest-control activities. This was the genesis of *Silent Spring*.

The American public awakened to the pesticide problem as a result of the Great Cranberry Scandal of 1959. The FDA placed a ban on cranberries just before Thanksgiving of that year. The USDA had approved the use of the chemical aminotriazole for use on cranberry bogs after the berries had been harvested. But in 1957, many cranberry growers applied the chemical prior to harvest, and some of it got into the berries. The manufacturer of the chemical, American Cyanamid, conducting its own studies, established that the herbicide was a carcinogen.

When these results became known, HEW banned all sales of cranberries or cranberry products produced in 1957, 1958, or 1959, until the cranberry industry could figure out a test for, separate, and destroy the contaminated berries. Cranberry growers demanded that President Eisenhower fire HEW secretary Arthur S. Flemming for this ruling. Flemming remained at his post. It also emerged that farmers were using the chemical widely on cornfields, and in apple and pear orchards to control poison ivy.[19]

The chemical assault on humans continued to dominate the news. In 1959, *Consumer Reports* found detectable levels of strontium 90, a chemical created from the fallout of nuclear bomb testing, in cows' milk. In August and September of that year, a two-part story in the *Saturday Evening Post*, "Fallout: The Silent Killer," conveyed scientists' concerns that radioactive materials in the atmosphere were causing leukemia, bone cancer, and genetic mutations.[20]

Health problems slowed Carson's research and writing beginning in early 1960. Doctors found two tumors in her left breast, one of which was "suspicious enough to require a radical mastectomy," she reported. But the doctors, unaccountably, did not refer her for further radiation treatment or surgery. Feeling that her doctors had deceived her, she flew to a Cleveland clinic, where tests confirmed breast cancer and that it had metastasized. She began a regimen of radiation therapy. The treatment left her alternately nauseated and fatigued, but more than ever she wanted to finish her book on pesticides.[21]

Excerpts from *Silent Spring* first appeared in three June 1962 issues of the *New Yorker*, prior to the book's publication that September. The articles created a sensation. Some of the reaction was negative, and often personal. A man from California wrote that her "reference to the selfishness of insecticide manufacturers probably reflects her Communist sympathies . . . We can live without birds and animals, but . . . we cannot live without business. As for insects, isn't it just like a woman to be scared to death of a few little bugs!"[22]

More measured attacks on the book focused on an implied cost-benefit analysis. Perhaps the chemicals would kill nonthreatening plants and animals. But by taking out weeds and pests that harmed crops, livestock, and humans, such results were acceptable. Edwin Diamond, editor of *Newsweek*, presented a version of that argument: "I mourn for the dead cats of Java and for the silent birds of the United States. I understand that the spraying of weed killer along roadsides also destroys some shelter for wildlife and therefore upsets the 'balance of nature' so mystically evoked in *The Silent Spring* [sic]. But is man to refrain from disturbing certain circumstances in nature that if kept in 'balance' may balance him right out of existence?"[23]

In fact, biological methods for attacking weeds and pests that did not upset the ecosystem already existed, and Carson devoted an entire chapter in her book to those ecologically friendly methods. She discussed the "male sterilization" technique developed by a USDA scientist that would create infertile eggs so a population of insects would eventually die out. Insects were also susceptible to fungi, protozoa, and microscopic worms. Unlike chemicals, insect pathogens were harmless to all but their intended targets. But sadly, biological control received little support, not surprising considering the cozy relationship between the chemical industry and the federal government.[24]

Diamond also failed to understand that collateral damage would ultimately adversely impact the very animals and humans chemicals were supposed to protect. He was incorrect in charging that Carson advocated "going back to a dark age of plague and epidemic" by eliminating pesticides. Carson stated clearly in the book, "It is not my contention that chemical insecticides must never be used. I do contend that we have put poisonous and biologically potent chemicals indiscriminately into the hands of persons largely or wholly ignorant of their potentials for harm."[25]

The book excerpts in the *New Yorker* rattled the chemical industry. Carson had identified two products of the Velsicol Chemical Company of Chicago, chlordane and heptachlor, as particularly dangerous pesticides. Company officials sent a threatening letter to Carson's publisher implying that the book was part of a conspiracy "to create the false impression that all business is grasping and immoral, and to reduce the use of agricultural chemicals in this country . . . so that our supply of food will be reduced to east-curtain parity." They charged that Carson had made disparaging and inaccurate statements about their product, suggesting that a lawsuit was possible. Nothing came of these threats.[26]

Silent Spring created obvious problems for the National Agricultural Chemicals Association (NACA). It was difficult to challenge the science, so NACA contacted magazine and newspaper editors hinting that a favorable review of Carson's book might adversely affect future advertising. The pressure worked on at least one popular publication. *Reader's Digest* dropped plans to publish a condensed version of the book. NACA wound up spending more than $250,000 on a campaign to discredit the book.[27]

What made Carson's work even more threatening was that she attacked the prevailing wisdom of the postwar era that technology was good, and that experts, in this case scientists, were infallible. A society that had conquered some of the most dreaded diseases and was conquering outer space certainly had the expertise to rearrange the planet's biology without adverse affects on humans. Unable to attack the book on its scientific merits, critics attacked the author.

Former Secretary of Agriculture Ezra Taft Benson sent a bitter letter to Dwight Eisenhower wondering "why a spinster with no children was concerned about genetics." Benson concluded that she was "probably a Communist." Carson's marital status was a topic of frequent comment. When asked, she simply said, "No time," and that she envied male writers who had wives to provide their meals and shield them from interruptions.[28]

Numerous policymakers and journalists, though, rallied to her cause. New York Republican congressman John V. Lindsay praised Carson's work and read into the *Congressional Record* the final paragraphs of the last *New Yorker* installment. A *New York Times* editorial praised "Rachel Carson's warning" and made clear that she did not advocate a total ban on pesticides, but rather cautioned against "the dangers of misuse and overuse by a public that has become mesmerized by the notion that chemists are the possessors of divine wisdom."[29]

As Congressman Lindsay's actions indicated, political leaders had a growing interest in Carson's work. At a press conference that summer, a reporter asked President Kennedy, "There appears to be a growing concern among scientists as to the possibility of dangerous long-range side effects from the widespread use of DDT and other pesticides. Have you considered asking the Department of Agriculture or the Public Health Service to take a closer look at this?" The president replied, "Yes, and I know that they already are. I think particularly, of course, since Miss Carson's book."[30]

Carson, although already well-known in scientific and literary circles prior to *Silent Spring*, became a national celebrity. *Life* magazine did a special feature on her, complete with Alfred Eisenstaedt photographs. Jane Howard, who wrote the piece for *Life*, assured readers that although Carson was single she was not a feminist, quoting her: "I'm not interested in things done by women or by men, but in things done by people."[31]

By 1963, *Silent Spring* had become an integral part of a growing national discourse focusing not only on the environment, but also on the assumption that technology and science would inevitably improve life. The crucial element remained human judgment to harness progress responsibly. Vice Admiral Hyman Rickover warned in March 1963 about the dangers of deferring judgment to science. "I suggest," he wrote, "we reject the notion that man is no longer master of his own and of his society's destiny. Let us put man back in the center of the stage and do some hard thinking about the kind of life that technology is currently creating for us." As a prime example: "Only now . . . are we beginning to realize that careless use of dangerous pesticides and weed killers may poison soil, vegetation, animals and humans."[32]

The ultimate danger of these chemicals, as Rickover implied, was that they had a cumulative effect on the human body. DDT in particular lodged in animal fats and formed residues on fruits and vegetables. Cooking did not destroy these residues. Carson lamented that "to find a diet free from DDT and related chemicals, it seems one must go to a remote and primitive land." Research had identified many of these chemicals as carcinogens. Carson wondered whether the recent spike in cancer among children was related to the increase of chemical use in agriculture. As she noted in her testimony before Senator Ribicoff's committee, "The problem of pesticides can be properly understood only in context, as part of the general introduction of harmful substances into the environment . . . In water and soil, and in our bodies, these chemicals are mingled with others, or with radioactive substances. There are little understood interactions and summations of effect."[33]

Carson did not merely sound the alarm in *Silent Spring*. She advanced solutions. Her years in government had schooled her in public policy. She recommended the elimination of tolerances on pesticides in food and a significant increase in FDA inspectors to enforce that regulation. She advocated the use of less toxic chemicals that already existed. She particularly emphasized the use of nonchemical methods such as the introduction of insect diseases.[34]

CBS Reports prepared to air a program devoted to "The Silent Spring of Rachel Carson," on April 3, 1963. Three of the five sponsors of the program withdrew, including Lehn & Fink Products, the makers of Lysol disinfectant spray, and two manufacturers of food products, Standard Brands Inc. and the Ralston Purina Company. Kiwi polish and Brillo stayed. The program went on and ended with an eloquent statement from Carson. She challenged Americans to question their invincibility, especially in their relation to nature. Humility and harmony were much more productive responses to the natural environment: "We still talk in terms of conquest. We still haven't become mature enough to think of ourselves as only a very tiny part of a vast and incredible universe. Now I truly believe that we in this generation must come to terms with nature, and I think we're challenged, as mankind has never been challenged before, to prove our maturity and our mastery, not of nature but of ourselves."[35]

Ten to 15 million people viewed the program. The next day, Senator Hubert Humphrey announced that he had asked Senator Ribicoff to conduct a wide-ranging inquiry into the use of pesticides and would hold hearings for that purpose. President Kennedy's Science Advisory Committee in the meantime released a report, *The Uses of Pesticides*, concluding, "The accretion of residues in the environment can be controlled only by orderly reductions of persistent pesticides." The report faulted equally federal agencies and the chemical industry.[36]

In November 1963, 5 million dead fish floated on the surface of the lower Mississippi River in Louisiana. The massive fish kill baffled state officials, and they called in PHS. Scientists from PHS discovered that all of the fish had ingested the pesticide endrin. Carson had identified endrin in *Silent Spring* as "the most toxic" of the chlorinated hydrocarbon pesticides, noting that in the decade of its use "it had killed enormous numbers of fish, fatally poisoned cattle that have wandered into sprayed orchards . . . [and] poisoned wells."[37]

Further investigation revealed that the source was a Memphis waste-treatment plant owned by none other than the Velsicol company, one of Carson's fiercest chemical-industry adversaries. This was enough for Senator Ribicoff, who prepared a Clean Water Bill for the Senate. When PHS officials held a news conference in Mississippi to announce their findings, a reporter asked one of the scientists, "How does Rachel Carson look now?" "She looks pretty good," he replied.[38]

Rachel Carson passed away on April 14, 1964. Senator Ribicoff attended the memorial service at Washington National Cathedral with his legislative assistant, Jerome Sonosky. Ribicoff recalled the last Christmas card he had received from Carson, a pen-and-ink sketch of the cathedral's south facade adorned with a traditional Scottish blessing. As Ribicoff and Sonosky emerged from the cathedral, they noticed that the trees around the church all had signs on them: NO PARKING 7 A.M. TO 4 P.M. TREES TO BE SPRAYED WITH PESTICIDES.[39]

JOHN F. KENNEDY HAD EXPRESSED interest in environmental issues early in his administration when he lobbied for an increase in federal aid for sewage-treatment plants. He noted that current plant construction, a program begun in the Eisenhower administration, would meet only about 50 percent of the nation's needs. Kennedy also sought to preserve certain seashore areas, and as Eisenhower had, Kennedy called for greater federal regulatory powers to address water and air pollution. "Our common goal," JFK declared, "is an America of open spaces, of fresh water, of green country—a place where wildlife and natural beauty cannot be despoiled." He succeeded in persuading Congress to increase grants for the construction of sewage-treatment works.[40]

Kennedy had a strong ally in the U.S. Senate in Maine Democratic senator Edmund S. Muskie. As governor of Maine, Muskie pioneered a program to improve water quality in the state's waterways, an effort that helped to boost the Maine lobster industry. The program demonstrated that environmental regulations and economic development were not mutually exclusive objectives. In the Senate, Muskie revived a proposal put forth by President Eisenhower in 1955 (but rejected by Congress that year) to have the federal government set and enforce water-quality standards. Kennedy did little to support the legislation, and it suffered the same fate as befell the Eisenhower administration's initiative.[41]

Stewart L. Udall, secretary of the interior, was the strongest advocate for federal environmental regulations in Kennedy's cabinet. He believed that material abundance did not define a successful nation if its people blighted the water, air, and land while developing economically. "One of the paradoxes of American society," Udall observed, "is that while our economic standard of living has become the envy of the world, our environmental standard has steadily declined. We are better housed, better nourished, and better entertained, but we are not better prepared to inherit the earth or to carry on the pursuit of happiness." The Kennedy White House made relatively little effort to transform Udall's ideals into public policy. Fortunately, Udall would remain on in the Johnson administration.[42]

On December 17, 1963, Lyndon Johnson signed the Clean Air Act of 1963. This limited law established a federal program within the PHS authorizing research into techniques for monitoring and controlling air pollution. LBJ viewed environmental protection as part of the commonwealth ideal, an endeavor for all Americans to enjoy the benefits of the natural environment while protecting that environment from human depredation.[43]

President Johnson addressed the environmental issues Rachel Carson's 1963 Senate testimony illuminated. He stated his determination to reduce water and air pollution, not only through cleanup operations, but also by setting water and air quality standards to prevent pollution in the first place. His objective was "to restore as well as to protect."[44]

LBJ's environmental program blended well with Lady Bird's highway beautification drive to restrict billboard advertising and provide attractive vistas for drivers while preserving the natural landscape. Their initiatives ran into stiff, if predictable, opposition from automobile manufacturers, chemical companies, and the billboard-advertising industry. Yet, the president succeeded in fulfilling all three objectives with the Water Quality and Clean Air acts and the Highway Beautification Act. They were not as strong as he would have preferred, but they were the most comprehensive environmental-protection initiatives undertaken by any administration since Teddy Roosevelt's.[45]

LBJ, working with an overwhelming Democratic majority beginning in January 1965, moved quickly on environmental legislation. Unlike President Kennedy, who gave only lukewarm support, Johnson not only backed Edmund Muskie's revived Clean Water bill, but also strengthened the original 1963 version. LBJ's main concern was that the earlier legislation did not provide for adequate enforcement procedures, specifically that it did not prevent pollution at its source, but only engaged the government long after pollution had actually occurred. Johnson, therefore, proposed to "provide through the setting of effective water quality standards, combined with a swift and effective enforcement procedure, a national program to prevent water pollution at its source rather than attempting to cure pollution after it occurs." Coupling standards with stiff enforcement in a national program meant that states could not sidestep federal standards without penalty. Muskie enthusiastically adopted the president's version of the revived bill.[46]

When Johnson signed the Water Quality Act of 1965, he made clear it was only the beginning of what would eventually become a comprehensive attack on water pollution: "Today, we begin to be masters of our environment . . . Additional, bolder measures will be needed in the years ahead. But we have begun."[47]

That was a cue to Senator Muskie to continue the fight for water-quality legislation in the Senate. Muskie now focused on closing the gap between the supply of and demand for sewage treatment facilities, authorizing $6 billion for that purpose. The bill received bipartisan support as Delaware Republican senator J. Caleb Boggs worked closely with Muskie in shaping the bill. The bill passed the Senate, 90–0, and the House by a vote of 313–0. The marriage of large public works projects with environmental protection proved a good union for bipartisan support. The result was the Clean Water Restoration Act of 1966.[48]

Muskie continued with the administration's blessing. Although the Clean Air Act of 1963 marked the beginning of the legislative assault on air and water pollution, it was a relatively weak law that did not address automobile emissions, which accounted for 52 percent of the nation's air pollution. Muskie's new bill prescribed emission standards for gasoline-powered vehicles, allowing the auto industry until 1967 to comply. Congress modified the bill, removing the 1967 deadline, opting instead for a compliance date set at the discretion of HEW. With this modification the bill sailed through both houses without opposition. The act represented the first active federal role in clean air policy. In October 1965, LBJ signed the amendment to the 1963 Clean Air Act, quoting Rachel Carson.[49]

These measures did not pass in a public-opinion vacuum. Nationally, more people were aware of and alarmed by air pollution and its health consequences. When a killer smog struck Donora, Pennsylvania, in 1948, Americans noticed, but the policy responses were weak and the episode was soon buried in the postwar rush to prosperity. By the mid-1960s, it did not require an especially deadly environmental incident to prompt public attention, nor to identify the culprits. As one editorial concerning the air in New York City observed, breathing that city's air was the "equivalent of smoking two packs of cigarettes a day." But the editor also pointed out, "The air is also foul in cities across the nation and the reason for it is the same everywhere. The air is filthy because of greed and apathy."[50]

The same was true with respect to water-quality legislation. Americans were experiencing serious problems with chemical pollutants in waterways. Rachel Carson's work highlighted the issue, and the frequent publicity of egregious examples of water pollution rallied public opinion behind congressional action. The lopsided votes may have reflected lawmakers' appetites for pork as well as the huge Democratic majorities in both houses, but they also indicated growing alarm and impatience among the general public.

Noted environmental journalist John Bird, an ally of Rachel Carson's, wrote a searing and widely read article under the alarming title "Our Dying Waters" in April 1966. He began his piece, "We have filled our streams with raw excrement and garbage, laden with disease. We have stained them with oil, coal, dust, tar dyes and chemical 'liquors' discharged by industries." After these opening sentences, it got worse. Bird walked along the Potomac as it flowed by the nation's capital. An early colonist called the river "the sweetest and greatest river I have seen," but when tourists visited George Washington's home at Mount Vernon and walked to the river landing below the mansion, they saw a sign: DO NOT COME INTO CONTACT WITH POLLUTED WATER. It was not a question of avoiding swimming or fishing; it was a matter of not touching the water at all.[51]

Honeymooners at Niagara Falls, New York, lost the romance of the place when the torrent of water filled the air with a stench similar to that of rotten eggs. Daily, nineteen thousand gallons of oil, more than two hundred thousand gallons of acid, and 2 million pounds of chemicals salts and one hundred thousand pounds of iron poured into the Detroit River. Added to that were partially treated human wastes. The entire concoction emptied into Lake Erie. The Hudson River flowing by New York City was little more than a swift-moving sewer. As Senator Bobby Kennedy (D-NY) quipped, "If you fall in here, you don't drown—you decay." More seriously, some children found a watermelon floating in the Hudson off 125th Street in Harlem. They took it home, washed it off, and eight of them came down with typhoid fever.[52]

A truly depressing litany, but Bird found some hope in the Water Quality Act of 1965. Bird urged lawmakers to heed the president's plea to "clean and preserve entire river basins from their sources to their mouths," a feature that would further strengthen the Water Quality Act. LBJ also asked for powers to take action against offenders regardless of whether the watercourse was intra- or interstate.[53]

U.S. Chamber of Commerce officials opposed federal environmental initiatives. They argued that federal intervention would constrict economic development. But James M. Quigley, LBJ's acting commissioner of the Water Pollution Control Administration, told them, "No one has the *right* to use America's rivers as a sewer" and "You must accept the principle that the cost of pollution control from now on is part of the cost of doing business."[54]

That equation was especially noticeable in the environmental footprint of suburban development. Suburbanization spurred the postwar economic boom and solved a good deal of the nation's housing shortage. Of necessity, it required relatively quick construction with often little regard to the surrounding natural environment. Fulfilling the dreams of homeownership came with an environmental cost. By 1965, the public discourse had grown through books, articles, and public policy debates to reframe an essential question. "The great issue in planning is not where to build," planner S. B. Zisman wrote that year, "but where not to build." This was especially true with respect to wetlands, sensitive environments that included a diverse array of plants and animals. Although the greatest threat to wetlands was agricultural runoff, development also played an important role in degrading those ecosystems.[55]

Between 1954 and 1964, developers and local governments had drained one third of Long Island's wetlands to provide housing, airports, industrial plants, parking lots, recreational facilities, and garbage dumps. In 1966, several New York congressmen introduced legislation to set aside sixteen thousand acres of wetlands on Long Island as a permanent reserve. Representative John Dingell (D-MI) thought this was such a good idea he introduced a bill to have the Department of Interior acquire a nationwide system of wetlands. In testi-mony supporting Dingell's legislation, it became apparent how thoroughly Rachel Carson's perception of the connectedness of natural and human envi-ronments had become embedded in the public discourse. A member of the Nassau County (Long Island) Planning Commission asserted, "Once we disturb one link in the chain of life, we endanger it all." In 1968, Congress passed a wetlands preservation law. Within ten years, fifteen states and a thou-sand local governments had passed regulations to protect wetlands. It was a good example of how federal legislation produced a synergy that inspired states to act.[56]

Johnson and the Eighty-ninth Congress were not yet finished with their environmental agenda. Lady Bird was determined to tilt at the billboard lobby. The Eisenhower administration sponsored billboard-control legislation in 1958 that offered states the carrot of a financial bonus if they controlled bill-boards on the new interstate highway network. Only about half the states took advantage of the program. Officials at the Outdoor Advertising Association of America, however, recognized the First Lady had successfully transformed a relatively minor esthetic issue into a national cause, and they sought a compromise. They agreed to a ban on billboards in scenic areas in exchange for unrestricted access in business areas. The resulting bill, known as Lady Bird's Bill, covered not only the interstate system, but also primary roads. The bill also revived a proposal advanced by the Eisenhower administration to withhold federal highway funds from any state that did not exclude billboards from noncommercial areas. In a ceremony with "America the Beautiful" as background music, LBJ signed the bill into law, stating, with some hyperbole, "This bill will bring the wonders of nature back into our daily lives."[57]

The Johnson administration emphasized beautification as a fulcrum to address a variety of environmental issues. LBJ emphasized that environmental degradation was not merely a rural problem: "We must not only protect the countryside and save it from destruction, we must restore what has been destroyed and salvage the beauty and charm of our cities." In 1965, he convened the White House Conference on Natural Beauty to discuss water and water-fronts and how cleaning up these areas could provide recreational pursuits for millions of urban residents, as well as the enjoyment of nature. Cities began to see the economic and environmental benefits of opening their waterfronts to recreational pursuits. These improvements also limited the damage from flooding.[58]

It would be too much to state that the flurry of federal environmental legis-lation following the publication of Rachel Carson's *Silent Spring* resulted from the public reaction to the book. Many of the ideas and issues surrounding environmental policy in the 1960s had aired during the Eisenhower administration, and some, such as the preservation and extension of public lands, dated from Teddy Roosevelt's presidency. But the book generated a widespread public discussion that engaged Congress and the Oval Office. Both Presidents Kennedy and Johnson were very much of aware of the book and used quotes from it in their speeches. But Johnson was the president who began to translate Carson's recommendations into public policy.

LBJ broadened the idea of environmental protection from an emphasis on conservation to also include restoration and innovation. "Its concern is not with nature alone, but with the total relation between man and the world around him. Its object is not just man's welfare but the dignity of man's spirit." The ideal had been confined primarily to ecologists such as Rachel Carson. Now, it would resonate with a broad constituency. And it would be called the New Conservation.[59]

Also apparent in the legislative advances during the Johnson years was the growing influence of a variety of environmental groups, from the older preservationist organizations such as the Sierra Club and the National Audubon Society to more recent activist groups such as Friends of the Earth, Zero Population Growth, and Ecology Action. Most of these organizations shared the idea that the best way to advance the agenda of the environment was through federal action. They provided an increasingly effective counterweight to industrial and development lobbyists.[60]

Johnson appointed no fewer than nine task forces to address various environmental issues. Between 1964 and 1968, he signed nearly three hundred conservation and beautification measures supported by congressional funding of more than $12 billion. The total number of environmental laws passed exceeded the number passed between the nation's founding and 1964. The sheer variety of the legislation was equally impressive, encompassing air and water quality, expansion and protection of wilderness areas, and the creation of urban open spaces. Although environmental historians identified the National Environmental Policy Act of 1969 (NEPA) as a seminal event in environmental policymaking, it was actually the culmination of government efforts during the Johnson administration.[61]

States and localities now looked to the federal government, not only for funding to clean up the environment, but also for expertise in rooting out current and potential problems. States that wanted but could not afford environmental policies or that succumbed to industry pressures now had a staunch ally in the federal government.[62]

In September 1967, Matt Perry of Havertown, Pennsylvania, wrote a brief letter to President Johnson: "When I grow up I want to be a famous fisherman.

But when I am that age all the water will be polluted." LBJ replied, assuring young Matt that he shared that concern and "that many brilliant and dedicated people are doing everything they possibly can to regain and preserve our great heritage . . . But one step we must take—all of us together—is to end the carelessness and selfishness which has so often spoiled our clean, pure waters." Environmental consciousness had reached well into the gifted generation, and it would be their good fortune to arrest and in some cases reverse the deterioration that had occurred through unmindful use of the national patrimony.[63]

Not only boys, but also governors of threatened states looked to Washington for assistance in halting and reversing adverse environmental trends. Funding for waste-treatment facilities was among the most popular federal environmental policies in the mid-1960s. This was especially true for rapidly growing states in the West. The governor of California howled in a letter to LBJ in June 1967 complaining about a cutback in waste-treatment-facilities funding. He reminded the president that his objective was not merely to prevent pollution but also to preserve and enhance the quality of California's waters. With a population growth of six hundred thousand persons a year, the $1 billion invested by the federal government thus far in the state for the construction of waste-treatment and disposal facilities had been invaluable. The governor beseeching LBJ for more federal aid was Ronald Reagan.[64]

By the time President Johnson left office in 1969, an array of new legislation both protected the environment and expanded the natural domain. Equally important, Americans in and out of government were much better informed in 1969 than they were in 1960. The impact of pesticides, the interrelationship of ecosystems and human dependence upon them, and the location and extent of particularly sensitive environmental areas and how to protect them became more common knowledge by the end of the decade. *Silent Spring* played a pivotal role in this education. Still missing from the legislative haul was an agency to apply the science and coordinate these disparate but related issues.

Two events in 1969 would close this gap quickly and give birth to a national grassroots movement, already under way, but only loosely organized. In January of that year a major oil spill occurred in the Santa Barbara Channel off the coast of that California city. The spill continued for ten days and dumped one hundred thousand gallons of oil into the channel and onto the beaches of Santa Barbara and other coastal cities. It was the largest oil spill yet in American history. The disaster devastated wildlife and provoked national outrage.

On a Sunday morning in June, Cleveland's Cuyahoga River, which fed into Lake Erie, caught fire. How water could burn was a mystery to many, except that it would stretch the definition to call the ooze that masqueraded as a river a waterway. Both incidents made clear that, despite the efforts of the Johnson administration, the legislative and regulatory frameworks to protect the national patrimony were thin and patchy.[65]

THE COMMONWEALTH IDEAL THAT informed public policy in the decades immediately following World War II meant that the good of the commonwealth exceeded the benefit to certain groups or individuals. The best policies would accommodate both, not to the fullest extent, of course, but where both views could live with each other and in harmony with their surroundings. The balance that previous administrations sought between government, the people, and business was skewed when it came to environmental issues in the early 1960s. The beginning of a comprehensive American environmental policy would address that. LBJ began the process.

CHAPTER 19

A WOMAN'S WORLD

IN 2005, THE EDITORS OF the conservative publication *Human Events* compiled a list of "the ten most harmful books of the nineteenth and twentieth centuries." Betty Friedan's *Feminine Mystique* (1963) ranked seventh, five spots below *Mein Kampf*. It was understandable. Betty Friedan's book upset the gender status quo, though she was hardly the first writer to articulate the tension between women's aspirations and society's expectations. In fact, her publisher warned on the eve of the book's publication, "One of our main problems is that much is being written these days about the plight (or whatever it is) of the educated American woman; therefore this one will have to fight its way out of a thicket."[1]

Friedan's synthesis of a voluminous literature and an array of personal accounts and surveys set her work apart. The book enabled American women to share what they had felt in isolation, to understand their frustrations, and to seek a remedy. Just as Thomas Paine's *Common Sense* stated the obvious about the relation between power and individual freedom, so *The Feminine Mystique* articulated what millions of women were feeling about their own relationship to power.

Bettye Goldstein's upbringing in Peoria, Illinois, hardly prefigured a career as one of the leading feminists of the twentieth century. Peoria was an industrial and transportation center on the Illinois River halfway between Chicago and the Mississippi River. The city had a Jewish population sufficient to support two synagogues. It had a small (3 percent) segregated black population. If Peoria had a national reputation, it was more likely as a vaudeville punch line.[2]

Bettye's father immigrated to Peoria from Ukraine in his teens. He supported himself selling collar buttons from a street-corner stand. Eventually, he opened Goldstein Jewelry Company, advertising it as the "Finest Jewelry Store in the Middle West." Bettye's mother was the daughter of Hungarian immigrants who initially settled in St. Louis, but moved to Peoria when her father became the city's public health commissioner.

She graduated from Bradley College (now University) in Peoria and took a job writing for the local newspaper. But her husband insisted that she quit and stay home to tend the house and three children. Bettye later attributed her feminism to her mother's being forced to quit her job when she married.[3]

In an era when appearance meant a great deal, not only for women, but also for girls, Bettye failed in that aspect, as her mother often reminded her. As a young child, she wore braces to straighten her legs, and then braces on her teeth when they emerged crooked. At age eleven, she wore eyeglasses. To make matters worse, she suffered from periodic respiratory illnesses. She also experienced anti-Semitism, denied membership in a high school sorority because of her religion. Years later, she acknowledged that her "passion against injustice . . . originated from my feelings of the injustice of anti-Semitism." All of these afflictions created a lonely and unhappy child.[4]

But during her last two years in high school, she excelled in academics and built a small but fulfilling group of friends. Bettye recited Abraham Lincoln's Gettysburg Address at a Memorial Day commemoration, receiving praise from Everett Dirksen, then a House representative.

Bettye's academic achievements secured her a spot at Smith College in 1938. She had always wanted to attend the college, mainly because her maternal grandparents had prevented her mother from enrolling. The school in Northampton, Massachusetts, boasted a first-rate faculty, 63 percent of whom were women, and an all-women student body where nonconformity flourished. Bettye thrived at Smith and participated in numerous campus activities, foremost of which was the campus newspaper, where she became editor in chief. The loneliness she had felt as a girl dissipated. The only clouds on her otherwise clear horizon were her persistent respiratory problems and her inability to meet and date young men.

Dorothy Wolff Douglas was Bettye's favorite faculty member. Her economics course "Theories and Movements for Social Reconstruction" introduced Bettye to a variety of progressive social movements, including feminism. Douglas was also a role model—Jewish, wealthy, radical, and politically engaged. She lived in a historic house in Southampton, Massachusetts, with her partner, the noted Southern writer Katharine Du Pre Lumpkin.

During the summer, at Professor Douglas's recommendation, Bettye spent several weeks at the Highlander Folk School in Monteagle, Tennessee. This was the school that would nurture and train Rosa Parks, and that provided inspiration for Pete Seeger. Highlander was noted for its emphasis on social justice for African Americans and women. Students learned about organizing demonstrations and picket lines, as well as learning and singing protest songs.

There were also writing workshops, in which Bettye enrolled, and classes on the labor union movement.

Returning to Smith for her senior year, 1941–42, Bettye joined the school theater, working with Nancy Davis, the future Mrs. Ronald Reagan, on a student production of *A Lady Tourist*. Although her Smith experience had been fulfilling, she had one regret: "I was that girl with all A's and I wanted boys worse than anything. With all that brilliance, I saw myself becoming the old maid college teacher."[5]

Bettye launched her graduate school career at UC-Berkeley in the fall of 1942 in the field of psychology. Here, she encountered her first serious male relationship with a graduate student in physics, David Bohm, who worked with the noted scientist Robert Oppenheimer on a project to make uranium 235 for atomic weapons. Bohm joined the Communist Party in 1942, and Bettye shared many of his political views.

But she missed the activism of her Smith years and promptly left Berkeley and Bohm to work in the labor movement. In 1943, she took a job with the Federated Press in New York, a left-wing labor publication for which she wrote articles, many from a feminist perspective. Three years later, she moved to another left-wing union publication, the *UE News*. In 1947, she married and became Betty Friedan and moved out of Manhattan to Queens. Her husband, Carl Friedan, was a war veteran, Jewish, and a New Englander. He pursued a career in theater as a producer of experimental plays.

The advent of the Cold War and the rise of anticommunism hurt left-wing unionism as well as the associated causes of civil rights for African Americans and women. One of the casualties was the Congress of American Women (CAW), formed in 1946 by a coalition of left-leaning women, including Nora Stanton Blatch Barney, the granddaughter of Elizabeth Cady Stanton, and Susan B. Anthony II. Friedan reported on the group in the *UE News*. By 1947, the CAW counted a membership of 250,000 women that cut across class and racial lines. Their program called for tenant rights, equal pay for equal work, government-sponsored day-care facilities, an antilynching law, and greater representation of women in unions and in the media. Some of the same issues that Friedan would explore in *The Feminine Mystique*—the myth of the happy housewife and the corrosive nature of consumption—found their way into magazine articles written by CAW women.

By 1952, Friedan had two children and found it difficult to maintain her position at the *UE News* and care for her children at the same time. Besides, most of her earnings went to child care. Ultimately, it was not her decision. Red-baiting had reduced United Electrical, Radio, and Machine Workers of America (UE) membership, and the union cut its staff, including Friedan.

Friedan's writing in the mid-1950s moved away from left-wing labor journalism to a wider discussion of issues confronting middle-class women. This was a politically safer topic, but it also reflected the significant expansion of the middle class in the decade following the end of the World War II. More personally, she felt trapped by what she began to call the feminine mystique—by the expectations of the home and the desire to be out in the world pursuing a rewarding career. *The Feminine Mystique* was born out of this frustration.

Her initial research for the book derived from responses to a questionnaire sent to her 1942 Smith College classmates in 1957. To supplement the material from her survey, Friedan read widely in women's magazines and in the behavioral science journals. She also conducted more than eighty interviews and scoured surveys of graduates of women's colleges. The book was thoroughly grounded in both the popular and scientific literature of the day.

One of Friedan's objectives in her book was to relate what she had experienced as a captive of the feminine mystique. The enemy in the book was not husbands, or men generally, but "society." It did not call for a war of the sexes; the book, rather, hoped to empower women to rebel against societal norms. "There was a strange discrepancy between the reality of our lives as women and the image to which we were trying to conform, the image that I came to call the feminine mystique." The message was that women could liberate themselves—that change did not require legislation, just education, for both women and society as a whole. "In the end," she wrote, "a woman, as a man, has the power to choose, and to make her own heaven or hell." Were it that simple.[6]

What especially saddened Friedan was that college women in the 1950s seemed in retreat from the ambitions of their sisters of the 1940s. Interviewing a group of Smith seniors in 1959, Friedan noted that they were similar in some respects to her own classmates seventeen years earlier, "except that many more of the girls wore rings on their left hands." She asked the women what they planned to be. "The engaged ones spoke of weddings, apartments, getting a job as a secretary while husband finished school. The others, after a hostile silence, gave vague answers about this job or that, graduate study, but no one had any real plans." She found a similar lack of career ambition among Vassar girls.[7]

Friedan cited statistics that two out of three girls who entered college in the 1950s dropped out before they finished. But even those who stayed "showed no signs of wanting to be anything more than suburban housewives and mothers." Friedan never assumed that this might be a legitimate and heartfelt objective of some women, not necessarily a society-directed choice or an absence of suitable options. The expectations of society *did* weigh heavily on women, perhaps more heavily on educated and highly motivated women, but domesticity could be a valid choice.[8]

Yet something was changing, and Friedan noticed it. The lure of education, of a career outside the home, beckoned to those women in their late thirties or forties who had raised a family, married young, and either never completed their college education or had not yet begun. In January 1962, a story in the *New York Times* reported that Sarah Lawrence College professor Esther Raushenbush had obtained a grant to help mature women finish their education or work for graduate degrees part-time. The response was so overwhelming it crashed the school's switchboard.[9]

Friedan concluded her book with a plea that still resonates today: "When enough women make life plans geared to their real abilities, and speak out for maternity leaves or even maternity sabbaticals, professionally run nurseries, and the other changes in the rules . . . they will not have to sacrifice the right to honorable competition and contribution anymore than they will have to sacrifice marriage and motherhood."[10]

The book provoked an avalanche of letters to Friedan from women who suddenly recognized themselves in its pages. One woman wrote, "I thought these problems and situations were only mine, and mine alone . . . and the knowledge that my neighbor-housewifes [*sic*] also have problems" came as such a "relief." A thirty-one-year-old homemaker with four children declared, "You have freed me from such a mass of subconscious and conscious guilt feelings, that I feel, today, as though I had been filled with helium and turned loose!"[11]

More than forty years after *The Feminine Mystique* appeared, women could still recall their relief and gratitude after reading the book. For some, the book relieved a sense of guilt over their feelings, as one reader related: "There were Negroes being beaten in the South. There were children with bellies swollen from hunger in Appalachia. And here I was with comforts my mother would have given her eye-tooth for. What right did I have to be so miserable?" Another woman recalled simply, "I got my mind back."[12]

Friedan also inspired members of the gifted generation, who had yet to make their choices in life. Linda Barker read the book in 1963 at the age of eighteen as she was about to enter college. She believed it steered her life toward a rewarding career. Friedan received a considerable number of letters from women who felt it was too late for them, but not for the gifted generation. As one such correspondent declared, "It would be a crime to let another generation go as mine had." She prayed that her daughter could "avoid becoming a miserable housewife!"[13]

There were, of course, negative notices of the book. Ridgely Hunt wrote a sarcastic review in the conservative *Chicago Tribune* mocking Friedan's notion of women wanting to do something meaningful with their lives. He described the contemporary man wondering, "Is there no worthier goal toward which I can direct my finely machined intelligence than this tawdry business of earning a living and supporting my family?" But "no one is listening to him. His wife is off to a painting lesson so she can express her inner self." Hunt eventually underwent a transformation, literally. He left his wife and three children several years later and, in the mid-1970s, had sex-reassignment surgery and became Nancy Hunt.[14]

Criticism did not only emanate from conservative writers. Critics noted that Friedan replicated the feelings of white middle-class women, but working-class women and especially African American women were invisible in her book. One white woman explained that Friedan's experiences were "utterly foreign to me as a working-class farm kid." Also, less educated housewives were happier staying home than educated housewives. Helen Gurley Brown's *Sex and the Single* Girl (1962) spoke more to working-class women and captured the growing candor with respect to women's sexuality, advancing a functional view of marriage that some (mostly men) found scandalous. She instructed that women should not see marriage as "the best years of your life." Rather, marriage "is insurance for the *worst* years of your life. During your best years you don't need a husband. You do need a man of course every step of the way and they are often cheaper emotionally and a lot more fun by the bunch."[15]

A black woman related that she and her friends "were too busy struggling to achieve the American dream to be concerned with women who appeared to have it all." It was also less likely that black women could marry a man who earned enough to enable her to withdraw from the workforce. In 1960, 60 percent of black middle-class families included two-earner households, compared to less than 40 percent for white middle-class families. Considering Friedan's early sympathies for the union movement and civil rights, these were ironic critiques.[16]

Despite these shortcomings, Friedan addressed a rapidly growing segment of the population in postwar America confronting dilemmas that were relatively new. In many ways the book was more valuable for the gifted generation than for her target audience. College opportunities and employment options opened for women. The growing number of articles in the popular press extolling women's intelligence, resourcefulness, and contributions to a prosperous, strong nation provided validation for exercising those options.

These young women also saw young men moving ahead rapidly and wanted to share in the bounty.

ROCHELLE "SHELLI" KANET LOVED math in high school, and her teachers encouraged her pursuit of a subject many felt too complex for girls. Like many working-class girls, she came from a home where out of necessity both parents worked. Her father was a cutter in the garment industry, and her mother was a secretary for the New York City Board of Education. Shelli went to Brooklyn College in 1961 because that was what she could afford: it was free, save a $30 general fee. She majored in math. "Sometimes I was the only girl in the class." But she did not give it a thought as nobody pointed out the anomaly of a female mathematician. At college, "I did lots of things that only men did." She did not perceive herself to be a feminist: "I really always followed what I loved and what I wanted to do and was unconscious of whether a woman could do that or not."[17]

Columbia University accepted Kanet in its M.A. program with a fellowship so she could afford to attend. But she never enrolled. Her idea was to obtain a master's degree and teach math in the public schools. However, she realized that the market for mathematicians had broadened considerably since she entered high school, especially in the new field of computers. She became a computer programmer for AT&T, a job that did not exist when she entered high school. She helped develop sonar equipment for the U.S. Navy, working on a team with engineers and psychologists. She subsequently worked with MIT on developing a time-sharing machine, which informed the creation of the Internet.[18]

Shelli did not read Betty Friedan's book, but the expanding options of the 1960s and 1970s, especially in science and technology, enabled her to pursue work that few women engaged in prior to this era. Although want ads remained segregated by gender until the late 1960s, and although most working women toiled at so-called pink-collar occupations, the employment vista was changing.

The Feminine Mystique initially had more impact on women (and on men's perception of women) than it had on public policy. It gave voice to a movement already under way. In 1956 President Eisenhower had urged Congress to pass legislation requiring equal pay for equal work, but Congress did not act, though Ike appointed more women to government posts than any other previous administration, a trend that continued with JFK and LBJ. In 1961, Kennedy created the President's Commission on the Status of Women "to develop plans for fostering the full partnership of men and women in our national life." States began to establish similar bodies. These organizations were important precursors of the National Organization for Women (NOW), which Friedan played a major role in creating in 1966.[19]

Bringing women into the commonwealth as equal members would only strengthen it. Lady Bird Johnson often expressed that message: "Today the nation cannot afford to waste the talents of American women." The prevailing image of the domesticated woman of yesteryear had even less relevance in a modern world that required all Americans to participate to their best potential. "A woman," Lady Bird explained, "can no longer simply rock the cradles, churn the butter, hem the skirts and leave everything else—all the change and difference between a pioneer society and our fast-moving world of today—for men to struggle with. *We must help. We must use our talents, our energies, our ambitions and our dreams.*"[20]

COLUMNIST SALLY KOHN, GROWING UP in the 1980s in a different gender context from the 1960s, enjoyed watching old sitcoms from the fifties and sixties. She particularly noticed the transition in her favorite television shows. In the 1950s shows "housewives in fancy dresses and high heels" populated the small screen. June Cleaver of *Leave It to Beaver* was typical of that era. But Kohn knew she did not want to grow up like June: "The dress. The hair. The pearls. The sense that she never had any fun, never broke the rules, possibly never even exhaled."

But in the 1960s, *Gidget* appeared. "Finally, a TV woman I wanted to be," Kohn related. "Smart. Independent. Even sarcastic at times." Then came a clutch of similar empowering women's shows: *That Girl*, with Marlo Thomas, Agent 99 from *Get Smart*, and Emma Peel from *The Avengers*—not just women, but spies. "Who kicked ass!" There was *Julia*, featuring an African American woman who was a single mother. The 1960s were not typically the years critics referred to as the Golden Age of Television, but for women leads, they were a bonanza.[21] When *The Mary Tyler Moore Show* debuted in 1970, featuring a thirtysomething single woman who was more concerned about advancing her career than finding a mate, it reflected a major transformation of public perceptions of women in the popular culture in less than a decade.

It was easier for the gifted generation to break the prescribed gender rules in the 1960s. The Pill was a liberation movement in itself. The development of the oral contraceptive was not merely a scientific breakthrough; it changed behaviors, laws, and the perception of women's sexuality. Margaret Sanger was America's great birth-control pioneer and founder of Planned Parenthood. Despite her tireless efforts for nearly half a century, contraception remained illegal in many states into the 1960s. Sanger envisioned a magic pill that would place birth control entirely within the hands of a woman. The problem was that scientists (almost all male) considered research on contraceptives "dirty, disreputable work." No government agency, pharmaceutical company, or foundation would support such research.[22]

But she was dedicated to the belief that women were entitled to enjoy sex just as much as men. Sanger was realistic about the chances of funding such research, though. She realized that "a movement centered on sexual pleasure would never get the support it needed, but a movement focused on health might have a chance." So she shrewdly pursued the Pill as a means to relieve the painful symptoms and irregularity of the menstrual cycle in certain women.[23]

Sanger found an angel in Katherine McCormick, who had married the heir to the International Harvester Company. McCormick was a biologist and suffragist who during her long lifetime identified with a range of feminist issues, including contraception, into which she poured a good deal of her fortune to support the work of Gregory Goodwin "Goody" Pincus at the Worcester (MA) Foundation for Experimental Biology. Changing attitudes in the 1950s took the research out of the shadows and into mainstream science.

In 1954, Pincus, along with Dr. John Rock, chief of gynecology and obstetrics at Harvard Medical School, began experimenting with a synthetic hormone developed by Searle Laboratory. Since 1900 scientists had known of the role of hormones in ovulation. In 1934, scientists isolated the hormone progesterone as an anti-ovulation hormone, and Pincus sought to imitate that chemical in an oral contraceptive. He was as much of a showman as a scientist, and he called his invention Pincus Pills for Prolific People. In 1957, the U.S. Department of Agriculture approved the pill for treatment of miscarriages and some menstrual disorders. And in May 1960, the federal Food and Drug Administration approved Enovid as a contraceptive.[24]

Charlotte, North Carolina, instituted one of the earliest pilot programs for the Pill in November 1960. Dr. Alan Guttmacher of Planned Parenthood reported a year and a half later, "There has not been a single pregnancy among" those who took the Pill. The results in Charlotte indicated that the Pill was both effective and safe.[25]

The rush for the Pill was on. By the end of 1961, 408,000 American women were using the Pill, and by 1963, the figure had climbed to 2.3 million and was rising. Clare Boothe Luce, a writer and politician, framed the Pill's importance for women: "Modern woman is at last free as a man is free, to dispose of her own body, to earn her living, to pursue the improvement of her mind, to try a successful career." In 1965, one year before Sanger's death, in a validation of her lifetime of work for feminist causes, former presidents Truman and

Eisenhower became cochairmen of Planned Parenthood's world population committee.[26]

The widespread acceptance of the Pill in the 1960s was somewhat surprising, given the fears that it would lead to unprecedented promiscuity and sexually transmitted diseases. The Pill fit into a growing concern, especially among mothers, that "little girls are too sexy too soon." As one mother put it, "Little girls today are not little girls at all but full-fledged females, with no time for anything in this life not oriented toward sex." She attributed the rise among teenagers of out-of-wedlock births to "earlier dating and the use of adult dress and makeup." The result was that "where once girls were groomed to be feminine, now girls are groomed to be sexy." Combine the Pill with early sexuality and you have a moral disaster in the making.[27]

But the sexual revolution was already well under way before the Pill. As one coed in the mid-1960s stated, "No, I don't think the Pill has changed campus morals. The change was there. The Pill just makes it easier." What changed was the power balance between the sexes. As Harvard dean John Munro explained, the Pill enhanced "the independence of women . . . Boys and girls are so much more companionable than ever before. Girls can do so much more."[28]

The Pill also created a dilemma for Roman Catholics, although many Catholic women simply ignored Church teaching and took it. Dr. John Rock was a devout Roman Catholic and had no difficulty in reconciling his work with his faith. Boston's Richard Cardinal Cushing also favored legalizing birth control. As early as 1958, Pope Pius XII, a doctrinal conservative, gave his approval for the Pill if doctors believed that its use would regularize ovarian cycles or prevent miscarriage in a woman. As a measure of how far we are today from the cultural consensus of the 1960s, an autographed portrait of Cardinal Cushing hung in the office of Dr. Alan F. Guttmacher, the president of Planned Parenthood at the time.[29]

But a number of states had long-standing bans against artificial contraception. Ten states that had such legislation, including New York State, threw out the laws by the early 1960s. Connecticut, however, held on to an eighty-six-year-old law prohibiting the sale and use of artificial contraceptives. Estelle Griswold had led Planned Parenthood in Connecticut since 1953 and had been trying to overturn that state's artificial-contraceptive ban ever since.

Drugstores throughout the state openly sold condoms, and those who wanted oral contraceptives could go out of state. But the ban was particularly difficult for poor women. Tired of driving around the state with boxes of diaphragms in the trunk of her car, Griswold decided to challenge the law in a direct and provocative manner. She opened a birth-control clinic in

New Haven. Authorities arrested and fined her. Griswold appealed, eventually to the U.S. Supreme Court, where, in *Griswold v. Connecticut* (1965), the justices in a 7-2 decision declared that the Connecticut statute was unconstitutional.[30]

Justice William O. Douglas, writing for the majority, ruled that the statute violated the right to privacy, a right "to protect[ion] from governmental intrusion." Although that right appears nowhere explicitly in the Constitution, it was implied in the "penumbras" and "emanations" of other constitutional provisions. The Connecticut law, Douglas observed, "in forbidding the use of contraceptives rather than regulating their manufacture or sale, seeks to achieve its goals by means having a maximum destructive impact upon [privacy]." He concluded, "We deal with a right of privacy older than the Bill of Rights—older than our political parties, older than our school system. Marriage is a coming together for better or worse, hopefully enduring and intimate to the degree of being sacred." The language was a preemptive strike against those who favored the statute on religious grounds. Douglas said, in effect, that the state's law violated the sanctity of marriage.

The *Griswold* decision was one of the greatest legal victories women had attained to that point. As one commentator noted, "They [women] have gained what for eons was denied the daughters of Eve—a secure means of planning the birth of their children. They are the beneficiaries of one of the most dramatic sociomedical revolutions the world has ever known."[31]

THE *GRISWOLD* CASE WOULD LOOM large in the landmark decision on abortion, *Roe v. Wade* (1973). As abortion advocates would argue, if the right to privacy protected the access to contraception, then access to therapeutic abortions, which enabled women to terminate pregnancies that endangered their physical or mental health, should fall under the same constitutional protection.[32]

In the more favorable judicial and cultural climate for women, abortion, long a subject in the shadows, became a matter for public discussion. Newspapers referred to abortion, when they found out about it, usually through a tragedy, as "illegal surgery." But public health officials, physicians, and attorneys in the 1950s began to explore how to liberalize prevailing abortion laws. In 1958, Planned Parenthood tasked the American Law Institute to draft a model abortion law that would decriminalize therapeutic abortions, the "hard" cases. Growing public sentiment for freedom of choice emerged in the 1950s, first as a medical issue and then as a matter of women's rights.[33]

Dr. Alan F. Guttmacher of Planned Parenthood campaigned for moderating abortion restrictions, though not eliminating them entirely. In a lengthy article for *Redbook* in August 1959, he criticized abortion laws for making "hypocrites of all of us—doctors and patients, legislators and law-enforcement officials." The difference between a legal and a "therapeutic" abortion, Guttmacher asserted, was often "three hundred dollars and knowing the 'right' person." It was the difference between a relatively safe procedure and a dangerous operation. But the law in New York (and similar ones in other states) provided an exception only to preserve the mother's life. A doctor soon realized, Guttmacher admitted, "that there is more to life than mere existence." Should doctors take account not only of the physical life, but also of the mental and emotional life and health of a patient?[34]

Guttmacher performed 147 abortions between 1953 and 1958, all approved by his hospital's protocol committee. But he estimated that about 90 percent of those abortions were illegal by the strictest interpretation of the law. There were probably anywhere from two hundred thousand to 1.2 million illegal abortions performed annually, an unknown number of those with dire consequences. The wide divergence in the statistics indicated a general ignorance about the subject.

Guttmacher's solutions to ending both the hypocrisy and the danger were, first, to improve sex education and begin that instruction in the fifth grade; second, to devise social welfare policies to improve the standard of living so that families could support additional children; third, to develop an effective and inexpensive contraceptive; and finally, to significantly expand the definition of therapeutic abortion.

On this last point, he held up Sweden as a model for the United States. In that Scandinavian country, women could obtain abortions legally for medical reasons, for the general health of the mother (including having too many children, or children too close together, and for economic hardship), if congenital diseases were detected, and for humanitarian reasons such as pregnancies resulting from rape, incest, or the impregnation of a girl less than fifteen years old. If states took these steps, Guttmacher assured, illegal abortions would disappear. He admitted, though, that few politicians would back such a plan, but he was hopeful that voters would become informed on the issue and lobby their representatives.

In 1965 the National Opinion Research Center conducted a poll showing 73 percent of respondents supporting abortion in "hard" cases, where the mother's life was endangered, 57 percent where there was a fetal deformity, and 59 percent in cases of rape. But in "soft" cases, such as where the woman was unmarried (18 percent), did not want additional children (16 percent), or could not afford more children (22 percent), the level of support declined significantly. By 1972, one year before Roe v. Wade, support for both the hard and soft cases had increased, with the latter up around the fortieth percentile.

By that date, New York had removed almost all restrictions on first- and second-trimester abortions.[35]

In October 1966, Dr. William B. Ober, director of laboratories at New York's Knickerbocker Hospital, wrote an article for the *Saturday Evening Post*, "We Should Legalize Abortion." It was a title, and an essay, that few if any major magazines would have published a decade earlier. It was a measure of how far the abortion debate had come, and of the success of women in moving that discussion along. Dr. Ober minced no words: "I have been a doctor for twenty years and it has become more and more obvious to me that our moral and legal attitudes toward abortion are absurd." He noted that of the million abortions performed annually, about 99 percent were illegal. Ober argued, "There is no moral difference among abortions, whether the fetus is the result of rape, incest or rich conjugal love. By what right does state or church claim a jurisdiction superior to that of the woman involved in pregnancy?" The woman's right to choose was becoming a core argument of the fight against laws prohibiting abortions.[36]

By the time Dr. Ober wrote this piece, several states were considering the modification of their abortion statutes. In 1967, California passed one of the earliest and most liberal abortion laws in the country. The Therapeutic Abortion Law allowed hospital review committees to sanction an abortion if the pregnancy would impair the mother's physical or mental health, following one of the key recommendations of Dr. Guttmacher. The new law also empowered local district attorneys to approve abortions in the case of rape or incest. Governor Ronald Reagan signed the bill into law.[37]

These developments reflected the growing visibility of women in public policy discussions that pertained directly to their well-being and status in American society. When the gifted generation began to enter college in the early 1960s, many did so with expectations different from those of the previous generation, particularly with respect to single-sex education. Young men at the elite schools, growing up in an increasingly egalitarian society, began to demand the gender integration of their institutions. In 1965, a Yale study indicated that the all-male character of the institution was a serious drawback in competing with other Ivy League schools. Princeton endorsed full coeducation in 1968. Yale established a quota for women with a target of fifteen hundred undergraduate women compared to four thousand men. But when the women came to campus in 1969, they pressed for full equality, and by 1974 the institution had adopted a sex-blind admissions policy.[38]

SHIFTING ATTITUDES ON SEX, abortion, and education reflected a general pattern in society trending toward greater gender equity by the late 1960s.

Between 1967 and 1972, support for the employment of married women rose dramatically from 44 percent to 64 percent, a remarkable increase in a relatively short time. It reflected the entry of the gifted generation into the job market. It also coincided with the abolition of gender-specific want ads. The trend was especially noticeable on the campuses of the elite universities, where the proportion of students agreeing with the statement "the activities of married women are best confined to the home and family" fell from 64 percent in 1967 to 46 percent in 1972.[39]

Public policy in the 1960s began to reflect these trends. In July 1962, President Kennedy ordered all federal agencies to become gender neutral in hiring, training, and promoting employees. In 1963, Congress passed the Equal Pay Act, the same year the President's Commission on the Status of Women issued its final report, which called for paid maternity leave, economic equality in marriage, and child-care facilities for families. The Feminine Mystique appeared at the crest of this wave of interest in gender issues.[40]

Lyndon B. Johnson was dedicated to increasing the number of women in all levels of government, and he pursued that objective more aggressively than any of his predecessors. The federal government already employed a fairly sizable number of women, but almost all served as secretaries or receptionists. LBJ's goal was to appoint women to better-paying and higher-profile positions. In January 1964, Johnson, in the White House a little over one month, convened a meeting of the heads of regulatory agencies, directing them to appoint more women. He vowed to make "stag government" a thing of the past by appointing at least fifty women to key policy positions.[41]

Johnson told the officials that the country was wasting a "national resource" and he intended to change that. "It is imperative that an intensive effort be made to fill top-level vacancies in your agency with women who, but for the historical bias against their sex, would be considered well qualified." The officials greeted LBJ's words with mild amusement, but his surveillance of their agencies over the next months convinced them that the president would reward or punish officials for their success or failure in carrying out his directive.[42]

By June 1964, LBJ had far exceeded his goal, having appointed more than 230 women to top-level government jobs, and promoting another 730 already holding government employment to positions paying more than $10,000 annually ($77,000 in current dollars). Included in this group were Katharine White, ambassador to Denmark; Dr. Mary I. Bunting, who left Radcliffe to become the first woman member of the Atomic Energy Commission; Virginia Mae Brown, the first woman commissioner of the Interstate Commerce Commission; Elizabeth S. May, the first woman director of the Export-Import

Bank; and Jane Hanna, deputy assistant secretary of defense. Notable among his hires were three black women appointed to top jobs, including Frankie Freeman, a Missouri attorney, as a member of the Civil Rights Commission.[43]

As Johnson declared, "A woman's place is not only in the home, but in the House, the Senate, and throughout government service." A local newspaper columnist warned that women strolling around Washington should be "extra careful" because "if they don't get mugged, they may get drafted for a job in Government." For those concerned about what this policy implied for men in the city, the president reassured them, "Men will always have a place in government, as long as there are no women to fill the jobs."[44]

When administration officials came to him with personnel requests, LBJ was likely to give them a lecture on how it would be a good idea to hire a woman for the position. In February 1964, when Secretary of Agriculture Orville Freeman spoke with the president about filling a vacancy in his department, Johnson pounced: "Why don't you find the greatest farm woman with an international background in this country and then give it to [her]?"[45]

LBJ expressed his frustration about the lack of women in government on a few occasions, most notably when he talked with Orville Freeman about a potential appointee to the Department of Agriculture. Johnson complained to Freeman, "We've got a cabinet made up *wholly* of men. We've got independent agencies made up *wholly* of men. The best thing we've got is sometimes we promote them to . . . a stenographer."[46]

This is not to say that LBJ was a model male feminist. Just as he used the N-word on occasion, particularly when talking with Southern colleagues, he also made inappropriate comments to women. In February 1964, for example, he scolded one of his secretaries, Vicki McCammon, "I don't like your dress. It's too dull. You're prettier than that." He was also particular as to the type of clerical staff he wanted around the White House. Competence and the ability to work long hours and on weekends were important. But he sought other attributes as well, as he explained to an aide in January 1964: "I want the five smartest, best-educated, fastest, prettiest secretaries in Washington . . . I want them to have a college degree if it's at all possible . . . I don't want any of your old, broke-down old maids—I want them from twenty-five to forty."[47]

But when it came to legislating for gender equity, the president was on the front line. Perhaps the most important legislative initiative of the early 1960s was more or less an afterthought. Members of Alice Paul's National Woman's Party, founded in 1916, contacted Virginia Democratic congressman Howard Smith, eighty-year-old chairman of the powerful House Rules Committee. Committee members were deliberating a bill that would eventually become the 1964 Civil Rights Act. The women reminded the conservative Southerner that Johnson's bill, if passed in its present form, would include protections for black men that were denied to white women. Shrewdly appealing to the congressman's racial and chivalric sensibilities, they suggested that Smith add one word—*sex*—to the bill as a protected class along with "race, color, religion, or national origin." He agreed, though he would later contend he did so more out of mischief than conviction, hoping such an inclusion would confuse and eventually sidetrack the bill.[48]

Smith's tone in placing the amendment before the House supported that interpretation, as eyewitnesses recalled his jocular comments. The mood in the House that day seemed especially lighthearted. Brooklyn Democratic congressman Emanuel Celler claimed he knew all about equality for women. He had been married for forty-nine years, and he usually had the last two words: "Yes, dear." More laughter and more jokes in the House. But then congresswoman Martha Griffiths (D-MI) stood up: "If there had been any necessity to have pointed out that women were a second-class sex, the laughter would have proved it."[49]

Female House members cheered the addition and the president supported it. The amendment to add the category of sex to Title VII of the civil rights bill passed the House by the relatively close vote of 168–133, given the overwhelming Democratic majority. The amendment drew considerable support from Republicans and Southern Democrats, the latter hoping the inclusion of sex would derail the bill in the Senate. But some prominent liberals, including Celler and John V. Lindsay, opposed the amendment, fearing for the overall civil rights bill. When the clerk registered the final tally, two women in the visitors' gallery shouted, "We've won! We've made it!" Guards removed them. The entire bill passed easily, 290–130. Contrary to Congressman Smith's hopes, the sex amendment provoked little debate in the Senate.[50]

The enforcement mechanism was another matter. The 1964 Civil Rights Act established the Equal Employment Opportunity Commission (EEOC) to adjudicate discrimination claims, though the law gave it no enforcement powers. The body was to use persuasion and mediation. The chair of the EEOC dismissed the Title VII provision as applied to women, explaining its inclusion was "a fluke . . . conceived out of wedlock." The liberal *New Republic* agreed: "Why should the mischievous joke perpetrated on the floor of the House of Representatives" be treated seriously by EEOC administrators?[51]

A *New York Times* editorial also made light of the sex-discrimination provision. Without gender divisions there would be "no more milkman, iceman, serviceman, foreman or pressman . . . The Rockettes may become bi-sexual, and a pity too . . . This is revolution, chaos. You can't even safely advertise for a wife any more." The Title VII provision also horrified the personnel director of a major airline, as he wondered what would happen "when a gal walks into our office, demands a job as an airline pilot, and has the credentials to qualify."[52]

Washington insiders jokingly referred to the amendment as the Bunny Law, imagining a hypothetical case in which a man was turned down for a job as a bunny in a Playboy club. But it was not a joke to women who took advantage of the new law. Of the 8,854 complaints filed in the EEOC's first year, nearly a third charged gender discrimination. To process these complaints, the commission hired the lawyer wife of a staff member. She was a temp.[53]

Martha Griffiths led the fight against the EEOC's indifference. Concerning gender-segregated help-wanted ads, she noted that the 1964 Civil Rights Act would likely prohibit a newspaper from listing such ads under "white" and "colored." Then why was it acceptable to list ads under "male" and "female"?[54]

The EEOC had already determined that certain jobs qualified as BFOQ— "bona fide occupational qualification"—meaning that they were naturally for men or women. Commission members had determined that flight attendants fell under that category as exclusively female. Again, Griffith rose to the attack: "Do they really think for one moment that men or women make plane trips for the sole purpose of having a female—or male—flight attendant serve them lunch or give them an aspirin?" On the other hand: "If you are trying to run a whorehouse in the sky, get a license."[55]

Griffith's comments received support at a conference in the summer of 1966 that led to the founding of NOW with Betty Friedan as its president. Her first initiative was to seek a writ of mandamus against the EEOC, compelling it to perform its legal function under Title VII of the 1964 Civil Rights Act. On Mother's Day in 1967, she mounted NOW's first picket line at the White House fence, with the sign RIGHTS NOT ROSES. The NOW demonstrators threw away chains of aprons, flowers, and mock typewriters and moved on to the offices of the EEOC, where they dumped bundles of newspapers on the floor to protest segregated help-wanted ads.[56]

NOW's efforts were central in pushing the EEOC to deny flight attendants BFOQ status in February 1968. In August the EEOC declared that listing jobs ads by gender was unlawful. In November, a federal district court ruled that state women's labor-protection laws violated Title VII and were unconstitutional. Henceforth, the states would apply protective legislation equally to both sexes. In a unanimous decision in the first gender-discrimination case to reach the U.S. Supreme Court, *Phillips v. Martin Marietta* in 1971, the justices held that Martin Marietta's policy of denying employment to women with preschool-aged children violated Title VII.[57]

In the 1970s the impact of the 1964 Civil Rights Act on gender equity would resonate beyond EEOC issues. In 1972, Congress, in a series of amendments to an education act, passed Title IX, using the exact language of Title VII of the '64 act, substituting only *sex* for *race* in authorizing the Office of Civil Rights in the Department of Health, Education, and Welfare to police gender discrimination in all public schools and colleges and universities receiving federal funds, which encompassed almost all of those institutions. The immediate result of Title IX was to open up a bonanza of athletic opportunities for women, including access to athletic scholarships at the college level.[58]

Martha Griffiths filed a successful discharge petition in 1970 to yank the Equal Rights Amendment legislation from Congressman Celler's Judiciary Committee. Celler had argued condescendingly that "neither the National Woman's Party nor the delightful, delectable, and dedicated gentlelady from Michigan can change nature." But Celler's dictum fell on deaf ears as both the House and Senate mustered the required two-thirds majorities to send the amendment to the states for ratification in 1972. A few months later, Celler lost the Democratic primary in his Brooklyn district to Elizabeth Holtzman, who became one of seven new women to join the House. Within a year twenty-eight states had ratified the ERA, seemingly well on the way to the required thirty-eight states. Gender equity seemed both inevitable and imminent.[59]

CHAPTER 20

THE GREAT AMERICAN BREAKTHROUGH

LYNDON B. JOHNSON KNEW about poverty. He grew up on the edge of it. He quit his first year of college to take a job to save money to complete his education. His teaching job in Cotulla, Texas, introduced him to a level of poverty and prejudice he had not before encountered. In Cotulla, he understood the connection between the two. Now that he was president, he vowed to use the mighty engine of the federal government to pull Americans to productive citizenship. In the commonwealth, none would rest until all prospered.

By the time President Johnson announced his War on Poverty in 1964, poverty, like gender equality and environmental protection, had assumed an important place in the national discourse. Americans did not discover poverty in the 1960s—anyone who had lived through the Great Depression knew about it, often firsthand. In fact, government attempts to address the issue dated from the colonial period. What was new in these confident years was the belief that through public policy Americans could not only conquer an age-old scourge, but perhaps even eliminate it.

The confidence derived from three factors. First, an array of experts believed that it was possible to attack poverty with public policies grounded in the social and behavioral sciences. Second, President Johnson believed that such a mission was possible. The third factor was the support of the American people—not all of them, but enough to render an assault on poverty generally popular. The nation was moving to put a man on the moon; it was addressing long-standing unequal treatment of African Americans, immigrants, and women; and it had a generation of young people fired by the possibilities not only of their future, but also of the opportunity to extend those choices to everyone. Confidence and idealism merged at Washington, D.C.

The idea of poverty as a target of public policy reemerged during a time of general prosperity, a dynamic very different from the attack on poverty in the Great Depression. Politicians, journalists, and academics took poverty in the midst of plenty as their theme. During the 1950s, they publicized the chronic poverty of Appalachia. Poverty entered the political discourse in the

1960 presidential campaign when former Democratic presidential candidate Adlai E. Stevenson wrote a long essay for *Life* magazine on the responsibility of the American political system to address poverty.[1]

Stevenson noted that government had a history of addressing inequality whether it was slavery, child labor, or minimum wages. It was no longer acceptable "that the many can smugly overlook the squalor and misery of the few." Stevenson believed that "the old idea of America and its government as a positive instrument for the common weal is being restored once again after all the cheap sarcasm about 'bureaucracy' and 'creeping socialism.'" More than a quarter century after New Deal legislation responded to the "one-third of a nation that is ill-clothed, ill-housed, and ill-fed," poverty persisted. As much as one fourth of the nation still fell below the poverty line by the late 1950s.[2]

Although the Eisenhower administration raised the minimum wage, a large body of workers remained outside its provisions. It covered, for example, only 33 percent of retail workers. One fourth of retail workers still earned less than $1 an hour as late as 1961. Social Security doled out a maximum benefit of $190.50 a month in 1961 (or $1,515 in current dollars), but only if the recipient earned an income well above the poverty line throughout his or her life. Other New Deal legislation such as unemployment compensation, the Wagner Act (which institutionalized collective bargaining), and various farm programs were directed at union workers or market farmers, not the poorest of the poor.[3]

WHEN *BUSINESS WEEK* PRESENTED an overview of poverty in America in February 1964, it stated, "The emergence of poverty as a major issue has been sudden" and attributed this revelation to Michael Harrington's book *The Other America* (1962). This was more a tribute to Harrington than to the facts, but it accurately reflected the impact of his book on public policy discussions. Much like *Silent Spring* and *The Feminine Mystique*, *The Other America* did not create something new. Rather, it captured and synthesized a great deal of information and analysis already circulating in the media and the academy on the issue of poverty.

Harrington was thirty-four years old when the book was published, though installments had appeared as early as 1959. He was born into a moderately prosperous family in St. Louis, the only child of devoutly Catholic Irish parents. He did his undergraduate work at the College of the Holy Cross in Worcester, Massachusetts and attended Yale Law School and the University of Chicago. In 1949, he relocated to New York City, determined to become a writer. In 1951, Harrington joined Dorothy Day's Catholic Worker movement, a group of left-wing Roman Catholics dedicated to working with the poor and applying Marxist principles to society. He joined the Socialist Party and, by the late 1950s, was probably the nation's best-known socialist, aside from that party's perennial standard-bearer, Norman Thomas.[4]

Harrington's greatest contribution in *The Other America* was to demonstrate how poverty generated an array of problems well beyond merely not having enough money. It affected education, housing, life expectancy, and aspirations. It also led to increasing isolation, which, in turn, reduced the opportunities for advancement. Harrington contrasted the poor of the late 1950s, primarily black, as his research focused on New York City, with immigrants from Europe and Asia. The latter may have dwelled in slums, but they were not slum dwellers. Mixed among an array of aspirational people with a variety of skills, the immigrants perceived their circumstances as temporary; and they saw frequently how neighbors improved themselves and left for better neighborhoods. Better neighborhoods meant more secure surroundings, and that led to better schools, and better schools meant upward mobility. It was still possible into the early 1950s to secure a decent job with a high school education. By the 1960s, the economy demanded more education. Between 1953 and 1959 alone, 1.5 million blue-collar jobs, or 11 percent of the total blue-collar workforce, were lost, and those jobs would not return.[5]

For African Americans, the structure of the urban housing market sealed them off from geographic and economic mobility. The poorest among them suffered the greatest isolation, set apart from the strivers and so-called middle-class values. If people in these neighborhoods worked, it was likely in jobs Harrington called "the economic underworld"—outside of trade unions and minimum-wage protections. Not surprisingly, a drug culture flourished, education was devalued, and crime and indifference were rampant. And it became increasingly difficult to escape.[6]

Harrington's analysis did not attribute poverty totally to the environment. In line with then-current sociology, he contended that these neighborhoods exhibited a culture of poverty, a set of values that diverged dramatically from those of mainstream society. Because of this culture, public policy had to address not only the environment, but also the person.[7]

The culture of poverty extended to the next generation. Young persons in poor families began life in a condition of "inherited poverty." Family structure—homes without fathers, fewer marriages, and more early pregnancies—was an especially destructive element of this culture. The result was that "hundreds of thousands, and perhaps millions, of children in the other America never know stability and 'normal' affection." Without these supports, extrication from poverty, let alone upward mobility, was unlikely.[8]

For Harrington, poverty wore primarily a black face. Increasing numbers of Americans, especially if they lived in cities, were coming to associate that color with poverty and dysfunction, Harrington moved African Americans to center stage of the poverty discussion, an emphasis that initially helped to focus public policy on the problems of black neighborhoods, but that ultimately weakened public support.

By the late 1950s, African Americans accounted for 16 percent of New York City's population, but more than 40 percent of the people who received public welfare assistance. Black unemployment was double white unemployment, and African Americans' wages were roughly half those of white workers. These circumstances helped to create dysfunctional neighborhoods. In Harlem, Harrington noted, the infant mortality rate was 45.3 per thousand, compared to city's white rate of 15.4 per thousand. Harrington concluded that Harlem, "as well as every other Negro ghetto, is the center of poverty, of manual work, of sickness, and of every typical disability which America's underdeveloped areas suffer. It is on this very real and material base that the ghetto builds its unique culture."[9]

Harrington noted that, to a greater extent than other ethnic groups, black Americans experienced "the double indignity of racial discrimination and economic oppression." While he was aware of the civil rights movement, he recognized, as many other Americans did not, that the removal of all the discriminatory laws would not remove the inherent racism of "the American economy, the American society, the American unconscious. If all the laws were framed to provide equal opportunity, a majority of the Negroes would not be able to take full advantage of the change." This idea would form the basis of President Johnson's famous Howard University speech of 1965, where he explained the necessity for affirmative action.[10]

Poor housing was "one of the most important facts about the other America. This is where the nation builds the environment of the culture of poverty." But twelve years after the passage of the 1949 Housing Act, Congress had authorized funding for only a fraction of the units Presidents Truman and Eisenhower had requested. Harrington called it "one of the greatest single domestic scandals of postwar America." He estimated that about 30 percent of Americans were living in substandard housing, or roughly equal to the one-third ill-housed that President Roosevelt identified nearly three decades earlier.[11]

Urban renewal had worsened the situation, demolishing dwelling units for the poor, but not always replacing them with affordable public housing. Harrington believed that the best strategy for public housing was to construct it outside the ghetto. Public housing, he wrote, "should avoid segregating the poor off in some corner of the metropolis . . . The projects and subsidized homes should be located as parts of neighborhoods, so that income groups, races, and cultures will mingle." The projects should also be modest in size, not "huge high-rise ghettos." There was no point in spending millions of dollars merely to perpetuate the isolation and pathology of the poor. Fifty years later, studies confirm the wisdom of this insight.[12]

But by merely moving the poor to a new environment, "the chances are that they will import the culture of poverty." A comprehensive approach involving education, home visits, health care, and employment opportunities was necessary to break that culture. It was unrealistic to expect the poor to "exhibit all kinds of gentle, middle-class virtues" simply by changing their geography.[13]

For Harrington, nothing less than a comprehensive plan would work because the ghetto's problems were interconnected. "The real emancipation of the Negro," Harrington concluded, "waits upon a massive assault upon the entire culture of poverty in American society: upon slums, inferior education, inadequate medical care, and all the rest." That was a task for government: "only one agency in America is capable of eradicating both the slum and slum psychology from this land: the federal government."[14]

BOTH KENNEDY AND JOHNSON were aware that the piecemeal approach was not working. Welfare programs rather than decreasing dependency seemed to have the opposite effect. Urban renewal was a bust, except in helping some cities recoup taxes by building sports venues or middle-income housing. Job-training programs faltered as many of the hard-core poor lacked basic skills to enter training. A month before he went to Dallas, Kennedy ordered his staff to develop a "comprehensive, coordinated attack on poverty."[15]

Johnson, at his very first meeting with the late president's White House staff, brought up the poverty initiative: "That's my kind of program . . . Move full speed ahead." The team came up with the idea of focusing on ten demonstration areas to determine if a comprehensive program was viable. Each poverty area would form a development corporation to plan and execute programs. The hope was, according to Johnson, that "organized local community action" would "help individuals, families, and communities to help themselves." Programs would include tax reductions, employment services, better educational facilities, an emphasis on youth employment, adult education and training, and health care for the elderly. The problem with these initiatives, however, was that, in the short run, they did not solve the basic problem of families in poverty: the lack of money to move beyond the daily struggle for subsistence.[16]

So why not just give the poor money and forget about trying to change their behavior? With a secure stipend, perhaps they could leave their impoverished neighborhoods and begin the upward climb themselves. The idea derived from conservative economist Milton Friedman, but also received support across the political spectrum. By 1968, one thousand academic economists had endorsed the idea. The direct subsidy to the poor would be a "negative income tax." Under this plan, everyone would file an income tax return. Those reporting incomes below the poverty line would then receive a payment from the government. That payment would lift all of the poor above the poverty line. Such a subsidy would reduce the federal bureaucracy and shift initiative and responsibility to the poor themselves. President Johnson's Council of Economic Advisers explored this idea and concluded that it would take an annual subsidy of $11 billion—or less than 2 percent of the GDP—to bring all of the poor above the poverty line. The total federal outlay for all welfare programs during the mid-1960s was $8 billion.[17]

But LBJ (and many lawmakers) remained wedded to the ideal of welfare as a hand-up rather than a handout: that welfare must connect to work, educational, or training components. Although the negative income tax made sense to many economists and lawmakers, "the only ones really against it are the people." An AFL-CIO official noted, "Support for this kind of plan just doesn't exist and could not exist in a work-oriented culture."[18]

The fear was that some families would use the direct subsidy and do nothing or spend it on frivolity or worse. Transfer payments might produce not only disincentives to work, but also to save, and to learn skills. More serious for those who believed that the culture of poverty, not poverty itself, submerged the poor, a guaranteed income would do little or nothing to exorcise "the extreme present-orientedness" of individuals living in that culture; in fact, such payments might make things worse.[19]

The idea that public policy should rehabilitate the poor, as well as provide temporary sustenance, governed social welfare policy in postwar America. LBJ believed in the rehabilitative role of poverty policy. In January 1964, he laid out some of his plans to a Texas friend in the vernacular he often used with Southerners skeptical about government welfare activities, especially those directed at African Americans: "I'm gonna try to teach these nigras that don't know anything how to work for themselves instead of just breedin'. I'm gonna try to teach these Mexicans who can't talk English to learn it so they can work for themselves . . . and get off of our taxpayer's back." By connecting his proposals to the American work ethic, he hoped to turn skeptics of his programs into supporters.[20]

Johnson declared war on poverty in his first State of the Union address on January 8, 1964: "This administration today, here and now, declares unconditional war on poverty in America . . . We cannot leave the further wearing away of poverty solely to the general progress of the economy." That unemployment stabilized at a then frustratingly high 5.5 percent despite prosperity and greater productivity strengthened the view that if the government could equip the long-term poor with skills and motivation, it could solve poverty.[21]

The bill sent to Congress (and it originated almost entirely in the White House, a relative rarity for a major piece of legislation) included provisions for a Job Corps, providing education and vocational training for youths aged sixteen through twenty-one; a Neighborhood Youth Corps, offering public service employment; a work-study program for college students; a loan program to spur small businesses; and a national service corps, Volunteers in Service to America, or VISTA.[22]

None of these initiatives represented new ideas, though they did fulfill LBJ's desire to focus on youth. The new feature of the bill was the Community Action Program (CAP), to involve the residents themselves in the development of their neighborhoods. Although poverty was a national problem, experts believed its solution lay at the local level, especially with residents. The provision was LBJ's strategy to address the culture of poverty: by involving the poor in their own elevation, they would shed the debilitating traits of their chronic existence. Johnson called his bill the Economic Opportunity Act (EOA), a good public relations title as postwar federal programs had emphasized broadening opportunities for Americans, not guaranteeing results. The Office of Economic Opportunity (OEO) would administer the act.[23]

None of the bill's provisions implied a strategy of redistributing income to the poor. There would be no tax increases. In fact, there was a tax cut, per President Kennedy's proposal. President Johnson's Council of Economic Advisers warned him that, when explaining how the government would fight poverty, he ought to "avoid completely the use of the terms 'inequality' or 'redistribution.'" He should refer to the poor as "targets of opportunity." The objective was to increase opportunity. Education and work would not only solve the economic problems of the poor, but would also induce middle-class values. It was an optimistic formula at a time of great optimism.[24]

Johnson budgeted the bill at $1 billion, hardly enough to fund a bare-bones version of its provisions. That mayors across the country would be clamoring for the funds meant that the funding would be spread so thin, its impact would be limited. Also, LBJ did not divide the funds among the programs in the bill, leaving it up to cities to determine how to allocate the grants. The bill passed Congress fairly easily, and the president signed the bill on August 20, 1964. Early returns from the program in 1965 and 1966 were positive. And so were Americans. In February 1966, a national poll found 72 percent of respondents in favor of the administration's domestic programs.[25]

The legislation did not resolve the philosophical issue Harrington had raised: a comprehensive attack on poverty required targeting both the individual and the community. Harrington had argued that changing the environment—removing individuals from debilitated neighborhoods—was as important as tending to their individual educational, vocational, and daily needs. Community Action Programs assumed that residents would remain in the community and that whatever environmental transformations occurred would happen in that neighborhood. But ghetto enrichment worked only if everyone in the neighborhood participated.

THE EOA WAS PART OF A BROADER initiative that Johnson called the Great Society in a speech at the University of Michigan on May 22, 1964, before a crowd of eighty thousand in the school's football stadium. LBJ had used the phrase prior to the Michigan speech, but did not fully articulate its meaning. It responded to rising concerns about the unfettered materialism of American society and how that might devolve into unbridled individualism that neglected the commonwealth. As with Truman and Eisenhower, Johnson sought to stake out the middle ground and balance individual ambition with collective objectives.[26]

"The Great Society," he explained in Ann Arbor, "rests on abundance and liberty for all. It . . . is a place where every child can find knowledge to enrich his mind and enlarge his talents . . . where the city of man serves not only the needs of the body and the demands of commerce but the desire for beauty and the hunger for community." Attaining this balance was a prerequisite for greater things: "The Great Society is not a safe harbor . . . It is a challenge constantly renewed, beckoning us toward a destiny where the meaning of our lives matches the marvelous products of our labor."

Johnson focused on three broad policy areas, which provided a blueprint for the nation fifty years ahead and beyond. He predicted with remarkable accuracy that by 2014 four fifths of the nation's population would live in urban areas (that occurred in 2012). The people in these areas would need homes, highways, and facilities "equal to all those built since this country was first settled." Therefore, "we must rebuild the entire urban United States." This required an integrated policy of transportation, environmental protection, and housing construction. The unbalanced growth of metropolitan areas had eroded "time-honored values of community with neighbors and communion with nature." The result: "The loss of these values breeds loneliness and boredom and indifference." It was not only the poor that required a behavioral reset. The diagnosis of anomie and disconnection apparently afflicted other Americans as well. Robert D. Putnam and others would make this diagnosis a half century later.

LBJ also addressed problems "in our countryside." In rhetoric reminiscent of Rachel Carson's *Silent Spring*, he warned that the beauty of the countryside was in danger. "The water we drink, the food we eat, the very air that we breathe, are threatened with pollution. Our parks are overcrowded, our seashores overburdened. Green fields and dense forests are disappearing."

Education was the third policy area. At a time when a high school diploma was becoming less marketable, "each year more than one hundred thousand high school graduates, with proved ability, do not enter college because they cannot afford it." In the primary and secondary grades, "classrooms are overcrowded and curricula are outdated." Poverty was the greatest threat to an educated population.

The solution to these problems rested, most of all, on the students in front of him, members of the gifted generation: "For better or for worse, your generation has been appointed by history to deal with those problems and to lead America toward a new age. You have the chance never before afforded to any people in any age. You can help build a society where the demands of morality, and the needs of the spirit, can be realized in the life of the nation."

In an extended essay in the *Saturday Evening Post* in October 1964, LBJ justified why the federal government should be leading this movement toward a Great Society. Many of the conservative magazine's readers questioned government activism, particularly on the scale posited by the Great Society initiatives.[27]

Johnson addressed the fear that "government has become a major menace to individual liberty," an idea he flatly rejected in terms familiar to both Truman and Eisenhower. "Does government subvert our freedom through the Social Security system . . . ? Does government undermine our freedom by bringing electricity to the farm, by controlling floods, or by ending bank failures? Is freedom lessened by efforts to abate pollution . . . by efforts to gain knowledge of the causes of heart disease and cancer . . . by banning the sale of harmful drugs, by providing school lunches for our children, by preserving our wilderness areas, or by improving the safety of our airways?" And finally, "Is freedom betrayed when . . . we redeem in full a pledge made a century ago by the Emancipation Proclamation?"

To the contrary, "government at its best liberates [the individual] from the enslaving forces of his environment." LBJ quoted Thomas Jefferson, hardly an advocate of big government, on this point: "The care of human life and happiness and not their destruction, is the first and only legitimate object of good government." To support his view of the commonwealth, Johnson recruited Aristotle: "If liberty and equality . . . are chiefly to be found in democracy, they will be best attained when all persons alike share in the government to the utmost."

Johnson took not only an expansive view of government, but also of time. He asked readers to look ahead to the 1990s and imagine how Americans then would look back upon "these 1960s as the time of the great American Breakthrough—toward the victory of peace over war; toward the victory of prosperity over poverty; toward the victory of human rights over human wrongs; toward the victory of enlightened minds over darkness." It would have been a stirring retrospective if only history had not intervened.

LBJ's comprehensive view of urban issues and his commitment to partnering with localities found their way into the 1966 Demonstration Cities and Metropolitan Development Act, which came to be known as Model Cities. It was his most significant legislative achievement in the area of urban policy. In his January 26, 1966, special message to Congress, Johnson declared, "We must set in motion the forces of change in great urban areas that will make them the masterpieces of our civilization . . . I recommend an effort larger in scope, more comprehensive, more concentrated, than any that has gone before." The act involved more than 150 five-year experiments to develop new antipoverty programs in the covered cities, to explore alternative forms of municipal government, and to increase the recruitment of minorities into city government.[28]

The act authorized the expenditure of $2.3 billion over the ensuing six years in federal matching grants (80 percent federal, 20 percent local) to cities. LBJ envisioned a close cooperative relationship between federal and local officials, much as he had posited in his education policy. The proliferation of civil disturbances in the nation's cities heightened the urgency. Cities would also seek to "reduce welfare rolls, lower crime rates," and achieve "greater participatory democracy." It was an ambitious agenda, particularly given the parochial political interests in the participating cities. But, like most of LBJ's proposals, he advanced Model Cities with confidence and optimism: the cities could become wholesome, governable, equitable, and beautiful environments. It was the most comprehensive urban policy effort in the nation's history.[29]

One of the more important results of Model Cities was to increase the visibility of African Americans in city government agencies. Roderick Juniel, chief of the Denver City Fire Department, recalled, "I ended up as the city's first African American fire chief. I would not even have been able to get a job with the city without Model Cities."[30]

OF ALL THE GREAT SOCIETY initiatives, education was probably closest to LBJ's heart. On March 6, 1965, on a call to Hubert Humphrey, his point man for the

Great Society, LBJ wanted to make sure his vice president had the arguments to persuade lawmakers to support Johnson's education package: "Now, by God, they [blacks] can't work in a filling station and put water in a *radiator* unless they can *read* and *write*. Because they've got to go and punch their cash register, and they don't know which one to *punch*. They've got to take a check, and they don't know which one to *cash*. They've got to take a *credit* card, and they can't pull the *numbers* . . . Now that *you* damn fellows better be working on. If these Republicans want to be for the nigras—and I hope they do, I want a two-party system—I hope some nigras vote for Republicans. But you make them vote for *education*!" It worked. Congress renewed the NDEA in 1964, increasing the authorization level for student loans, raising the number of graduate fellowships, and supporting the purchase of instructional equipment not only in the sciences but also for English, reading, history, geography, and civics.

Johnson was familiar with the concept of an urban companion to the Civil War–era Morrill Act, which established federally funded land-grant colleges. The Morrill Act expanded higher-education opportunities for rural and small-town youths and promoted scientific agriculture. An "urban grant" bill would enable urban universities to address the problems of their cities. The result was the Higher Education Act (HEA) of 1965. The act provided $70 million annually to universities for scholarships to students of "exceptional financial need," and below-market-interest loans for other students. It also allotted funds for the construction of instructional facilities, including targeted grants to upgrade campus libraries. It was the first time in U.S. history that the federal government provided scholarships to undergraduate students. The act also established the National Teacher Corps. On November 8, 1965, Johnson traveled to his alma mater, now known as Southwest Texas State College in San Marcos, to sign the Higher Education Act.[31]

Education legislation directed at the primary and secondary levels had confounded previous administrations on the twin obstacles over what to do about parochial schools and the persistent fear of federal intrusion into an area normally reserved for states and localities. Also, some liberals now opposed such aid as it could go to segregated schools. With the 1964 Civil Rights Act linking federal funding to desegregation, at least in theory this last concern vanished. Also, local governments found themselves financially overextended from the flood of students descending on their public schools. Since most communities relied on property taxes to fund the schools, and considering such taxes had increased by 200 percent from the late 1940s to the early 1960s, federal assistance suddenly seemed less threatening.[32]

On the church-state issue, the Johnson administration constructed a bypass by targeting programs to children rather than to schools. LBJ recommended a billion-dollar-a-year package for "the special educational needs of educationally deprived children." The federal government would provide the funds in proportion to the number of children in families with incomes under $2,000 a year; in other words, the hard-core poor. As one of the bill's sponsors, Senator Wayne Morse (D-OR), noted, "We are going into federal aid for elementary and secondary schools . . . through the back door."[33]

The Elementary and Secondary Education Act of 1965 (ESEA) was the greatest educational triumph of Johnson's presidency. The act also included Head Start, an acknowledgment that early interventions prior to regular schooling could enhance long-term educational attainment, and Follow Through, an extension of Head Start, passed in 1967. Johnson signed the ESEA in the one-room school in Stonewall, Texas, where he began his education in 1913, as his first teacher, Katherine Deadrich Loney, looked on.[34]

As part of his education package, LBJ also championed the creation of the National Endowment for the Arts (NEA) and the National Endowment for the Humanities (NEH). The administration emphasized the importance not only of science and technology programs, but also of the liberal arts. It did not perceive an antagonism between these broad disciplinary areas; rather, the administration viewed them as complementary. Heretofore, community theaters and dance groups, orchestras and opera companies, and artists and sculptors relied heavily on private philanthropy and support. Now, in line with policies in Western Europe, the U.S. government would subsidize creativity for the benefit not only of the artists and actors, but also for the esthetic tastes of Americans. As Johnson explained, "Pursuit of artistic achievement, and making the fruits of that achievement available to all its people, is also among the hallmarks of a Great Society." In one year, as the president noted, Congress "did more for the wonderful cause of education in America than all the previous 176 regular sessions of Congress did, put together."[35]

The federal share of all expenditures for education by all levels of government rose from less than 3 percent to 10 percent by the end of the 1960s. Also by that date, ESEA was assisting 9 million children from low-income families. Head Start had enrolled 716,000 children by January 1968, and Follow Through an additional 63,500 children. By 1970, the Higher Education Act of 1965 had funded 2 million grants, loans, and interest subsidies for guaranteed loans. These funds reached one out of every four college students. By 1970, $9 billion in federal funds had built classrooms, libraries, laboratories, and other instructional facilities.[36]

As the gifted generation streamed onto college campuses in the 1960s, the federal government directly assisted their tuition and instruction. Between 1955 and 1974, the number of college students soared from 2.5 million to 8.8 million.

The percentage of eighteen- to twenty-four-year-olds attending college jumped from 17.8 to 33.5 during this period. This was a broad trend throughout the country. The number of African Americans attending college rose from 95,000 to 814,000 between these years, and the number of women from one third of all students to one half. Federal education policy did not account for these trends by itself, but the measures inaugurated by the Johnson administration made attendance at an institution of higher education more attainable.[37]

LBJ TURNED TO HEALTH CARE, another key element in forging a Great Society. The idea of universal health insurance had been around at least since the administration of Franklin D. Roosevelt. Harry Truman revived it, but the Democratic Party platform of 1952 dropped the proposal. Dwight D. Eisenhower resurrected a version of the plan that included the participation of private health insurers, but strong Republican opposition and the lobbying efforts of the American Medical Association (AMA) removed any chance of passage. The day after Ike's proposal suffered an embarrassing defeat in the House, 238–134, he stated testily, "There is nothing to be gained by shutting our eyes to the fact that all of our people are not getting the kind of medical care to which they are entitled." But the people would have to wait.[38]

Johnson, like Eisenhower, recognized that universal health insurance was a nonstarter, even in the supercharged Eighty-ninth Congress. He was also aware that even a moderate proposal like Eisenhower's would face stiff opposition from the medical community and from Republicans. Medicare evolved as a strategy when studies demonstrated that retirees were the least protected class for health insurance. They were typically ineligible for group plans designed for employed persons. If they had belonged to such a plan, it had usually ended upon their retirement. Obtaining health insurance privately became prohibitive for retirees, especially the vast majority of those living on fixed incomes. Yet, their health care needs grew as their income declined and coverage disappeared.[39]

In 1952, Senators James Murray (D-MT) and Hubert Humphrey (D-MN) hit upon the idea of tying health care for the elderly to Social Security simply by amending the latter. They calculated that they could accomplish this without raising the payroll taxes that financed Social Security, especially with increased numbers of Americans entering the job market. But their idea went nowhere. The elderly were not yet a burgeoning cohort, nor were they well organized politically.

Public support for some version of Medicare grew in the early 1960s. A Gallup poll in 1962 indicated that 67 percent of voters favored it. The Democratic landslide in 1964 settled the matter—voters defeated thirty-seven legislators identified as "friends of the AMA." Medicare covering all the elderly, financed by mandated increases in Social Security taxes (paid by both employer and employee) passed Congress on July 28, 1965. Included in the Medicare bill was a provision inserted by Wilbur Mills (D-AR), chairman of the powerful House Ways and Means Committee. Called Medicaid, it offered federal matching grants to states for poor individuals already qualified for welfare programs.[40]

Two days later, the president traveled to Independence, Missouri, as a tribute to Harry Truman, who had worked hard but futilely for universal health insurance during his administration. Although Medicare covered only a portion of Americans, it was, many hoped, an important step toward Truman's ultimate objective. LBJ, in Truman's presence, signed the bill into law on July 30, 1965. "No longer will older Americans be denied the healing miracle of modern medicine," the president stated. "No longer will illness crush and destroy the savings that they have so carefully put away over a lifetime so that they might enjoy dignity in their later years." Within a decade, both Medicare and Medicaid reached one fifth of Americans.[41]

IMMIGRATION REFORM INITIALLY was not a priority of the Johnson administration, nor of the people. A Harris poll conducted in the spring of 1965 and published in the *Washington Post* found that Americans, by a margin of 56 percent to 24 percent, objected to "changing immigration laws to allow more people to enter this country." The *Post* concluded, "Americans prefer people from Canada and northern and western Europe as immigrants and tend to oppose immigrants from Latin America, southern and Eastern Europe, Russia, the Middle East, and Asia." Emanuel Celler, the most vigorous proponent of immigration reform in the House, admitted, "There is no burning desire in the grass roots of this country to change our immigration policy." Which meant that presidential leadership would play a significant role if a new immigration policy was to emerge.[42]

As a senator, Johnson had opposed amending or scrapping the McCarran-Walter Act. But when he was president, immigration quotas clashed with his vision of a Great Society as a nation free from ethnic and religious exclusion. In the midst of the Cold War, quotas damaged America's image abroad. In the midst of a civil rights movement, their presence seemed perverse. As Johnson confided to House Speaker John McCormack, "There is no piece of legislation before the Congress that in terms of decency and equity is more demanding of passage than the immigration bill."[43]

Working with Michigan Democratic senator Philip Hart, and Celler in the House, the Kennedy administration crafted a bill in 1963 that failed to reach a vote by the time of Kennedy's assassination in November. Even when Johnson took it on, his advisers were pessimistic that he could ever get a reform bill passed given the persistent opposition of Southern Democrats.[44]

As with so many of LBJ's initiatives, the landslide election of 1964 proved fortuitous. Also by that date, the American Immigration and Citizenship Council (AICC), a coalition of ethnic groups, provided a strong lobbying apparatus to counter nativist sentiment in Congress. Joining the AICC were a number of liberal religious organizations, such as the National Catholic Welfare Conference, the National Council of Jewish Women, and the National Council of Churches of Christ. Labor unions and business organizations also supported change.

The very groups the 1924 act had sought to restrict had grown in size and strength to demand a change. Opposition was weak, coming primarily from the National Association of Evangelicals and the anticommunist Liberty Lobby. In the U.S. Senate, North Carolina Democrat Sam Ervin, a longtime opponent of civil rights for African Americans, led the meager forces opposed to immigration reform.[45]

The new immigration law repealed the controversial quotas set in 1924. It allowed the entry of 290,000 immigrants annually, roughly the number admitted yearly up to that time. The law emphasized family reunification, a priority for Jewish and Catholic groups concerned about religious intolerance in the Iron Curtain countries of Eastern Europe. The law also privileged skilled applicants. For the first time, an immigration law set limits—120,000— on the numbers of immigrants from the western hemisphere, with 170,000 coming from Europe, and smaller numbers for Africa and Asia, with a cap of 20,000 people from any single nation, except those in the western hemisphere, which had no limit.

Every Jewish member of Congress in both Houses supported the bill, as did all Catholics in the Senate and all but three of ninety-two in the House. When President Johnson signed the Immigration and Naturalization Act of 1965 at the foot of the Statue of Liberty on October 3, 1965, he declared that the new law repaired "a very deep and painful flaw in the fabric of American justice." Commentators hailed the new immigration law as on a par with the civil rights acts of 1964 and 1965.[46]

Most observers expected the new law to redress the inequities of the quota system. Initially, they were correct. In the late 1960s, most immigrants came to the United States from Southern and Eastern Europe. The largest arriving groups were Italian, Greek, and Portuguese immigrants. But in a textbook example of unintended consequences, over the next decade an average of 100,000 additional immigrants (over the 290,000 total) arrived annually, benefiting from a provision of the law that permitted the admission of close relatives of U.S. citizens. Between 1961 and 1970, 3.3 million immigrants arrived in the United States. That swelled to 4.5 million in the following decade, and continued to rise thereafter. The new flows were very different from the old.[47]

The overwhelming majority of these individuals came from Latin America and Asia. During the McCarran-Walter years after World War II, 42.6 percent of the annual total of immigrants came from Latin America, the West Indies, Asia, and Africa. By the early 1970s, that had climbed to 71.7 percent and remained steady at 75 percent for the next two decades.[48]

The family-unification provision affected Irish immigrants in particular. Since Irish immigration peaked in the nineteenth century, family connections to the old country were rarely close enough to qualify people for immigration. Immigration from Europe fell from 113,400 in 1965 to an annual average of 65,000 in the late 1970s. Latin American immigration, on the other hand, increased from 88,400 in 1965 to almost 3.5 million by the early 1980s.[49]

By 1976, more than half of all legal immigrants to the United States came from seven nations: Mexico, the Philippines, Korea, Cuba, Taiwan, India, and the Dominican Republic. By 1980, the number of foreign-born in the United States had increased to 14 million, compared with 9.7 million in 1960, and 730,000 legal immigrants were arriving annually, only one tenth of whom came from Europe. In the last third of the twentieth century, the nation's foreign-born population tripled and underwent a significant change in composition. Lawmakers had hoped that the new law would curb illegal immigration. Instead, the opposite occurred.[50]

The immigration revival made the United States younger and more diverse. Individuals born abroad founded 25 percent of the nation's fastest-growing companies in the twenty-first century. By 2010, more than 50 percent of technical employees in Silicon Valley had come there from Asia. Google, Adobe Systems, Motorola, Microsoft, and even Pepsi-Cola have immigrant chief executives. Immigrants, in other words, have provided a spark of renewal, a different perspective on issues and technology, and a drive to succeed in a relatively unfettered environment. Had Donald Trump's immigration ban on six predominantly Muslim countries been in effect several decades ago, Steve Jobs's father, a Syrian, would have been barred from entry.[51]

LBJ was especially sensitive to the status of Mexican immigrants to the United States. Federal policy toward Mexican migrants up to his administration had ranged from indifference to cruelty. Under the Bracero Program, begun in 1942 to provide vetted contract laborers for farmers, 200,000 to 450,000 laborers came to the United States annually. But the demand for farmworkers after World War II soared, and many large farms employed undocumented workers to till and harvest the fields. The exploitation of these laborers led church and union groups to press the federal government for a solution. The result, in 1954, was a deportation program called Operation Wetback.

Though humanitarian concerns provided the initial impetus for the program, Cold War hysteria and prejudice were motivating factors too, as the very name of the program indicated. In 1954, the *Teamster Magazine* alleged that "more than 100 Communists a day are coming across the sparsely patrolled border." Attorney General Herbert Brownell scoffed at this assertion, stating there was "no evidence" of such an invasion. But the Republican Congress overruled him and authorized the militarization of the border with jeeps and planes corralling over 1 million migrant workers in 1954 and another 242,000 the following year, often transported in packed cargo ships to Veracruz in conditions akin to an "eighteenth-century slave ship," according to a congressional investigation. In one roundup in 112-degree heat, eighty-eight braceros died of heatstroke before the Red Cross intervened. Because *wetback* was an ethnic slur and not a legal term, a number of legal migrants were also swept up in the raids.[52]

LBJ's upbringing in Texas and, particularly, his experience teaching Mexican American students in Cotulla sensitized him to the particular needs of this group. He knew their history. In July 1967, LBJ established a Cabinet Committee on Mexican American Affairs and named Vicente T. Ximenes of New Mexico, a teacher and war hero, to head it.[53]

The appointment was part of a broader effort to connect Mexican Americans more directly with the government. It included the placement of Mexican Americans in key positions in government agencies and targeting existing programs to benefit their communities where knowledge of such benefits might not have been widespread.[54]

On November 7, 1966, LBJ went to the Welhausen School in Cotulla, Texas, to deliver a speech to honor National Education Week. He had taught there as a twenty-year-old in 1928. In his speech, with some of his former students and local dignitaries in the audience, he noted that during the nearly three years of his administration, he had initiated more than forty new programs for the health and education of children. The president listed how, specifically, the Welhausen School and its students had benefited from reading programs, child nutrition programs, and after-hours education centers.[55]

Given the occasion, it was not surprising that LBJ's remarks were celebratory. However, midway in the address, he changed direction to focus on the challenges confronting Mexican Americans in Texas. "Three out of every four

Mexican American children now in a Texas school will drop out before they get to the eighth grade," Johnson related. "One out of every three Mexican Americans in Texas who are older than fourteen have had less than five years of school." The president wondered, "How long can we pay that price?" In the Southwestern states, 19 percent of the total population had less than eight years of school. But the Mexican American rate was 53 percent. LBJ's hope was that the Great Society would help to fully integrate Mexican Americans into the national mainstream.[56]

To accelerate this process, Johnson sponsored the Bilingual Education Act of 1968 as Title VII of the revised Elementary and Secondary Education Act. Bilingual education was (and is) a controversial issue, but LBJ believed that such instruction would enhance competence in a wide variety of subjects without necessarily limiting competency in English. In 1974, the U.S. Supreme Court, in *Lau v. Nichols*, provided an endorsement of the act by ruling that school districts serving substantial numbers of children with English-language deficiencies must do something special for these students.[57]

ALMOST ALL OF JOHNSON'S initiatives had emerged in the three previous administrations. Kennedy might have eventually accumulated an admirable legislative record had he lived, but in some cases he did not take advantage of growing public opinion on his side, such as Medicare legislation. In other cases, such as in ending racial segregation, that only a minority of Americans favored federal legislation on the subject (though by 1963, 55 percent of those outside the South supported some form of government action) gave him pause. That LBJ worked with JFK's agenda initially does not diminish LBJ's legacy. Unlike his predecessors, he succeeded in transforming these proposals into law.[58]

If one measures the success of an administration by legislation, then Lyndon Johnson was one of the most successful chief executives of all time. Some of the credit goes to the remarkable Eighty-ninth Congress, swept in with Johnson's landslide victory in November 1964. Between February and August of 1965, that Congress passed the voting rights bill; the Medicare bill; the education bill, which, for the first time, authorized federal funds for the general support of local schools; a housing bill that included rent supplements to poor families; an Appalachia bill targeting more than $1 billion for the economic development of that eleven-state region; and a series of environmental bills including clean-air legislation, the establishment of parks and national-wilderness areas, and the control of billboard advertising on interstate highways. Those were merely the highlights. It would be an understatement to say that the Johnson administration "introduced" a wide range of legislation to the Congress. It was more like a bombardment.[59]

Johnson's former Senate colleagues stood back in admiration. Senate majority leader Mike Mansfield (D-MT) asserted, "Johnson has outstripped Roosevelt, no doubt about that. He has done more than FDR ever did or ever thought of doing." Which was exactly what LBJ hoped to do.[60]

Americans approved of the expansive (and expensive) government activism. A Harris poll in January 1966 asked respondents if they supported specific federal initiatives. On voting rights, 95 percent of respondents approved; federal aid to education received an approval rating of 90 percent; 89 percent approved the college scholarship program; 82 percent approved Medicare; 79 percent endorsed highway beautification; and the antipoverty program, which, by the date of the poll, most Americans perceived as directed toward African Americans, received an approval rating of 73 percent. Overall, LBJ's popularity stood at 67 percent, with only 21 percent disapproving of his performance. The commonwealth ideal of a level playing field and a balance of disparate interests overseen and protected by the federal government seemed triumphant.[61]

In September 1965, as Congress was winding down its record legislative run, Larry O'Brien, the president's Special Assistant for Congressional Relations, commented to a reporter, "I have the feeling of a curtain being rung down." More triumphs would come, most notably in immigration and the establishment of the Model Cities program, but some recognized that the legislative haul was more a climax than a beginning. Starting with the New Deal of the 1930s, a thirty-year run of legislation had planted the federal government as the prime guarantor of the nation's and the individual's general welfare.[62]

The extraordinary legislative bonanza had required a presidential assassination and a gifted, if deeply flawed, president to overcome lobbyists, Congress, and even public opinion. These elements could not sustain themselves for long. The tragedy of Lyndon Johnson was not that, like some American Icarus, he soared and crashed. It was, simply, that he ran out of time.

CHAPTER 21

BLOOD

FOLLOWING HIS HISTORIC ELECTORAL VICTORY in November 1964, LBJ assembled his staff and warned them that, despite significant Democratic majorities, they had about six months to get all of his programs through Congress. He was not far off. In September 1965, he suffered his first major legislative setback when Congress refused to pass a bill giving home rule to the District of Columbia. In the aftermath of a series of riots in American cities over the summer, conservative Republicans and Southern Democrats expressed their frustration over a string of defeats during the previous year by scuttling the District bill. "It only takes one for them to see they can cut us and make us bleed," Johnson confided to his aides. "They'll bleed us to death on our other legislation." It was a portent of the backlash that would occur in 1966 and beyond. The violence in the nation's cities and, later, the contention over Vietnam eroded his support in Congress and in the country. Presidential credibility and faith in the federal government suffered. The greatest casualty was America's confidence in itself.[1]

Blood became more than a metaphor by the mid-1960s. Five days after Lyndon B. Johnson signed the historic Voting Rights Act on August 6, 1965, the Watts section of Los Angeles erupted into a violent racial confrontation following a police stop in the neighborhood. The riot and those that followed over the next three years of long hot summers exposed numerous fissures in American society that would not heal anytime soon. The uprisings underscored the disconnect between the civil rights movement in the South and the lives of African Americans in the rest of the country. The Great Migration had reshuffled the nation's demography, resettling 8 million African Americans in the cities of the North and West. Confined to deteriorating neighborhoods that already housed an indigent black population, limited in job prospects through a combination of economic transition, inadequate education, and discrimination, and ill-served by declining public school systems, hostile law enforcement, and city hall indifference, the right to vote and the right to check into a hotel hardly seemed relevant.

LBJ hoped his Great Society initiatives would address these problems. The attempt was laudable, and some of the policies attained a measure of success. Many of these programs provided employment for African Americans who were already upwardly mobile. But local officials commandeered some of the funds to support their own projects and political ambitions, as well as to reward supporters. The trickle-down theory did not work in economics and it did not work in public policy.

Observers said that LBJ had set the bar too high, that he set himself up for the inevitable fall when funds and goodwill became scarce. But it was courageous to forge a society based upon equity and justice. Though it did not come out quite that way, America was a better place in 1965 than it was in 1945. The gifted generation—their education, their ideals, and the work they would accomplish over the next fifty years—reflected the transformation in American society. Educational institutions, employment opportunities, and the political system were much more open and accommodating in 1965 than in 1945. More people were engaged with their country, and more people wanted to have a voice in its future. The nation had apparently achieved that balance between individual striving and collective responsibility, between government action and private enterprise. But it was a tenuous equilibrium.

White Americans, a majority of whom supported both the 1964 Civil Rights Act and the 1965 Voting Rights Act, reacted incredulously when Watts exploded in August 1965. Rochester, Harlem, and Brooklyn had seen racial disturbances the previous year, but few foresaw that these conflicts would touch off four years of racial violence that would scar many American cities and kill more than 250 people, most of them African Americans. Another casualty of the riots was white support for race-specific policies, ironically maintaining a racial divide that LBJ had hoped to bridge with his civil rights and Great Society initiatives.

The disturbances in 1964 and the apparent rise in violent crime portended a backlash that quickly became full blown. An editorial in the *Saturday Evening Post* in June 1964 related several troubling incidents that had occurred in recent weeks. In Washington, D.C., an elderly white man was sitting on his porch when two black youths passed by and allegedly shouted, "There's a white man. Let's get him." They beat him badly enough to hospitalize him. The editorial spoke of a "wave of racial violence" in New York City, as a gang of black teenagers mugged two Columbia University professors, and another mob of twenty blacks terrorized a subway car, beating and robbing passengers. Two dozen African American youths "ran amok" on the Staten Island ferry, robbing the concession stand and destroying property. And on it went.

African Americans had generated a great deal of sympathy from their challenge to white supremacy in the South. Now that goodwill receded.[2]

Ironically, conditions seemed to be improving among Northern blacks. A survey of African American public opinion in non-Southern metropolitan areas late in 1964 indicated that 81 percent of the respondents agreed that things were getting better for blacks; 70 percent believed that a day would come when whites would fully accept blacks; and 59 percent agreed that the police treated African Americans either fairly well or very well. But the survey may have oversampled middle- and working-class African Americans, whose economic status had indeed improved in Northern cities since the end of World War II. Still, these results seemed to confound the idea that the riots occurred because of seething outrage in black neighborhoods.[3]

Some experts provided empirical support for the views expressed in the survey. Nathan Glazer and Daniel Patrick Moynihan, in their 1963 book *Beyond the Melting Pot*, asserted that "New York has good race relations," owed primarily to the "mellowness" of the city's Irish and Italian populations. So good, in fact, that the authors predicted, "New York will very likely in the end be an integrated city . . . where people find homes and neighborhoods according to income and taste . . . We see the signs everywhere." They dismissed Southern-style violence erupting in New York as "hardly possible." (The authors removed both assertions in the second edition, published in 1970.)[4]

Similarly, a walk through Watts before August 1965 would not have predicted a major conflagration there. It was not a neighborhood of decrepit dwellings or dysfunctional apartment towers. For the most part, the neighborhood consisted of well-kept pastel bungalows with poinsettia and hibiscus adorning the yards. Los Angeles had a fairly good reputation among blacks nationally. The Urban League in 1964 rated the city first among sixty-eight urban areas based on a series of statistics concerning African American well-being. But three quarters of the adult black males in Watts were unemployed, and more than two thirds of the residents had less than a high school education. Nearly a third of the families had incomes below the poverty level. Bus service was sporadic, and the two hospitals serving Watts, reachable only by auto, were seriously overcrowded. A closer inspection of the neighborhood revealed few playgrounds, no movie theaters, several "hot-pillow" motels renting rooms for $3 for four hours, and families of eight to ten people crowding into two-room apartments.[5]

THE TROUBLE IN WATTS began on August 11, 1965, when a white highway patrolman arrested a twenty-one-year-old black man for drunken driving.

The suspect's complaints at being stopped drew a crowd of black boys and young men, and the arrival of Los Angeles police turned the bystanders into an angry mob that eventually grew to five thousand people hurling whiskey and beer bottles and pieces of asphalt and cement at motorists. One disgusted black observer noted, "These were just young hoodlums working off their frustration. They were out to do destruction. They just wanted to hurt anybody, black or white."[6]

Then it got worse. The official state investigation reported how rioters "looted stores, set fires, beat up white passersby whom they hauled from stopped cars, many of which were turned upside down and burned, exchanged shots with law enforcement officers, and stoned and shot at firemen." Martin Luther King Jr. walked through the neighborhood urging nonviolence. The rioters ignored him. Looting, sniping, and arson spread throughout the neighborhood for several more days until 13,900 National Guard troops cordoned off the trouble spots and occupied the neighborhood on August 14 and 15.[7]

Some black commentators called it a "rebellion," not a riot. Civil rights leader Bayard Rustin asserted that the rebels "would no longer quietly submit to the deprivation of slum life." That interpretation took hold when the disturbances spread to other cities, many beginning with a provoking incident. Almost all originated in neighborhoods with high concentrations of boys and young men. Black comedian Dick Gregory was probably one of the few who could extract some humor from the strife. He called the Watts riot "urban renewal without the graft."[8]

LBJ was relaxing at his ranch when he learned about Watts. The news threw him into despair. He cut himself off from all communication and spent the day boating on Lake Lyndon B. Johnson and riding around the ranch in his white Lincoln. LBJ's top domestic adviser, Joseph Califano, recalled, "He just couldn't accept it. He refused to look at the cable from Los Angeles describing the situation . . . He refused to take the calls from the generals who were requesting government planes to fly in the National Guard. I tried to reach him a dozen times." It was Califano who gave the "presidential approval" to send the army into Watts to maintain order. Johnson understood that the greatest casualty of Watts was the Great Society.[9]

LBJ feared that Watts would kill the chances for more progress on civil rights and would sour the country on uplifting the poor. It recalled to him the fate of Reconstruction. Blacks, he told Califano, are going to "end up pissing in the aisles of the Senate" and make "fools" of themselves out of "frustration, impatience, and anger." The one order he gave that day was to demand an investigation of whether a "Communist conspiracy" had incited the Watts rioters. He could think of no other cause. He had considerable company in this theory as 45 percent of the nation's whites blamed "outside agitators," including Communists, for the uprising.[10]

Watts mystified the president. "What do they want? I'm giving them boom times and more good legislation than anybody else did, and what do they do? Attack and sneer. Could FDR do better? Could anybody do better? What do they want?"[11]

The Justice Department launched an investigation. It confirmed LBJ's worst fears. The report stated that the white population of California was now "far less sympathetic to and has greater difficulty trying to understand the needs of the poverty areas than before the riots." The public demanded more law enforcement and a crackdown on welfare. Agreement was widespread that the administration should "not yield to demands related to violence," and that "assistance to the riot areas rewards lawlessness."[12]

It seemed unlikely that the racial polarization evident in the aftermath of Watts resulted exclusively, or even primarily, from that episode. Antagonisms were on both sides for many years prior to August 1965. Journalist Stewart Alsop toured Watts three months after the riot and revealed a still-seething community, especially toward law enforcement. Quoting a resident: "A Negro kills a cop, it's murder. A cop kills a Negro, it's justifiable homicide."[13]

In Watts, Alsop noted, "The Negroes killed during the rioting are not hoodlums but martyrs." What about the civil rights legislation over the past year? "The civil rights law?" asked one man. "Just words." Another was more critical: "Martin Luther King is just a sellout black man—his job is to guide the Negro masses into a trap." A local black newspaper editorial denounced "the whole civil rights movement [as] a branch of Zionism." Alsop, shocked by the responses, concluded, "In Watts it began to seem to me, for the first time, that the racial problem in this country is wholly insoluble—that is like some incurable disease, with which both whites and Negroes must learn to live in pain all the days of our lives." The confidence that had characterized America in the postwar years seemed seriously in jeopardy, suddenly and unexpectedly.[14]

Only the president could resolve the crisis, Alsop concluded: "The President must find a way out." He had to convince white voters to spend "a vastly disproportionate amount of their tax money to help the Negroes," while at the same time he had to "persuade the Negroes that not all their troubles are the fault of 'whitey,' that they must work out their own salvation."[15]

A year after the Watts riot, in the midst of another long hot summer, the neighborhood still boiled with resentment, but also a sense of pride in the riot that had captured national and world attention. Novelist and literary critic John Gregory Dunne visited the neighborhood in July 1966 and, in an awkward metaphor, reported, "It is as if the riots were a mass *bar mitzvah* in which the entire black population of Los Angeles gained its manhood . . . The rubble still piled along parts of Central Avenue might just as well be triumphal arches and parks."[16]

Dunne also noted that the Johnson administration had spent $16 million in Watts since the riot, including $2.7 million for improved bus service. But, as one federal official admitted, the money did little more than "shovel sand against the tide." Voters in Los Angeles County defeated a bond referendum that would have built a new hospital for Watts residents. The neighborhood lacked decent shopping prior to the riot. A year later that absence persisted. A retail renaissance was more unlikely in 1966 than in 1965 as insurance companies hiked their rates by as much as 500 percent.

What united the Watts community most of all a year later was "an endemic hatred of the LAPD, the white Gestapo in the black community." One young black man told Dunne, "Even if the people got nothing else out of it, they can always say, 'We beat the LAPD, beat them to the ground. They had to call in the National Guard to stop us.'"[17]

A report written by Daniel Patrick Moynihan released in September 1965, one month after the Watts riot, raised additional questions about race and public policy. He was serving in the Johnson administration as assistant secretary of labor. In that capacity, he prepared a report for LBJ, *The Negro Family: The Case for National Action*. The report discredited color-blind poverty policies, stating that the eradication of black poverty required a different set of strategies. Moynihan cited the distinctive history of African Americans, the chronic unemployment in the midst of a prosperous economy, and the matriarchal structure of the black family. Although Moynihan did not employ the phrase *culture of poverty*, he argued that black neighborhoods suffered from a "tangle of pathology." The key to federal policy, he believed, was to provide incentives to black family stability and jobs.[18]

Moynihan supported his conclusion with an array of historical sources. "The fundamental problem" was family breakdown. "From the wild Irish slums of the nineteenth-century Eastern seaboard, to the riot-torn suburbs of Los Angeles, there is one unmistakable lesson in American history: a community that allows large numbers of young men to grow up in broken families . . . never acquiring any stable relationship to male authority, never acquiring any set of rational expectations about the future—that community asks for and gets chaos."[19]

The report and whether to release it generated considerable discussion in the administration. A Labor Department official expressed concern that releasing the report "could be used to job the Negro." Another aide disagreed:

"With this stress on the importance of improving the Negro family, should we fail to make full use of a report that provides facts concerning the condition of the Negro family because some of them are unpleasant and may be misused by a few? I do not believe so . . . We can never solve the problems that exist if we are afraid to face up to the facts." In the end, the administration released the report, but ignored its research and findings.[20]

Ironically, conservatives barely addressed the report; the greatest criticism came from liberals. James Farmer, head of the Congress of Racial Equality (CORE), called the report a "massive academic cop-out for the white conscience." Black leaders also objected to Moynihan's implication that African Americans should follow a white middle-class ideal of the family. Floyd McKissick of CORE protested, "My major criticism of the report is that it assumes that middle-class American values are the correct values for everyone in America." What values, then, did McKissick have in mind? Liberals also argued that personal immorality had nothing to do with the plight of African Americans; the discrimination and policies of white society were primarily to blame. The idea that victims had only rights and society had only obligations would create significant fissures in liberal ranks and embolden conservatives in future years.[21]

The liberal attack on the Moynihan report was a mistake. True, it stated some unpleasant facts, but they were indeed facts, and they contributed to the conditions in the ghetto. Understanding this was a prerequisite to formulating policy. The sharp reaction against the report discredited both the culture of poverty and family structure as legitimate research topics in the academic community for at least two decades. It took a prominent black scholar, William Julius Wilson, to expose the folly of abandoning the Moynihan report and the issues it raised. In 1987, Wilson praised the report as "a prophetic document" for revealing that family structure matters a great deal for low-income children, regardless of color. Today, many in the academy accept Moynihan's conclusions as both prescient and valid. A 2015 article by Sara McLanahan of Princeton and Christopher Jencks of Harvard noted, "A father's absence increases antisocial behavior, such as aggression, rule-breaking, delinquency and illegal drug use," and that these effects lay heaviest on boys.[22]

THE RIOTS SHOCKED AND saddened the president, but they did not deter him from pressing his Great Society agenda, despite mounting opposition in Congress and among white Americans. He knew, as he had predicted, that time was running out. Studies of the riots illuminated housing discrimination as a key grievance in black communities. It limited residential choices, made wealth accumulation more difficult, and consigned ambitious blacks to crime-ridden neighborhoods, substandard schools, and poor access to good jobs. In 1962, President Kennedy signed an executive order barring discrimination in housing guaranteed or insured by the FHA and the VA. But it did not include a retroactive feature, which meant it excluded all existing homes and about 80 percent of new housing.[23]

LBJ, in his 1966 State of the Union address, asked for a much more comprehensive fair housing bill. But the persistence of riots that summer killed any chance for legislation barring discrimination in housing. Dan Rostenkowski, a Chicago congressman and normally a reliable ally of the president's, called the White House and informed an aide that his constituents were "extremely heavy in opposition" to fair housing legislation. LBJ's open housing bill failed in the liberal Eighty-ninth Congress, and again in the more conservative Ninetieth Congress following the midterm elections.[24]

LBJ's legislative options narrowed after the 1966 midterm elections. Democrats retained control of both houses of Congress, but the Republicans—a party badly defeated and in disarray just two years earlier—made a strong comeback. The riots, the deteriorating situation in Vietnam, and government programs that were both expensive and seemingly ineffective enabled Republicans to gain forty-seven House and three Senate seats. The results reflected the erosion of support for the Great Society, especially for those programs identified as "black." Great Society legislation had not purchased peace, despite the generous price tag. In 1960 there were 3.1 million welfare recipients. A decade later 9.7 million people were on welfare, and this during a decade of widespread prosperity. And the cost had ballooned from $3.8 billion to $14.5 billion during this time.[25]

Democrats retained an impressive edge in the House, 247–187, and 64–35 in the Senate, though that masked the still-potent Southern Democratic and conservative Republican coalition. *Newsweek* summarized the results in colorful but accurate language: "In the space of a single autumn day . . . the 1,000 day reign of Lyndon I came to an end: The Emperor of American politics became just a President again."[26]

Still, the Democratic majorities enabled Johnson to eventually get his fair housing legislation, though with a much weaker enforcement mechanism than his original bill. He added anti-riot provisions to that bill (an indication of how much the riots had affected the political process). The bill passed easily in both houses. On April 11, 1968, one week after a series of riots in the aftermath of Martin Luther King Jr.'s assassination, President Johnson signed the Fair Housing Act of 1968. It was more a symbolic gesture than a redress of racial discrimination in housing. Not until 2015 would the law receive stronger enforcement provisions.[27]

THAT LBJ WAS SUCCESSFUL even in this modest proposal was all the more remarkable because the riots persisted well beyond the 1966 midterm elections. In 1967, 164 civil disturbances occurred. The worst were in Newark and Detroit. In the former city, rioters systematically looted and torched white businesses. The riot caused twenty-five deaths.[28]

The timing of the Newark riot reflected to some degree what had happened to the city during the postwar era. During the 1950s, Newark public schools had a fine reputation. Philip Roth graduated from the predominantly Jewish Weequahic High School and Amiri Baraka (then LeRoi Jones), the noted black poet and playwright, attended the predominantly Italian Barringer High School. But Newark's industrial base cratered in the 1960s just when the migration of poor blacks from the South reached its peak. Urban renewal programs, rather than adding to the housing stock, displaced a higher percentage of poor residents than in any other city. Office towers and civic plazas replaced the housing, moving poor families into five massive housing projects in one section of the city.[29]

As poor black residents poured into Newark, middle-class whites streamed out. Between the early 1950s and the mid-1960s, the city had shifted from two-thirds white to two-thirds black, the fastest population turnaround of any American city except for Detroit and Gary, Indiana. The school system deteriorated, with substitute teachers instructing one quarter of the classes. The NAACP reported, "In schools with high Negro enrollments, textbooks were either not available or so outmoded and in such poor condition as to be of no value." Comic books were the only reading materials in some classrooms.[30]

The most serious conflagration occurred in Detroit in the summer of 1967, with forty-three dead, seven thousand arrested, thirteen hundred buildings destroyed by fire, and twenty-seven hundred businesses looted. Jerome Cavanaugh, the city's mayor, remarked dejectedly, "It looks like Berlin in 1945." The National Guard and the deployment of units from the 82nd and 101st Airborne divisions of the U.S. Army ended the siege. The 101st was the same division that had protected the nine black high school students in Little Rock ten years earlier. The blocks of blazing buildings in the Motor City stunned television viewers as much as the unmerited suffering of African Americans in Selma, Alabama, in March 1965. But the target of public disgust had changed.[31]

The riots provoked a reaction in Congress against additional funding for existing Great Society programs and any new initiatives. In the aftermath of the Newark and Detroit riots, the House approved a strong anticrime bill overwhelmingly, 377–23. At the same time, a seemingly noncontroversial administration bill to eradicate rats in ghetto neighborhoods drew derision and opposition. House conservatives playfully denounced it as a "civil rats" bill. Representative George H. Mahon (D-TX) drew loud applause after demanding that legislators "stop crouching in the corner" and admit that their liberalism had contributed to the unrest: "The more we have appropriated for these programs, the more violence we have [had]." What was needed now were "discipline, self-respect, and law and order."[32]

Some lawmakers attacked existing antipoverty programs. Wilbur Mills (D-AR) proposed freezing welfare payments at their current levels and requiring adult recipients of program funds—Aid to Families with Dependent Children (AFDC)—to accept opportunities for work or training. When spokesmen from the National Welfare Rights Organization (NWRO), representing welfare recipients, loudly objected, Missouri Democratic senator Edward V. Long denounced "female broodmares" and suggested that "people who have that much time available to them should have time to do some work."[33]

In April 1968 following the assassination of Martin Luther King Jr. in Memphis, riots erupted in dozens of cities, the most destructive in Baltimore and Washington, D.C. Then it more or less ended. No city experienced a second riot. It was as if ghetto residents loosed their frustrations in a circus of destruction and then retreated to life as before. Only a little worse, a little more isolated, and a little more despised. There was no further talk of a Marshall Plan to rebuild America's cities. There were precious few rewards for destroying one's own neighborhood. As far as white America was concerned, "Burn, baby! Burn!" had replaced "We Shall Overcome." The toll of the riots by the end of 1968 stood at 250 African Americans dead, eight thousand wounded, and fifty thousand arrested in more than three hundred civil disturbances since 1965.

THE RISE OF BLACK POWER, combined with the racial turmoil in the cities, further alienated whites. The militancy of young black leaders shocked some African American civil rights veterans as well. Venerable black labor leader A. Philip Randolph expressed concern at "the rise of demagogic Negro leadership in a number of cities and their determined effort to sow confusion and compound frustration while offering the Negro masses no concrete alternative." The riots not only shattered what black-white amity existed, but they also fractured the black community along class and generational lines.[34]

Polls reflected rising white resistance to racial equality. A Louis Harris poll conducted in August 1966 indicated that 46 percent of white Americans would object to a black family living next door, and 70 percent agreed "Negroes were trying to move too fast." Other polls indicated a drastic drop in Johnson's popularity, attributed mainly to the riots. In September, George P. Mahoney won an upset victory in the Democratic gubernatorial primary in Maryland. His single issue: "Your home is your castle—protect it." There was little need for reading between the lines; voters understood he meant protect your home from black people. A disconsolate Senator Edward Kennedy (D-MA) stated it was a "frightening argument" that "because the actions of some Negroes deserve condemnation," all should be denied the full rights of citizenship.[35]

To increasing numbers of Americans, the Great Society programs began to look more like protective legislation against further unrest than efforts to build an equitable nation. As early as August 1964, when Johnson signed the Economic Opportunity Act, some called it "an anti-riot bill," as it followed closely the riots in Harlem and Bedford-Stuyvesant. LBJ understood that if Americans viewed his legislative initiatives on behalf of the poor as measures of appeasement, the program was doomed.[36]

Great Society programs became more closely identified with African Americans and, therefore, suspect. As Moynihan's report indicated, there were good reasons for such targeting. But for a nation imbued with the ideas of a level playing field and equal opportunity for all, such a focus seemed like favoritism.

The president admitted, "There are other answers that are still to be found, nor do we fully understand even all of the problems." To get at those answers, LBJ proposed a White House conference, "To Fulfill These Rights." The conference produced its recommendations in June 1966 as another summer of civil disturbances unfolded. Proposals included a massive acceleration of housing construction to 1 million units a year, extensive public works projects of a size similar to Eisenhower's interstate highway program, free community colleges, and higher welfare benefits. The conference proposed a "freedom budget" of $185 billion over ten years. Given the political and racial climate at the time, both the budget and the programs were fanciful.[37]

Republicans viewed the recommendations as a series of bribes to keep black youths off the streets for the upcoming summer. Spending, they argued, would not prevent riots. Instead, they demanded "law and order." House Republican leader Gerald Ford of Michigan, a moderate, asked, "How long are we going to abdicate law and order—the backbone of any civilization—in favor of a soft social theory that the man who heaves a brick through your window or tosses a firebomb into your car is simply the misunderstood and underprivileged product of a broken home?" Even some Democrats wondered if LBJ was departing too far from the fundamental government responsibility of safeguarding citizens and was instead reducing them to the status of "clients." Voters answered the question in November, adding forty-seven Republicans to the House.[38]

LBJ remained unmoved. On the evening of July 27, 1967, in the wake of the disastrous race riots in Newark and Detroit, he addressed the nation. He believed his Great Society programs were more necessary than ever. The president reminded viewers that the conditions in these ghettos bred the riots, and the conditions included "ignorance, discrimination, slums, poverty, disease, not enough jobs." He vowed to continue to attack these nemeses "not because we are frightened by conflict, but because we are fired by conscience." He also cataloged the massive government efforts to date to address the problems of these communities: Model Cities, the Voting Rights Act, the Civil Rights Act, Medicare and Medicaid, Head Start, the Job Corps, and many other programs. But viewers could rightly wonder, with all of these government efforts, why did the riots persist? And if all of these initiatives had not stemmed the violence, then why did LBJ believe continuing, even redoubling, these efforts would produce different results?[39]

INDEED, THE PRESIDENT INHABITED the worst of all possible worlds by the summer of 1967: both the Vietnam War and the racial situation in America's cities seemed beyond the ministrations of a beneficent government. The hostility toward government mounted from both the right and the left. But race, most of all, eroded support for LBJ's Great Society initiatives. In October 1964, well before Vietnam became a contentious political issue, but shortly after the first of many long hot summers of racial violence, a Gallup poll found that 73 percent of Americans agreed that blacks should end their protests "now that they have made their point." One year later, political commentator Stewart Alsop predicted, "If the feelings among whites in the North on the racial issue began to approach in intensity the feelings [among whites] in the South, the President would be badly hurt." What would it take for that to happen? "A few more episodes like the Los Angeles riots." The rioting persisted, urban crime rose, and white support for the administration plummeted. Richard Nixon would exploit these elements of revolt in his successful 1968 campaign for the presidency.[40]

LBJ encouraged his aides to brainstorm to come up with a strategy to address the domestic crisis. Perhaps the most detailed advice came from James Q. Wilson, professor of government at Harvard University, and it was unsolicited. His solution appeared in the September 1967 issue of *Encounter*, an intellectual and cultural journal published in the United Kingdom. He shared the piece with LBJ's top domestic adviser, Joseph Califano, and urged him to show it to the president.[41]

Newark and Detroit destroyed three basic hypotheses of postwar America, Wilson argued. Gone was the "confident generalization of liberals about what must be done for the Negro." Also vanished was "the hope of some Negroes that 'equal opportunity' alone would change the lives of many." This had formed the basis of the Truman, Eisenhower, and, initially, the Johnson domestic policies: that the federal government, by leveling the playing field, would provide opportunity for all. That was no longer a valid concept, at least as applied to African Americans. The final casualty, and perhaps the greatest loss, was "the belief of working- and middle-class whites that the government could insure order whatever happened."[42]

Wilson observed that the riots seemed to vindicate those whites who resisted residential integration and believed that blacks were not yet "ready" for full citizenship. He also cast doubt on a favorite theory of academics that the riots resulted from a "revolution of rising expectations." If that was true, Wilson argued, then the best way to prevent riots was to cease all federal programs in these neighborhoods.[43]

Wilson recognized the role of unemployment, poor education, inadequate housing, and unreliable public services in generating grievances in these communities. But, he argued, these conditions had existed for decades and were, for the first time, being addressed. So, why did the riots occur at this particular time?

Here, Wilson elaborated a controversial theory. He claimed that the riots occurred because "rioting has been made legitimate." From the president on down, administration officials had predicted the riots, saying, in effect, "If I were in their position I would riot, too." Civil rights leaders, in turn, used the threats of violence to push their proposals: "Do this, or there will be a long, hot summer." Television gave riots and rioters "an audience, an immediacy, and a dramatic impact." Riots had occurred before in American history, but they were sporadic. Now, a pictorial mass media had nationalized the violence.[44]

Wilson asserted that the federal programs aimed at the ghetto were "aimless, impossible to administer well (or at all), and irrelevant to the lives of the masses." He hoped that the policy dysfunction would generate new solutions, such as Daniel Patrick Moynihan's idea of a federal program of guaranteed employment, where anyone, white or black, could walk into a local office and get a permanent job linked to vocational training. Connecting the program directly to work made it more politically feasible than the negative income tax. It also ensured that the beneficiaries of the program would be the unemployed, "not social workers, university researchers, and local bureaucrats," who invariably rode handsomely on the federal gravy train.[45]

But Wilson was skeptical Moynihan's proposal would change anything in the short run. Wilson wondered why unparalleled prosperity plus multi-billion-dollar welfare and antipoverty programs had not mitigated poverty. Discrimination was part of the answer, but not the whole answer. The culprit, although Wilson did not use the term, was the culture of poverty: "It is now quite apparent that a modern economy, however affluent, has great difficulty in doing much for anybody who finds life on the street corner more attractive than life in the factory." And jobs in the factory were disappearing. Wilson alleged "a substantial fraction of Negro men" operate "big-city hustles—pimping, petty gambling, pushing dope, defrauding tourists (and each other)." The only solution in the short run, lamented Wilson, was that "we are going to have to garrison our major metropolitan areas, at least during the summer months, with National Guard units stationed in armories or available on one hour's notice." The militarization of black neighborhoods would come in time.[46]

None of these nostrums would help LBJ. Providing a job was possible in federal policy; changing behavior or, even more, a culture was beyond even a Johnson administration. In the meantime, black leaders pressured Johnson, demanding new legislation to stave off future long hot summers.

Martin Luther King Jr., as if to ratify Wilson's assertion, fired off a telegram to LBJ in August 1967 warning that unless Congress acted IMMEDIATELY UPON SOME CREATIVE AND MASSIVE PROGRAM TO END UNEMPLOYMENT, the rioting would spread. Some in Congress viewed this as blackmail. King also proposed THE CREATION OF A NATIONAL AGENCY THAT SHALL PROVIDE A JOB TO EVERY PERSON WHO NEEDS WORK, a variation of Moynihan's proposal. King expressed particular frustration with congressional inaction: THE SUICIDAL AND IRRATIONAL ACTS WHICH PLAGUE OUR STREETS DAILY ARE BEING SOWED AND WATERED BY THE IRRATIONAL, IRRELEVANT AND EQUALLY SUICIDAL DEBATE AND DELAY IN CONGRESS. Congress remained unimpressed, and Johnson noted despairingly, "I'm now master of nothing . . . We cannot make this Congress do one damn thing that I know of."[47]

Johnson hoped that by appointing a National Advisory Commission on Civil Disorders in July 1967, he would relieve, for a time at least, the pressures from both right and left. In his statement creating the committee, the president warned against the "apostles of violence, with their ugly drumbeat of hatred," while at the same time urging Americans not to turn away from social justice: "This is not a time for angry reaction. It is a time for action starting with legislative action to improve the life in our cities." LBJ acknowledged, "There is a danger that the worst toll of this tragedy will be counted in the hearts of Americans: in hatred, in insecurity, in fear, in heated words which will not end the conflict, but prolong it. So let us acknowledge the tragedy, but let us not exaggerate it."[48]

Otto Kerner, the Democratic governor of Illinois, chaired the commission, which became known as the Kerner Commission. Kerner had a great deal of bipartisan respect. The vice chairman was John V. Lindsay, a liberal Republican, former congressman, and current mayor of New York City. The two African Americans, Roy Wilkins of the NAACP and Senator Edward Brooke (R-MA), were both moderates, whose appointments immediately generated charges of a "whitewash" from the left. Senator Fred Harris, a populist Democratic senator from Oklahoma, also served, along with two moderate congressmen, James Corman (D-CA) and William McCulloch (R-OH). I. W. Abel, a vice president of the AFL-CIO, represented labor interests. Charles B. Thornton, CEO of Litton Industries, and Katherine Graham Peden, a broadcasting executive and Kentucky's commerce commissioner, represented the business community. Police Chief Herbert Jenkins of Atlanta (a city that had seen little violence during the long hot summers) represented law enforcement. Given the broad representation and moderation of the commission, many assumed its report would be fair and balanced.[49]

The commission released its report in February 1968, before the King riots of April that year. It did not make LBJ happy in a period of his life that was already depressing. A month later, he would announce his decision not to run for reelection. The Kerner Report was not the immediate cause. An accumulation of woes headed by the quagmire of Vietnam had driven LBJ to that decision. But the Kerner Report was a blow upon many blows as it either repudiated or marginalized the effectiveness of the Great Society programs. The commission's proposals endorsed the ideas of the most liberal members of Congress and many younger African Americans in calling for the creation of 2 million jobs over the next three years, six hundred thousand housing starts, and a guaranteed income along the lines that conservative economist Milton Friedman had suggested a decade earlier. These proposals were not significantly different from the recommendations of the White House conference two years earlier, and they were just as unrealistic.

But the most controversial section of the report was its summary, authored by Mayor Lindsay. Its tone differed substantially from the measured analysis of the report's body. Lindsay had threatened to issue a minority report if commission members voted to exclude the summary, so they accepted it. Most of the media attention would focus on this summary, rather than on the recommendations. The "basic conclusion," Lindsay wrote, was that "our nation is moving toward two societies: one black, one white—separate and unequal." Lindsay explained:

> Reaction to last summer's disorders has quickened the movement and deepened the division. Discrimination and segregation have long permeated much of American life; they now threaten the future of every American ... To pursue our present course will involve the continuing polarization of the American community and, ultimately, the destruction of basic democratic values.[50]

Many Americans and the media interpreted the summary as laying this apocalyptic scenario at the feet of whites with no action required from the black community. In fact, the summary stated, "White racism is essentially responsible for the explosive mixture which has been accumulating in our cities since the end of World War II." Some of Lindsay's charges were generally true, though overdrawn. For example: "What white Americans have never fully understood—but what the Negro can never forget—is that white society is deeply implicated in the ghetto. White institutions created it, white institutions maintain it, and white society condones it." Kerner seemed to endorse this perspective when he stated that a principal goal of the report was "to educate the white, rather than the Negro."[51]

The commission's report, however, had data problems, depicting an African American community in greater distress than was the reality. The commission, for example, persistently noted the ineffectiveness of Great Society programs. In doing so, it cited statistics from the 1960 census. The earliest initiatives of the Johnson administration did not occur until 1964. In fact, African Americans made substantial gains in income and employment during the Johnson years. Fresher data were available as the Census Bureau had compiled statistics on these categories in the fall of 1967. Equally troublesome, the commission surveyed only three riot cities in assessing the impact of antipoverty programs.[52]

To many Americans in the mid- and late 1960s, it seemed as if their society was breaking apart. The growing protests on college campuses, the marches and demonstrations against the Vietnam War, the rise of Black Power, and the annual summer riots in the nation's cities lent credence to the belief that the center could not hold, that LBJ, regardless of his legislative bonanza, could not buy peace, either at home or abroad, nor could he placate the growing numbers of the gifted generation who rebelled on campuses, in the streets, or in the political arena. Feminism was upsetting traditional gender relations. The national homicide rate doubled between 1963 and 1970, and the face of crime to many white Americans was now black. Television brought the carnage of Vietnam and Detroit into millions of living rooms. In movie theaters, *Bonnie and Clyde* was the most popular film in 1967. The society many Americans thought they knew was somehow different now, more threatening, more fluid, and with the federal government seeming to play a major role in orchestrating this transformation.

The nation of immigrants fell back on its immigrant narrative when asked about special privileges or affirmative action for African Americans. A white man wondered, "Who will pay the Jews for two thousand years of slavery? Who will compensate the Italians for all the ditches they dug?" Another white man posed a different question: "What happened four hundred years ago, all those whites who whipped them and beat them, are we responsible for it? I don't even have anything to do with slavery. What's past is past." Call it white backlash, but many whites would argue it was the black backlash that started the vicious spiral.[53]

While some might dismiss these complaints as bigotry, more than a few academics and Northern Democrats worried about liberal excuses for black rioters. Daniel Patrick Moynihan, in a 1967 speech, "The Politics of Stability," warned liberal Democrats that stability of the social order was a key concern of voters. Indeed, in the presidential election campaign the following year, both George Wallace and Richard M. Nixon would exploit that theme. Moynihan also suggested that perhaps the federal government was not always the likeliest candidate for ameliorating social problems, and that liberals needed to stop "defining and explaining away" the problems in black neighborhoods as the product of white racism.[54]

What often went unexplored was that, daily, the greatest victims of ghetto crime were the poor themselves. A walk through these neighborhoods in the late 1960s uncovered an architecture of fear: metal bars on windows, windowless and doorless buildings, razor wire everywhere, bulletproof Plexiglas separating customers from service workers, and perhaps the saddest indication of the daily disorder, a padlocked Virgin Mary in front of a South Bronx home. What both left and right could agree on was the loss of faith in the federal government to right society's wrongs and create a more equitable nation.[55]

But LBJ would not fade quietly into the shadows during the last year of his presidency. He was a veritable dervish during the last half of 1968, badgering Congress to implement natural gas pipeline safety, the vote for eighteen-year-olds, a mass transit proposal, a tenfold increase in low- and moderate-income housing, funds for family planning, stronger air-pollution regulations, more aggressive conservation of natural resources, and additional support for black economic progress. By early September, he had signed bills eliminating barriers to the handicapped in buildings, and regulations protecting Americans from toxic gases. Into the fall, he secured legislation providing early-childhood education for handicapped children, extending the food stamp program, expanding opportunities via three education bills for veterans in higher and vocational education, and establishing the Woodrow Wilson International Center for Scholars at the Smithsonian Institution. The vigorous legislative activity could not overcome Johnson's own sense of despair and frustration. In an interview in November 1968, LBJ admitted, "I know we're leaving office pretty well repudiated."[56]

ON DECEMBER 11–12, 1972, a familiar crowd gathered at the LBJ Presidential Library on the campus of the University of Texas at Austin. Civil rights stalwarts such as U.S. Supreme Court justice Thurgood Marshall, Roy Wilkins of the NAACP, former chief justice Earl Warren, and former vice president Hubert H. Humphrey were joined by a younger generation of activists including Barbara Jordan, Julian Bond, and Henry González for a two-day civil rights conference. These were not propitious times for civil rights amid Southern strategies, white flight, and racially polarized voting. The president who had done more for the cause than any other chief executive struggled to the podium to deliver the keynote address. He was ill and would be dead within six weeks.[57]

Despite his present infirmities, LBJ did not want the conference to turn into a nostalgia-fest. He did not want to "spend two days talking about what we have done." Instead of summarizing all that he had accomplished during his more than five years in office, he regretted he had not "done nearly enough." He observed, "The progress has been much too small." "So," he implored, "let no one delude themselves that our work is done . . . The black problem today, as it was yesterday and yesteryear, is not a problem of regions or states or cities or neighborhoods. It is a problem, a concern, and a responsibility of this whole nation . . . To be black in a white society is not to stand on level and equal ground. While the races may stand side by side, whites stand on history's mountain and blacks stand in history's hollow. Until we overcome unequal history, we cannot overcome unequal opportunity."[58]

It was instinctively what Harry Truman believed, the unfairness of it, as did Dwight David Eisenhower. They not only saved the New Deal from the forces of regression, but they also began the slow but inexorable national engagement with the issue of race. Truman, Eisenhower, and Johnson saw government as a positive force in people's lives, that it could make a difference; all three men perceived that the nation could not be whole until everyone had the opportunity to succeed. They knew from personal experience that government was not only good but also necessary to address society's inequalities. The accomplishments in the two decades after World War II in civil rights, in immigration reform, in reducing poverty, in constructing housing, in building infrastructure, in cleansing the environment, in breakthroughs in science, medicine, and technology, and in expanding educational opportunities and health care testified to the wisdom of this view.

We owe these accomplishments to many forces—to private citizens, organizations, and writers such as Rachel Carson, Betty Friedan, and Michael Harrington. But organizations and individuals do not make national public policy, however much their work is important toward that end. Their cause must become the cause of public officials and especially of presidents. These accomplishments resulted above all from the commitment of these three presidents, who overcame their own limitations, often in the face of public hostility, ridicule, or indifference.

These were imperfect men. Truman was sometimes too obstinate, Eisenhower equivocated too much in public, and Johnson alternated between deep insecurity and flights of messianic conviction. They were nineteenth-century men, boys of small towns and limited means. Yet each held a gift to see beyond the border, to a new nation with liberty and justice for all. To them, the federal government and its laws and sacred documents were the instruments of redemption, redeeming the promise of our founding creed that all men are created equal. In incredibly confident vision, and in appealing to our better selves, they were ensuring a better nation.

PART IV

THE GREAT REGRESSION

CHAPTER 22

PARTY LINES

AS THE JOHNSON PRESIDENCY was coming to an end, and with it the postwar confidence that had sustained a remarkable legislative era, the four-party political system was undergoing a major shift. The events were not unrelated. Over the next four decades, the Republicans moved right and the Democrats moved up. Government that utilized its powers to balance the nation's competing interests, both individual and collective, receded and reoriented its priorities. The party realignment produced a government, but not governance.

The four-party political system—with liberal and conservative factions in each of the two major parties—had frustrated presidents and political analysts from the late 1930s to the late 1960s. In 1944, Franklin D. Roosevelt pitched a plan to his 1940 Republican presidential opponent, Wendell Willkie: "We ought to have two real parties—one liberal and the other conservative." One of FDR's aides pointed to an ancillary benefit of such a rearrangement: it would "get rid of [the] reactionary element in the South, and . . . attract . . . liberals in the Republican Party." The effort, though, remained speculative, and Roosevelt was dead within the year. He would not be the last president to contemplate party realignment. Both Presidents Truman and Eisenhower, similarly stymied by the coalition of Southern Democrats and Republican conservatives, also articulated wishes for party realignment. The Republican Eisenhower and the Democrat Johnson often found it easier to construct legislative majorities across party lines rather than within their respective parties.[1]

The American Political Science Association published a report in 1950, "Toward a More Responsible Two-Party System," equally critical of the current party system. Noted political scientist E. E. Schattschneider oversaw the project and concluded in unusually direct terms that a political party that "does not capitalize on its successes by mobilizing the whole power of the government is a monstrosity reflecting the stupidity of professional politicians." Schattschneider pinned the disgrace on both the Republican and Democratic parties, calling them "probably the most archaic institutions in the United States." The members of both parties were effective in delivering pork to constituents back home, but not in governing the country. Neither party had a coherent agenda or a distinct ideological focus.[2]

An equally nefarious trend in party politics was the undue influence of outside groups on legislating. The disease afflicted both parties. Schattschneider cited President Truman's ill-fated proposal for universal health care, which ran into well-funded opposition from the American Medical Association. The two parties, Schattschneider wrote, "let themselves be harried by pressure groups as a timid whale might be pursued by a school of minnows."[3]

Despite the frustrations, this four-party system actually worked fairly well between 1900 and the 1970s. The Progressive movement, the New Deal, and the cornucopia of postwar legislation resulted from a bipartisan effort that usually, though not always, overcame conservative opposition. Its replacement coincided with and contributed to the devolution of public policy on behalf of the commonwealth.

The upheavals of the 1960s reshuffled the parties, though ideological differences remained within each. The transformations were the culmination of trends emerging in the 1940s and 1950s. In 1948, the Dixiecrat revolt against Harry Truman portended the Democrats' later fracturing over civil rights. Southern whites defected to the Republican Party following the passage of the 1964 Civil Rights Act and the Voting Rights Act of 1965. By the time Ronald Reagan captured the Republican presidential nomination in 1980, the exodus of the white South was almost complete. But the groundwork for the Reagan insurgency that combined small government, favorable tax and regulatory policies for business, social and cultural conservatism, and racial and xenophobic bigotry was prepared in the 1950s. Reagan was less the initiator than the culmination of the reconstructed Republican coalition.

NUMEROUS ALLIES OF CONGRESSIONAL conservatives emerged after World War II that would help to reshape the Republican Party. The anticommunist movement energized the religious right and young ideologues who feared that Washington had settled into an irrevocable New Deal mind-set that would eventually destroy individual liberty by creating dependence and over-regulating the economy.

Religious fundamentalism had coursed in and out of political discourse since the early nineteenth century. Fundamentalists were hardly a monolithic group, but most were hostile to the cultural changes sweeping postwar America. They viewed government ambivalently. While they feared that government encouraged cultural change, they also attempted to use that same government to safeguard traditional values in race, religion, ethnicity, and gender.

The emerging political power of the religious right gained from the anti-communist crusade. But it also benefited from the dynamics of postwar American life. The geographic mobility motivated migrants to create new communities in their transplanted homes, much as the westward movement in the early nineteenth century spawned the Second Great Awakening. They joined clubs, neighborhood associations, and especially churches. Membership in religious organizations grew from 49 percent in 1940 to an all-time high of 69 percent by 1959.[4]

Billy Graham became the most prominent avatar of the evangelical revival. In a one-room office with one employee, Graham founded the Evangelistic Association in 1950. Graham's message was apolitical: he preached against materialism and secularism. His crusades attracted millions of Americans who heeded his altar call, though some in the theological community doubted that such conversions had much staying power.[5]

Evangelicals also expressed hostility to science. As one evangelical journalist wrote in 1950, "A major tragedy of our day is the drift of our country, particularly in intellectual and scientific circles, away from the basic religious concepts which bind men of all ages and races together." The editorial represented part of a growing wedge in society between experts and laypeople that would become more pronounced in the 1960s and beyond.[6]

The Cold War against "godless" Communism inspired numerous expressions of public religion, such as the establishment of a National Day of Prayer in 1952, the addition of "under God" to the Pledge of Allegiance in 1954, and the creation of "In God We Trust" postage stamps that same year. Also evident during the immediate postwar era were "faith drives." By the early 1950s, private organizations began to champion religious programs as part of what one historian called "the spiritual-industrial complex." Together they formed the Committee to Proclaim Liberty (CPL) on July 4, 1951, to promote God as the true guarantor of American freedom. The CPL included such Hollywood luminaries as Ronald Reagan, Walt Disney, and Cecil B. DeMille, publisher Henry Luce, and business moguls Conrad Hilton and J. C. Penney. The group's pitch was that Independence Day began as a religious holiday that secularization had regrettably overwhelmed.[7]

Several Protestant denominations opened offices in Washington after the war to lobby the government more directly. If General Motors had a presence in the nation's capital, why not God? In 1946 the Northern branch of the Presbyterian Church sent a part-time observer to Washington, reassuring those concerned about mingling church and state that the move was "for the

purpose of securing information rather than the purpose of influencing legislation." The Baptist Joint Conference Committee was more forthright in its
reason for opening a Washington office in 1947: "to watch the Catholics." In
1948, the Methodist Women's Division appointed a full-time Washington
lobbyist. By 1951, sixteen churches had Washington, D.C., offices. These developments were nonpartisan, though eventually they would find a welcome
home within the Republican Party.[8]

Religious and ideological conservatism found fertile ground in the West
during the 1950s, especially in California. Conservatives discovered receptive
audiences among the thousands who'd arrived from the South and Southwest
during the war to work in defense plants and the booming oil and gas facilities. One result was a demand for institutions to build communities in the new
environment. Many of the migrants came from places where churches played
key roles in developing a sense of community and fellowship. Churches were
one of the first institutions the migrants created. They also sought to reestab-
lish their conservative politics as well.[9]

The communities the migrants built prided themselves on low taxes, homogeneity (primarily white Protestants), no labor unions, and active evangelical
Protestant churches. They blended well with local entrepreneurs who abjured
government regulations, especially zoning, environmental rules, and tax laws.
Bolstered by a theology that emphasized individual redemption and brought
up with a distrust of central government, the migrants provided the early
cadre of what would become a burgeoning conservative movement in the
1950s and beyond.

ONE OF THE EARLIEST CONSERVATIVE victories in California occurred in 1946
with the defeat of Proposition 11, backed by an interracial coalition that
included the NAACP and the Congress of Industrial Organizations (CIO).
Proposition 11 would have established a state version of the federal Fair
Employment Practices Committee to ban discrimination in job hiring. Agricultural interests that employed large numbers of Mexican laborers opposed
the measure, arguing that Hispanics were most suited for crop labor. Many of
the newcomers staunchly believed that hiring was a matter of individual
choice, a position also advanced by the Los Angeles Times. For good measure,
Proposition 11 opponents also charged that it was Communist inspired.
Proposition 11 went down to resounding defeat as 70 percent of California
voters cast ballots against it.[10]

One aspect of the transplants' political habits changed in California. Many
of the newcomers had never voted for Republican candidates before. But in
California, working- and middle-class whites found a home in the GOP, with

its entrepreneurial ideology and its white Protestant ethos. They prefigured the "great white switch" to the Republican Party in the South in the 1960s.

Southern California was amenable not only for political conservatism, but also for its evangelical religion, and often the two merged. Billy Graham's Los Angeles crusade in 1949 was a key moment in the launch of his career as America's premier evangelist. Although his preaching was initially apolitical, he became entwined with conservative political movements in the 1960s. Billionaire Texas oilman Sid Richardson bankrolled Graham and encouraged his incursion into politics, a move that paved the way for Jerry Falwell and the Moral Majority of the 1970s. The gospel of wealth contrasted sharply with the voice many Christian pastors in the late-nineteenth century raised against the evils of unfettered capitalism, but it fit well with evangelical pastors who ran their ministries like lucrative businesses with their upwardly mobile suburban congregations.[11]

The religious and philosophical developments of the 1950s appealed to a relatively narrow audience with little impact on party politics or national public policy during the moderate Eisenhower years. That would change with the emergence of William F. Buckley's *National Review* in 1955. Buckley also played a role in the rise of Arizona senator Barry Goldwater to Republican prominence. In 1960, *The Conscience of a Conservative* appeared, ostensibly authored by Goldwater, but actually ghostwritten by Buckley's brother-in-law, L. Brent Bozell. Patrick Buchanan, a Buckley acolyte, referred to the book as the "New Testament," and it did indeed serve as the bible of the conservative movement. By the following year, Goldwater had appeared on the cover of *Time* magazine, and conservatives launched a Draft Goldwater Committee well in advance of the 1964 presidential campaign.[12]

The book articulated the main points of the Tea Party fifty years before that movement emerged. The connection was not only ideological. One of the early financial backers of the book was Fred Koch, the father of Tea Party funders Charles and David Koch. Government was the villain of Goldwater's book, destroying American freedoms through entitlement programs such as Social Security that subsidized dependence, and federal aid to schools and farms that wasted taxpayer dollars and usurped individual rights. Goldwater also opposed labor unions and the desegregation of public education—he believed the *Brown* decision was unconstitutional—and called for America's withdrawal from the United Nations. His positions seemed so out of the mainstream that few initially took his presidential ambitions seriously. Yet he received the Republican nomination in 1964. When he suffered a landslide defeat at the hands of Lyndon B. Johnson, pundits wrote the obituary for the conservative insurgency in the Republican Party.

It was a premature burial. Advocates of small government and fiscal conservatism, and those who were hostile to globalism and averse to racial, religious, and ethnic diversity, had this in common: dedication to restricting government from challenging both discrimination and corporate predation. Goldwater was unstinting in his hostility toward government: "My aim is not to pass laws, but to repeal them. It is not to inaugurate new programs, but to cancel old ones." In the next decade, Ronald Reagan would pick up the government-bashing refrain, though in characteristically more polite terms.[13]

But neither Goldwater nor his followers were libertarians. It was the function of government as an umpire that irked conservatives the most. They had no difficulty with government fashioning favorable legislation for business and industry or devising tax reforms that favored the wealthy. Government protecting Americans from corporate avarice or assisting the most vulnerable, particularly minorities, were illegitimate functions, according to conservatives.

The conservative factions of the Republican Party shared a common desire to shrink government, reduce its regulatory footprint, limit social services, and cease social engineering on behalf of minorities and women. The result, they believed, would unleash business investment, create jobs, remove dependence, and guarantee individual liberty. Government would still play a role, but mostly as a protector of free enterprise, national defense, and individual freedom.

The business elite looked to government for tax and regulatory relief and to negotiate lucrative trade deals. The social conservatives hoped government would rein in abortion and gender equity and restore school prayer. The war hawks fought for a muscular defense establishment, lobbying for resources to build up the military. The racists and xenophobes sought government overhauls of immigration legislation, release from Justice Department protocols, and funding to enhance local police functions.

The factions of the new Republican Party mounted a vigorous opposition to the federal effort to expand the definition of *American*, to extend basic rights to all Americans regardless of gender, race, religion, or sexual orientation. The party abandoned its equanimity on civil rights it had carried through the early 1960s, a loss that eventually paid political dividends. Not only Southern whites but also Northern white working men energized by Richard Nixon's 1968 "law and order" campaign, voted for Republican candidates. By 1980, Republicans were hailing them as "Reagan Democrats," though many had fled that party years earlier.

Black Republicans, by contrast, became ever more rare. While Eisenhower had openly courted African Americans, and Nixon did the same in his 1960 presidential run, the party of Lincoln effectively abandoned black voters after 1970. In 1960, Nixon received 32 percent of the black vote; that dropped to 6 percent in 1964 when Goldwater, who had opposed the 1964 Civil Rights Act, ran for president. Since 1980, Republican presidential candidates have received between 6 and 12 percent of the black vote. At the 2016 Republican National Convention in Cleveland, only 18 of the 2,472 delegates were black, a percentage even lower than in 1964 when Goldwater received the nomination. Donald Trump won 8 percent of black voters in 2016.[14]

The revised party also fought against feminism from the 1970s onward. Just as they opposed the aspirations of black Americans, the conservatives did not endorse the expansion of women's roles in American society, particularly in the workplace. They favored the more traditional role of women as stay-at-home mothers and challenged legislation that in any way eased life for working mothers. The United States came close to achieving universal preschool in 1971 when Senator Walter Mondale (D-MN) introduced a bill to make quality preschool available to every family in the nation that wanted it.

The Comprehensive Child Development Act enjoyed bipartisan support and easily passed the Senate, 63–17. But President Nixon, influenced by his conservative domestic policy adviser Patrick Buchanan, vetoed it, claiming Congress was proposing "communal approaches to child rearing," an effective allegation in the midst of the Cold War with the Soviet Union. When Mondale attempted to resurrect the plan during the Ford administration, thousands of letters poured into Congress warning that such a proposal would destroy the American family. Mondale contended later, "That was really the beginning of the Tea Party . . . They said it was a socialist scheme." That was the last concerted attempt at universal preschool.[15]

It was not foreordained that the Democrats, though, would become the women's party. Betty Ford, the wife of President Gerald Ford, campaigned heartily for the ERA and supported abortion rights. At the 1972 Republican National Convention in Miami, women succeeded in restoring support for the Equal Rights Amendment to the platform. It proved a hollow victory as Phyllis Schlafly founded STOP ERA immediately following the convention. By 1980, the party was openly hostile to feminism. Even a moderate such as George Romney called supporters of the ERA "moral perverts." Republican feminists condemned the "Republican War against Women" as a reversal of ideology for the party of Lincoln and Susan B. Anthony. The party's hardening stance on abortion also played a role in turning women away from the GOP. In fact, prior to 1980, the gender gap worked in favor of the Republicans. In that year's presidential election, more women than men supported the Democratic candidate, Jimmy Carter, by eight percentage points. Since that election, women have never favored the GOP presidential candidate.[16]

THE DECADE OF THE 1970S was a transitional period for the Republican Party as its governing philosophy became increasingly hostile toward the federal government's role as an umpire and as a nonpartisan advocate for all of the people. The good-government party of the immediate postwar era would become a partisan advocate for corporate interests. Richard M. Nixon was an important bridge in this. Nixon, like Johnson, was not an ideologue, despite his virulent anticommunist campaigning in the 1940s. His opening to China was less a stroke of genius than his assessment that it was a practical political move for both himself and the United States. For the same reason, unlike conservative Republicans, who'd dreamed of dismantling the New Deal since the end of World War II, he did not oppose the Great Society welfare state as much as he sought to rein in what he viewed as its excesses. Besides, like JFK, Nixon was more interested in foreign policy, which meant that he was likely to defer to the Democratic Congress on some domestic issues.[17]

Nixon faced serious economic challenges during his first two years in office. The unemployment rate doubled, more a reflection of the American economy transforming away from manufacturing than of specific government missteps. To end the economic slide, he resorted to Keynesian policies that were heretical to most Republicans: increasing government spending during an economic downturn and clamping on wage and price controls to reduce the threat of inflation. Nixon also devalued the dollar to stimulate foreign trade, a move no president had attempted since Franklin D. Roosevelt. In January 1971, Nixon startled ABC television anchor Howard K. Smith by announcing, "I am now a Keynesian in economics." Smith later quipped that Nixon's conversion to Keynesianism was "a little like a Christian crusader saying, 'All things considered, I think Muhammad was right.'"[18]

Nixon's domestic policies in his first term reflected his accommodation to a Democratic Congress as well as a desire to expand the social safety net during a time of economic uncertainty. He promoted the Family Assistance Plan (FAP) as a major overhaul of public welfare. The plan would have set the minimum income for a family of four at $1,600 a year (slightly over $10,000 in 2016), plus at least $800 in food stamps (for a total of over $15,000 in current dollars). The proposal also required able-bodied recipients to accepts jobs or vocational training, but did not reduce or suspend payments if the recipient obtained low-paying employment. The FAP, in other words, did not penalize work. But it had few friends across the political spectrum.[19]

Nixon was more successful with the Basic Opportunity Grant program—popularly known as Pell grants—which established a billion-dollar fund for outright grants to low-income students. The Pell grants, named after U.S. senator Claiborne Pell (D-RI), remain as one of the more important progressive legacies of the postwar era.[20]

President Nixon also supported the Supplemental Security Income program, which Congress passed in 1972. The measure replaced a joint federal-state effort to assist the elderly poor, and the blind and disabled, with national payments, which meant that recipients were not at the mercy of states that limited funding for these programs. Congress also approved substantial increases in Social Security benefits. These payments grew from $27.3 billion in 1969 to $64.7 billion by 1975. The social safety net grew stronger in the Nixon administration. Poverty declined from 12.8 percent of the population in 1968 to 11.1 percent in 1973, a figure that represented an all-time low in American history. Some of this decline reflected a recovering economy. But it also indicated that the Great Society and its continuation under President Nixon were winning the war on poverty.[21]

Nixon's greatest domestic accomplishment was environmental protection. By the time he took office, the environmental movement, led by an army of the gifted generation and inspired by Rachel Carson, was well under way. The number of members in the major environmental organizations grew from 124,000 in 1960 to 1,127,000 by 1972. Polls in 1970 identified the environment as the top domestic issue, despite the media emphasis on campus unrest, rising crime, and unmanageable cities. *Time* magazine in 1970 viewed environmental issues as benefiting more than the planet's ecology. The environment "may well be the gut issue that can unify a polarized nation."[22]

Nixon had not demonstrated much interest in the environment during his political career. According to journalist Tom Wicker, Nixon's attitude toward the environment prior to entering the Oval Office was "when in doubt, make it a park." But, keenly attuned to political winds, the momentum and enthusiasm of the environmental movement caught his attention. And the fire on the Cuyahoga River in Cleveland as well as the Santa Barbara oil spill, both in 1969, offered more immediate alarm about the environmental consequences of unregulated industrial development.[23]

On January 1, 1970, Nixon proclaimed the 1970s the "Environmental Decade" and established the Environmental Protection Agency (EPA). Nixon also singled out the environment as the nation's top domestic priority in his 1970 State of the Union address three weeks later: "The great question of the '70s is, shall we surrender to our surroundings, or shall we make our peace with nature and begin to make reparations for the damage we have done to our air, to our land, and to our water?"[24]

That same month, Nixon signed the National Environmental Policy Act, which firmly placed the federal government as the primary institution responsible for protecting and restoring environmental quality. It required officials on federally funded projects to submit environmental impact assessments and also created a Council on Environmental Quality (CEQ) to advise the president. When Nixon forwarded the first CEQ report to Congress seven months later, he called it "a historic milestone." For the first time, Americans had paused to consider carefully "the state of the Nation's environment."[25]

On April 22, 1970, millions of Americans, many of them members of the gifted generation, gathered to celebrate the nation's first Earth Day. In September 1969, Senator Gaylord Nelson (D-WI), a leading environmental advocate, had given a speech in Seattle, stating, "I am convinced that the same concern the youth of this nation took in changing this nation's priorities on the war in Vietnam and on civil rights can be shown for the problem of the environment." Nelson called for "a national teach-in" to dramatize the issue. Earth Day generated more than twelve thousand events across the country, many on high school and college campuses. The popular NBC-TV morning show *Today* covered the event live. Millions eventually participated, though it was a largely unscripted affair.[26]

Legislation followed, including the creation of the Occupational Safety and Health Administration (OSHA) to protect workers from environmental and other workplace hazards. Nixon's support of the revised Clean Air Act of 1970 sped its passage, though the Democratic majority in Congress was already receptive to the administration's efforts. The act identified 189 pollutants that caused smog and set standards to regulate their emissions. Factories installed scrubbers—smokestack filters—to comply with the new regulations.[27]

As with much other federal legislation in the postwar era, these measures inspired state action. In some cases, states instituted regulations that were more rigorous than federal air- and water-quality standards. The prediction of the first CEQ report that the establishment of the EPA marked a turning point would prove true. Within twenty years of the passage of the revised Clean Air Act, for example, the evidence was overwhelming that the air quality of the United States had improved. Restrictions on the use of leaded fuel resulted in a decline in the release of lead into the air from more than two hundred thousand tons annually to less than ten thousand tons.[28]

But by 1975, the environmental movement flagged at the federal level. The Arab oil embargo of 1973 and the economic stress that followed turned attention to the economy. Some believed that environmental regulations stifled economic growth and contributed to rising unemployment. After Nixon's resignation in August 1974, conservative Republicans claimed environmentalism was a luxury the nation could no longer afford. They argued that the federal government heaped costs and regulations on businesses that consumed profits and jobs. Labor unions, a key constituency for the Democratic Party, also raised concerns that environmental regulations cost jobs. A popular union bumper sticker read IF YOU'RE HUNGRY AND OUT OF WORK, EAT AN ENVIRONMENTALIST.[29]

Political scientist Theodore Lowi called Richard Nixon the last Democratic president of the twentieth century. This may be more of a reflection of the retrenchers who succeeded him than of any genuine New Deal proclivities on Nixon's part. But his record demonstrated an appreciation for government activism to further the common good, or at the least a skepticism of fiscal conservatism for its own sake. As with his predecessor Lyndon B. Johnson, it was difficult to discern whether Nixon's support for social and environmental initiatives came from deep-seated personal beliefs or from political expediency, or a combination of both. What mattered were the results.[30]

But Nixon's veto of the Comprehensive Child Development Act in 1971 and the Clean Water Act of 1972 reflected the growing influence of conservatives within the Republican Party, particularly the influence of Patrick Buchanan, who blended populism with religious and fiscal conservatism. Events in the 1970s energized conservative Republicans and opened the way for Ronald Reagan's ascension. Supreme Court decisions expanding the rights of the accused, upholding provisions of the Voting Rights Act, ordering busing to achieve school desegregation, sustaining affirmative action, and, above all, the *Roe v. Wade* ruling in 1973 legalizing abortion on demand fueled a sense that the nation was under attack by renegade forces that required a strong and patriotic response.

In 1976, conservatives' efforts on behalf of their preferred candidate, Ronald Reagan, nearly upended the nomination of the sitting president, Gerald Ford, in what would have been a historic rebuke. But if Reagan lost the nomination, he won the platform with "pro-life, pro-gun, pro-God, and anti-détente planks" that heralded the Republican Party to be. It was not the Tea Party that reshaped the Republican Party; it was Ronald Reagan.[31]

The closeness of the 1976 Republican convention alarmed moderate party members because it signaled the ascendancy of a group of rabid ideologues at odds with the compromising, give-and-take nature of American government since the end of World War II. One Ford aide worried, "We are in real danger of being outorganized by a small number of highly motivated *right wing nuts.*" His concern was hardly mollified by Patrick Buchanan's triumphal declaration, "The liberal wing of the Republican Party is a spectator now . . . The civil war in the GOP is between conservatives—militant and moderate." The scene appalled the most prominent conservative at the convention, Barry Goldwater. The former presidential candidate allowed that some of Reagan's aides were among "the most vicious people I have ever known."[32] In 1980, when now presidential candidate Reagan opened his campaign in Philadelphia, Mississippi, the scene of the heinous murder of three civil rights workers sixteen years earlier, and when the candidate subsequently vowed fealty to a conclave of evangelical ministers, the triumph of the conservative factions in the Republican Party seemed complete.

Ronald Reagan's administration marked a reorientation of government away from the commonwealth and toward a narrow, well-financed, and well-positioned group of donors and corporate and financial moguls. Evangelicals, Northern white, predominantly Catholic working-class ethnics, racial and ethnic bigots, and fiscal hawks would be disappointed by Reagan's two terms, despite their ardent support and his frequent rhetorical nods in their direction. The merger of the various Republican factions was still a work in progress. What held them together was their visceral opposition to the Democrats and government activism on behalf of groups such as the poor and blacks, and causes such as education and the environment.

Although unemployment stood at a relatively high 7.5 percent when Reagan took office, his first budget eliminated the public service component of Richard Nixon's jobs program, the Comprehensive Employment and Training Act (CETA). Reagan preferred to rely on the private sector rather than on local governments to provide employment in a new measure, the Job Training and Partnership Act (JTPA). CETA had funded more than three quarters of a million full-time public service jobs during its lifetime. The JTPA funded training, but not wages, and it reached a much smaller clientele. Altogether, spending on employment and training programs fell from $22 billion to $8 billion between 1979 and 1982. The Reagan administration also reduced spending for food stamps, school lunches, and legal services. Reagan's emphasis during these years was to bring down inflation, not support social services. His tax cuts favored the wealthy. As one economist noted, "Reagan achieved a dramatic redistribution of the federal tax burden from corporations and high-income classes to moderate- and low-income groups."[33]

By the end of Reagan's second term, his tax and economic policies had enabled the top 1 percent of the population to obtain a 60 percent increase in its income *after* taxes. Those Americans in the middle-income levels remained stagnant, while American wage earners in the bottom fifth saw their earnings decline by 10 percent. Coupled with freezing federal welfare programs for the poor (which actually translated into an inflation-adjusted decline), their losses were greater. This was especially so for African Americans. The bottom 10 percent of blacks experienced an 18 percent decline in family income during the 1980s, which meant that the average black family subsisted on less than $98 a week (or $205 in current dollars). That figure included not only direct welfare, but also the value of food stamps and housing and medical assistance.[34]

By 1990, African Americans in the bottom 20 percent of the nation's population were poorer in relation to whites than at any time since the 1950s. In their case, the gifts from the 1950s and 1960s not only stalled, but regressed. By the time Reagan entered the White House, Republicans figured (correctly) that they had lost the African American vote. There would be no negative political repercussions from these economic policies.

ONE OF THE FIRST THINGS Ronald Reagan did when he took office in January 1981 was to remove Jimmy Carter's solar panels. The act was more than symbolic. It represented his disdain for environmental regulation and reflected the growing skepticism about science in the Republican Party. Reagan entrusted the nation's environmental bureaucracy to three individuals whose antienvironmental credentials were impeccable: James Watt, who headed the Department of the Interior; Anne Gorsuch Burford, who led the EPA; and Donald Hodel as energy secretary. Among Hodel's more interesting comments was that the best way to deal with ozone depletion was to apply stronger suntan oil.[35]

Reagan slashed the budgets of environmental regulatory agencies and attempted to repeal (mostly unsuccessfully) a range of environmental legislation. Democratic Congresses, however, stood as sentinels to not only block Reagan's worst depredations but also to pass new legislation such as stronger regulations on water purity and the reduction of pesticide use. Although no major new environmental laws were enacted during Reagan's tenure, Congress renewed and strengthened several existing laws.[36]

By the mid-1980s, the depletion of the earth's protective ozone layer was no longer a matter for uninformed humor. In 1986, scientists discovered a hole in the ozone over the Antarctic and concluded it resulted from man-made chlorofluorocarbon (CFC) gases. The report prompted twenty-three nations, including the United States, to ban CFC production and use by 1999.[37]

In 1988, scientists from NASA warned that rising carbon dioxide levels primarily from gasoline-powered vehicles were at least contributing to if not causing global warming by trapping the sun's radiation close to the earth. The scientists called this the greenhouse effect. Scientists had sounded the alarm

"See How Much Better Things Are Without the Heavy Hand of Government?"
Ronald Reagan. Washington Post, *December 22, 1988. Herblock Collection.*
Library of Congress, Prints & Photographs Division.

on global warming more than thirty years earlier, yet a comprehensive plan for addressing it remained elusive. The EPA predicted that, at current emissions rates, rising sea levels would inundate 30 to 80 percent of the nation's coastal wetlands by the end of the next century.[38]

In March 1989, the *Exxon Valdez* ran aground off Alaska's Prince William Sound, spilling 11 million gallons of crude oil into the water, polluting six hundred acres of coastal habitats and killing thousands of sea otters and birds. President George H. W. Bush called it a "major tragedy," but did not restrict offshore oil exploration and drilling.[39]

ALTHOUGH RICHARD NIXON HAD acknowledged, "We will all have to be education presidents now," the message did not travel far. By 1981, Ronald Reagan cut federal aid to public education, a move that particularly hurt poor school districts, as states had reduced funding to disadvantaged districts expecting the federal government to cover those areas. As two educators noted at the time, "To weaken the federal partnership with states and local districts that has prevailed for the past fifteen years is to harm a largely powerless constituency." But it was not Reagan's constituency. Pell grants no longer kept pace with the climb in tuition, and private lenders became more central to the student-loan business. Students who wanted a college education but had to balance that with work increasingly turned to for-profit colleges, which often left them deeper in debt ($32,700) than their counterparts attending private colleges ($17,600). Student loans are now the second-largest source of debt behind mortgages for individuals under the age of thirty-five as college tuition has increased faster than inflation every year since 1981, the year Reagan began the education cuts.[40]

Student debt hurt not only the poorest, but also constituencies that voted for Reagan, especially blue-collar voters. Working-class Americans did not vote for what political analyst George Packer called "the destruction of blue-collar America . . . or the creation of a new plutocracy, or the rigging of legislation in favor of organized money." But that is what they got.[41]

If working-class whites received little in the way of substantive economic gains, they achieved at least a sense of redemption. The Nixon voters of the 1960s, the Reagan Democrats of the 1980s, and the Trumpers of 2016 voted their "emotional self-interest," a release from the frustration of an upended social and racial order. They had borne the brunt of school desegregation, open housing, and affirmative action and took out their resentment in favor of candidates who seemingly understood their plight. George Wallace and Richard Nixon had inaugurated a politics of resentment, Ronald Reagan expanded upon it, and Donald Trump perfected it.[42]

Because Reagan did it with a shrug and a smile, rather than a scowl, the dark import of his message was submerged. But it was there. As he said of Medicare, it was "the first step toward serfdom" and would lead to "other federal programs that will invade every area of freedom as we have known it in this country until one day . . . we will wake to find that we have socialism." Reagan made *government* a synonym for *toxic* and rendered any action in favor of the commonwealth, as opposed to corporate interests and the military, suspect.[43]

In August 1986, Reagan quipped, "The nine most terrifying words in the English language are 'I'm from the government, and I'm here to help.'" The response was so positive he repeated it on several subsequent occasions. Yet, he did not perceive the irony of presiding over a government that he tossed off as a punch line. His greatest success was in passing down this view to his successors. Federal impotence on behalf of the commonwealth would turn out to be a rueful legacy.[44]

But Reagan did not so much dismantle the federal government as unleash its power in favor of corporate interests. The Federal Trade Commission receded as a consumer protection agency and as a bulwark against corporate concentration. The Federal Communications Commission permitted greater concentration of media ownership. The Environmental Protection Agency declined to weigh in on acid rain. The U.S. surgeon general said little or nothing about the blooming AIDS epidemic. The Federal Savings and Loan Insurance Corporation ignored the risky lending and investment strategies of savings institutions. In a real sense, government fulfilled Reagan's narrative: it had indeed become terrifying, most especially to the interests of the people.[45]

Reagan was less a departure from Republican Party politics than its logical conclusion. Between 1945 and 1968, the era when the federal government bestowed its greatest gifts on the American population, Republicans controlled Congress only twice: 1946–48 and 1952–54. Together with Southern Democrats on both occasions, they accomplished virtually nothing except to block the proposals of Presidents Truman and Eisenhower, respectively. The sole major contribution of the Republican Congress of 1946–48 was to pass the Taft-Hartley Act, which restricted the rights of trade unions.

A Russell Sage Foundation study in 2008 found that, over the previous fifty years, real incomes of middle-class families have grown twice as fast under Democratic administrations as they have under Republicans, while the real incomes of the working poor have grown six times as fast under Democrats. The Sage report also found that between 1948 and 2005, unemployment has been almost 30 percent higher under Republican presidents than in

Democratic administrations. Despite Republicans' emphasis on curbing infla
tion, the rate of inflation was similar under both Republican and Democratic
presidents over this period.[46]

The minimum wage, for example, has declined by more than 40 percent in
real value since the late 1960s. In the 1950s and 1960s, families in all income
categories experienced robust growth; since the mid-1970s, income growth
has slowed, and it is significantly less evenly distributed. The dramatic gains
over the past forty years have been among the extremely wealthy.[47]

Although Bill Clinton provided a major expansion of the earned income
tax credit (EITC) for the working poor, his focus was on cutting the deficit.
His successor, George W. Bush, inherited a budget surplus. Bush resurrected
Reagan's policy of reducing the tax burdens of corporations and the wealthy.
During his first term, Bush presided over a 2 percent increase in the real
incomes of families in the 95th percentile of income distribution, a 1 percent
decline in the real incomes of middle-class families, and a 3 percent decline
among working poor families. Those families at the 99th percentile saw their
real incomes increase by more than 7 percent, and in the 99.99th percentile
by almost 18 percent. The Sage report estimated that had Al Gore been president during those four years, the real incomes of working poor families would
have likely grown by about 6 percent and the real incomes of middle-class
families would have grown by 4.5 percent, while those in the 95th percentile
would have seen their real incomes unchanged.[48]

But to place the blame for the fading American dream solely on Republicans is unfair. The abnegation of federal responsibility has been a bipartisan
affair. The Democrats were complicit in reorienting the federal government.
As Southern white Democrats exited the party in the late 1960s and early
1970s, another transformation occurred within it.

Nixon's landslide victory in the 1972 election prompted a major reset for
Democrats. They understood that the nation was moving away from its industrial base and expanding its technological and professional white-collar
workforce. Blue-collar workers, a declining demographic, seemed less likely
to return to the party fold. Nixon had successfully played on their resentment
and racism to detach them from their traditional political home. Instead, the
party would cast its lot with educated professionals and build on their base of
African American and Latino voters acquired during the Johnson years.
Senator Gary Hart of Colorado and Governor Bill Clinton of Arkansas would
become leaders in this new Democratic Party.[49]

Former Georgia governor Jimmy Carter was a transition figure for the
Democrats, as Nixon was for the Republicans. He was a moderate with a
strong record of racial reconciliation and a technocratic bent. As a Southerner,

he could also hold some of the states in his native region, and as an outsider, he drew back into the party some of the defecting white workers who had spurned the professorial and antiwar candidacy of George McGovern.

Carter favored fiscal austerity, promoted deregulation, limited government social spending, and championed Paul Volcker for the Federal Reserve Board for his inflation-fighting policies, hang the social costs. But he had only a weak response to an economy suffering from inflation and unemployment— "stagflation"—and a strong attack from the left within the Democratic Party led by Massachusetts senator Edward M. Kennedy wounded Carter's reelection bid in 1980.[50]

Carter, however, provided the prototype for the Democrats' centrist politics. When they finally won the presidency again in 1992, they did so with another Southern governor and one of the major architects of the new Democratic Party. Bill Clinton proceeded to govern, like Carter, "as a moderate Republican." Deregulation, welfare reform, and free-market trade deals highlighted his administration. Clinton's notable declaration in 1996 "The era of big government is over" would have worked well in a Reagan speech. In fact, Clinton was two decades behind that reality.[51]

Clinton's welfare reform fit well within this strategy. He promised to "end welfare as we know it," and he was true to his vow. Reagan would have been comfortable making that promise. The Republican-controlled Congress went along with Clinton's plan to send block grants to the states with wide latitude on how and to whom they would distribute the funds. The plan, Temporary Assistance for Needy Families, or TANF, emphasized the "temporary." Congress funded the program at $16.5 billion, and twenty years later, it is still at that amount despite inflation. According to the Center on Budget and Policy Priorities, the grant has lost more than a third of its buying power. States had to meet job-participation benchmarks, but they could bypass that requirement by simply reducing the welfare rolls and deploy the money for other purposes, which many states under Republican rule did.[52]

Until TANF, single mothers without income were eligible for Aid to Families with Dependent Children (AFDC), the program begun during the Eisenhower years. AFDC regulations required states to fashion federally approved standards for eligibility and forbade states from using welfare funds for other purposes. TANF was much more lenient on the states and restrictive for the poor; its benefits were more difficult to obtain, and those who could not find a job lost the payments. In 2009 the unemployment rate was twice as high as in 1996, yet the number of families on TANF was less than half of the number receiving AFDC in 1996. "What we lost," one economist explained, "is a commitment to the poor who face significant barriers to work, whether

Portrait of LBJ's mother, Rebekah Baines Johnson, 1917. She had a significant influence on LBJ. LBJ PRESIDENTIAL LIBRARY, PHOTO BY UNKNOWN

LBJ (second row, center) with his students at the Welhausen School in Cotulla, Texas, where he first confronted extreme poverty and ethnic prejudice, 1928. LBJ PRESIDENTIAL LIBRARY, PHOTO BY UNKNOWN

LBJ meeting with Martin Luther King Jr. in the Oval Office, December 3, 1963. Johnson's top initiative in his first ten days in office was civil rights legislation.

LBJ PRESIDENTIAL LIBRARY, PHOTO BY YOICHI OKAMOTO

President Johnson's special address to Congress on voting rights on March 15, 1965. This was probably LBJ's most eloquent speech as president, setting out the need for voting rights legislation as a fulfillment of the nation's ideals for all Americans. LBJ PRESIDENTIAL LIBRARY, PHOTO BY CECIL STOUGHTON

THIS PAGE: Michael Harrington, 1969. LIBRARY OF CONGRESS, PRINTS & PHOTOGRAPHS DIVISION

PRECEDING PAGES - TOP LEFT: An estimated thirty thousand civil rights marchers fill the street in front of the Alabama State Capitol in Montgomery at the completion of the march from Selma, March 21, 1965. *NEW YORK WORLD TELEGRAM & SUN* COLLECTION, LIBRARY OF CONGRESS, PRINTS & PHOTOGRAPHS DIVISION

BOTTOM LEFT: Officer aids Bruce Williams, shot during Watts rioting, August 15, 1965. Ambulances had a difficult time reaching victims because rioters attacked the vehicles. Watts was one of the key events in shifting white public support away from President Johnson's Great Society agenda. *HERALD-EXAMINER* COLLECTION, LOS ANGELES PUBLIC LIBRARY

RIGHT: LBJ at the podium on Liberty Island, October 3, 1965, at the signing of the immigration bill that banished the discriminatory quotas for immigrants.
LBJ PRESIDENTIAL LIBRARY, PHOTO BY YOICHI OKAMOTO

TOP: Rachel Carson at her microscope, 1951. Carson spent most of her professional career with the federal government. Her research provided the basis for award-winning books, including *Silent Spring*.
RACHEL CARSON COUNCIL

BOTTOM: Rachel Carson (far left) meeting with the president's Science Advisory Committee, 1962. The committee released a pathbreaking report in 1963 incorporating many of Carson's findings in *Silent Spring*.
RACHEL CARSON COUNCIL

Smog obscures view of lower portion of downtown high-rises, Los Angeles, November 22, 1966.
LIBRARY OF CONGRESS, PRINTS & PHOTOGRAPHS DIVISION

Councilman Henry Sinkiewicz (left) and John Pilch examining a cloth dipped in the Cuyahoga River, Cleveland, July 1964. MICHAEL SCHWARTZ LIBRARY, CLEVELAND STATE UNIVERSITY, CLEVELAND PRESS COLLECTION

because of child care or physical or mental disabilities." Extreme poverty doubled between 1996 and 2012.[53]

In fairness to Clinton, he reflected the views of a majority of Democrats. In 1994, when Republicans were poised to take over the Congress, 59 percent of Democrats agreed that government was almost always wasteful, and 44 percent of the party of the common man believed that the poor had it too easy. By 2016, only 40 percent of Democrats believed government is almost always wasteful, and only 25 percent agreed that the poor have it too easy. The impact of millennials coupled with the Great Recession has recalibrated the perspective on government, at least for some Democrats. Whether the party's leadership will respond to these changes is another matter.[54]

Clinton's presidency reaffirmed the Democrats' commitment to the rising professional class in the new postindustrial economy and to identity politics appealing particularly to African American and Latino voters. Barack Obama continued that orientation during his two presidential terms. The employees of the University of California, Microsoft, Google, the U.S. government, and Harvard were the top five contributors to Barack Obama's 2012 election campaign. These professional and tech workers had little connection to the white working class—in education, where they lived, what they earned, and their social perspectives. The Democratic Party is ostensibly a liberal party, which, as journalist Nicholas Lemann noted, "does not make economic justice its overriding concern, and . . . includes well-off professionals in its core constituency."[55]

Political analyst Thomas Frank argued that the elites of both parties have more in common with each other than they do with voters down the economic scale: "The leadership of the two parties presents two classes. The GOP is a business elite; the Democrats are a status elite, the professional class." Their playground includes "Wall Street, Big Pharma, energy, [and] Silicon Valley." Their respective policies reflect those interests rather than the broader needs of the commonwealth. Those left behind are not only white working-class men, but also young people burdened with college debt and limited job prospects. Government no longer worked for the commonwealth, no longer provided a balance between major economic interests and individual Americans.[56]

CHAPTER 23

THE POPULIST MOMENT

ENTER THE POPULISTS. "POPULISM" became a favorite label of media and pundits to describe the Trump phenomenon during the 2016 presidential election campaign. Into this empty vessel was poured all sorts of political meaning. Hillary Clinton's Democratic primary rival Bernie Sanders also received the populist designation, calling the party back to its roots as the party of common men and women. That appeal did not work, but Trump's did. At the core of both visions was the perception that government had failed; Washington had become exclusionary—for the elites, for Wall Street—and no longer worked for the people. Sanders talked often of a "rigged system," a phrase that also found resonance among Trump supporters. Sanders's appeal harked back to the class-based rhetoric of Harry Truman and the commonwealth ideal expressed in the policies of Dwight D. Eisenhower and Lyndon B. Johnson. Trump's populism, framed by the slogan "Make America Great Again," also looked back to the immediate postwar era. But Sanders looked to restore the good government that had opened so many opportunities for the gifted generation.

Trump dealt more with resentment than regeneration. The nation he and his followers had in mind was the white, Christian, male-dominated country that good government had thrown open to the broader American public. In that, he appealed to a portion of the Republican Party, loyal but often ignored, disappointed by Reagan and the Bushes but energized by Tea Party successes. They identified with a presidential candidate who articulated not only their fears and resentments, but also their dream of chasing the usurpers from the American temple and reinstalling their status, uplifting their defeated towns, and restoring their dignity.

The original Populists, the Southern and Western farmers and town merchants in the 1890s, had little use for the two major political parties. They believed that their government had abandoned them in favor of a cabal of railroad, financial, and industrial interests. They were not, however, opposed to government activism. To the contrary, they looked to Washington for help.[1]

They wanted a good government, not a dismantled government. They wanted political leaders to limit the powers of monopolies and trusts that were driving middle-class farmers and merchants to economic peril. The Populists wanted their fair share of the bounty from the new economy. They wanted their government to represent their interests as opposed to skewing toward the big-money interests. They wanted a commonwealth, a nation where everyone could share prosperity and indulge in the opportunity to succeed. Many of their demands were forward-looking: a federal income tax, direct election of U.S. senators, railroad regulation, and antitrust laws. All of them eventually became law, and we are a better nation for that.

The Populists, though, were not simply progressives in overalls or gingham. Some of them believed that they were victims of a conspiracy between government and corporate management. They engaged in what historian Richard Hofstadter called "the paranoid style" of politics, imagining a deep well of shadowy institutions and individuals who financed the cabal and controlled the media. Some Populists fingered international Jewish bankers as the masterminds of corporate dominance over "the people." Southern populists came to view African Americans as dupes of the Republican Party. Tom Watson, the prominent Georgia Populist, at first welcomed African Americans into the ranks. But as the movement faltered, Watson's views curdled and he became a prominent voice for racism, anti-Catholicism, and anti-Semitism into the first two decades of the twentieth century.[2]

In the 1930s, listeners flocked to Father Charles Coughlin, the populist radio priest, and thrilled to his vicious anti-Semitic attacks, and also to the "minister of hate," Gerald L. K. Smith, who demanded a "leadership with guts" and matched Coughlin's anti-Semitism. Smith became a leader in the America First movement, which opposed war against Nazi Germany. Arthur Schlesinger Jr.'s description of the Americans in the 1930s who were drawn to these populist orators presaged that of the enthusiasts for Trump. Writing in *The Politics of Upheaval* (1960), Schlesinger noted that in the 1930s extremists "came from provincial and traditionally nonpolitical groups in the population, jolted from apathy into near-hysteria by the shock of economic collapse." Many also "came from the evangelical denominations; years of Bible reading and fundamentalist revivalism had accustomed them to millennial solutions." It was "Old America in resentful revolt against both contemporary politics and contemporary economics." Smith's publication, *The Cross and the Flag*, blended patriotism and religion in fashioning a muscular and righteous message for white Christian America.[3]

The populists of the 1890s and 1930s emerged during eras of catastrophic economic failure. They had once formed the backbone of the country—hardworking farmers and small-town shopkeepers. Suddenly, they had become obsolete, ignored by their government, and thrown into a national economy stacked against them. Their identification of culprits—corporations, railroads, banks, a colluding government—held some validity. But they often sought to put a face, a religion, an ethnicity, on these enemies to deepen the conspiratorial narrative and to champion leaders who would restore the nation to its rightful owners.

Populism persisted because of the rapid demographic, economic, and legal changes in American life after World War II. It was as if the nation collapsed a century into two decades for all of the transformations that occurred in American life: for African Americans, women, immigrants, and minority religious and ethnic groups. Add to that a booming new cohort—the gifted generation—that changed popular culture, the economy, educational institutions, and politics as no group previously in American history. For those Americans accustomed to a more homogeneous nation with fixed hierarchies and set values, the result was ideological whiplash. As with the earlier populists, the 1960s versions identified government and assorted minorities as the main offenders.

Alabama's Governor George Wallace was the populist prototype of the 1960s. In both his 1964 and 1968 presidential runs, he articulated the resentments of the "forgotten men"—the white workingmen of the North and the South, bypassed by the changing economy and rising educational expectations, demoted below the rising minorities—religious and racial—and overcome by new cultural norms fashioned by the gifted generation. Wallace struck responsive chords in Northern working-class districts. They were losing their neighborhoods, their schools, and their country. His plain talking and open disdain for the media and the Washington elites resonated deeply. He was unafraid to call out the enemies of his supporters, the "hippies, pornographers, sophisticated intellectuals who mocked God, traitorous anti–Vietnam War protesters, welfare bums, cowardly politicians . . ." His supporters understood the barely veiled code phrases of "forced busing," "the bloc vote," and "inner-city thugs." It was us versus them. And "them" were dragging down a great country. Only a strong government, not an indulgent one, could suppress enemies both domestic and foreign. The more the mainstream media attacked Wallace for seeking "political profit in fear and hate," the more his popularity rose. As Wallace noted, "I could care less what *Time* magazine thinks; I only use it once a day in the outhouse."[4]

When journalists questioned Wallace supporters why they flocked to his rallies and keened to rhetoric no mainstream politician would dare utter, they replied, "George doesn't give us some mealymouth 'on the one hand and on the other' spiel. He tells it like it is, and if it offends some government bureau-crats and loudmouth civil rights agitators, so what? He's standing up and fighting for real Americans." In twenty-first-century parlance, Wallace was being politically incorrect, and the crowds loved it.[5]

Wallace failed, but succeeded in handing Republican candidate Richard Nixon some valuable talking points in the 1968 presidential race against the Democrats' Hubert H. Humphrey. As Wallace biographer Dan T. Carter put it, Nixon adopted "a housebroken version" of the governor's populist rhetoric and policies, and they have been part of the Republican repertoire and appeal ever since. They helped elect Ronald Reagan and provided the ideological basis for the Tea Party, and the electoral army that propelled Donald J. Trump to the presidency in 2016.[6]

The populist insurgency that helped to carry Ronald Reagan to the White House did not produce a populist legislative agenda, however. Reagan talked a great deal about social and cultural issues dear to evangelicals and the white working class, but focused primarily on scaling back the regulatory state as demanded by the more traditional elements of the Republican Party. Reagan's successor, George H. W. Bush, similarly used populist imagery in his campaigns—most notably the Willie Horton ad that implied his Demo-cratic opponent, Michael Dukakis, was soft on crime and too indulgent of minorities. But, like Reagan, his main focus was to keep the regulatory state at bay as best he could given Democratic congressional majorities.

The populist element within the Republican Party persisted, even if their presidents frustrated them. Perhaps the best articulation of their views prior to the Trump insurgency was Patrick Buchanan's speech to the 1992 Repub-lican National Convention. Though disappointed by the failure to implement a populist agenda during the Reagan years, he believed the Republican Party provided the best opportunity to establish, as he put it, a nation abiding by "Judeo-Christian principles." Buchanan's role at the convention was to endorse George H. W. Bush's renomination and energize the populist factions within the party to work for the ticket. While he made occasional references to Bush, the core of his speech was unalloyed populism, laying down a stark gauntlet of class, cultural, and racial perils.

Buchanan admonished the delegates to favor people over profits, a remon-strance not often heard at Republican conclaves. And then he said, "The agenda Clinton & Clinton would impose on America—abortion on demand, a litmus test for the Supreme Court, homosexual rights, discrimination against religious schools, women in combat—that's change, all right. But it is not the kind of change America wants . . . And it is not the kind of change we can tolerate in a nation that we still call God's country."

As populists often did, he portrayed a nation in dire peril: "There is a religious war going on in our country for the soul of America. It is a cultural war, as critical to the kind of nation we will one day be as was the Cold War itself." It was time, Buchanan declared, to choose sides. "And in that struggle for the soul of American, Clinton & Clinton are on the other side, and George Bush is on our side."

Buchanan recalled his time in New Hampshire earlier that year during the Republican primary. He talked with workers at a paper mill—"hard, tough men, one of whom was silent, until I shook his hand. Then he looked up in my eyes and said, 'Save our jobs!'" Buchanan met a women, a legal secretary, at the Manchester airport on Christmas Day, who broke down crying: "I've lost my job, I don't have any money; they're going to take away my daughter. What am I going to do?" Buchanan roared to the delegates, "They are our people. And we need to reconnect with them. We need to let them know we know they're hurting. They don't expect miracles, but they need to know we care." This was not an antigovernment manifesto. It was a plea for a government that cared, at least for the white working class.

Buchanan then pivoted to the Rodney King riots in Los Angeles earlier that year, one of the bloodiest racial disturbances in American history, leaving more than fifty people dead, and more than two thousand injured. He recounted his visit to the army compound in south Los Angeles, where two young soldiers told their story. They had come to Los Angeles on the second day of the riot and walked through a ruined Koreatown, "where the mob had looted and burned every building but one, a convalescent home for the aged." As the crowd moved on that structure, the troopers arrived, "M16s at the ready. The mob threatened and cursed, but the mob retreated. It had met the one thing that could stop it: force, rooted in justice, backed by courage." Buchanan added, "And as they [the army] took back the streets of LA . . . so we must take back our cities, and take back our culture, and take back our country." Here was the blueprint for the 2016 Republican presidential campaign, eloquently stated twenty-four years earlier.[7]

Buchanan's rhetoric rested well within the populist tradition. Without using those terms, he evoked Wallace's "forgotten man" and Nixon's "silent majority," burdened by economic anxiety, political impotence, and held in disdain by elites, bureaucrats, and liberals. The populists sought a cleansing of the government, not its destruction. A common populist theme articulated by Buchanan was that they no longer recognized their country. In 2010, Tea Party placards would declaim WE WANT OUR COUNTRY BACK—back from immigrants, back from feminists, back from the government, and back especially from a black president. Donald Trump would energize this faction,

helped by the uneven recovery from the Great Recession and the tone deaf-
ness of the Democratic Party to their erstwhile working-class constituency.

The Republican populists were more complementary than antagonistic to
mainstream conservatives in their party. This was especially the case with
respect to racial issues. Barry Goldwater had opposed the 1964 Civil Rights
Act, and even earlier, William F. Buckley Jr. deployed his *National Review*
consistently against racial equality. In a 1957 editorial, "Why the South Must
Prevail," unadorned with code words or softened by qualifications, Buckley
declared, "The central question that emerges . . . is whether the White
community in the South is entitled to take such measures as are necessary to
prevail, politically and culturally, in areas where it does not predominate
numerically? The sobering answer is *Yes*—the White community is so entitled because for the time being, it is the advanced race." Less than a quarter
century later, Buckley's views on race were becoming core ideals in the
revised Republican Party under Ronald Reagan, if considerably sanitized.[8]

The populist insurgencies reflected the view that government no longer
worked for the commonwealth, but only for a select group or groups who
benefited inordinately from public policy. Resentment motivated the populist
minions, with a strong dose of nostalgia for a time when they counted for
something. They were correct in interpreting their reduced circumstances and
constricted futures as somehow related to public policy. But they often chose
to support leaders who promised them the carcasses of scapegoats rather than
a path to better education, child care, job training, infrastructure, and a
reformed tax structure. The former made them feel better for a time; but
without the latter, their lives would remain the same, or worse.

The Trump populists are somewhat different from their counterparts in the
1890s, 1930s, and 1960s. Trump voters tend to be unmoored from community
institutions such as churches, volunteer organizations, and government. Their
lack of higher education has isolated them from the technological and professional economy headquartered in the metropolitan centers, limiting their
opportunities. Trump provided them with a community. They are generally
in poorer health than the rest of the population, and they worry that their
children will be even worse off. The issues of globalism, race, and immigration matter to these Americans, but mostly they compare themselves to their
parents and grandparents and find that the American dream is ever more
elusive.[9]

The Trump populist moment has been building for at least the past forty
years. Children are no longer exceeding their parents' careers and incomes;
over 90 percent of Americans born in 1940 at the start of the baby boom
earned more than their parents. Only 50 percent of those born in 1980 will do

the same. The Great Recession, and especially the federal government's tepid response to it, will have an impact on wealth accumulation for decades beyond 2008. That black families have suffered particularly from these events—they will have 40 percent less wealth by 2031 as a result of losses from the Great Recession—has been well publicized. But white families will have 31 percent less wealth.[10]

And that is not all: life expectancy is declining among some white working-class cohorts, income inequality is rising, infrastructure is crumbling, and higher education is increasingly out of the financial reach of even middle-class students. The nation's lead in entrepreneurship and innovation built up over a century since the end of the Civil War is eroding as well. It is not the global economy nor the flight of manufacturing that have caused this reversal. It is the devolution of government, its failure to balance society, that has limited national and personal advance. The devolution has not only affected Trump's white working-class base, but has infected families further up and down the economic hierarchy, and the economy itself.

New-business formation has declined in every decade since the 1970s. Correspondingly, competition in manufacturing, construction, retail, and service enterprise has shrunk due to mergers. The corporate concentrations that bedeviled the 1890s Populists and worried Keynes, Schlesinger, and the three postwar presidents have returned with a vengeance. The share of all businesses that are new fell 50 percent between 1978 and 2016. The Roosevelt Institute, a think tank, concluded, "Markets are more concentrated and less competitive than at any point since the Gilded Age." The situation is not merely the working of "the market." It reflects government policies since the Reagan administration that have allowed large companies to dominate their respective markets. The Reagan administration eased rules on company mergers, especially if the new entity promised lower prices for the consumer. These concentrations restrict innovation, harm start-ups, and attack the economic security of the middle class. Elizabeth Warren (D-MA) predicted, "Left unchecked, concentration will pervert our democracy into one more rigged game."[11]

Concentration of economic activities into "superstar firms," in manufacturing, retailing, and technology, with the government's blessing, have contributed mightily to wage stagnation and to huge corporate profits. In the six industries that account for 80 percent of the private employment in the United States, all experienced "a remarkably consistent upward trend in concentration." In 1982, the top four manufacturing companies, for example, controlled 38 percent of sales; by 2012, that share had increased to 43 percent. In finance, the growth went from 24 percent to 35 percent, and in retail from 15 percent to 30 percent. The faster concentration proceeded, the greater the decline in labor's share of the profits. Only state intervention can free the market and boost wages. As columnist David Brooks noted, "If you are pro-market, you have to be pro-state."[12]

Analysts of the 2016 presidential election focused attention on the role of the white working class in securing Donald Trump's victory as they responded to his populist rhetoric. But the message also drew considerable support from middle-class voters holding on precariously to their status, their jobs, and their homes. A 2016 Princeton study asked individuals if they could come up with $2,000 within thirty days for an unforeseen expense. More than 25 percent could not, and an additional 19 percent would need to pawn valuables or obtain payday loans to meet that expense. The study concluded that nearly half of American adults are "financially fragile" and "living very close to the financial edge." These are not individuals or families on the brink of poverty; these are members, statistically at least, of the middle class.[13]

In 2010, the U.S. Commerce Department defined "middle class" by aspiration rather than as a specific number on an economic scale. Aspiration included homeownership, a car for each adult, health insurance, a college education for each child, a retirement fund, and an annual family vacation. This middle-class lifestyle required an income of more than $130,000 a year. The median family income was half that.[13]

Upward mobility has stalled generally, but the middle class has fallen. In a 2012 report, the Pew Research Center's sobering conclusion about the first decade of the twenty-first century was "America's middle class has endured its worst decade in modern history. It has shrunk in size, fallen backward in income and wealth, and shed some—but by no means all—of its characteristic faith in the future." While the poor and rich extremes have expanded since 2000, the middle class is a much smaller part of the population than it used to be.[14]

Blue-collar workers were among the first to slip out of the middle class. In 1967, 97 percent of thirty- to fifty-year-old American men with only a high school diploma were working. In 2010, that figure had fallen to 76 percent. That reflected the disappearance of "men's work"—manual-labor jobs in construction and factories. With that decline, other difficulties followed, such as divorce and births outside of marriage. An increasing disengagement with community occurred from the 1990s on. The cultural chasm, which did not exist prior to the 1980s, between the traditional middle class (or its exiles) and the top 30 percent of society is growing.[15]

The housing crisis, which triggered the Great Recession, hit the middle class hard as a great deal of its wealth resided in their homes. The mean net worth of middle-class families plunged 28 percent during that first decade. But the hit on salaries was even greater. For the first time since World War II, the middle class experienced the greatest decline in median income for a four-person household, greater than for the wealthy and the poor. By 2011, 51 percent of the population was middle-class, compared to 61 percent in 1971. Only 23 percent of the respondents were very confident that they would have enough money for retirement, and only a minority—43 percent—believed their children's standard of living would be better than their own.[16]

The diminished middle class affects the entire economy. The middle class has historically been an engine for consumer spending, as the immediate postwar era demonstrated. They are less able today to invest in their future by educating themselves and their children. A smaller middle class also means fewer tax receipts for governments.[17]

According to a *Forbes* magazine survey in 2014, the middle 60 percent of earners' share of the national economic pie has fallen from 53 percent in 1970 to 45 percent in 2012. In the four decades since 1971, the percentage of Americans earning between two thirds of and twice the national median income has fallen from 61 to 51 percent of the population. The rise of part-time work, the "offshoring" American jobs, technology, and the expansion of the service sector have played roles, as has the absence of federal policy to address these issues.

The decline of manufacturing has been a common narrative in American economic discourse, but it is jobs, not production, that have fallen, and this trend began in the late 1950s. The jobs that are disappearing now include traditional white-collar occupations in sales, administrative support, and nonmanagerial office work. One out of twelve jobs in those fields vanished during the Great Recession, inflicting further harm on the middle class. It is unlikely that these jobs will return. Computer software can now do many of these white-collar jobs.[18]

Forbes criticized business leaders and conservatives for offering "little more than bromides about low taxes" as a solution to the vanishing middle class: "The country's rise to world preeminence and admiration stemmed from the fact that its prosperity was widely shared." In the two decades after World War II, the percent of households earning middle incomes doubled to 60 percent. To address both economic inequality and the erosion of the middle class, *Forbes* concluded, the federal government should encourage high-wage industries such as construction and energy. Tax reform would shift burdens from employers and employees to those "who simply profit from asset infla-tion." And job training should focus on practical skills connected to jobs at the end of the training.[19]

The basic premise of the article is correct: the rise in inequality and the shrinking middle-class are connected and derive from a narrow public policy. The gifted generation was gifted because of a robust federal government that cast a wide net. Most children growing up today no longer have an advocate in Washington. Between 1945 and 1973, incomes converged and living standards for average Americans increased steadily. In the 1950s, the average American CEO's income was twenty times as much as his employees'. In 2014, average CEO compensation was two hundred times greater than that of the firm's employees. This is a symptom, not the cause of income inequality. In 2010, the wealthiest 10 percent of households owned 70 percent of the nation's wealth, with the top 1 percent owning 35 percent of American wealth. The bottom 50 percent of households owned just 5 percent. The disparity grows. Since 2009, corporate profits, dividend payouts, and the stock market have risen sharply, but wages have remained flat. The top 1 percent garnered 95 percent of the nation's income growth between 2010 and 2012.[20]

Since the alleged recovery after 2009, the middle-class regression has continued. In June 2014, the median household income was $53,891, down from $55,589 in June 2009. The purchasing power of the average American family was 3.1 percent lower in 2014 than in 2009. In the meantime, health-care spending per person, adjusted for inflation, doubled between 1988 and 2013, pushing up health-insurance premiums. As the cost of college rises faster than inflation, 66 percent of students now rely on loans, up from 45 percent two decades ago.[21]

The tax structure exacerbates both isolation and inequality. Taxes were never meant to reward political allies or punish foes. As historian Jill Lepore remarked, "Taxes are what we pay for civilized society, for modernity, and for prosperity. The wealthy pay more because they have benefited more. Taxes, well laid and well spent, insure domestic tranquility, provide for the common defense, and promote the general welfare." They also pay for infrastructure, protect the environment, and support schools and public service employees. They pay for medical care and emergency services. The nonpartisan Congressional Research Service reported in 2012, "Changes over the past sixty-five years in the top marginal tax rate and the top capital gains tax rate do not appear correlated with economic growth," but "appear to be associated with the increasing concentration of income at the top of the income distribution." Federal economic policy skewed in favor of one group tilts the playing field and is antagonistic to the idea that we share a common mission as a people and a nation.[22]

President Reagan signed the last major overhaul of the tax code in 1986. He set tax rates on capital gains at the same level as ordinary income, both topping out at 28 percent. Bill Clinton reduced the tax rate on capital gains, and his successor, George W. Bush, lowered them even further to 15 percent. The result was that between 1985 and 2008, the wealthiest four hundred Americans saw the percentage of their income paid in federal taxes shrink from 29 percent to 18 percent. Billionaire Warren Buffett admitted that the low rates for investment income had allowed him to pay only about 17 percent of his income in federal taxes, less than the effective rate paid by his secretary.[23]

The government policies of the Truman, Eisenhower, and Johnson administrations contributed to a more equitable economy. The U.S. Census Bureau has measured income inequality since 1947. Between that date and 1968, inequality dropped to the lowest ever recorded; then it began to rise, and today it is greater than in any other democracy in the developed world.[24]

Between 1973 and 2012 productivity in the United States expanded by 93 percent, but the median American family's real income rose by only 12 percent. Technology accounted for some of this outcome, but the balance of income from work and income from wealth has shifted, with the latter benefiting inordinately from a beneficent tax policy. Wealth holding is much more highly concentrated than labor income.[25]

Today's economy, which depends on the spending of the few—5 percent of the wealthiest Americans account for 37 percent of all consumer purchases—is more prone to boom-and-bust cycles. When the very wealthy took home a much smaller proportion of total income, as between 1947 and 1977, the economy grew faster and median wages surged. As Keynes had predicted, government policies that promoted good wages for workers benefited not only the workers, but the economy generally. This circumstance created, former secretary of labor Robert B. Reich contended, "a virtuous cycle in which an ever growing middle class had the ability to consume more goods and services, which created more and better jobs, thereby stoking demand. The rising tide did in fact lift all boats."[26]

It was not a coincidence that, in two periods when the wealthy took home a larger proportion of income—between 1918 and 1933, and from 1981 to the present—growth slowed, median wages stagnated, and severe economic downturns occurred. The respective peak years for income distortion, 1928 and 2007, presaged economic debacles.[27]

Reich traced the weakening of the middle class to the 1970s as wages flattened in the face of new technologies. These technologies provided great rewards to those who could harness them for innovative purposes. Some were product entrepreneurs, and others were financial entrepreneurs. The middle class did not reduce its spending during the 1970s and 1980s, but its members went deeper into debt. Between the late 1990s and 2007, the average household debt grew by one third. This was not necessarily dangerous as long as housing values continued to rise. But they did not.[28]

Given the lengthy arc of the middle-class slide, Reich wondered why public policy in the last two decades of the twentieth century could not have addressed it. Such policies as early-childhood education, improved public schools, greater access to higher education, and more efficient public transportation might have ameliorated some of the middle-class decline. A broader safety net, similar to those of European nations—which have not experienced middle-class contraction—could have extended unemployment insurance to cover part-time work. It could have created insurance for communities that lost a major employer and provided Medicare for everyone. Requiring major corporations to pay severance to workers, raising the minimum wage, and stronger negotiations with our foreign trade partners were other policies that could have cushioned a downturn. Raising taxes on the wealthy and lowering them for the poor would have been an additional strategy.[29]

But, beginning in the late 1970s, the federal government did almost the opposite. The government "deregulated and privatized." It slashed spending on infrastructure as a percentage of the national economy. It shifted the financial burdens of higher public education to families, and it cut big holes in the safety net as only 27 percent of the unemployed came to be covered by unemployment insurance. The government facilitated companies' flight offshore and did nothing to stem the union-busting tactics of employers. The top income tax rate was halved to 35 percent and on capital gains to 15 percent. And the federal government deregulated Wall Street.[30]

This was not the case in other Western democracies. While Americans' average hourly pay increased only 6 percent between 1985 and 2011, German workers' pay rose almost 30 percent. The top 1 percent in Germany take home about 11 percent of all income—the same as in 1970. The real reason for what Reich called "America's Great Regression" was the failure of public policy. Marriner S. Eccles was chairman of the Federal Reserve Board during the Roosevelt and Truman administrations. He described the 1920s as an era when people "with great economic power had an undue influence in making the rules of the economic game." It is not that much different today.[31]

Improving economic conditions typically result in advances in political and social conditions, as the immediate postwar era demonstrated. The reverse may also be true: a stagnant economy can result in political and social regression. Benjamin M. Friedman, a Harvard political economist, supports that view: "Today's constipated politics, the eroding civility of our public life, and the virtual disappearance of generosity from our policy debates are the predictable pathologies that emerge whenever most of the population loses its sense of getting ahead, and loses as well any optimism that renewed gains are on the horizon." But these "pathologies" did not emerge in a vacuum. They arose because the federal government ceased its role as a vigorous and impartial arbiter of domestic policy. A vicious cycle replaced the virtuous cycle, resulting in a dysfunctional government that fueled economic stagnation, which fed the political dysfunction that failed to address the imbalances in American economic and social life.[32]

By emphasizing globalization and technology as the major culprits in the decline of the American middle class, analysts miss two things. First, globalization and technology are hardly new phenomena, and second, successful societies have negotiated both well—think of England overtaking Spain by the seventeenth century. Public policy can enhance or mitigate globalization and technology; they are not independent variables. As economist Anthony Atkinson noted, globalization and technology are susceptible to laws, such as regulating unions, trusts, banks, wages, and taxes. The problem of America is less economic than it is political.[33]

The Scandinavian countries have confronted similar technological and globalization challenges, but they have experienced the same or greater growth in per capita incomes as the United States, with far greater equality, according to Nobel Prize–winning economist Joseph E. Stiglitz. He argues that welfare in the United States has not so much disappeared as shifted its target significantly in favor of the wealthy. While Congress subsidizes rich farmers, it has reduced nutritional support for the poor. Drug companies receive hundreds of billions of dollars, while Medicaid benefits remain crimped. During the Great Recession, the banks received billions, while little went to homeowners and victims of those same banks' predatory lending practices. Stiglitz believes that what is needed is not only a war on poverty, but also a war to protect the middle class. He called for "ending the special privileges of speculators, corporations, and the rich," particularly in terms of taxes. "We are not embracing a politics of envy if we reverse a politics of greed."[34]

Income inequality has political consequences. The wealth of the top 1 percent enables them to "take control of the political system," according to one economist. They have the purchasing power to maintain the political status quo, which means the income gap may continue to grow and, with it, the other disparities as well. A majority of respondents to a 2014 Pew Research Center survey—69 percent—agreed, "The government should do a lot/some to fix the gap between the rich and everyone else." And 60 percent believed that the United States unfairly favors the wealthy.[35]

Perceptions that the rich are getting richer are an American commonplace. A 1940 Gallup poll revealed that 60 percent of the respondents agreed that too much power was in the hands of a few rich people and large corporations in the United States. In 1987, another poll showed that 75 percent thought the "rich are getting richer and the poor are getting poorer." The difference today is the growing awareness that these differences result from public policy, which 61 percent say unfairly favors the wealthy.[36]

When the gifted generation graduated college, the employment landscape was different from what it is today. The gig economy barely existed. They also had the luxury of selecting the job or career they wanted, rather than the job that was available. Many of them benefited from state and federal programs that lowered or remitted the cost of higher education. Many were the first generation in their families to attend a college or university. They were not born into a privileged family or neighborhood. They earned their degree and the bright future that often followed, but they had a great deal of support along the way, from their families and from the federal government. They and their offspring would enjoy the benefits of upward mobility.[37]

For the first time since the end of World War II, children are now less likely to best their parents economically. In 2016, for the first time in a century, more eighteen- to thirty-four-year-olds are living with their parents than with a romantic partner. While Republicans waged culture wars and attacked federal spending, Democrats waxed eloquent about prosperity, globalization, and innovation. Until 2016, neither party seemed to want to address the economic reality of life for millions of middle- and working-class Americans in the second decade of the twenty-first century.

On the precarious lower edge of the middle class and below, life is especially difficult for men without college degrees. The economic transformations over the past half century, as well as the withdrawal of government from educational and job-creating initiatives, have constricted options for these men. Median earnings for men with only a high school diploma have fallen by 28 percent since 1980. For these men, the American middle-class dream is becoming more elusive. A thirty-five-year-old white male construction worker admitted, "It's much harder for me as a grown man than it was for my father."[38]

THE ECONOMIC DECLINE OF white blue-collar workers and the erosion of the middle class seem puzzling given that the economy has performed fairly well since 2000. Between 2000 and the end of 2016, the net worth of the nation's households and nonprofit institutions has more than doubled, from $44 trillion to $90 trillion, a robust increase. But that good news masked that the recovery from the Great Recession has been uneven. It took the United States more than six years—until mid-2014—to attain its late-2007 per capita production levels. By the end of 2016, output was only 4 percent higher than it was in 2007. Call it the lost decade of the American economy. Or, as political economist Nicholas Eberstadt named it, "America's Second Gilded Age," with strong wealth creation for a tiny proportion of Americans and little accumulation or a good deal of regression for everyone else.[39]

As the figures imply, the slow rate of growth preceded the Great Recession. Between 2000 and 2007, per capita GDP growth averaged less than 1.5 percent annually. Had the nation's economy performed at pre-twenty-first-century rates, the GDP would be more than 20 percent higher than it was in 2016.

Labor trends since 2000 are even worse, with the work rate for those aged twenty or older falling from 64.6 percent to 59.7 percent by the end of 2016, a decline greater than for any similar period in the postwar twentieth century. Although the unemployment rate fell to 4.7 percent by the end of Barack Obama's presidency, that figure does not include workforce dropouts. One estimate is that for every unemployed male between twenty-five and fifty-five, another three are neither working nor looking for work. Eberstadt summarized the situation: "The plain fact is that 21st-century America has witnessed a dreadful collapse of work."

But the collapse did not begin in 2000. It dates from the 1960s, when more knowledge- and service-based employment overtook a manufacturing sector beset by declining unionization, increasing mechanization, and foreign competition. The blue-collar army failed to keep pace with these changes because government failed to address the transformation. Instead, they were told that government was not the answer to their plight but a reason for it. The politics of resentment may have been a salve for their souls, but it did not return them to their previous living status. And women in pink-collar occupations have not fared better. Their work rates have slid to what they were when Reagan took office.

The impact of the decline of work is far-reaching. Life expectancy today is higher in the former East Germany than it is in the United States. Death rates for middle-aged white men and women rose slightly between 1999 and 2013, but more sharply for those with a high school degree or less, precisely the population cohort most affected by the economic transformation and public policy neglect. Suicides, alcohol, and drugs were the main culprits, a sure sign of despair and hopelessness in blue-collar America. These men don't "do civil society," meaning volunteer work and religious activities. They spend their hours in front of screens. They go nowhere. Geographic mobility has declined since the 1980s; what is called labor market fluidity—changing jobs to get ahead—has also declined. Most disheartening, the odds of a thirty-year-old today earning more than his parents at the same age is 51 percent; in the 1970s, it was 86 percent. For all the talk and print about economic inequality, this disparity between what is, and what was, is the most difficult to parse.[40]

Debates over the size of government, and fealty to tax and spending cuts, are irrelevant to resolving the real problems of struggling middle- and working-class Americans, particularly those with only high school degrees. The need for good government is particularly evident given the trend of employers to slash benefits for their workers, including health insurance, medical leave, workers' compensation insurance, unemployment insurance benefits, and pensions and contributions to 401(k) plans. Management could do this because of the weakness of labor unions, the indifference of government, and the changing nature of work, which related to the first two trends. It was more profitable to hire workers on contract—the gig economy—and to transfer the burdens of these benefits to the workers themselves. So when things go wrong for workers, such as being laid off, ill health, and family emergencies, the safety net is threadbare.

Most of the individuals caught in this snare are not impoverished; many still earn something, if not in middle-class terms, then sufficient to support their families. But they are not getting anywhere, and neither are their children. Instead, they see minorities in the great cities benefiting from government entitlement programs—food stamps, housing assistance, and education programs such as Head Start—that they cannot access because they are above the poverty line. Sixty-one percent of the poor draw from these and other means-tested government programs, while only 13 percent of families with incomes above the poverty line qualify. They see how affirmative action benefits well-to-do African Americans or immigrants from Latin America or Asia who never experienced slavery or Jim Crow, yet the Polish, Italian, or Irish ancestors of these white men and women suffered deep prejudice from which no government offered rescue. And they also see the liberal cheerleaders in the Democratic Party pushing for more entitlements while ignoring the needs of their erstwhile white working-class constituents. Little wonder that whites without a college degree favored Trump over Hillary Clinton by 39 percentage points. The issue is not big government versus small government, but on whose side the government works, the commonwealth or the corporation. The issue, in other words, is good government.[41]

Twelve percent of men twenty-five to fifty-four years of age in the United States were neither working nor looking for work in 2014. It is easy to blame this situation on globalization and technology. But Spain, France, and Japan were subject to the same structural phenomena, yet the comparable figures of working-age men neither working nor looking for work were 7 percent in the two European countries and 4 percent in Japan. And these three countries have a much stronger social safety net, which might make it easier to drop out of the labor market. But what these international comparisons suggest is that good government is the remedy. According to the White House Council of Economic Advisers, "a successful labor market requires, at the very least, more than just flexibility but also policies or institutions that help connect workers with jobs or facilitate their taking jobs through subsidized child care or flexible workplaces." Education and job training help as well. Few of these policies are available for American workers, certainly not to the extent that they exist in other places of the industrialized world.[42]

The fissures in the labor market reflect the growing isolation of certain communities and workers from the more affluent areas of the country. Contrast the ailing Rust Belt heartland with the thriving coastal cities. Between 1980 and 2013, the per capita income of Washington, D.C., jumped from 29 percent above the national average to 68 percent; that of San Francisco, from 50 percent to 88 percent; and in New York City, from 80 percent to 172 percent.[43]

The "Big Sort" worked not only for cities and towns, but also for people. Since the Reagan administration, Americans have sorted themselves increasingly into income enclaves. The share of upper-income households residing in census tracts that are majority upper income has doubled since 1980. It is segregation both by class and by geography. The red-state/blue-state phenomenon is not only a political divide. It represents a division of lifestyles, outlooks, and prospects.

Non-Hispanic whites comprise 62 percent of the population, but account for 78 percent in nonmetropolitan areas, while making up only 56 percent in the country's one hundred largest urban areas. Many of the new jobs created in the recovery were in the service sector located mainly in large metropolitan areas, not in the towns and rural areas that once housed factories. In 2016, American households experienced the fastest economic growth on record, but the median household income outside metropolitan areas fell 2 percent.

Until Donald Trump came along, there was little public sympathy for these white workers and their struggling Rust Belt towns. The white working class, polls indicate, are the most pessimistic of Americans, and Trump played to that gloom. Government and the political parties had abandoned them. Little wonder that Trump appeared as a savior. Even conservative commentators such as Kevin Williamson of the *National Review* who wrote about these left-behinds in 2016 find little of value either in the communities or in the people who reside there:

> The truth about these dysfunctional downscale communities is that they deserve to die. Economically, they are negative assets. Morally, they are indefensible . . . Forget your sanctimony about struggling Rust Belt factory towns . . . The white American underclass is in thrall to a vicious, selfish culture whose main products are misery and used heroin needles.[44]

THE ASSESSMENT RESEMBLES what some commentators have said about impoverished black districts. It implies that the condition of these down-and-out white workingmen is their fault, when, in fact, the government bears a great deal of the responsibility.

J. D. Vance, in *Hillbilly Elegy* (2016), a bittersweet memoir of growing up in a gritty Rust Belt town in southern Ohio, chronicles the resentment toward neighbors who engage in welfare fraud, petty crime, and drugs—afflictions that descended on a community bereft of jobs and institutions. Vance allowed, "Public policy can help, but there is no government that can fix these problems for us." But he is wrong to imply that moral failure is the primary cause of the misery. It is yet another tale of corporate concentration and government neglect. The government benignly presided "over the rise of new monopolies, the effect of which has been to concentrate wealth in a handful of companies and regions." The government-corporate combine weakened organized labor. The government also precipitated the decline of coal, a good thing for the environment to be sure, but without providing remedies for thousands of families affected by such policies.[45]

The solutions proposed by the Trump administration thus far of erecting a tariff wall, further deregulating businesses, and cutting taxes for the wealthy and corporations will worsen economic prospects for the middle and working classes and widen income inequality. Promises to bring back coal and labor-intensive manufacturing jobs are simply fanciful. More productive would be policies such as greater tax credits for children of lower earners, universal preschool, educational and job-retraining subsidies, and relocation assistance. Upper-income parents are able to seed the next generation of upper-income earners with music lessons, travel, tutoring, and other investments in their children's future. Without the intervention of public policy, these gaps will increase.[46]

The class gap manifests itself early in a youngster's educational life. Starting kindergarten, children from families of low economic status are already more than one year behind the offspring of college grads in both reading and math. By high school that gap will have widened by one half to two thirds. Even if economically disadvantaged students enter kindergarten on the same educational level as their well-off peers, they will inevitably fall behind. The disparities have less to do with race than with class. Children from poor backgrounds are seven times more likely to have a teenage mother. Only 50 percent of these children live with both parents, compared with 83 percent of the children of college graduates.[47]

The children with less educated parents suffer a myriad of other handicaps that retard their intellectual development: their obesity rates are higher, they have more emotional and physical-health issues, and they are much less likely to experience enrichment opportunities, such as tutors, music and art exposure, and sports, that well-off parents provide for their children. The result is that the proficiency gap between the poor and the well-to-do is nearly twice as great as that between black and white children.

The electoral polarization reflects the increasing separation and isolation of those, regardless of color, who lack access to good education and good work. Many who reside in Rust Belt towns face dim futures, few institutions, a declining sense of community, and high rates of opioid addiction, suicide, and premature death. The Okies packed their household wares into rickety jalopies and left for California in the 1930s. But these folks seem stuck, unwilling or unable to move. The grown children more likely live with their parents. These places have an air of suspended animation, as if a paralysis of the soul has settled in. The culture of poverty is color-blind, and these mostly white people, white men in particular, share the anomie and restless nothingness of their black peers in the equally blasted inner cities. Things were better back when. Sure, these white enclaves can be racist and xenophobic, but what hurts the most is that the parents and the grandparents of these folks had it better, had good work, led meaningful lives, and prospered. The residents now feel like strangers in the land because this is not the country into which they were born. Donald Trump tapped into this sentiment, as Hillary Clinton ignored it and, worse, dismissed it.

Populists have historically exploited economic, ethnic, and racial anxieties and have pitted the cosmopolitan frame of mind against the more traditional rural and small-town ideals, what former Republican vice-presidential candidate Sarah Palin called "the real America." The divide on this last point was especially notable in the 2016 election. The Democrat Hillary Clinton carried only 472 of more than 3,000 counties nationwide. The Clinton counties were predominantly urban and accounted for about two thirds of the nation's economic output. As a Brookings report concluded, "No election in decades has revealed as sharp a political divide between the densest economic centers and the rest of the country."[48]

The threat to democracy is palpable because the economic, ethnic, and racial anxieties, and "the growing economic inequality between urban centers and rural hinterlands," drain confidence in our government at a time when government activism is more necessary than ever. The erosion has been going on for a long time, and both political parties have been complicit. We have lost sight of what good government can do. Before the cities exploded, before Vietnam, and before Watergate, most Americans embraced their government. They believed that the partnership between Washington and the people would fulfill the promise of American life. As writer Karl Marlantes explained, "You don't finish the world's largest highway system, build huge numbers of public schools and universities, institute the Great Society, fight a major war, and go to the moon, which we did in the 1960s—simultaneously—if you're cynical about government and politicians." The way to "make America great again" is to make our government work for all the people as it did in the two decades after World War II.[49]

CHAPTER 24

STALL

NEARLY FIFTY YEARS AGO, psychologist Abraham H. Maslow, rare among his colleagues at the time, believed that society should not force women to make a choice of either family or a career. Women should make that choice, and if they selected both options, neither role should suffer. As Maslow wrote, "It is possible for a woman to have all the specifically female fulfillments (being loved, having the home, having the baby) and *then*, without giving up any of the satisfactions already achieved, go on beyond femaleness to the full human-ness that she shared with males . . . , the full development of her intelligence, of any talents that she may have, of her own particular idiosyncratic genius, of her own individual fulfillment." Most Americans today would agree with this assertion. By 2015, 58.1 percent of mothers with infant children worked outside the home; 74.8 percent of mothers with children under the age of eigh-teen were in the labor force. Public opinion about these developments has changed drastically over the past half century. In 2015, 92 percent of Ameri-cans support the idea of working mothers.[1]

Consider that when Betty Friedan's book appeared in 1963, most Ameri-cans believed that a woman could not pursue a career and be a fulfilled wife or successful mother. In a 1962 University of Michigan survey, two thirds of the female respondents agreed that most important family decisions "should be made by the man of the house." The transformation was not instantaneous. As late as 1977, two thirds of Americans believed that it was "much better for everyone involved if the man is the achiever outside the home and the woman takes care of the home and family." But by 1994, the women of the gifted generation had changed that perception: two thirds of Americans rejected that statement.[2]

By the early 2000s, more women had more choices in work, in marriage, and in family creation than at any other time in American history. The differ-ence between marriage rates for college-educated women and women with less education has mostly disappeared, but other gaps have emerged. College-educated women are marrying later, having fewer divorces, and having children later than other women. In 1992–94, 30 percent of forty- to forty-four-year-old women with a master's degree and 34 percent of women with a doctoral degree were childless. By 2006–8, the figures had fallen to 25 percent and 23 percent respectively in this age group.[3]

The immediate postwar perspective that successful career women were more likely to be "spinsters" has changed considerably. Eighty-eight percent of women thirty to forty-four years of age earning more than $110,000 per year are married compared to 82 percent of women earning less than that amount. Their marriages were more stable as well. As late as 1980, a wife working outside the home was more likely to experience marital problems than marriages where only the husband had a job outside the home. By 2000, the reverse was true. These figures confirm Betty Friedan's assertion that independence is good for women and good for their partners. Married women with high-prestige jobs reported greater well-being than any other group of women.[4]

Journalist Gail Collins in *When Everything Changed* (2009) marked the progress women have made since the 1960s. She called the changes between that decade and the first years of the twenty-first century an "amazing journey." In 1970, the dean of the University of Texas Dental School limited female admissions to 2 percent of the students because "girls aren't strong enough to pull teeth." Perhaps as a result of women's greater participation in college athletics, thanks to Title IX of the Civil Rights Act, they were apparently much stronger by 2000, when they comprised 40 percent of that dental school's graduates.[5]

By 2008, "the long-standing gap between high school boys and girls on standardized math tests had disappeared." Now, women earn a majority of bachelor's degrees in chemistry, biology, and agricultural science. In 1970, less than 8 percent of physicians in the United States were women; by 2010 that figure stood at 25 percent and women composed nearly one half of all medical school students.[6]

The negative stereotypes of women who have children and work outside the home, or of single career women, have diminished considerably. If anything, stereotypes of stay-at-home mothers have replaced the older perspectives, as Americans rate them "low in competence, often classing them with other stigmatized groups, such as the disabled and elderly."[7]

Women have also gained greater legal status since the 1960s. A 1961 Florida law made jury service mandatory for men but optional for women. A challenge to that statute wound up before the Warren Court, a body intimately associated with advancing the civil rights of African Americans. But not of women. The Court ruled unanimously in the state's favor in *Hoyt v. Florida*.

The justices agreed that Florida could have this rule for jury service because "woman is still regarded as the center of home and family life." As current Supreme Court justice Ruth Bader Ginsburg noted of the case, "I don't think they [the justices] regarded discrimination against women as discrimination at all." But, as Ginsburg observed, when the women's movement built momentum in the 1960s, laws began to change.[8]

That momentum was evident in a case Ginsburg argued before the Supreme Court in 1971, a court now headed by Chief Justice Warren Burger. Sally Reed was a single mother who cared for disabled people in her Idaho home. On March 29, 1967, Reed's teenage son, Skip, shot and killed himself during a visit with his father. Sally was suspicious because her former husband had taken out a life-insurance policy on the boy. She petitioned to become the administrator of Skip's estate. Idaho courts denied her claim because of a state law that said "males must be preferred to females" in such disputes.[9]

Ginsburg, who would become the first tenured woman at Columbia University Law School in 1972, based her case on the equal protection clause of the Fourteenth Amendment, asserting that it prohibited discrimination not only on the basis of race, but also of sex. Her brief before the Court summarized the evolution of the women's movement up to that point: "In very recent years, a new appreciation of women's place has been generated in the United States. Activated by feminists of both sexes, courts and legislatures have begun to recognize the claim of women to full membership in the class 'persons' entitled to due process guarantees of life and liberty and the equal protection of the laws."[10]

Chief Justice Burger, a Nixon appointee, ruling for a unanimous court, struck down the Idaho law as "the very kind of arbitrary legislative choice forbidden by the Equal Protection Clause of the Fourteenth Amendment." Sex discrimination was unconstitutional. Building on the success of *Reed v. Reed* (1971), Ginsburg launched a series of legal attacks against government laws that treated men and women differently. As one legal scholar noted, "The most important thing she [Ginsburg] did was persuade legislatures that they just couldn't write laws anymore that drew distinctions between men and women."[11]

The most momentous decision concerning women and the Burger Court was *Roe v. Wade* (1973). The issue concerned the constitutionality of a Texas law that banned all abortions except those to save the life of the mother. In a 7–2 opinion striking down the Texas law, Harry Blackmun (another Nixon appointee) wrote for the majority. Blackmun went considerably beyond banishing the Texas statute by declaring unconstitutional virtually any law banning early-term abortions. The Court invoked the "right to privacy," established in the *Griswold* birth-control case in 1965, as the main constitutional support for its ruling.[12]

The sweeping ruling, which effectively nullified numerous state laws, opened a major front on the culture wars that would infest the political process going forward. Although she applauded the sentiment behind the decision, its broad strokes concerned Ginsburg, who favored a more cautious approach to the issue. Prior to *Roe v. Wade*, Planned Parenthood was a bipartisan cause. Barry Goldwater and his wife, Peggy, were major supporters of the group, and when George H. W. Bush was a congressman from Texas during the 1960s, he was such an enthusiastic backer that colleagues nicknamed him Rubbers. President Nixon was also a supporter, and in 1970, he signed into law Title X of the Public Health Service Act, which made contraceptives available to women who could not afford them. But after *Roe v. Wade*, abortion became an issue that would seriously divide the parties and many Americans, and the divisions leached into other women's issues, such as the Equal Rights Amendment, which lost momentum after *Roe*.[13]

YOUNG, CHILDLESS WOMEN WITH good educations have benefited most from the transformations over the past half century. They generally have an educational advantage over men between the ages of twenty-one and thirty; they tend to earn more than men of the same age; and overall, the gender wage gap has almost disappeared in this cohort. The greatest progress has occurred with women in the top 20 percent of wage earners. The gifted generation passed their gifts along to their daughters and granddaughters.[14]

The gifts are especially evident in the long view—looking back at the status of women in American society only fifty years ago, compared to their position today. In contemporary America, women are much more than tokens in the upper echelons of government, business, and the professions. They earn more than one half of all college degrees. By 2020, it is likely that women will comprise a majority of physicians, attorneys, and college faculty. In the early 1960s, a typical woman's path to security and status was to make a "good" marriage and as early as possible. Women derived their social standing from their husbands. Marriage, to a great degree, was a transactional institution: the husband provided security, protection, and social standing, while the wife provided sex, children, and household management. The Pill wrecked this equation and the gifted generation accomplished the rest.[15]

None of these landmarks suggest that the fight for gender equality is nearly complete, especially on issues related to work. In 1994, women comprised 46 percent of the workforce; that figure barely budged over the next twenty years.

During the prime working ages of twenty-five to fifty-four, 82.5 percent of men, but only 69.5 percent of women, had jobs in 2013. The narrowing of the wage gap stalled during the 1990s as well. Women's earnings were 76 percent of men's in 2001; it moved slowly upward to 79 percent by 2013. In the twenty years since 1994, "there has been little change in the level of agreement with the statement, 'It is much better for everyone involved if the man is the achiever outside the home and the woman takes care of the home and family.'"[16]

While many women have moved into fields once dominated by men, the opposite has not occurred. Although male nurses are not unusual anymore, women still comprise 90 percent of all nurses. Whether men feel the cultural stigma of moving into these occupations, or whether the relatively lower pay dissuades them, there appears to be little movement. To some extent it reveals that, as Princeton political scientist Anne-Marie Slaughter indicated, "the way we view women changed radically" over the past fifty years. "The way we view men not at all."[17]

The majority of the pay gap comes from differences within occupations, not between them, and the gap widens with the highest-paying jobs, such as those in business, law, and medicine. Women who are financial specialists, for example, earn 66 percent of what men in that field earn. The jobs that require long hours at the office, significant face time, and being on call—fields such as business, law, and medicine—have the greatest pay gaps because employers value flexibility and the people who spend longer hours at the office. A lawyer working eighty hours a week is likely to receive double the compensation of a lawyer at the same firm working the "normal" forty-hour week. Women who have children or other caregiving responsibilities generally cannot match the hours men invest in these fields.[18]

It may be, as younger, better-educated women enter the workforce, some of these disparities will disappear. Already the wages of younger women are much closer to those of younger men than the overall averages indicate. This reflects the extent to which younger women are obtaining college degrees. In 1980, only 13.6 percent of adult women had graduated from college compared with 20 percent of men; by 2012, these figures had changed to 30.6 percent and 31.4 percent, and by now, women may well have surpassed men.[19]

The more serious problem is the absence of work-family policies enjoyed by the rest of the industrialized world that would help women avoid the motherhood penalty reflected in salary and promotion disparities with men. Such policies would add at least 5 percent to the gross domestic product. By the late 1990s, married women with children under the age of three were leaving the workforce. By 2004, a smaller percentage of these women were in the labor force than in 1993. This interruption in career was a factor in income disparity. Ann Crittenden, in *The Price of Motherhood: Why the Most Important Job in the World Is Still the Least Valued* (2001), estimated that the typical college-educated woman lost more than $1 million in lifetime earnings and retirement benefits after opting out of the workforce.[20]

Sometimes the opt-out became an obstacle to getting back in. Nearly 30 percent of mothers who opted out, according to Crittenden, could not return to work; and of those who did return, only 40 percent landed full-time professional jobs. Progress in gender equity depends less on changing attitudes and relationships today than on persistent structural obstacles. As Stephanie Coontz concluded, "The gender revolution is not in a stall. It has hit a wall."[21]

If highly educated American mothers can afford to do so, they will leave the workforce more than in any other industrialized nation. Almost 30 percent of mothers with MBAs, for example, no longer work outside the home. Part of the reason for shunning reentry is that the average workweek for educated workers has significantly expanded. No national law prohibits employers from working their salaried employees well beyond the traditional forty-hour workweek without paying overtime. Mothers could perhaps adjust to this new economic reality, but their spouses are not picking up the slack at home. A 2010 study indicated that partnered women scientists did 54 percent of the cooking, cleaning, and laundry, while partnered male scientists carried only 28 percent of the load.[22]

Crittenden argued that this gendered work-home culture reflected Americans' ambivalence about a mother's proper role that "still socializes women to be the ones who care for others; and that has elevated 'work' to the status of a religion." Had President Nixon signed the universal child care bill in 1971, it could have changed the context of this perception.[23]

The absence of a federal child-care policy has negatively affected the status of women in the workplace, a status that lags far behind that of women in other industrialized countries. Jason Furman, former chair of President Obama's Council of Economic Advisers: "When it came to women in the workplace, the United States used to be seventh. And now we're twentieth." This adversely affects the competitiveness of the American economy as some women simply leave the workforce rather than maintain a difficult balance between home and work. As American society has increasingly relied upon women in the workforce, little provision has been made by the government for child care. The cost of child care for a family with a four-year-old and an eight-year-old can exceed the cost of housing. For a single mother with those same two children, child care could consume one third of her income. In many states, infant care is more expensive than college tuition. And even then, at least 12 percent of child-care facilities are so poor that they are harmful to the children who attend them.[24]

THE UNFORTUNATE SAGA OF family-leave policy underscores yet again the federal government's failure to maintain the type of support other industrialized countries afford to families. Lawmakers and presidents have protected corporate interests from such policies. With the diminishing bargaining power of unions, the system is skewed against parents.

What the United States has is the Family and Medical Leave Act (FMLA), passed in 1993, which guarantees to both men and women twelve weeks of *unpaid* leave. Stipulations for eligibility, however, include the size of company, the length of time on the job, and the position of the employee on the company pay scale. As a result, FMLA covers only about 60 percent of the workforce. But at the time, its sponsors hailed it as a breakthrough. No wonder; the elements of the act had been circulating in congressional committees since 1984, and when the House and Senate passed a version of it in 1990, President George H. W. Bush vetoed it, as he opposed mandating coverage. He believed companies should come to that conclusion voluntarily. Bush vetoed a similar bill in 1992. When President Clinton signed the bill in 1993, advocates believed that it was a first step toward expanded coverage to bring the United States up to the standard of the rest of the industrialized world. But that has not occurred. Instead, a handful of states and cities have stepped in to devise their own family-leave policies.[25]

The policy shortcomings are even more glaring considering that the dynamics of the American family have changed considerably in the past fifty years, but public policy, at least in the United States, lags considerably behind the demographic realities. In 2015, in 46 percent of all two-parent households, both parents worked full-time, up from 31 percent in 1970. Sixty percent of the nation's children now live in households where the parents work at least part-time, up from 40 percent in 1965. Simply put, conditions in the workplace, especially the wage gap, the absence of family leave, and the "weak infrastructure of care" hinder the career advancement of any woman who wishes to combine career and children. Forty-one percent of working mothers stated that being a parent made it harder to advance in their careers; only 20 percent of fathers felt that way.[26]

Today, only about 20 percent of American families with children under the age of fifteen follow the old postwar model of a working father and a stay-at-home mother. The United States, like Liberia, Papua New Guinea, and Swaziland, does not have federal legislation guaranteeing paid leave for families with newborn children. Among the world's twenty-one wealthiest nations, the United States is the only country in which sick days are not required by law. Great Britain, not a paragon for family-friendly legislation (compared to the Scandinavian countries and Germany), offers mothers a maximum of one year of paid family leave, six months of which can be transferred to fathers. Britain also guarantees employees the right to request a flexible work schedule.[27]

This is not simply a matter of political philosophy or checkbook politics. It hurts the economy. Family-leave policies enable men and women to participate in the workforce more completely and encourage a shared responsibility between husband and wife, especially since men tend to take leave when it is paid. An indication of how far this issue has remained from implementation: in 2015, President Obama became the first chief executive to call for paid family leave in his State of the Union address. An estimated 79 percent of respondents in one poll agreed with the president, but implementation remains illusory.[28]

The result of the public policy vacuum for families is that unmarried, childless women have been the major beneficiaries of feminism and federal protections. They now earn 96 percent of what men earn. Mothers, on the other hand, are not doing as well, earning 76 percent of what men do. Mothers today talk of a "time bind." The forty-hour work week is long gone for professionals, and union protections and set schedules and benefits have disappeared for blue-collar workers. Mothers in professional occupations, as Judith Shulevitz has noted, "siphon off time and money to hand-raise children who can compete in a global economy." This raises the levels of stress and anxiety at home that can affect marriages and the very children parents are eager to benefit. Aimee Barnes, who works at California's Environmental Protection Agency in Sacramento, has a fifteen-month-old son with her husband, Jakub Zilkiewicz, who also works at the agency. Although they have household and child-care help, flexible schedules, and family in the vicinity, the balance between work and parenting is still hard. "You basically just always feel like you're doing a horrible job at everything," Barnes stated. Working-class mothers rarely have the opportunity to provide those benefits to their children. The result is that the gap between socioeconomic classes widens even further.[29]

The growing class divide between the lives of upper-middle-class women—the top 15 to 20 percent—and those below that status reflects and reinforces class divisions in American society generally in the twenty-first century. Upper-middle-class women are likely to return to work full-time after childbirth, while women further down the economic scale typically do not. Part of the reason for this quick return is that upper-middle-class couples can afford nannies and other forms of child care. Though they tend to have fewer children, upper-middle-class couples also devote more time than other couples to interacting with their children, despite the demands of their jobs. They are enmeshed in what journalist James Surowiecki called "the cult of overwork." Or, as columnist Margaret Carlson put it in *Time*, "Sleep is the new sex."[30]

These parents send their children to the best day cares, the best schools, hire athletic coaches, tutors, music and drama instructors, arrange playdates, and expose their offspring to museums, concerts, and foreign travel. The advantages for these children are not available to others, and that both increases the separation of the affluent from everyone else and extends income inequality to the next generation. The advances of women in work and education, and their success in partnering with spouses in childrearing, are incomparable gains over the historical obstacles that confronted women just a few decades ago. But the progress has not been without costs.

Margaret Carlson asserted that perhaps the greatest cost is the loss of civic engagement. "Earlier generations of educated women worked largely in schools or volunteered in the community, because little else was on offer." Paid employment has replaced community activism, and most ambitious women dismiss teaching, except at the university level.[31]

These women are separated from their sisters by income and by lifestyle. And they are separated from their communities by paid work and child care. Economist Alison Wolf's theme is the "fracturing of sisterhood." But did men evince a particular "brotherhood" with other men? Perhaps it was unnecessary, and perhaps the fracturing of sisterhood reflects the great advances women have experienced over the past fifty years. Like blacks, they were united in their second-classness, regardless of income or residence. Now, that is dissipating. Women such as Jill Considine and Heni Nunno and others of the gifted generation who came from modest backgrounds were able to pass along their success to the next generation and beyond. Should they be faulted for "separation," or should we look to the withdrawal of a good government for the failure to provide a wider range of Americans with the opportunities to do the same?[32]

Although childrearing strategies and career decisions are individual choices, the void in government policy has restricted women's options.

Feminist writer Judith Shulevitz notes, "What we [women] are not talking about in nearly enough detail, or agitating for with enough passion, are the government policies, such as mandatory paid maternity leave, that would truly equalize opportunity."[33]

The good news, however limited, is that several states have stepped up to fill the void of a faltering federal government. California, New Jersey, and Rhode Island offer paid family and medical leave; Connecticut, Massachusetts, and California have passed laws requiring paid sick leave for private-sector employers with more than fifty employees. A number of states, including California, Illinois, Louisiana, Massachusetts, Minnesota, North Carolina, Rhode Island, and Vermont, provide for a limited number of hours annually for parents to attend school-related events and activities for their children.[34]

States, of necessity, have also begun to address the needs of the most vulnerable women, the poor. In 2014, Judith Shulevitz outlined the legislative agenda for American women. It included both traditional concerns and relatively new issues. She noted the continuing lack of equal opportunity for women. Such inequality manifested itself in the lack of adequate child care, the absence of family leave and equal-pay protections, the incoherent policies concerning sexual and domestic violence, the lack of respect for both paid and unpaid domestic labor, the increasing limits on access to reproductive health care, and, especially, the importance of equal pay for equal work. She targeted the 1976 Hyde Amendment in particular (named after its author, Congressman Henry Hyde, an Illinois Republican), which barred the use of federal funds to pay for abortions for poor women, including Medicaid recipients, unless the pregnancy resulted from rape or incest, or if the mother's life is in danger. These are precisely the women who are most in need of such services.[35]

About 42 percent of women who have abortions live below the poverty line. The unintended pregnancy rate among poor women is five times the rates for higher-income women, as is the abortion rate. Poor women tend to have limited access to contraception, particularly given the recent assault on Planned Parenthood in several states and now, perhaps, at the federal level. Four states have stepped in to fill the federal void: Hawaii, Maryland, New York, and Washington. Thirteen other states provide funds as a result of court order. President Obama agreed to retain the Hyde Amendment in exchange for votes for the Affordable Care Act.[36]

JILL CONSIDINE WAS TWO YEARS OLD when Gwyned Filling came from Missouri to make her way in New York City at the age of twenty-one. In the seventy years since Filling came to New York, the options for women in America have soared. Many were, like Considine, from modest backgrounds, but with extraordinary talent—talent that could at last find a place in American life and, in turn, make the country better and stronger. The agenda for what remains to be done in the continuing battle for gender equity is indeed extensive, and it requires an affirmative state to implement. But it proceeds in a nation that has grown significantly since Filling took her job at the advertising agency. Perceptions of women's roles and protections of their rights have defined that growth. That the movement has stalled, and in some cases regressed, is cause for concern, but not despair. The constrained lives of American women in the early 1960s, the legal restrictions, the limitations in education and work, and the demands of a society predicated on male work and female nurture are gone for the most part. That alone should give heart and confidence for the future. But hope and heart can only persist if Americans can revive the partnership between a good government and all of the people.

CHAPTER 25

THE COLOR LINE

HARVEY GANTT GREW UP POOR in Charleston, South Carolina. Not an unusual circumstance for an African American in the South during the 1940s. He was born on Young's Island, one of several islands surrounding Charleston, in 1943. His father was twenty-one and his mother was eighteen. As an infant, Harvey moved with his family to public housing in Charleston. The future prefigured for their young son was not bright.[1]

Harvey described his family as "lower, lower income," but quickly added that they showered him with love and attention, and they expressed "a great deal of belief in America as the land of opportunity if you work hard and you get an education." As Harvey explained, they may have been poor in economic terms, but they "were middle class in concept."

There was work in Charleston during the war as federal contracts funded defense industries. Harvey's father found a job at the naval shipyard as a carpenter and mechanic. He supplemented his modest income by assisting a small contractor on weekends, and by a third job, picking up laundry for a dry-cleaning business. Harvey's father earned and saved enough so that by 1947 he could build a house in the city for his family. The family grew to five children—four sisters and Harvey. The father eventually obtained a supervisory position at the shipyard at a higher salary and much less hard labor. The father's steady income allowed Harvey's mom to remain home to take care of the five children.

Naturally bright, Harvey skipped the first grade of his segregated elementary school. In the ninth grade at a segregated high school, he decided he wanted to be an architect, an unusual aspiration for a black child at the time. His father was his role model. Harvey enjoyed watching him put the house together, and that, plus his own aptitude for drawing, pushed him in that direction.

As a child growing up in the strictly segregated environment of Charleston, Harvey's family, school, and church kept him somewhat sheltered from the more humiliating aspects of Jim Crow. He admitted, "For the first ten years of my life I paid no attention to it." It was just the way things were—walking past the white school on the way to his black school; sitting in the back of the bus when his mother took the family shopping on Saturdays; and drinking from the COLORED fountains. His life, like that of many ten-year-olds, revolved around the drugstore on the corner and his street, a playground for football and stickball, with the familiar neighbors always watching out for one another's kids. He never felt "disadvantaged." The words he used to describe his childhood were "comfortable," "love," "secure."

But at age eleven in 1954, Harvey's life changed. In that year, the U.S. Supreme Court handed down its decision in *Brown I*, declaring laws mandating segregated education unconstitutional. Separate was no longer equal. Harvey became more interested in civil rights, and it jolted him out of his acceptance of racial segregation in Charleston. "I never questioned it before, and then I started."

Harvey's father joined the local NAACP and brought home materials his son devoured. His father led parents' efforts to allow Harvey's high school to use the white high school stadium for football games because the field at the black school was decrepit.

Harvey called his high school education "excellent," though he had no idea at the time that the textbooks were out of date. He recalled that the competition to do well was considerable, though almost all of the students came from "relatively low income" families. His parents were actively involved with the Parent-Teacher Association. Parents made a significant difference in an environment that rendered academic achievement for African American youngsters difficult.

Harvey was a senior in high school in 1960 when he led a sit-in with fellow students at the lunch counter of the S. H. Kress department store in Charleston. His colleagues were all youth members of the NAACP, and they had read about Dr. King and the gospel of nonviolence. Although sit-ins were going on all over the South that spring, inspired by the Greensboro, North Carolina, protests in February, high school students didn't usually lead such actions. Several of Harvey's fellow protesters went on to distinguished careers, including Delano Meriwether, who became the first African American to graduate from Duke University Medical School and who headed up the federal government's swine flu immunization program in 1976.

Harvey and his cohorts were arrested but not put into jail. He recalled that Charleston authorities, unlike officials in some other cities, handled the demonstrators "in a very civil manner." The magistrate confined them to the courtroom until their parents came for them. Although the sit-ins did not

Williams, Cecil. Harvey Gantt with architecture model as a requirement for entrance into Clemson University. N.d. Photograph. Clemson, SC. ETV South Carolina. PBS. Web. 2 May 2013. ca 1962.

change Charleston's racial customs immediately, they did inspire protests across the city that eventually ended segregation in public accommodations.

Harvey's college choices were limited, given the segregation of higher education, even at many Northern institutions. Although he applied to Howard University in Washington, D.C., a historically black institution, Harvey had already made up his mind: "I was going to go somewhere to get an integrated education." He wanted to be an architect, a profession with mostly white practitioners. He wanted the experience of an integrated education, and as a National Merit Scholarship student he could afford to attend at least the state universities. He decided to enroll at Iowa State University in

Ames, Iowa. The school had a fine architecture program, but Harvey was not prepared for life in rural Iowa.

Other African Americans attended Iowa State, but most were student athletes. During Harvey's first days at the school, everyone assumed he was on the football team, an assumption that he found degrading. Harvey also did not like the bitter-cold Iowa winters. He considered transferring. But where?

Clemson became his preferred choice. It was in his home state; the winters were relatively mild; and it had a good architectural school. On a day when the temperature plunged to twenty-three degrees below zero, Harvey decided to enroll at Clemson. Except that Clemson, a state university, was all-white and intended to remain that way.

But South Carolina authorities, hoping to avoid the violence and adverse publicity that had occurred in Alabama and Mississippi, accepted Harvey, and he enrolled peacefully in January 1963. On his first visit to the Clemson campus, he felt more at home than he ever had in Iowa. African Americans were throughout the campus: they were janitors, servers in the cafeteria, and maintenance workers. But still, it gave him a sense of belonging. And it paid some dividends. Walking through the cafeteria line, Harvey recalled, "I got the biggest piece of apple pie." He was the only black student at Clemson, but he did not feel alone. Gantt's experience at Clemson was mostly positive. By the time of his senior year in 1965, other black students at were at Clemson, including his future wife, Lucinda (Cindy) Brawley.

Gantt was grateful for the education he received at Clemson. When he opened an architectural firm in Charlotte, he hired a number of students from Clemson's School of Architecture. The university, in turn, has honored Gantt's loyalty by establishing the Harvey and Lucinda Gantt Multicultural Center, committed to "creating diverse learning environments that foster the holistic development of our students."

Gantt's interest in city planning and in coordinating land use and transportation as Charlotte expanded rapidly into undeveloped areas allowed him to network with leaders in the city's business and political communities. His progress in Charlotte reflected the relative openness of race relations in the city and the desire of civic leaders to help the city grow and prosper. In 1974, Democrats tapped him to fill the term of Fred Alexander, Charlotte's first black city councilman, who had taken a seat in the North Carolina State Senate.

In 1983, Harvey Gantt became Charlotte's first black mayor and served two terms. He did not measure his success as mayor in racial terms; as with any other mayor, the standards were economic development, infrastructure, and community relations. He worked with North Carolina National Bank (now

Bank of America) CEO Hugh McColl and Senior Vice President Dennis Rash to transform derelict downtown neighborhoods into thriving residential communities that ultimately attracted more residents and commercial activities. And Gantt ensured a diverse racial mix in several new downtown residential developments.

For Harvey Gantt, the civil rights movement, as he put it, "had its purpose." From the *Brown* decision forward, the federal government, prodded by young African Americans like Gantt and like-minded young whites, provided the gifts that enabled him and many others to succeed. He could climb out of the segregated and impoverished black South and pass his success to the next generation. These are the gifts that keep giving. One daughter, Sonja Gantt, is a news anchor for a Charlotte television station and, since 2015, has headed the Charlotte-Mecklenburg Schools Foundation, dedicated to raising money in the corporate and community sectors for the public school system.

A second daughter, Dr. Erika Gantt, is an orthopedic surgeon in Charlotte. Dr. Angela Gantt, another daughter, is an obstetrician/gynecologist in Raleigh, North Carolina, and son Adam Gantt is head of financial technology for Stott and May, an executive-search recruitment agency specializing in technology, finance, and cybersecurity, headquartered in London with a U.S. office in Brooklyn. These are the legacies not only of Harvey and Cindy Gantt, but also of the civil rights movement.

GANTT'S STORY REFLECTED THE broad ascent and expansion of a black middle class over the past fifty years. By 2014 the percentages of white and black households earning between $50,000 and $75,000 were the closest they had ever been: 18.7 percent for whites and 15.1 percent for blacks. The black middle class tripled in size between 1960 and 2000, growing at a faster rate than the white middle class.[2]

Middle class blacks moved not only up, but out. African American families exited the ghetto and moved into working-class neighborhoods and suburbs. These new neighborhoods were often as segregated as the districts they left, but had improved schools, services, and security. The neighborhoods they left behind, though, suffered further from deepening isolation and the removal of positive role models.[3]

The persistence of housing discrimination has inhibited greater upward mobility among middle-class African Americans. They have been less able than whites to take advantage of the great postwar surge in housing equity. In 1984, the Pew Research Center released the first of its wealth-gap studies. That year, white wealth was twelve times that of black wealth. It remained much the same ratio for the next decade. By the late 1990s, however, the gap had closed to seven to one. But in 2011, after the Great Recession, median white wealth was twenty times that of black households, the highest discrepancy since the survey began. In practical terms, what this meant was that if property taxes went up, or if someone lost a job (as happened often during that time), or if the roof leaked, the car broke down, or a child became ill, white households could draw on $92,000 to tide them over the rough times, while black families had to stretch a nest egg of $4,900.[4]

African Americans experienced a double loss during the Great Recession. The collapse of the housing market hit them especially hard since they were often the targets of the worst subprime loans. In Detroit, more than one third of black homeowners lost a home to foreclosure. The second blow, a higher unemployment rate among blacks than whites—13.6 percent versus 7.4 percent—during the downturn, compounded the first loss.[5]

The expansion of the black middle class from the 1960s onward produced a cruel irony. African Americans were significantly underrepresented in the stock market until the 1990s, when, after thirty years of capital accumulation, they had sufficient resources to invest in wealth-building vehicles such as stocks. Then came the crash of 2008. Blacks lost 71 percent of the value on their investments, from a median of $27,468 in 2005 to $8,000 in 2009. Whites experienced a loss of 9 percent on their investments, from a median of $30,984 to $28,043. The wide disparity in losses reflected that many African Americans purchased stocks at or near their highest value, and because of thin wealth reserves, they sold at the bottom of the market. The most common reason African Americans gave for investing in the stock market in the first place was to send their children to college.[6]

Public policy since the 1970s has only exacerbated racial wealth-accumulation disparities. Adjustments in the federal tax code and other financial policies aimed these asset-building measures at people who already had assets. At the same time, federal cuts in safety-net programs have retarded black wealth accumulation. The relatively small financial cushion of African Americans meant that black first homebuyers relied much less on inheritance and gifts from parents for down payments. They waited, on average, eight years longer than whites to purchase their first homes, which meant that they accumulated less equity. They missed out on the great home bonanza between 1970 and 1985, when home prices rose 230 percent, or twice the rate of inflation. White ownership has held steady at 70 percent or higher for decades, while black homeownership, a more recent trend, peaked at 49 percent in the mid-1980s and has not risen above 50 percent since.[7]

The policy solutions lay in vigorous enforcement of existing fair housing legislation and in an overhaul of the mortgage credit system. In 2012, the federal government spent $270 billion on housing subsidies. Nearly all that sum went to individuals who owned homes, with the wealthiest receiving the most through the home-interest write-off. Individuals making less than $20,000 a year received $1,471 in housing benefits, while those making more than $200,000 received $7,014.[8]

The U.S. Supreme Court ruling in *Texas Department of Housing and Community Affairs v. Inclusive Communities Project* in June 2015 may have a salutary impact on wealth accumulation for African Americans. The Fair Housing Act of 1968 prohibited state and local governments from spending federal housing funds in ways that perpetuated racial segregation. State and local governments have mostly ignored that provision, and the federal government has not enforced it. Considering that poor schools are really a housing problem, and that many of the ghetto pathologies—crime, unemployment, and family disintegration—result from the concentration of the poor in "hyperghettos," the failure to employ the Fair Housing Act for nearly fifty years has reinforced those pathologies and has restricted upward mobility.[9]

The case concerned a federal tax credit program Texas used to build affordable housing. The plaintiff, a nonprofit, sued the state arguing that Texas allocated too many tax credits to projects in black inner-city areas and too few in white suburbs. In a 5–4 opinion the Court interpreted the Fair Housing Act as enabling plaintiffs to challenge local housing policies that have a discriminatory effect without having to prove that the discrimination was intentional. Justice Anthony Kennedy, writing for the majority, provided a good history lesson to support his decision. Going back to the 1950s, he cited such common practices as redlining, restrictive covenants, and government-sponsored mortgage discrimination that severely constrained black wealth accumulation and hastened the isolation and dysfunction of black districts. The presidents after LBJ allowed states and localities to interpret the Fair Housing Act however they wished.[10]

Within weeks of the decision, the Obama administration attached new rules to the Fair Housing Act directing HUD to furnish local governments with data on segregated living patterns and concentrations of poverty. The new rules "encourage" local governments to partner with surrounding jurisdictions to resolve segregation.[11]

DESPITE THE ADVANCES OF MIDDLE-CLASS African Americans, poverty, for many whites, still has a black face. *Welfare*, a benign term in the 1940s and 1950s, assumed negative connotations by the 1960s. A 1949 editorial in the *Saturday Evening Post* cautioned opponents of President Truman's initiative to expand benefits: "The opponents of such a system have an excellent case, but they do not help it by adopting precisely the words which put it in a favorable light. 'Welfare' is the key word. Who's against welfare? Nobody . . . Fighting an election by opposing welfare is on a par with taunting an opponent for being born in a log cabin."[12]

But in the 1950s, Cold War propaganda linked government-sponsored welfare with European socialism and therefore as inherently un-American. By the early 1960s, *welfare* and *race* became synonymous as unmarried black women with children dominated public assistance rolls in the nation's cities. The confluence of War on Poverty legislation and the riots fed the perception that welfare recipients (mostly black in the public view) looked upon the assistance check as an entitlement rather than as a temporary bridge to self-sufficiency. When Ronald Reagan talked of "welfare queens" in 1976 (the *Chicago Tribune* actually coined the phrase), everyone knew whom he had in mind.[13]

The issue of poverty is then also a race problem. When Congress established Aid to Dependent Children in 1935 (it eventually became Aid to Families with Dependent Children), it excluded African Americans. By the 1960s, most Americans identified AFDC as a black program, and national support plummeted. The "tax revolt" of the late 1970s, highlighted by Proposition 13 in California in 1978, had strong associations with race for white voters. Proposition 13 cut taxes supporting social welfare programs that many white Californians identified as handouts to blacks.[14]

Ronald Reagan made tax cuts the centerpiece of his 1980 presidential campaign. The motivation was purportedly economic, but it contained a considerable racial component. His administration argued that programs such as AFDC and Medicaid supported dependency and immorality. Reagan engineered huge cuts in these programs. More than 1 million poor people lost food stamp benefits. Reagan also slashed taxes for the wealthy. During the Eisenhower administration, the top income-tax rate was above 90 percent. In Reagan's administration, it fell to 28 percent. When Reagan took office, the national debt was $930 billion; when he left, it was $2.6 trillion. If fiscal probity was a major conservative Republican tenet, Ronald Reagan was a poor steward of that principle.[15]

Today, most social welfare policies, regardless of their color-blind nature, are likely to provoke opposition because of race. President Obama's Affordable Care Act (ACA) makes no mention of race, but radio commentator Rush Limbaugh denounced it as reparations. Although the ACA expanded Medicaid, the U.S. Supreme Court made expansion optional for states in *National Federation of Independent Business v. Sebelius* (2012) with the result that many poor African Americans in the South do not benefit from it as many Republican-controlled Southern states refused to pick up that option.[16]

Ideological motives also drove welfare policy, though they were often inextricably if only implicitly connected to race. The belief was widespread that welfare support ruined initiative, though farm subsidies and corporate tax breaks did not apparently affect the work ethic of mostly white farmers and executives. The perspective is built into American culture. A World Values Survey in 2014 indicated that, while 60 percent of Europeans believed "the poor are trapped in poverty," only 29 percent of Americans agreed, and 60 percent of Americans thought "the poor are lazy," compared to just 26 percent of Europeans. Given these beliefs, formulating public policy to both address poverty and comply with cultural norms is difficult. Often, the norms have taken precedence.[17]

In October 1988, President Ronald Reagan signed a welfare reform bill, the Family Support Act, sponsored by Daniel Patrick Moynihan, then a Democratic senator from New York, that the Senate passed by a vote of 96–1. Reagan believed the Family Support Act (FSA) would "lead to lasting emancipation from welfare dependency." One of the most forceful statements in favor of the bill came from the spokesman of the National Governors Association, Bill Clinton of Arkansas. He envisaged a "new covenant" between the welfare recipient and the state, "setting forth not only the recipient's right to receive benefits but responsibilities that go along with those benefits." For those—and there were many—who believed that the social legislation of the 1960s had generated a catalog of welfare rights, but little or nothing in the way of responsibilities, these were encouraging words.[18]

The FSA was the forerunner of the 1996 welfare reform. The former law encouraged mothers to work outside the home provided that adequate child care was available (it rarely was). The subtext of the discussion surrounding this law was that welfare mothers lacked motivation or at least preferred to stay home rather than work. That was not often the case.[19]

President Bill Clinton's 1996 welfare law, Temporary Assistance for Needy Families (TANF), reflected this limited perspective, reversing sixty years of federal social policy by ending welfare as an entitlement program. It placed a five-year limit on receipt of benefits, required most of the recipients to seek and obtain work, and stepped up enforcement of child support. Without a supporting network of child care or family leave, and without adequate public transportation systems in many cities, the new policy created hardships for both single parents and their children. It also perpetuated the lack of coordination between welfare and the labor market.[20]

Only with President Barack Obama's fiscal stimulus package in 2009 did the connection between state-provided jobs and public assistance reemerge. Thirty-nine states used $1.3 billion from the stimulus package to create more

than 260,000 jobs by subsidizing private employers. Roughly two thirds of
these jobs would not have existed without the subsidy, and many were filled
by the hard to employ, including those with criminal records and former
workers who had been jobless for a long time or had been on welfare. The
program ended in September 2010, but 37 percent of the subsidized workers
kept their jobs.[21]

A SHELF OF SOCIAL SCIENCE literature provided intellectual support for the
shrinking federal safety net, especially as the culture of poverty concept
enjoyed a renaissance from the 1980s onward. Charles A. Murray's *Losing
Ground* (1984) focused on the culture of poverty in poor black neighborhoods:
the "young ghetto black on his way up was not cheered on his way, as the
young Jewish or Chinese . . . youth has been." Murray contended that social
policy in the 1960s broadcast an unfortunate message to African Americans:
"It's not your fault."[22]

But why was this the case? Murray and his coauthor, Richard Herrnstein,
believed they had found at least a partial answer in their controversial book,
The Bell Curve (1994). Their argument was that a hierarchy of intelligence
existed, with East Asians and Ashkenazi Jews at the top and blacks at the very
bottom. The authors insisted that this was not a racist argument as they were
not asserting that *all* blacks were inferior to *all* whites. The upshot was that
public policy was futile to resolve the multitude of ills that plagued the lives
of poor African Americans. In a particularly controversial chapter, "Coming
of the Custodial State," the authors conjured privileged middle and upper
classes creating a "high tech and more lavish version of the Indian reserva-
tion" to contain and control a rapidly breeding black underclass. Some would
agree that this already describes today's isolated and dysfunctional black
districts whose residents pose greater threats to themselves than to anyone or
anything beyond the districts' boundaries.[23]

In *The End of Racism* (1995), the conservative educator Dinesh D'Souza also
elaborated on the concept of the culture of poverty. He depicted the ghetto as
a place of unrestrained hedonism, violence, and social irresponsibility where
black men were twice as likely to be unemployed as white men, eight times
more likely to die by homicide, and ten times more likely to be in prison or on
parole. Given these conditions, government policy, as Charles Murray had
argued, was not only ineffective, but actually harmful as it reinforced deviant
behavior by protecting welfare recipients from the consequences of their
actions. For D'Souza the circumstances of ghetto life were less a factor
of genetics or of the environment than of choice. Residents had the option
of continuing their willful depravity or they could emulate the values of

middle-class society. But the isolation of these areas and the separation of their residents from middle-class institutions such as decent schools and role models rendered the availability of such an option unlikely.[24]

THESE WORKS BOTH SUPPORTED and contributed to the increasingly restrictive federal policy toward poverty since the Reagan administration. Statistics tend to support the view that some blacks are indeed apart from American society, though the respective roles of discrimination and culture and their interaction remain a matter of debate, the literature notwithstanding. According to the Pew Research Center, the share of American children living in poverty fell to 20 percent in 2013, down from 22 percent in 2010. The falling poverty rate was true for all groups except for African American children. Their poverty rate remained unchanged at 38.3 percent, or nearly four times the rate for white children, at 10.7 percent. About 30.4 percent of Hispanic children and 10.1 percent of Asian children lived in poverty. For the first time since the federal government began collecting poverty data, the absolute *number* of black children in poverty exceeded the number of impoverished white children—4.2 million to 4.1 million, respectively. What is especially troubling about black poverty rates over the years have been their persistence, contrasted with improving rates among other nonwhite ethnic groups, including African and Caribbean immigrants.[25]

Young African Americans fare poorest in a range of indices in comparison with other groups. In an era when the job market demands a higher level of skills, black youngsters lag behind significantly in their educational attainment and employment. As a consequence, they are also worse off mentally and physically than their peers. Nationally, 21.6 percent of black youths between the ages of sixteen and twenty-four are neither working nor in school, compared with 16.3 percent of Latinos, 11.3 percent of whites, and 7.9 percent of Asians. In some metropolitan areas, the figure for blacks exceeds 25 percent. These are youths who live "wholly apart from the mainstream." In Chicago, for instance, where African American crime rates are notoriously high, and where the nation's most defined segregated residential pattern exists, black youths perform worse than the national average for African Americans on standardized tests, while white and Hispanic youths in Chicago rate better than the national average for their respective groups.[26]

The policies of so-called ghetto enrichment—of improving housing and services in existing black neighborhoods—have had only marginal success, though local politicians like the strategy because it either concentrates their political base, or for districts outside the ghetto, it keeps black people away. Reducing residential segregation is perhaps the most crucial objective in attacking the culture of poverty. Housing location is intimately connected with schools and social pathology.

African American sociologist Orlando Patterson observed that the majority of blacks in the nation's inner cities "labor incredibly hard, advocate fundamental American values and aspire to the American dream for their children." But they expend considerable energy avoiding the violence around them. Helping this group evacuate the ghetto would matter significantly. But, Patterson notes, that still leaves "a problem minority, ranging from 12 percent to 28 percent who are not in school, not at work, and subsist through an underground economy." Many of these are young men who belong to gangs. And many of their neighborhoods have turned into what Patterson called "the Wild West."[27]

These districts are often the flash points for confrontations between aggressive law enforcement and young black men. But to attribute these conflicts solely to white racism misses an important point. In the early 1970s, New York governor Nelson A. Rockefeller introduced tough new drug laws to combat rising violence in New York City. The city's black leaders fully supported his initiative, as black street gangs and drug addicts were destroying their neighborhoods. Black mayors coming to power in other cities also promoted strict sentencing guidelines and rigorous policing. But the draconian sentencing and incarceration rates that followed in New York and, by the 1990s, nationally went well beyond what African American leaders had contemplated. The black homicide rate fell after these drastic interventions, but it remains at eight times the national rate and has been rising steadily since 2002.[28]

A comprehensive public policy attack on these neighborhoods, as posited more than a half century ago by Michael Harrington, involving education, job training, housing options, and early-intervention programs, may break the culture of poverty, but this expensive experiment lacks an effective constituency. And the problems are daunting. For example, the percentage of black children currently born to single, poor black women stands at 72 percent. The result of this alarming figure, according to Patterson, is "greatly increased risk of prolonged poverty, child abuse, education failure, and youth delinquencies and violence, especially among boys." As one gang member told an interviewer, "I grew up looking for somebody to love me in the streets. You know, my mother was always working, my father used to be doing his thing. So I was by myself. I'm here looking for some love. I ain't got nobody to give me love, so I went to the streets to find love."[29]

If money was the answer, then Baltimore's wretched public school system would be among the nation's best. It is among the worst. In 2011 that city ranked second among the nation's largest one hundred school districts in annual per pupil expenditure: $15,483. In the late 1980s, Baltimore's first elected African American mayor, Kurt Schmoke, decided to make Sandtown a model community. Sandtown was a decaying black neighborhood where two decades later riots erupted over the death of a resident, Freddie Gray, following a "rough ride" in a police van. The mayor partnered with new-town developer James Rouse and Habitat for Humanity, raising $130 million to build new homes, develop curricula for the schools, provide job-training programs, and open health-care centers. The partnership built town houses for $87,000 and sold them to residents for $37,000.[30]

By 2000 the poverty rate in Sandtown had declined by 4.4 percent, and the percentage of residents living in owner-occupied dwellings had risen by 8.3 percent. But that was all the improvement Sandtown could boast. Today, the neighborhood has no grocery stores or restaurants, and crime and unemployment are rampant. Freddie Gray was a victim of this neighborhood, despite the millions poured into it. He suffered from lead-paint poisoning. His mother was an illiterate heroin addict. Gray was four grade levels behind in reading and had been arrested more than a dozen times.[31]

The pathology of Sandtown did not reside in bricks and mortar. It lay elsewhere, in part in the quality of relationships in the home, and in the lack of future-oriented thinking in its residents, but also in educational, housing, and employment opportunities. In Freddie Gray's neighborhood, half the high school students do not show up in school on any given day. Would it matter if they did?

As Freddie Gray's story (and so many others) attests, Moynihan was correct about the impact of black family disintegration on the lives of their children. Children raised by single parents are three times as likely to live in poverty as kids in two-parent homes. Despite the dispiriting environment of these neighborhoods, policies do indeed exist to address, if not the present, then hopefully the future of these blasted places. Programs that emphasize early intervention are especially important. Public preschool, for children as young as twelve months, and home visitations to ensure the nutritional, educational, and nurturing qualities that are extremely important for very young children are also helpful.[32]

Orlando Patterson recommended a significant expansion of already-existing federal programs to extract children from their toxic environments as early as possible: child care from prenatal to pre-K stages, such as Head Start and the nurse-family partnership program; after-school programs to keep boys, especially, off the streets; programs that provide male role models; and expansion of the charter-school system. But Patterson noted that the success of federal policies required fundamental changes in the behavior of recipients: "Those to whom such policies are directed must . . . both accept personal responsibility and courageously make transformative choices for them and their future—including assimilation" in the middle-class nation.[33]

Such expressions of caution on the reach of public policy were prevalent at the outset of the Great Society. James Coleman's government-sponsored report on education in 1966 emphasized that the key to educational success was the relationships at home and in the neighborhood. He noted that LBJ's programs were transferring huge sums to the poor, but the poor neighborhoods improved relatively little as families continued to disintegrate. "At root," he wrote, "in almost every area of important concern, we are seeking to induce persons to act virtuously," but virtue was scarce in the ghetto.[34]

In *The Moral Sense* (1993), James Q. Wilson addressed the subject of virtue, which, he argued, was attained through "practicing good manners, being dependable, punctual and responsible day by day." In other words conforming to middle-class values. Wilson believed that order exists "because a system of beliefs and sentiments held by members of society sets limits to what those members can do." The limits in these neighborhoods were, if not absent, at least so distinctive from the rest of society as to contribute to the dysfunction of both place and person. This returns us to Michael Harrington's assertion more than fifty years ago that the culture of poverty—distorted norms and aspirations—trapped poor (mainly black) people as much if not more than material deprivation. The saddest aspect of this culture, according to Harrington, was that parents passed it along to their children, and children passed it along to their children. It was generational.[35]

STILL, LBJ's WAR ON POVERTY worked better than most observers today admit. The programs continued with his immediate successors, Richard Nixon, Gerald Ford, and Jimmy Carter, as the Democrats retained control of Congress for twelve years after 1968. The harvest was impressive. Some of today's most important antipoverty programs, including food stamps, Supplemental Security Income (a guaranteed minimum income for the elderly and disabled), and Section 8 rent subsidies (enabling the poor to access private housing and, therefore, remove themselves and their families from bad neighborhoods) either came online or were significantly expanded between 1969 and 1980.[36]

Christopher Jencks, a Harvard social-policy expert, calculated in 2015 that the absolute poverty rate declined significantly since the mid-1960s, from 19.0 percent in 1964 to 4.8 percent in 2013. At the least, it discredits Ronald Reagan's quip that "we fought a war on poverty, and poverty won." While it did not follow that LBJ's War on Poverty was responsible for the decline, food stamps, rent subsidies, and refundable tax credits had a measurable impact on

improving rates. But food stamps did not become a national program until
the end of the Nixon administration, the rent-subsidy program grew slowly
through the 1980s, and refundable tax credits were not significant until after
1993. Jencks argued, however, that LBJ's programs inspired Democrats to
champion such legislation from both a political and a moral perspective.[37]

Studies of the long-term impact of Head Start on its participants have
found moderate effectiveness. A 2002 analysis indicated that black students
who attended Head Start were twelve percentage points less likely to have
been arrested and charged with a crime than those who had not been in Head
Start. Academically, though, test score advantages of Head Start students
tended to decline over time relative to students who did not attend the
program. Neither the public schools nor the neighborhoods built on the
educational gains of Head Start's early intervention.[38]

Title I funding assessments showed similarly mixed outcomes. Title I
expenditures—funding to improve the academic performance of disadvantaged students—helped to reduce spending disparities between wealthy and
impoverished school districts in the 1960s and 1970s, but not after 1990, when
the program lacked sufficient funding. But greater funding parity did not
reduce the differences in math and reading scores between poor and wealthy
schools. In the South, however, Title I gave the federal government more
leverage in forcing Southern school districts to desegregate in the 1970s, and
there, black students' academic performance experienced gains.[39]

Black youngsters have benefited from an array of programs initiated or
inspired by War on Poverty measures that stressed interventions even before
they were born. As a result of federal family-planning assistance for at-risk
teenage girls, the teenage birthrate has fallen by one half since the mid-1990s.
Parent-coaching programs have educated expectant mothers on the dangers
of smoking, drinking, and doing drugs during pregnancy. Programs such
as Nurse-Family Partnership, Healthy Families America, Child First, Save
the Children, and Thirty Million Words Project, many of them public-
private initiatives, have recognized that the earliest years of childhood are the
most important.[40]

Despite these efforts, nearly four in ten black children live in poverty, the
highest poverty rate of any cohort in America. The shockingly high poverty
rate among black children derives from the high poverty rate of black single
mothers—30 percent. The Clinton welfare reform legislation requiring
single mothers to work was ill conceived without a support network of child-care
facilities. Single mothers turned over most of their paychecks to child care.[41]

The earned income tax credit, enacted during the Ford administration
in 1975 to provide relief for the working poor, has addressed some of the

problems generated by the Clinton welfare reform as it has increased employment among single mothers, keeping 6 million Americans above the poverty
line. Food stamps have kept 4 million recipients above the poverty line. If
Congress raised the federal minimum wage from a historic low of $7.25 an
hour to only $10.10 an hour, it would lift 5 million people out of poverty. Full-
time work offers the best opportunity for escaping poverty. The poverty rate
for full-time workers is only 3 percent; for those out of work, it is 33 percent.[42]

At the college level, administrations in the 1970s and later did not sustain
the generosity of the Johnson administration, even if they maintained the
programs. The program providing federal grants to needy college students
grew from $800 million in 1963–64 to $157 billion in 2010–11. Of that sum, $35
billion went to students from families below the poverty line through the Pell
grants. The objective of this program was to enable poor children to increase
their rate of college attendance. Instead, the college gap has widened. Among
students from the top 25 percent of income, the percentage entering college
rose from 51 percent to 66 percent between 1972 and 1992. For the bottom
quarter, the percentage rose only from 22 percent to 30 percent. Graduation
rates have exhibited a similar gap. Jencks attributed this disappointing
outcome to rising college costs, especially as state legislatures have reduced
support for public institutions of higher education. Student loans are an alternative, but an expensive one.[43]

Legislation targeting the elderly in the War on Poverty fared better. Between
1965 and 1973, Congress raised Social Security's average monthly benefits by
about 50 percent, accounting for inflation. Many of the elderly poor were
relying on middle-aged children for support, and some of those children had
financial difficulties themselves. The Social Security upgrade helped to cut the
poverty rate among the elderly from 30 percent in 1964 to 15 percent in 1974.
By 2014, the elderly poverty rate was less than 9 percent.[44]

Overall, the War on Poverty was successful. Investments in education,
housing, health care, and nutrition for working families have had significant
long-term benefits for children. Moving to Opportunity, a HUD demonstration program begun during the Clinton administration in 1994, is an example
of public policy following good social science research. It is generally agreed
that moving the poor out of ghettos is a positive step. Moving to Opportunity
provided two sets of rental vouchers for families: traditional rental vouchers
and experimental rental vouchers, the latter requiring people to move to less
poor neighborhoods. Fifteen years later, the children of families with conventional vouchers had increased their earnings as adults by 15 percent, but in
those families that had obtained vouchers that required them to move to less
poor neighborhoods, children's earnings had increased by 31 percent. The

additional tax revenue from these higher earnings more than paid for the program.[45]

Some of the antipoverty programs produced positive unintended consequences. The earned income tax credit has also reduced the incidence of low birth weight, raised math and reading scores, and increased college enrollment for children whose parents benefited from the program. The multiplier effect of Medicaid is another success story, as children of families who qualified for the program are more likely to graduate from high school and complete college, and it's less likely that a black youngster will die in his late teens. For women, Medicaid participation in childhood typically leads to increased earnings as an adult. Programs that help families pay for basic needs such as food, shelter, and health care reduce the intense economic pressure they confront. By decreasing family stress, young children's cognitive development improves. The greater earnings achieved by these children as adults result in additional tax revenue, reducing the programs' costs.[46]

These are long-term benefits mainly supporting the future of children. But there are short-term benefits as well. In 2013, for example, federal income and nutrition programs lifted 46 million people, including 10 million children, out of poverty. The falling percentages of Americans who are poor and uninsured reflect this safety net. Nor do these programs discourage work. The EITC, for example, rewards low-income parents for working. Child-care and pre-K programs, though they are underfunded, make it easier for parents to work.[47]

Poverty has fallen by three quarters since the mid-1960s. Studies have suggested that without the War on Poverty, mass incarceration, the increase in the number of single mothers, and the decline in trade unions would have pushed the poverty rate much higher. Genuine successes include the significant decline of poverty among the elderly. The EITC has reduced poverty among single mothers. Medicaid has benefited the poor as well. Head Start has helped equip poor children with social skills, though the academic benefits remain uncertain.[48]

Poverty might have eroded faster if wages had risen along with worker productivity, but that linkage ended around 1980. The bottom third of the American workforce has experienced little or no rise in inflation-adjusted wages since the early 1970s, and male workers in that group have actually experienced a sharp wage decline. Given these doleful figures, the successes of the War on Poverty are even more impressive. Christopher Jencks's conclusion is accurate: "We did not lose the War on Poverty. We gained some ground. Quite a lot of ground."[49]

More successes might have occurred had the momentum from the 1960s carried over more vigorously during the next half century. The retreat from attacking poverty resulted from what historian Michael Katz called "the war on dependence." From the Nixon presidency onward, administrations transferred political authority from the federal government to the states, reversing the enhancement of federal power that began with the New Deal. In the 1990s, states with Republican governors, such as Michigan's John Engler and Wisconsin's Tommy Thompson, battled federal regulations of public assistance programs and implemented their own welfare systems, which invariably cut benefits. And the increased policy emphasis on the connection between work and welfare ignored the challenges of a job market transitioning away from low-skilled full-time work to part-time employment.[50]

The failure to protect the neediest should have become an international embarrassment for the United States. In 1980, the United States ranked thirteenth among the thirty-four industrialized nations of the Organisation for Economic Co-operation and Development (OECD) in life expectancy for newborn girls. Thirty-five years later, it ranked twenty-ninth. In 1980, the infant mortality rate in the United States was roughly equivalent to that in Germany. In 2015, American babies died at almost twice the rate of German babies. The United States in 2015 had the highest teenage birthrate—seven times the rate in France—among OECD countries. More than 25 percent of this country's children live with one parent, again the highest among OECD nations. More than 20 percent of children live in poverty, ranking the United States twenty-eighth among the thirty-four OECD nations. Seven out of every one thousand American adults are in prison, five times more than in any other OECD nation, and more than three times the rate in the United States in the 1970s. These figures fall disproportionately on the black poor.[51]

IN AUGUST 1963, MORE THAN one hundred thousand people rallied in front of the Lincoln Memorial in Washington, D.C., stretching out beyond the Reflecting Pool as far as the eye could see. They came together, black and white, for "Jobs and Freedom." Martin Luther King Jr. electrified the crowd and millions of television viewers with his stirring "I Have a Dream" speech. The March on Washington did not push a civil rights bill through Congress; Lyndon B. Johnson did. But the ideals enumerated by King, and the obvious justice of the cause, made the president's job a little easier.

In June 1968, after an unusually wet spring, the Mall in Washington, D.C., was mostly a muddy mess. A scattering of plywood and canvas tentlike structures anchored loosely in the quagmire were all that remained of a hopeful encampment called Resurrection City. On June 24, police cleared the area and dismantled the structures without incident.

A contingent of twenty-eight hundred people had gathered there a month earlier to demand economic justice for the poor. The Poor People's March, the last major event King organized before his assassination on April 4, presented a stark contrast to the soaring rhetoric and expectations of that day five years earlier. But five years might have been five decades for the contrast between the two events. The March on Washington was a righteous voice demanding justice. The Poor People's Campaign was a poorly organized, mostly African American affair that drew more scorn than sympathy from whites. The campaign generated no new legislation.

Many felt that all that federal money in the intervening five years had purchased unrest, not peace. There had always been fissures in American society, but in the two decades after the end of World War II, federal leadership was able to bridge the differences and move toward a more egalitarian society. Now, it seemed, the federal government was a major perpetrator in casting that consensus asunder. Nineteen sixty-eight was a different time from 1963. It is still that time.

In 1903, the great black leader W. E. B. Du Bois wrote, "The problem of the Twentieth Century is the problem of the color-line." It has been a long century.[52]

CHAPTER 26

THE OLD COUNTRY

VIETNAM, LIKE NO OTHER EVENT in the 1960s, exposed the serious fissures in American society and the plunge in national confidence. Many in the gifted generation protested the war in Vietnam. The opposition was personal as the draft accelerated after 1964, placing the gifted generation in the crosshairs of a conflict they despised, though only 2.1 million of the 26.8 million early boomers (born between 1943 and 1949) served in Vietnam. But the mere chance that one might fight in an increasingly unpopular and unwinnable war created significant anxiety. The protests were also firmly grounded in moral objections to the war. By 1968, one third of young men born in 1948 were in the armed forces. But those who actually fought in Southeast Asia were predominantly from poor or working-class backgrounds—80 percent—not the college-educated draftees. When the draft changed over to a lottery system in 1969, that created more anxiety and fueled more protests.[1]

The opposition to the Vietnam War culminated a decade of questioning of the prevailing way of doing and thinking, whether in government, school, or at home, by members of the gifted generation. Steve Kelman was born in 1948 and graduated with honors from high school in Great Neck on Long Island. As a member of the gifted generation, Kelman set his thoughts down for the *Saturday Evening Post* in November 1966 during his freshman year at Harvard. The essay was primarily a defense of rebellion—not scorched-earth rebellion, but thoughtful opposition to what he and his cohorts perceived as discordant with American values. Bob Dylan was a particular inspiration for Kelman, who explained that Dylan's songs were often about skepticism, "about what's really going on in the world as compared to what we're being taught is going on in the world." Rather than merely accepting received wisdom, Kelman and his cohorts preferred to test it for validity to their present world. "When we take a look for ourselves, the facts we see are so different from what we've been taught that we have no choice but to turn into rebels." Kelman's generation had seen what Truman and Eisenhower perceived in the immediate postwar years: that America was coming into a new time, with a more complex economy, a more diverse population, and greater aspirations.[2]

As Kelman explained to adult readers, "hypocrisy" was a big issue with the gifted generation. His first glimpse of the disconnect between reality and what was being taught came in the first grade when he opened textbooks populated with "white tots living in suburbia with a dog running around the lawn." His first bout of skepticism occurred when he learned about slums and figured that "when slum kids are taught about a world that has nothing to do with the world in which they live," they become skeptics too. The gifted generation grew up in a less insular world than their predecessors, despite their experience of world war. Television and a multitude of accessible media informed them of the world that was, rather than the world that was not.[3]

Steve turned to a discussion about sex, hardly surprising for an eighteen-year-old boy. He and his high school classmates had quickly discovered that sex was very much a part of the real world, their world. But his high school ignored it. His high school also ignored student government. Steve was active along with other student leaders, but their role, from the administration's perspective, was primarily to plan social events. When they tried to do something meaningful, such as a fast during lunch hour in sympathy with people in India, the administration vetoed it.

The teaching of history reflected similar hypocrisy. The 1960s was a landmark decade for revising American history's old myths, from slavery to the Civil War and Reconstruction, as well as uncovering the stories of men and women who lived less public lives than prominent politicians and entrepreneurs. These changes proffered dignity and a voice to their subjects. Steve's high school curriculum (and that of many other school systems) did not yet reflect such revisions.[4]

Steve's high school history text was advanced enough to cover the history of American cities, but that coverage ended at the turn of the twentieth century. He figured that these texts were at least thirty years behind the latest historical interpretations and offered as an example the treatment of American intervention in Latin America in the early 1900s, the main purpose of which, according to the text, was to "lend a helping hand" to build roads, bridges, and hospitals.[5]

More egregious was the interpretation of the American Civil War. Quoting from the textbook, Steve shared this excerpt of African American history, which the book covered in four paragraphs: "During the War Between the States, all Negro slaves were set free. Since then American Negroes have gone through a difficult period of adjustment to new ways of life. They have made remarkable progress in a short time."[6]

Steve derided the fetish of objectivity, especially in political science, a subject, he argued, that was not objective. "Politics are not objective. Love is not objective. People are not objective." He urged schools to replace objectivity with democracy. "Democracy means trusting us to make up our minds." Here is an essential characteristic of the gifted generation: the refusal to accept received wisdom. Steve suggested trusting his generation to conduct their own empirical research into the world around them and derive conclusions based on that reality regardless if those conclusions clashed with or overturned conventional viewpoints.[7]

Steve Kelman went on to a distinguished public service and academic career, serving as administrator of the Office of Federal Procurement Policy in the Office of Management and Budget during the first Clinton administration, 1993–97. Kelman is currently the Weatherhead Professor of Public Management at Harvard's John F. Kennedy School of Government.

Freedom was a consistent theme among the Tilden High School class of 1961, as it was for Steve Kelman: the freedom to explore, to engage in new pursuits, to become involved in a variety of causes, and, above all, to make up their own minds. These were not junior anarchists as much as pioneers charting new courses, a very American tradition. Perhaps the greatest gift of the good government was freedom. Freedom enabled one to look hopefully to the future. The members of the gifted generation believed in themselves, in their country, and especially in their prospects. As Herman Melville wrote, "The Past is the textbook of tyrants; the future the Bible of the free."[8]

Jay Griffiths, a British writer, in *A Country Called Childhood: Children and the Exuberant World* (2014), contended, "If happiness is a result of freedom then surely the unhappiness of modernity's children is caused in part by the fact that they are less free than any children in history . . . Today's children are enclosed in school and home, enclosed in cars to shuttle between them, enclosed by fear, by surveillance and poverty and enclosed in rigid schedules of time." It is a more ordered world than in the 1950s and, especially, the 1960s, when the gifted generation came of age. But as writer Andrew Solomon noted, "The true opposite of order is not disorder but freedom. The true opposite of control is not chaos but self-control."[9]

The current generation has grown up in more constrained times. They have reaped the fallout from a diminished government and a sense of national drift. The gifted generation was in a hurry—to finish school, to sample careers, to start families. No sense lingering when the bright future beckoned. Today's generation delays adulthood. Twice as many college graduates per capita are living at their parents' homes today as there were in the 1960s. As for work, they're advised, "Follow your dream! The possibilities are limitless!" But that does not reflect the reality of the contemporary job market. In a sample of recent college graduates, 53 percent were unemployed, underemployed, or making less than $30,000 a year. In the 1960s, a college education was a sure ticket to a rewarding career or, more likely, careers.[10]

If mobility, both economic and geographic, characterized the gifted generation, then the current cohort may be the Go-Nowhere Generation. Todd G. Buchholz, White House director of economic policy under George H. W. Bush, wrote in 2012 that the likelihood of twentysomethings moving to another state has dropped well over 40 percent since the 1980s, regardless of educational level. Young people want to remain connected to their hometowns rather than to experience other parts of the country or the world. John Della Volpe of Harvard's Institute of Politics said, "I spoke with a kid from Columbus, Ohio, who dreamed of being a high school teacher. When he found out he'd have to move to Arizona or the Sunbelt, he took a job in a Columbus tire factory." This reflects wariness about striking out on one's own. The gifted generation was bold, motivated by opportunity rather than constrained by fear.[11]

What has happened since the late 1960s is a loss of confidence. The first two decades after World War II were America's confident years. The conquest of polio, the attempt to ameliorate if not demolish racial, ethnic, and gender prejudice, and nothing less than saving the planet from environmental ruin imbued young men and women with the idea that the future was limitless and progress was everlasting. That is no longer the case.

The later boomers were the first victims of this psychological deflation. On April 30, 1970, the Nixon administration announced the American invasion of Cambodia, triggering a wave of protests on college campuses. The following night students at Kent State University in Ohio hurled bottles at police cars and smashed store windows. On the next night, students firebombed the university's ROTC building, prompting Ohio governor James Rhodes to deploy the National Guard. On May 4, about five hundred protesters gathered on campus, some of whom threw stones at the guardsmen, who retaliated with tear gas. Although some of the demonstrators stood less than twenty yards from the troops, a few of the guardsmen opened fire with live ammunition. Two students walking to class were among the four killed. A presidential Commission on Campus Unrest condemned the "indiscriminate firing" as "unnecessary, unwarranted and inexcusable."[12]

One of the Kent State victims, Allison Krause, was 343 yards from the nearest guardsman, hardly a threat to the soldiers. Her sister Laurel still recalls the episode with bitterness: "My sister bled to death, for forty-five minutes, before an ambulance came, yet ambulances were available over the hill, reserved for guard and authority injuries only." A police officer from Madison, Wisconsin, reported, "Everyone on the Madison police force celebrated after we heard about the Kent State shootings."[13]

On May 14, Jackson, Mississippi, police killed two students and wounded nine others at predominantly black Jackson State College (now University) during a protest. By that time demonstrations and strikes had spread to 350 campuses around the country, engaging about 25 percent of all university students in America. At least thirty ROTC buildings were burned or bombed. A banner hung outside a dorm window at New York University declared THEY CAN'T KILL US ALL! But a key fact of these outbursts was that the American public had pretty much abandoned the boomers. A *Newsweek* poll taken a few days after the killings at Kent State showed that 58 percent of the respondents blamed the students, and only 11 percent blamed the national guardsmen.[14]

On May 8, New York's Mayor John V. Lindsay set aside the day to memorialize the victims of Kent State. Hundreds of people, most of them students, gathered near Wall Street to protest peacefully. Suddenly about two hundred construction workers descended on the gathering, using their hard hats as weapons to beat the demonstrators. The workers marched to City Hall, where they raised the American flag, which had been flying at half-staff. For good measure, they stormed into nearby Pace College (now University) to attack students, most of whom were not involved in the protest.[15]

Divisions were common in postwar America. Just ask Harry Truman, who tried to push through an array of progressive legislation, or Dwight D. Eisenhower, who struggled to bring Republicans into the twentieth century. In the two decades after World War II, many believed the nation was heading in the wrong direction. There had been individuals like this throughout American history—fearful of change, of new groups asserting themselves for full citizenship, of new economic forces, of new ethnic and religious ideas, of new music and literature, and of just about anything that smacked of divergence from the status quo or deviated from a mythical era of harmony somewhere in the recent past. Vietnam was the capstone of a decade that experienced foundational changes, and the reaction against those changes generated a visceral animosity that has persisted. Neither political party proved capable of healing these fissures. In fact, both the Republicans and the Democrats would exploit them. We are still dealing with the crack-up.

Opinion polls in the 1960s chronicled the separation between the gifted generation and their elders, between the new society an activist government was creating and the old nation that had gone before. A *Saturday Evening Post* editorial in November 1965 expressed concern that "a phenomenal number of citizens seem to think that virtually any kind of unusual behavior is a dire peril to the American Way of Life." The editor was responding to a recent Louis Harris poll where 89 percent of the respondents rated the American Communist Party (a small and fractured group by this time) as a threat, along with "People who don't believe in God" (72 percent). One half of the respondents condemned "working career women with young children" as harmful, and 36 percent felt the same way about "women who wear bikini bathing suits."[16]

Two years later, HEW Secretary John W. Gardner wrote a memo to LBJ that "something is eating people" and suggested a National Service Foundation consisting of various community-service activities to connect citizens "to some meaningful social effort, to be a part of something, to belong." Gardner feared that generational differences, the Vietnam War, and racial unrest were atomizing American society. He concluded that the nation's gravest crisis "is not Vietnam, nor the Negro, nor the city. It is the national mood of bitterness, distrust, and hostility; that mood is creating unparalleled divisiveness."[17]

Gardner prefigured the argument of Robert D. Putnam in *Bowling Alone: The Collapse and Revival of American Community* (2000), identifying the decline in civic participation as a serious obstacle both to national purpose and unity and to family cohesiveness. Putnam attributed the trend to the privatization of leisure, the growth of commuting, and two-career families. But these trends were evident by the late 1960s, and as Gardner understood, it was not only that people felt alone, it was that they felt increasingly disconnected from a nation they no longer trusted or understood.

Conservative political analyst George Will in *Statecraft as Soulcraft* (1983) commented on these trends nearly two decades before Putnam identified them, noting that the upheavals of the 1950s and 1960s, particularly the impact of the gifted generation, had profound implications for American society generally. Will explained this in terms that might have come directly from Putnam's work: "The institutions that once were most directly responsible for tempering individualism—family, church, voluntary associations, town governments—with collective concerns have come to seem more peripheral." Will, who generally is not a strong advocate of federal activism, suggested that the best way out of this situation is "using government discriminatingly but energetically to strengthen these institutions." He urged that this should be "the natural program of conservatives."[18]

Arthur Schlesinger Jr. addressed the same issue as Will in *The Vital Center* (1949) in a very different era. Then, at the dawn of postwar America, when the prospects for world peace seemed unclear and when a prosperous but uncertain America hoped for a future free from the turmoil of economic dislocation and war, Schlesinger presented his argument for an active federal government presence in the lives of Americans: "No one would argue that steering more resources into the public sector would cure the spiritual ailments of the affluent society; but it seems possible that the resulting improvements in opportunities in education, medical care, social welfare, community planning, culture and the arts will improve the chances for the individual to win his own spiritual fulfillment." Thus, government activism had both an economic and a moral dimension. Strengthening the collective elevated the individual.[19]

Some leaders today recognize the disconnect between the people and their government and among people as well. Senator Elizabeth Warren (D-MA) conceives of society "as an organic, mutually dependent whole" and supports government activism to foster this idea. It is the commonwealth ideal, that all Americans are interconnected and, in turn, connected to their government. President Barack Obama articulated this idea at a campaign stop in Roanoke, Virginia, in June 2012. A Mitt Romney campaign surrogate had said that the government had no role in helping her build her business, which, she claimed, she had accomplished on her own. Obama demurred:

> If you were successful, somebody along the line gave you some help.
> There was a great teacher somewhere in your life. Somebody helped to
> create this unbelievable American system that we have that allowed
> you to thrive. Somebody invested in roads and bridges. If you've got a
> business, you didn't build that. Somebody else made that happen.[20]

THE IDEA THAT CONSENSUS dominated politics prior to the 1960s is a convenient but incorrect view of history. The fractures in society—generational, class, racial, and ethnic—were visible before the early 1960s. The difference was that America had a good government attuned to building the commonwealth by creating opportunities for individuals. A thriving economy and a broad public faith in the efficacy of government after coming out of a depression and a successful war played important roles as well. But these features did not exist in isolation from public policy. The policies pursued by the three presidents reinforced and built upon these inherent advantages. That was not the case in the 1970s, nor later. The gifted generation grew up with leadership that embraced national rather than parochial interests; that had a sense of history enabling the leaders to see change as an opportunity, rather than as a threat; and that viewed diversity as an asset, not as a burden.

The later boomers missed these gifts, and perhaps they knew it. The suicide rate for fifteen- to nineteen-year-olds experienced its greatest increase in

1970–71; then the twenty- to twenty-four-year-old age group took its biggest jump in suicides a few years later. Those boomers born between 1953 and 1957 were three times as likely to kill themselves as those born in 1944 to 1948. A Louis Harris poll in 1978 revealed that the most alienated group in society were boomers between the ages of eighteen and twenty-two with only a high school education. Less than 50 percent agreed with the statement "the average man is probably better off today than he ever was." They had inherited the expectations from the gifted generation, but not an active and engaged federal government and the economic prosperity that accompanied it.[21]

The American bicentennial in 1976, for all its hoopla and pyrotechnics, seemed flat to many observers, a celebration of past greatness at a time when Americans were not feeling particularly good about themselves or their country. Journalist Frank Rich captured the feeling: "The mood of the union was not so much volatile as defeated, whiny and riddled by self-doubt."[22]

Three years later, a pollster asked the Princeton class of 1969 at their tenth reunion to identify the person in public life they most admired. The leading selection, by far, was "Nobody." That same year, President Jimmy Carter gave a speech in which he identified the illness as a "national malaise," but what Americans needed was less a diagnosis than a shot of confidence.[23]

In 2012, Michael F. Ford, director of Xavier University's Center for the Study of the American Dream, found "a stunning lack of confidence in American institutions" from a survey he conducted. Of those surveyed, 65 percent believed that the United States was in decline; 83 percent had less trust in "politics in general" than even fifteen years earlier; 79 percent had less trust in major corporations; 78 percent had less trust in government; and 72 percent had less trust in media. Compare these results to a Gallup poll from the early 1970s indicating that 70 percent of Americans had "trust and confidence" that the government could handle domestic problems.[24]

Perhaps the residue from the economic collapse of 2008–9 accounted for these pessimistic responses. But by the end of 2014, the mood had not changed. A *New York Times* poll found that only 64 percent of respondents believed in the American dream, the lowest result in two decades, and even lower than in the depths of the financial crisis in 2009. Especially discouraging, young adults between the ages of eighteen to thirty-four were most likely to feel the dream was unattainable.[25]

Some have argued such pessimism failed to consider how far the nation had come since the end of World War II: "the emancipation of women and their integration on equal terms in education, the granting of civil rights to homosexuals, the removal, at least formally, of racial discrimination," as one journalist cataloged the advances. But few people compare their present situation to national historical events. They compare their current condition to their own previous status and that of their parents and grandparents. They might manufacture a past, a mythical Valhalla of good times and good jobs, but the gains in human rights are beside the point if jobs, housing, and educational opportunities become illusive.[26]

People also care about their children's future; that has always been the case, but the concerns are more fraught now than they were in the 1950s and 1960s. In 2014, a *Wall Street Journal*/NBC poll indicated that 76 percent of Americans did not feel confident that "life for our children's generation will be better than it has been for us." Not only was that the worst rating ever recorded on that issue, but it was also ten percentage points worse than the poll had ever before recorded. A similar poll, conducted by the *National Journal*, indicated that only 20 percent of Americans expected today's children to have more opportunities to get ahead than their parents had, while 45 percent expected them to have fewer.[27]

In August 2014, columnist Frank Bruni lamented the nation was "surrendering to a new identity and era, in which optimism is quaint and the frontier anything but endless." That same *WSJ*/NBC poll also showed that 71 percent of Americans thought the country was on the wrong track. The federal government in particular drew a harsh assessment from those polled: only 30 percent expressed confidence in the Supreme Court, 29 percent in the presidency, and a record low 7 percent in Congress, except for their own representative, though even there 51 percent of respondents disapproved of the job their member of Congress was doing.[28]

As Bruni noted, this was not only a reaction to a lagging economy. At least three major recessions occurred in the two decades after World War II, yet they did not throw the country into despair and paralysis. But the federal government was considerably more active then, and large public works projects, tax adjustments, and aid to education and housing smoothed the economic bumps.

What Bruni detected was fear, a feeling of impotence, both at home and abroad, a tired nation unable or unwilling to move with alacrity and purpose. An age of negativity had replaced the era of confidence. We "can't find common ground and peace at home, can't pass needed laws, can't build necessary infrastructure, can't, can't, can't." Philosopher Leon Wieseltier wondered, "When did we fall in love with discouragement?" It was quite a contrast from the can-do spirit of the immediate postwar era.[29]

Quite a contrast also from the sense after the war that America was new—with smooth, wide highways, shiny new air terminals, tunnels that burrowed deep into riverbeds to carry traffic into and out of booming cities, and bridges that arched high above rivers and bays, graceful structures that excelled in both beauty and strength. And today? "American bridges crumble. American trains crawl. American flights leave from terminals that pale next to many Asian and European counterparts." Europe used to be the Old World, and Asia, especially China, was not even on the radar of competition. Now, these places are the new. If great building projects reflect optimism, it is little wonder that pessimism has taken hold so deeply in the United States. We have become old without the accompanying wisdom of age, with merely its decrepitude. Decline is a choice, not an inevitability.[30]

We live in an era of "reduced expectations," and that has become a self-fulfilling prophecy. On the international "social progress index," which includes 132 countries, the United States in 2014 ranked thirty-ninth in basic education, thirty-fourth in access to water and sanitation, and sixteenth overall, just two notches above Slovenia. Work, that great elixir of upward mobility, has also regressed. Today, labor-force participation is at its lowest in decades.[31]

The outlines of defeat and pessimism were already visible by the late 1960s and early 1970s. Vannevar Bush, the imaginative scientist who had a hand in much of the technology we take for granted today, looked around his troubled nation in 1970, with the images of riot-torn cities and a ruinous war flickering incessantly on his television screen, and lamented, "We have lost our bright spirit and with it our perspective." But the man who wrote *Science: The Endless Frontier* was not ready to succumb to despair: "The times are tough, but let us look back and see if we can recover balance." That balance, between government, the people, and economic institutions, grew increasingly askew in the decades after 1970. The vital center eroded, and dysfunction and inequality seeped into the body politic.[32]

The major difference between the time the gifted generation came of age and the present is that the federal government's role as the great umpire, the leveler, has diminished. The federal government today has a great opportunity to borrow money at relatively low interest rates to build infrastructure and improve public transportation to enable workers to have access to better jobs. The federal government can increase wage subsidies to employers who hire the long-term unemployed. Federal tax reform could produce a genuinely progressive income tax structure. The best federal investment in human capital is through education. If a two-earner high-school-educated couple, for example, obtained college degrees, their income would increase by $58,000 annually. These and other solutions to address what has become an "emotional recession" are available, but not implemented.[33]

Political scientist Francis Fukuyama argues that democracy and state building are directly connected: the more active and efficient the federal government, the greater the democracy. In the nineteenth century, the United States had a weak and often corrupt national government. But beginning in the Progressive era at the end of the nineteenth century and especially during the New Deal, the state became a strong and effective independent actor. The transformation to an industrial economy played an important role in federal activism, not only because it brought new constituencies into politics, but also because of the necessity of balancing the interests of the commonwealth with the new power of large corporations.

This trajectory is well-known to historians and political scientists. Fukuyama asserts, however, that beginning in the 1970s American political development not only stalled, but began to regress. The American state has become "weaker, less efficient and more corrupt," a closer resemblance to its nineteenth-century forebear. The reason is the growing wealth inequality and its concentration, "which has allowed elites to purchase immense political power and manipulate the system to further their own interests." These influences "are collectively unrepresentative of the public as a whole." The result, Fukuyama concludes, is a vicious cycle where the state cannot address major challenges, which in turn produces greater public distrust in the federal government, leading to a decline in both resources and authority, which results in even worse performance. It is a persuasive analysis, though "wealth inequality and its concentration" did not corrupt the government; rather, the government, particularly from the Reagan administration forward, facilitated the economic coup.[34]

THE UNITED STATES, WITH THE OLDEST continuing form of government in the developed world, has always been a young country, charting new territory, whether in geography or technology, and providing opportunities for perhaps the most diverse array of ethnic and racial groups in the industrialized world. In the nineteenth century, political leaders often referred to the nation as an "experiment" because there was nothing like it on the face of the earth. There was always the hope that enlightened peoples in the Western world would eventually insist on a government by the consent of the governed.

The experiment proved resilient enough to survive a bloody civil war. With the administrations of Teddy Roosevelt, Woodrow Wilson, and then FDR, America established a precedent of government activism for the common good. That sensibility carried us through the Great Depression and World War II, from which we emerged strong and confident because our government was strong and confident. We were a young country again and so were, increasingly, our people. The gifted generation seized the promise this confidence and activism sustained. But by the 1970s, the United States became increasingly an old country—more cautious, less confident, and looking to an imagined golden past instead of building for a promising future.

CHAPTER 27

THE GREAT REGRESSION

FEDERAL DEVOLUTION WAS NOT A sudden phenomenon. The government was unlikely to maintain the extent of activism it had during the two decades after World War II, particularly in the face of racial, military, and economic challenges that emerged after 1965. But as the Nixon administration demonstrated, especially with environmental legislation, government was still a relatively robust presence in the early 1970s.

In 1971, two years before the Arab oil embargo, the Nixon administration asked Congress to fund a department of natural resources to unify energy resource development. Congress did not see the need for such an agency at that time. With the embargo in 1973, Congress approved the establishment of the Federal Energy Administration. Over the next two years the Ford administration funded the Energy Research and Development Administration to support basic research in energy to lessen dependence on Middle East oil.[1]

In the twenty-first century, government research funding for science and technology has declined. During the depths of the Great Recession, 2008–9, it was understandable that funding levels would drop, but they continued to recede in the years that followed. Between 2011 and 2013, federal funding for science and technology research fell 13 percent. The shortsightedness of such cutbacks is evident by what the government accomplished in this field prior to 2000. Some of Apple's most significant achievements, such as the mouse, a graphical user interface, the touch screen, and Siri, came about with the support of federal funds. Google's search engine derived from a $4.5 million digital-libraries research grant from the National Science Foundation. Federal funding has been essential for the pharmaceutical industry. According to the Congressional Budget Office, sixteen of the twenty-one "most influential drugs" introduced between 1965 and 1992 depended on federally funded research.[2]

The list of everyday technology connected to government funding is long: lasers, transistors, semiconductors, microwave ovens, communication satellites, cellular phones, and the Internet, to name a few. Almost any major application related to geospatial information, such as the GPS network and climate-change-monitoring systems, benefited from government funding. NIH initiated the Human Genome Project. These projects were too new, too large, and too risky for private investors. The government took the risk, paid the bill, and benefited a nation.[3]

As a good example of the unfortunate difference between then and now, journalist James Fallows pointed to the contrast between President Eisenhower's response to *Sputnik* in 1957 and President George W. Bush's handling of 9/11. In the former instance, Eisenhower "set our foreign policy and our domestic economy on a path for another fifty years of growth." He invested in science and technology. Bush, on the other hand, "created problems that will probably take another fifty years to correct." Bush went to war.[4]

Many in the gifted generation had a direct hand in scientific and technological innovations, and a willing partner in the federal government. Innovation was the greatest American industry of the twentieth century, yet government support is now dwindling. Without innovation, as journalist John B. Judis argued, "you have an economy dependent on tourism, the tottering superstructure of big finance, and the export of raw materials and farm products." The result is a weaker nation, not only in comparison with competitors, but also "in its ability to provide its citizens with richer, longer, more imaginative lives."[5]

In the immediate postwar era, federal support for innovation in science and technology was bipartisan, beginning with the Truman administration. Federal support increased significantly during the Eisenhower administration.

Ronald Reagan, hardly an advocate of government spending, nevertheless saw the value of continued support for scientific and technological research. In 1982, he established a new program, the Small Business Innovation Research (SBIR), which, by 2006, was spending $2.1 billion on more than fifty-eight hundred research grants. SBIR led to the formation of Sematech, a joint government-industry nonprofit to develop new methods of chip manufacturing and also fund research in nanotechnology.[6]

The major shift in science and technology funding did not occur until the Tea Party victory in the 2010 midterm elections. The new Congress slashed the NIH budget by $1.6 billion—to the level that existed in 2000. NSF budget cuts led to a thousand fewer research projects funded, and Congress gutted programs for renewable energy and climate change. Republicans proposed an 81 percent cut in the Energy Department's Advanced Research Projects Agency.[7]

Judis attributed the growing Republican opposition to funding scientific research to partisan politics, but more specifically to the growing antigovernment and anti-intellectual sentiment of the party's base. The great innovations initiated by federal programs in the immediate postwar era reflected a confidence in the future, not the fear of change, the nostalgia for a lost past, or adherence to superstition and myth.[8]

In a 2015 op-ed in the *New York Times*, Newt Gingrich, the former House Speaker and budget hawk, set out the case for doubling the NIH budget to $60 billion. Congress had not increased that budget since 2003, though grant applications grew by almost 50 percent over the next decade. Gingrich's argument was that only government possessed the resources to both cure and treat the most expensive diseases. He charged, "It's irresponsible and shortsighted, not prudent, to let financing for basic research dwindle."[9]

The chances of doubling the NIH budget may be gauged by the comment of Representative Raúl Labrador (R-ID): "I think whatever we do to increase NIH funding has to be offset with cuts somewhere . . . I just don't buy the argument that government spending actually creates growth." Senator Labrador is obviously not a student of Alexander Hamilton, who urged government support for the new nation's nascent industries—the "high-tech sector of its day." Hamilton's great insight was "that the enormous economic value that innovative industries could offer the nation merited public efforts to enable their success."[10]

Government cutbacks in research funding have resulted in closed labs, laid-off scientists, and postponed projects. The regression of government has placed a higher premium on private financing of scientific research, but such funding reflects the research priorities of the specific donors, rather than what is necessary from a national perspective, or even what is good. Since the conservative takeover of Congress after the 2010 elections, federal spending on basic research has fallen by a quarter, the sharpest decline in history. What is at stake "is the social contract that cultivates science for the common good."[11]

In the postwar era, an activist federal government encouraged scientific and technological research. The United States got to the future first. That attribute is now threatened. By 2023, China could pass the United States in funding for scientific research and development. A warning of how much we have slipped is that in 2011, only one U.S. corporation, Qualcomm, made it into the world top ten for international patent filings.[12]

The false economy in cutting spending for research in science and technology has its parallels in other areas where government excelled in the immediate postwar era. James Fallows wondered why President Obama's stimulus package had no funds to upgrade and build ports, highways, and air terminals and provide for an educated populace. Perhaps Obama was wary that Republican opposition might scuttle the entire package, but he barely tried to make his case. In transportation, we have hardly advanced at all during the past forty years, which means we have regressed. Fallows noted, "It should have been possible to build all those things, in a contemporary, environmentally aware counterpart" to President Eisenhower's interstate-highway plan. Pushing it off to the next generation is hardly the "gift" we should bequeath to our children and grandchildren.[13]

THE GIFT OF EDUCATION WAS among the most important supports of the postwar era. It helped the gifted generation—especially the children of working-class families profiled in this book—to achieve economic and social mobility (and, therefore, independence) almost unimagined by their parents. Ironically, their success has widened the chasm between them and those who live in high-school-educated America.

Robert D. Putnam's *Our Kids* (2015) noted that educational differentials result in other shortcomings. About 10 percent of children born to college graduates now grow up in single-parent households. Nearly 70 percent of children of the high school educated are raised in such households. High-school-educated parents read to their children less than their college-educated counterparts. They also take them to church less and do not talk to them as much, or spend as much time on developmental activity. The culture of poverty is apparently advancing upward from the very poor to the working class. As columnist David Brooks explained, "It's not only money and better policy that are missing in these circles; it's norms."[14]

These debilities often pass to the next generation. More than 70 percent of children who grew up in a family ranked in the top quarter of income earners will earn a college degree, compared with less than 15 percent of those born into a family ranking in the bottom half of wage earners. That has long-term adverse consequences for children today. In 2012, two-year-degree holders earned close to $7,000 more annually than those who held only a high school diploma. Those with a four-year degree earned $15,000 more annually than individuals with an associate degree, and a professional-degree holder earned $35,000 more annually than someone with a college degree. The stall in upward mobility reflects that birth is increasingly a predictor of access to higher education.[15]

Yet, that stall could be mitigated if middle- and lower-income students could afford to attend four-year institutions. During the past two decades, those born into the middle three income quintiles were more than twice as likely to attain the top income quintile if they possessed a college degree compared to those without such a degree. But the greatest boost occurred among students in the second-poorest quintile who obtained a college diploma, as nearly two thirds jumped to the richest quintile.[16]

Visit any elite university today and the diversity is impressive, at least in terms of race and ethnicity. "Never mind," as one educator observed, "that all of their parents are doctors or bankers." Not quite, but it reflects the lack of class diversity on most elite campuses. It underscores the increasing isolation of lower- and even some middle-class families from a key element in upward mobility. In 1985, 46 percent of incoming freshmen at the 250 most selective colleges came from the top quarter of the income distribution. By 2000 that had risen to 55 percent, and by 2006, only 15 percent of students at these schools came from the bottom half of wage-earning families. Although cause and effect are circumstantial, the increasing exclusivity of universities tracked the decline of federal support for less affluent students. It also extends the class divide into subsequent generations.[17]

Equally important in educational disparities is the ability of affluent parents to equip their children with competitive advantages such as music lessons, sports, foreign travel, and SAT preparation. Performance on the SAT exam and family income are directly correlated. But even if low-income students do well on the exam, fewer than 50 percent will enroll in a four-year institution. The result today is that the education system does not mitigate the class system as it once did. It reproduces it.[18]

Despite the well-documented advantages in contemporary America of a college education, more men ages twenty-five to twenty-nine had college degrees in 1976 than in 2006. Today, almost 60 percent of adults over the age of twenty-five do not have a degree beyond a high school diploma. That is not only a drag on the economy, but also on those in that group, particularly men. The peak earnings year for men with a high school diploma was 1973.[19]

The so-called college premium soared after 1970, which allowed the gifted generation to pursue a variety of well-remunerated careers. This reflected the postwar economic transition that placed a high demand on technical and communication skills and devalued unskilled and semiskilled workers. The G.I. Bill and low tuitions at public universities made low-cost education accessible in the two decades after World War II, a time when the United States led the world in college completion. By 2013, the United States ranked sixteenth.[20]

In 2013, the pay gap between college graduates and everyone else reached a record high, as those with a four-year degree earned 98 percent more an hour on average than people without a degree. The figure was 64 percent in the early 1980s. It is not that wages for college graduates have soared—they increased only 1 percent between 2004 and 2014—but that the average wage for everyone else has fallen 5 percent. The real cost of a college degree is about negative $500,000—that is, not going to college will cost you half a million dollars.[21]

Yet the expense of going to college continues to be a major obstacle for many students. Public universities were once a great bargain, but tuition increases have squeezed even middle-class families. For students coming from the richest fifth of the population, the annual cost of attending a public four-year institution has increased slightly from 6 percent of family income in 1971 to 9 percent in 2011. For everyone else, the bite out of family income is at least in double digits, with the costs for the poorest fifth jumping from 42 percent to 114 percent of family income. In the 1970s, the Pell grants for low-income students covered nearly 80 percent of the costs at a public university; by 2013–14, they covered just 31 percent. State governments are complicit as well. Between 1990–91 and 2009–10, spending per full-time public university student fell by an average of 26 percent.[22]

The public school system below the collegiate level is seriously bifurcated, making a college education more elusive as one descends the economic scale. The United States provides very good to excellent education for affluent students, reflecting the key role of parents and the support of prosperous local governments. But that is not the case for poorer students, especially African Americans. One of the greatest predictors of academic success is household income, which perpetuates the advantages of more affluent students through generations. But as the gifted generation demonstrated, federal activism, family engagement, and low-cost higher education provided genuine paths for upward mobility. It is a model followed by most European nations today.[23]

Educators agree that learning is lifelong and must start in early childhood, very early. By the time poor children reach kindergarten, it is already too late. They have typically suffered from inadequate nutrition, limited reading at home, and no preschool experience. Across the OECD, an average of 70 percent of three-year-olds are enrolled in educational programs; in the United States the figure is 38 percent, a reflection of the paltry child-care infrastructure in this country. Also paltry are teacher salaries. American teachers earn 68 percent as much as the average college-educated worker; in the OECD countries, the average is 88 percent. The basic funding mechanism of American education—the local property tax—contributes to these disparities. Other developed countries have the benefit of generous state and national subsidies. Columnist Nicholas Kristof has argued, "Fixing the education system is the civil rights challenge of our era." It is not only an African

American or even an immigrant issue. It is a matter of our future prosperity in a competitive world.[24]

MEMBERS OF THE GIFTED GENERATION retained their gifts, for the most part, and built upon them. Yes, they grew up in a different economic era, but they also grew up in a different political era. Today, supported by income from Social Security, pensions, investments, and, for some, salaries from continuing to work, they not only weathered the Great Recession, but have been doing quite well since 2007. As recently as the late 1990s, one in five Americans in their late sixties held a job now it is one in three. Some might argue that this trend reflects the need to work, rather than the choice to continue. But many in the gifted generation enjoy their work, and some, as profiled here, have embarked on new projects in their sixties and seventies. This leading edge of the baby boom is better off than any previous generation at this time in their lives. Bucking the trend of the eroding middle class, more seniors fall into this category now than ever before.[25]

According to a Pew survey in May 2015, nearly half of seniors age sixty-five and older consider themselves in excellent or good shape financially, compared to younger boomers, who perceive their status less favorably. Consumer data confirms these impressions. The gifted generation spent 18 percent more per household in 2013 than in the late 1980s, while spending for other age groups remained relatively flat. Health costs were part of the reason for increased spending, but these seniors spent 57 percent more on entertainment, and considerably more than that on homes, rental cars, and alcohol.[26]

The Great Regression has not been as unkind to the gifted generation as to the millennial generation. The arc of the gifted generation's lives demonstrated the lasting impact of their gifts, which they passed along to their children. What will today's children be able to bequeath to the next generation? The answer is unknowable, but its uncertainty should be a matter of national concern and action.

IN THE 1960S, THE GIFTED GENERATION engaged in the most American pastime of holding the nation to its ideals. The members of this group helped to forge a new path to full participation in American society. Many of the stories here chronicled the lives of immigrants' children who grew up and beyond the attainments of their parents. The parents applauded the ambitions of both their sons *and* daughters and sacrificed for them as well. Those who opposed immigration as damaging to the republic were unaware that these sons and daughters and grandsons and granddaughters of immigrants were the most American of all. Their families came here for freedom, an opportunity to attain an education and a livelihood, and to pass along those blessings to their children. It is the story of America. Some have gifted the country with innovations and inventions that have made our lives better and our nation stronger.

They sang and marched to support the cause of civil rights; they sang and marched to protest a useless war; and they demanded a new accountability on their campuses in curricula, student rights, and diversity. They were flag bearers much more than flag burners. Unlike the New Left, they did not disintegrate in a tidal wave of identity politics, white guilt, or black nihilism. The media paid less attention to them, but they built useful lives and a more equitable nation from the gifts they received.

Despite growing economic and social inequality, America today is better off than it was in 1945. Better off for women, for African Americans, for gays, and for all who share in the belief that expanding freedom for one expands freedom for all. What is missing today and has been for at least three decades is a good federal government ensuring opportunity for the greatest number as opposed to the relatively few.

Federal activism per se has not diminished as much as its role as an impartial umpire, providing opportunity for the commonwealth, not only for specific individuals or economic categories. The key commonalty about federal policy in the quarter century after World War II was its universality—policies that helped the entire nation even if a particular measure, such as civil rights legislation, targeted a particular group. Postwar legislation tended, as journalist George Packer observed, to establish "collective structures, not individual monuments, that channeled the aspirations of ordinary people. Among these structures were state universities, progressive taxation, interstate highways, collective bargaining, and Medicare." It was never a zero-sum game. As the federal government broadened opportunities, everyone benefited. It was rarely the individual versus the collective; each reinforced the other to build a nation. The role of government was to maintain both the synergy and the balance.[27]

In 1994, journalist Jonathan Rauch coined the word *demosclerosis*, which he defined as "government's progressive loss of the ability to adapt," a process "like hardening of the arteries, which builds up stealthily over many years." Symptoms of this disease frustrated Truman and Eisenhower, and even LBJ at times. But these leaders cobbled together enough allies in each party to pass key legislation. Often these measures were merely a "step," but they led to greater things and put the nation on record as dedicated not only to the principle of "all men are created equal," but also that the people could pursue happiness unencumbered by the restrictions on their race, ethnicity, gender, or sexual orientation that marked the first half of the twentieth century. The winnowing of the parties from the 1970s forward played some role in forging a sclerotic government, but neither party has been effective in addressing the aspirations of the nation as opposed to appeasing narrow constituencies.[28]

That dedication to that broader vision has regressed. Perhaps the best snapshot of the shift in public policy since the Nixon administration is the change in federal nonmilitary discretionary spending. That includes such programs as housing vouchers, veterans' health benefits, highway maintenance, and the Food and Drug Administration. It excludes domestic social programs that are mandatory, such as Social Security, Medicare, or Medicaid. When Nixon resigned the presidency in 1974, discretionary spending accounted for 4 percent of the GDP, or roughly similar to the figure at the end of Johnson's administration. Discretionary spending increased during the Ford and Carter administrations, peaking at 5.2 percent of the GDP in 1980. Then discretionary spending began its decline to a record postwar low of 3.6 percent of GDP in 2008, just at the onset of the Great Recession.[29]

Americans' support for and respect of their government has receded since the 1960s, almost in direct proportion to the decline in federal activism and personal mobility, and the increase in economic inequality. In 1965, during one of the most remarkable legislative sessions in history, 71 percent of Americans stated they trusted Washington most or all of the time. "The Congress of Fulfillment," House Speaker John W. McCormack (D-MA) called it. It was the Congress that began to ameliorate poverty, that assured health care for the elderly, that created jobs for the unemployed, that began to clean the air and water and beautify the environment, and to outlaw racial, ethnic, and gender discrimination. LBJ stood on the podium conducting the ensemble in works mostly of his own composition. But by 2013 only 20 percent of Americans trusted Washington most or all of the time. The majority of Americans believed that the government did not work for them.[30]

AMERICANS IN THE LATE 1940s, having recently defeated fascism and now immersed in the Cold War with the Soviet Union, understood the distinctions between totalitarian regimes and their own, though occasionally in their battle with the former they threatened the latter. Arthur Schlesinger Jr., writing in 1949, placed the distinction in the proper perspective: "The thrust of the democratic faith is away from fanaticism; it is toward compromise, persuasion and consent in politics, toward tolerance and diversity in society . . . Its love of variety discourages dogmatism, and its love of skepticism discourages hero-worship. In place of theology and ritual, of hierarchy and demonology, it sets up a belief in intellectual freedom and unrestricted inquiry."[31]

Compromise, tolerance, diversity, and intellectual freedom were the dominant ideals shaping public policy, especially during the 1960s. In the contentious environment of the late 1940s and onward, presidential leadership proved essential in enhancing the federal government's role as the torchbearer of "democratic faith." America did so for a quarter century after World War II. The benefits bestowed on the gifted generation, and on the country as a whole, remain with us today, though some are threatened or diminished. It will take a renewed faith in our government and the right leadership to resume that journey so that all Americans can benefit from the gifts inherent in our founding ideals.

The failure of our politicians should not lead to an overall indictment of the institution of government. The issue is not big government versus small government. The issue is good government. Politicians have fanned antigovernment sentiment not only for political gain, but also to satisfy their financial supporters. Voters know this. In 1964, 29 percent of voters believed that the government was "run by a few big interests looking out for themselves." By 2013, that was up to 79 percent. The record is clear: the United States has prospered in times of broad government activism; the nation has faltered when it has failed to live up to its people.[32]

Arthur Schlesinger Jr. expressed a common belief in the basic goodness and efficiency of government, thwarting a basic tenet of Marxism (a subject of considerable discussion in that era) that the capitalist state would become a tool of "the possessing class." Schlesinger argued that in the United States the state initiated the redistribution of wealth and fostered economic stabilization. "What the democratic parties of the developed nations have done," Schlesinger concluded, "has been to use the state to force capitalism to do what both the classical capitalists and the classical Marxists declared was impossible: to control the business cycle and to reapportion income in favor of those whom [Andrew] Jackson called the 'humble members of society.'"[33]

It seemed that way for the next two decades. The "affirmative state," as Schlesinger called it, had indeed narrowed economic inequality, expanded civil rights, and maintained a prosperous economic order. The role of the state is to maintain a balance in public policy, not privileging one part of society over another. Good government strengthens each citizen and, with it, the nation. The gifted generation is the abiding proof of that maxim. The policies to regenerate the nation and the people are well-known. The accomplishments of government in the decades after World War II provide a blueprint. What is lacking is leadership to implement the policies to grow and energize the many—the commonwealth—rather than just the few, and the people to demand it.

ACKNOWLEDGMENTS

Writing, it's often remarked, is a solitary enterprise. Good writing, though, is always a collaborative effort. If I have succeeded in that, it is because of the helpful (and patient) people in archives and libraries, the craftsmanship of editors, and the encouragement, support, and forbearance of friends, colleagues, and family.

Amanda Binder at UNC-Charlotte is simply the best librarian I have ever worked with. She obtained the digitized Eisenhower Papers for me and led me to a number of other sources that were useful to my work. I lived a great deal through Interlibrary Loan, and Ann Davis, the director of that operation, provided expert and efficient service.

I also benefited from a supportive and congenial group of colleagues, led by my supportive department chair, Jürgen Buchenau. The university administration provided time off and financial support for my work, as well as constant encouragement. For these benefits, I would like to thank Nancy Gutierrez, the dean of the College of Liberal Arts & Sciences, and Provost Joan Lorden.

I also received a great deal of help and advice from archivists and librarians around the country. This was especially so at the LBJ Presidential Library in Austin, Texas. Archivist Allen Fisher offered consistently good advice and assistance during my various visits to the library. Allen saved me a great deal of time and effort by directing me to the appropriate collections.

When the LBJ Library closed at five P.M., I had two good friends in Austin to help me relax before my next all-day foray into the archives. Cara DeDominicis and Barbara Formichelli served as my hosts at the Texas Book Festival in 2011 and made certain in subsequent years that I would not get into too much trouble during my downtime in Austin.

Kathy Struss at the Eisenhower Presidential Library and Tammy Williams at the Truman Presidential Library also provided valuable services to me. I received responsive and knowledgeable advice and assistance from Lynn M. Duchez Bycko and Donna Stewart at the Cleveland State University Library, Terri Garst at the Los Angeles Public Library, Thomas Lisanti and David Rosado at the New York Public Library, Diana Carey at the Schlesinger Library of Harvard University, Ross Feldner of the Rachel Carson Council, and Patricia L. Adams at the National Association for the Advancement of Colored People. I would especially like to single out Kia Campbell of the Library of Congress for expediting my requests and providing good advice on how best to secure my materials. I have also relied on the work of a broad array of academics, journalists, and government officials whose contributions I've identified in the endnotes.

The team at Bloomsbury, headed by my editor, Anton Mueller, helped to shape and reshape the book. Anton was a particularly perceptive voice during the various iterations of the manuscript, and any faults therein result from my stubbornness, not from his suggestions. Anton's colleagues at the publisher, Grace McNamee, Sara Kitchen, Nicole Jarvis, and Sara Mercurio, also played significant roles in the book's development and publication. I also benefited from the copyediting skills of Steve Boldt. My literary agent, Geri Thoma, was always available for advice, admonition, and support. She is truly a collaborator on this effort and also a good friend.

I have been fortunate through the years to have a group of wonderful friends who are not afraid to tell me what they think of me or my work at any given time. They have kept me grounded, but have also elevated me. Although I attended the University of Maryland a while ago—my son tells me Lord Baltimore was governor at the time—my close friendship with Pete Daniel, Jimbo Lane, and Ray Smock has never wavered. My mentor at Maryland, George H. Callcott, drilled into me the idea that the key to writing good history is a good story, and that people, not theories, paradigms, or "hidden hands," drive the narrative. It is something I've never forgotten.

After I left Maryland, I had to the good fortune to meet three more lifelong friends, Betsy Jacoway, Peter Kolchin, and, most of all, Blaine Brownell. We have shared many meals, many family stories, a few heartaches, and much laughter over the years. I am eternally grateful for these friendships.

A special thanks to Bill Wertheim, who periodically gathered several alumni of Samuel J. Tilden High School's Class of 1961 for lunches and my always intrusive interviews. I could not fit all of their stories into this book, but they are all in my heart. Their lives provide the best evidence of how an activist government can build a prosperous and equitable nation.

Any historian is aware of the importance of context in framing events and individual lives. The most important context in my life is my family. They render my work easier to perform and more meaningful. I rely on the good judgment of my artistic wife, Marie-Louise, and the creativity and sense of humor of my daughter Eleanor, son Erik, and daughter-in-law Beth, and on the example of my aunt, Mary Gainor, approaching her ninety-ninth birthday and who published her first book of poetry two years ago. Eleanor, the family activist and television personality, provided invaluable insights on the contrasts between the country I inherited and the one she and Erik grew up in.

I hope this book will be a compelling brief for government activism on behalf of all Americans. In that spirit, I am dedicating this work to Abigail Sofia Goldfield, my first (and thus far, only) grandchild, born in June 2015. May she enjoy the benefits I had growing up in a nation brimming with confidence and possibility.

NOTES

INTRODUCTION: GOOD GOVERNMENT

1. Pew Research Center, "Trust in Government, 1958–2015," http://www.people-press.org/2015/11/23/1-trust-in-government-1958-2015/trust-1/.

2. *Time* magazine, on the other hand, dated the baby boom from 1942. The Census Bureau's own figures (as opposed to its formal definition) placed the origin of the boom in 1941 when the United States registered the highest birth rate in more than a decade. Thomas A. DiPrete, a Columbia University sociologist, offered the most sensible explanation for these differences: "I think the boundaries end up getting drawn to some extent by the media." "The Under-25 Generation," *Time*, January 6, 1967; David Brooks, "Time for a Realignment," *New York Times*, September 9, 2016; Robert D. Grove and Alice M. Hetzel, *Vital Statistics Rates in the United States, 1940–1960* (Washington, DC: Government Printing Office, 1968), 60–61; quote in Philip Bump, "Here Is When Each Generation Begins and Ends, According to Facts," http://www.theatlantic.com/national/archive/2014/03/here-is-when-each-generation-begins-and-ends-according-to-facts/359589/.

3. Grove and Hetzel, *Vital Statistics*, 60–61; "Our Boom in Babies," *Redbook*, August 1948, 78; William Fielding Ogburn, "Marriages, Births, and Divorces," *ANNALS of the American Academy of Political and Social Science* 229 (January 1943): 20–29; Ray E. Baber, "Marriage and Family After the War," *ANNALS of the American Academy of Political and Social Science* 229 (January 1943): 164–75.

4. Jan Van Bavel and David S. Reher, "The Baby Boom and Its Causes: What We Know and What We Need to Know," *Population and Development Review* 39 (June 2013): 257–88; Walter T. K. Nugent, e-mail to author, April 26, 2012. See also Nugent's *Structures of American Social History* (Bloomington, IN: Indiana University Press, 1981), 126–35, and *Into the West: The Story of Its People* (New York: Knopf, 1999), 231, 255, 269–74, 311–15.

5. Harold Rosenberg, *The Tradition of the New* (Cambridge, MA: Da Capo Press, 1994; first published in 1959), 244.

6. Richard Pérez-Peña, "I May Be 50, but Don't Call Me a Boomer," *New York Times*, January 12, 2014; quote in Michael Medved and David Wallechinsky, *What Really Happened to the Class of '65* (New York: Random House, 1976), 285.

7. John Maynard Keynes set out his economic theories most completely in *The General Theory of Employment and Money* (London: Palgrave Macmillan, 1936).

8. Arthur M. Schlesinger Jr., *The Vital Center: The Politics of Freedom* (Boston: Houghton Mifflin, 1962; first published in 1949), 183.

9. John Maynard Keynes, "Liberalism and Labour," in Keynes, *Essays in Persuasion* (London: Macmillan, 1931; essay originally published in 1926), 230, https://www.gutenberg.ca/ebooks/keynes-essaysinpersuasion/keynes-essaysinpersuasion-00-h.html#Footnote_33_33.

10. First quote in Keynes, *General Theory*, 159; second quote in "The End of Laissez-Faire," in Keynes, *Essays of Persuasion*, 186 (originally published in 1926); Lincoln quote in http://housedivided.dickinson.edu/sites/lincoln/fragment-on-government-july-1-1854/.

11. Paul Starr, "How Gilded Ages End," *American Prospect*, Spring 2015, http://prospect.org/article/how-gilded-ages-end.

12. Nicholas Lemann, "Notorious Big," *New Yorker*, March 28, 2016, 74.

13. On the mutually reinforcing nature of individual achievement and collective improvement, see Abraham H. Maslow, *Motivation and Personality*, 2nd ed. (New York: Harper & Row, 1970; first published in 1954), 68, 100, 165, 177.

14. I am borrowing the concept of the hierarchy of needs from the work of psychologist Abraham H. Maslow. He contended that when individuals' basic needs are met, they can focus on attaining more advanced accomplishments, not only for themselves, but also for society generally. See Maslow, *Motivation and Personality*, 31, 38, 157, 160, 171.

15. See Senator John F. Kennedy, "Speech," Eastern Parkway Avenue [*sic*], Brooklyn, NY, October 27, 1960, http://www.presidency.ucsb.edu/ws/index.php?pid=74241.

16. Sam Roberts, "When Tilden Was the World," *New York Times*, December 17, 2006.

17. "Under-25 Generation."

18. James Truslow Adams, *The Epic of America* (New York: Blue Ribbon Books, 1931), 404, 405.

19. George Packer, "The Great Leveling," *New York Times*, May 19, 2013.

20. Schlesinger, *Vital Center*.

21. Ibid., 171, 176.

22. Vice Admiral H. G. Rickover, "The Decline of the Individual," *Saturday Evening Post*, May 30, 1963, 13.

23. Franklin D. Roosevelt, "Annual Message to Congress," January 3, 1936, http://www.presidency.ucsb.edu/ws/?pid=15095.

24. Schlesinger, *Vital Center*, 183, 256.

25. John Quincy Adams, "First Annual Message," December 6, 1825, http://www.presidency.ucsb.edu/ws/?pid=29467.

26. Woodrow Wilson, "First Inaugural Address," March 4, 1913, http://www.bartleby.com/124/pres44.html.

27. Interview with Arnold Fleischer, June 27, 2012.

28. Interview with Lewis Coopersmith, June 27, 2012; interview with Jane Goren, September 12, 2012.

29. Interview with Edwin Goodgold, June 26, 2012; interview with Anthony Scarfone, December 16, 2015.

30. James Stocker, Securities and Exchange Commission Historical Society, interview with Jill Considine, August 1, 2011, http://3197d6d14b5f19f2f440-5e13d29c4c016cf96cbbfd197c579b45.r81.cf1.rackcdn.com/collection/oral-histories/20110801_Considine_Jill_T.pdf.

31. Interview with Jerry Rosenbaum, October 2, 2013.

32. Interview with Henrietta Margolis Nunno, September 27, 2012.

CHAPTER 1: MOVING

1. First quote in David M. Oshinsky, *Polio: An American Story* (New York: Oxford University Press, 2005), 81; second quote in James T. Patterson, *Grand Expectations: The United States, 1945–1974* (New York: Oxford University Press, 1996), 5.

2. "What's the Score?," *Life*, September 9, 1946, 36.

3. Baber, "Marriage and the Family after the War," 174.

4. Bernard DeVoto, "The Easy Chair," *Harper's*, December 1944, 33.

5. "How U.S. Cities Can Prepare for Atomic War," *Life*, December 18, 1950, 77–82, 85–86.

6. "Shall We Have a Depression?," *Life*, October 7, 1946, 32.

7. First quote in "Christmas Rush," *Life*, December 23, 1946, 33–34; W. S. Woytinsky's analysis in "Prosperity?," *Life*, December 29, 1947, 28–29; second quote in "American Production," *Life*, October 4, 1948, 71.

8. First quote in "Homecoming Tourists Break Travel Record," *Life*, September 26, 1949, 38; second quote in "The Boom Goes On," *Life*, April 24, 1950, 38. See also Maslow, *Motivation and Personality*, 100; U.S. Department of Commerce, "Current Population Reports: Consumer Income," January 15, 1960, https://www2.census.gov/prod2/popscan/p60-033.pdf. As the government helped to satisfy the basic needs of its citizens in postwar America, civic consciousness flourished. Again, individual fulfillment led to collective achievement.

9. "What Have We Got Here?," *Life*, 46–50, 92; quote on 48; see Maslow, *Motivation and Personality*, 100.

10. Patterson, *Grand Expectations*, 64.

11. "Where Do We Go From Here?," *Life*, January 5, 1953, 86–92.

12. "The New South," *Life*, October 31, 1949, 79–80. See also David Goldfield, *Cotton Fields and Skyscrapers: Southern City and Region* (Baton Rouge: Louisiana State University Press, 1982), 182–83.

13. "The Northwest," *Life*, October 13, 1947, 121–36.

14. Arthur F. Burns, "Looking Forward," National Bureau of Economic Research, 1951, http://www.nber.org/chapters/c4147.pdf.

15. Peter F. Drucker, "Look What's Happened to Us!," *Saturday Evening Post*, January 19, 1952, 30, 83–86; quote on 83.

16. Ibid., 86.

17. Paul Krugman, "The Twinkie Manifesto," *New York Times*, November 19, 2012.

18. Both quotes in Hedrick Smith, "When Capitalists Cared," *New York Times*, September 2, 2012.

19. Ibid.

20. Jefferson Cowie, *The Great Exception: The New Deal & the Limits of American Politics* (Princeton, NJ: Princeton University Press, 2016), 156.

21. James Surowiecki, "Moaning Moguls," *New Yorker*, July 7, 2014, 36.

22. "How Top Executives Live (*Fortune*, 1955)," *Fortune*, May 6, 2012, http://fortune.com /2012/05/06/how-top-executives-live-fortune-1955/

23. Smith, "When Capitalists Cared."

24. Quote in David Halberstam, *The Fifties* (New York: Villard Books, 1993), 496.

25. Landon Y. Jones, *Great Expectations: America and the Baby Boom Generation* (New York: Coward, McCann & Geoghegan, 1980), 37–39; quote on 37.

26. Patterson, *Grand Expectations*, 70–71.

27. Ibid., 62–63.

28. Ferkauf's story appears in Halberstam, *Fifties*, chap. 10, and in Douglas Martin, "Eugene Ferkauf, 91, Dies; Restyled Retail," *New York Times*, June 6, 2012.

29. Quote in Halberstam, *Fifties*, 69.

30. Martin, "Eugene Ferkauf."

31. The McDonalds' story appears in Halberstam, *Fifties*, chap. 11.

32. Ibid., 73.

33. See John Kenneth Galbraith, *American Capitalism: The Concept of Countervailing Power* (New York: Routledge, 1993; first published in 1952).

34. John Kenneth Galbraith, *The Affluent Society* (Boston: Houghton Mifflin Company, 1984; first published in 1956), 264.

35. Ibid.

36. Interview with Rosenbaum.

37. Interview with Nunno.

CHAPTER 2: PIONEERS

1. Theodore Draper, "There Are No G.I.'s Any More," *Saturday Evening Post*, January 31, 1948, 26–27, 84, 86.

2. Ibid.

3. Quoted in Susan Mettler, *Soldiers to Citizens: The G.I. Bill and the Making of the Greatest Generation* (New York: Oxford University Press, 2005), 7.

4. Ibid., 106.

5. J. W. Hotchkiss, "How Some G.I.'s Are 'Reconverting,'" *Redbook*, November 1946, 62–63, 142.

6. Peter F. Drucker, "The New Society of Organizations," *Harvard Business Review*, September–October 1992, https://hbr.org/1992/09/the-new-society-of-organizations.

7. Mettler, *Soldiers to Citizens*, 16–22.

8. Quote, ibid., 22.

9. Quoted in Glenn C. Altschuler and Stuart M. Blumin, *The G.I. Bill: A New Deal for Veterans* (New York: Oxford University Press, 2009), 76.

10. Mettler, *Soldiers to Citizens*, 67.

11. Ibid., 70.

12. Quotes, ibid., 50, 54.

13. Altschuler and Blumin, *G.I. Bill*, 108.

14. Mettler, *Soldiers to Citizens*, 105.

15. Ibid., 7; quote on 8.

16. Ibid., 96.

17. "The Cost Squeeze Is On in the Colleges," *Saturday Evening Post*, May 17, 1947, 196.

18. Ibid.

19. "Revolution on the Campus," *Life*, February 2, 1948, 24.

20. Ibid.

21. Ibid.

22. Paul Engle, "In Defense of the State University," *Saturday Evening Post*, February 13, 1960, 22–23, 64, 66; quote on 64.

23. Quoted in Altschuler and Blumin, *G.I. Bill*, 106.

24. Quoted in Mettler, *Soldiers to Citizens*, 64.

25. Quoted in Altschuler and Blumin, *G.I. Bill*, 112. See also "Revolution on the Campus," 24.

26. First quote, U.S. Department of Labor, *Construction during Five Decades: Historical Statistics, 1907–1952* (Washington, DC: Government Printing Office, 1954), iv; Halberstam, *Fifties*, 134; final quote in Adam Rome, *The Bulldozer in the Countryside: Suburban Sprawl and the Rise of American Environmentalism* (Cambridge, UK: Cambridge University Press, 2001), 18.

27. Rome, *Bulldozer*, 23–28.

28. Both quotes, ibid., 32, 35.

29. Quote in "U.S. Tackles Its Housing Shortage," *Life*, April 15, 1946, 29.

30. "The U.S. in 1946," *Life*, November 25, 1946, 36.

31. "National Housing Emergency, 1946–1947," *CQ Researcher*, http://library.cqpress.com/cqresearcher/document.php?id=cqresrre1946121700.

32. "How Do We Get Housed?," *Life*, June 9, 1947, 36.

33. The following sources were most useful in detailing the life and career of William J. Levitt: "Nation's Biggest Housebuilder," *Life*, August 23, 1948, 75–77; Eric Pace, "William

J. Levitt, 86, Pioneer of Suburbs, Dies," *New York Times*, January 29, 1994; Altschuler and Blumin, *G.I. Bill*, 192; Susan Kirsch Duncan, *Levittown: The Way We Were* (Huntington, NY: Maple Hill Press, 1999); Halberstam, *Fifties*, 131–42; Jones, *Great Expectations*, 39; Patterson, *Grand Expectations*, 72; Rome, *Bulldozer*, 16–17.

34. Rome, *Bulldozer*, 35.

35. "Up from the Potato Fields," *Time*, July 3, 1950, 72.

36. Altschuler and Blumin, *G.I. Bill*, 184.

37. First quote in "Levitt," *New York Times*, January 29, 1994; second quote in Edward Humes, *Over Here: How the G.I. Bill Transformed the American Dream* (New York: Harcourt, 2006), 25.

38. Herbert J. Gans, *The Levittowners: Ways of Life and Politics in a New Suburban Community* (New York: Columbia University Press, 1967), 45.

39. Daniel Horowitz, *Betty Friedan and the Making of* The Feminine Mystique: *The American Left, the Cold War, and Modern Feminism* (Amherst: University of Massachusetts Press, 1998), 166.

40. Bernadette Hanlon, *Once the American Dream: Inner-Ring Suburbs of the Metropolitan United States* (Philadelphia: Temple University Press, 2010), 56.

41. Arnold Nicholson, "Are You Outgrowing Your House?," *Saturday Evening Post*, January 10, 1959, 26–27, 54–56.

42. Barbara M. Kelly, *Expanding the American Dream: Building and Rebuilding Levittown* (Albany: SUNY Press, 1993), 226.

43. David Riesman, *The Lonely Crowd* (New Haven, CT: Yale University Press, 2001; first published in 1950).

44. William H. Whyte, *The Organization Man* (New York: Simon & Schuster, 1956); Richard E. Gordon, Katherine K. Gordon, and Max Gunther, *The Split-Level Trap* (New York: B. Geis Associates, 1961); John Keats, *The Crack in the Picture Window* (Boston: Houghton Mifflin, 1956).

45. See Eric Avila and Mark H. Rose, "Race, Culture, Politics, and Urban Renewal: An Introduction," *Journal of Urban History* 35 (March 2009): 335–47.

46. Duncan, *Levittown*, 8, 12.

47. Peter Wyden, "Suburbia's Coddled Kids," *Saturday Evening Post*, October 8, 1960, 44.

CHAPTER 3: THE PLOWBOY

1. Truman biographies are numerous, but I found the following particularly helpful in creating the biographical narrative that informs this chapter: Aida D. Donald, *Citizen Soldier: A Life of Harry S. Truman* (New York: Basic Books, 2012); Robert H. Ferrell, *Harry S. Truman: A Life* (Columbia: University of Missouri Press, 1994); Michael R. Gardner, *Harry Truman and Civil Rights: Moral Courage and Political Risks* (Carbondale: Southern Illinois University Press, 2002); Alonzo L. Hamby, *Man of the People: A Life of Harry S. Truman* (New York: Oxford University Press, 1995); and David McCullough, *Truman* (New York: Simon & Schuster, 1992).

2. James R. Fuchs, "Oral History Interview with Jonathan Daniels," October 4, 1963, Harry S. Truman Presidential Library and Museum, https://www.trumanlibrary.org/oralhist/danielsj.htm.

3. McCullough, *Truman*, 86.

4. Quote, ibid., 116.

5. Donald, *Citizen Soldier*, 80.

6. Ibid., 74.

7. McCullough, *Truman*, 162.

8. Harry S. Truman to Bess W. Truman, May 11, 1933, Harry S. Truman Library and Museum, http://www.trumanlibrary.org/whistlestop/study_collections/trumanpapers/fbpa/index.php?documentid=HST-FBP_8-03_01&documentVersion=both.

9. Quoted in Donald, *Citizen Soldier*, 78.

10. Quoted in McCullough, *Truman*, 253.

11. Quotes from Donald, *Citizen Soldier*, 93. See also Robert H. Ferrell, *Truman & Pendergast* (Columbia: University of Missouri Press, 1999).

12. Truman to Bess W. Truman, December 12, 1937, in *Dear Bess: The Letters from Harry to Bess Truman, 1910–1959*, ed. Robert H. Ferrell (Columbia: University of Missouri Press, 1983), 409.

13. McCullough, *Truman*, 275.

14. Donald, *Citizen Soldier*, 107.

15. McCullough, *Truman*, 247.

16. Ibid., 332.

17. Quote, ibid., 335.

18. First quote in *Pittsburgh Courier*, July 29, 1944; second and third quotes in Raymond H. Geselbracht, *The Civil Rights Legacy of Harry S. Truman*, vol. 2 (Kirksville, MO: Truman State University Press, 2007), 190.

19. Both quotes in McCullough, *Truman*, 330.

20. Donald, *Citizen Soldier*, 126.

21. Hugh E. Evans, *The Hidden Campaign: FDR's Health and the 1944 Election* (Armonk, NY: M. E. Sharpe, 2002), 101.

22. Quotes in McCullough, *Truman*, 350.

23. Quotes, ibid.

24. Ibid., 353.

25. Quote in Gary A. Donaldson, *Truman Defeats Dewey* (Lexington: University Press of Kentucky, 1999). See also, Alden Whitman, "Harry Truman: Decisive President," *New York Times*, December 27, 1972.

26. First quote in William F. Felice, *Taking Suffering Seriously: The Importance of Collective Human Rights* (Albany: SUNY Press, 1996), 7; second quote in Harry S. Truman, "Address at the Jefferson-Jackson Day Dinner," February 19, 1948, Harry S. Truman Library and Museum, http://trumanlibrary.org/publicpapers/viewpapers.php?pid=1396.

27. All quotes in William E. Leuchtenburg, *The White House Looks South: Franklin D. Roosevelt, Harry S. Truman, Lyndon B. Johnson* (Baton Rouge: Louisiana State University Press, 2005), 162.

28. Ibid.

29. Quote, ibid., 163.

30. See, for example, Thomas J. Sugrue, *The Origins of the Urban Crisis: Race and Inequality in Postwar Detroit* (Princeton, NJ: Princeton University Press, 1996).

31. Harry S. Truman, "Letter to the Chairman, House Rules Committee, Concerning the Committee on Fair Employment Practice," June 5, 1945, http://www.presidency.ucsb.edu/ws/?pid=12214.

32. Quoted in Leuchtenburg, *White House Looks South*, 164.

33. Cabinet meeting, May 18, 1945, in Robert H. Ferrell, ed., *Off the Record: The Private Papers of Harry S. Truman* (Columbia: University of Missouri Press, 1980), 29.

34. Andrew E. Busch, *Horses in Midstream: U.S. Midterm Elections and Their Consequences, 1894–1998* (Pittsburgh: University of Pittsburgh Press, 1999), 124.

35. First quote in Patterson, *Grand Expectations*, 142; second and third quotes in William E. Leuchtenburg, *In the Shadow of FDR: From Harry Truman to Barack Obama* (Ithaca, NY: Cornell University Press, 2009), 8.

36. "Record of the 80th Congress," http://library.cqpress.com/cqresearcher/document .php?id=cqresrre1948080700.

37. First quote in Patterson, *Grand Expectations*, 145; second quote, "How Able a Man Is Truman?," *Saturday Evening Post*, February 2, 1946, 100.

38. First quote in Ferrell, *Dear Bess*, 540; second quote in Donald, *Citizen Soldier*, 173.

39. All quotes in Patterson, *Grand Expectations*, 145.

40. First quote in "The G.O.P. Trend," *Life*, November 4, 1946, 45; second quote in Robert A. Caro, *The Years of Lyndon Johnson: Master of the Senate* (New York: Random House, 2002), 100; third quote in Leuchtenburg, *Shadow of FDR*, 23.

41. Patterson, *Grand Expectations*, 28.

42. Quote, ibid., 156. See also, "Truman Wrote of '48 Offer to Eisenhower," *New York Times*, July 11, 2003.

43. Jerry N. Hess, "Oral History Interview with James H. Rowe," September 30, 1969, and January 15, 1970, https://www.trumanlibrary.org/oralhist/rowejhap.htm.

44. Ibid.

45. Harry S. Truman, *1946–52: Years of Trial and Hope. Memoirs*, vol. 2 (New York: Smithmark Publishers, 1996); first published in 1955), 172.

46. For a good overview of labor policy, including Taft-Hartley, see Harry A. Mills and Emily Clark Brown, *From the Wagner Act to Taft-Hartley: A Study of National Labor Policy and Labor Relations* (Chicago: University of Chicago Press, 1950).

47. Harry S. Truman, "Radio Address to the American People on the Veto of the Taft-Hartley Bill," June 20, 1947, *Public Papers of the Presidents of the United States* (Washington, DC: Government Printing Office, 1963), 299.

48. Ibid., 301.

49. For a good discussion of Truman's health-care policy and the opposition to it, see Sean J. Savage, *Truman and the Democratic Party* (Lexington: University Press of Kentucky, 1997), 154–57. See also a hostile editorial, "Health by Compulsion," *Life*, May 2, 1949, 40; James L. Sundquist, *Politics and Policy: The Eisenhower, Kennedy, and Johnson Years* (Washington, DC: Brookings Institution, 1968), 290.

50. First quote in Atul Gawande, "State of Health," *New Yorker*, October 7, 2013, 25; second quote, Harry S. Truman to Dr. Sam E. Roberts, September 8, 1949, Ferrell, *Off the Record*, 166.

51. Truman, "Rear Platform and Other Informal Remarks in Texas," September 27, 1948, *Public Papers of the Presidents of the United States: Harry S. Truman, Volume 4, 1948*, 581.

CHAPTER 4: TO SECURE THESE RIGHTS

1. For a good summary of the Woodard episode, see "Southern Schrecklichkeit," *Crisis*, September 1946, 276; Leuchtenburg, *White House Looks South*, 165–66; Andrew Myers, "The Blinding of Isaac Woodard," *Proceedings of the South Carolina Historical Association*, 2004, 63–73.

2. Robert A. Caro has a good summary of this incident in *Master of the Senate*, 194–95. See also "Southern Schrecklichkeit," 277; Greg Bluestein, "FBI Investigated Ga. Gov in Old Lynching," *Washington Post*, National News Wires, June 15, 2007, http://www.washingtonpost .com/wp-dyn/content/article/2007/06/15/AR2007061501356.html.

3. Leuchtenburg, *White House Looks South*, 169.

4. Ibid., 166.

5. Quote, ibid., 165.

6. Ibid., 167.

7. The Rowe/Webb Memo, September 18, 1947, http://www.ksg.harvard.edu/case/3pt/rowe .html.

8. Ibid.

9. Leuchtenburg, *White House Looks South*, 75–78.

10. Michael R. Gardner, "A President Who Regarded Civil Rights as a Moral Imperative," in Geselbracht, ed., *Civil Rights Legacy of Truman*, 2:21.

11. Leuchtenburg, *White House Looks South*, 171.

12. Ibid., 171–72.

13. "President Truman's Orders," *Crisis*, September 1948, in *60ᵗʰAnniversary Issue*, November 1970, 221.

14. "A Program of Action: The Committee's Recommendations," chap. 4, in *To Secure These Rights: The Report of the President's Committee on Civil Rights*, http://www.trumanli brary.org/civilrights/srights4.htm.

15. Both quotes in Leuchtenburg, *White House Looks South*, 173.

16. All quotes, ibid., 177.

17. Harry S. Truman to Ernest W. Roberts, August 18, 1948, in *Dear Harry . . . Truman's Mailroom, 1945–1953: The Truman Administration Through Correspondence with "Everyday Americans,"* ed. D. M. Giangreco and Kathryn Moore (Mechanicsburg, PA: Stackpole Books, 1999), 60–61.

18. For a good discussion of Southern power in the U.S. Senate in 1949, see Caro, *Master of the Senate*, chap. 3.

19. First quote, "Special Message to the Congress on Civil Rights," February 2, 1948, *Public Papers of the Presidents*, 4:121; second quote, Leuchtenburg, *White House Looks South*, 178.

20. First quote, Jason Morgan Ward, *Defending White Democracy: The Making of a Segregationist Movement & the Remaking of Racial Politics, 1936–1965* (Chapel Hill: University of North Carolina Press, 2011), 100; second quote, Kari Frederickson, *The Dixiecrat Revolt and the End of the Solid South, 1932–1968* (Chapel Hill: University of North Carolina Press, 2001), 77.

21. Leuchtenburg, *White House Looks South*, 191.

22. John C. Culver and John Hyde, *American Dreamer: The Life and Times of Henry A. Wallace* (New York: W. W. Norton, 2000), 456.

23. For two solid accounts of the 1948 presidential election campaign, see Zachary Karabell, *The Last Campaign: How Harry Truman Won the 1948 Election* (New York: Vintage, 2007); and David Pietrusza, *1948: Harry Truman's Improbable Victory and the Year That Transformed America* (New York: Union Square Press, 2011). Quote in Patterson, *Grand Expectations*, 155.

24. Quote in Caro, *Master of the Senate*, 454.

25. "Senator Hubert H. Humphrey's 1948 Speech on Civil Rights," Minnesota Historical Society, http://www.mnhs.org/library/tips/history_topics/42humphreyspeech/transcript.php.

26. Schlesinger quote in Schlesinger, *Vital Center*, 190; on the national reaction, see Sam Tanenhaus, "The Power of Congress," *New Yorker*, January 19, 2015, 71.

27. Quote in Charles Lloyd Garrettson III, *Hubert H. Humphrey: The Politics of Joy* (New Brunswick, NJ: Transaction Publishers, 1993), 94.

28. Quote in Leuchtenburg, *White House Looks South*, 195.

29. Quote in "The Line Squall," *Time*, July 26, 1948, 14.

30. Quote in Philip White, "The Secret Weapon That Helped Win the White House in 1948 & Establish the Political 'War Room,'" *Huffington Post*, October 27, 2014, http://www.huffington post.co.uk/philip-white/cold-war_b_6048336.html.

31. Quote in McCullough, *Truman*, 642, 703.

32. All quotes in Patterson, *Grand Expectations*, 160.

33. "Whistlestop Tour in Chariton, Iowa," September 18, 1948, Harry S. Truman Library and Museum, http://www.trumanlibrary.org/publicpapers/index.php?pid=1812&st=&st1=.

34. Karabell, *Last Campaign*, and Pietrusza, *1948*, offer a detailed account of the 1948 presidential campaign and election.

35. McCullough, *Truman*, 724.

36. Samuel Lubell, "Who Really Elected Truman?," *Saturday Evening Post,* January 22, 1949, 15–17, 54, 56, 58, 61, 64.

37. Senator J. Howard McGrath, "The Case for President Truman," *Saturday Evening Post,* October 2, 1948, 20–21, 77, 79–80, 82.

38. Quote in Halberstam, *Fifties,* 6.

39. Quotes, Patterson, *Grand Expectations,* 159.

40. "Rear Platform and Other Informal Remarks in Texas," September 27, 1948, *Public Papers of the Presidents. Harry S. Truman, 1945-1953,* Harry S. Truman Library and Museum, http://www.trumanlibrary.org/publicpapers/index.php?pid=1962. See also Gardner, *Truman and Civil Rights,* 129.

41. *Newsweek,* October 25, 1948, 32.

42. Henry Cabot Lodge Jr., "Does the Republican Party Have a Future?," *Saturday Evening Post,* January 29, 1949, 23, 81–82.

43. Lubell, "Who Really Elected Truman?," 61

44. Bernard DeVoto, "The Next Ten Years," *Redbook,* July 1949, 36–37, 83–86; quote on 83.

45. Quote in Leuchtenburg, *White House Looks South,* 214.

46. See Gardner, *Truman and Civil Rights*; and Robert Shogan, *Harry Truman and the Struggle for Racial Justice* (Princeton, NJ: Princeton University Press, 2013).

47. "Executive Order 9981," https://www.trumanlibrary.org/9981a.htm.

48. https://www.law.cornell.edu/supremecourt/text/339/637. See also David Goldfield, *Black, White, and Southern: Race Relations and Southern Culture, 1940 to the Present* (Baton Rouge: Louisiana State University Press, 1990), 58–59; Shogan, *Racial Justice,* 170–76.

49. Richard Kluger, *Simple Justice: The History of* Brown v. Board of Education *and Black America's Struggle for Equality* (New York: Vintage, 2004), 259.

50. Gunnar Myrdal, *An American Dilemma: The Negro Problem and Modern Democracy* (New York: Harper & Brothers, 1944).

51. Quote in Juan Williams, *Thurgood Marshall: American Revolutionary* (New York: Crown, 1998), 183.

52. https://www.law.cornell.edu/supremecourt/text/339/629; quote in Williams, *Thurgood Marshall,* 185.

53. For Briggs's life and the background of his case, see Ophelia De Laine Gona, *Dawn of Desegregation: J. A. De Laine and* Briggs v. Elliott (Columbia, SC: University of South Carolina Press, 2011).

54. Quote in John Egerton, *Speak Now Against the Day: The Generation Before the Civil Rights Movement in the South* (Chapel Hill, NC: University of North Carolina Press, 1995), 590.

55. https://scholar.google.com/scholar_case?case=17196258935977715010&hl=en&as_sdt =6&as_vis=1&oi=scholar.

56. Ibid. See also Tinsley E. Yarbrough, *A Passion for Justice: J. Waties Waring and Civil Rights* (New York: Oxford University Press, 1987).

57. Quote in Leuchtenburg, *White House Looks South,* 221.

58. *Life,* May 8, 1950; quote in Caro, *Master of the Senate,* 695.

59. Quote in George Streator, "Truman Defended by Negro Students," *New York Times,* April 24, 1949.

CHAPTER 5: SOUTH BY NORTH

1. First quote in Joe W. Trotter and Jared N. Day, *Race and Renaissance: African Americans in Pittsburgh since World War II* (Pittsburgh: University of Pittsburgh Press, 2010), 46; second quote in Isabel Wilkerson, *The Warmth of Other Suns: The Epic Story of America's Great Migration* (New York: Random House, 2010), 63.

2. See Leah P. Boustan and Robert A. Margo, "A Silver Lining to White Flight? White Suburbanization and African-American Homeownership, 1940–1980," *Journal of Urban Economics* 78 (2013): 71–80.

3. Robert Halpern, *Rebuilding the Inner City: A History of Neighborhood Initiatives to Address Poverty in the United States* (New York: Columbia University Press, 1995), 61.

4. Quote in Stacey Close, "Fire in the Bones: Hartford's NAACP, Civil Rights and Militancy, 1943–1949," *Journal of Negro History* 86 (Summer 2001): 228–63.

5. Matthew J. Countryman, "Why Philadelphia?," http://northerncity.library.temple.edu /content/historical-perspective/why-philadelphia.

6. Jacqueline Jones, *Labor of Love, Labor of Sorrow: Black Women, Work, and the Family from Slavery to the Present* (New York: Basic Books, 2010; first published in 1985), 210.

7. Ibid., 156.

8. Andrew Wiese, *Places of Their Own: African American Suburbanization in the Twentieth Century* (Chicago: University of Chicago Press, 2004), offers a thorough discussion of discrimination in new housing in chapter 4, "Forbidden Neighbors: White Racism and Black Suburbanites, 1940–1950."

9. Ta-Nehisi Coates, "The Case for Reparations," *Atlantic*, June 2014, 54–59.

10. https://supreme.justia.com/cases/federal/us/334/1/case.html.

11. Williams, *Thurgood Marshall*, 149–51; quote on 151.

12. Mettler, *Soldiers to Citizens*, 100–103.

13. "Statement by the President Upon Signing the Housing Act of 1949," July 15, 1949, http://www.presidency.ucsb.edu/ws/?pid=13246; Samuel Zipp, "The Roots and Routes of Urban Renewal," *Journal of Urban History* 39 (May 2013): 366–91.

14. Quote in "What Kind of America?," *Life*, July 25, 1949, 18.

15. Alonzo L. Hamby, *Liberalism and Its Challengers: FDR to Reagan* (New York: Oxford University Press, 1985), 65–66; Norman Krumholz, "The Reluctant Hand: Privatization of Public Housing in the U.S.," City Futures Conference, Chicago, July 8–10, 2004; Don Parson, "The Decline of Public Housing and the Politics of the Red Scare: The Significance of the Los Angeles Public Housing War," *Journal of Urban History* 33 (March 2007): 400–417.

16. Janet L. Abu-Lughod, *New York, Chicago, Los Angeles: America's Global Cities* (Minneapolis: University of Minnesota Press, 1999), 222; Dominic J. Capeci and Martha Frances Wilkerson, *Layered Violence: The Detroit Rioters of 1943* (Jackson, MS: University of Mississippi Press, 1991).

17. Quote in Arnold R. Hirsch, *Making the Second Ghetto: Race & Housing in Chicago, 1940–1960* (Chicago: University of Chicago Press, 1998; first published in 1983), 40; second quote in Patterson, *Grand Expectations*, 28.

18. Both quotes in Sugrue, *Origins of the Urban Crisis*, 215.

19. Quotes, ibid.

20. Ibid., 211.

21. Ibid., 233.

22. Ibid., 84.

23. Thomas J. Sugrue, "Crabgrass-Roots Politics: Race, Rights, and the Reaction against Liberalism in the Urban North, 1940–1964," *Journal of American History* 82 (September 1995): 551–78.

24. "Night Watch," *Life*, November 9, 1953, 57, 59–60. See also Arnold R. Hirsch, "Massive Resistance in the Urban North: Trumbull Park, Chicago, 1953–1966," *Journal of American History* 82 (September 1995): 522–50.

25. Quote in Martha Biondi, *To Stand and Fight: The Struggle for Civil Rights in Postwar New York City* (Cambridge, MA: Harvard University Press, 2003), 123. The following discussion of Lee Lorch's extraordinary life relies mostly on two articles in the *New York Times*:

Charles V. Bagli, "A New Light on a Fight to Integrate Stuyvesant Town," November 21, 2010; and David Margolick, "Lee Lorch, Desegregation Activist Who Led Stuyvesant Town Effort, Dies at 98," March 1, 2014.

26. Quote in Bagli, "New Light on a Fight."

27. Quote in "Integration Troubles Beset Northern Town," *Life*, September 2, 1957, 43.

28. Altschuler and Blumin, *G.I. Bill*, 118, 198; quote on 118.

29. Quote in Catherine M. Lewis and J. Richard Lewis, eds., *Jim Crow America: A Documentary History* (Fayetteville, AR: University of Arkansas Press, 2009), 193; Bruce Lambert, "At 50, Levittown Contends with Its Legacy of Bias," *New York Times*, December 28, 1997; Andrew Wiese, "Suburbia: Middle Class to the Last?," *Journal of Urban History* 23 (September 1997): 757.

30. Quote in Coates, "Case for Reparations," 65.

31. "Juvenile Delinquency: War's Insecurity Lifts Youthful Crime 100%," *Life*, April 8, 1946, 85.

32. Quote in Carl T. Rowan, "The Negro in the North," *Saturday Evening Post*, October 19, 1957, 88.

33. See Hirsch, *Making the Second Ghetto*. See also Beryl Satter, *Family Properties: Race, Real Estate, and the Exploitation of Black Urban America* (New York: Henry Holt and Company, 2009).

34. Quote in Altschuler and Blumin, *G.I. Bill*, 134; Hilary Herbold, "Never a Level Playing Field: Blacks and the GI Bill," *Journal of Blacks in Higher Education* 6 (Winter 1994): 104–8.

35. Ira Katznelson, *When Affirmative Action Was White: An Untold History of Racial Inequality in Twentieth-Century America* (New York: W. W. Norton, 2005).

36. Biondi, *To Stand and Fight*, 79; Joe W. Trotter, "African American Urban Life since the Atlantic Slave Trade," unpublished ms. in author's possession, 320.

37. First quote in Biondi, *To Stand and Fight*, 72; second quote in Quintard Taylor, *The Forging of a Black Community: Seattle's Central District from 1870 through the Civil Rights Era* (Seattle: University of Washington Press, 1994), 178.

38. Quote in Biondi, *To Stand and Fight*, 36.

39. Quotes in "The Negro and the North," *Life*, March 11, 1957, 151.

CHAPTER 6: THE SCARLET LETTER

1. Abraham H. Maslow wrote, "It is possible for a woman to have all the specifically female fulfillments (being loved, having the home, having the baby) and *then*, without giving up any of the satisfactions already achieved, go on beyond femaleness to the full humanness that she shared with males, for example, the full development of her intelligence, of any talents that she may have . . . of her own individual fulfillment." *Motivation and Personality*, xvii.

2. Gwyned Filling's story appeared in "The Private Life of Gwyned Filling," *Life*, May 3, 1948, 103–14.

3. For Gwyned Filling's post-1948 life, see Jacqueline Fitzgerald, "A Career and a Life," *Chicago Tribune*, May 7, 2003, http://articles.chicagotribune.com/2003-05-07/features/030 5070029_1_apartment-building-essay-moment; "Gwyned Filling Straus," *Newport Daily News*, July 31, 2005, http://www.newportdailynews.com/ee/newportdailynews/?pageToLoad=show Obits.php&obit_date=200507&obit_file=0940-straus.txt.

4. Quote in "Private Life," 114.

5. Mae N. Junod and W. B. Waldkirch, letters to the editor, *Life*, May 24, 1948, 14.

6. Patterson, *Grand Expectations*, 32.

7. Stephanie Coontz, *A Strange Stirring: The Feminine Mystique and American Women at the Dawn of the 1960s* (New York: Basic Books, 2011), 47.

8. First quote in Baber, "Marriage and Family After the War," 168; second quote on 169.

9. First quote, ibid., 170; second and third quotes, 172.

10. Coontz, *Strange Stirring*, 50.

11. Quote in Betty Friedan, "In France, de Beauvoir Had Just Published 'The Second Sex,'" *New York*, December 30, 1974/January 6, 1975, 52.

12. First quote in Stephanie Coontz, *The Way We Never Were: American Families and the Nostalgia Trap* (New York: Basic Books, 1992), 32; second and third quotes in Patterson, *Grand Expectations*, 36.

13. First and fourth quotes in Friedan, *Feminine Mystique*, 188, 195; second and third quotes in Coontz, *Strange Stirring*, 49.

14. Coontz, *Strange Stirring*, 67.

15. Altschuler and Blumin, *G.I. Bill*, 119, 120; Jerome Karabel, *The Chosen: The Hidden History of Admission and Exclusion at Harvard, Yale, and Princeton* (Boston: Houghton Mifflin Harcourt, 2005), 410.

16. Karabel, *Chosen*, 412.

17. Henry F. Pringle and Katharine Pringle, "What About Federal Aid for Schools?," *Saturday Evening Post*, April 16, 1949, 32–33, 149–51; quote on 32.

18. Halberstam, *Fifties*, 272–81; quote on 272.

19. Ernest Havemann, "The Kinsey Report on Women," *Life*, August 24, 1953, 41–42, 45–46, 48, 54, 56, 59–60, 62; quote on 60.

20. First and second quotes in Halberstam, *Fifties*, 280; last quote in James H. Jones, *Alfred C. Kinsey: A Life* (New York: W. W. Norton, 2004), 723.

21. Quote in Patterson, *Grand Expectations*, 357.

22. Frances Levison, "American Woman's Dilemma," *Life*, June 16, 1947; "The American Woman: Her Achievements and Troubles," *Life*, special issue, December 24, 1956; quote on 109.

23. "American Woman: Her Achievements," 361; Coontz, *Strange Stirring*, 51.

24. Coontz, *Strange Stirring*, 51.

25. Rufus Jarman, "It's Tougher Than Ever to Get a Husband," *Saturday Evening Post*, February 23, 1952, 30, 152–54; quotes on 151, 152.

26. Quote in Jones, *Great Expectations*, 22.

27. Ibid., 35.

28. Karabel, *Chosen*, 410.

29. Quote in Horowitz, *Making* Feminine Mystique, 124.

30. Quotes in Friedan, *Feminine Mystique*, 84, 85.

31. Quotes in Robert Coughlan, "How to Survive Parenthood," *Life*, June 26, 1950, 123, 126.

32. Maxine Margolis, *Mothers and Such: Views of American Women and Why They Changed* (Berkeley, CA: University of California Press, 1984), 52.

33. Jones, *Great Expectations*, 49.

34. Quotes in Bertram Vogel, "A Divorce Every Minute!," *Redbook*, January 1947, 34–37, 108.

35. Quote, ibid., 37.

36. "Working Wives," *Life*, January 5, 1953, 74–76; quote on 74.

37. Quote in Michael Harrington, *The Other America: Poverty in the United States* (New York: Simon and Schuster, 2012; first published in 1962), 179.

38. Coontz, *Strange Stirring*, 59.

39. Ibid.

40. Ibid.

41. Ibid., 120.

42. Elise Morrow and Sylvia Brooks, "The Lady Who Told Off the President," *Saturday Evening Post*, July 7, 1951, 28, 108–10.

43. Quote, ibid., 108.

44. Ibid.

45. Bess Furman, "Equal Rights Fails to Get Two-Thirds in Vote in Senate," *New York Times*, July 20, 1946.

46. Hila Colman, "Can a Man Have a Career and a Family, Too?," *Saturday Evening Post*, August 30, 1947, 20, 98; Elizabeth Pope, "How to Be a Successful Father," *Redbook*, July 1948, 34–35, 79–82; quote on 79.

47. Margaret Moon Loutit, "Memorandum," *Saturday Evening Post*, August 30, 1947, 36.

48. Covers of the following *Saturday Evening Post* issues: January 8, 1949; July 19, 1952; March 27, 1954.

49. Friedan, *Feminine Mystique*, 343. See also Stephanie Coontz, "Why Gender Equality Stalled," *New York Times*, February 16, 2013; Alison Wolfe, "Excerpt from *The XX Factor: How the Rise of Working Women Has Created a Far Less Equal World* (New York: Crown, 2013)," *Atlantic*, November 2013, 32.

50. Quote in Patterson, *Grand Expectations*, 5.

CHAPTER 7: THE ENDLESS FRONTIER

1. The biographical details of Bush's life come from G. Pascal Zachary, *Endless Frontier: Vannevar Bush, Engineer of the American Century* (New York: Free Press, 1997); quote on 4.

2. Quote, ibid., 8.

3. Quote, ibid., 19

4. Ibid., 25

5. Quote, ibid., 51.

6. Ibid., 76.

7. Ibid., 150.

8. Ibid., 220.

9. Vannevar Bush, *Science: The Endless Frontier*. A Report to the President by Vannevar Bush, Director of the Office of Scientific Research and Development, July 1945 (Washington, DC: Government Printing Office, 1945).

10. Quote in Zachary, *Endless Frontier*, 259.

11. For a good discussion of the creation of NSF, see Alfred K. Mann, *For Better or for Worse: The Marriage of Science and Government in the United States* (New York: Columbia University Press, 2000), 49–97.

12. See William Aspray, *John von Neumann and the Origins of Modern Computing* (Cambridge, MA: MIT Press, 1990).

13. The best work on Bell Labs is Jon Gertner, *The Idea Factory: Bell Labs and the Great Age of American Innovation* (New York: Penguin Press, 2012).

14. Quote in Walter Isaacson, "Inventing the Future," *New York Times Book Review*, April 8, 2012, 20–21. See also Jon Gertner, "True Innovation," *New York Times*, February 26, 2012.

15. Interview with Harvey Rubin, March 15, 2012.

16. Alva Johnston, "Television: Boom or Bubble?," pt. 1, *Saturday Evening Post*, March 9, 1946, 9–11, 134–35; quote on 9.

17. "Bigtime Television," *Life*, December 6, 1948, 131–41, first quote on 131; James Poling, "So This Is Television," *Redbook*, May 1949, 46–47, 91–93; second quote in Halberstam, *Fifties*, 180.

18. "Bigtime Television," 131; Poling, "So This Is Television," 92; Halberstam, *Fifties*, 185–87.

19. Quote in Poling, "So This Is Television," 91.

20. Mann, *Better or Worse*, 16–17.

21. Frederick Seidel, "Polio Days," *New York Review of Books*, April 3, 2014. From "Widening Income Inequality" by Frederick Seidel. Copyright © 2016 by Frederick Seidel. Reprinted with the permission of Macmillan, Inc. All rights reserved.

22. Quote in David M. Oshinsky, *Polio: An American Story* (New York: Oxford University Press, 2005): 71.

23. Morris Fishbein, "What You Can Do to Protect Your Child If POLIO [caps in original] Appears in Your Neighborhood," *Redbook*, August 1946, 28–29, 93–99.

24. "Polio," *Life*, August 15, 1949, 46–48, 51; Oshinsky, *Polio*, 128.

25. Interview with Millie (Dalton) Cox, October 9, 2014.

26. Grace Reiten, "Our Daughter Had Polio," *Saturday Evening Post*, August 21, 1954, 17–19, 60, 62, 64, 66, 68, 70–71; quote on 18.

27. Quote, ibid., 84.

28. Ibid., 98.

29. Quotes, ibid., 101.

30. Ibid., 161–62.

31. Quotes, ibid., 172.

32. On the Salk trials, see ibid., 188–207.

33. Quotes, ibid., 203. See also "Polio Vaccine Gets Go-Ahead," *Life*, April 25, 1955, 36–37.

34. Howard A. Rusk, M.D., "Turmoil Over Salk Shots," *New York Times*, May 8, 1955.

35. Oshinsky, *Polio*, 236.

36. "Polio Specter Stalks Chicago," *Life*, August 13, 1956: 24–25.

37. Milton Lehman, "In Search of Medical Miracles," *Saturday Evening Post*, March 31, 1956: 34–35, 102–04.

38. Jones, *Great Expectations*, 58.

39. Patterson, *Grand Expectations*, 318–19.

CHAPTER 8: "TO HELL WITH JEWS, JESUITS, AND STEAMSHIPS!"

1. "Child Immigrant," *Life*, June 10, 1946, 53–56.

2. See Robert N. Rosen, *Saving the Jews: Franklin D. Roosevelt and the Holocaust* (New York: Basic Books, 2007).

3. Quote in Aristide R. Zolberg, *A Nation by Design: Immigration Policy in the Fashioning of America* (Cambridge, MA: Harvard University Press, 2006), 216.

4. "Send Them Here!," *Life*, September 23, 1946, 36.

5. Quote in Zolberg, *Nation by Design*, 305.

6. Edward Angly, "Should We Open Our Doors to Immigrants?," *Life*, February 8, 1947, 26–27.

7. Ibid.

8. "Statement and Directive by the President on Immigration to the United States of Certain Displaced Persons and Refugees in Europe," December 22, 1946, Harry A. Truman Library and Museum, http://trumanlibrary.org/publicpapers/viewpapers.php?pid=515; Angly, "Open Our Doors," 125.

9. For a good summary and analysis of *Gentleman's Agreement*, see Bosley Crowther, "Gentleman's Agreement," *New York Times*, November 12, 1947, http://www.tabletmag.com/jewish-arts-and-culture/172526/gentlemans-agreement-tcm.

10. "Anti-Semitism," *Life*, December 1, 1947, 44.

11. Ibid.

12. Zolberg, *Nation by Design*, 297.

13. Ibid.

14. Quotes, ibid., 297–298.

15. Quote in Altschuler and Blumin, *G.I. Bill*, 92.

16. The definitive work on Jewish exclusion in the Ivies is Karabel, *Chosen*.

17. Ibid., 51.

18. Ibid., 194–95.

19. Ibid., 197.

20. For a summary of the musical see http://www.theatrehistory.com/american/musical 012.html.

21. Angly, "Open Our Doors," 126.

22. Zolberg, *Nation by Design*, 307–8.

23. "America Gets First of 200,000 DPs," *Life*, November 22, 1948, 33–37.

24. Quote, ibid., 33.

25. The Bronnys' story appeared in "New Americans One Year Later," *Life*, December 26, 1949, 11–15; quote on 15.

26. Patterson, *Grand Expectations*, 240.

27. Quote in Zolberg, *Nation by Design*, 311.

28. Quote, ibid.

29. Harry S. Truman, "Veto of Bill to Revise the Laws Relating to Immigration, Naturalization, and Nationality," June 25, 1952, Harry S. Truman Library and Museum, http://trumanlibrary.org/publicpapers/viewpapers.php?pid=2389.

30. Zolberg, *Nation by Design*, 311–15; quote on 316.

31. Hugh Davis Graham, *Collision Course: The Strange Convergence of Affirmative Action and Immigration Policy in America* (New York: Oxford University Press, 2002), 54.

32. "Before Attacking Immigration Law, Why Not Read It?," *Saturday Evening Post*, February 21, 1953, 10.

33. "The U.S.A. Owes a Lot to Immigrants—and Vice Versa!," *Saturday Evening Post*, October 27, 1956, 10. See Roger Daniels and Otis L. Graham, eds., *Debating American Immigration, 1882–Present* (London, UK: Rowman and Littlefield Publishers, 2001), 80.

34. Quote in Harry S. Truman, "Longhand Note," April 15, 1952, Truman Papers, President's Secretary's Files, https://www.trumanlibrary.org/whistlestop/study_collections/trumanpapers/psf/longhand/index.php?documentVersion=both&documentid=hst-psf_naid735309-01.

35. Ibid.

36. Quote in Neil Foley, *Mexicans in the Making of America* (Cambridge, MA: The Belknap Press, 2014), 48. This book is a good introduction into U.S. immigration policy with respect to Mexican immigrants.

37. Quote in Neil Foley, *The White Scourge: Mexicans, Blacks, and Poor Whites in Texas Cotton Culture* (Berkeley, CA: University of California Press, 1997), 212.

38. Quote in Foley, *Mexicans in the Making*, 78.

39. Julia Preston, "The Truth About Mexican Americans," *New York Review of Books*, December 3, 2015, http://www.nybooks.com/articles/2015/12/03/truth-about-mexican-americans/.

40. Quote, ibid.

41. Henry Steele Commager, "A Few Kind Words for Harry Truman," *Look*, August 28, 1951, 63–66.

42. Harry S. Truman to Ethel Noland, June 4, 1952, in Ferrell, *Off the Record*, 252.

43. Harry S. Truman, "Address at the Jefferson-Jackson Day Dinner," March 29, 1952, http://www.presidency.ucsb.edu/ws/?pid=14439.

44. "Address in New York City at the Convention of the Columbia Scholastic Press Association," March 15, 1952, http://millercenter.org/president/truman/speeches/speech-3352.

CHAPTER 9: THE SWEDISH JEW

1. I found the following works on Eisenhower most helpful: Herbert Brownell with John P. Burke, *Advising Ike: The Memoirs of Attorney General Herbert Brownell* (Lawrence, KS:

University of Kansas Press, 1993); Robert Frederick Burk, *The Eisenhower Administration and Black Civil Rights, 1953–1961* (Knoxville, TN: University of Tennessee Press, 1984); Jim Newton, *Eisenhower: The White House Years* (New York: Doubleday, 2011); David A. Nichols, *A Matter of Justice: Eisenhower and the Beginning of the Civil Rights Revolution* (New York: Simon & Schuster, 2007); and Jean Edward Smith, *Eisenhower in War and Peace* (New York: Random House, 2012).

2. Halberstam, *Fifties*, 247.

3. Quote, ibid.

4. Nichols, *Matter of Justice*, 6.

5. Quote in Smith, *Eisenhower*, 10.

6. Halberstam, *Fifties*, 247.

7. Quote in Smith, *Eisenhower*, 12.

8. *The 1915 Howitzer* (West Point, NY, 1915), 80.

9. Quote in Quentin Reynolds, "Mr. President Eisenhower," *Life*, April 17, 1950, 144.

10. Quote in Smith, *Eisenhower*, 117.

11. Quote in Robert Griffith, "Dwight D. Eisenhower and the Corporate Commonwealth," *American Historical Review* 87 (February 1982): 90.

12. *New York Times*, September 6, 1949.

13. Quote in Reynolds, "Mr. President Eisenhower," 146.

14. "Text of General Eisenhower's Address Before Bar Association," *New York Times*, September 6, 1949.

15. Dwight D. Eisenhower to George Arthur Sloan, March 1, 1952, Alfred D. Chandler, Louis Galambos, et al., eds., *The Papers of Dwight David Eisenhower* (21 vols.; Baltimore, 1970–2001), http://eisenhower.press.jhu.edu, 13:1037; second quote in Griffith, "Eisenhower," 91.

16. Hamby, *Liberalism*, 106–16.

17. Quotes in Griffith, "Eisenhower," 99.

18. Dwight D. Eisenhower to Edgar Newton Eisenhower, November 8, 1954, *Papers of DDE*, 15:1386.

19. Dwight D. Eisenhower to Eric Harlow Heckett, October 18, 1958, *Papers of DDE*, 19:1154. See also Sundquist, *Politics and Policy*, 419.

20. Nichols, *Matter of Justice*, 7. On Brownell's clandestine trip to Paris, see, Brownell, *Advising Ike*, 91–97.

21. Dwight D. Eisenhower to General George Catlett Marshall, January 7, 1945, *Papers of DDE*, 4:2408–10.

22. Quote in Shogan, *Racial Justice*, 146.

23. Dwight D. Eisenhower to Milton Stover Eisenhower, March 15, 1946, *Papers of DDE*, 7:942–44 (quotation on 942; emphasis in original).

24. Quote in Nichols, *Matter of Justice*, 11.

25. Ibid., 17.

26. Quote in Brownell with Burke, *Advising Ike*, 126.

27. http://www.livingroomcandidate.org/commercials/1952.

28. For a good concise discussion of the 1952 presidential campaign, see Patterson, *Grand Expectations*, 250–60.

29. Quotes, ibid., 255.

30. Dwight D. Eisenhower to Bernard Mannes Baruch, February 28, 1959, *Papers of DDE*, 19:1383.

31. Quotes in Samuel Lubell, "Who Elected Eisenhower?," *Saturday Evening Post*, January 10, 1953, 75.

32. Ibid., 26–27, 74–75, 78.

33. Ibid., 78.

34. Quotes in Nichols, *Matter of Justice*, 17, 19.

CHAPTER 10: THE WHEELS OF JUSTICE

1. Dwight D. Eisenhower to Frank Willard, March 7, 1951, *Papers of DDE*, 12:102–4; quote on 103.

2. Ibid., 103.

3. Patterson, *Grand Expectations*, 393.

4. http://www.presidency.ucsb.edu/ws/?pid=9829.

5. Nichols, *Matter of Justice*, 25.

6. Ibid., 29.

7. Quote in Nichols, *Matter of Justice*, 33.

8. First quote in http://www.presidency.ucsb.edu/ws/?pid=9603; second quote in Nichols, *Matter of Justice*, 33.

9. "A Head Start on Racial Equality," *Life*, May 31, 1954, 16.

10. Quote, ibid., 16.

11. Quote in Carolyn Marie Wilkins, *Damn Near White: An African American Family's Rise from Slavery to Bittersweet Success* (Columbia, MO: University of Missouri Press, 2010), 114.

12. Quote in Nichols, *Matter of Justice*, 38.

13. Ibid., 43.

14. First quote in Smith, *Eisenhower*, 11; second quote in Dwight D. Eisenhower to James Francis Byrnes, August 14, 1953, *Papers of DDE*, 14:473.

15. Quotes in Nichols, *Matter of Justice*, 49.

16. Dwight D. Eisenhower to James Francis Byrnes, August 14, 1953, *Papers of DDE*, 14:470.

17. Williams, *Thurgood Marshall*, 214.

18. Ibid., 218.

19. Ibid.

20. Quote in Shogan, *Racial Justice*, 185.

21. For biographical details on Earl Warren, see Ed Cray, *Chief Justice: A Biography of Earl Warren* (New York: Simon & Schuster, 1997).

22. Quote in Beverly Smith, "Earl Warren's Greatest Moment," *Saturday Evening Post*, July 24, 1954, 53.

23. Quote in Smith, *Eisenhower*, 604.

24. Dwight D. Eisenhower, *Papers of DDE*, 14:568.

25. Smith, *Eisenhower*, 606.

26. Nichols, *Matter of Justice*, 63–64.

27. Dwight D. Eisenhower to James Francis Byrnes, December 1, 1953, *Papers of DDE*, 15:712.

28. https://supreme.justia.com/cases/federal/us/347/483/case.html.

29. Ibid.

30. Quote in Williams, *Thurgood Marshall*, 229.

31. First quote in Michael J. Klarman, "Why Massive Resistance," in *Massive Resistance: Southern Opposition to the Second Reconstruction*, ed. Clive Webb (New York, 2005), 21; second quote in Williams, *Thurgood Marshall*, 230.

32. Quote in Williams, *Thurgood Marshall*, 231.

33. Quote in Patterson, *Grand Expectations*, 393. The story may have its origins in *The Memoirs of Chief Justice Earl Warren*, (New York: Doubleday, 1977), 291–92. On this

controversy, see http://abcnews.go.com/US/historian-stephen-ambrose-lie-interviews-president
-dwight-eisenhower/story?id=10489472.

34. Nichols, *Matter of Justice*, 66.

35. Smith, *Eisenhower*, 712.

36. Nichols, *Matter of Justice*, 69.

37. Quotes, ibid., 70.

38. Brownell with Burke, *Advising Ike*, 196.

39. Quote in Nichols, *Matter of Justice*, 70.

40. Quote, ibid., 71.

41. Quotes, ibid.

42. Ibid.

43. https://www.nationalcenter.org/cc0725.htm.

44. Ibid.

45. Quote in Nichols, *Matter of Justice*, 72. See also Brownell with Burke, *Advising Ike*, 197.

46. Quote in Caro, *Master of the Senate*, 700.

47. Goldfield, *Black, White, and Southern*, 88–89.

48. Brownell with Burke, *Advising Ike*, 204.

49. http://brooklynology.brooklynpubliclibrary.org/post/2015/01/16/The-Mystery-of-PS
-125.aspx.

50. http://www.pbs.org/wnet/supremecourt/rights/sources_document2.html.

51. *Public Papers of the Presidents of the United States: 1956: Containing the Public Messages, Speeches, and Statements of the President*, January 1 to December 31, 1956 (Washington, DC: Government Printing Office, 1956), 56.

52. Quote in Goldfield, *Black, White, and Southern*, 85.

53. William Faulkner, "A Letter to the North," *Life*, March 5, 1956, 51–52.

54. Ibid.

55. Quote in Goldfield, *Black, White, and Southern*, 85.

56. I have taken the following discussion of Rosa Parks and the Montgomery bus boycott from Goldfield, *Black, White, and Southern*, 95–96.

57. Dwight D. Eisenhower to William Franklin Graham, March 22, 1956, *Papers of DDE*, 16:2086–88.

58. Ibid., 16:2086–87.

59. Dwight D. Eisenhower to William Franklin Graham, March 30, 1956, *Papers of DDE*, 16:2104–5.

60. Dwight D. Eisenhower to Arthur Ellsworth Summerfield, March 24, 1956, *Papers of DDE*, 16:2095.

61. "Emmett Till's Day in Court," *Life*, October 3, 1955, 36–38.

62. "A Fair Climate at Home," *Life*, August 22, 1955, 32.

63. http://www.presidency.ucsb.edu/ws/?pid=10593.

64. For a discussion of the provisions in the civil rights bill, see Sundquist, *Politics and Policy*, 227.

65. Nichols, *Matter of Justice*, 132.

66. Ibid., 134.

67. "President Names Jersey Democrat to Supreme Court," *New York Times*, September 30, 1956.

68. Nichols, *Matter of Justice*, 138.

69. Ibid., 139.

70. On how contemporary observers misread Eisenhower, see John Lewis Gaddis, "He Made It Look Easy," *New York Times Sunday Book Review*, April 22, 2012, http://query.nytimes.com/gst/fullpage.html?res=9A04EEDE1F31F931A15757C0A9649D8B63.

CHAPTER 11: YESTERDAY

1. "The Case for Ike," *Life*, January 7, 1952, 12.

2. Quote in Garry Wills, "The Triumph of the Hard Right," *New York Review of Books*, February 11, 2016, 4, https://www.eisenhower.archives.gov/all_about_ike/speeches/1953_state_of_the_union.pdf; "The State of the Union," *Life*, July 6, 1953.

3. James L. McConaughy Jr., "While Eisenhower Proposes the Old Guard Disposes," *Life*, June 21, 1954, 125.

4. Dwight D. Eisenhower to Hugh Meade Alcorn, August 30, 1957, *Papers of DDE*, 18:396–99; quote in "A National Meeting on Schools Rings the Bell for Federal Aid," *Life*, December 12, 1955, 39.

5. "Blight on the Land of Sunshine," *Life*, November 1, 1954, 17–19.

6. See "Our Parks in Peril," *New York Times*, April 5, 1954; Seth S. King, "Influx Is Awaited by Yellowstone," *New York Times*, April 6, 1954.

7. Sundquist, *Politics and Policy*, 334.

8. First quote in "Texts of Gen. Eisenhower's Addresses at Waldorf-Astoria Dinner and in Paterson Armory," *New York Times*, October 17, 1952; second quote in https://www.eisenhower.archives.gov/all_about_ike/speeches/1953_state_of_the_union.pdf.

9. "Immigration: The Real Issue Is an Evil Law," *Life*, April 25, 1955, 45.

10. All quotes in "Legislative Background: Immigration Law," *Presidential Papers of LBJ* (LBJ Library), 1965, Box 1.

11. William Brinkley, "The Agonizing Odyssey of Two People in Love," *Life*, March 5, 1956, 160–68, 171–74.

12. Patterson, *Grand Expectations*, 328.

13. " 'National Origins' Should Be Kept in Immigration Law," *Saturday Evening Post*, April 20, 1957, 10.

14. "What's So 'Illiberal' and 'Inhumane' About Our Immigration Requirements?," *Saturday Evening Post*, January 4, 1958, 10; "Before We Weaken the Immigration Laws, Let's Study the Facts," *Saturday Evening Post*, October 10, 1959, 12.

15. Dwight D. Eisenhower to Joseph Morrell Dodge, November 5, 1953, *Papers of DDE*, 14:643–44.

16. Dwight D. Eisenhower to Aksel Nielsen, January 28, 1953, *Papers of DDE*, 14:14.

17. Dwight D. Eisenhower, *Diary*, October 26, 1953, *Papers of DDE*, 14:607.

18. Dwight D. Eisenhower to Aksel Nielsen, January 5, 1954, *Papers of DDE*, 15:802.

19. Quote in Parson, "Decline of Public Housing," 410.

20. See Jeffrey Helgeson, "The State of Blame in American Cities: Race, Wealth, and the Politics of Housing," *Journal of Urban History* 37 (November 2011): 992–99.

21. Oscar Lewis was the first scholar to use the phrase in a monograph, *The Children of Sanchez: Autobiography of a Mexican Family* (New York: Random House, 1961). The book was banned in Mexico for several years after its publication. Several writers had employed the idea of poverty's generating a separate and isolated culture before Lewis without using the phrase. Lewis presented a detailed perspective of the controversial concept in "The Culture of Poverty," a 1966 paper, http://www.ignaciodarnaude.com/textos_diversos/Lewis,Oscar,The%20Culture%20of%20Poverty.pdf. Some scholars misinterpreted the concept as "blaming the victim."

22. All quotes and statistics in the previous four paragraphs are in Carl T. Rowan, "Are Negroes Ready for Equality?," *Saturday Evening Post*, October 22, 1960, 21, 48–49, 51, 54, 56.

23. Goldfarb's story is in "School Problem—and a Suicide," *Life*, February 10, 1958, 86–87.

24. http://dlib.nyu.edu/undercover/sites/dlib.nyu.edu.undercover/files/documents/uploads/editors/NYWorldTelegramSun_1958November14_1.pdf.

25. http://www.washingtonpost.com/wp-dyn/content/article/2007/11/15/AR2007111502394 .html.

26. http://insideschools.org/component/schools/school/747.

27. Quotes in Carl T. Rowan, "The Negro in the North," *Saturday Evening Post*, October 12, 1957, 32, 33, 74, 76, 78.

28. Quote in Rowan, "Negro in the North," October 19, 1957, 86.

29. Ibid., 78.

30. First quote, ibid., 45; second quote in Rowan, "Negro in the North," October 12, 1957, 32.

31. Quotes in Rowan, "Negro in the North," October 12, 1957, 126, 128, 133.

32. Smith, *Eisenhower*, 648.

33. Transcript of radio interview, January 17, 1955, *Senate Papers of LBJ* (LBJ Library), Office Files of George Reedy, Box 412.

34. Dwight D. Eisenhower to Sid Williams Richardson, July 10, 1956, *Papers of DDE*, 17:2199.

35. "Are We Moving Toward a New Party Line-Up?," December 25, 1954, 6; "Eisenhower's Program Gets off the Drawing Board," *Saturday Evening Post*, February 13, 1954, 12.

36. "New Party Line-Up?," 6.

37. Quote in "There's No Demand for a G.O.P. New Deal," *Saturday Evening Post*, August 11, 1956, 10.

38. Dwight D. Eisenhower to Bradford Grethen Chynoweth, July 13, 1954, *Papers of DDE*, 15:1185–86.

CHAPTER 12: TOMORROW

1. Dwight D. Eisenhower, *Diary*, November 20, 1954, *Papers of DDE*, 15:1402–5.

2. Smith, *Eisenhower*, 654.

3. Ibid.

4. Mark H. Rose, *Interstate: Express Highway Politics, 1939–1989* (Knoxville, TN: University of Tennessee Press, 1979), 15–35.

5. Dwight D. Eisenhower to Gabriel Hauge, February 4, 1953, *Papers of DDE*, 14:23–24. See also Eric Avila and Mark H. Rose, "Race, Culture, Politics, and Urban Renewal: An Introduction," *Journal of Urban History* 35 (March 2009): 335–47.

6. Herbert Brean, "Dead End for the U.S. Highway," *Life*, May 30, 1955, 105.

7. Quote in Rose, *Interstate*, 78.

8. Richard Thruelsen, "Coast to Coast Without a Stoplight," *Saturday Evening Post*, October 20, 1956, 23.

9. Richard Thruelsen, "The Case of the Obsolete Highways," *Saturday Evening Post*, February 5, 1955, 29.

10. Rose, *Interstate*, 69–85; Thruelsen, "Coast to Coast," 23, 54, 59, 61.

11. Dwight D. Eisenhower to Lucius Du Bignon Clay, January 26, 1955, *Papers of DDE*, 16:1528.

12. Thruelsen, "Coast to Coast," 54.

13. Rose, *Interstate*, 92–94.

14. For a concise narrative of Wilson's story, see Halberstam, *Fifties*, 174–79.

15. For a concise narrative of Johnson's story, see Jack Alexander, "Host of the Highways," *Saturday Evening Post*, July 19, 1958, 16–17, 48–50.

16. Smith, *Eisenhower*, 650.

17. "The Key That Opens the Continent to the Sea," *Life*, July 14, 1958, 101–2; Smith, *Eisenhower*, 650.

18. Harold H. Martin, "Flying Can be Safer," *Saturday Evening Post*, November 10, 1956, 23, 50–51, 54–56.

19. Ibid., 51.
20. Ibid.
21. Lyndon B. Johnson, "Memorandum," n.d., ca 1957–58, *Senate Papers of LBJ*, Box 408; "Fine New Front Door for Jet-Age America," *Life*, December 16, 1957, 102–4.
22. "Off for Paris in Jet Time," *Life*, November 10, 1958.
23. Jack Kerouac, *On the Road* (New York: Viking, 1957), 54.
24. Ibid., 79.
25. Ibid., 125, 154.
26. Ibid., 158, 167.
27. My favorite Dodger books are too many to note here, but two of the best are by Roger Kahn—*The Boys of Summer* (New York: Harper & Row, 1972) and *The Era, 1947–1957: When the Yankees, the Giants, and the Dodgers Ruled the World* (Boston: Houghton Mifflin, 1993).
28. For a concise perspective on the Dodgers' exit from Brooklyn, see Sam Anderson, "Exorcising the Dodgers," *New York*, September 16, 2007, http://nymag.com/news/sports/37643/.
29. http://espn.go.com/mlb/jackie/news/story?id=2830342.
30. Martin Tolchin, "Coney Island Slump Grows Worse," *New York Times*, July 2, 1964. For an insightful view of similar decline, see Eric Avila, "Popular Culture in the Age of White Flight: Film Noir, Disneyland, and the Cold War (Sub)Urban Imaginary," *Journal of Urban History* 31 (November 2004): 3–22.
31. Avila, "Popular Culture," 10–15.
32. Jones, *Great Expectations*, 70; Frank McCulloch, "Will the West Take Over?," *Saturday Evening Post*, July 8, 1961, 18, 46, 49, 51.
33. McCulloch, "Will the West Take Over?," 49.
34. Ibid., 51.
35. Quotes in Robert A. Caro, *The Years of Lyndon Johnson: Master of the Senate* (New York: Alfred A. Knopf, 2002), 843.
36. Quote in Stewart Alsop, "What We Learned about the American People," *Saturday Evening Post*, January 12, 1957, 65.
37. James Reston, "Politics and Civil Rights," *New York Times*, July 24, 1957. See also Alsop, "What We Learned," 25, 63, 65–66.
38. John F. Kennedy, "A Democrat Says Party Must Lead—or Get Left," *Life*, March 11, 1957, 164–66, 171–72, 175–76, 179.

CHAPTER 13: STEPS

1. William S. White, "President Pushes Civil Rights Plan at G.O.P. Parley," *New York Times*, January 1, 1957, http://www.presidency.ucsb.edu/ws/?pid=11029.
2. Quote in Nichols, *Matter of Justice*, 144.
3. First quote in Tris Coffin, "How Lyndon Johnson Engineered Compromise on Civil Rights Bill," *New Leader*, August 5, 1957, 3; second quote in Caro, *Master of the Senate*, 853.
4. Quote in Caro, *Master of the Senate*, 868.
5. Brownell with Burke, *Advising Ike*, 224–25.
6. For a good discussion of this strategy and how it played out, see ibid., 220–21.
7. Quote in Caro, *Master of the Senate*, 916.
8. Quotes in Douglass Cater, "How the Senate Passed the Civil-Rights Bill," *The Reporter*, September 5, 1957, 9, *Senate Papers of LBJ*, Box 290.
9. Dwight D. Eisenhower to James Francis Byrnes, July 23, 1957, *Papers of DDE*, 18:328–30.
10. Caro, *Master of the Senate*, 988.
11. First two quotes, ibid., 13; last quote in Nichols, *Matter of Justice*, 161.
12. Caro, *Master of the Senate*, 990, 995.

13. Quote in Nichols, *Matter of Justice*, 167.

14. First quote in "The Eighty-Fifth [Congress] to Date," *New York Times*, September 1, 1957; second quote in David L. Stebenne, "Thomas J. Watson and the Business-Government Relationship, 1933–1956," *Enterprise and Society* 6 (March 2005): 45–75.

15. Dwight D. Eisenhower to Carol Beane, September 7, 1957, *Papers of DDE*, 18:418.

16. Clarence Mitchell to Lyndon B. Johnson, August 29, 1957, *Senate Papers of LBJ*, Box 290; C. Vann Woodward, "The Great Civil Rights Debate: The Ghost of Thaddeus Stevens in the Senate Chamber," *Commentary*, October 1, 1957, https://www.commentarymagazine.com /articles/the-great-civil-rights-debatethe-ghost-of-thaddeus-stevens-in-the-senate-chamber/.

17. H. William Culver to Lyndon B. Johnson, n.d., ca 1957; Mrs. Margaret Hales to Lyndon B. Johnson, January 21, 1958; Mr. and Mrs. W. D. Waltman Jr. to Lyndon B. Johnson, ca 1957; E. B. Sloss to Lyndon B. Johnson, September 23, 1957; *Senate Papers of LBJ*, Box 289.

18. Quote in Leuchtenburg, *White House Looks South*, 265.

19. For background to Little Rock, see Goldfield, *Black, White, and Southern*, 106–9; quote on 107.

20. Quote, ibid., 107.

21. Quote, ibid., 109.

22. Dwight D. Eisenhower, "Statement by the President Following a Meeting with the Governor of Arkansas," September 14, 1957, *Public Papers of the Presidents of the United States: Dwight D. Eisenhower. 1957. Containing the Public Messages, Speeches, and Statements of the President, January 1 to December 31, 1957* (Washington, DC: Government Printing Office, 1958), 188.

23. Dwight D. Eisenhower to Woodrow Wilson Mann, September 26, 1957, *Papers of DDE*, 18:460–61.

24. Ibid., 461; quote in Nichols, *Matter of Justice*, 194.

25. Dwight D. Eisenhower, "Radio and Television Address to the American People on the Situation in Little Rock," September 24, 1957, *Public Papers of the Presidents*, 691.

26. Smith, *Eisenhower*, 726–27.

27. Dwight D. Eisenhower to Richard Brevard Russell, September 27, 1957, *Papers of DDE*, 18:463.

28. Ibid.

29. Lyndon B. Johnson, "Comment" on Little Rock troop deployment, n.d., ca September 1957, *Senate Papers of LBJ*, Box 22.

30. "Integration Won't Be Hastened by Military Action," *Saturday Evening Post*, October 26, 1957, 10.

31. Nichols, *Matter of Justice*, 213.

32. Dwight D. Eisenhower to Ralph Emerson McGill, September 3, 1958, *Papers of DDE*, 19:1087.

33. https://supreme.justia.com/cases/federal/us/358/1/case.html; quotes in Nichols, *Matter of Justice*, 228.

34. Nichols, *Matter of Justice*, 228.

35. Ibid., 236.

36. Ibid., 239.

37. Ibid., 241.

38. Ibid., 242.

39. https://www.eisenhower.archives.gov/all_about_ike/speeches/1960_state_of_the _union.pdf.

40. Nichols, *Matter of Justice*, 250.

41. Quote in Goldfield, *Black, White, and Southern*, 119.

42. Quote, ibid.

43. Ibid., 120.

44. Dwight D. Eisenhower, "The President's News Conference of March 16, 1960," *Public Papers of the Presidents of the United States, Dwight D. Eisenhower, 1960-61* (Washington, DC: Government Printing Office, 1961), 293.

45. Nichols, *Matter of Justice*, 251–52.

46. Quotes in Robert Dallek, *Lone Star Rising: Lyndon Johnson and His Times, 1908-1960* (New York: Oxford University Press, 1991), 562.

47. Ibid., 563–64; quote on 564.

48. For a full discussion of the 1960 Civil Rights Act, see ibid., 235–63.

49. Ibid., 83.

50. Brownell with Burke, *Advising Ike*, 182. See also Jack Bass, *Taming the Storm: The Life and Times of Judge Frank M. Johnson and the South's Fight over Civil Rights* (New York: Doubleday, 1993); Anne Emanuel, *Elbert Parr Tuttle: Chief Jurist of the Civil Rights Revolution* (Athens, GA: University of Georgia Press, 2011); and Joel William Friedman, *Champion of Civil Rights: Judge John Minor Wisdom* (Baton Rouge: Louisiana State University Press, 2009).

51. "The New Congress and You," *Redbook*, February 1959, 29.

CHAPTER 14: CONFIDENCE

1. Patterson, *Grand Expectations*, 420; Dwight D. Eisenhower to Ralph Emerson McGill, November 17, 1957, *Papers of DDE*, 18:574.

2. First quote in Caro, *Master of the Senate*, 1024; second and fourth quotes in Zachary, *Endless Frontier*, 387; third quote in George R. Price, "Arguing the Case for Being Panicky," *Life*, November 18, 1957, 125–26, 128.

3. First quote in "The President's News Conference of October 9, 1957," *Public Papers of the Presidents of the United States, Dwight D. Eisenhower, 1957* (Washington, DC: Government Printing Office, 1957), 730–31; second quote in https://history.state.gov/historicaldocuments/frus1955–57v19/d152.

4. Address to the American Society of Newspaper Editors and the International Press Institute, April 17, 1958, http://www.presidency.ucsb.edu/ws/?pid=11357.

5. https://www.eisenhower.archives.gov/all_about_ike/speeches/chance_for_peace.pdf.

6. "Radio and Television Address to the American People on Science in National Security," November 7, 1957, http://www.presidency.ucsb.edu/ws/?pid=10946.

7. Ibid.; text of National Defense Education Act: http://wwwedu.oulu.fi/tohtorikoulutus/jarjestettava_opetus/Troehler/NDEA_1958.pdf, quote on 1581; Hugh Davis Graham, *The Uncertain Triumph: Federal Education Policy in the Kennedy and Johnson Years* (Chapel Hill, NC: University of North Carolina Press, 1984), 224.

8. Robert Bendiner, "What's Really Happening in Our Schools," *Redbook*, September 1959, 46–47, 98–100, quote on 98; "Tryouts for Good Ideas," *Life*, April 14, 1958, 117–25, quote on 119.

9. Graham, *Federal Education Policy*, xviii.

10. Quote in Hugh Davis Graham and Nancy Diamond, *The Rise of American Research Universities: Elites and Challengers in the Postwar Era* (Baltimore: Johns Hopkins University Press, 1997), 34, 48.

11. "Science vs. Culture: A Phony War," *Life*, February 17, 1958, 38.

12. Congressional Budget Office, "Federal Support for Research and Development" (Washington, DC: Government Printing Office, June 2007), 2. See also Mariana Mazzucato, *The Entrepreneurial State: Debunking Public vs. Private Sector Myths* (London: Anthem, 2013).

13. Galbraith, *Affluent Society*, 207.

14. Zachary, *Endless Frontier*, 389.

15. John B. Judis, "Steve Jobs's Angel: The Republicans Want to Kill It," *New Republic*, September 2, 2013, 4, 6–7.

16. Graham and Diamond, *Research Universities*, 28–33.

17. Interview with Rubin.

18. "An American Necessity," *Life*, November 30, 1959, 36.

19. Dwight D. Eisenhower to Stanley Hoflund High, October 29, 1957, *Papers of DDE*, 18:524.

20. Quote in Sundquist, *Politics and Policy*, 252.

21. Quote, ibid., 253.

22. The Right Reverend James A. Pike, "Should a Catholic Be President?," *Life*, December 21, 1959, 78–80, 83–85; quote on 79.

23. Ibid., 85.

24. "Transcript: JFK's Speech on His Religion," September 12, 1960, http://www.npr.org/templates/story/story.php?storyId=16920600.

25. First quote in Patterson, *Grand Expectations*, 436; second quote in Halberstam, *Fifties*, 733.

26. Patterson, *Grand Expectations*, 437.

27. Quote, ibid.

28. Ibid.

29. A good concise history of the 1960 presidential election is W. J. Rorabaugh, *The Real Making of the President: Kennedy, Nixon, and the 1960 Election* (Lawrence, KN: University Press of Kansas, 2009).

30. Alsop, "What We Learned," 25, 63, 65–66; quotes on 66.

31. Patterson, *Grand Expectations*, 311–13.

32. John Gardner, "Can We Count on More Dedicated People?," *Life*, June 13, 1960, 98.

33. Archibald MacLeish, "We Have Purpose . . . We All Know It," *Life*, May 30, 1960, 86, 88, 93; quote on 93.

34. Sundquist, *Politics and Policy*, 442–43.

35. Ibid., 449–50.

36. Mettler, *Soldiers to Citizens*, 134. See also Robert E. Lane, "The Politics of Consensus in an Age of Affluence," *American Political Science Review* 59, no. 4 (1965): 874–95.

37. "New Congress and You," 29.

38. Ibid.

39. Ibid.

40. Dallek, *Lone Star Rising*, 514.

41. Clinton Rossiter, "We Must Show the Way to Enduring Peace," *Life*, June 13, 1960, 99, 112, 115–16, 118; quote on 116.

42. Ibid., 116.

CHAPTER 15: THE COWBOY

1. I drew biographical details on Lyndon B. Johnson from the following sources: "Chronological Material on President Lyndon B. Johnson," Box 94, Names in Honor of the President, Presidential Papers, LBJ Presidential Library, Austin, Texas (hereinafter cited as LBJ Library); Robert A. Caro's four volumes (to date) of *The Years of Lyndon Johnson* (New York: Alfred A. Knopf, 1982–2012): *The Path to Power* (1982); *Means of Ascent* (1990); *Master of the Senate* (2002); and *The Passage of Power* (2012); and Robert Dallek's two volumes—*Lone Star Rising: Lyndon Johnson and His Times, 1908–1960* (1991), and *Flawed Giant: Lyndon Johnson and His Times, 1961–1973* (New York: Oxford University Press, 1998).

2. Quote in Dallek, *Lone Star Rising*, 23.

3. Quote, ibid., 30; "As Student and Teacher, LBJ Was Go-Getter," *Kansas City Times*, May 25, 1965, Box 108, Presidential Papers, 13-4, LBJ Library.

4. Ibid.

5. Quotes in Caro, *Master of the Senate*, 720; last quote in Dallek, *Lone Star Rising*, 23.

6. Quote in "As Student and Teacher."

7. Quotes in Dallek, *Lone Star Rising*, 106.

8. Ibid., 107.

9. First two quotes in Caro, *Path to Power*, 275; last two quotes in Dallek, *Lone Star Rising*, 111.

10. Aubrey Williams (Executive Director, NYA) to LBJ, July 25, 1935, Box 73, LBJA Subject File, LBJ Library.

11. LBJ to John Corson (Assistant Director of NYA), September 22, 1935, Box 73, LBJA Subject File, LBJ Library.

12. Ibid.

13. Quotes in Dallek, *Lone Star Rising*, 142, 143.

14. Quote, ibid., 142.

15. *Austin American*, January 30, 1938, Box 73, LBJA Subject File, LBJ Library.

16. Quote in Dallek, *Lone Star Rising*, 161.

17. Ibid., 169.

18. Ibid., 258.

19. Quote, ibid., 276.

20. Quote in Caro, *Path to Power*, 125.

21. Quote in Dallek, *Lone Star Rising*, 145.

22. Ibid., 346.

23. Robert A. Caro has a good discussion of the Russell-Johnson relationship in *Master of the Senate*. See especially 363–66.

24. Ibid., 452.

25. Ibid., 459.

26. Quote in Hamby, *Liberalism*, 250.

27. Remarks of Senate Democratic Leader Lyndon B. Johnson to the Democratic Conference, January 7, 1959, https://www.gpo.gov/fdsys/pkg/CDOC-105sdoc20/pdf/CDOC-105sdoc20.pdf.

28. Quote in Dallek, *Lone Star Rising*, 447.

29. Quote in Alfred Steinberg, *Sam Rayburn: A Biography* (New York: Hawthorn Books 1975), 236.

30. Quote in Dallek, *Lone Star Rising*, 541.

31. See Goldfield, "Border Men," 7–38.

32. Quote in Leuchtenburg, *White House Looks South*, 234, 236.

33. Dallek, *Lone Star Rising*, 366, 404.

34. Ibid., 257.

35. Quote in Dallek, *Flawed Giant*, 589.

36. Quote in Leuchtenburg, *White House Looks South*, 249.

37. Ibid., 280.

38. Stewart Alsop, "Lyndon Johnson: How Does He Do It?," *Saturday Evening Post*, January 24, 1959, 13–14, 38, 43; quotes on 14 and 43.

39. Leuchtenburg, *White House Looks South*, 281.

41. Quote in Dallek, *Lone Star Rising*, 583.

42. Quote in Leuchtenburg, *White House Looks South*, 284.

43. Quote in Dallek, *Lone Star Rising*, 585.

44. All quotes in Leuchtenburg, *White House Looks South*, 285.

45. Quotes in Dallek, *Lone Star Rising*, 589.

46. Quote in Leuchtenburg, *White House Looks South*, 290.

47. Dallek, *Lone Star Rising*, 589.

48. Quote in David Pietrusza, *1960: LBJ vs. JFK vs. Nixon: The Epic Campaign That Forged Three Presidencies* (New York: Union Square Press, 2008), 401.

CHAPTER 16: INTERLUDE

1. Quote in Leuchtenburg, *White House Looks South*, 292.

2. See Robert Dallek's comments in "When Lofty Words from the President Also Led to Swift Action," *New York Times*, June 9, 2013.

3. Louis Menand, "The Sex Amendment: How Women Got In on the Civil Rights Act," *New Yorker*, July 21, 2014, 74–81; quotes on 76.

4. Ibid.

5. The discussion of the Freedom Rides relies on Goldfield, *Black, White, and Southern*, 124–32.

6. Louis Menand, "The Color of Law: Voting Rights and the Southern Way of Life," *New Yorker*, July 8 and 15, 2013, 80–88; quote on 82.

7. Ibid.

8. "No Time for Boldness?," *New York Times*, January 3, 1962; second quote in "Mr. Kennedy's Deliberate Speed," *Saturday Evening Post*, February 24, 1962, 98.

9. "Mr. Kennedy's Deliberate Speed," 98.

10. Goldfield, *Black, White, and Southern*, 114.

11. David Blight and Allison Scharfstein, "King's Forgotten Manifesto," *New York Times*, May 18, 2012.

12. Williams, *Thurgood Marshall*, 306; quote in Caitlin Flanagan, "Jackie and the Girls: Mrs. Kennedy's JFK Problem and Ours," *Atlantic*, July 2012, http://infoweb.newsbank.com .librarylink.uncc.edu/resources/doc/nb/news/13FBB4B4E5009C48?p=WORLDNEWS.

13. Stewart Alsop, "The Mood of America," *Saturday Evening Post*, September 22, 1962, 13–21; quote on 16.

14. Graham, *Collision Course*, 28.

15. Ibid., 28.

16. Quote, ibid., 96.

17. Dallek, *Flawed Giant*, 30.

18. For an overview of the Birmingham campaign, see Goldfield, *Black, White, and Southern*, 134–41.

19. Ibid., 136.

20. "Federal Funds and Mississippi," *Saturday Evening Post*, May 18, 1962, 82.

21. Menand, "Sex Amendment," 76.

22. JFK, "Report to the American People on Civil Rights, 11 June 1963," http://www.jfklibrary .org/Asset-Viewer/LH8F_0Mzvoe6Ro1yEm74Ng.aspx.

23. Patterson, *Grand Expectations*, 482.

24. LBJ, "Remarks at Gettysburg on Civil Rights (May 30, 1963)," http://millercenter.org /president/lbjohnson/speeches/speech-3380.

25. Quote in Patterson, *Grand Expectations*, 465.

26. Ibid., 474.

27. Quote in Graham, *Federal Education Policy*, 3.

28. Ibid., 11–12.

29. Ibid., 13.

30. Ibid., 18–25.

31. "The President and the Congress," *Saturday Evening Post*, August 25, 1962, 86.

32. "Many in Congress Decry Its Record; Voice Frustration over Lag in Legislative Output; Few Final Actions, Reforms Proposed," *New York Times*, November 12, 1963.

33. Hamby, *Liberalism*, 207–8.

34. Robert Schlesinger, "The Myth of JFK as Supply Side Tax Cutter," *US News & World Report*, January 26, 2011, https://www.usnews.com/opinion/articles/2011/01/26/the-myth-of-jfk-as-supply-side-tax-cutter.

35. See "John F. Kennedy: The American Franchise," http://millercenter.org/president/biography/kennedy-the-american-franchise.

36. See the discussion between Cynthia Harrison and Caitlin Flanagan on this point in the Letters to the Editor section, *Atlantic*, October 2012, 10.

37. Stewart Alsop, "They Hate Kennedy," *Saturday Evening Post*, October 5, 1963, 18.

38. Quotes in Dallek, *Flawed Giant*, 44.

39. Ibid., 46–47.

40. Theodore H. White, "For President Kennedy: An Epilogue," *Life*, December 6, 1963.

CHAPTER 17: BEING LINCOLN

1. Quote in Leuchtenburg, *White House Looks South*, 302.

2. David Niven, *The Politics of Injustice: The Kennedys, the Freedom Rides, and the Electoral Consequences of a Moral Compromise* (Knoxville, TN: University of Tennessee Press, 2003), 36.

3. LBJ, Address to Joint Session of Congress, November 27, 1963, http://millercenter.org/president/lbjohnson/speeches/speech-3381.

4. Leuchtenburg, *White House Looks South*, 298, 301, 302.

5. Quote, ibid., 307.

6. Ibid.

7. Quotes in Michael O'Donnell, "How LBJ Saved the Civil Rights Act," *Atlantic*, April 2014, http://www.theatlantic.com/magazine/archive/2014/04/what-the-hells-the-presidency-for/358630/.

8. First quote in David Farber, *The Rise and Fall of Modern American Conservatism: A Short History* (Princeton, NJ: Princeton University Press, 2010), 112; second quote in Leuchtenburg, *White House Looks South*, 300.

9. First quote in Dallek, *Flawed Giant*, 113; second and third quotes in Leuchtenburg, *White House Looks South*, 303.

10. LBJ, "Annual Message to the Congress on the State of the Union," January 8, 1964, http://www.presidency.ucsb.edu/ws/?pid=26787.

11. Quote in Sundquist, *Politics and Policy*, 266.

12. Quotes in O'Donnell, "How LBJ Saved the Civil Rights Act."

13. LBJ to Roy Wilkins, January 6, 1964, 5:12 P.M., in *The Presidential Recordings. The Kennedy Assassination and the Transfer of Power, November 1963–January 1964, Volume III*, ed. Robert David Johnson and Kent B. Germany (New York: W. W. Norton, 2005), 190–94.

14. Quotes in O'Donnell, "How LBJ Saved the Civil Rights Act."

15. LBJ to Hubert Humphrey, February 25, 1964, 11:00 A.M., in *The Presidential Recordings. Lyndon B. Johnson: Toward the Great Society. Volume IV, February 1, 1964–March 8, 1964*, ed. Robert David Johnson and Kent B. Germany (New York: W. W. Norton, 2007), 713–14.

16. Sundquist, *Politics and Policy*, 265.

17. Quote in Dallek, *Flawed Giant*, 119.

18. Ibid., 119–21.

19. LBJ to Roy Wilkins, June 19, 1964, 5:20 P.M., in *Taking Charge: The Johnson White House Tapes*, ed. Michael Beschloss (New York: Simon & Schuster, 1997), 420.

20. Lady Bird Johnson's diary entry, June 19, 1964, ibid., 420

21. LBJ, Remarks upon Signing the Civil Rights Act, July 2, 1964, http://millercenter.org/president/speeches/speech-3525.

22. Quote in Goldfield, *Black, White, and Southern*, 145., ibid.

23. Menand, "Color of Law," 80–88.

24. LBJ to Allen J. Ellender, July 23, 1964; LBJ to Richard B. Russell, July 23, 1964; Box 67, Presidential Papers, LBJ Library.

25. Harry Golden to Jack Valenti, July 30, 1965, Box 67, Presidential Papers, LBJ Library.

26. Dallek, *Flawed Giant*, 114; quote in "Now That the Bill Has Passed," *Saturday Evening Post*, July 11, 1964, 88.

27. Quote in Dan T. Carter, *From George Wallace to Newt Gingrich: Race in the Conservative Counterrevolution* (Baton Rouge: Louisiana State University Press, 1996), xiii.

28. Quote in Patterson, *Grand Expectations*, 549.

29. M. Margaret Conway, "The White Backlash Re-examined: Wallace and the 1964 Primaries," *Social Science Quarterly* 49 (December 1968): 710–19.

30. Ibid., 555–56; quote in Leuchtenburg, *White House Looks South*, 314.

31. Quotes in Leuchtenburg, *White House Looks South*, 314.

32. Lisa McGirr, *Suburban Warriors: The Origins of the New American Right* (Princeton, NJ: Princeton University Press, 2001), 113, 135–36.

33. Quotes in Dallek, *Flawed Giant*, 133.

34. Ibid., 167.

35. Quote in Leuchtenburg, *White House Looks South*, 323.

36. Quotes, ibid., 558.

37. Ibid., 560.

38. Bill Moyers to LBJ, September 5, 1964, in *Reaching for Glory: Lyndon Johnson's Secret White House Tapes, 1964–1965*, ed. Michael Beschloss (New York: Simon & Schuster, 2001), 33.

39. "Why Lyndon Johnson Must Be Elected," *Saturday Evening Post*, September 19, 1964, 80.

40. LBJ to Bill Moyers and McGeorge Bundy, November 4, 1964, in Beschloss, *Reaching for Glory*, 113.

41. Quote in "Civil Rights Act Leaves Deep Mark on the American Political Landscape," *New York Times*, July 2, 1989.

42. Barry Goldwater, "The G.O.P. Invades the South," *Saturday Evening Post*, April 13, 1963, 10, 12.

43. Ibid.

44. On Selma, see Goldfield, *Black, White, and Southern*, 161–67.

45. Menand, "Color of Law," 80–88; quote in Goldfield, *Black, White, and Southern*, 152.

46. Menand, "Color of Law," 85.

47. On voting-rights drives before Selma, see Goldfield, *Black, White, and Southern*, 153–57. Quote, ibid., 154.

48. Quote, ibid., 157.

49. Ibid., 159.

50. Ibid., 161.

51. Quote, ibid., 162.

52. Quote, ibid., 164.

53. The description of the Johnson-Wallace confrontation derives from the transcription of the meeting between LBJ and George Wallace, with Nicholas Katzenbach and Buford Ellington (former governor of Tennessee) in attendance, March 18, 1965, in Beschloss, *Reaching for Glory*, 233–34.

54. LBJ, Speech Before Congress on Voting Rights, March 15, 1965, http://millercenter.org/president/speeches/speech-3386.

55. Quote in Leuchtenburg, *White House Looks South*, 330.

56. Quote, ibid.

57. Quote, ibid.

58. Quotes in Kent B. Germany, "When History Is Not Good Enough for Hollywood: *Selma*, Lyndon B. Johnson, and Martin Luther King Jr.," *AHA Perspectives on History*, May 2015, 31–32.

59. Martin Luther King Jr., "Our God Is Marching On!," March 25, 1965, https://kingin stitute.stanford.edu/our-god-marching.

60. LBJ, Remarks on the Signing of the Voting Rights Act, August 6, 1965, http://miller center.org/president/speeches/speech-4034.

61. LBJ, Press Conference at the White House, August 25, 1965, http://millercenter.org/pres ident/lbjohnson/speeches/speech-5911.

62. Dallek, *Flawed Giant*, 220–21.

63. Goldfield, *Black, White, and Southern*, 176.

64. Quote, ibid., 178.

65. John W. Macy Jr. to Marvin Watson, June 14, 1967, Box 2. Presidential Papers, LBJ Library.

66. Charles E. Silberman, "Beware the Day They Change Their Minds," *Fortune*, November 1965, 150–58; quote on 150.

CHAPTER 18: PATRIMONY

1. Ben H. Bagdikian, "Death in Our Air," *Saturday Evening Post*, October 8, 1966, 31–35, 106, 108–10; quote on 110.

2. Ibid., 33.

3. Quote, ibid.

4. Ibid.

5. Ibid.

6. Quotes in Linda Lear, *Rachel Carson: Witness for Nature* (New York: Henry Holt, 1997), 454.

7. Biographical details on Rachel Carson, ibid.

8. Quote, ibid., 16.

9. Ibid., 18–20.

10. Ibid., 34.

11. Ibid., 78.

12. Quote, ibid., 163.

13. Ibid., 206.

14. Ibid., 226.

15. Ibid., 233, 260.

16. Rachel Carson, *Silent Spring* (Boston: Houghton Mifflin, 1962), 163–64.

17. Ibid., 161–71.

18. Ibid., 157–58.

19. Lear, *Rachel Carson*, 358–60.

20. Steven M. Spencer, "Fallout: The Silent Killer," *Saturday Evening Post*, August 29, 1959, 26–27, 87, 89, 90; Steven M. Spencer, "Fallout: The Silent Killer (How Soon Is Too Late)," *Saturday Evening Post*, September 5, 1959, 25, 84–85.

21. Quote in Lear, *Rachel Carson*, 367.

22. Ibid., 409.

23. Edwin Diamond, "The Myth of the 'Pesticide Menace,'" *Saturday Evening Post*, September 28, 1963, 16, 18.

24. Carson, *Silent Spring*, 283.

25. Ibid., 12.

26. Quote in Lear, *Rachel Carson*, 417.

27. Ibid., 423.

28. Both quotes, ibid., 429.

29. "Rachel Carson's Warning," *New York Times*, July 2, 1962.

30. Quote in Lear, *Rachel Carson*, 419.

31. Jane Howard, "The Gentle Storm Center: A Calm Appraisal of *Silent Spring*," *Life*, October 12, 1962, 105–6, 109–10; quote on 109.

32. Rickover, "Decline of the Individual," 11–13; quote on 12.

33. First quote in Carson, *Silent Spring*, 179; second quote in Rome, *Bulldozer*, 109.

34. Carson, *Silent Spring*, 183–84.

35. Lear, *Rachel Carson*, 448–50; quote on 450.

36. Ibid., 451.

37. Carson, *Silent Spring*, 27.

38. Lear, *Rachel Carson*, 471.

39. Ibid., afterword.

40. Quote in Sundquist, *Politics and Policy*, 346.

41. Ibid., 349.

42. Quote in Benjamin Kline, *First Along the River: A Brief History of the U.S. Environmental Movement* (Lanham, MD: Rowman & Littlefield, 1997), 85.

43. Sundquist, *Politics and Policy*, 363.

44. Quote in Dallek, *Flawed Giant*, 229.

45. Ibid., 229–30.

46. Quote in Memorandum from Kermit Gordon, Director, Bureau of the Budget, March 6, 1965, Box 24, Presidential Papers, LBJ Library.

47. LBJ, Remarks at the Signing of the Water Quality Act of 1965, October 2, 1965, http://www.presidency.ucsb.edu/ws/?pid=27289.

48. Sundquist, *Politics and Policy*, 366–67.

49. Ibid., 371.

50. "Don't Breathe Deeply," *Saturday Evening Post*, July 31, 1965, 88.

51. John Bird, "Our Dying Waters," *Saturday Evening Post*, April 23, 1966, 29–35, 66–67; quotes on 31.

52. Quote, ibid., 31.

53. Quote, ibid., 32.

54. Ibid., 34.

55. Quote in Rome, *Bulldozer*, 153.

56. Quote, ibid., 164.

57. Ibid., 375–79.

58. Quote, ibid., 140.

59. Quote in Kline, *First Along the River*, 86.

60. Martin V. Melosi, "Environmental Justice, Political Agenda Setting, and the Myths of History," *Journal of Policy History* 12, no. 1 (2000): 43–71.

61. Ibid.

62. Memorandum from Matt Nimetz (the White House) to Joe Califano, December 4, 1967, Box 38, Presidential Papers, LBJ Library.

63. Matt Perry to LBJ, September 24, 1967; LBJ to Matt Perry, October 7, 1967; Box 24, Presidential Papers, LBJ Library.

64. Ronald Reagan to LBJ, June 1, 1967, Box 26, Presidential Papers, LBJ Library.

65. On the Santa Barbara oil spill, see "1969 Oil Spill," http://www.presidency.ucsb.edu/ws/?pid=27289; on the Cuyahoga River fire, see Jonathan H. Adler, "The Fable of the Burning River, 45 Years Later," *Washington Post*, June 22, 2014. Adler's piece emphasizes the importance of timing in public policy.

CHAPTER 19: A WOMAN'S WORLD

1. Quotes in Stephanie Coontz, *Strange Stirring*, xv, 144.

2. Biographical details of Betty Friedan are in Horowitz, *Betty Friedan*.

3. Ibid., 17–19; quote on 17.

4. Quote, ibid., 23.

5. Ibid., 86.

6. Friedan, *Feminine Mystique*, 50, 56.

7. Ibid., 125.

8. Ibid., 228.

9. Fred M. Hechinger, "Sarah Lawrence Plans New Center," *New York Times*, January 11, 1962.

10. Friedan, *Feminine Mystique*, 509.

11. Ibid., 26, 27.

12. Ibid., 114, 116.

13. Ibid., 95.

14. Ibid., 31.

15. Ibid., 102, 136.

16. Quote, ibid., 102.

17. Interview with Rochelle "Shelli" Cohen Kanet, September 27, 2012.

18. Ibid.

19. Quote in Coontz, *Strange Stirring*, 151.

20. "Mrs. Lyndon B. Johnson's Challenge to Women," *Saturday Evening Post*, June 27, 1964, 88–89; quote on 88; italics in original.

21. Sally Kohn, "How Gidget Broke the Rules in '60s TV," *CNN News*, August 25, 2014, http://www.cnn.com/2014/05/29/opinion/kohn-tv-women-60s-gidget/.

22. The most helpful account of the Pill and its creation is Jonathan Eig, *The Birth of the Pill: How Four Crusaders Reinvented Sex and Launched a Revolution* (New York: W. W. Norton, 2014), quote on 4.

23. Quote, ibid., 51.

24. Steven M. Spencer, "New Case-History Facts on Birth-Control Pills," *Saturday Evening Post*, June 30, 1962, 13–19.

25. Ibid., 14.

26. Quote in Halberstam, *Fifties*, 605.

27. First quote in Jonathan Rinehart, "Mothers Without Joy," *Saturday Evening Post*, March 23, 1963, 33; remaining quotes in Cleo Shupp, "Little Girls Are Too Sexy Too Soon," *Saturday Evening Post*, June 29, 1963, 12, 16.

28. Steven M. Spencer, "The Birth Control Revolution," *Saturday Evening Post*, January 15, 1966, 21–25; 66–70; quote on 67.

29. Spencer, "New Case-History Facts," 13–19.

30. *Griswold v. Connecticut*, June 7, 1965, https://www.law.cornell.edu/supremecourt/text/381/479.

31. Quote in Spencer, "Birth Control Revolution," 22.

32. Rosemary Nossiff, "Abortion Policy Before *Roe*: Grassroots in Interest-Group Mobilization," *Journal of Policy History* 13, no. 4 (2001): 463–78.

33. John Bartlow Martin, "Abortion," *Saturday Evening Post*, May 20, 1961, 19–21, 72, 74; quote on 19.

34. Alan F. Guttmacher, "The Law That Doctors Often Break," *Saturday Evening Post*, August 1959, 23–24, 95–98; first quote on 25; second quote on 95; third quote on 96.

35. Nossiff, "Abortion Policy," 465.

36. William B. Ober, "We Should Legalize Abortion," *Saturday Evening Post*, October 8, 1966, 14, 20; quotes on 14.

37. Rebecca Traister, "Women Before Fetuses," *New Republic*, November 24, 2014, 26–27.

38. Karabel, *Chosen*, 415–28.

39. Quote, ibid., 423.

40. Coontz, *Strange Stirring*, 151.

41. LBJ cabinet meeting, January 17, 1964, in Johnson and Germany, *Presidential Recordings*, 3:593.

42. Peter Lisagor and Marguerite Higgins, "LBJ's Hunt for Womanpower," *Saturday Evening Post*, June 27, 1964, 86–87; quote on 87.

43. Ibid., 87.

44. Quotes, ibid., 86.

45. Orville Freeman to LBJ, February 19, 1964, in Johnson and Germany, *Presidential Recordings*, 4:591–92.

46. Ibid., 592.

47. Before taking a call from Clinton Anderson, February 4, 1964, 9:37 A.M., Johnson and Germany, *Presidential Recordings*, 4:160; LBJ to John Macy, January 6, 1964, 3:30 P.M., ibid., 3:167–68.

48. Menand, "Sex Amendment," 74–81.

49. Quotes, ibid., 80.

50. Quote, ibid.

51. First quote in ibid.; second quote in Coontz, *Strange Stirring*, 155.

52. Quote in Coontz, *Strange Stirring*, 155.

53. Menand, "Sex Amendment," 80.

54. Ibid.

55. Ibid.

56. Deborah Siegal, *Sisterhood, Interrupted: From Radical Women to Grrls Gone Wild* (New York: Palgrave Macmillan, 2007), 83.

57. Menand, "Sex Amendment," 81.

58. Graham, *Collision Course*, 81.

59. Quote in Menand, "Sex Amendment," 81.

CHAPTER 20: THE GREAT AMERICAN BREAKTHROUGH

1. Adlai Stevenson, "Extend our Vision . . . to All Mankind," *Life*, May 30, 1960: 87, 94, 97, 99–100, 102.

2. Ibid., 94, 97.

3. Leonard Silk, "The Vicious Cycle of Poverty," *Business Week*, February 1, 1964, 39–40, 42–43.

4. See Herbert Mitgang, "Michael Harrington, Socialist and Author, Is Dead," *New York Times*, August 2, 1989; Harold Meyerson, "The (Still) Relevant Socialist," *Atlantic*, August 2000, http://www.theatlantic.com/magazine/archive/2000/08/the-still-relevant-socialist/378331/.

5. Michael Harrington, *The Other America: Poverty in the United States* (New York: Macmillan, 1962), 31.

6. Ibid., 21.

7. Ibid., 13.

8. Ibid., 187, 16.

9. Ibid., 63.

10. Ibid., 71.

11. Ibid., 139, 140.

12. Ibid., 155, 156.

13. Ibid., 156.

14. Ibid., 79, 154.

15. Quote in Sundquist, *Politics and Policy*, 136.

16. Quotes, ibid., 137, 139.

17. Silk, "Vicious Cycle of Poverty," 42–43.

18. Quote in Edwin L. Dale Jr., "A Guaranteed Income; Idea Gains Ground Among Leaders, but to Many People It's a 'Handout,'" *New York Times*, May 28, 1968.

19. Quote in Edward C. Banfield, *The Unheavenly City: The Nature and the Future of Our Urban Crisis* (Boston: Little Brown, 1968), 125.

20. Quote in Dallek, *Flawed Giant*, 113.

21. Quote in Gareth Davies, *From Opportunity to Entitlement: The Transformation and Decline of Great Society Liberalism* (Lawrence, KN: University Press of Kansas, 1996), 36.

22. Russell M. Lawson and Benjamin A. Lawson, *Poverty in America: An Encyclopedia* (Westport, CT: Greenwood Press, 2008), 145.

23. Sundquist, *Politics and Policy*, 142–46; Davies, *Opportunity to Entitlement*, 34–35.

24. Quotes in Jill Lepore, "Tax Time," *New Yorker*, November 26, 2012, 28.

25. Sundquist, *Politics and Policy*, 145–50.

26. LBJ, "Great Society" speech, University of Michigan Commencement, May 22, 1964, http://www.pbs.org/wgbh/americanexperience/features/primary-resources/lbj-michigan/.

27. Lyndon B. Johnson, "The Great Society," *Saturday Evening Post*, October 31, 1964, 30–31.

28. Quote in Bret A. Weber and Amanda Wallace, "Revealing the Empowerment Revolution: A Literature Review of the Model Cities Program," *Journal of Urban History* 38 (November 2012): 173–92; quote on 175.

29. Quote, ibid., 175.

30. Ibid., 173.

31. For a good discussion of this legislation, see Graham, *Federal Education Policy*, 80–83.

32. Sundquist, *Politics and Policy*, 188–216.

33. Quotes, ibid., 211, 215.

34. Graham, *Federal Education Policy*, 76–79.

35. Graham and Diamond, *Research Universities*, 44. The numbers of Americans patronizing museums, symphonies, ballet, opera, and other "high" cultural activities skyrocketed during the 1960s. Public policy toward achieving a more equitable society and the prosperity generated by such policies opened up new cultural vistas for millions of Americans. Their basic needs satisfied, Americans developed a strong sense of civic consciousness that supported these cultural activities. Individual independence solidified the commonwealth. See Abraham H. Maslow's discussion of these points in *Motivation and Personality*, 100; LBJ, "Statement by the President," March 10, 1965, Statements of LBJ, March 8, 1965–March 25, 1965, Box 141, Presidential Papers, LBJ Presidential Library; quote in Sundquist, *Politics and Policy*, 216.

36. Sundquist, *Politics and Policy*, 217–19; Graham, *Federal Education Policy*, 202.

37. Graham, *Federal Education Policy*, xi–xiv.

38. Quote in Sundquist, *Politics and Policy*, 292.

39. Ibid., 294.

40. Julian E. Zelizer, *The Fierce Urgency of Now: Lyndon Johnson, Congress, and the Battle for the Great Society* (New York: Penguin, 2015). See especially chapter 6, "The Fabulous Eighty-Ninth Congress."

41. LBJ, Remarks with President Truman at the Signing in Independence of the Medicare Bill, July 30, 1965, http://www.lbjlib.utexas.edu/johnson/archives.hom/speeches.hom/650730.asp.

42. "U.S. Public Is Strongly Opposed to Easing of Immigration Laws," *Washington Post*, May 31, 1965; quote in Graham, *Collision Course*, 60.

43. Quote in Dallek, *Flawed Giant*, 227.

44. Henry H. Wilson Jr. to Lawrence F. O'Brien, July 11, 1964, Office Files of Henry W. Wilson, Box 3, Presidential Papers, LBJ Library.

45. A good discussion of the efforts to recast immigration is in Graham, *Collision Course*, 55–64.

46. Zolberg, *Nation by Design*, 329–34; LBJ, Remarks at the Signing of the Immigration Bill, Liberty Island, New York, October 3, 1965, http://www.lbjlib.utexas.edu/johnson/archives .hom/speeches.hom/651003.asp.

47. Zolberg, *Nation by Design*, 336–43.

48. Ibid., 336.

49. Graham, *Collision Course*, 93–96; "Immigration Visas Table," *New York Times*, May 26, 1966.

50. Patterson, *Grand Expectations*, 577–78; Zolberg, *Nation by Design*, 10.

51. Ted Widmer, "The Immigration Dividend," *New York Times*, October 6, 2015.

52. Quoted in Jeet Heer, "Operation Wetback Revisited," *New Republic*, June 2016, 5.

53. Felix E. Salinas, Special Assistant to the Chairman, Inter-Agency Committee on Mexican Affairs, the White House, to Committee Members, July 21, 1967, Box 94, Presidential Papers, LBJ Library.

54. LBJ to Edward R. Roybal, May 9, 1967, Box 421, Presidential Papers, LBJ Library.

55. LBJ, Remarks at the Welhausen Elementary School, Cotulla, Texas, November 7, 1966, http://www.presidency.ucsb.edu/ws/?pid=28003.

56. Ibid.

57. Graham, *Federal Education Policy*, 218; *Lau v. Nichols*, January 21, 1974, https://scholar .google.com/scholar_case?case=5046768322576386473&hl=en&as_sdt=6&as_vis=1&oi =scholar.

58. Sundquist, *Politics and Policy*, 484.

59. Quote, ibid., 3.

60. Quote in Dallek, *Flawed Giant*, 231.

61. Sundquist, *Politics and Policy*, 496–97.

62. Quote in Stewart Alsop, "Where Do We Go from Here?," *Saturday Evening Post*, September 25, 1965, 14.

CHAPTER 21: BLOOD

1. LBJ to unidentified aides, n.d., in Beschloss, *Reaching for Glory*, 426.

2. "Extremism and the Negro Revolution," *Saturday Evening Post*, June 24, 1964, 78.

3. Edward C. Banfield, *Unheavenly City*, 195.

4. Quotes in Davies, *Opportunity to Entitlement*, 55.

5. John Gregory Dunne, "The Ugly Mood of Watts," *Saturday Evening Post*, July 16, 1966, 83–87.

6. Quote in Banfield, *Unheavenly City*, 195.

7. Quote in Davies, *Opportunity to Entitlement*, 78.

8. Quotes in Banfield, *Unheavenly City*, 196.

9. First quote in Joseph A. Califano Jr., *The Triumph & Tragedy of Lyndon Johnson: The White House Years* (New York: Simon & Schuster, 1991), 49; second quote in Davies, *Opportunity to Entitlement*, 78.

10. Quote in Rick Perlstein, *Nixonland: The Rise of a President and the Fracturing of America* (New York: Scribner, 2008), 17.

11. Quote in Patterson, *Grand Expectations*, 589.

12. Stewart Alsop, "Watts: The Fire Next Time," *Saturday Evening Post*, November 6, 1965, 18. For a comprehensive analysis of the riot, see Gerald Horne, *Fire This Time: The Watts Uprising and the 1960s* (Charlottesville, VA: University Press of Virginia, 1995).

13. Alsop, "Watts," 20.

14. Ibid.

15. Stewart Alsop, "Johnson the Genius," *Saturday Evening Post*, January 29, 1966, 18.

16. Dunne, "Ugly Mood of Watts," 84.

17. Quotes, ibid., 85.

18. Daniel Patrick Moynihan, *The Negro Family: The Case for National Action* (Washington, DC: Government Printing Office, 1965). The title of chapter 4 is "The Tangle of Pathology."

19. Quote in Nicholas Kristof, "When Liberals Blew It," *New York Times*, March 12, 2015.

20. Bill Moyers to Joe Califano, July 30, 1965; and John W. Leslie to Frank Erwin, July 30, 1965; Box 67, Presidential Papers, LBJ Library.

21. Quote in Kristof, "When Liberals Blew It."

22. Quote, ibid.

23. Peter Beinart, "Why America Is Moving Left," *Atlantic*, January/February 2016, 62. See also Thomas Edsall and Mary Edsall, *Chain Reaction: The Impact of Race, Rights, and Taxes on American Politics* (New York: W. W. Norton, 1991).

24. Jake [?] to LBJ, August 10, 1966, Box 4, Presidential Papers, LBJ Library.

25. Ibid., 672.

26. Quoted in Andrew E. Busch, "1966 Midterm Foreshadows Republican Era," http://ashbrook.org/publications/oped-busch-06-1966/2.

27. D. Bradford Hunt, "Rethinking the Retrenchment Narrative in U.S. Housing Policy History," *Journal of Urban History* 32 (September 2006): 937–50; Hugh Davis Graham, "The Surprising Career of Federal Fair Housing Law," *Journal of Policy History* 12, no. 2 (2000): 215–32.

28. Davies, *Opportunity to Entitlement*, 180.

29. Dale Russakoff, "Schooled," *New Yorker*, May 19, 2014, 58–73.

30. Quote, ibid., 61.

31. Quote in Patterson, *Grand Expectations*, 663.

32. Quote in Davies, *Great Society*, 180.

33. Quote, ibid.

34. Quote, ibid., 63.

35. Quotes in Sundquist, *Politics and Policy*, 281, 282.

36. Quote in Davies, *Opportunity to Entitlement*, 65.

37. Sundquist, *Politics and Policy*, 285.

38. First quote, ibid.; second quote in Sam Tanenhaus, "The Power of Congress," *New Yorker*, January 19, 2015, 69–75; quote on 75.

39. LBJ, Speech to the Nation on Civil Disorders, July 27, 1967, http://millercenter.org/president/lbjohnson/speeches/speech-4040.

40. Stuart Alsop, "What the People Really Think," *Saturday Evening Post*, October 23, 1965, 27–31.

41. Memorandum from the Vice President to the President, July 27, 1967, Box 2, Presidential Papers, LBJ Library.

42. James Q. Wilson to Joseph Califano, August 8, 1967, Box 6, Presidential Papers, LBJ Library.

43. Ibid.

44. Ibid.

45. Ibid.

46. Ibid.

47. First quotes in "Dr. King Urges LBJ to Stop Riots with Jobs," *Jet*, August 10, 1967, 8, https://books.google.com/books?id=OroDAAAAMBAJ&pg=PA9&lpg=PA9&dq=LBJ%27s+r at+bill&source=bl&ots=iEvky9Hctw&sig=Dy8Ore4HOwGi5IMqT3EnI8on764&hl=en&sa=X &ved=oahUKEwjHl6yJx_3MAhWRdSYKHV6aD_MQ6AEIHjAA#v=onepage&q=LBJ's%20 rat%20bill&f=false; final quote in Tanenhaus, "Power of Congress," 75.

48. LBJ, Speech to the Nation on Civil Disorders, July 27, 1967, www.presidency.ucsb.edu/ws /?pid=28368.

49. Report of the National Advisory Commission on Civil Disorders, February 29, 1968, https://archive.org/stream/kernerreportreviooasse/kernerreportreviooasse_djvu.txt.

50. Report of the National Advisory Commission on Civil Disorders. Summary of Report, http://www.eisenhowerfoundation.org/docs/kerner.pdf.

51. Ibid.

52. Davies, *Opportunity to Entitlement*, 206.

53. Quotes in Patterson, *Grand Expectations*, 676.

54. Carter, *Wallace to Gingrich*, 37.

55. James Borchert, "Viewing the 'Underclass' and Ghetto from the Top Down," *Journal of Urban History* 25 (May 1999): 583–93.

56. LBJ, Remarks to the National Governors Conference, July 23, 1968, 46–53, http://www .nga.org/files/live/sites/NGA/files/pdf/1968NGAAnnualMeeting.pdf; LBJ, Remarks Upon Signing the Housing and Urban Development Act of 1968, August 1, 1968, http://www.presi dency.ucsb.edu/ws/?pid=29056; last quote in Dallek, *Flawed Giant*, 593.

57. LBJ, Remarks of Former President Lyndon B. Johnson at Civil Rights Symposium, Presidential Library, Austin, Texas, December 12, 1972, http://www.c-span.org/video/?320205- 1/lyndon-johnson-civil-rights.

58. Ibid.

CHAPTER 22: PARTY LINES

1. Quoted in Kevin Baker, "Political Party Meltdown," *New York Times*, December 20, 2015.

2. Quotes in Tanenhaus, "Power of Congress," 71.

3. Ibid., 72.

4. Mettler, *Soldiers to Citizens*, 123.

5. Selwyn James, "Billy Graham: God's Angry Young Man," *Redbook*, June 1954, 26–27, 75–78.

6. "If People Ever Required Religious Faith, It's Now," *Saturday Evening Post*, November 11, 1950, 10, 12; quote on 10.

7. The best source for the connection between business and religion is Jonathan P. Herzog, *The Spiritual-Industrial Complex: America's Religious Battle against Communism in the Early Cold War* (New York: Oxford University Press, 2011), quote on 84. See also Jonathan Herzog, "America's Spiritual-Industrial Complex and the Policy of Revival in the Early Cold War," *Journal of Policy History* 22, no. 3 (2010): 337–65.

8. A. James Reichley, "Faith in Politics," *Journal of Policy History* 13, no. 1 (2001): 137–80; quotes on 164.

9. For a full accounting of the West's key role in the resurgence of conservative religion and politics in postwar America, see Darren Dochuk, *From Bible Belt to Sunbelt: Plain-Folk Religion, Grassroots Politics, and the Rise of Evangelical Conservatism* (New York: W. W. Norton, 2011).

10. Mark A. Noll, "Jesus and Jefferson," *New Republic*, June 9, 2011, 38.

11. Elizabeth Stoker Bruenig, "Profits of God," *New Republic*, May 2015, 86–89.

12. Quote in Matthew Dallek, "The Conservative 1960s," *Atlantic*, December 1995, https://www.theatlantic.com/magazine/archive/1995/12/the-conservative-1960s/376506/.

13. Quote in Murray Kempton, "Barry Goldwater," *Spectator*, July 11, 1963, http://archive.spectator.co.uk/article/12th-july-1963/6/barry-goldwater.

14. Leah Wright Rigueur, "Why the G.O.P. Can't Win Black Votes," *New York Times*, August 4, 2016.

15. Quotes in Gail Collins, "The State of the 4-Year-Olds," *New York Times*, February 13, 2013.

16. Quote in Jill Lepore, "The Woman's Card," *New Yorker*, June 27, 2016, 26.

17. Hamby, *Liberalism*, 299.

18. Quotes in Patterson, *Grand Expectations*, 740.

19. Hamby, *Liberalism*, 318–19.

20. Richard Nixon, "Special Message to the Congress on Higher Education," March 19, 1970, http://www.presidency.ucsb.edu/ws/?pid=2915.

21. Patterson, *Grand Expectations*, 721–22.

22. Ibid., 726–27.

23. Quote in Allen Barra, "Female Athletes, Thank Nixon," *New York Times*, June 17, 2012.

24. Richard Nixon, "Remarks on Signing the National Environmental Policy Act of 1969," January 1, 1970, http://www.presidency.ucsb.edu/ws/?pid=2446; "Annual Message to the Congress on the State of the Union," January 22, 1970, http://www.presidency.ucsb.edu/ws/?pid=2921.

25. Richard Nixon, "Message to the Congress Transmitting the First Annual Report of the Council on Environmental Quality," August 10, 1970, http://www.presidency.ucsb.edu/ws/?pid=2618.

26. First quote in Bill Christofferson, *The Man from Clear Lake: Earth Day Founder Sen. Gaylord Nelson* (Madison, WI: University of Wisconsin Press, 2004), 87; second quote in Nicholas Lemann, "When the Earth Moved: What Happened to the Environmental Movement?," *New Yorker*, April 15, 2013, 73–76; quote on 73.

27. For an excellent and concise overview of U.S. environmental policy, see Michael E. Kraft, "U.S. Environmental Policy and Politics: From the 1960s to the 1990s," *Journal of Policy History* 12, no. 1 (2000): 17–42.

28. Kline, *First Along the River*, 119.

29. Rome, *Bulldozer*, 238–247; quote in Patterson, *Grand Expectations*, 729.

30. Theodore J. Lowi, *The End of the Republican Era* (Norman, OK: University of Oklahoma Press, 2006; first published in 1995), 268.

31. George Packer, "The Uses of Division," *New Yorker*, August 11 and 18, 2014, 86.

32. Robert G. Kaiser, "Our Conservative, Criminal Politicians," *New York Review of Books*, November 6, 2014, 54–56; quotes on 56. See also Rick Perlstein, *Invisible Bridge: The Fall of Nixon and the Rise of Reagan* (New York: Simon & Schuster, 2014).

33. Larry M. Bartels, *Unequal Democracy: The Political Economy of the New Gilded Age* (New York: Russell Sage Foundation, 2008), 47–55; quote on 55.

34. Carter, *Wallace to Gingrich*, 63.

35. Ibid., 114.

36. Ibid., 117.

37. Ibid.

38. Ibid.

39. Ibid., 118.

40. Quotes in Graham, *Federal Education Policy*, 215. See also Suzanne Mettler, *Degrees of Inequality: How the Politics of Higher Education Sabotaged the American Dream* (New York: Basic Books, 2014).

41. Packer, "Uses of Division," 86.

42. Quote in Jason DeParle, "Why Do People Who Need Help from the Government Hate It So Much?," *New York Times Book Review*, September 19, 2016, https://www.nytimes.com /2016/09/25/books/review/strangers-in-their-own-land-arlie-russell-hochschild.html?_r=0. The quote came from Arlie Russell Hochschild's book *Strangers in Their Own Land: Anger and Mourning on the American Right* (New York: New Press, 2016).

43. Quotes in Sam Tanenhaus, "The Leftist Origins of the Rabid Right," *Atlantic*, March 2016, 43.

44. Ronald Reagan, "The President's News Conference," August 12, 1988, http://www.pres idency.ucsb.edu/ws/?pid=37733.

45. Nicholas Lemann, "Reagan: The Triumph of Tone," *New York Review of Books*, March 10, 2016, 8, 10, 12.

46. Bartels, *Unequal Democracy*, 1–3, 32–41, 47–55.

47. Ibid., 6–12.

48. Ibid., 65–66.

49. George Packer, "The Unconnected," *New Yorker*, October 31, 2016, 48–61.

50. Lemann, "Reagan," 12.

51. First quote, Packer, "Unconnected," 52; second quote, Bill Clinton, "Address Before a Joint Session of the Congress on the State of the Union," January 23, 1996, http://www.presidency .ucsb.edu/ws/?pid=53091.

52. Clinton first promised to "end welfare as we know it" in a 1992 campaign ad. *Washington Post*, August 30, 2016, https://www.washingtonpost.com/video/national/rep-nunes-apologizes -for-handling-of-trump-surveillance-claim/2017/03/23/96ce9424-100c-11e7-aa57-2ca1b05c41b8 _video.html.

53. Quote in Eduardo Porter, "Discredited Notions Still Guide Policy on Aid to the Poor," *New York Times*, October 21, 2015. See also Christopher Jencks, "Why the Very Poor Have Become Poorer," *New York Review of Books*, June 9, 2016, 15–17.

54. Eduardo Porter, "The Case for More Government, Not Less," *New York Times*, August 3, 2016.

55. Nicholas Lemann, "Can We Have a 'Party of the People'?," *New York Review of Books*, October 13, 2016, 48.

56. Quote in Packer, "Unconnected," 58.

CHAPTER 23: THE POPULIST MOMENT

1. The best overview of the populist political movement in the United States is Michael Kazin, *The Populist Persuasion: An American History* (Ithaca, NY: Cornell University Press, 1998). A fine work on the 1890s Populists is Lawrence Goodwyn, *The Populist Moment: A Short History of the Agrarian Revolt in America* (New York: Oxford University Press, 1978).

2. C. Vann Woodward, *Tom Watson: Agrarian Rebel* (New York: Oxford University Press, 1963; first published in 1938); Richard Hofstadter, "The Paranoid Style in American Politics," *Harper's*, November 1964, 77–86.

3. Quotes in Sam Tanenhaus, "Why Populism Now?," *New York Times Book Review*, June 26, 2016, 15.

4. Quotes in Dan T. Carter, "What Donald Trump Owes George Wallace," *New York Times*, January 10, 2016. See also Carter's superb study *The Politics of Rage: George Wallace, the Origins of the New Conservatism, and the Transformation of American Politics* (New York: Simon & Schuster, 1995).

5. Quote in Carter, "What Trump Owes Wallace."

6. Ibid.

7. Patrick Buchanan, "1992 Republican National Convention Speech," August 17, 1992, http://buchanan.org/blog/1992-republican-national-convention-speech-148.

8. Quote in Wills, "Triumph of the Hard Right," 4, 6. See also E. J. Dionne, *Why the Right Went Wrong: Conservatism—from Goldwater to the Tea Party and Beyond* (New York: Simon & Schuster, 2016).

9. Packer, "Unconnected," 30.

10. Tracie McMillan, "White Resentment on the Night Shift at Walmart," *New York Times*, December 18, 2016.

11. Quotes in Derek Thompson, "America's Monopoly Problem," *Atlantic*, October 2016, 26, 27.

12. Patricia Cohen, "More Work for Less Pay," *Atlantic*, March 9, 2017; David Brooks, "The G.O.P. Health Care Crackup," March 10, 2017.

13. Quotes in Neal Gabler, "My Secret Shame," *Atlantic*, May 2016, 57.

13. Ibid., 60.

14. Quote in Aaron Smith, "The Middle Class Fall Further Behind," *CNN Money*, August 22, 2012, http://money.cnn.com/2012/08/22/news/economy/middle-class-pew/.

15. Don Peck, "Can the Middle Class Be Saved?," *Atlantic*, September 2011, 60–78.

16. Ibid.

17. Joseph E. Stiglitz, "Inequality Is Holding Back the Recovery," *New York Times*, January 20, 2013.

18. Ibid.

19. Joel Kotkin, "The U.S. Middle Class Is Turning Proletarian," *Forbes*, February 16, 2014, http://www.forbes.com/sites/joelkotkin/2014/02/16/the-u-s-middle-class-is-turning-proletarian/#5fd471f2f293.

20. Peck, "Can the Middle Class Be Saved?"

21. Eduardo Porter, "America's Sinking Middle Class," *New York Times*, September 19, 2013; Eduardo Porter, "A Simple Equation: More Education = More Income," *New York Times*, September 11, 2014.

22. Lepore, "Tax Time," 24–29; quote on 28.

23. David Kocieniewski, "Since 1980s, the Kindest of Tax Cuts for the Rich," *New York Times*, January 18, 2012.

24. Jill Lepore, "Richer and Poorer," *New Yorker*, March 16, 2015, 26–32.

25. Benjamin M. Friedman, " 'Brave New Capitalists' Paradise': The Jobs?," *New York Review of Books*, November 7, 2013, 74–76.

26. Robert B. Reich, "Limping Middle Class," *New York Times*, September 4, 2011.

27. Ibid.

28. Ibid.

29. Ibid.

30. Ibid.

31. Quote, ibid.

32. Friedman, " 'Brave New Capitalists' Paradise,' " 76.

33. Lepore, "Richer and Poorer." See also Anthony B. Atkinson, *Inequality: What Can Be Done?* (Cambridge, MA: Harvard University Press, 2015).

34. Joseph E. Stiglitz, "Inequality Is Not Inevitable," *New York Times*, June 29, 2014.

35. First quote in Eduardo Porter, "A Search for Answers on Income Inequality," *New York Times*, March 26, 2014; second quote in Charles M. Blow, "We Can't Grow the Gap Away," *New York Times*, March 15, 2014.

36. Andrew Kohut, "Don't Mind the Gap," *New York Times*, January 27, 2012.

37. Ben Carpenter, "Is Your Student Prepared for Life?," *New York Times*, September 1, 2014.

38. Quote in Andrew J. Cherlin, "Why Are White Death Rates Rising?," *New York Times*, February 22, 2016.

39. All quotes and figures in this paragraph and the succeeding four paragraphs derive from Nicholas Eberstadt, "Our Miserable 21st Century," *Commentary*, February 15, 2017, https://www.commentarymagazine.com/articles/our-miserable-21st-century/.

40. Quote and figures in this paragraph and the succeeding paragraph are in Neil Irwin, "Job Growth in Past Decade Was in Temp and Contract," *New York Times*, March 31, 2016.

41. Eduardo Porter, "A Budget Reflecting Resentments," *New York Times*, March 8, 2017; Ross Douthat, "A Different Bargain on Race," *New York Times*, March 5, 2017.

42. Quote and figures in Neil Irwin, "How Being More Like France Might Help Labor Markets," *New York Times*, June 21, 2016.

43. Figures in this paragraph and the succeeding two paragraphs from Eduardo Porter, "President-Elect Found Votes Where the Jobs Weren't," *New York Times*, December 14, 2016.

44. Quote in Jelani Cobb, "Working-Class Heroes," *New Yorker*, April 25, 2016, 34.

45. Quote in Alec MacGillis, "The Original Underclass," *Atlantic*, September 2016, 100.

46. Tyler Cowen, "How a Marriage of Equals May Promote Inequality," *New York Times*, December 27, 2015.

47. The figures in this paragraph and the succeeding paragraph are from Eduardo Porter, "Education Gap Widens Between Rich and Poor," *New York Times*, September 23, 2015.

48. Quote in Jonathan Rauch, "Containing Trump," *Atlantic*, March 2017, 63.

49. Karl Marlantes, "The War That Killed Trust," *New York Times*, January 8, 2017.

CHAPTER 24: STALL

1. Maslow, *Motivation and Personality*, xvii. The quote comes from the preface of the new edition. Statistics from Claire Cain Miller, "Signs of a Truce in the Mommy Wars," *New York Times*, December 10, 2015.

2. Quotes in Coontz, "Why Gender Equality Stalled."

3. Coontz, *Strange Stirring*, 169.

4. Ibid., 172.

5. Quote, ibid., 173.

6. Ibid., 174.

7. Ibid.

8. Jeffrey Toobin, "Heavyweight: How Ruth Bader Ginsburg Has Moved the Supreme Court," *New Yorker*, March 11, 2013, 38–47; quotes on 41.

9. Ibid., 42.

10. Ibid.

11. Ibid.

12. *Roe v. Wade* (1973), http://caselaw.findlaw.com/us-supreme-court/410/113.html.

13. Jeffrey Toobin, "Daughters of Texas," *New Yorker*, August 5, 2013, 24–29; Jeffrey Toobin, "Our Broken Constitution," *New Yorker*, December 9, 2013, 64–73.

14. Coontz, *Strange Stirring*, 178.

15. Marcia Angeli, "The Women at the Top," *New York Review of Books*, March 20, 2014, 18, 20–21.

16. Ibid.; Eduardo Porter, "To Address Gender Gap, Is It Enough to Lean In?," *New York Times*, September 25, 2013.

17. Philip N. Cohen, "How Can We Jump-Start the Struggle for Gender Equality," *New York Times*, November 23, 2013; quote in Porter, "Gender Gap."

18. Claire Cain Miller, "Pay Gap Is Because of Gender, Not Jobs," *New York Times*, April 24, 2014.

19. Porter, "Gender Gap."

20. Ibid.; Coontz, "Why Gender Equality Stalled."

21. Coontz, "Why Gender Equality Stalled."

22. Ann Crittenden, "On Top of Everything Else," *New York Times Book Review*, March 30, 2014, 15.

23. Quote, ibid.

24. Ibid. Statistics in Gail Collins, "Where Did Our Working Women Go?," *New York Times*, October 17, 2015.

25. Megan A. Sholar, "The History of Family Leave Policies in the United States," *American Historian*, November 2016, 41–45.

26. Quote in Judith Shulevitz, "It's Payback Time for Women," *New York Times*, January 10, 2016. See also Claire Cain Miller, "Stressed, Tired, Rushed: Portrait of the Modern Family," *New York Times*, November 5, 2015.

27. Judith Warner, "Family Way," *New York Times*, May 10, 2012.

28. Sholar, "Family Leave Policies," 43.

29. First quote in Shulevitz, "Payback Time"; other quotes in Miller, "Stressed, Tired, Rushed."

30. Quotes in James Surowiecki, "The Cult of Overwork," *New Yorker*, January 27, 2014, http://www.newyorker.com/magazine/2014/01/27/the-cult-of-overwork. See also Wolf, *The XX Factor*.

31. Quote in Angeli, "Women at the Top."

32. Wolf, *XX Factor*, 77.

33. Judith Shulevitz, "The Corporate Mystique: Sheryl Sandberg and the Folly of Davos-Style Feminism," *New Republic*, March 25, 2013, 6–8; quote on 8.

34. National Council of State Legislatures, "State Family and Medical Leave Laws," July 19, 2016, http://www.ncsl.org/research/labor-and-employment/state-family-and-medical-leave-laws.aspx.

35. Ibid.

36. On the Hyde Amendment, see John Light, "Five Facts You Should Know About the Hyde Amendment," *Moyers and Company*, January 25, 2013, http://billmoyers.com/content/five-facts-you-should-know-about-the-hyde-amendment/.

CHAPTER 25: THE COLOR LINE

1. Lynn Haessly interview with Harvey B. Gantt, January 6, 1986, Southern Oral History Program Collection (#4007), University of North Carolina, Chapel Hill.

2. Dean Starkman, "The $236,500 Hole in the American Dream," *New Republic*, July 14, 2014, 30–35.

3. Norman Fainstein and Susan Nesbitt, "Did the Black Ghetto Have a Golden Age? Class Structure and Class Segregation in New York City, 1949–1970, with Initial Evidence for 1990," *Journal of Urban History* 23 (November 1996): 3–28.

4. Ibid.; Isabel Wilkerson, "Race to the Bottom," *New Republic*, March 1, 2012, 10–11.

5. Wilkerson, "Race to the Bottom,"

6. Ibid.

7. Starkman, "American Dream," 30–35.

8. Ibid.

9. "Affordable Housing, Racial Isolation," *New York Times*, June 29, 2015.

10. *Texas Department of Housing and Community Affairs et al. v. Inclusive Communities Project, Inc., et al.*, June 25, 2015, http://www.supremecourt.gov/opinions/14pdf/13-1371_m640.pdf.

11. "The End of Federally Financed Ghettos," *New York Times*, July 12, 2015.

12. Michael B. Katz, "The American Welfare State and Social Contract in Hard Times," *Journal of Policy History* 22, no. 4 (2010): 509–29; quote on 509.

13. Josh Levin, "The Welfare Queen," *Slate*, December 19, 2013, http://www.slate.com/articles /news_and_politics/history/2013/12/linda_taylor_welfare_queen_ronald_reagan_made_her_a _notorious_american_villain.html.

14. David O. Sears, "Black-White Conflict: A Model for the Future of Ethnic Politics in Los Angeles?," in *New York & Los Angeles*, ed. David Halle (Chicago: University of Chicago Press, 2003), 367–79; quote on 373.

15. Lepore, "Tax Time," 24–29.

16. Coates, "Case for Reparations," 54–71. See also *National Federation of Independent Business v. Sebelius* (2012). https://supreme.justia.com/cases/federal/us/567/11-393/

17. Franklin D. Roosevelt, "Annual Message to Congress," January 4, 1935, http://www .presidency.ucsb.edu/ws/?pid=14890; Benjamin M. Friedman, "What's in a Name? Every-thing," *Atlantic*, July and August 2014, 40–41.

18. Ronald Reagan, "Remarks on Signing the Family Support Act of 1988," October 13, 1988, http://www.presidency.ucsb.edu/ws/?pid=35013; "Welfare Reform," Hearings Before the Committee on Finance, U.S. Senate, 100th Cong., 1st sess., October 14 and 28, 1987, http:// njlaw.rutgers.edu/collections/gdoc/hearings/8/88601411b/88601411b_1.pdf.

19. "The Family Support Act of 1988," http://www.irp.wisc.edu/publications/focus/pdfs /foc114e.pdf.

20. Peter Wehner, "Government Is Not the Enemy," *New York Times*, February 28, 2015; Michael B. Katz, "Segmented Visions: Recent Historical Writing on American Welfare," *Journal of Urban History* 24 (January 1998): 244–55.

21. Eduardo Porter, "Confronting Old Problem May Require a New Deal," *New York Times*, January 20, 2014.

22. Charles A. Murray, *Losing Ground: American Social Policy, 1950–1980* (New York: Basic Books, 1984), 191.

23. Richard J. Herrnstein and Charles Murray, *The Bell Curve: Intelligence and Class Structure in American Life* (New York: Free Press, 1994), 526.

24. Dinesh D'Souza, *The End of Racism: Principles for a Multiracial Society* (New York: Free Press, 1995).

25. Sabrina Tavernise, "Black Youth Lag as Peers Progress on Poverty," *New York Times*, July 15, 2015.

26. "The Cost of Letting Young People Drift," editorial, *New York Times*, June 21, 2015.

27. Orlando Patterson, "The Real Problem with America's Inner Cities," *New York Times*, May 10, 2015.

28. Ibid. Michael Javen Fortner, *Black Silent Majority: The Rockefeller Drug Laws and the Politics of Punishment* (Cambridge, MA: Harvard University Press, 2015). See also James Forman Jr., *Locking Up Our Own: Crime and Punishment in Black America* (New York: Farrar, Straus & Giroux, 2017).

29. Quote in Patterson, "Real Problem."

30. Ibid.

31. Ibid.

32. Nicholas Kristof, "Where the G.O.P. Gets It Right," *New York Times*, April 10, 2014.

33. Ibid.; quote in Orlando Patterson, "The Content of Character," *New York Times Book Review*, March 8, 2015, 12.

34. Quote in Vishaan Chakrabarti, "America's Urban Future," *New York Times*, April 17, 2014.

35. Quotes in David Brooks, "The Rediscovery of Character," *New York Times*, March 6, 2012.

36. Christopher Jencks, "The War on Poverty: Was It Lost?," *New York Review of Books*, April 2, 2015, 82–85; Christopher Jencks, "Did We Lose the War on Poverty?—II," *New York Review of Books*, April 23, 2015, 37–39.

37. Ibid.

38. Jencks, "War on Poverty," April 23, 2015, 37.

39. Ibid.

40. Nicholas Kristof, "Progress in the War on Poverty," *New York Times*, January 9, 2014.

41. Annie Lowrey, "50 Years Later: War on Poverty Is a Mixed Bag," *New York Times*, January 5, 2014.

42. Eduardo Porter, "In the War on Poverty, a Dogged Adversary," *New York Times*, December 13, 2013.

43. Jencks, "War on Poverty," April 23, 2015, 37–39.

44. Kristof, "Progress in the War on Poverty."

45. Jason Furman, "Smart Social Programs," *New York Times*, May 11, 2015.

46. Ibid. Again Abraham H. Maslow's theory on the hierarchy of needs is instructive here. With government providing basic needs, recipients can focus on satisfying higher-level needs such as education, meaningful work, and civic engagement. Maslow, *Motivation and Personality*.

47. Furman, "Smart Social Programs."

48. Paul Krugman, "The War over Poverty," *New York Times*, January 10, 2014.

49. Ibid., 39.

50. Jennifer Frost, "Social Citizenship and the City," *Journal of Urban History* 30 (January 2004): 289–98; quote on 290.

51. Eduardo Porter, "Income Inequality Is Costing the Nation on Social Issues," *New York Times*, April 29, 2015.

52. W. E. B. Du Bois, "The Forethought," in *The Souls of Black Folk* (Chicago: A. A. McClurg & Co., 1903).

CHAPTER 26: THE OLD COUNTRY

1. Patterson, *Grand Expectations*, 597–99, 616–21, 633.

2. Steve Kelman, "You Force Kids to Rebel," *Saturday Evening Post*, November 19, 1966, 12, 14; quotes on 12.

3. Ibid., 12.

4. Ibid.

5. Ibid., 14.

6. Ibid.

7. Ibid.

8. Quote in Andrew Delbanco, *Melville: His World and Work* (New York, 2013), 304.

9. Quote in Andrew Solomon, "Go Play Outside," *New York Times Book Review*, December 14, 2014, 26–27.

10. Jeffrey Jensen Arnett and Elizabeth Fishel, *Getting to 30: A Parent's Guide to the 20-Something Years* (New York: Alfred A.Knopf, 2013), 3.

11. Quote in Todd G. Buchholz and Victoria Buchholz, "The Go-Nowhere Generation," *New York Times*, March 11, 2012.

12. The Report of the President's Commission on Campus Unrest (Washington, DC: Government Printing Office, 1970), http://files.eric.ed.gov/fulltext/ED083899.pdf.

13. Quote in Jon Wiener, "Something Happening Here," *New York Times Book Review*, June 12, 2016, 11. See also Clara Bingham, *Witness to the Revolution: Radicals, Resisters, Vets, Hippies, and the Year America Lost Its Mind and Found Its Soul* (New York: Random House, 2016).

14. Patterson, *Grand Expectations*, 755.

15. Ibid.

16. "Our Threatened Way of Life," *Saturday Evening Post*, November 6, 1965, 98.

17. John Gardner to LBJ, "Memorandum," December 27, 1967, Presidential Papers, Box 8, LBJ Library.

18. George F. Will, *Statecraft as Soulcraft: What Government Does* (New York: Simon & Schuster, 1983), 151.

19. Schlesinger, *Vital Center*, xv.

20. Quotes in John Cassidy, "Elizabeth Warren's Moment," *New York Review of Books*, May 22, 2014, 4, 6, 8.

21. Quote in Jones, *Great Expectations*, 253.

22. Frank Rich, "A Distant Mirror," *New York Times Book Review*, August 3, 2014, 1, 16–17.

23. Quote in Jones, *Great Expectations*, 256.

24. Michael F. Ford, "Five Myths About the American Dream," *Washington Post*, January 6, 2012.

25. Andrew Ross Sorkin and Megan Thee-Brenan, "Many Feel the American Dream Is Out of Reach, Poll Shows," *New York Times*, December 10, 2014.

26. Adam Gopnik, "Decline, Fall, Rinse, Repeat," *New Yorker*, August 29, 2011, 40–47; quote on 47.

27. Arthur C. Brooks, "We Need Optimists," *New York Times*, July 26, 2015; Frank Bruni, "America the Shrunken," *New York Times*, May 4, 2014.

28. Frank Bruni, "Lost in America," *New York Times*, August 28, 2014.

29. Ibid.; Leon Wieseltier, "Xu's Gift," *New Republic*, February 17, 2014, 55.

30. Bruni, "America the Shrunken."

31. Ibid.

32. Quote in Zachary, *Endless Frontier*, 403.

33. David Brooks, "The Working Nation," *New York Times*, October 23, 2014.

34. Sheri Berman, "As the World Turns," *New York Times Book Review*, September 14, 2014, 1, 22; quotes on 22. See also Francis Fukuyama, *Political Order and Political Decay: From the Industrial Revolution to the Globalization of Democracy* (New York: Farrar, Straus, and Giroux, 2014).

CHAPTER 27: THE GREAT REGRESSION

1. Mann, *For Better or for Worse*, 138.

2. James Fallows, "How America Can Rise Again," *Atlantic*, January/February 2010, 38–55; quote on 52.

3. Ibid.

4. Ibid., 55.

5. Judis, "Steve Jobs's Angel," *New Republic*, September 2, 2013, 4, 6–7.

6. Ibid.

7. Ibid.

8. Ibid.

9. Newt Gingrich, "Double the N.I.H. Budget," *New York Times*, April 25, 2015.

10. First quote in Sam Stein, "Newt Gingrich Wants to Double the NIH Budget; Some of His Old Colleagues Aren't So Sure," *Huffington Post*, April 22, 2015, http://www.huffingtonpost.com/2015/04/22/newt-gingrich-nih_n_7121750.html; second quote in Joe Nocera, "Government Nurtures Innovation," *New York Times*, May 3, 2014.

11. William J. Broad, "Billionaires with Big Ideas Are Privatizing American Science," *New York Times*, March 16, 2014.

12. Eamonn Fingleton, "America the Innovative?," *New York Times*, March 31, 2013.

13. Fallows, "How America Can Rise Again," 55.

14. Robert D. Putnam, *Our Kids: The American Dream in Crisis* (New York: Simon & Schuster, 2015); David Brooks, "The Cost of Relativism," *New York Times*, March 10, 2015.

15. Gary Rivlin, "B.A.s and I.O.U.s," *New York Times Book Review*, June 6, 2014. See also Mettler, *Degrees of Inequality*.

16. Jonathan Cowan and Jim Kessler, "The Middle Class Gets Wise," *New York Times*, October 19, 2013.

17. William Deresiewicz, "I Saw the Best Minds of My Generation Destroyed by the Ivy League," *New Republic*, August 4, 2014, 24–29; quote on 29.

18. Ibid.

19. Cowan and Kessler, "Middle Class Gets Wise."

20. Robert J. Gordon, "The Great Stagnation of American Education," *New York Times*, September 8, 2013.

21. David Leonhardt, "Is College Worth It? Clearly, New Data Says," *New York Times*, May 27, 2014.

22. Suzanne Mettler, "College, the Great Unleveler," *New York Times*, March 2, 2014.

23. Louis Menand, "Today's Assignment," *New Yorker*, December 17, 2012, 25–26.

24. Nicholas Kristof, "The American Dream Is Leaving America," *New York Times*, October 26, 2014.

25. Dionne Searcey and Robert Gebeloff, "U.S. Seniors Prosper, Finding 'Sweet Spot' in Middle Class," *New York Times*, June 15, 2015.

26. Ibid.

27. George Packer, "Celebrating Inequality," *New York Times*, May 20, 2013. See also E. J. Dionne Jr., *Our Divided Heart: The Battle for the American Idea in an Age of Discontent* (New York: Bloomsbury, 2012).

28. Fallows, "How America Can Rise Again," 38–55; quote on 49.

29. Ibid.

30. Sundquist, *Politics and Policy*, 3–6.

31. Schlesinger, *Vital Center*, 245.

32. David Cole, "How Corrupt Are Our Politics?," *New York Review of Books*, September 24, 2014, 46, 48.

33. Schlesinger, *Vital Center*, xii.

BIBLIOGRAPHY

PRIMARY SOURCES

COURT CASES, LETTERS, MEMOIRS, DIARIES, PAMPHLETS, BOOKS, ARTICLES, AND SPEECHES

"1969 Oil Spill," http://www.presidency.ucsb.edu/ws/?pid=27289.

Adams, John Quincy. "First Annual Message." December 6, 1825. http://www.presidency.ucsb.edu/ws/?pid=29467.

Beschloss, Michael, ed. *Reaching for Glory: Lyndon Johnson's Secret White House Tapes, 1964–1965.* NY: Simon & Schuster, 2001.

Beschloss, Michael, ed. *Taking Charge: The Johnson White House Tapes.* NY: Simon & Schuster, 1997.

Briggs v. Elliott (1951). https://scholar.google.com/scholar_case?case=17196258935977715010&hl=en&as_sdt=6&as_vis=1&oi=scholarr.

Buchanan, Patrick. "1992 Republican National Convention Speech," August 17, 1992. http://buchanan.org/blog/1992-republican-national-convention-speech-148.

Clinton, Bill. "Address Before a Joint Session of the Congress on the State of the Union," January 23, 1996. http://www.presidency.ucsb.edu/ws/?pid=53091.

Daniels, Roger and Otis L. Graham, eds. *Debating American Immigration, 1882–Present.* London: Rowman & Littlefield, 2001.

Eisenhower, Dwight D. *Papers of Dwight David Eisenhower.* [DDE] http://eisenhower.press.jhu.edu.librarylink.uncc.edu/index.html.

Eisenhower, Dwight D. "Address to the American Society of Newspaper Editors and the International Press Institute." April 17, 1958. http://www.presidency.ucsb.edu/ws/?pid=11357.

———. "Radio and Television Address to the American People on Science in National Security," November 7, 1957. http://www.presidency.ucsb.edu/ws/?pid=10946.

Ferrell, Robert H. ed. *Off the Record: The Private Papers of Harry S. Truman.* Columbia, MO: University of Missouri Press, 1980.

———. ed. *Dear Bess: The Letters from Harry to Bess Truman, 1910–1959.* Columbia, MO: University of Missouri Press, 1983.

Giangreco, D.M. and Kathryn Moore. eds. *Dear Harry . . . Truman's Mailroom, 1945–1953: The Truman Administration Through Correspondence with "Everyday America."* Mechanicsburg, PA: Stackpole Books, 1999.

Griswold v. Connecticut, June 7, 1965. https://www.law.cornell.edu/supremecourt/text/381/479.

Johnson, Robert David and Kent B. Germany, eds. *The Presidential Recordings. Lyndon B. Johnson: Toward the Great Society. Volume IV. February 1, 1964–March 8, 1964.* NY: W.W. Norton, 2007.

Johnson, Lyndon Baines. *Presidential Papers of LBJ.* LBJ Presidential Library. Austin, Texas.

————. *Senate Papers of LBJ*. LBJ Presidential Library. Austin, Texas.

————. Remarks Upon Signing the Housing and Urban Development Act of 1968. August 1, 1968. http://www.presidency.ucsb.edu/ws/?pid=29056.

————. Remarks to the National Governors Conference, July 23, 1968: 46–53. http://www.nga .org/files/live/sites/NGA/files/pdf/1968NGAAnnualMeeting.pdf.

————. Speech to the Nation on Civil Disorders, July 27, 1967. www.presidency,ucsb.edu/ws /?pid=28368.

————. Remarks at the Welhausen Elementary School, Cotulla, Texas, November 7, 1966. http:// www.presidency.ucsb.edu/ws/?pid=28003.

————. Remarks at the Signing of the Water Quality Act of 1965, October 2, 1965. http://www .presidency.ucsb.edu/ws/?pid=27289.

————, Press Conference at the White House, August 25, 1965. http://millercenter.org/president /lbjohnson/speeches/speech-5911.

————. Speech Before Congress on Voting Rights, March 15, 1965. http://millercenter.org/presi dent/speeches/speech-3386.

————. Remarks Upon Signing the Civil Rights Act, July 2, 1964. http://millercenter.org/presi dent/speeches/speech-3525.

————. "Great Society" speech, University of Michigan Commencement, May 22, 1964. http:// www.pbs.org/wgbh/americanexperience/features/primary-resources/lbj-michigan/.

————. "Annual Message to the Congress on the State of the Union." January 8, 1964. http://www .presidency.ucsb.edu/ws/?pid=26787.

————. "Address to Joint Session of Congress." November 27, 1963. http://millercenter.org/presi dent/lbjohnson/speeches/speech-3381.

————. "Remarks at Gettysburg on Civil Rights." May 30, 1963. http://millercenter.org/president /lbjohnson/speeches/speech-3380.

Kennedy, John F. "Report to the American People on Civil Rights." June 11, 1963. http://www .jfklibrary.org/Asset-Viewer/LH8F_oMzvoe6Ro1yEm74Ng.aspx.

————. "Speech on Religion." September 12, 1960. http://www.npr.org/templates/story/story .php?storyId=16920600.

————. "Speech." October 27, 1960. http://www.presidency.ucsb.edu/ws/index.php?pid =74241.

King, Martin Luther, Jr.. "Our God is Marching On!" March 25, 1965. https://kinginstitute .stanford.edu/our-god-marching.

Lau v. Nichols, January 21, 1974. https://scholar.google.com/scholar_case?case=5046768322576 386473&hl=en&as_sdt=6&as_vis=1&oi=scholarr.

Lewis, Catherine M. and J. Richard Lewis, eds. *Jim Crow America: A Documentary History*. Fayetteville, AR: University of Arkansas Press, 2009.

McLaurin v. Oklahoma State Regents (1950). https://www.law.cornell.edu/supremecourt/text /339/637.

Nixon, Richard. "Remarks on Signing the National Environmental Policy Act of 1969," January 1, 1970. http://www.presidency.ucsb.edu/ws/?pid=2446.

————. "Annual Message to the Congress on the State of the Union," January 22, 1970. http:// www.presidency.ucsb.edu/ws/?pid=2921.

————. "Special Message to the Congress on Higher Education," March 19, 1970. http://www .presidency.ucsb.edu/ws/?pid=2915.

————. Message to the Congress Transmitting the First Annual Report of the Council on Envi- ronmental Quality," August 10, 1970. http://www.presidency.ucsb.edu/ws/?pid=2618.

Reagan, Ronald. "The President's News Conference," August 12, 1988. http://www.presidency .ucsb.edu/ws/?pid=37733.

Reagan, Ronald. "Remarks on Signing the Family Support Act of 1988." October 13, 1988. http://www.presidency.ucsb.edu/ws/?pid=35013.

Roe v. Wade (1973). http://caselaw.findlaw.com/us-supreme-court/410/113.html.

Roosevelt, Franklin D. "Annual Message to Congress," January 4, 1935. http://www.presidency.ucsb.edu/ws/?pid=14890.

Rowe/Webb Memo. September 18, 1947. http://www.ksg.harvard.edu/case/3pt/rowe.html.

"Senator Hubert H. Humphrey's 1948 Speech on Civil Rights." Minnesota Historical Society. http://www.mnhs.org/library/tips/history_topics/42humphreyspeech/transcript.php.

Sweatt v. Painter (1951). https://www.law.cornell.edu/supremecourt/text/339/629.

Texas Department of Housing and Community Affairs et al. v. Inclusive Communities Project, Inc., et al (2015). http://www.supremecourt.gov/opinions/14pdf/13-1371_m640.pdf.

Truman, Harry S. "Veto of Bill To Revise the Laws Relating to Immigration, Naturalization, and Nationality," June 25, 1952. Harry S. Truman Library & Museum. http://trumanlibrary.org/publicpapers/viewpapers.php?pid=2389.

———. "Address at the Jefferson-Jackson Day Dinner," March 29, 1952. http://www.presidency.ucsb.edu/ws/?pid=14439.

———. "Address in New York City at the Convention of the Columbia Scholastic Press Association," March 15, 1952. http://millercenter.org/president/truman/speeches/speech-3352.

———. "Statement and Directive by the President on Immigration to the United States of Certain Displaced Persons and Refugees in Europe," December 22, 1946. Harry S. Truman Library & Museum. http://trumanlibrary.org/publicpapers/viewpapers.php?pid=515.

———. "Letter to the Chairman, House Rules Committee, Concerning the Committee on Fair Employment Practice," June 5, 1945. http://www.presidency.ucsb.edu/ws/?pid=12214.

Wilson, Woodrow, "First Inaugural Address," March 4, 1913. http://www.bartleby.com/124/pres44.html.

INTERVIEWS

Coopersmith, Lewis. June 27, 2012.

Cox, Millie Dalton. October 9, 2014.

Fleischer, Arnold. June 27, 2012.

Fuchs, James R. Interview with Jonathan Daniels. October 4, 1963. Harry S. Truman Presidential Library and Museum. https://www.trumanlibrary.org/oralhist/danielsj.htm.

Goodgold, Edwin. June 26, 2012.

Goren, Jane. September 12, 2012.

Lynn Haessly interview with Harvey B. Gantt, January 6, 1986. Southern Oral History Program Collection (#4007). University of North Carolina, Chapel Hill.

Hess, Jerry N. "Oral History Interview with James H. Rowe." September 30, 1969 and January 15, 1970. https://www.trumanlibrary.org/oralhist/rowejhap.htm.

Kanet, Rochelle (Shelli) Cohen. September 27, 2012.

Nunno, Henrietta Margolis. September 27, 2012.

Rosenbaum, Jerry. October 2, 2013.

Rubin, Harvey. March 15, 2012.

Scarfone, Tony. December 16, 2015.

Stocker, James. Securities and Exchange Commission Historical Society. Interview with Jill Considine. August 1, 2011. http://3197d6d14b5f19f2f440-5e13d29c4c016cf96cbbfd197c579b45.r81.cf1.rackcdn.com/collection/oral-histories/20110801_Considine_Jill_T.pdf.

NEWSPAPERS AND MAGAZINES

The Atlantic
Crisis
Fortune
Harper's
Life
Look
New York Times
Newsweek
Pittsburgh Courier
Redbook
Saturday Evening Post
The New Republic
The New Yorker
Time
Washington Post

GOVERNMENT DOCUMENTS

Bush, Vannevar. *Science: The Endless Frontier.* A Report to the President by Vannevar Bush,
     Director of the Office of Scientific Research and Development, July 1945. Washington:
     GPO, 1945. https://www.nsf.gov/od/lpa/nsf50/vbush1945.htm.
"The Family Support Act of 1988." http://www.irp.wisc.edu/publications/focus/pdfs/foc114e.pdf.
Grove, Robert D. and Alice M. Hetzel, *Vital Statistics Rates in the United States, 1940–1960.*
     Washington: GPO, 1968.
Moynihan, Daniel Patrick. *The Negro Family: The Case for National Action.* Washington: GPO,
     1965.
National Council of State Legislatures. "State Family and Medical Leave Laws." July 19, 2016.
     http://www.ncsl.org/research/labor-and-employment/state-family-and-medical-leave
     -laws.aspx.
National Defense Education Act. http://wwwedu.oulu.fi/tohtorikoulutus/jarjestettava_opetus
     /Troehler/NDEA_1958.pdf.
President's Commission on Civil Rights. *To Secure These Rights* (1947). http://www.truman
     library.org/civilrights/srights4.htm.
President's Commission on Campus Unrest (1970). http://files.eric.ed.gov/fulltext/ED083899
     .pdf.
Public Papers of the Presidents. http://presidency.proxied.lsit.ucsb.edu/ws/.
Report of the National Advisory Commission on Civil Disorders, February 29, 1968. https://
     archive.org/stream/kernerreportrevi00asse/kernerreportrevi00asse_djvu.txt.
Truman, Harry S. "Statement by the President Upon Signing the Housing Act of 1949." July 15,
     1949. http://www.presidency.ucsb.edu/ws/?pid=13246.
U.S. Congress. "Record of the 80th Congress." http://library.cqpress.com/cqresearcher/docu
     ment.php?id=cqresrre1948080700.
U.S. Senate. "Welfare Reform." Hearings Before the Committee on Finance. United States
     Senate. 100th Congress; First Session, October 14 and 28, 1987.
U.S. Department of Labor. *Construction during Five Decades: Historical Statistics, 1907–1952.*
     Washington: GPO, 1954. http://njlaw.rutgers.edu/collections/gdoc/hearings/8/88601411
     b/88601411b_1.pdf.

"Welfare Reform," Hearings Before the Committee on Finance, U.S. Senate, 100th Cong.,
    1st sess., October 14 and 28, 1987, http://njlaw.rutgers.edu/collections/gdoc/hearings/8
    /88601411b/88601411b_1.pdf.

SECONDARY SOURCES

BOOKS

Abu-Lughod, Janet L. *New York, Chicago, Los Angeles: America's Global Cities*. Minneapolis:
    University of Minnesota Press, 1999.
Adams, James Truslow, *The Epic of America*. NY: Blue Ribbon Books, 1931.
Altschuler, Glenn C. and Stuart M. Blumin, *The G.I. Bill: A New Deal for Veterans*. NY: Oxford
    University Press, 2009.
Ambrose, Stephen E. *Eisenhower: Soldier and President*. NY: Simon & Schuster, 1990.
Arnett, Jeffrey Jensen and Elizabeth Fishel. *Getting to 30: A Parent's Guide to the 20-Something
    Years*. NY: Workman Publishing Co. 2013.
Aspray, William. *John von Neumann and the Origins of Modern Computing*. Cambridge, MA:
    MIT Press, 1990.
Atkinson, Anthony B. *Inequality: What Can Be Done?* Cambridge, MA: Harvard University
    Press, 2015.
Banfield, Edward C. *The Unheavenly City: The Nature and the Future of Our Urban Crisis*.
    Boston: Little, Brown, 1968.
Bartels, Larry M. *Unequal Democracy: The Political Economy of the New Gilded Age*. NY:
    Russell Sage Foundation, 2008.
Bass, Jack. *Taming the Storm: The Life and Times of Judge Frank M. Johnson and the South's
    Fight over Civil Rights*. NY: Doubleday, 1993.
Bingham, Clara. *Witness to the Revolution: Radicals, Resisters, Vets, Hippies, and the Year
    America Lost Its Mind and Found Its Soul*. NY: Random House, 2016.
Biondi, Martha. *Stand and Fight: The Struggle for Civil Rights in Postwar New York City*.
    Cambridge, MA: Harvard University Press, 2003.
Brownell Herbert with John P. Burke. *Advising Ike: The Memoirs of Attorney General Herbert
    Brownell*. Lawrence, KN: University of Kansas Press, 1993.
Burk, Robert Frederick. *The Eisenhower Administration and Black Civil Rights, 1953–1961*.
    Knoxville, TN: University of Tennessee Press, 1984.
Califano, Joseph A., Jr. *The Triumph & Tragedy of Lyndon Johnson: The White House Years*. NY:
    Simon & Schuster, 1991.
Capeci, Dominic J. and Martha Frances Wilderson. *Layered Violence: The Detroit Rioters of
    1943*. Jackson, MS: University of Mississippi Press, 1991.
Caro, Robert A. *The Years of Lyndon Johnson: The Passage of Power*. NY: Alfred A. Knopf,
    2012.
———. *The Years of Lyndon Johnson: Master of the Senate*. NY: Alfred A. Knopf, 2002.
———. *The Years of Lyndon Johnson: Means of Ascent*. NY: Alfred A. Knopf, 1990.
———. *The Years of Lyndon Johnson: The Path to Power*. NY: Alfred A. Knopf, 1982.
Carter, Dan T. *From George Wallace to Newt Gingrich: Race in the Conservative Counterrevo-
    lution*. Baton Rouge: Louisiana State University Press, 1996.
———. *The Politics of Rage: George Wallace, the Origins of the New Conservatism, and the
    Transformation of American Politics*. NY: Simon & Schuster, 1995.
Carson, Rachel. *Silent Spring*. Boston: Houghton Mifflin, 1962.
Christofferson, Bill. *The Man from Clear Lake: Earth Day Founder Sen. Gaylord Nelson*.
    Madison, WI: University of Wisconsin Press, 2004.

Coontz, Stephanie. *A Strange Stirring: The Feminine Mystique and American Women at the Dawn of the 1960s.* NY: Basic Books, 2011.

————. *The Way We Never Were: American Families and the Nostalgia Trap.* NY: Basic Books, 1992.

Cowie, Jefferson. *The Great Exception: The New Deal & the Limits of American Politics.* Princeton, NJ: Princeton University Press, 2016.

Cray, Ed. *Chief Justice: A Biography of Earl Warren.* NY: Simon & Schuster, 1997.

Crittenden, Ann. *The Price of Motherhood: Why the Most Important Job in the World Is Still the Least Valued.* NY: Metropolitan Books, 2001.

Culver, John C. and John Hyde. *American Dreamer: The Life and Times of Henry A. Wallace.* NY: W. W. Norton, 2000.

Dallek, Robert. *Flawed Giant: Lyndon Johnson and His Times, 1961–1973.* NY: Oxford University Press, 1998.

————. *Lone Star Rising: Lyndon Johnson and His Times, 1908–1960.* NY: Oxford University Press, 1991.

Davies, Gareth. *From Opportunity to Entitlement: The Transformation and Decline of Great Society Liberalism.* Lawrence, KN: University Press of Kansas, 1996.

Delbanco, Andrew. *Melville: His World and Work.* NY: Alfred A. Knopf, 2013.

Dionne, E. J. *Why the Right Went Wrong: Conservatism—from Goldwater to the Tea Party and Beyond.* NY: Simon & Schuster, 2016.

————. *Our Divided Heart: The Battle for the American Idea in an Age of Discontent.* NY: Bloomsbury, 2012.

Dochuk, Darren. *From Bible Belt to Sunbelt: Plain-Folk Religion, Grassroots Politics, and the Rise of Evangelical Conservatism.* NY: W.W. Norton, 2011.

Donald, Aida D. *Citizen Soldier: A Life of Harry S. Truman.* NY: Basic Books, 2012.

Donaldson, Gary A. *Truman Defeats Dewey.* Lexington, KY: University Press of Kentucky, 1999.

D'Souza, Dinesh. *The End of Racism: Principles for a Multiracial Society.* NY: Free Press, 1995.

Du Bois, W. E. B. *The Souls of Black Folk.* Chicago: A. A. McClurg & Co., 1903.

Duncan, Susan Kirsch. *The Levittown: The Way We Were.* Huntington, NY: Maple Hill Press, 1999.

Edsall, Thomas and Mary Edsall. *Chain Reaction: The Impact of Race, Rights, and Taxes on American Politics.* NY: W.W. Norton, 1991.

Egerton, John. *Speak Now Against the Day: The Generation Before the Civil Rights Movement in the South.* Chapel Hill, NC: University of North Carolina Press, 1994.

Eig Jonathan. *The Birth of the Pill: How Four Crusaders Reinvented Sex and Launched a Revolution.* NY: W.W. Norton, 2014.

Emanuel, Anne. *Elbert Parr Tuttle: Chief Jurist of the Civil Rights Revolution.* Athens, GA: University of Georgia Press, 2011.

Evans, Hugh E. *The Hidden Campaign: FDR's Health and the 1944 Election.* Armonk, NY: M.E. Sharpe, 2002.

Farber, David. *The Rise and Fall of Modern American Conservatism: A Short History.* Princeton: Princeton University Press, 2010.

Felice, William F. *Taking Suffering Seriously: The Importance of Collective Human Rights.* Albany: SUNY Press, 1996.

Ferrell, Robert H. *Harry S. Truman: A Life.* Columbia, MO: University of Missouri Press, 1994.

————. *Truman & Pendergast.* Columbia, MO: University of Missouri Press, 1999.

Foley, Neil. *Mexicans in the Making of America.* Cambridge, MA: The Belknap Press, 2014.

————. *The White Scourge: Mexicans, Blacks, and Poor Whites in Texas Cotton Culture.* Berkeley, CA: University of California Press, 1997.

Forman, James, Jr. *Locking Up Our Own: Crime and Punishment in Black America*. NY: Farrar, Straus & Giroux, 2017.

Fortner, Michael Javen. *Black Silent Majority: The Rockefeller Drug Laws and the Politics of Punishment*. Cambridge, MA: Harvard University Press, 2015.

Frederickson, Kari. *The Dixiecrat Revolt and the End of the Solid South, 1932–1968*. Chapel Hill: University of North Carolina Press, 2001.

Friedan, Betty. *The Feminine Mystique*. NY: W.W. Norton, 1997; first published in 1963.

Friedman, Joel William. *Champion of Civil Rights: Judge John Minor Wisdom*. Baton Rouge: Louisiana State University Press, 2009.

Fukuyama, Francis. *Political Order and Political Decay: From the Industrial Revolution to the Globalization of Democracy*. NY: Farrar, Straus, and Giroux, 2014.

Galbraith, John Kenneth. *American Capitalism: The Concept of Countervailing Power*. Boston: Houghton Mifflin, 1993; first published in 1952.

———. *The Affluent Society*. Boston: Houghton Mifflin, 1984; first published in 1952.

Gans, Herbert J. *The Levittowners: Ways of Life and Politics in a New Suburban Community*. NY: Columbia University Press, 1967.

Gardner, Michael R. *Harry Truman and Civil Rights: Moral Courage and Political Risks*. Carbondale, IL: Southern Illinois University Press, 2002.

Garrettson, Charles Lloyd, III. *Hubert H. Humphrey: The Politics of Joy*. New Brunswick, NJ: Transaction Publishers, 1993.

Gertner, John. *The Idea Factory: Bell Labs and the Great Age of American Innovation*. NY: Penguin Press, 2012.

Geselbracht, Raymond H. ed. *The Civil Rights Legacy of Harry S. Truman*. Volume 2. Kirksville, MO: Truman State University Press, 2007.

Goldfield, David. *Black, White, and Southern: Race Relations and Southern Culture, 1940 to the Present*. Baton Rouge: Louisiana State University Press, 1990.

———. *Cotton Fields and Skyscrapers: Southern City and Region*. Baton Rouge: Louisiana State University Press, 1982.

——— and Blaine A. Brownell. *Urban America: A History*. Boston: Houghton Mifflin, 1990; second edition.

Gona, Ophelia De Laine. *Dawn of Desegregation: J. A. De Laine and Briggs v. Elliott*. Columbia, SC: University of South Carolina Press, 2011.

Goodwyn, Lawrence. *The Populist Moment: A Short History of the Agrarian Revolt in America*. NY: Oxford University Press, 1978.

Gordon, Richard E. Katherine K. Gordon, Max Gunther. *The Split-Level Trap*. NY: B. Geis Associates, 1961.

Graham, Hugh Davis. *Collision Course: The Strange Convergence of Affirmative Action and Immigration Policy in America*. NY: Oxford University Press, 2002.

———. *The Uncertain Triumph: Federal Education Policy in the Kennedy and Johnson Years*. Chapel Hill, NC: University of North Carolina Press, 1984.

Graham, Hugh Davis and Nancy Diamond. *The Rise of American Research Universities: Elites and Challengers in the Postwar Era*. Baltimore: Johns Hopkins University Press, 1997.

Griffiths, Jay. *A Country Called Childhood: Children and the Exuberant World*. Berkeley, CA: Counterpoint Press, 2014.

Halberstam, David. *The Fifties*. NY: Villard Books, 1993.

Halpern, Robert. *Rebuilding the Inner City: A History of Neighborhood Initiatives to Address Poverty in the United States*. NY: Columbia University Press, 1995.

Hamby, Alonzo. *Man of the People: A Life of Harry S. Truman*. NY: Oxford University Press, 1995.

———. *Liberalism and Its Challengers: FDR to Reagan*. NY: Oxford University Press, 1985.

Hanlon, Bernadette. *Once the American Dream: Inner-Ring Suburbs of the Metropolitan United States*. Philadelphia: Temple University Press, 2010.

Harrington, Michael. *The Other America: Poverty in the United States*. NY: Scribner, 2012; first published in 1962.

Herrnstein, Richard J. and Charles Murray. *The Bell Curve: Intelligence and Class Structure in American Life*. NY: Free Press, 1994.

Herzog, Jonathan P. *The Spiritual-Industrial Complex: America's Religious Battle against Communism in the Early Cold War*. NY: Oxford University Press, 2011.

Hirsch, Arnold R. *Making the Second Ghetto: Race & Housing in Chicago, 1940–1960*. Chicago: University of Chicago Press, 1998; first published in 1983.

Hochschild, Arlie Russell. *Strangers in Their Own Land: Anger and Mourning on the American Right*. NY: The New Press, 2016.

Horne, Gerald. *Fire this Time: The Watts Uprising and the 1960s*. Charlottesville, VA: University Press of Virginia, 1995.

Horowitz, Daniel. *Betty Friedan and the Making of* The Feminine Mystique: *The American Left, the Cold War, and Modern Feminism*. Amherst: University of Massachusetts Press, 1998.

Humes, Edward. *Over Here: How the G.I. Bill Transformed the American Dream*. NY: Harcourt, 2006.

Jones, Jacqueline. *Labor of Love, Labor of Sorrow: Black Women, Work, and the Family from Slavery to the Present*. NY: Basic Books, 2010; first published in 1985.

Jones, James H. *Alfred C. Kinsey: A Life*. NY: W.W. Norton, 1997.

Jones, Landon Y. *Great Expectations: America and the Baby Boom Generation*. NY: Coward, McCann & Geoghegan, 1980.

Kahn, Roger. *The Era, 1947–1957: When the Yankees, the Giants, and the Dodgers Ruled the World*. Boston: Houghton Mifflin, 1993.

———. *The Boys of Summer*. NY: Harper & Row, 1972.

Karabel, Jerome. *The Chosen: The Hidden History of Admission and Exclusion at Harvard, Yale, and Princeton*. Boston: Houghton Mifflin, 2005.

Karabell, Zachary. *The Last Campaign: How Harry Truman Won the 1948 Election*. NY: Vintage, 2007.

Katznelson, Ira. *When Affirmative Action Was White: An Untold History of Racial Inequality in Twentieth-Century America*. NY: W. W. Norton, 2005.

Kazin, Michael. *The Populist Persuasion: An American History*. Ithaca, NY: Cornell University Press, 1998.

Keats, John. *The Crack in the Picture Window*. Boston: Houghton Mifflin, 1956.

Kelly, Barbara M. *Expanding the American Dream: Building and Rebuilding Levittown*. Albany: SUNY Press, 1993.

Kerouac, Jack. *On the Road*. NY: Viking, 1957.

Keynes, John Maynard, *The General Theory of Employment and Money*. London: Palgrave Macmillan, 1936.

Kline, Benjamin. *First Along the River: A Brief History of the U.S. Environmental Movement*. Lanham, MD: Rowman & Littlefield, 1997.

Kluger, Richard. *Simple Justice: The History of* Brown v. Board of Education *and Black America's Struggle for Equality*. NY: Vintage, 2004.

Lawson, Russell M. and Benjamin A. Lawson, eds. *Poverty in America: An Encyclopedia*. Westport, CT: Greenwood Press, 2008.

Lear, Linda. *Rachel Carson: Witness for Nature*. NY: Henry Holt, 1997.

Leuchtenburg, William E. *The White House Looks South: Franklin D. Roosevelt, Harry S. Truman, Lyndon B. Johnson*. Baton Rouge: Louisiana State University Press, 2005.

——. *In the Shadow of FDR: From Harry Truman to Barack Obama*. Ithaca, NY: Cornell University Press, 2009.

Lewis, Oscar. *The Children of Sanchez: Autobiography of a Mexican Family*. NY: Random House, 1961.

——. "The Culture of Poverty." 1966. http://www.ignaciodarnaude.com/textos_diversos/ Lewis,Oscar,The%20Culture%20of%20Poverty.pdf.

Lowi, Theodore J. *The End of the Republican Era*. Norman, OK: University of Oklahoma Press, 2006; first published in 1995.

Mann, Alfred K. *For Better or for Worse: The Marriage of Science and Government in the United States*. NY: Columbia University Press, 2000.

Margolis, Maxine. *Mothers and Such: Views of American Women and Why They Changed*. Berkeley, CA: University of California Press, 1984.

Maslow, Abraham H. *Motivation and Personality*. NY: Harper & Row, 1970; first published in 1954.

Mazzucato, Mariana. *The Entrepreneurial State: Debunking Public vs. Private Sector Myths*. London: Anthem, 2013.

McCullough, David. *Truman*. NY: Simon & Schuster, 1992.

McGirr, Lisa. *Suburban Warriors: The Origins of the New American Right*. Princeton, NJ: Princeton University Press, 2001.

Medved, Michael and David Wallechinsky, *What Really Happened to the Class of '65*. NY: Random House, 1976.

Mettler, Susan. *Degrees of Inequality: How the Politics of Higher Education Sabotaged the American Dream*. NY: Basic Books, 2014.

——. *Soldiers to Citizens: The G.I. Bill and the Making of the Greatest Generation*. NY: Oxford University Press, 2005.

Mills, Harry A. and Emily Clark Brown. *From the Wagner Act to Taft-Hartley: A Study of National Labor Policy and Labor Relations*. Chicago: University of Chicago Press, 1950.

Murray, Charles A. *Losing Ground: American Social Policy, 1950–1980*. NY: Harper & Brothers, 1984.

Myrdal, Gunnar. *An American Dilemma: The Negro Problem and Modern Democracy*. NY: Harper & Brothers, 1944.

Newton, Jim. *Eisenhower: The White House Years*. NY: Doubleday, 2011.

Nichols, David A. *A Matter of Justice: Eisenhower and the Beginning of the Civil Rights Revolution*. NY: Simon & Schuster, 2007.

Niven, David. *The Politics of Injustice: The Kennedys, the Freedom Rides, and the Electoral Consequences of a Moral Compromise*. Knoxville, TN: University of Tennessee Press, 2003.

Nugent, Walter T. K. *Structures of American Social History*. Bloomington, IN: Indiana University Press, 1981).

——. *Into the West: The Story of Its People*. NY: Alfred A. Knopf, 1999.

Oshinsky, David M. *Polio: An American Story*. NY: Oxford University Press, 2005.

Patterson, James T. *Grand Expectations: The United States, 1945–1974*. NY: Oxford University Press, 1996.

Perlstein, Rick. *Invisible Bridge: The Fall of Nixon and the Rise of Reagan*. NY: Simon & Schuster, 2014.

——. *Nixonland: The Rise of a President and the Fracturing of America*. NY: Scribner, 2008.

Pietrusza, David. *1948: Harry Truman's Improbable Victory and the Year that Transformed America*. NY: Union Square Press, 2011.

——. *1960: LBJ vs. JFK vs. Nixon: The Epic Campaign That Forged Three Presidencies*. NY: Union Square Press, 2008.

Putnam, Robert D. *Bowling Alone: The Collapse and Revival of American Community*. NY: Simon & Schuster, 2000.

———. *Our Kids: The American Dream in Crisis*. NY: Simon & Schuster, 2015.

Riesman, David. *The Lonely Crowd*. New Haven, CT: Yale University Press, 2001; first published in 1950.

Rome, Adam. *The Bulldozer in the Countryside: Suburban Sprawl and the Rise of American Environmentalism*. Cambridge, UK: Cambridge University Press, 2001.

———. *The Genius of Earth Day: How a 1970 Teach-in Unexpectedly Made the First Green Generation*. NY: Hill and Wang, 2013.

Rorabaugh, W. J. *The Real Making of the President: Kennedy, Nixon, and the 1960 Election*. Lawrence, KN: University Press of Kansas, 2009.

Rose, Mark H. *Interstate: Express Highway Politics, 1939–1989*. Knoxville, TN: University of Tennessee Press, 1979.

Rosen, Robert N. *Saving the Jews: Franklin D. Roosevelt and the Holocaust*. NY: Basic Books, 2007.

Rosenberg, Harold *The Tradition of the New*. Cambridge, MA: Da Capo Press, 1994; first published in 1959).

Satter, Beryl. *Family Properties: Race, Real Estate, and the Exploitation of Black Urban America*. NY: Picador, 2009.

Savage, Sean J. *Truman and the Democratic Party*. Lexington, KY: University Press of Kentucky, 1997.

Schlesinger, Arthur M., Jr. *The Vital Center: The Politics of Freedom*. Boston: Houghton Mifflin, 1962; first published in 1949.

Shogan, Robert. *Harry Truman and the Struggle for Racial Justice*. Princeton, NJ: Princeton University Press, 2013.

Siegal, Deborah. *Sisterhood, Interrupted: From Radical Women to Grrls Gone Wild*. NY: Palgrave Macmillan, 2007.

Sitkoff, Harvard. *Toward Freedom Land: The Long Struggle for Racial Equality in America*. Lexington, KY: University Press of Kentucky, 2010.

Smith, Jean Edward. *Eisenhower in War and Peace*. NY: Random House, 2012.

Spruill, Marjorie J. *Divided We Stand: The Battle Over Women's Rights and Family Values That Polarized American Politics*. NY: Bloomsbury, 2017.

Steinberg, Alfred. *Sam Rayburn: A Biography*. NY: Hawthorn Books, 1975.

Sugrue, Thomas J. *The Origins of the Urban Crisis: Race and Inequality in Postwar Detroit*. Princeton, NJ: Princeton University Press, 1996.

Sundquist, James L. *Politics and Policy: The Eisenhower, Kennedy, and Johnson Years*. Washington, D.C.: The Brookings Institution, 1968.

Taylor, Quintard. *The Forging of a Black Community: Seattle's Central District from 1870 through the Civil Rights Era*. Seattle: University of Washington Press, 1994.

Teaford, Jon C. *The Metropolitan Revolution: The Rise of Post-Urban America*. NY: Columbia University Press, 2006.

Trotter, Joe W. and Jared N. Day, *Race and Renaissance: African Americans in Pittsburgh since World War II*. Pittsburgh: University of Pittsburgh Press, 2010.

Ward, Jason Morgan. *Defending White Democracy: The Making of a Segregationist Movement & The Remaking of Racial Politics, 1936–1965*. Chapel Hill: University of North Carolina Press, 2011.

Wiese, Andrew. *Place of Their Own: African American Suburbanization in the Twentieth Century*. Chicago: University of Chicago Press, 2004.

Whyte, William H. *The Organization Man*. NY: Simon & Schuster, 1956.

Wilkerson, Isabel. *The Warmth of Other Suns: The Epic Story of America's Great Migration*. NY: Random House, 2010.

Wilkins, Carolyn Marie. *Damn Near White: An African American Family's Rise from Slavery to Bittersweet Success.* Columbia, MO: University of Missouri Press, 2010.

Will, George F. *Statecraft as Soulcraft: What Government Does.* NY: Simon & Schuster, 1983.

Williams, Juan. *Thurgood Marshall. American Revolutionary.* NY: Times Books, 1998.

Wolf, Alison. *The XX Factor: How the Rise of Working Women Has Created a Far Less Equal World.* NY: Crown, 2013.

Woodward, C. Vann. *Tom Watson: Agrarian Rebel.* NY: Oxford University Press, 1963; first published in 1938.

Yarbrough, Tinsley E. *A Passion for Justice: J. Waties Waring and Civil Rights.* NY: Oxford University Press, 1987.

Zachary, G. Pascal. *Endless Frontier: Vannevar Bush, Engineer of the American Century.* NY: Free Press, 1997.

Zelizer, Julian E. *The Fierce Urgency of Now: Lyndon Johnson, Congress, and the Battle for the Great Society.* NY: Penguin, 2015.

Zolberg, Aristide R. *A Nation by Design: Immigration Policy in the Fashioning of America.* Cambridge, MA: Harvard University Press, 2006.

ARTICLES AND BOOK CHAPTERS

Anderson, Sam. "Exorcising the Dodgers." *New York Magazine.* September 16, 2007. http://nymag.com/news/sports/37643/.

Angeli, Marcia. "The Women at the Top." *New York Review of Books.* March 20, 2014: 18, 20–21.

Avila, Eric. "Popular Culture in the Age of White Flight: Film Noir, Disneyland, and the Cold War (Sub)Urban Imaginary." *Journal of Urban History* 31 (November 2004): 3–22.

Avila, Eric and Mark H. Rose, "Race, Culture, Politics, and Urban Renewal: An Introduction." *Journal of Urban History* 35 (March 2009): 335–47.

Baber, Ray E. "Marriage and Family After the War," *The ANNALS of the American Academy of Political and Social Science* 229 (January 1943): 164–75.

Berman, Sheri. "As the World Turns." *New York Times Book Review.* September 14, 2014: 1, 22.

Borchert, James. "Viewing the 'Underclass' and Ghetto form the Top Down." *Journal of Urban History* 25 (May 1999): 583–93.

Boustan, Leah P. and Robert A. Margo. "A Silver Lining to White Flight? White Suburbanization and African-American Homeownership, 1940–1980." *Journal of Urban Economics* 78 (November, 2013): 71–80.

Burns, Arthur F. "Looking Forward." Washington: National Bureau of Economic Research, 1951. http://www.nber.org/chapters/c4147.pdf.

Busch, Andrew E. "1966 Midterm Foreshadows Republican Era." http://ashbrook.org/publications/oped-busch-06-1966/.

Cassady, John. "Elizabeth Warren's Moment." *New York Review of Books.* May 22, 2014: 4, 6, 8.

Cater, Douglass. "How the Senate Passed the Civil-Rights Bill." *The Reporter.* September 5, 1957: 9.

Close, Stacey. "Fire in the Bones: Hartford's NAACP, Civil Rights and Militancy, 1943–1949." *The Journal of Negro History* 86 (Summer 2001): 228–63.

Coffin, Tris. "How Lyndon Johnson Engineered Compromise on Civil Rights Bill." *The New Leader.* August 5, 1957: 3–4.

Cole, David. "How Corrupt Are Our Politics?" *New York Review of Books.* September 24, 2014: 46, 48.

Countryman, Matthew J. "Why Philadelphia?" http://northerncity.library.temple.edu/content/historical-perspective/why-philadelphia.

Crittenden, Ann. "On Top of Everything Else" *New York Times Book Review.* March 30, 2014: 15.

"Dr. King Urges LBJ to Stop Riots with Jobs." *Jet*, August 10, 1967: 8. https://books.google.com /books?id=OroDAAAAMBAJ&pg=PA9&lpg=PA9&dq=LBJ%27s+rat+bill&source=bl &ots=iEvky9Hctw&sig=Dy8Ore4HOwGi5IMqT3EnI8on764&hl=en&sa=X&ved=oah UKEwjHl6yJx_3MAhWRdSYKHV6aD_MQ6AEIHjAA#v=onepage&q=LBJ's%20rat %20bill&f=false.

Drucker, Peter F. "The New Society of Organizations." *Harvard Business Review* (September-October 1992). https://hbr.org/1992/09/the-new-society-of-organizations.

Eberstadt, Nicholas. "Our Miserable 21st Century." *Commentary* (February 15, 2017). https:// www.commentarymagazine.com/articles/our-miserable-21st-century/.

Fainstein, Norman and Susan Nesbitt. "Did the Black Ghetto Have a Golden Age? Class Structure and Class Segregation in New York City, 1949–1970, With Initial Evidence for 1990." *Journal of Urban History* 23 (November 1996): 3–28.

Friedan, Betty. "In France, de Beauvoir Had Just Published 'The Second Sex'," *New York Magazine*. December 20, 1974/January 6, 1975: 52.

Frost, Jennifer. "Social Citizenship and the City." *Journal of Urban History* 30 (January, 2004): 289–98.

Gaddis, John Lewis. "He Made It Look Easy." *New York Times Sunday Book Review*. April 22, 2012. http://query.nytimes.com/gst/fullpage.html?res=9A04EEDE1F31F931A15757C0A 9649D8B63.

Germany, Kent B. "When History Is Not Good Enough for Hollywood: *Selma*, Lyndon B. Johnson, and Martin Luther King Jr." *AHA Perspectives on History* (May 2015): 31–32.

Goldfield, David. "Border Men: Truman, Eisenhower, Johnson, and Civil Rights." *Journal of Southern History*. LXXX (February 2014): 7–38.

Graham, Hugh Davis. The Surprising Career of Federal Fair Housing Law." *Journal of Policy History* 12 (#2, 2000): 215–32.

Griffith, Robert. "Dwight D. Eisenhower and the Corporate Commonwealth." *The American Historical Review* 87 (February 1982): 87–122.

Helgeson, Jeffrey. "The State of Blame in American Cities: Race, Wealth, and the Politics of Housing." *Journal of Urban History* 37 (November 2011): 992–99.

Herbold, Hilary. "Never a Level Playing Field: Blacks and the G.I. Bill." *Journal of Blacks in Higher Education* 6 (Winter 1994): 104–08.

Herzog, Jonathan. "America's Spiritual-Industrial Complex and the Policy of Revival in the Early Cold War." *Journal of Policy History* 22 (#3: 2010): 337–65.

Hirsch, Arnold R. "Massive Resistance in the Urban North: Trumbull Park, Chicago, 1953–1966." *Journal of American History* 82 (September 1995): 522–50.

Hofstadter, Richard. "The Paranoid Style in American Politics." *Harper's* (November 1964): 77–86.

Hunt, D. Bradford. "Rethinking the Retrenchment Narrative in U.S. Housing Policy History." *Journal of Urban History* 32 (September 2006): 937–50.

Isaacson, Walter. "Inventing the Future." *New York Times Book Review*. April 8, 2012: 20–21.

Jencks, Christopher. "The War on Poverty: Was It Lost?" *New York Review of Books*. (April 2, 2015): 82–85.

———. "Did We Lose the War on Poverty?—II." Ibid. (April 23, 2015): 37–39.

———. "Why the Very Poor Have Become Poorer." Ibid. (June 9, 2016): 15–17.

Kaiser, Robert G. "Our Conservative, Criminal Politicians." *New York Review of Books* (November 6, 2014): 54–56.

Katz, Michael B. "Segmented Visions: Recent Historical Writing on American Welfare." *Journal of Urban History* 24 (January 1998): 244–55.

———. "The American Welfare State and Social Contract in Hard Times." *Journal of Policy History* 22 (#4: 2010): 509–29.

Kempton, Murray. "Barry Goldwater." *The Spectator* (July 11, 1963). http://archive.spectator.co .uk/article/12th-july-1963/6/barry-goldwater.

Keynes, John Maynard. "Liberalism and Labour." In *Essays in Persuasion*, edited by Keynes. 1931. https://www.gutenberg.ca/ebooks/keynes-essaysinpersuasion/keynes-essaysin persuasion-00-h.html#Footnote_33_33.

———. "The End of Laissez-Faire," ibid.

Klarman, Michael J. "Why Massive Resistance." *Massive Resistance: Southern Opposition to the Second Reconstruction.* Clive Webb., ed. NY: Oxford University Press, 2005: 21–38.

Kohn, Sally. "How Gidget Broke the Rules in '60s TV." *CNN News.* August 25, 2014. http:// www.cnn.com/2014/05/29/opinion/kohn-tv-women-60s-gidget/.

Kraft, Michael E. "U.S. Environmental Policy and Politics: From the 1960s to the 1990s." *Journal of Policy History* 12 (#1, 2000): 17–42.

Lane, Robert E. "The Politics of Consensus in an Age of Affluence." *American Political Science Review* 59 (#4, 1965): 874–95.

Levin, Josh. "The Welfare Queen." *Slate.* December 19, 2013. http://www.slate.com/articles/news _and_politics/history/2013/12/linda_taylor_welfare_queen_ronald_reagan_made_her_a _notorious_american_villain.html.

Light, John. "Five Facts You Should Know About the Hyde Amendment." *Moyers and Company.* January 25, 2013. http://billmoyers.com/content/five-facts-you-should-know-about-the -hyde-amendment/.

Melosi, Martin V. "Environmental Justice, Political Agenda Setting, and the Myths of History." *Journal of Policy History* 12 (#1, 2000): 43–71.

Myers, Andrew. "The Blinding of Isaac Woodard." *Proceedings of the South Carolina Historical Association* (2004): 63–73.

"National Housing Emergency, 1946–1947." *CQ Researcher.* http://library.cqpress.com/cqre searcher/document.php?id=cqresrre1946121700.

Nickerson, Michelle. "Beyond Smog, Sprawl, and Asphalt: Developments in the Not-So-New Suburban History." *Journal of Urban History* 41 (January 2015): 171–80.

Nossiff, Rosemary. "Abortion Policy Before *Roe*: Grassroots in Interest-Group Mobilization." *Journal of Policy History* 13 (#4 2001): 463–78.

Ogburn, William Fielding, "Marriages, Births, and Divorces," *The ANNALS of the American Academy of Political and Social Science.* 229 (January 1943): 20–29.

O'Hagan, Andrew. "Jack Kerouac: Crossing the Line." *New York Review of Books.* March 21, 2013: 15–17.

Parson, Don. "The Decline of Public Housing and the Politics of the Red Scare: The Signifi- cance of the Los Angeles Public Housing War." *Journal of Urban History* 33 (March 2007): 400–17.

Preston, Julia. "The Truth About Mexican Americans." *New York Review of Books* December 3, 2015. http://www.nybooks.com/articles/2015/12/03/truth-about-mexican-americans/.

Reichley, A. James. "Faith in Politics." *Journal of Policy History* 13 (#1: 2001): 137–80.

Rich, Frank. "A Distant Mirror." *New York Times Book Review.* August 3, 2014: 16–17.

Sears, David O. "Black-White Conflict: A Model for the Future of Ethnic Politics in Los Angeles?" *New York & Los Angeles.* David Halle, ed. (Chicago: University of Chicago Press, 2003): 367–79.

Seidel, Frederick. "Polio Days." *New York Review of Books.* April 3, 2014: 16.

Sholar, Megan A. "The History of Family Leave Policies in the United States." *American Histo- rian* (November 2016): 41–45.

Silk, Leonard. "The Vicious Cycle of Poverty." *Business Week.* February 1, 1964: 39–40, 42–43.

Solomon, Andrew. "Go Play Outside." *New York Times Book Review.* December 14, 2014: 26–27.

Starr, Paul. "How Gilded Ages End." *American Prospect*. Spring 2015. http://prospect.org/article
    /how-gilded-ages-end.
Stebenne, David L. "Thomas J. Watson and the Business-Government Relationship, 1933–1956."
    Enterprise and Society 6 (March 2005): 45–75.
Sugrue, Thomas J. "Crabgrass-Roots Politics: Race, Rights, and the Reaction against Liberalism
    in the Urban North, 1940–1964." *Journal of American History* 82 (September 1995): 551–78.
Tanenhaus, Sam. "Why Populism Now?" *New York Times Book Review* (June 26, 2016): 15.
Van Bavel, Jan and David S. Reher, "The Baby Boom and Its Causes: What We Know and What
    We Need to Know." *Population and Development Review* 39 (June 2013): 257–88.
Weber, Bret A. and Amanda Wallace. "Revealing the Empowerment Revolution: A Literature
    Review of the Model Cities Program." *Journal of Urban History* 38 (November 2012):
    173–92.
White, Philip. "The Secret Weapon That Helped Win the White House in 1948 & Establish the
    Political 'War Room'." *Huffington Post*. (October 27, 2014). http://www.huffingtonpost
    .co.uk/philip-white/cold-war_b_6048336.html.
Wiener, Jon. "Something Happening Here." *New York Times Book Review* (June 12, 2016): 11.
Wiese, Andrew. "Suburbia: Middle Class to the Last?" *Journal of Urban History* 23 (September
    1997): 750–59.
Wills, Garry. The Triumph of the Hard Right." *New York Review of Books* (February 11, 2016):
    4, 6.
Woodward, C. Vann. "The Great Civil Rights Debate: The Ghost of Thaddeus Stevens in the
    Senate Chamber." *Commentary*. October 1, 1957. https://www.commentarymagazine
    .com/articles/the-great-civil-rights-debatethe-ghost-of-thaddeus-stevens-in-the-senate
    -chamber/.
Zipp, Samuel. "The Roots and Routes of Urban Renewal." *Journal of Urban History* 39 (May
    2013): 366–91.

Index

A NOTE ON THE AUTHOR

David Goldfield is the Robert Lee Bailey Professor of History at the University of North Carolina, Charlotte. He is the lead author of the cornerstone textbook *The American Journey*, now in its eighth edition, and is the author of many works on Southern history, including *Still Fighting the Civil War*; *Black, White, and Southern*; and, most recently, *America Aflame*. He lives in North Carolina.